25. 00

H45

D0519329

Hertfordshire

-9 JAN 2006   BICRO
7/12   OWE

0 7 MAY 2004

2 7 MAY 2004

2 4 SEP 2004
0 5 NOV 2004

2 5 AUG 2005
1 3 SEP 2005

CIRCULATING STOCK ROUTE 22

HOD

Please renew/return this item by the last date shown.

So that your telephone call is charged at local rate,
please call the numbers as set out below:

	From Area codes 01923 or 020:	From the rest of Herts:
Renewals:	01923 471373	01438 737373
Enquiries:	01923 471333	01438 737333
Textphone:	01923 471599	01438 737599

L32   www.hertsdirect.org/librarycatalogue

Lord Cromer

Lord Cromer

Victorian Imperialist, Edwardian Proconsul

ROGER OWEN

OXFORD

UNIVERSITY PRESS

OXFORD

UNIVERSITY PRESS

Great Clarendon Street, Oxford OX2 6 DP

Oxford University Press is a department of the University of Oxford.
It furthers the University's objective of excellence in research, scholarship,
and education by publishing worldwide in

Oxford New York

Auckland Bangkok Buenos Aires Cape Town Chennai
Dar es Salaam Delhi Hong Kong Istanbul Karachi Kolkata
Kuala Lumpur Madrid Melbourne Mexico City Mumbai Nairobi
São Paulo Shanghai Taipei Tokyo Toronto

Oxford is a registered trade mark of Oxford University Press
in the UK and in certain other countries

Published in the United States
by Oxford University Press Inc., New York

© Roger Owen 2004

The moral rights of the author have been asserted
Database right Oxford University Press (maker)

First published 2004

All rights reserved. No part of this publication may be reproduced,
stored in a retrieval system, or transmitted, in any form or by any means,
without the prior permission in writing of Oxford University Press,
or as expressly permitted by law, or under terms agreed with the appropriate
reprographics rights organization. Enquiries concerning reproduction
outside the scope of the above should be sent to the Rights Department,
Oxford University Press, at the address above

You must not circulate this book in any other binding or cover
and you must impose this same condition on any acquirer

British Library Cataloguing in Publication Data

Data available

Library of Congress Cataloging in Publication Data

Data available

ISBN 0-19-925338-2

1 3 5 7 9 10 8 6 4 2

Typeset by Kolam
Printed in Great Britain
on acid-free paper by
Biddles Ltd. Guildford & King's Lynn

COMMUNITY INFORMATION:

LIBRARIES

H45 213 074 9

Macaulay	31/03/04
	£25.00

To my children, Kate, Ben, and Isabel,
and my grandchildren, Charlotte and Natalia

PREFACE

In the heyday of Empire, just before the First World War, two British proconsuls stood head and shoulders above the rest in fame and public esteem: Lord Curzon, the former viceroy of India, and Lord Cromer, whose name was firmly identified with the British occupation of Egypt. In the days when Cairo and Calcutta represented the twin poles of the British power in Asia and Africa, Cromer's commanding presence and Curzon's brilliance, seemed to radiate the essential spirit of imperial rule.

Yet, while Curzon has remained very much in the historical limelight, Cromer's huge pre-First World War reputation has been largely forgotten. Even his one official biography, written by the Marquess of Zetland, an Indian provincial governor, and published in 1932, has a rather apologetic air about it as though Cromer's trenchant approach to what he himself called 'the government of subject races' was no longer appropriate in the post-1914 world.[1] For the rest, Lord Cromer has mainly been reduced to the role of stage villain in the long story of Britain's unhappy relationship with Egypt. The real ruler of the country for most of a quarter of a century, 1883–1907, he stands four-square across the period as someone British writers have to come to terms with and the man most Egyptians have been taught to love to hate. 'Where is this Cromer buried?', a party of young students from Egypt asked the local archivist in the small Norfolk town of Cromer in 1998, 'We would like to spit on his grave.'

Why is it worth trying to resurrect the life of someone whose name is hardly remembered outside the Egyptian context and whose once mighty reputation has now almost totally disappeared? One obvious reason stems directly from the times we live in and the many resemblances between our present wave of globalization and the previous one in which Lord Cromer was a major participant in the forty years or so before the First World War. Both periods can be characterized by a growing economic interconnectedness in which international financial management and global orthodoxies concerning fiscal practice, openness, loans, and national indebtedness were, or are, essential ingredients.

---

[1] This is the title of Cromer's article published in the *Edinburgh Review* (Jan. 1908).

There are, however, other factors which made the first wave different from the second, though not always quite so radically different as is sometimes supposed. One is that it took place during the high tide of empire when military, political, and economic expansion went hand in hand in ways which still elude final explanation in spite of all the efforts of a line of influential theorists of Victorian imperialism, from Hobson, through Robinson and Gallagher, to Cain and Hopkins.[2] The second is the conscious identification between empire and racial superiority embodied in the notion that it was Europe's duty to promote what the British referred to as the moral and material progress of the colonized peoples, whether they liked it or not.

Cromer, as a member of the famous City banking family of Baring Brothers, as a Commissioner of the Public Debt in Egypt, as the Finance Minister in India, played a significant role in all these nineteenth-century developments, combining liberal economic ideas about low tariffs and taxes and balanced budgets with the changing political and cultural principles and prejudices of his own white governing class. Brought up in a Whig family, and fancying himself a radical in his young days, he made the not unfamiliar passage from the liberal, free-trade internationalism of the Bright–Gladstone wing of the Liberal Party of the 1870s and early 1880s to the more power- and race-conscious nationalism of the Liberal Imperialists in the two decades before the First World War. And he did this against a background of public service, first in the old empire of island fortresses like Corfu and Malta, of the West Indian sugar colonies, and of India, and then of the new empire in Africa following the occupation of Egypt in 1882 and Sudan in 1898. Few imperial administrators had quite this range of experience. And none had his long practice of ruling different non-European peoples at a time when the whole notion of Empire itself entered more and more into the metropolitan political debate.

Other reasons for writing Cromer's life are more purely personal. Cromer and the residence he built by the Nile—now the British Embassy—have always been part of the Cairo I first visited in June 1956, when the streets were hung with banners announcing the final evacuation of the last British troops from the Canal Zone, where they had been stationed since 1882. He was also the subject of my first published

[2] J. A. Hobson, *Imperialism: A Study* (London: James Nesbit, 1902); Ronald Robinson and John Gallagher with Alice Denny, *Africa and the Victorians: The official Mind of Imperialism* (London: Macmillan, 1961) P. J. Cain and A. G. Hopkins, *British Imperialism: Innovation and Expansion, 1688–1914* (London: Longman, 1993), esp. chs. 3 and 4.

academic article, 'The Influence of Lord Cromer's Indian Experience on British Policy in Egypt 1883–1907'.[3] More recently I have followed him to Malta, Calcutta, and Simla, visiting the houses in which he lived, and the offices in which he worked, to get a better idea of the life of a man who chose to make his home in hot and humid cities, where great rewards were accompanied by great discomfort, where large projects like the first Aswan Dam could be constructed and large natural disasters like the Indian famines confronted, where there was little check on the exercise of great personal power, and where the presence of an alien government inevitably excited growing resistance from the governed.

Lastly, having written and taught the economic and political history of the Middle East for most of my working life, I was anxious to try my hand at other aspects of the historian's craft. There is not a great deal of room in economic history for an exercise of such traditional and still vital skills as that of the historical imagination needed to think yourself into particular periods of time and to recapture some of the sensibilities, ways of life, and world-views that characterized them. Biography is also, and of necessity, less determinist than economic and much social history. Lives have to be written forward, just as they were lived. They are ruled by contingency, randomness, and much muddled choice. Nothing is preordained. For the most part, 'Things don't just happen,' as Paul Bowles once wrote in an autographed copy of his *The Sheltering Sky*: 'it depends on who comes along.'[4] The way lives are lived also turns out, at least to the apprentice biographer, to be surprisingly social. You begin by looking for your subject's personal contribution to the formation of policies and ideas only to discover that the authorship of almost every one of his or her initiatives is shared with so many others that ultimate responsibility becomes difficult if not impossible to pin down. Hence Cromer, like so many imperial administrators of his kind, is better seen as an energizer, a coordinator, an implementer, a problem-solver, and an apologist, rather than as original thinker in his own right.

Writing such a life presents a number of obvious challenges. As far as its public aspect is concerned, Cromer's legacy, and particularly the impact of his policies on the lives of millions of Egyptians (and before that, 200 million Indians) must remain controversial. As Professor André Raymond remarked on the two hundredth anniversary of the French conquest of

[3] Roger Owen, *St Antony's Papers*, 17: *Middle Eastern Affairs*, 4, ed. Albert Hourani (London: Oxford University Press, 1965).

[4] Quoted in *New York Times*, Book Review, 19, Dec. 1999, 39.

Egypt in 1798, 'il n'y a pas d'occupation heureuse'.[5] Nevertheless, at the beginning of the twenty-first century, with formal empire a thing of the past, it is now easier to discuss such matters in the less heated manner in which analysis precedes, rather than follows, judgement. The writing of history remains, as always, a process which combines a never-ending dialogue with previously held positions, with the intrusion of 'incremental revelations'.[6] My aim is to interrogate past interpretations with the use of as much new primary source material as I have been able to find.

Meanwhile, as far as the craft of biography itself is concerned, for all the excitement caused by the writings of the new biographers, such as Richard Holmes, Hermione Lee, Michael Holroyd, and others, the basic problems involved in writing the life of another human being remain more or less the same as they always were. In shaping your story, you have to impose an order which would almost certainly be unrecognizable to your subject. You deal with public and private records which, inevitably, reflect fleeting moods, partial understandings, temporary points of view. You have to track the moving target created by your subject's growth and physical and emotional change. You have to contend with what has been called the 'invented self', that is the subjects' own attempts, implicitly or explicitly, to present themselves in a particular way to their family, friends, and colleagues, as well as, of course, to themselves. And you have to attend to what still remains the most essential task of a good biographer: to make your subject live upon the page.

It is, of course, an impossible task, and all biographers should keep some statement to this effect from one of the great sceptics about the craft constantly in front of them. To W. M. Thackeray, for example, the whole attempt to understand another human being was simply 'futile'. 'Ah Sir,' he once explained to a questioner, 'a distinct universe walks about under your hat and under mine . . . you and I are but a pair of infinite isolations, with some fellow islands a little more or less near.'[7] Nevertheless, the engagement with individual historical figures, and the attempt to see them whole and to explain their impact on the specific situations in which they found themselves, will always remain part of the biographer's task, and often a particularly rewarding one at that.

---

[5] André Raymond, *Égyptiens et françaises au Caire, 1798–1801* (Cairo: Institut Français d'Archéologie Orientale, 1998), 365.

[6] The term is Diane Johnson's, *New York Review of Books*, 19 Oct. 2000, 21.

[7] Quoted in John Sutherland's review of D. J. Taylor, *Thackeray: 'Wife Overboard'*, *London Review of Books*, 20 Jan. 2000, 35–6.

In the case of Evelyn Baring, who became Lord Cromer in 1892, the challenge is of particular interest because of the deliberate attempt he made in his early sixties, when both newly remarried and thinking himself close to death, to set out his personal records in ways which would provide a clear structure to anyone wanting either to understand him or to write a posthumous biography. Central to this effort was his 'Biographical Notes'. These are contained in a single bound volume of just over 400 pages, with an original date of 12 November 1905, which, I assume, is when the process of having it typed up by a Mrs Springett of 5 Salters Court, London EC, was finally complete. There are also several short appendices (including a pastiche of a Lear nonsense poem written by Cromer himself) and four brief additions inserted in the back, three dated 2 August 1910, 26 July 1911, and 15 February 1915, respectively, with the last, undated, but referring directly to the death of his successor in Egypt, Sir Eldon Gorst, in the summer of 1911.

The 'Notes' are dedicated to Rowland, the eldest of his three sons. According to the preface, they were 'composed' at Strathmore Lodge in Scotland in August 1905, partly that the children should know something of their father's career, partly that they might be of use to a biographer 'if ever my life is written'.

The material in the 'Notes' provides almost all that is known about Evelyn Baring's private life up to the moment he first went to India in 1872 at the age of 31. It demonstrates few signs of introspection or of a willingness to examine personal choices or analyse motives. But it is presented in a form which gives powerful shape to these first thirty-one years: describing the transition from an indifferent schoolboy with little formal education, to a hedonistic, spendthrift young army officer, and then to personal reformation as a result of the love of a good woman and the example of fellow officers and friends much better educated than he. Although this seems to have been shaped largely in order to act as a piece of moral instruction for his sons, the form is so seductive that it exercised a decisive influence on the organization of the Marquess of Zetland's official biography written fifteen years after his death.[8] Indeed, Zetland's project provides an extra meaning to the term 'ghost-written' in that it gives off a very strong sense of having been directly inspired from beyond the grave.

[8] Zetland was asked to write the biography by Cromer's son Rowland, the second Earl; Zetland to Boyle, 19 Feb. 1931, CP/3, file 1/4.

I have done my best not to fall into the same trap. However, given the overwhelming weight of the material Baring provided about his own early life, it is very difficult to avoid. The challenge has been to write both with Lord Cromer's account of his own life and against it. One way has been to use evidence which he himself suppressed; for example, information concerning his illegitimate daughter or his near-disastrous row with the viceroy, Lord Ripon, in India in 1881. Another has been to focus on the alternative, and more general, structures which sustained or informed his life, notably the conventional notion of a career leading to recognition and reward and then a public-spirited retirement. Yet another has been to follow Cromer's Egyptian version of the Victorian yearly round, with the high season from December to May as Cairo filled with foreign visitors, and the annual summer flight home, first to London for official business, then to Scotland for shooting and fishing and other forms of upper-class recreation. However, the structure I have tried to pay most attention to is that of the colonial residency, the house which contained not just the domestic quarters of a governor or a viceroy but also his own private offices, allowing him to mix with family, staff, official visitors, and guests on a daily basis. I found this of particular importance in trying to find space to write in his two wives, partners, and companions, who, like the vast majority of Victorian women, passed through their lives leaving little trace in either official or even family records. Privately schooled, they emerge only at the time of their marriage and then disappear from the historical records again, rarely mentioned by their husbands in either diaries or correspondence with male friends and relatives. Such was the fate of Evelyn Baring's sister Cecilia; such was the fate of his wives, Ethel and Katherine.

A final word to my Egyptian friends. I am well aware that by writing about someone as well known and well hated as Lord Cromer I run the risk of appearing as an apologist of empire, which I am certainly not. My main excuse is that, as Indian historians have already discovered, a country's history under colonialism can only be properly understood in terms of a process of related experience, however unwillingly it may have been entered into by the colonized themselves. This was recognized by many of Cromer's Egyptian contemporaries, who were much more ready to acknowledge some of the positive effects of his rule than most of those who followed. For better, and often worse, Lord Cromer is as much a part of Egypt's history as he is of Britain's.

A NOTE ON VOCABULARY

It is now widely accepted that people like Evelyn Baring, Lord Cromer, thought of themselves as English, even though they lived in a state which contained Scotland, Ireland, and Wales and, in his case, served in something called the British Army and was later much connected with another entity called the British Empire. In what follows I have tried to preserve this linguistic distinction between then and now, leaving him and his contemporaries to talk of England, of Constantinople, of the Moham-medans, etc., while I myself write of Britain, Istanbul, and the Muslims.

R.O.

Cambridge, Massachusetts
May 2003

ACKNOWLEDGEMENTS

This biography would have been impossible without the generous and wholehearted cooperation of members of the Baring family, in particular the Dowager Countess of Cromer, the Earl of Cromer, the Honourable Mrs Vivian Baring, and Lord Howick. My most grateful thanks.

For the rest, biography is above all a team effort and I should like also to thank the following for their help in providing information, in suggesting sources, in helping with editing and copy-editing the text, and, in general, by providing a sympathetic ear, a critical eye, and general moral and intellectual support: Geoffrey Adams, Roger Adelson, Shahid Amin, Dr Tom Andrews, Mona Anis, Paul Auchterlonie, Gillian Barratt, Martin Barratt, HE Graham Boyce, Helen Calloway, Dr J. Stewart Cameron, John Chalcroft, Jill Christie, Uma Dasgupta, Ayman El-Desouky, John Fox, Nicholas Frayn, Martin Gilbert, Marwan Hanania, Robert Harrison, Fayza Hassan, the Reverend Terence V. Healey, Jane Horton (Archives and Special Collections, Durham University), David Jones (House of Lords Library), Ruth Kershaw, Zachary Lockman, S. R. Mehrotra, Peter Mellini, John Orbell (ING Barings), Margaret Owen, Ursula Owen, John Parker, Susan Pederson, Carol Kinsey Pope, Sally Richmond, Gowher Rizvi, Eugene Rogan, John Roper, Father George Rutler, George Scanlon, Kath Shawcross (Borough of Sutton County Archives), Relli Shechter, Jenny Sneddon, Alison Weir, Richard Wilson, and David Wolton.

Finally, I should like to thank the following for giving me permission to publish illustrations from their collections or to quote from documents they possess: the Baring–Cromer family and in particular the Dowager Countess of Cromer and Lord Howick, ING Barings, the British Library, the Houghton Library (Harvard University)—for permission to cite from the diaries of Edward Lear and the Wilfrid Blunt Papers—the University Library (Durham), St Antony's College Middle East Centre (Oxford University), the Cromer and Walsingham Museums, and the London Borough of Sutton, the Illustrated London News, Corbis, and Robert J. Baxter.

CONTENTS

PART I. *The Training of an Officer and a Gentleman, 1841–1872*

PART II. *An Apprenticeship in Imperial Government and International Finance, 1872–1883*

PART III. *Governing Egypt, 1883–1907*

PART IV. *Reimmersion in British Political Life, 1907–1917*

LIST OF ILLUSTRATIONS
(between pp. 232–233)

ABBREVIATIONS

AR	*Annual Reports* (Egypt)
BA	ING Barings Historical Archives
BL	British Library, London
BN	'Biographical Notes' (Cromer), CP/1
BowP	Humphrey Bowman Papers, Middle East Centre, St Antony's College, Oxford
BP	Boyle Papers (Harry Boyle), Middle East Centre, St Antony's College, Oxford
CAB	Cabinet Papers, PRO
C-BP	Campbell-Bannerman Papers (Henry Campbell-Bannerman), BL
CP/1	Cromer Papers, in private possession of Cromer–Baring family
CP/2	Cromer Papers, PRO
CP/3	Cromer Papers, Middle East Centre, St Antony's College, Oxford
CP/4	Cromer Papers, Notes from Dr Peter Mellini
CP/5	Cromer Papers, Durham University Library
DBB	*Dictionary of Business Biography: A Biographical Dictionary of Business Leaders Active in the Period 1860–1986*, 5 vols. (London: Butterworths, 1984–6)
DNB	*Dictionary of National Biography*
DP	D'Abernon Papers (Edgar Vincent), BL
FO	Foreign Office, London
GC	Greville Correspondence (Charles C. Greville), BL
GD	Gorst Diaries (Eldon Gorst), Notes provided by Gorst's Biographer, Dr Peter Mellini
GladP	Gladstone Papers (W. E. Gladstone), BL
GP	Gordon Papers (Charles Gordon), BL
GrenP	Grenfell Collection (General Francis Grenfell), Middle East Centre, St Antony's College, Oxford
H(B)MG	His/Her (Britannic) Majesty's Government
H.C. Deb.	Hansard, *Parliamentary Debates*, Commons, 5th ser. (1909–)

H.L. Deb.	Hansard, *Parliamentary Debates*, House of Lords, 5th ser. (1909–)
HMSO	His/Her Majesty's Stationery Office, London
HP	Sir Charles Hardinge Papers, Cambridge University Library
KP	Kitchener Papers (Herbert Horatio Kitchener), PRO
LP	Lyall Papers (Alfred Lyall), Oriental and India Office Collections, BL
MBL	Moberley Bell Letters, TA
MP	Milner Papers (Alfred Milner), Bodleian Library, Oxford
NAI	National Archives of India, New Delhi, India
NP	Northbrook Papers (Thomas George, first Earl Northbrook), Oriental and India Office Collections, BL
Parl. Deb.	Hansard, *Parliamentary Debates* (Lords and Commons) (1907–1908)
PP	*Parliamentary Papers* (London)
PRO	Public Record Office (London)
RL	Richmond Letters (Ernest Tatham Richmond), in private possession of Richmond family
RMA	Royal Military Academy, Woolwich
RP	Ripon Papers (George Frederick Robinson, Marquess of Ripon), BL
SP	Salisbury Papers, Hatfield House, Hertfordshire (formerly in Christ Church, Oxford)
SPCA	Society for the Prevention of Cruelty to Animals
TA	Times Archive, London
TC	Temple Correspondence (Richard Temple), Oriental and India Office Collections, BL

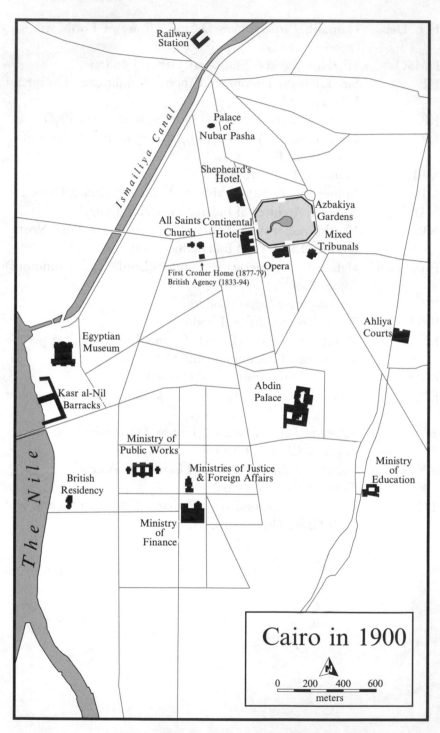

Cairo in the Time of Cromer

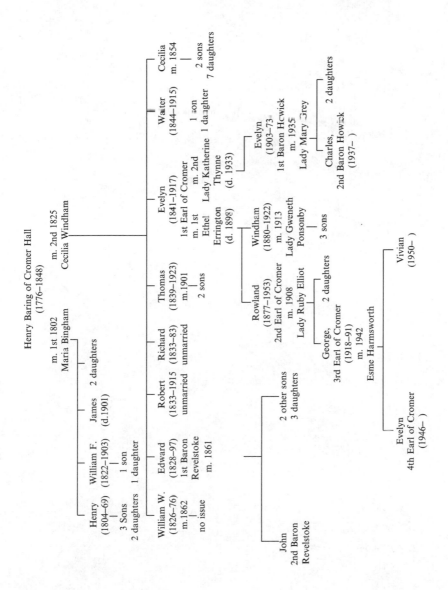

Henry Baring of Cromer Hall
(1776–1848)

m. 1st 1802
Maria Bingham

m. 2nd 1825
Cecilia Windham

Henry
(1804–69)
3 Sons
2 daughters

William F.
(1822–1903)
1 son
1 daughter

James
(d.1901)
2 daughters

William W.
(1826–76)
m.1862
no issue

Edward
(1828–97)
1st Baron
Revelstoke
m. 1861

Robert
(1833–1915)
unmarried

Richard
(1833–83)
unmarried

Thomas
(1839–1923)
m.1901
2 sons

Evelyn
(1841–1917)
1st Earl of Cromer

m. 1st
Ethel
Errington
(d. 1898)

m. 2nd
Lady Katherine
Thynne
(d. 1933)

Walter
(1844–1915)
1 son
1 daughter

Cecilia
m. 1854
2 sons
7 daughters

Rowland
(1877–1953)
2nd Earl of Cromer
m. 1908
Lady Ruby Elliot

Windham
(1880–1922)
m. 1913
Lady Gweneth
Ponsonby
3 sons

Evelyn
(1903–73)
1st Baron Howick
m. 1935
Lady Mary Grey

Charles,
2nd Baron Howick
(1937–)
2 daughters

John
2nd Baron
Revelstoke

2 other sons
3 daughters

George,
3rd Earl of Cromer
(1918–91)
m. 1942
Esme Harmsworth

2 daughters

Vivian
(1950–)

Evelyn
4th Earl of Cromer
(1946–)

The Baring Family Tree

PART I

---

*The Training of an Officer
and a Gentleman
1841–1872*

I

———◆———

A Norfolk Childhood
1841–1852

Family and Absent Parents

On 8 June 1841 census enumerators visited Cromer Hall, a newly built neo-Gothic house just a mile and a half from the little fishing town of Cromer in Norfolk. There they collected the form showing that the house contained two little boys, Master Thomas Baring, aged 2, and Master Evelyn Baring, aged 5 months, together with five female house servants, including Ann Cox, the boys' nurse. The boys' parents, Mr and Mrs Henry Baring, were away, as they very often were, staying at their London House at 11 Berkeley Square with their one daughter, Cecilia, aged 8, and the twins, Robert and Richard, aged 7, looked after by fourteen live-in servants. Two older sons, William Windham and Edward (Ned), were absent from home that census day, most probably at school.

As the youngest of a large family, and with a father of sixty-five, it must have been clear even then that young Evelyn, the future Earl of Cromer, was going to suffer from lack of parental attention. This was to force him to make his own way in the world with little education and an early reputation for wildness well captured by his family nickname of Mina (pronounced 'Myna'), given to him because of the way he would pick up objects and rush around saying 'mine-a', 'mine-a'.

Evelyn's father, Henry (1776–1848), was a somewhat eccentric member of the German merchant family of Johann (later John) Baring, who moved to Exeter in 1717. John's third son, Francis, founded the banking house of John and Francis Baring & Co. in London in 1762. It quickly prospered, first through the growing issue of the acceptances, the letters of credit used to finance late eighteenth-century trade, then by an ever-increasing web of political and business connections which allowed the house to make large profits from loans issued during the Napoleonic Wars. By the early nineteenth century Barings had become the premier banking house in London, although it was soon to face great competition from another set of German immigrants, the Rothschilds.[1]

Like so many other successful merchant bankers, the Barings began to marry well, to send their sons to good schools, to build or buy country houses, to have their portraits painted by Gainsborough and Lawrence, to make strategic political connections, to enter Parliament, to obtain knighthoods, and in every way to become central figures in that world of 'gentlemanly capitalism' which, as Cain and Hopkins assert, animated the expansion of England's empire in the nineteenth century.[2] Their position within the class structure was now secure. But whether, in spite of the increasing number of peerages—Francis Baring's son Alexander, who received the title of Lord Ashburton in 1793, being the first—they could be said to have entered the aristocracy is less clear. To Edgar Vincent, Evelyn Baring's young financial adviser in Egypt in the mid-1880s, Evelyn and his cousin Lord Northbrook were still 'good hard-working men of business' with only the 'imagination of ordinary middle class merchants', or so he wrote in the privacy of his diary.[3] Unlike the members of the old aristocracy, the source of their money could not be conveniently forgotten.

A more useful way of describing the Barings is as 'gentlemen', that is, as people who, when young, 'passed through a long process of education' based on a code of honour, part Christian, part feudal in origin, which placed duty before self-advancement, and who, when older, 'commanded positions in society which provided them with sufficient leisure to practice the gentlemanly arts, namely leadership, light administration and competitive sports'.[4] Gentlemen, as Cain and Hopkins also note, held a common view of the world and how it should be ordered. Their inevitable disputes were seen as being within the larger family. 'Disagreements were expressed freely because the values underlying them were not in question' and because they were aware that what they were arguing about was the best route to a common goal.[5]

---

[1] For a family history of the Barings, see Philip Ziegler, *The Sixth Great Power: A History of One of the Greatest of All Banking Families, the House of Barings, 1762–1929* (New York: Alfred Knopf, 1988). For the Rothschilds, Niall Ferguson, *The World's Banker: The History of the House of Rothschild* (London: Weidenfeld & Nicolson, 1998).

[2] Cain and Hopkins, *British Imperialism*, ch. 1.

[3] Note, 29 Aug. 1884, DP, Add. MS 48948, 112.

[4] Cain and Hopkins, *British Imperialism*, 23.   [5] Ibid. 28–9.

Evelyn's father, Henry, was Francis Baring's third son. His brilliance with figures was soon accompanied by a great deal of waywardness of behaviour and he was sent to China in his mid-teens. It does not seem to have worked as a cure and, on his return, he became a passionate and successful gambler, something which discouraged his family from allowing him to play a prominent role in the work of the bank, although he remained technically a partner until 1823.[6] According to Evelyn, Henry acquired his town house in Berkeley Square as the result of winning a playing-card bet against Lord Orford.[7] Henry soon gained further notoriety by marrying, and then divorcing, the daughter of an American senator, William Bingham of Philadelphia, with whom he had three sons and two daughters. He remarried in July 1825, taking as his new bride Cecilia Anne, one of the daughters of Admiral William Windham (sometimes Wyndham) of Fellbrigg Hall near Cromer. She was 20 at the time, he nearly 50. Their first child, William, was born in April 1826 and their second, Ned, a future head of the House of Barings, in 1828. Evelyn, the sixth, arrived on 26 February 1841, and the last, Walter, in 1844.

In spite of the disparity in their ages, Henry and Cecilia seem to have formed an unusual partnership based largely on a vigorous London social life. They had a wide circle of close political friends, including the Tory Prime Minister Sir Robert Peel, whom they, as Whigs, supported strongly through the fierce debates over the repeal of the Corn Laws, putting them in the opposite camp to most of their Tory landowning friends and neighbours. Henry had long been a popular figure in the London clubs. Nevertheless, a great deal of their social success was also due to Cecilia. She was an unusually well-educated woman, fluent in French, German, and Italian, and with a good knowledge of Latin and Greek. She loved to travel. She also had what Evelyn later described as a 'magnificent' contralto voice, which had been trained by Rossini and other leading Italian singers and composers.[8]

Perhaps because of all this Mrs Baring was accepted as a close confidante by Charles Greville, the major diarist and political commentator of his age, talking to him often in London and carrying on a spirited correspondence when she was back at Cromer Hall. His letters to her are full of lively discussions of political and religious matters as well as often scandalous gossip about the leading figures of the day, including frequent reference to

[6] Ziegler, *Sixth Great Power*, 40–7.   [7] BN 10.   [8] BN 46–7.

5

adulterous liaisons and bitterly conducted divorce cases among members of the aristocracy. They also include worldly, and no doubt very welcome, advice about the upbringing of her children. As he wrote on 10 January 1842, not quite a year after Evelyn's birth: 'I am very glad to hear that your boys give you satisfaction and promise well for the future. I have no doubt they will do well and be all you desire. Don't expect too much—don't require them to be paragons of much purity and you will not be disappointed.'[9]

Cromer Hall, where Evelyn Baring spent much of his first seven years, was rented from his mother's sister the Countess of Listowel. The original had burned down in 1829 and it was then rebuilt out of flintstone in the fashionable neo-Gothic style. Much later, when it was locally supposed to have provided the visiting Sir Arthur Conan Doyle with an idea for the gloomy Baskerville Hall, it might well have seemed more like the classic dark, crenellated Gothic country house designed, as one art historian has put it, to illustrate a kind of 'dramatised decay'.[10] The same somewhat forbidding aspect continues today. However, a lithograph from some time around 1850 shows it standing alone, with fine, rolling country in front and a distant view of Cromer church and the sea behind: a handsome two-storey house with five central bays and a mass of turret-like chimneys. To young Evelyn it must have seemed a magic, mysterious sort of a place, full of indulgent servants and interesting visitors but lacking, for long periods of time, the warmth of any kind of parental attention.

Cromer itself was a small fishing port of some 1,200 inhabitants, known mainly for its herrings, lobsters, and crabs. In the early 1840s it was also beginning to become popular as a 'bathing place of some celebrity' on account of its sandy beaches and beautiful scenery.[11] Like most Norfolk seaside towns it was also fighting a fierce battle against the sea. Large portions of its cliff and the houses built upon it had been washed away in a particularly fierce storm in 1837, and the new groyne built to protect it a year later was still something of an untested defence. There was little to recommend it to the Barings, however: no hotel, just a church and a circulating library. They found their entertainment in London, in the local great houses, and in visits from friends during the shooting season.

---

[9] Greville to Mrs Baring, 10 Jan. 1842, GC, Add. MS 41184.

[10] Review of Richard Davenport-Hines, *Gothic*, *Times Literary Supplement*, 22 Jan. 1999, 12.

[11] Samuel Lewis (ed.), *A Topographical Dictionary of England*, 7th edn., vol. i (London: Samuel Lewis, 1848), 730.

We are almost completely dependent on Evelyn's own 'Biographical Notes' for an account of his early years. Not surprisingly, one has to try to read between the lines for hints of his relationship with his parents. As he puts it, his father was old and distant, an invalid towards the end of his life of whom he saw very little. Moreover, in Evelyn's eyes, he very obviously belonged to another age: 'an old gentleman with a stiff white choker and nankeen trousers which buttoned at the ankle, who took snuff from an old-fashioned gold snuff-box and went out shooting on a rough but well-trained pony'.[12] Evelyn was very much more in awe of his mother. She, for her part, seems to have maintained a distance between them by regarding him as something of a dunce and, in his own words, 'the fool of the family'.[13] Nevertheless, Greville's replies to some of her letters seem to imply that she felt some concern about her boys' upbringing and well-being. And, according to Evelyn himself, she did keep one of his early poems in her scrapbook. It was entitled 'The Siege of Gibraltar' and began:

> When the Spanish appeared before Gibraltar,
> Brave Eliot shot them hot balls.
> And they were all drowned in the water,
> Except for a few men who were saved.[14]

Without really being able to know anything about the actual situation it seems likely that Evelyn found himself increasingly forced to vie with his older siblings, as well as his younger brother, Walter, for his mother's attention, and soon learned, like many others, that one way to do so was to combine youthful disingenuousness with naughtiness and playing the fool.

Looking back on it at the end of his life, Evelyn writes that he thinks that his mother guided him more 'by example than precept'. Her idea of forming the character of her children was to leave them a great deal alone. 'No one ever corrected me much as a boy. I had to find out from experience what I ought and what I ought not to say.'[15] Such neglect must often have been painful at the time, the more so as Cecilia often used to laugh at her children, something which the older Evelyn thought a great mistake. 'Youth is sensitive and cannot stand ridicule,' he wrote in the 'Biographical Notes', a very telling remark. Nevertheless, he never ceased wanting her respect. 'She thought me extremely ignorant and so I made an effort to learn.'[16] Just when this attempt began is less clear. It only really

---

[12] BN 10.   [13] BN 15.   [14] BN 11.   [15] BN 47–8.   [16] BN 49.

seems to have made any headway when he began learning classical Greek while an officer in the garrison on Corfu in the early 1860s, and could show this off to his mother when she came to the island on visits.

Evelyn's main companion was his older brother Tom, with whom he remained close for the whole of his life. They were given lessons together by their nurse, Ann Cox. She seems to have been something of a 'character'. Evelyn mentions that her husband was a recruiting sergeant and that she taught the boys many recruiting songs.[17] To Charles Greville she was an endless source of what he called 'nursiana', odd and amusing sayings of which he often begged Cecilia to send more.[18] Later the boys were placed in charge of a governess, Fräulein Ilhardt, a 'clever but bad-tempered woman' who left after a time to become a governess to Queen Victoria's children at Windsor.[19] The appearance of the Fräulein is one of the many examples of the way the Barings sought to maintain their German connections by encouraging an early knowledge of both the country and its language. There was also some attention to literature, particularly of Sir Walter Scott, whose *Ivanhoe* and *Bride of Lammamoor* Evelyn had read by the age of 8. He also responded eagerly to stirring tales like *The Last of the Mohicans* or stories of Red Indian life on the Midwestern plains, which were major influences on his play. Tom was always Red Eagle, Evelyn remembered, while he, as the younger, was forced to play the Osage chief, 'a thoroughly abominable character'.[20]

Another source of instruction was the long sermons given by the vicar of the family church, St Peter and St Paul, in Cromer. The Reverend Sharp talked in a broad Norfolk accent. He was what Evelyn calls a 'strong Protestant' and considered the 'Pope o' Rome' the embodiment of all the evil in the world.[21] Otherwise a great deal of time was spent outside with the gamekeepers, feeding the pheasants in summer and hunting rabbits and ferrets in the winter. This was enough to give both brothers a taste for shooting which lasted the rest of their lives.

Information about the outside world was provided by the frequent visitors both to Cromer Hall and then, when Evelyn was a bit older, during the family's summer migration to London. Local visitors included members of his mother's family such as her brother Henry, who was in the Navy and whom Evelyn remembered making him sing 'Hearts of oak are our ships, jolly tars are our men, we'll fight and we'll conquer again and again.'[22] Others came from further afield, like Sir Robert Peel, who gave

[17] BN 8–9.   [18] BN 9.   [19] BN 16.
[20] Ibid.   [21] BN 21–2.   [22] BN 5–6.

Evelyn a book, *Peter Parley's Tales*, with his name on the title page, or Lord Auckland, who was so short-sighted that he once shot at one of the keepers thinking his black leather gaiters were a hare.[23]

Visits to the London house were more exciting. There was no railway from Cromer until 1877 and the family travelled the 130 miles through Norfolk, Ipswich, and Colchester by road, with the parents in an open carriage called a britschka, and the children, servants, and luggage following in a horse-drawn van. Once in London, Evelyn remembered the Battle of Waterloo being refought almost every night at the dinner table. He also remembered meeting the Duke of Wellington as he and Tom and their nurse were passing Apsley House on their way back from playing in Hyde Park. Suddenly the nurse made a profound curtsy to a bent old white-haired man, who asked them who they were and then, on being told that they were the sons of Henry Baring, patted each of them on the head and said that he knew their father.[24]

It was on a visit to London in 1846 that he saw crowds standing in the streets waiting for a sight of a man they called Ibrahim Parker, actually Ibrahim Pasha, the eldest son and heir of Mehmet Ali (Muhammad Ali), the longtime ruler of Egypt.[25] And it was in London too that Evelyn's father died on 13 April 1848, just as the capital's elite were bracing for the huge Chartist demonstration in Hyde Park, with some, like Greville, defending their offices with piled copies of Privy Council registers as fortifications over which they proposed to fire their shotguns at any menacing crowd.[26] Life was never to be the same again.

A Wild Boy Sent Away to School

One of Cecilia's first responses to her husband's death was the decision that both Tom and Evelyn should be sent off to school. Clearly the events were connected. In a letter to Greville written just over a year later she mentions her worries about her older sons. 'It is awful work', he replied, 'finding positions for boys and settling their affairs—to say nothing of their scrapes.' William, the eldest, at 22, was 'an embarrassment' and, even though about to try the Church, would probably 'do nothing'. The twins were another problem. Only Edward, aged 20 when his father died, looked

[23] BN 21.   [24] BN 6.   [25] BN 7.
[26] Charles Greville, *Greville Memoirs: Reign of Queen Victoria 1837–1852*, vol. iii (London: Longmans, Green, 1885), 164–5.

set for a career, in banking. 'Ned will be a millionaire sooner or later,' Greville averred, and would 'in all probability become head of [the banking] house'.[27] Comforting though this prediction might be, Evelyn and Tom were made to pay some of the price. Evelyn was only seven and half when the decision was made and, in his own words, 'much too young'. However, he also adds that he had become 'rather unmanageable', one of his last feats being to chase the German governess round the conservatory with a red-hot poker.[28]

The school chosen by his mother was in the house of a clergyman, the Reverend Frederick Bickmore, who, like many of the early Victorian rural clergy, took in the children of some of their richer neighbours as pupils. Evelyn mentions the sons of Admiral Woodhouse, Lord Shaftesbury, and the Lambtons, as well as his own first cousin Frederick Windham.[29] Others recorded as resident by the 1851 census included the son of John Mott, a local Cromer justice of the peace. Bickmore had previously acted as tutor to the sons of Sir John Boilieu, who had bought an estate at Ketteringham near Norwich in 1841. Not only had he married the Boilieu children's governess, a Miss Paramond, but he had also found sufficient favour to be lodged in one of the estate's finer houses, Hethel Hall, a well-proportioned late eighteenth-century building with a substantial kitchen garden. A century later it was used as an officers' mess by American airmen during the Second World War and then pulled down shortly after. In 1851 it housed the two Bickmores, Evelyn, and seven other male pupils aged between 8 and 13, a cook, a coachman, and three housemaids.

It is not surprising that, in later years, Evelyn had few fond memories of the place. Mr Bickmore, he noted, was a fair classical scholar but he 'did not teach me much'. He based his lessons on Arnold's *Latin Grammar* and 'thrashed me unmercifully on the theory that I could learn but would not do so'. Meanwhile, Mrs Bickmore, 'armed with a stout ruler', tried vainly to teach him the piano.[30] Things certainly did not get off to a good start: Evelyn was involved in a fist fight with Albert Woodhouse after he had only been there for an hour.[31] There was little improvement after that, with Evelyn, like so many small boys, treating his teachers as his 'natural enemy'.[32] It was small comfort when, in later life, Evelyn was to come into contact with a number of colleagues who had had roughly similar Dickensian experience of early Victorian vicarage schools. Lord Salisbury, for example, recalled unhappily that his life at the Reverend Francis Faithfull's

[27] Greville to Mrs Baring, 15 Dec. 1849, GC, Add. MS 41185.
[28] BN 25.   [29] BN 30–1.   [30] BN 30.   [31] BN 26.   [32] BN 30.

establishment, where he was sent at the age of 6, was an 'a existence among devils'.[33]

Evelyn was also present during part of a now famous feud between Sir John Boilieu and the local vicar, the Reverend William Andrew, who had been evicted from Hethel Hall to make way for the Bickmores.[34] Perhaps in revenge, Andrew refused to live within the parish boundaries, as he was supposed, and added further injury to Sir John by refusing to preach sermons of which the lord of the manor approved. His version of their long struggle is recorded in great detail in his diaries.[35] Bickmore, wisely from his point of view, stayed doggedly on Sir John's side, often being called on to perform duties which Andrew might refuse.

Evelyn was witness to one of the more sensational events which marked the struggle, beginning with the 1849 murder of a local farmer. In his 'Biographical Notes' he remembers being given news of the murder by Bickmore himself, who was putting on his greatcoat in the school hall before rushing off in a state of great agitation.[36] Later, after the murderer had been apprehended, Andrew preached what was to become a nationally famous sermon in Ketterham church in April 1849, which Evelyn and the other boys might possibly have attended. Andrew had visited the condemned man in gaol just before his public execution and spoken with him about the need for repentance. This, in turn, became the subject of a 140-minute sermon in which he set out the gloomy doctrine that redemption rested not on individual will but on free grace, that Christians must continually be aware of the world and its temptations (he specifically mentioned the ballroom, the theatre, and the Sunday newspaper), and must always be searching in themselves to see if their lives were rushing them down the path taken by the Gadarine swine. The sermon caused a local sensation and was then published in pamphlet form for the wider national audience.[37] If the 8-year old Evelyn were indeed present, it must certainly have given him considerable pause for thought.

Another memory is that of the 'grown-ups' in Hethel Hall waiting for the arrival of each monthly instalment of David Copperfield with 'great excitement'. The fact that much of the early part was set locally, in Norfolk, clearly added to the sense of anticipation. For Evelyn, Barkis, the gloomy carter was later to remind him vividly of his own coachman,

---

[33] Andrew Roberts, *Salisbury: Victorian Titan* (London: Weidenfeld & Nicolson, 1999), 8.
[34] Owen Chadwick, *Victorian Miniature* (London: Hodder & Stoughton, 1960), 46.
[35] These are used extensively by Chadwick, ibid.   [36] BN 26.
[37] Chadwick, *Victorian Miniature*, 113–18.

Dan, who drove him and Tom along the Norfolk-to-Cromer toll road for their school holidays. They vied with each other as to who should sit next to him up on the driver's box.[38]

Evelyn's last term was greatly affected by his mother's decision, taken after a great deal of hivering and hovering and much advice from Charles Greville, to vacate Cromer Hall in 1852 and to spend all her time in Berkeley Square. Under the new dispensation Tom, who was clearly thought the brighter of the two, was to go to Eton, and Evelyn to the newly established Ordnance School at Carshalton, Surrey, in preparation for entry into the Royal Military Academy at Woolwich. It was necessary to pass an entrance examination first, and it was to this end that the Reverend Bickmore darkened Evelyn's last months at the school by trying to teach him decimal fractions just when he had been about to start Greek.[39]

So ended Evelyn's first eleven years spent largely in Norfolk. The fact that he chose the title of Lord Cromer, when raised to the peerage in 1892, shows that his early life there must have made a strong impression, even if he never lived there again and rarely returned. He left with a pronounced Norfolk accent, a number of useful social connections, and memories which, however mixed, seem to have provided him with a kind of emotional anchor for the rest of his life. Part of it must have been the pleasurable recollections of roaming the estate at Cromer Hall. Part may also have been the powerful effects of the views of the flat, rich countryside under the large Norfolk sky, observed at leisure during the long, slow, cart rides to London and to Bickmore's school, and then of the wild, elemental scenes along the North Sea coast. A century later, as a national service officer proceeding in crawling convoys between Colchester in Essex and the training area at Stanford in Norfolk in the hot summer of 1955, I felt something of the physical strength of the landscape myself, with its huge, rich agricultural estates, its distant views of great, solid houses, and, along the coast, its ceaseless battle against the encroaching sea. The spirit and tenacity of a Cromwell seemed to haunt the place, as did the vivid, stoical presence of Dickens's Ham, Peggotty, and all the others who made their precarious living along the water's edge.

In Evelyn's days there was also what many born in Norfolk experienced as a pre-industrial simplicity of social relations. Master and servant seemed to exist in a purely agricultural setting with none of the vulgar competition

[38] BN 29.   [39] BN 31.

for wealth, none of the overt class tensions, to be found in England's factory towns. Those who left often found it again, or, rather, imagined they had found it, in the villages and among the tribes of Africa and Asia, making life among those distant peoples something like an agreeable home from home. In Cain and Hopkins's apt phrase, they took to the paternalism of Empire 'as squires to the manor born'.[40]

[40] Cain and Hopkins, *British Imperialism*, 34. The idea itself comes from Joseph Alois Schumpeter, *Imperialism and Social Classes*, trans. Heinz Norden (New York: A. M. Kelley, 1951).

2

A Military Education
1852–1858

Carshalton Ordnance School

The military school to which Evelyn Baring was sent in 1852 at the age of 11 had been started only a few years earlier as an experiment to prepare young boys for a cadetship at the Royal Military Academy, Woolwich (RMA). It was not a success and came to an end in 1859 after only ten years owing to a disagreement between the masters. It was quartered in Carshalton House, most parts of which had been built by an East India Company merchant in the eighteen century, and leased to the Board of Ordnance in 1847. A drawing of 1850 shows it to have been an imposing, three-storey structure. It was built in a brownish-yellow brick, with decorations of better-quality red brick and stone window sills. There was also a large formal garden with a lake, an island, and an ornamental bridge. The same drawing shows groups of boys in Eton jackets, white shirts, and caps, sitting or standing by the lake or rowing in two boats on it. The house still exists as the home of St Philomena's Roman Catholic Girls' School.

At the time of Evelyn's arrival the establishment consisted of a headmaster, two assistant masters, and twelve servants.[1] There was room for about a hundred boys, although in the mid-1850s there were only 'some eighty' actually in residence.[2] According to the *Regulations for Admission* published in October 1849, it was necessary both to be nominated by the Master-General of the Ordnance (who happened to be an old friend of the Barings) and to pass an examination and a medical. As far as the examination was

[1] Captain F. G. Guggisberg, *'The Shop': The Story of the Royal Military Academy*, 2nd edn. (London: Cassell, 1892), 69.   [2] BN 32.

concerned, there were only two subjects. One was English. Candidates had to be able to spell correctly, to write from dictation, and to possess a 'good, legible hand'. The second subject, arithmetic, required a candidate to work regularly and correctly to the four rules of addition, subtraction, multiplication, and division. The examination was conducted personally by the Headmaster. Given the fact that Evelyn Baring was later unable to remember ever taking such a thing, it may be that, for boys with his connections, a brief interview was considered sufficient.[3]

The period of study was limited to three years, at the end of which there was a final examination upon which entry to the RMA depended. This consisted of English, arithmetic, algebra, geometry, painting and drawing, and history, the last to include a 'competent knowledge' of English and 'general acquaintance' with the leading points of ancient and modern history. There was a graduated level of fees, those for boys in Evelyn's category (i.e. 'sons of noblemen who were not officers in the army or navy') being set at £110 a year. In the school's first years the compulsory clothing consisted of a greatcoat, three jackets, three pairs of dark-coloured trousers, ten pairs of white shorts, nine pocket handkerchiefs, three pairs of boots or shoes, and six towels. However, in Evelyn's second year, a new headmaster, Captain Peter Maclean, reorganized training on a military basis and required boys to dress in army uniform. Pocket money was set at a shilling a week, except for monitors, who were allowed 1s. 6d. No boy was allowed to have more than a sovereign (£1) in his possession.

Evelyn's memories of the time he spent at Carshalton were mixed. Discipline, he wrote in the 'Biographical Notes', was very severe, with birching of the bare flesh and the cane in constant use. He himself was never birched. But he was once given twenty strokes of the cane with all the strength of the Headmaster's arm and bore the marks for weeks. This was 'far too cruel a punishment', he writes, 'for a boy of twelve'.[4] He did not think that he was a popular boy with the masters, being 'undisciplined, far from industrious, full of animal spirits and up to all the tricks of the hour'. As a result he was often punished. To make matters worse, the food was 'detestable', so much so that, according to the Baring family doctor, Sir Henry Holland, it was responsible for a bad eruption which broke out on his face. Sir Henry sagely recommended drinking port as a cure. However, Baring also adds that his 'lot was lightened when Lord Raglan, another family friend, visited the school and asked after him'.[5]

---

[3] Ibid.   [4] Ibid.   [5] BN 32–4, 39.

On the brighter side, the boys were encouraged to play the usual games, not only cricket, which Evelyn never took to, but also football and hockey, the latter made particularly enjoyable when played on the frozen lake.[6] There was also bathing in the lake in summer, which he found more pleasant than the weekly winter bath every Saturday night, in which three boys were required to share the same water.[7]

The 'Biographical Notes' also provide a few glimpses of the process of growing up and taking notice of the world. For example, there is Baring's comment that he was the only boy who took, and read, a daily newspaper, something which suggests an interest in the progress of the Crimean War, the main political and military event of his years at Carshalton.[8] Another refers to a rather unusual event which took place during his summer holidays in 1853, when he was 12. As part of his mother's kill-or-cure promotion of self-reliance, she left him to find his own way back from Salzburg to London. It seems to have worked. Even though he found that he had left his money and his passport in the diligence between Salzburg and Munich while it stopped for lunch, he says he was 'not the least perturbed'. He simply went to the best hotel in Munich and waited until he had recovered both of the missing items before continuing on his way.[9] Clearly both mother and son had all the confidence of the European moneyed elite to which they belonged. It also seemed to bear out Greville's 1849 assertion that, though the Baring boys had many problems, 'your boys are well disposed and not paupers' and so 'you are better off than most mothers'.[10]

Altogether, Evelyn's treatment of the incident is an interesting example of the way the 'Biographical Notes' are structured, accentuating his process of individual self-education and self-reliance while downplaying the importance of family and money. Nevertheless, his mother's use of her connections is not entirely ignored. Evelyn also tells the story of how, having been rejected for the RMA on the grounds of his defective eyesight, Cecilia simply got in a carriage and drove down to Army Headquarters in Horse Guards Parade, where she quickly persuaded the new Master-General of the Ordnance, Lord Raglan, to get the case reconsidered.[11] Meanwhile, Evelyn himself does not seem to have had any problem with the entrance examination, although, as he himself notes,

---

[6] BN 35.   [7] Marquess of Zetland, *Lord Cromer* (London: Hodder & Stoughton, 1932), 25.
[8] Ibid. 26.   [9] BN 48.
[10] Greville to Mrs Baring, 15 Dec. 1849, GC, Add. MS 41185.   [11] BN 38–9.

he had never heard of anyone not passing.[12] The fact that, given the demands of the Crimean War, the army then needed all the young officer cadets it could find was no doubt another important factor.

The Royal Military Academy, Woolwich

The RMA, Woolwich, for boys wishing to enter the Engineers or the Artillery, was one of the two nineteenth-century establishments for officer training, the other being the Royal Military College, Sandhurst, for those opting for a career in the infantry or cavalry. Evelyn arrived in 1855 just as the first winds of change were affecting the Army after all the military and organizational failures revealed in the Crimea. As a result of the initiatives begun by Lord Panmure, Florence Nightingale's fellow reformer Sidney Herbert, it was made possible to enter by an open exam and then to proceed straight into the Senior 'practical' class without passing through the first two years of what were known as 'theoretical' studies. Before this the only method of entry was either by nomination or by passing through Ordnance School. In 1855 thirty-one of the candidates entered by the new way, as opposed to thirty by direct nomination to the practical class, and ninety-one, like Evelyn, either from Carshalton or under the old nomination system.[13]

According to Evelyn Baring's military records, he was appointed a gentleman cadet on 7 August 1855, aged 14 years and 5 months, and on 17 August joined the bottom of the four classes.[14] His uniform was a double-breasted, blue tailcoat faced with red, a stiff leather stock under the collar, and a white, pipe-clayed belt. He wore a forage cap on weekdays and a tall black shako on Sundays, its white, horse-hair plume reminding him of a 'shaving brush'.[15] According to Guggisberg's history of the RMA, this style of uniform was changed the next year to a busby and tunic.[16] First- and second-year cadets were paid 2s. 8d. a day, which was supposed to cover mess expenses and clothing. This was raised to 3s. in 1857.[17]

Guggisberg gives a detailed account of life in the RMA by a cadet who joined from Carshalton two years after Evelyn. It coincided with the new regime introduced by the commandant, General Wilford, who was against anything he felt was a luxury. Each day began at 7.55 a.m. with a breakfast

[12] BN 38.   [13] Guggisberg, 'The Shop', 88.
[14] RMA, Cadet Register of Royal Military Academy at Woolwich, PRO, WO 149/6.
[15] BN 40.   [16] Guggisberg, 'The Shop', 91.   [17] Ibid. 96.

of coffee, sausages, brown bread, and butter. This was followed by three hours of study, a rushed snack of bread, cheese, and beer in the mess hall, and then drill from 11.15 to 1 p.m. 'Dinner' (lunch) consisted of a joint of meat with potatoes and beer, with apple pie on Tuesdays and plum duff on Sundays. There was more study from 2.30 to 4.00, another hour of drill, two more hours of classes from six to eight, and finally a supper of sausages with bread, butter, and tea. The day ended with a 10 p.m. roll-call. As General Wilford did not approve of providing lights to go to bed by, they were extinguished as soon as the roll of names had been called and the cadets had to undress as best they could in the dark.[18]

The cadets slept four to a room with a corporal ('head of room') in charge. Baths were in the yard and supplied with cold-water taps only. First-year cadets (known as 'snookers') had to fill the baths every morning with cans. It was a very cold business when wearing only a pair of trousers, a dressing gown, and slippers. In summer the cadets bathed in a nearby pond and were taught to swim after a fashion by 'more or less repeated duckings'. There was a great deal of forbidden drinking and smoking, which the authorities tried to control by a system of spies.

According to the same former cadet, the snookers were forced to obey each and every command of an older cadet, as well as to pay strict attention to a number of unwritten laws. For example, they could not use the library or the racquets courts, had to wear their chinstrap down, to keep coats buttoned up, and their stocks round their necks, at all times. Not surprisingly, there was a great deal of bullying. Snookers were 'terribly fagged' and frequently thrashed with belts and tennis bats. A crisis arose at this time when a cadet revealed that some of the older cadets who had been kept back for failing exams demanded that the younger ones answer only half the questions in their end-of-year exams, presumably to keep the average scores down. News of some excessively heavy thrashings by the older cadets also leaked out. The authorities tried to make enquiries, but when none of the younger cadets would reveal the names of their oppressors, all the snookers were marched off to hospital, where they were examined by medical officers. Anyone with bruises was required to reveal how he had got them. This led to some of the older cadets being dismissed and others rusticated for a period of time.

Evelyn Baring does not write directly about these events in his 'Biographical Notes'. What he remembered was the unwise division between

---

[18] Ibid. 91–4.

the civilian instructors and the military officers, with the latter in charge of training and discipline although having no experience of managing boys. There was no flogging by members of the staff, he notes, but the award of an extra drill for the slightest offence. It involved marching up and down the barrack yard in the early morning and all recreation periods carrying a heavy old flintlock musket.[19] He was, however, once given a 'licking' with a racquet handle by an Old Cadet called Price for throwing a jackboot at his head.[20]

After two years of classwork and drill, Baring joined the first ('practical') class in September 1857. This meant a move to the Sapper Barracks nearby, with the senior cadets only returning to the RMA itself for special occasions. One such was the visit of Queen Victoria to inspect the artillery siege train on its return from the Crimea. Baring was Number Two on one of the three-pounder gun crews which fired the official salute.[21] The practical side involved digging trenches and gun emplacements, building temporary bridges, moving guns around the Essex Marshes, and taking riding lessons at the Royal Artillery Barracks. There were also some more classroom lessons and lectures. Although he passed his final exams in all subjects, Baring does not seem to have done so with distinction. He never became a cadet corporal, nor is there any record of him having won a prize.[22] If he broke out of barracks to spend a night in London, as many did, or even if he started to smoke at Woolwich, he does not say.

Evelyn Baring was commissioned as a lieutenant in the Royal Artillery on 22 June 1858. He chose the gunners over the sappers (Royal Engineers) because he thought the work of the latter 'too sedentary'. Interestingly, he notes that his mother could not possibly have exercised any influence over his choice as she had only the vaguest notion of the difference between the two corps.[23] In spite of the fact that Woolwich was so close to Mrs Baring's residence in Berkeley Square, and that he must certainly have returned to her London home on most of his leaves, it does not suggest that they could have spent very much time discussing either his training or his future career.

Baring, or perhaps his mother, then used the influence of their former Norfolk neighbour Colonel Wodehouse, the Adjutant-General of the Artillery, to obtain a posting to the garrison battery on Corfu, one of the seven Greek islands which had been under British control since the Napoleonic Wars. Baring gives as his reason the fact that he had heard

[19] BN 40–1.   [20] Cromer to Major Leslie, 17 Mar. 1913, CP/2, FO 633/24.
[21] BN 42.   [22] RMA, Cadet Register.   [23] BN 43.

good accounts of the shooting to be had on the mainland coast, just a few miles away by boat.[24] On the way out he spent some time with his mother travelling through Europe to Venice, where he was to take the boat on to Corfu. On parting, she gave her now grown-up son a gold locket, which he was to wear on his watch-chain for the rest of his life. Inside was her portrait and the inscription 'Evelyn Baring. In memory of Venice. September 1858'.[25]

It is clear that Baring did not have much of a schooling, not even the 'Classics only and the Classics taught badly', which Edward Bulwer Lytton described as the standard diet of the contemporary English public school.[26] It was something he bitterly regretted in later life. Even history and geography were struck from the RMA syllabus in 1856, and there were no classics at all, leaving him with just the Latin he had learned from the Reverend Bickmore. It seems that he had no special teacher to inspire him or to encourage him to extend himself, no one to help him develop any intellectual discipline. What he did have, though, was an experience of a small part of the British Army's attempt to come to terms with the short-comings exposed by the Crimean War, something which made him quick to join the ranks of the military reformers when he was seconded to work at the War Office ten years later.

Evelyn Baring's years at Carshalton, and then at Woolwich, were also the period of what would now be called his adolescence. Apart from puberty itself, these years are also supposed to be a time when, in John Mack's words, 'the establishment of a firm personal identity occurs, when questions of adult sexuality are being faced, when a comfortable emotional distance for one's parents is being established, childhood ideals are brought into harmony with adult realities and most childhood fantasies are given up'.[27] Whether this could possibly have worked out in quite such an orderly way for the bulk of early Victorian males hurried so quickly from childhood to adult responsibilities seems highly unlikely. Certainly some rearrangement of Evelyn's relationships with his mother and his brothers must have taken place at this time.

As a Baring, Evelyn was also in a good position to learn something about the great world of politics and banking. He tells us, for example, that he

---

[24] Zetland, *Lord Cromer*, 27.   [25] BN 44–5.

[26] Edward Lytton, *England and the English*, new edn. (Chicago: Chicago University Press, 1970), 7.

[27] John Mack, *A Prince of Our Disorder: The Life of T. E. Lawrence* (Boston: Little, Brown, 1976), 476 n.

went to hear John Bright give a speech some time towards the beginning of his ten-year campaign to extend the franchise to include parts of the working class, and was much impressed by Bright's reference to the importance of bridging the gap between 'Belgrave Square and Bethnal Green'.[28] As John Vincent points out, 'Bright made young Whigs more radical', adding that, during the 1860s, so many were attracted to this path that, for men like Baring's cousin Lord Northbrook, radicalism became a high road 'not [to] the wilderness but to office'.[29] Nevertheless, my impression is that, when Baring first went to Corfu, he still had a great deal of growing up to do and that, for a while at least, the boy and the young man coexisted quite easily within the context of the comfortable way of life permitted to any well-connected army officer with plenty of leisure time on his hands.

[28] BN 37.
[29] John Vincent, *The Formation of the Liberal Party 1857–1868* (London: Constable, 1966), 15–16, 205.

3

Garrison Life in Corfu
1858–1864

A Subaltern's Delight

Corfu is the most southerly of the string of seven Ionian Islands which stretch north–south at the point where the Adriatic meets the Ionian Sea between the Italian and Albanian–Greek coasts. The islands had been under Venetian control for many centuries until they were occupied, first by the French, then by the British, during the Napoleonic Wars. Their putative independence was acknowledged at the Congress of Vienna in 1814. A year later, as a result of the Treaty of Paris, they were recognized by the British, the French, and the Russians as a 'single', 'free', and 'independent' state, known as the United States of the Ionian Islands, under the protection of Great Britain.

A British Lord High Commissioner was instructed to provide the islands with a constitution. Unfortunately for the islanders, the first High Commissioner, Sir Thomas Maitland, thought them unfit for parliamentary government and drew up a document which placed as little power as possible in the hands of the elected members of a bicameral legislature containing representatives from all seven islands.[1] Nevertheless, as time went on, a small group of local politicians learned to use the new machinery to their advantage, as well as to embark on an increasingly vociferous campaign for union with Greece. The notion of 'Greece for the Greeks', a patriotic slogan which Evelyn Baring was to come across in other forms throughout his overseas life, was much in evidence by the late 1850s and was warmly supported by the hierarchy of the Greek Orthodox

---

[1] H. Jervis-White, *History of the Island of Corfu and of the Republic of the Ionian Islands* (Chicago: Argonaut, 1970; first pub. London, 1852), 200–5.

Church.[2] The islands' 200,000 or so inhabitants were mostly Greek Orthodox but with some Roman Catholics. The country folk spoke Greek, the urban population generally Italian.

Corfu was the largest of the seven islands. Shaped like an elongated lamb chop with the meaty part to the north-east, it was about 60 miles long and 30 miles across at its widest point. Corfu town, the capital, was situated about halfway down the eastern side, facing the mainland. In 1860 it contained some 17,700 inhabitants, of whom 4,450 were foreigners. Its main feature, the palace of the High Commissioner, was built in 1816. Next to it stood the residence of the President of what was known locally as the Septinsular Republic. Both stood at one end of the Esplanade, a long open space with a tree-shaded walkway on one side and a handsome, colonnaded row of houses on the other.[3] The island itself was known for its great beauty. The Venetians had succeeded in turning it into a vast orchard with olive groves on the slopes of the hills, lemons, oranges, peaches, apricots, and pears in the shallow valleys and across the plains. It had its own mountain, Panrator, which rose nearly 3,000 feet, as well as magnificent views of the yet higher mountains, snow-capped in winter, on the mainland. Its spectacular scenery attracted large numbers of visiting artists, including Edward Lear, who painted there for three winters, 1856–8.

As a member of a garrison which was engaged in largely ceremonial duties, Lieutenant Baring did not have a great deal to do apart from making sure that the guns under his command remained in good working order. He was asked to undertake the management of the Artillery Officers' Mess accounts, which had got into some disorder, perhaps his first real opportunity to demonstrate a latent skill at finance.[4] He was a frequent contributor to the garrison newspaper, which had been started by his close friend Arthur Ponsonby, who was aide-de-camp to General Sir George Buller, the Garrison Commander and whose sister later married Evelyn's eldest brother, William.[5] For the rest, he was free to enjoy what one contemporary British resident described as a 'kind of earthly paradise' for army subalterns: 'excellent shooting in Greece and Albania, delightful yachting excursions and [mounted] paper chases for the ladies and gentlemen'.[6]

[2] Edmond Spencer, *Travels in European Turkey in 1850*, vol. ii (London: Colbourn, 1851), 222.
[3] Jervis-White, *History of the Island of Corfu*, 263.
[4] Sir Henry Drummond Wolff, *Rambling Recollections*, vol. i (London: Macmillan, 1908), 291–2.
[5] BN 63.
[6] Viscount Kirkwall (ed.), *Four Years in the Ionian Islands: Their Political and Social Condition with a History of the British Protectorate*, vol. ii (London: Chapman & Hall, 1864), 17.

Baring's particular interest was in the shooting. His father had left him £1,200 in his will and he used most of it to maintain a yacht, which allowed him to make hunting expeditions to the Gulf of Arta, a long, landlocked inlet on the mainland, about 50 miles, sailing south-east of Corfu town.[7] There he shot birds, wild boar, and deer, as well as a few chamois, which had to be stalked with great difficulty because of lack of local assistance. His brother Tom came out to join him on at least one of these expeditions, and extracts from their gamebook suggest a huge slaughter of woodcock and not a few ducks.[8] It was Baring's love of hunting that accounts for his one major misdemeanour. In a hurry to be off, he decided to speed up the return salute to an Ottoman warship that was just entering Corfu harbour. Instead of firing the twenty-one-gun salute at the regulation 15-second intervals, he ordered three quick salvoes of seven shots each. Such a cannonade could not fail to arouse the attention of General Buller, whose house was just below the battery.[9] Baring's own account does not mention the nature of the reprimand. Perhaps because it affected only a Turkish vessel, the crime was not considered very great.

It is also very likely that Baring took a local Corfiote mistress. This was common practice among military officers of his class as well as trainee diplomats. Posted to the Madrid Embassy in 1862, his future rival Wilfrid Blunt engaged a Spanish Irishman to procure him what his biographer calls a 'respectable mistress' who would instruct him in her language 'and anything else he needed to know'. The result was a period of cohabitation with a 23-year-old woman who had been abandoned by her husband and who was forced to earn a living by sewing.[10] In Baring's case, evidence comes from the fact that he acknowledged the existence of an illegitimate daughter, Louisa Sophia, born some time in the summer of 1863. Proof is to be found in a file of his correspondence with the Catholic Archbishop of Corfu while in India in 1880–2, when Louisa Sophia was just about to come of age. It is clear from this exchange that, at some time, the girl had been placed in the care of nuns.[11] What the letters do not make clear is whether this was done out of social or economic necessity or because her mother had died.

[7] BN 68–9.

[8] BN 54.

[9] Zetland, *Lord Cromer*, 27–8.

[10] Elizabeth Longford, *A Pilgrimage of Passion: The Life of Wilfrid Scawen Blunt* (London: Granada, 1982), 31–2.

[11] CP/1, file marked 'Letters about the girl Louisa Sophia' (in Evelyn Baring's hand) and '1st Earl's correspondence about his illegitimate daughter Louisa' (in another).

Baring must have returned to Britain on leave some time in 1860 because this is the year of a photograph taken in London of the 'Sons of Mrs Henry Baring'.[12] There are only five in the picture, William, Edward (Ned), Richard, the 19-year-old Evelyn, and Walter. Missing are Tom, who was most probably in America, and Robert, the other twin. They are wearing almost identical dark frock coats, white shirts, black cravats, and well-polished black shoes. The photographer had them carefully posed round two chairs, and equally carefully made them look in different directions. Evelyn, on the extreme right, has one knee on one of the chairs and his head in profile to reveal a fine straight Roman nose. He looks slim and taller than at least two of his brothers. One much later observation puts his height at 6 feet.[13]

Baring took another home leave the following year and was given permission to travel back through the Ottoman provinces, which still stretched from northern Greece to the Austro-Hungarian border along the Danube at Belgrade. His route took him from Durazzo (now Durrës) on the Albanian coast near Tirana to Whiddin (Vidin), halfway between Belgrade and Bucharest, about 160 miles as the crow flies. There he had his first real experience of Ottoman government. He did not much like what he saw. 'Wherever the Turk was supreme,' he later observed, 'there was squalor, desolation and the absence of almost every trace of civilization.' However, as he also pointed out, 'order was preserved'. It was a result of this experience, he says, that he began to question the traditional policy of upholding the Ottoman Empire as a barrier to Russian expansion into the Mediterranean, still a rare point of view at the time, although one that was to gain increasing strength, particularly among Whigs and Liberals, in the 1870s.[14]

At some point in his early years in Corfu, Baring began to be aware of his lack of learning and became determined to do something about it. In the 'Biographical Notes' he explains that this was the result of his association with officers who were much better educated than himself and the discovery that 'he was extremely ignorant of a number of things which they knew and I ought to have known'. He had no Greek, he writes, and very little Latin. And while he remembered some German, his French was 'extremely bad'.[15] As a result he began to learn Italian (possibly from his

---

[12] A copy can be found in BA, DEP 272.

[13] Quoted in Peter Mellini, *Sir Eldon Gorst: The Overshadowed Proconsul* (Stanford, Calif.: Hoover Institution Press, 1977), 54.

[14] BN 65.   [15] BN 55.

mistress) until he could read and speak it fluently. He also devoted a good deal of time to playing the piano and achieved a 'fair degree of proficiency'. But the achievement that gave him greatest satisfaction was learning first modern, then some ancient, Greek from a local tutor, although without ever mastering the grammar properly.[16] He certainly did well enough to impress his mother when she came out to visit him in 1863 or 1864.[17] Thinking back on it when writing the 'Notes', he imagines that 'the first incident that caused her to take any real interest in me was when she visited Corfu and found that I could put her right over translating the chorus from the Agamemnon of Aeschylus which I happened recently to have studied'.[18]

Aide-de-Camp to the High Commissioner

Two people whom Baring got to know in Corfu in 1862 contributed greatly to his drive for self-education. The first was the High Commissioner, Sir Henry Storks, who asked him to become one of his two aides-de-camp (ADCs) when his previous aide was in too much pain from his Crimean War wounds to continue his work.[19] This not only saved Baring from a return to Britain with the rest of his unit but also gave him the beginnings of a new career as a military administrator. Not for the last time, he was to benefit from some of the fallout from the war in the Crimea.

Sir Henry was a career officer who had served in the Ionian Island garrison in the late 1830s and early 1840s. He was later made High Commissioner after William Gladstone, still a relatively young member of the British Parliament, had been asked to conduct an inquiry into what was perceived as a serious crisis in the islands in October 1858. This stemmed from the grant of a new constitution in 1848 which had greatly diminished the powers of the High Commissioner vis-à-vis the islands' president and parliament. The result was a struggle between successive commissioners and the legislative assembly, leading to growing problems with tax collection, an increasing deficit, and so a shortage of the funds

[16] BN 56.
[17] Drummond Wolff, *Rambling Recollections*, i. 358. Drummond Wolff mentions that Mrs Baring and one of her sons came out 'towards the end of our stay' (which ended in June 1864).
[18] BN 49.
[19] Drummond Wolff, *Rambling Recollections*, i. 291.

needed to maintain the islands' crumbling infrastructure. Gladstone visited all seven islands between November and Christmas 1859, gauging local opinion and trying to find a way out of the impasse. In the end he found himself unable to recommend either union with Greece, as the most vocal of the politicians demanded, or a suspension of the 1848 Constitution. All he could do was advocate ways of turning what he believed to be 'the mockery of free government' into more of a reality.[20]

Gladstone also came to the conclusion that the then High Commissioner was unable to cooperate with the members of the legislative assembly and so attempted briefly to act in his place. This proved to be a particularly tense time as the assembly itself immediately passed a resolution stating that it was the unanimous will of the Ionian people that they be united with Greece. Gladstone replied by suggesting that it be sent in the form of a petition to Queen Victoria. Excitement mounted further. Town bells were rung for two days, the Roman Catholic archbishop, a leading unionist, ordered a *Te Deum*, and there was yet another lengthy set of speeches in the assembly. In the midst of all this Gladstone discovered that it was impossible to combine management of the island with his British parliamentary duties and decided to return home. It was then that Storks was named as his successor.

Sir Henry was born in 1811. During his first period of service on the islands he had married an Italian woman who had helped him gain a fluent command of her language. His wife died in 1848 and they had no children. This encouraged Storks to keep a bachelor household with his ADCs and a few army friends for company. He often faced criticism for not inviting local people to the High Commissioner's palace, something which his private secretary, Henry Drummond Wolff, and his wife tried for a while to remedy.[21] However, he did manage to bring the political furore under temporary control by proroguing the assembly for most of 1859 and then again from March 1861 to March 1862. He used the resulting breathing space to bring the budget back into balance while finding small sums of money for the most pressing of the much-needed public works.[22]

Such was the situation when Lieutenant Baring joined the palace staff. No doubt his new knowledge of Italian and Greek were regarded as points in his favour. However, his Greek was not anything of the same standard as

[20] John Morley, *The Life of William Ewart Gladstone*, vol. i. (New York: Macmillan, 1903), 602, 610–17.

[21] Kirkwall (ed.), *Four Years in the Ionian Islands*, ii. 5, 7, 23.

[22] Ibid. i, 248, 250, 265.

the other ADC, another artillery officer called George Strahan, who had been chosen by Gladstone himself because of great proficiency in the language. Baring writes that they were used more as administrative private secretaries than as mere military aides.[23] They lived with the High Commissioner in the palace, which doubled as the centre of government. On the ground floor were the offices of the islands' second chamber, the senate, on one side, and those of the chief secretary, in charge of the civil administration, and the chief of police, on the other. Storks and his aides worked in rooms on the first floor, which was reached by a fine double staircase. From their windows they had a marvellous view of the Corfu channel and the Albanian mountains beyond. The palace had a large garden at the front, with palms and evergreen shrubs, and a smaller, private one at the back.[24] It was transformed into a museum of archaeology in 1935.

The political situation continued to be tense. Storks ran into serious trouble later in 1862 for dismissing several local judges. He then had to deal with the situation produced by the popular revolt against King Otho of Greece in October with the King being forced to flee Athens in a British ship and arriving in Corfu angry and in a state of great disarray. Baring remembered the King's fustanella (Greek kilt) as very dirty, and the Queen, in tears, telling him a very long story designed to demonstrate that she and her husband were entirely blameless for all that had occurred.[25] In the event this provided a way forward for the British Government. The vacant throne was offered to Prince William George of Denmark, someone regarded as very much more liberal and open-minded than his dictatorial and often brutal predecessor. Once the Prince had accepted, the British announced the election of special representatives to ascertain the wishes of the Ionian people with regard to union.

This was the beginning of yet more excitement in Corfu. No sooner had the new King been officially accepted by the Greek people in June 1863 than the Catholic archbishop invited Storks to join him for another *Te Deum*. The High Commission asked Drummond Wolff to act as his representative with Baring as his aide. As Drummond Wolff was later to describe the scene,

We were greeted with cheers, and on our arrival at the church, 'God Save the Queen' was played. I was placed between the Consuls of France and Russia [two of

[23] BN 66.
[24] D. N. Anstead, *The Ionian Islands in the Year 1863* (London: W. H. Allen, 1863), 23.
[25] BN 79.

the other signatories of the Treaty of Paris]. A prayer was offered for the King of the Greeks and that was followed by the Danish National Anthem and cries of 'Zhtw' ['union' in Greek]. A prayer was then offered to Her Majesty. 'God Save the Queen' was again played, and there was more shouting. Then came a prayer for unity and the Greek Hymn. Vast crowds, carrying Greek and English flags, marched to the Palace, where the High Commissioner was warmly cheered; and the town was afterwards illuminated.[26]

There was no going back, and in October 1863 a freely elected assembly voted unanimously for union with Greece. Even though the assembly itself was then prorogued for refusing to agree to the conditions laid down for union, a process of international negotiation had been set in train which no one wished stopped. Finally, as a result of a treaty signed in London between the three co-signatories of the Treaty of Paris, Britain, France, and Russia, and Greece on 29 March 1864, the terms and conditions were agreed for a handover to take place in a little over two months' time.

All this provided a very useful apprenticeship for Baring in administration, politics, and diplomacy, as well as in dealing with a popular nationalist movement. Storks, as he observed in the 'Biographical Notes', though not a good soldier, was a first-rate civil administrator and diplomat. He also commended himself to the young Baring by being a 'rigid economist' when it came to dealing with public money.[27] Baring almost certainly shared Storks's low opinion of the local Ionian politicians.[28] Nevertheless, he was sure that if the Ionians wanted to join Greece, they should be allowed to do so. This was much in keeping with a youthful radicalism characterized by his support for John Bright's wing of the Liberal Party at home and for nationalists like Cavour and Garibaldi abroad.[29] Whereas his political views became more conservative as he grew older, his belief that it had been right to return the islands to Greece never wavered.[30]

Ethel

Evelyn Baring's second significant encounter in 1862 was with the 17-year-old Ethel Errington, brought to the island with her two sisters by her father, Sir Rowland Errington, after the untimely death of her mother,

---

[26] Drummond Wolff, *Rambling Recollections*, i. 384–5.   [27] BN 68.
[28] Drummond-Wolff, *Rambling Recollections*, i. 375–9.
[29] BN 37.   [30] BN 87–8.

Julia, in 1861.[31] Sir Rowland had accepted an invitation from his deceased wife's sister Henrietta Buller, the wife of the commanding officer, to spend part of the winter on Corfu. Sir Rowland came from the old Catholic branch of the Cheshire Stanleys and owned a house at Puddington in the Wirrall. He had recently inherited his baronetcy from his brother, and his name, and a second estate at Sandhoe near Hexham in Northumberland, from his great-uncle Henry, who, having no close relatives of his own, had left his property to Rowland on condition that he assumed his own family name of Errington.[32] Early in life he had been one of the London dandies or, as Evelyn was to put it, a considerable 'man of fashion'.[33] However, after inheriting Sandhoe, he had settled down to manage his lands and to act as the Master of the Quorn hunt and as a local justice of the peace. He rebuilt Sandhoe Hall without changing too much of its original Elizabethan style. He improved the gardens.[34] And he devoted himself wholeheartedly to the annual August shooting on his estates.

Sir Rowland had married in 1839. His bride was the daughter of Sir John Macdonald, for many years Adjutant-General of the British Armed Forces. She was known as a celebrated 'beauty' and, like Evelyn's mother, was intimate with much of the fashionable and literary world of her time.[35] The Erringtons had three daughters, Claudine, who was to die of diphtheria soon after leaving Corfu, Ethel, and the youngest, Venetia, who later married Viscount Pollington, the only son of the Earl of Mexborough, and who remained a confidante of Baring for the rest of her life.

Storks lent the Errington party his official country residence, a 'beautifully-situated house' known as The Casino.[36] Baring was a frequent visitor. He writes in the 'Biographical Notes' that the episode he remembered 'most vividly' was acting charades with the Errington girls, in one of which they appeared as angels 'in the full bloom of their youth and beauty'. His own contributions were more down to earth. In one charade his friend Ponsonby played King Alfred, and Evelyn the woman who scolded him for burning the cakes while in disguise and hiding from the Danes. He was soon 'desperately in love'.[37] Zetland, following Baring's own lead, makes it

---

[31] Zetland, *Lord Cromer*, 34, gives the date of Lady Errington's death as 1861, but the *Northumberland County History*, iv. 194, gives it as 1859.

[32] *Northumberland County History*, iv. 194, 205.

[33] BN 71.

[34] *Bulmer's History and Directory of Northumberland* (1886), 403–4.

[35] BN 72.

[36] BN 92.

[37] Ibid.

the turning point of his life. But for meeting Ethel, he might easily have become 'a man of pleasure'. As it was, it turned him decisively in the direction of work. He had not enough money to be married. He had spent most of his father's legacy. And all he possessed was a trust fund yielding an income of £300 a year, in addition to his pay of £100. Hence he was determined to find a way of gaining a livelihood in order to 'render myself worthy... of the woman I had chosen'.[38] In Zetland's romantic gloss, Ethel becomes Baring's 'destiny', the 'decisive event in his life'. In his words,

The urge to definite endeavour, hitherto lacking, now became a driving force of incalculable power. An irresistible ambition now seized him and became the absorbing passion of his waking life—the ambition not merely of making marriage possible, but of rendering himself and his life's work worthy of the woman whose companionship he craved. It was one of the inestimable gifts of providence to Evelyn Baring that, having brought within his purview a woman capable of devotion of the finest texture, she should have endowed him with the capacity for appreciating and reciprocating it.[39]

Well, yes: this would seem to be the truth, but not the whole truth. Zetland's beguiling portrait of the rake reformed, based on the moral which Baring himself chose to draw from the event, and, we must also remember, for his sons, for whom the 'Biographical Notes' were intended, is all right as far as it goes. However, it also suggests quite a bit of shaping from a literary, as well as an ethical, point of view. For one thing, it is not at all clear that Evelyn and Ethel did get formally engaged at this time. The 'Biographical Notes' certainly assert that this was the case, before going on to commend the 'virtue of long attachments'. There is also some very special pleading. 'I know of nothing more calculated to keep a young man surrounded by all sorts of serious temptations out of serious harm, and to give stimulus to work, than to form a deep attachment to a good woman.'[40] Against this later view, there is the fact that there is no mention of a prior engagement in the letter containing the firm statement of his commitment which he finally sent to Ethel just before leaving for what he thought would be a five-year stint in India in 1872.[41] What seems more accurate is that there was indeed something of an 'attachment' significant enough to allow Evelyn to be invited to shoot at the Erringtons' Sandhoe estate when he was back in England in the summer of 1864.[42]

[38] BN 68–9.   [39] Zetland, *Lord Cromer*, 33–4.   [40] BN 69.
[41] Baring to Ethel Errington, 26 Feb. 1872, CP/1, file marked 'Letters and papers of the 1st Lady Cromer'.   [42] BN 24.

There is also the question of the existence of Baring's Corfiote mistress, with whom he must have continued to sleep until at least the autumn of 1862 for their joint child to have been born the following summer. We can only speculate that the passage about 'serious temptations' and the role of a 'good woman' might refer to another aspect of his moral reformation at this time. Whether or not he confessed all this to Ethel, either then or when they finally got married in 1876, cannot be known. Perhaps the most charitable comment is that while life is lived forward with its multitude of ambiguities and confusions, autobiography is written backwards with the all-too-human desire to tidy up an untidy past.

Lastly, there is the difficult question of their different religions. One possible scenario is that Sir Rowland, who himself seems to have married a non-Catholic, would have agreed to the match, at this stage at least, provided that any children were brought up as Catholics like Ethel and her sisters. Later, however, he definitely seems to have turned against it. All the evidence suggests that his opposition grew over the years to such an extent that, when Baring sent his 1872 declaration of feelings, he gave it to his brother to deliver personally to Ethel's house for fear of interception if it went by ordinary post. Circumstantial support for such a hypothesis comes from the fact that the British Catholic Church's opposition to mixed marriages increased greatly in the early 1870s. This is sometimes put down to the impact of the First Vatican Council in 1870. Baring himself seems to have blamed it personally on the head of the British Church, the powerful and influential Cardinal Manning.[43] Others have pointed to the underlying trend towards greater exclusivity which was characteristic of all the British denominations at this time, but of the Catholic Church above all.[44]

Last Months with Edward Lear on Corfu

The last months of the British protectorate were particularly difficult. For one thing, the British had given in to Austrian and Turkish pressure to destroy the islands' fortifications before they left, something which was deeply resented by the local people. For another, there were vocal protests from the Corfu social and political clubs against the prorogation of the assembly. For some weeks every little incident of friction became instantly magnified, as when one of the last of the British community's cross-

[43] BN 39–41.
[44] Mary Heimann, *Catholic Devotion in Victorian England* (Oxford: Clarendon Press, 1995), 123.

country paper hunts was blamed for damaging Greek-owned vines.[45] All this caused great concern among the resident British population as to whether they would be welcome if they stayed on after the troops withdrew.

Baring himself must also have been closely involved in the plans for the official handover and the departure of the High Commissioner and his staff. Nevertheless, all was not work and worry: his last months on the island were considerably enlivened by his growing friendship with the painter and nonsense poet Edward Lear. Lear was then in his early fifties and an old friend of Baring's cousin Thomas Baring, later Lord Northbrook, whose own love of painting had led him to support the artist with commissions. Another patron was Sir Henry Storks, to whom Lear's *Views in the Seven Ionian Islands*, published in December 1863, was specially dedicated. Indeed, Lear had a particular fondness for the Ionian scene, describing the view from Corfu towards the Albanian mountains as 'one of the loveliest in the world'. As for the islands' ubiquitous olive tree, he extolled 'the perpetual framing of beautiful scenes by its twisted branches and the veil-like glitter it throws around by its semi-transparent foliage'.[46] A photograph of him taken in 1865 shows him as a burly, avuncular-looking man with a big bushy beard, a rather bulbous nose, and shrewd-looking eyes behind round, rimless spectacles.[47] His own cartoon-like drawings of himself generally make him look small and portly, almost rotund, although he was in fact quite tall and heavily built. The gentle melancholy of most of his rhymes was also a little deceptive, hiding as they did his regular depressions, his hypochondria, and a considerable amount of self-loathing.[48]

According to Lear's diary, he first met Baring at Storks's palace in December 1862. They got to know each other better in the early months of 1863, although not, it would seem, on a very firm basis.[49] As Lear noted in April, he liked Baring less than George Strahan, the other ADC. Their friendship only blossomed when Lear returned to Corfu in January 1864. The painter was now so much part of the winter scene that he was always invited to the special Sunday dinners which the High Commissioner ate

[45] Kirkwall (ed.), *Four Years in the Ionian Islands*, ii. 272.

[46] Edward Lear, *Views in the Seven Ionian Islands* (London, 1 Dec. 1863), introd.

[47] *Edward Lear: Selected Letters*, ed. Vivian Noakes (Oxford: Clarendon Press, 1988), frontispiece.

[48] I have relied mainly on the observations in Vivian Noakes, *Edward Lear: The Life of a Wanderer* (Boston: Houghton Mifflin, 1969).

[49] Lear's yearly Diaries are in the Houghton Library, Harvard University, MS Eng 797.3.

only with his close personal staff. Lear's diagram of the seating arrangements, which usually accompanied his somewhat bare description of any social occasion, show him placed between Storks and Strahan on 10 January and Storks and Baring on 17 January. Two weeks later he notes that he went to both Strahan's and Baring's rooms after dinner, no doubt for a further drink and a smoke. After that it seems to have been his custom to spend an hour or two every Sunday evening with Baring before walking home to his lodgings.

Their growing friendship was quickly marked by a weekly nonsense note from Lear in reply to the dinner invitations which Baring either brought or sent on behalf of Sir Henry. One dated 'Toosdy' (12 January 1864), and accompanied by a drawing of Lear's head protruding from a bag, began:

Dear Baring,

Disgustical to say, I must beg you to thank His Excellency from me, & relate that I cannot come. I was engaged to dine with the De Veres, but am too unwell with an awful cold in the head & eyes to go out at all.

I have sent for two large tablecloths to blow my nose on, having already used up all my handkerchiefs. And altogether I am so unfit for company that I propose getting into a bag and being hung up in the bough of a tree until this tyranny is overpast.[50]

A second note, sent sometime later in January 1864, was accompanied by a sketch of Lear as a large bird and began:

Beneficial and brick-like Baring,

Thank you for your note. I will come to his Excellency tomorry. Meanwhile, please give him the accompanying note & book, which I hope you and Strahan will like. Give my love to Strahan. I have some frightfull bad books for you both to read.

It ended, in Greek letters, 'goodbye . . . my friend. Edwardos Lear'.[51]

In a third, sent on 4 February, the writing goes round and round in ever smaller circles and is accompanied by a picture of Lear as a rotund insect. It begins, 'my dear Baring how beautifully you write! every letter is better than t'other & I wish eye could right as well!' It concludes:

Do not bother about trying to cawl on me, for you must have lots to do,—but when Strahan comes back [from Syria], come & dine some evening. Why did Jacob sleep five in a bed? When he slep with his 4 = fathers. Say to his Excellency that I will most gladly come on Sunday if so be as I have no relapps.[52]

---

[50] *Edward Lear: Selected Letters*, 192.   [51] Ibid. 191.   [52] Ibid. 193–4.

A fourth suggested an exchange of photographs of each other:

dearbaringiphowndacuppelloffotografsthismawningwir[?] chisendjoo thereiswu-
nofeecg[?]sortsoyookankeepbothifyooliketodoosoanwenyou = = haveabetterwu
nofyourselflet mehaveit.

(Dear Baring I found a couple of photographs this morning which I send you.
There is one of each sort so you can keep both if you like to do so. And when you
have a better one of yourself let me have it.)[53]

Clearly Baring responded to Lear's quirky sense of humour with its
mixture of the playful and the melancholic. He too enjoyed puns and
jokes involving accidental or deliberate misunderstandings between
words in different languages. According to Baring, they were 'tremendous
gigglers together'.[54] However, there can also be little doubt that he was
also responding to the interest taken in him by someone old enough to be
his father, particularly one so well travelled and well-read and with such an
excellent, though self-taught, knowledge of classical Greek. Better still,
there were things which he, young as he was, could offer in return. Lear
was notoriously disorganized and always grateful to people like the 'brick-
like Baring' who were willing to look after him and to sort out some of his
personal difficulties and muddles. Lear's own testimony is quite clear on
this point: not only was Evelyn 'the sweetest, kindest and funniest of young
men', he was also a 'Godsend of efficiency'.[55]

Later evidence from when Baring and Lear met again in India in 1873–4
shows that Baring was nicely sensitive to Lear's moods and bouts of
melancholia. However, even at this earlier stage in their relationship he
seems to have been helpful in coping with his friend's mounting sadness as
the time for the handover to the Greeks drew close, with Lear believing
that this would end his visits to the enchanted isle for ever. A wistful entry
in his diary for 19 January 1864 notes that 'a certain placidity in this Corfu
life is a charm—never before attained to except in early Roman days—and
never more to be found on leaving this'. And on 10 March, 'it is difficult to
fancy a place where one could be happier than here'. There can be little
doubt that it was due to Lear's sense of being cast out of paradise that
Storks asked Baring to accompany him to Athens when he finally left the
island in early April. There was a final small dinner at the palace on Sunday
3 April, after which Lear wrote that he had 'sat singing until 11 with the
ADCs'.

[53] Ibid. 195.
[54] Peter Levi, *Edward Lear: A Biography* (New York: Scribner, 1995), 246.   [55] Ibid. 194.

Lear and Baring then boarded a ship for Piraeus the next evening, with Lear writing that he was in better spirits than he had been when leaving a year before because Evelyn was with him. They had dinner on the ship together, after which they walked on deck and talked until 8 p.m. It was in the early hours of the next morning that Lear wrote his strangely disturbing poem which begins:

> She sits upon her Bulbul
> Through the long hours of night
> And the dark horizon gleams
> O'er the Yashmak's fitful light,
> The lone yaourt sinks slowly down
> The deep and craggy dell
> And from his lofty nest loud screams
> The white plumed asphodel.[56]

The couple reached Piraeus on 6 April and spent the next day sightseeing, visiting the Acropolis and the newly excavated Temple of Bacchus together before finishing up at a theatre. They had dinner at the British Legation on 8 April, and then sat talking until 11.30 p.m. The next day they went their separate ways, Lear by ship to Crete, Baring back to Corfu to assist Storks with the final arrangements for the handover. The tension was now even greater than before. The British were blowing up the fortifications in earnest, so that the loud bangs could be heard all over the islands. There was also a new row, this time about the fact that the Greeks were being forced to pay large indemnities to British officials whose services were no longer required. Drummond Wolff, for example, received a handsome lifetime pension of £576 13s. 4d. a year.[57]

On 19 May M. Zainis, the Commissioner Extraordinary of the King of the Hellenes, arrived in Corfu to arrange the form and manner of the final ceremonies due to take place on 2 June. He received a warm welcome from a large crowd waving Greek flags. On 24 May there was a levée in honour of Queen Victoria's birthday, followed by a last parade of British troops along the esplanade outside the palace. The troops themselves began to embark on 27 May.[58] Finally, on 2 June, Storks said a few words of farewell to some assembled friends and took ship on HMS Marlborough to sail to Catacola to meet the new King. The British colours were ceremonially

---

[56] Lear, 1864 Diary, 5–8.
[57] Stefanos Xenos, *East and West: A Diplomatic History of the Annexation of the Ionian Islands to the Kingdom of Greece* (London: Trubner, 1865), 33.
[58] Ibid. 193–6.

lowered and the Greek flag run up on the flagstaffs of the remaining forts.[59]

Baring himself set off a few hours after Storks with some last dispatches. Now 23, he faced the prospect of a return to barrack-room life in Britain. However, for the moment he had two exciting things to look forward to. One was a trip to the United States and Canada with his brother Tom, the other was the thought of seeing Ethel again, either in London or when he went north in August for the shooting.

[59] Drummond Wolff, *Rambling Recollections*, i. 390–1.

4

Helping to Govern Malta
with Many Excursions
1864–1867

Shooting in America

After leaving Corfu, Baring returned quickly to England and then on to North America for a shooting trip and to see his brother Tom, who was working for Baring Brothers in New York. 'Now don't get shot and marry a squaw,' wrote Lear.[1] It proved to be sage advice as Baring's first act was to hasten down to Washington to observe some of the Civil War, then in its last stages, following General Grant's wilderness campaign in southern Virginia. This was part of Grant's juggernaut drive into the Confederate heartland, which had just ground to a halt after encountering Robert E. Lee's army in an area of thick shrub and swamps outside the town of Petersburg, some 30 miles south of the Confederate capital of Richmond. Baring got permission from Lord Lyons, the British Ambassador, to visit Grant's camp, and spent several days there observing and commenting on the military tactics being used after the armies had settled down to months of trench warfare.[2]

Skirmishing from fixed lines inevitably included a great deal of mining, one of the subjects he had been taught in the Royal Military College at Woolwich. Just before the famous Battle of the Crater he walked far enough along the underground passage dug out by the coal miners of

---

[1] Lear's letter of 30 June 1864 is quoted in Baring's introduction (written as the Earl of Cromer) to Edward Lear, *Queery Leary Nonsense: A Lear Nonsense Book*, ed. Lady Strachey (London: Mills & Boon, 1911), 17.

[2] BN 95–7, 99.

the 48th Pennsylvania Regiment to hear the guns of a Confederate artillery battery being run out just above his head. But he was gone before its use to explode a charge of 8,000 pounds of black gunpowder on 30 July under the Confederate front line and the subsequent failure of the Union troops to exploit the confusion in order to break through the enemy's secondary defences.[3]

Baring was allowed a short interview with Grant himself, who, as he writes in the 'Biographical Notes', 'fully maintained his character for taciturnity by scarcely uttering a word'.[4] He wore his Royal Artillery officer's uniform throughout, even though it was 'singularly unsuited to hot July weather'. He also wore his own forage cap except on visits to advanced posts, where it was replaced by a US officer's plain cloth cap as his cap's gold band tended to glitter in the sun, making it a tempting target for the expert Confederate sharpshooters. Once, when he hoisted it above the sheltering parapet, it was instantly pierced by several bullets. It was, he wrote, the only time he had ever experienced a shot fired in earnest.[5] Later he visited the Northern troops blockading Charleston, South Carolina, some 350 miles to the south.

The whole experience of modern battle, with its new weaponry and huge casualties, obviously made a great impression on him and was one of the many things which was to turn him into a convinced military reformer just a few years later. He seems to have been specially impressed by the quality of the staff officers and the intelligence work that went into planning a campaign. But whether he was capable of realizing the real import of what he saw as far as the underlying changes which were taking place in the art of warfare is unlikely. Only a few foreign military observers seem to have understood that the introduction of breech-loading rifles had given such an enormous advantage to the defence that trenches, rather than massed cavalry and infantry charges, were now to be the order of the day. Interestingly, the one British officer who drew the correct lesson, Colonel Patrick MacDougall, did not visit the American battlefields at all. The author of the influential work *Modern Warfare as Influenced by Modern Artillery*, he was later to be Baring's Commandant at the Staff College in Camberley at the end of the 1860s.[6]

[3] The Earl of Cromer, 'Reminiscences of the American Civil War', pt. 1, *The Spectator*, 3 June 1916, copy in CP/2, FO 633/33.

[4] BN 98.

[5] BN 106.

[6] Jay Luvaas, *The Education of an Army: British Military Thought, 1815–1940* (Chicago: University of Chicago Press, 1964), 109–12.

What was more characteristic of the young Baring at this time was his continued willingness to take the unfashionable side of a political argument by becoming an open advocate of the Northern cause at a time when most members of the British elite still supported the South. As he was to write to the editor of *The Times* over twenty-five years later, his belief in the paper's pro-Confederate line had not lasted a week once he had actually reached America.[7] This was to make him particularly resentful when he was shown part of an exploded Whitworth shell fired from a southern battery in Charleston, which he believed had been brought in by a blockade-runner from England.[8]

After this intense experience Baring went off to shoot moose in the Canadian province of New Brunswick at the mouth of the St Lawrence. However, in spite of spending six weeks in the woods with two Indian guides he got in only one shot, and that missed. Another event he records is that when his canoe capsized, he had to rescue one of his guides, who could not swim, by holding him above the water by his long hair.[9] Baring then took the German steamer *Hansa* from New York to Southampton before returning immediately to the United States on 'family business', spending three days with Tom in New York before they both sailed back to England together.[10]

With Storks in Malta

When Baring finally got back to London, it was to find that Sir Henry Storks had been appointed Governor of Malta in November 1864. Storks immediately asked him and George Strahan to act once again as his aides-de-camp. Storks and Strahan arrived in Valletta on 30 November and Baring soon followed.

Once again Baring found himself as part of the government of a Mediterranean island captured during the Napoleonic Wars. Once again the administration was shared between British officials and a local council, although, in the case of Malta, only eight of its members were elected with the other ten nominated by the governor, five of them Maltese. And once again too there had been friction between the various elements, leading to the reassignment of the previous governor, Sir John Le Marchant. As a result, Storks was appointed with special instructions from Lord Cardwell

---

[7] Baring to Moberley Bell, 3 Apr. 1890, MBL, TA (1890).   [8] BN 39.
[9] BN 108–9, 111.   [10] BN 111–12.

at the Colonial Office to win the cooperation of the elected members, and
to ensure that no allocation of money was made without their approval
except in the most special of circumstances.[11]

Malta was even smaller than Corfu, only 17 miles long and 8 miles wide.
At the time of the 1861 census it contained just under 120,000 inhabitants,
of whom 1,263 were British (not counting members of the armed forces)
and 1,126 foreign. The main features of its capital, Valletta, were the
Grand Harbour, the palaces of the Grand Masters of Knights of St John
of Jerusalem, the Cathedral of St John, and the Opera House. The Governor had his own palace there, as well as a country (summer) palace at San
Antonio, 4 miles inland, a rural retreat which the poet Coleridge had found
greatly to his liking with its high, cool rooms, exotic gardens, and magnificent panoramas.[12]

Storks's first order of business was the general election to be held under a
new electoral law between 9 and 14 January 1865. He himself described it
as being 'orderly and peaceful'. Of the eight Maltese elected, all but one
belonged to the so-called 'opposition party'.[13] Baring was not there to
witness this event, however. A fragment of a diary he kept in the early
months of 1865 shows that, on 10 January, he had just arrived in Naples
after an eight-hour journey.[14] The account of his next three months in
Naples and then of his journey back to London will be taken entirely from
this source. It is only possible to speculate why he was able to spend so
much of his first half-year as an ADC away from his post. Clearly it had
Storks's own approval. Perhaps, as we shall see, the fact that his mother,
and, possibly, Ethel too, joined him in Naples had persuaded the Governor
to relieve him of his duties. Perhaps he had simply accumulated this much
leave as a result of his six years in Corfu.

Once in Naples, Baring rented an 'appartamento au premier' at the
Grand Britannique Hotel, which overlooked the gardens of the Villa
Nationale and the Riviera di Ciaja, where the fashionable visitors could
be seen driving in their carriages every evening near the sea. In the ten days
before his mother arrived, he engaged in a non-stop social round. It began
with visits with cards and flowers. As is clear from the diary, he was already

---

[11] Edith Dobie, *Malta's Road to Independence* (Norman: University of Oklahoma Press, 1967),
18, 21–2.
[12] Richard Holmes, *Coleridge: Darker Reflections, 1804–1834* (New York: Pantheon Books,
1998), 19.
[13] Storks to Cardwell, 24 Jan. 1865, PRO, CO 156/206.
[14] BA, DEP 121.10. The handwriting is tiny, full of personal shorthand, and often difficult to
understand.

well acquainted with a number of people who had come to spend the winter there, like a Mrs de Burgh, the Duchess de St Arpino, and Lady Holland. Other acquaintances quickly appeared as he made his rounds from one 'at home' to another. He was clearly a presentable, good-looking, well-connected young man from a well-known European family. It must have helped too that by now he spoke good Italian as a result of his time in Corfu. It is also possible that Naples was one of the cities his mother had visited before her marriage to learn singing in the Italian manner, and that she still had a number of friends there.

Baring went to his first big evening out on 16 January at the huge San Carlo Opera House, where he sat in the Gabriellis' box. The performance was of Rossini's *Mosè in Egitto*, which he thought 'beautifully sung' but with a 'bad ballet'. Two days later he attended his first ball at Lady Backhaus's, a woman also known as Marguerite de Salza, whom he clearly liked a great deal. There he was introduced to a great many Italian members of Neapolitan society. The next evening he was at Mme Gabrielli's as one of a party of fifteen. He danced after dinner until midnight.

His mother seems to have arrived the following Saturday, 21 January. She was accompanied by a companion, a 'Miss D' and someone else the diary refers to simply as 'E'. If this was indeed Ethel Errington, his writing gives no clues. It is true that on 3 March there is mention that someone called Ethel was ill. But whether this is the same person as the 'E' who was also a member of the party is unclear. There is also the larger question of whether Sir Rowland would have allowed his now 19- or 20-year-old daughter to go off to meet a young man to whom she was not officially engaged, even if the young man's mother had agreed to act as a chaperone. It is possible, of course, that some such plan had been agreed to when Baring was staying with his mother in London, and then the Erringtons at Sandhoe, at the end of the previous year. That is about as far as one can go and it remains a tantalizingly open question.

Baring spent much of the next few days with his mother and her party. It was carnival time and there were many parades and other festivities to be seen from the balconies of the hotel. Women who seem to have been close friends of the Baring family came by to visit: Edith de Burgh and a Mary Fox, who invited them to play croquet, an appointment that Baring could not keep because he was 'ill all day'. By the end of January, however, he had begun his old social rounds again, although whether with or without the members of his mother's party the diary does not say. On the 29th he went to hear Flatow's *Martha* at the Opera House. And the next day he was at a ball at the Duchess de St Arpino's, at which he danced past 4 a.m. and enjoyed it 'beyond anything'. He danced, he says, every dance including a waltz (he calls it a 'valse') with Granotte de Parraga, another woman of whom he seemed to see quite a lot at this time. On 2 February he attended his first court ball, dancing a great deal but also sitting out with the Duchess and enjoying it 'excessively'. And on 4 February he was at a charity ball dancing what he called an 'excellent cotillion', followed by another turn with Granotte.

Meanwhile, his mother's naval connections were being attended to as a result of the arrival in the harbour of the British warship HMS *Revenge*. The Admiral came to dine with her on 7 February and the next day the Baring party had lunch aboard the ship itself, after which there was more dancing on deck. Baring himself also attended two more operas, *Mosè in Egitto* again, and Francesco Perugina's *Morina* with a diva called La Greca. The week then ended with a spectacular eruption from Mount Vesuvius, which 'broke into fire' on the night of 10 February, and dinner at the former King of Naples's palace on the 12th.

After that both Evelyn and some of the rest of the party fell ill. His fortnight of bad health began with headaches and repeated fever. On one very bad day a doctor had to be called no less than four times. It caused Baring's birthday celebrations to have to be postponed until he felt a bit better in early March. The delayed celebrations included an invitation to sit in the Duchess de St Arpino's box at the opera on 6 March and a return visit the next evening to hear *The Barber of Seville*, which he thought 'very badly sung'. Unfortunately, he then fell ill again and was unable to visit the palace to celebrate King Victor Emmanuel's birthday. He does not seem to have recovered until he (and perhaps his mother) took a short trip to Salerno, Amalfi, and Pompeii towards the end of March.

Baring's last few days in Naples were spent at the races and then in leaving cards and in saying his goodbyes. On the first day of racing he won the lottery of £3 10s. on the first horse, called Justice, in a gentleman riders' race. On the second, he took Mrs De Burgh and, in spite of 'excellent places', they lost all their bets. On 31 March he said a special goodbye to the Duchess, got into the train for Rome, and was 'very, very sorry to leave'. He was accompanied by his mother, 'Miss D', who managed to lose one of her boxes a few days later, and the still mysterious 'E', who had not been mentioned in the diary for the whole of March. In Rome they went sightseeing, including visits to St Peter's Cathedral and the galleries at the

Doria Palace. Baring also went to the races and to a cricket match in the gardens at Pamphili.

The Barings left Rome by train on 14 April and travelled to Paris via Leghorn, Pisa, Florence, Bologna, Turin, and then Mâcon and Dijon. In Paris they dined with their friends the Stanleys, where they met the very old M. Talleyrand. They attended a ball given by the Empress at the Tuileries, at which Baring danced a 'great deal' until 2 a.m. And they drove home from a visit to Versailles and St Cloud, the château on the left bank of the Seine a few miles from Paris where the Emperor Napoleon III and his wife, Eugénie, spent most of the spring and summer, through the Bois de Boulogne in the moonlight, which they thought 'charming'. Thanks to the efforts of the Emperor and Baron Haussmann, the Bois now had 40 miles of bridle paths and carriage roads, as well as lakes and wide avenues. Finally, Baring, if not the whole party, reached Folkestone on 20 May and London the next day. There he met two new ADCs going out to Malta. And there too the fragment of diary ends. There is no mention of the trip in the 'Biographical Notes'.

It is unclear exactly when Baring returned to Valletta. If he got there by the beginning of June, it would have been to witness the last of the thirteen sessions of the new council, which was then adjourned from 5 June to 29 December. Storks himself was obviously pleased with the way things had gone. He had also made certain innovations of a kind which Baring himself was to use himself when he was at the War Office in 1870. These included associating the elected members of the council with all government proposals by a process of appointing them to all the relevant select committees, on which they were generally given a majority of the votes.[15] If Baring had returned by August, it would have been to experience three months of a serious outbreak of cholera in which 1,600 people died.[16] All that is certain is that he was there in January 1866, when Storks received a summons to proceed at once to Jamaica to head a royal commission of inquiry into the methods used by the Governor, John Eyre, to quash an armed uprising by some of the former plantation slaves. The telegram from London was deciphered at 8 a.m., and by 3 p.m. Storks, Baring, and Strahan had boarded a navy vessel and set off for the West Indies.

---

[15] Storks to Cardwell, 6 Jan. 1865, PRO, CO 158/206.
[16] Storks to Cardwell, 11 Nov. 1865, PRO, CO 158/207.

The Governor Eyre Inquiry

The reason for Storks's hasty departure was that the conduct of Governor Eyre had become a cause célèbre in London. The uprising took place the previous October. News of the month-long process of brutal pacification which followed soon reached London and gave rise to a great deal of heated discussion, as well as to demands from rival parties, either for the governor's instant dismissal or for an inquiry which his supporters hoped would exonerate him. Not only had some 500 black Jamaicans been killed by the police and army, but also thousands of their homes had been set on fire. Meanwhile, Eyre himself had used the occasion to secure the court martial, and then speedy execution, of his most significant local opponent, George William Gordon, who also happened to be a member of the Jamaican house of assembly. All this was bitterly attacked by much of the London press, stirred up by the publication of the militia commanders' dispatches appended to the Governor's report, with their bloody accounts of hangings, shootings, and house burnings, mostly without any kind of trial.[17]

Lord Cardwell, now Secretary of State for the Colonies, clearly felt the need to act quickly. Eyre was put on leave for the course of the inquiry and Storks made temporary Acting Governor in his place.

The Commission met for the first time on 20 January at the King's House in Spanish Town and began hearing evidence on the 25th. Baring and Strahan acted as assistants to its secretary, Charles Roundell. Their main task was to take down summaries of evidence, something which, according to Baring, caused them to bear the brunt of 'much hard swearing'.[18] It was also extremely tiring work. The Commission sat for fifty-one days, until 21 March, including visits by Baring and some of the commissioners to the districts which had been most affected by the uprising around Morant Bay on the south-east tip of the island. All in all it listened to 730 witnesses.[19]

The Commission's Report gives a graphic description of the problems it faced. Witnesses, both black and white, educated as well as uneducated,

---

[17] Bernard Semmel, *Jamaican Blood and Victorian Conscience: The Governor Eyre Controversy* (Westport, Conn.: Greenwood Press, 1976), 13–23.

[18] BN 127.

[19] *Report of the Jamaican Royal Commission 1866*, 9 Apr. 1866, 10; Baring's own copy can be found in CP/2, FO 633/98.

were 'irregular in their attendance'. Many of them had a 'singular ignorance of the nature and value of evidence' and had to be repeatedly cautioned against introducing hearsay. Others shared a general misconception of the purpose of the inquiry, which they believed had come either to award compensation for their damaged property or to inflict on-the-spot punishment on their attackers. As for what the Report called the 'negroes', it was enough to recall, it said, that 'they were for the most part uneducated peasants, speaking in strange accents to the ear, often in a phraseology of their own, with vague conceptions of time and number, unaccustomed to definiteness or accuracy of speech, and, in many cases, still smarting under a sense of injuries sustained'.[20] The reams of personal testimony came to several thousands of pages when finally printed. It was then carefully sifted and discussed for several weeks before final conclusions were drawn.

In spite of all the difficulties, there was a general feeling among the members themselves, warmly underlined by most subsequent historians, that they had managed as well as anyone could possibly have done to get at the truth, both 'in fact and in the estimation of persons'.[21] Indeed, most histories continue to rely almost entirely on the findings of the Report when it comes to their analysis of what actually happened. After presenting a narrative record of the event the Commission drew three major conclusions. First, the uprising had been a planned resistance to authority with the object of securing rent-free land, and that 'not a few' of the conspirators contemplated the achievement of this end by the 'death or expulsion of the white inhabitants of the Island'. Secondly, the original disorder had spread with 'singular rapidity' and, if allowed to go further, its ultimate defeat would have been attended with 'still more fearful loss of life and property'. Thirdly, in spite of some praise for Governor Eyre's vigour in the early stages, martial law had been abused by too many executions and reckless floggings, and by a burning of houses, which was 'wanton and cruel'.[22] The Report was also critical of the way the courts martial had been conducted, especially that of Gordon, a prisoner who, in the commissioners' opinion, was not himself involved in the original conspiracy.

The commissioners then proceeded to London, where their Report was issued on 18 June giving Eyre time to read all the evidence for and against him. It was an exciting moment. Not only was there a huge reaction to the Commission's findings, but its Report appeared in the middle of the Second Reform Bill crisis. Such was the strength of popular feeling that

[20] Ibid. 7–8.   [21] Ibid. 8.   [22] Ibid. 40–1.

Eyre was soon put on trial for 'high crimes and misdemeanours', although eventually acquitted. One must suppose that the young Baring, still only 25 years of age, was forced to defend the Commission's findings in what was now a highly polarized London political climate, with many of the capital's most illustrious writers, for example Ruskin, Tennyson, Carlisle, and Dickens, taking part in the campaign in Eyre's defence. Unfortunately, we know nothing of Baring's own views at the time. All we have are his much later thoughts as expressed in the 'Biographical Notes'. Governor Eyre was at fault, he writes, because he had no special knowledge of West Indian affairs. Furthermore, there was one feature of his character which alone should have been sufficient to prevent his appointment and that was his outspoken championship of the Church of England on an island where the majority of the ex-slaves were ardent Methodists.

For the rest, Baring's experiences in Jamaica were used to support his belief that two centuries of British rule had failed to produce any 'negro' of an 'intellectual standard ... higher than that of a somewhat ill-informed village schoolmaster'.[23] Such a judgement was very much in line with the general assumption in London that the emancipation of the West Indian slaves had been a notable failure owing to the freed slaves' own unwillingness to do more than practice a limited subsistence agriculture. Whether it also represented his position in 1866 cannot be known. Nevertheless, it seems likely that his few months in Jamaica did act to reinforce Baring's already quite low opinion of the quality of the representative to be found in the three colonial assemblies he had now witnessed at first hand, those in Corfu, Valletta, and now Spanish Town.

Sir Henry Storks did not resume his governorship in Malta until December 1866. He travelled there with two ADCs, although whether one of them was actually Baring is impossible learn from the request he made to the Colonial Office for a reimbursement of his expenses from London to Marseilles.[24] The Governor had four busy months establishing the district committees, each with three elected and two official members to provide the local consultation, the lack of which he felt had hampered efforts to deal with the cholera epidemic of 1865. He hoped that it might encourage the inhabitants to look more after their own affairs such as street-cleaning, lighting, and the water supply.[25] There were also eleven sittings of the council before it was adjourned for the year in April. These, he wrote to the new Colonial Secretary, the Duke of Buckingham, had been conducted

[23] BN 131–2.   [24] Storks to Sir Frederick Rogers, 27 Dec. 1866, PRO, CO 158/208.
[25] Storks to Caernarvon, 2 Feb. 1867, PRO, CO 158/211.

with 'great good feeling', partly as a result of some 'judicious management'.[26] Storks left Malta a few days later to assume his new post at the
War Office as surveyor-general, followed some months later by promotion
to under-secretary and controller-in-chief. Baring, with nothing better to
do, returned to England to reassume his regimental duties at the Royal
Artillery depot at Warley in Essex.

Many years later, when writing his 'Biographical Notes', Baring claims
not to have been impressed by the local Maltese politicians, whom he
describes as 'a few agitators who strutted on [Valletta's] minuscule stage'
and who 'represented very imperfectly the views and interests of the mass
of the population'. He also made the significant distinction between
freedom for the Ionian Islanders and his belief that Malta was of such
strategic importance that he was not prepared to see Britain's vital naval
and military interests subordinated to a futile attempt to 'conciliate a
factious, unrepresentative and irreconcilable opposition'.[27] It seems unlikely that, even in his radical days, Baring was ever a real democrat in the
sense of believing that the election of representatives was the best way of
finding out where a people's real interests lay. What was needed instead
was some other method by which the weight and privilege of the upper
class should be balanced against the needs of those further down the social
scale. In the British case, it could have been a reformed House of Commons, as he seems to have believed in the 1860s, or it could be the work of a
small, disinterested, and, above all, intelligent cadre of selfless administrators, which was the Whig ideal. Transferred outwards to the Empire, he
saw this same ideal as the model for imperial government from the 1870s
onwards.[28]

[26] Storks to Buckingham, 13 Apr. 1867, PRO, CO 158/211.   [27] BN 114.
[28] For the Whig view, see Vincent, *Formation of the Liberal Party*, 16–17.

5

Staff Officer and Military Reformer
1867–1872

Staff College

Baring soon found his return to army life 'uncongenial'.[1] It must also have
been a considerable anticlimax after his nine years in Corfu and Malta. And
though nearer to Ethel geographically, he was no nearer to be being able to
afford to marry. The only incident of any interest which he records in the
'Biographical Notes' about his life at this time was also unlikely to have
made him feel better about the problems posed by a mixed marriage. This
was the visit of the Catholic Archbishop of Westminster, Henry Edward
Manning, to preach to a congregation which consisted mainly of soldiers.
Baring was shocked, he said, because instead of urging his audience to live
at peace with its neighbours, Manning launched into a 'violent and bitter
tirade against Protestantism in general'.[2]

Within a short period of time Baring decided to become a candidate for
the new Staff College which had been established in 1858, and moved to a
permanent home in Camberley, Surrey, in 1862. There was an entrance
examination, which involved a few weeks of concentrated cramming in
French with one of the many private tutors making a living out of the
growing importance of competitive examinations. Baring came second out
of almost twenty candidates and was immediately admitted to the two-year
course beginning in February 1868.

The Staff College had been established as part of the general concern
with the improvement of military education after the Crimean War.
First-year courses included military history, topographical drawing,

---

[1] BN 139.   [2] BN 139–41.

mathematics, astronomy, and French, with an examination at the end. Compulsory second-year courses included military history, military administration and law, fortifications, and military surveying and reconnaissance. It was also necessary to choose three more subjects from maths, modern languages (French, German, or Hindustani), and natural and experimental sciences.[3] The course in military engineering was assisted by a detachment of Royal Engineers, who gave demonstrations in throwing up fieldworks, constructing bridges, and other activities which the Staff College students watched but took no part in. The study of military administration took up only a week and involved such subjects as the activities of the commissariat, manoeuvring troops and supplies on and off boats, and the layout of camps. The languages were taught in three-weekly periods of one and a half hours a week.[4] Baring almost certainly chose German, although he appears to have regretted this later when he noted that Hindustani would have been useful to him when he went to Calcutta in 1872.[5] The year ended with an examination by outside assessors in seven of these subjects. There were also three internal exams a year.[6] In addition, student officers had to take compulsory lessons in riding. For most officers, the atmosphere was much too much 'like school'.[7]

The students were housed in a new Italianate building designed by James Pennethorne. It was planned to accommodate forty students but in 'Spartan style'. There were minimal provisions for bathing, and the only running hot water was provided by a small boiler in the mess kitchen which could heat just enough for a small can for each officer. Those wanting to have a proper bath had to get their servant to boil water on a range in the kitchen on the second floor.[8] For recreation there were occasional cricket matches and at least one ball a term. Some officers hunted. As outside servants were not allowed, the students had to make do with the services provided at the college itself. The result of these and other charges meant that they required a private income of about £100 above their regimental pay to live in 'anything like the style expected'.[9]

[3] Brian Bond, *The Victorian Army and the Staff College 1854–1914* (London: Eyre Methuen, 1972), 88–92.

[4] Brevet-Major A. R. Godwin-Austin, *The Staff and the Staff College* (London: Constable, 1927), 130–7.

[5] BN 151.

[6] Bond, *Victorian Army*, 88–92.

[7] Ibid. 92.

[8] Godwin-Austin, *Staff and the Staff College*, 129–30.

[9] Ibid. 142, 144.

Fortunately for the biographer, a royal commission was appointed in June 1868 to examine how the College was developing. Baring and a number of his fellow students came before it to give evidence. There was still a considerable controversy about military education in the Army at this time, with a powerful group around the Duke of Cambridge, the Queen's uncle and commander-in-chief, who thought that anything but on-the-job training in the regiment was a waste of time. Others, notably a group which included Lord Cardwell, soon to be appointed Minister of War, and Sir Henry Storks, believed that a well-trained corps of staff officers like those in Germany or the United States was now an absolute necessity. Lord Dufferin, a future Ambassador to the Ottoman Empire and Viceroy of India, was appointed chair of the Commission. Another member was Baring's older cousin Thomas Baring, now the second Earl of Northbrook following the death of his father in 1866.

For someone who had been at the College for little more than half a year, Baring's observations and criticisms seem to have been expressed with surprising confidence and self-assurance. He told the Royal Commission that 'officers cram up for the examination just a few hours before it comes on and then forget all about it'. He said he regarded military administration as the most important subject and urged that it be more practical. And how could a staff officer be trained for rapid decision-making under the present system, he asked, when, for example, he had been given a month to prepare a plan of defence for a village which was supposed to be attacked in just six hours?[10] Nevertheless, he believed strongly that the Staff College,

imperfect though it may be, is much better than no College at all. A large proportion of the officers [in the British Army] . . . receive their commissions direct; they know nothing of their profession beyond their ordinary military duties. [And apart from the College] scarcely any opportunity is afforded them for [gaining theoretical knowledge] should they be willing to do so.[11]

Baring's other contribution to encouraging a more professional attitude among army officers was to publish a series of three papers in a small volume called *Staff College Essays*.[12] They were written, he notes in a brief

[10] *Royal Commission on Military Education: Minutes of Evidence*, First Report (1869), quoted in Bond, *Victorian Army*, 92.

[11] Bond, *Victorian Army*, 103.

[12] (London: Longmans, Green, 1870) 'by Lt. Evelyn Baring, RA (11 Berkeley St. 19 March 1870)'. This was his mother's address.

introduction, as part of his 1868 and 1869 studies, and their chief aim was to show the public and officers unacquainted with the College the 'nature of the work done at the institution'. These essays were encouraged by the College's lecturer in military history, Major Adams, who had served in the Austrian Army in 1848. Their titles, 'Changes in the Art of War from 1792 to 1815', 'Campaign in Ulm and Comments on the Campaign', and 'Operations in Poland from Dec. 1 to 26, 1866 and Comments on the Campaign', clearly reflect Adams's own interests. Taken together, they constitute a general argument for the importance of military history. They also show Baring responding to the enormous changes in the con-duct of war which were taking place at this period, from the American Civil War through the Prussian campaigns of 1864 and 1866 and culminating in the German defeat of the French Army in 1870. In every case success, so Baring firmly believed, was due primarily to the excellent work of each general staff.

Baring performed well enough to allow him to pass out of Camberley at the head of his class in December 1869. He then had a very short spell with a cavalry regiment at Aldershot before being appointed to the Topograph-ical and Statistical Department of the War Office in March 1870, a forerunner of the soon-to-be-created Intelligence Branch. This was a move which took him right into the heart of the battle for military reform then being conducted by Lord Cardwell, who had arrived at the War Office at the end of 1868 with Lord Northbrook as his under-secretary of state. Baring was now just 29. He was close to the centres of power in London. And he had a strong possibility of making a name for himself as a rising young man close to the reforming wing of the governing Whig–Liberal Party.

The Cardwell Reforms

The Topographical and Statistical Department had been created in 1855 to remedy one of the many deficiencies produced by the Crimean War, the absence of adequate military maps. In 1870 it underwent the first of its several reorganizations as the result of one of the recommendations of Lord Northbrook's Commission of Inquiry into the workings of the War Office, which produced its final report in February 1870. It was now to become a branch of the commander-in-chief's Military Department, with the task of providing information about foreign armies and foreign orders of battle.[13]

Baring's personal contribution seems to have begun with a comparison between the French and German armies, which allowed him to predict, even before the campaign had begun, that the French would be defeated in a great battle somewhere near Châlons and that the Prussians would probably seize Paris. As his predictions went against most of the conventional military opinion of the time, his near-accuracy—the decisive battle was fought not on the Marne but at Sedan some 60 miles to the north—must have given him great pleasure as well as a certain amount of kudos among his colleagues.[14] Then, in November 1870, he was given the task of preparing an appreciation of both the Russian and the Turkish armies at a time when there was a brief possibility that Britain might have to go to war with Russia after its repudiation of the clauses in the 1856 treaty concerning the Black Sea.[15] A third task, conducted directly at Cardwell's request, was a study of the German Army, including its practice of regular peacetime manoeuvres, leading to the publication of abridged translations of W. von Tschischwitz's *Anleitung zum Kriegspiel*, under the title *Rules for the Conduct of the War-Game* (1872), and H. F. W. Perizonius's *The Elementary Tactics of the Prussian Infantry* (1871).[16]

Baring's knowledge of the German military system also led to his close involvement in the British Army's first manoeuvres in Berkshire and parts of Hampshire and Surrey in the autumn of 1871. He was appointed secretary to the Commission consisting mainly of the lords-lieutenant and local Members of Parliament which was given the task of arranging matters between the soldiers and the civilian population of the area, notably the local landowners whose estates and fields might easily be ridden and marched over and their standing crops destroyed. One of Baring's duties was to go round the districts explaining the situation to the local farmers. Here he employed a tactic, surely learned from Storks in Malta, of offering anyone who raised objections membership of the Commission. When recalling this initiative, he remarked that 'nothing calms opposition so much as to take an opponent into council and, if possible,

---

[13] Michael Roper, *The Records of the War Office and Related Departments 1660–1964* (London: Public Record Office Publications, 1998), 213.

[14] Zetland, *Lord Cromer*, 45–6.

[15] Ibid. 46.

[16] The former was published by the Topographical and Statistical Department of the War Office and the latter by HMSO.

render him to some extent responsible for the action to which he is inclined to object'.[17] It was a tactic he was to employ in many other situations abroad, most notably with his invitation to one of his major Egyptian critics, Saad Zaghlul, to become Minister of Education in 1906. In southern England it worked so well that the moneys paid out with respect to unavoidable damage came to only £1,200.[18]

The Topographical Department was reorganized again in 1871. Its duties were now defined as 'to collect and classify all possible information relating to the strength and organization of foreign armies, including the preparation of orders of battle [and] to keep in touch with the progress made in foreign countries in military arts and sciences'.[19] To do this it was divided into three sections, each of which was to draw up a complete account of the military formations of the countries assigned to it. Baring was given responsibility for Great Britain and Ireland, northern Germany, Spain, Portugal, and Italy.[20] One result may well have been a rise in pay. Another committee report of 24 January 1871 proposed that the salaries of Baring and his two colleagues should be increased from their present £232 13s. 9d. to £450 a year. It is interesting to compare this with the pay of the office cleaner, a Mrs Farrell, which the committee proposed should remain at an annual £39 2s. 6d.[21]

Baring's personal experience was called upon in other areas of military reform as well. For example, he was a member of yet another commission appointed in October 1870 to recommend a suitable war establishment specifying the men and equipment needed for a variety of the different types of units envisaged for the new British Army including a battalion of infantry, a regiment of cavalry, and a battery of artillery.[22] However, his most significant activity was the assistance he provided Cardwell, Northbrook, and his old chief Sir Henry Storks in their campaign to persuade the Duke of Cambridge to permit the abolition of the system allowing officers to purchase senior posts for themselves simply by the

[17] Quoted in Zetland, *Lord Cromer*, 47.

[18] General Sir Robert Biddulph, *Cardwell at the War Office: A History of His Administration* (London: John Murray, 1904), 189.

[19] Roper, *Records of the War Office*, 214.

[20] Captain E. H. H. Collen, 'Report on the Intelligence Branch, Quarter-Master-General's Department, Horse Guards', Oct. 1878, PRO, WO 33/23, 6.

[21] 'Report of a Committee on the Topographical and Statistical Department', 241/1871, Appendix 255–7, PRO, WO 33/22.

[22] The Commission was appointed on 30 Oct. 1870, PRO, WO 33/32.

payment of a large sum of money. This was the subject of a bitter debate in Parliament all through the early months of 1871.[23]

Two of the main spokesmen for the new policy were Northbrook in the Lords, and Storks, who had just entered Parliament as member for Ripon, in the Commons. They, in turn, were provided with information and general support by a small group of younger officers, including Baring and his fellow Staff College graduate Garnet Wolseley, later the commander of the British Expeditionary Force to Egypt in 1882. Baring himself wrote a memorandum entitled 'Arguments For and Against the Purchase System', in which he makes the statement that the abolition of the system was the 'key to army reform'.[24] This was then used as a brief for the military reformers in Parliament.[25] As in the case of the Jamaican Royal Commission, he found himself involved in a highly controversial set of recommendations. In this case he also ran a considerable risk to his own career by going against the express wishes of the Army's commander-in-chief. The matter was finally settled in July 1871 with the issue of a Royal Warrant by which all regulations fixing the prices at which commissions might be sold, purchased, or exchanged were to be cancelled as of 1 November that year. To judge from his lengthy comments in the 'Biographical Notes', his role in this affair continued to be source of real pride.[26]

London Life, Ethel, and India

The offices of the Topographical Department were in Horse Guards Parade, not far from 11 Berkeley Square, to which Baring had returned to live with his mother after leaving the Staff College. According to the 1871 census, their household consisted of the two of them, his brother Richard (now a merchant of 38), and a staff of eight including a butler, a cook, a lady's maid, and two footmen. Ned, Evelyn's elder brother, now only a few years away from taking over as head of the family firm, lived just round the corner at 37 Charles Street with his wife, Louisa, and three sons and three daughters.

One advantage of living at his mother's was his proximity to Ethel's aunt Lady Buller, who lived in Bruton Street, just off Berkeley Square. Meanwhile, Sir Rowland Errington himself had town houses first in Grosvenor

[23] Biddulph, *Cardwell at the War Office*, 108–41.   [24] Quoted in Zetland, *Lord Cromer*, 48.
[25] Cromer to Major Leslie, 20 Mar. 1913, CP/2, FO 633/24.   [26] BN 151–4, 161–73.

Street, then in Curzon Street, also nearby. But whether Ethel herself was much in London is unclear. By now her father's opposition to their possible marriage had become a great deal more of a problem. Meanwhile, Ethel's remaining sister, Venetia, had married Viscount Pollington, a Catholic, in April 1867. Later evidence suggests that she was able to act as a useful go-between when Evelyn experienced difficulties in trying to make direct contact with the Errington–Stanleys in Cheshire or Northumberland.

The Baring family must also have seen a lot of Lord Northbrook, whose town house was in nearby Hamilton Place, Piccadilly. A widower since 1867, he was then doubly cast-down by the loss of his second son, Arthur, when his ship went down in a storm off Finisterre in September 1870. These sorrows had accentuated his already grave, serious, pensive de-meanour, making him look much older than his little more than 40 years. He had a profound sense of duty, worked extremely long hours, and seems only to have been able to relax with close friends and family. Altogether he was a perfect representative of that influential band of Whig administrators who, though rich, 'felt themselves bound in common by ability alone, to represent the ascendancy of intelligence alone and not of property'.[27]

Northbrook, like everyone else, was completely surprised by his sudden offer of appointment as Viceroy of India in February 1872 following the assassination of Lord Mayo. Once he had said yes, he immediately asked Evelyn to accompany him as either his private or military secretary. Baring, feeling once again that he had no wish to push on with his military career, chose the first rather than the second of these two options. It was yet another example of the role of the totally unexpected in human life, and paved the way for an entirely new career as a colonial administrator with a special expertise in political economy, the master science of the Gladsto-nian age.

Baring wrote at once to tell Ethel the news and, in effect, to ask her to wait for him until he returned from the East:

February 26, 1872
Dear Miss Errington,

I am about to go to India for 5 years. I should very much like to write to you before I go but I am so afraid of not getting an answer which is really your own, that I prefer to leave this with my brother, who will take an opportunity of giving it to you.

[27] Vincent, *Formation of the Liberal Party*, 15–16.

You know how deeply I have been attached to you for many years; I have never spoken to you on the subject nor do I at all know what is your *personal* feeling about it; this is what I really care most about: it is a matter which lies entirely between you and me, neither shall I ever abandon the idea which I have cherished for so long a time, unless I hear from your own lips that I must do so. Bitter as the disappointment would be to me—for I can assure you that I have worked hard [for?] this one idea of my life—I hope that you will not for one moment hesitate to tell me the truth however disagreeable it may be. But if your answer is favourable, as I earnestly hope it may be, would it be too much to ask you to write me a line of encouragement? I should not then despair but look forward to the end of my 5 years with new hope. Understand that I am not selfish to ask you to make any promise. On the contrary whatever answer you make I shall consider that you in no way bind yourself to anything, but are quite free to act as you please for the future. All I want is that I should know once for all whether I am living on false hopes, or whether I may still hope on? In any case I hope you will not be offended with me for writing this letter. I have been silent so long that I can no longer forbear to speak out whatever may happen.

Believe me that I shall always be most sincerely yours

Evelyn Baring.[28]

This powerful expression of his feelings was written, with much obvious trepidation, on Baring's thirty-first birthday.[29] It suggests a real fear that Ethel would not be free to make up her own mind. Nevertheless, it seems almost certain that she gave him a favourable response before he and Northbrook set off to India. Among Ethel's small collection of her most treasured letters is a note from Mrs Henry Baring to 'My Dear Ethel' informing her that 'I have a small party tomorrow and every Friday', which suggests a recognition that she was now considered to be a close friend of the family.[30] Unfortunately it is undated. However, it must have been sent before Baring's mother's death in 1874. Even more to the point is the way Baring himself greeted her as 'My Darling Ethel' in a letter written from India on 20 July 1873.[31]

[28] CP/1, Letters and Papers of the 1st Lady Cromer.
[29] Ibid.   [30] Ibid.   [31] Ibid.

PART II

---

*An Apprenticeship in Imperial
Government and International Finance
1872–1883*

6

The Vice-Viceroy: India
1872–1876

Learning to Govern India from Calcutta and Simla

Lord Northbrook and Evelyn Baring travelled out to India together in March–April 1872, leaving Northbrook's two surviving children, Frank (21), who had been appointed as one of the Viceroy's aides-de-camp, and Emma (18), to join them later, when the weather was less hot. They took the train to Marseilles, a boat to Alexandria, and another train to Cairo, where they were entertained in great style by the ruler, the Khedive Ismail Pasha. It was Baring's first visit to the city in which he would live for so much of the rest of his life. Then on to Suez and the SS *Glasgow*, which transported them to Bombay via the island of Perim and the British colony of Aden. Life on board for the new Viceroy consisted of long periods spent studying 'blue and other books' about India, starting lessons in Hindustani, the Indian 'language of command', and reading a Life of the Prophet Muhammad.[1] We can be sure that his equally industrious cousin followed much the same routine.

The Viceroy and his party landed in Bombay on 29 April. After being introduced to various officials and Indian princes, they set off on the long, hot journey along the Great Indian Peninsula, and then the East Indian Railway, to Calcutta, a trip which, even without the obligatory stops any viceroy had to make along the way, generally took some sixty-five hours. There they stayed for only a few days before setting off again on a tour of northern India—Lord Northbrook wanted to see the state of India 'for

[1] Bernard Mallet, *Thomas George Earl of Northbrook G.C.S.I.: A Memoir* (London: Longmans, Green, 1908), 54–5; Bernard Cohn, *Colonialism and Its Forms of Knowledge: The British in India* (Princeton: Princeton University Press, 1996), 33–45.

himself', as Baring wrote to one of his local correspondents—finishing up in the summer capital of Simla in the Himalayan foothills north of Delhi on 28 May.[2] The year ended with a second tour beginning on 17 October, which took them to Lahore, Karachi, and then by boat south to Bombay, before getting back to Calcutta on 13 December just before Christmas.

Calcutta had a population of some 500,000, of whom 7,265 were classi-fied in the 1872 census as European, the majority divided into the civil service, the military, and the business and professional elites, with marked cleavages between them. The city had originally been built on swampy land beside the sacred River Ganges, a river which the Europeans per-versely persisted in calling the Hooghly. In spite of certain recent improve-ments in the 1870s, such as the introduction of piped water and underground sewers, it enjoyed a murderous reputation as far as its bad health and great heat were concerned. Rudyard Kipling, who visited it in 1888, wrote at length about the ever present 'stink' from the river which permeated all quarters of the town.[3] And Lord Macaulay, who lived and worked there in the 1830s, had summed it up well in his complaint that 'we are annually baked for four months, boiled four more, and allowed the remaining four to become cool if we can. Insects and undertakers are the only living creatures which seem to enjoy the climate.'[4]

Government House, the official residence of the Viceroy, stood close to the river, between the government offices around Dalhousie Square and the long open piece of parkland, the Maidan, which stretched along the left bank of the Ganges, past the cricket ground, and on down to the military headquarters at Fort William and the racecourse beyond. The house had been built at great expense by the Marquess of Wellesley in 1799–1803, in the heyday of the East India Company's rule in Bengal, and had a marked resemblance to Kedlestone Hall in Derbyshire, with a two-storey central block connected to four wings by crescent-shaped galleries. The former contained the great marble banqueting hall (with seating for a hundred and a ceiling so high that whole palm trees could be used for decoration), the throne room (for receiving members of the Indian aristocracy), two ball-rooms, and the grand drawing room, while the wings provided space for the Viceroy's offices and private apartments, bedrooms with connecting bathrooms for guests, and the council chamber. It was well designed to

[2] Baring to Routledge, 17 May 1872, *Letters from Capt. Baring to Persons in India* (Simla: Private Secretary's Office Press, 1873), copy in CP/2, FO 633/1.

[3] Rudyard Kipling, *City of Dreadful Night* (New York: H. M. Caldwell, 1899), ch. 1.

[4] Quoted in the foreword to *Official History of the Bengal Club, Calcutta* (May 1997), 35–6.

attract whatever breeze might be blowing, and had been much improved by the addition of gas lighting in 1863 and hot and cold running water in 1872 just as Northbrook and Baring had arrived. The stables were across the road from the front gates. On official occasions the Viceroy would sweep out of his residence in his open carriage, surrounded by his mounted bodyguards in their long, bright-scarlet tunics and hessian boots, long lances at rest.

The domestic arrangements were run by the Viceroy's ADCs, each of whom administered a different department—household, kitchen and cook, invitations, and stables—and a very large number of Indian servants. Lady Dufferin, the wife of the Viceroy in the second half of the 1880s, wrote of the jemadars, who acted as the private servants to the major members of the household, the sentries standing outside each person's bedroom door, the kitmutgars wearing long, red cloth tunics, white trousers, and white turbans, who waited at table, and the army of cleaners, some seven or eight to a room.[5] Northbrook himself put up with all pomp and circumstance of viceregal life as best he could, although likening himself to a 'gold fish in a glass bowl on a dinner table without so much as a weed or a bit of mud to get under'.[6] Edward Lear, who stayed there as a guest of Northbrook over Christmas and New Year's Eve 1873, was even less amused. He wrote of his 'artificial life in dark rooms and Punkah air', and later noted that there was no rest in what he called 'Hustlefussabad'.[7] He thought better of the peace provided by the six acres of gardens, even though they had lost most of their shady trees as a result of a cyclone in 1864.

The Viceroy also had a country residence up the river at Barrackpore, reached either by steam launch or by 12 miles of road. It was here that Northbrook went every Sunday he was resident in Calcutta for quiet and rest. It was simply furnished by viceregal standards, with few rooms, and the staff put up in bungalows in the grounds. Visiting it in January, Lear complained of how cold and draughty it was.[8] But it had pleasant gardens by the river—'quite like an English park', according to Lady Dufferin—with a summer house and plenty of shade under a huge banyan tree.[9]

[5] The Marchioness of Dufferin and Ava, *Our Viceregal Life in India: Selections from My Journal 1884–1888* (London: John Murray, 1890), 8–9.

[6] Mallet, *Thomas George Earl of Northbrook*, 81.

[7] Ibid. 271–2.

[8] 27 Dec. 1873, Edward Lear, Journal in India, vol. i (Oct. 1873–May 1874), Houghton Library, Harvard University.

[9] Marchioness of Dufferin, *Our Viceregal Life*, 14.

Visiting it myself on another cold, rainy day in March 1997, I found that it had been turned into the headquarters of an Indian police training college, with rows of the equestrian statues of old viceroys and British commanders-in-chief lined up just outside the summer house after their post-independence removal from Calcutta's main squares.

Simla was something else again. A jumble of gabled cottages with lace-curtained windows, corrugated-iron roofs, and names like Oakover, Ravenswood, and Kelvin Grove, clinging to the thin spine of a ridge 7,000 feet above sea level, it had only become the summer capital at the insistence of a previous Viceroy, Lord Lawrence, in the 1860s. It was difficult of access and extremely uncomfortable. By 1873 the railway system reached only as far as the military cantonment of Umballa (now Ambala), 1,100 miles from Calcutta, after which it was necessary to take a post carriage to Kalka, at the foot of the mountains, and then ride either 57 miles by winding road—a journey which took Alfred Lyall, a member of the Viceroy's Council, eleven hours in 1873—or 41 miles by mountain path.[10] Carriages took longer to get up, perhaps as much as three days, but could come down in much less. Once you reached Simla, the views were spectacular, particularly towards the Tibetan mountains to the north-east, as the sight of ridge after ridge carries the eye to the snow-covered peaks beyond.

Almost every official was put up in rented accommodation, from Northbrook, who squatted in a house owned by the Maharaja of Nahan, to the more lowly officials and the multitude of some 20,000 or so Indian servants brought up from the plain. To the wife of Lord Northbrook's successor, Lord Lytton, the Peterhoff, as the Viceroy's residence was known, was 'like a large rectory', but one attended by 300 servants and no fewer than 100 cooks. Rain seeped into every room, and there was so little space that it was necessary to put up a large tent on the lawn for the ceremonial durbars with Indian princes or for local receptions.[11] The ADCs lived in little bungalows down the steep hill to the north and, as Lady Dufferin noted, had to 'go through the most perilous adventures to come to dinner'.[12] They also suffered from an unusually high mortality, owing, it was rumoured, to the fact that the house was built on the site of a former graveyard. To make matters worse for the inhabitants of Simla, it rained incessantly in the spring, necessitating fires most of the time and causing an ever present problem with mud slides, which regularly took

[10] Lyall to Sibylla, 17 Apr. 1873, LP, MS Eur. F132/5.
[11] Quoted in E. J. Buck, *Simla Past and Present*, 2nd edn. (Bombay: Times Press, 1925), 39–40.
[12] Quoted ibid. 46.

away houses, shops from the bazaar, and, occasionally, at least according to Rudyard Kipling's short story 'At the Pit's Mouth', horses and their riders as well.

Apart from official work, there was an intense social life consisting of picnics, parties, amateur theatricals, and cricket and horse racing at Annandale (a small piece of flat ground in the valley just to the north). Recreations included shooting and fishing, long horseback rides for the men, or, for women, outings in the ubiquitous canvas portable chairs carried by two pairs of men known as jompons along paths through the forests of deodars and other trees which covered the mountain slopes. For most of the British community it seems that all the obvious discomforts were well justified by the pleasure of getting away from Calcutta during the hottest months of the year, together with the opportunity to create a replica of the English way of life, including its mists and drizzle, with as little contact with Indian society as possible. It all produced an enormous sense of solidarity among the members of this well-paid elite, never more so than on Sundays, when they prayed together at Christ Church at the top of the Mall, the Viceroy and his family at the front on one side of the aisle, the commander-in-chief of the Army on the other. The small brass plaques indicating their pews remain, even though the church has long lost all of its European Christian parishioners.

From the beginning the annual remove to Simla excited considerable criticism on the grounds of expense as well as for taking the government too far from its base in Calcutta and regular contact with the mercantile community there. For Alfred Lyall, and no doubt for many other officials who had come through the searing experience of the sepoy rebellion in 1857, it was 'dangerously cut off from the vast country that lies below'.[13] However, for Lord Lawrence, as well as for both Northbrook and Baring, the move was readily justified in terms of the greater amount of work which could be got through away from all the day-to-day distractions of city life. According to Baring, the Viceroy saw it as a 'time for study and deliberation', while he himself welcomed the opportunity to thrash out difficult subjects before taking any public steps.[14] His use of words here is interesting and may well indicate another, equally powerful motive: the possibility of getting away from the extremely intrusive presence of the Anglo-Indian press, which lived off scoops about the government's future intentions and whose correspondents were well practised at bribing lowly

---

[13] Lyall to Sibylla, 17 Apr. 1873, LP, MS Eur. F132/5.
[14] Baring to Dr G. Smith, 3 June 1873, *Letters from Capt. Baring.*

officials and loitering around government offices, making official secrecy something of a nightmare.[15] Not that Simla itself was entirely proof against such practices. As Kipling was later to note in his poetical parody of the ultra-secretive proceedings of the Finance Council in 1886, 'the hills are full of little birds what need of compromising words'.[16] As an apprentice journalist, he was certainly in a good position to know.

So much did Northbrook appreciate Simla's quiet remoteness that in 1873, and then, after missing a year because of the Bengal–Bihar famine, in 1875, he took care to arrive in April and not to leave until mid-October, spending half the year there. As for Calcutta, the practice of taking an extensive autumn tour on the way back meant that he was in official residence only from Christmas to Easter. The fact that he much enjoyed sketching and botany as well as riding, trekking, and fishing may also have had something to do with it. As his daughter Emma reported to her great-aunt in England, 'Directly tours began out came the sketch books, especially at Simla where Lord Northbrook was less watched and also allowed his favourite exercise of walking.'[17]

As the Viceroy's private secretary, and, just as important, as his cousin, Baring lived with the Northbrooks as a member of the family, whether in Calcutta, Simla, or in the tented camps which they used on their official tours. Like most Victorians, Northbrook kept to a rigid daily routine, albeit one dictated by the Indian climate. As he described it to his sister Hannah, he would get up between 6 and 7 a.m., drink a cup of tea, take a quick round of the garden, and then read the Bible or a short sermon until official work began at 8.15 with a visit from Evelyn Baring with the day's programme.[18] Such a routine also had the great advantage of allowing him to remain in his dressing gown until just before family prayers and break-fast at 9.15, when he was finally forced to don the trousers and frock coat which was the standard uniform of the Calcutta official. He then worked until tiffin at 2 p.m., a meal consisting usually of just a little soup but augmented for visitors like Edward Lear to include two hot meat dishes, a sirloin of beef, and two fowls.[19] The Viceroy took the afternoon off, before

---

[15] The same thing could also happen at the India Office in London. See Salisbury to North-brook, 26 Aug. 1874, NP, MS Eur. C144/11.

[16] Rudyard Kipling, 'Parturiunt Montes', 26 Apr. 1886, in *Early Verses by Rudyard Kipling 1879–1889: Unpublished, Uncollected and Rarely Collected Poems* ed., Andrew Rutherford (Oxford: Clarendon Press, 1986).

[17] Quoted in Mallet, *Thomas George Earl of Northbrook*, 78.

[18] Ibid. 80–1.

[19] 24 Dec. 1873, Lear, Journal in India, vol. i.

going out for a ride, usually along the Maidan, with one of his ADCs, between six and seven.

Dinner was at 8.30 p.m. and might involve anything from just North-brook's immediate family and one or two of the ADCs to a larger affair with some fifty to sixty guests. His daughter Emma generally acted as hostess during their first two winters before being sent back to England when Northbrook feared for her health should she have to remain in Calcutta through the 'famine' summer of 1874. She did not return until late in 1875, and her place was taken by the wife of the Viceroy's military secretary. Cooking for major events was supervised by Northbrook's own French chef, M. Bonsard. The day ended with brandy and a cigar before bed between eleven and midnight. Only the Sundays spent at Barrackpore were different, permitting what Northbrook called 'a complete rest', generally spent sleeping a great deal and writing private letters quietly in his room.[20]

India in 1872

Northbrook's appointment came at a time when Lord Mayo's assassination had revived more general fears of a larger plot, or even preparations for a second mutiny. This was on top of earlier fears produced by the murder of the Acting Chief Justice of Bengal on his courtroom steps, as well as by the publication of W. W. Hunter's book *The Indian Musalmans: Are They Bound in Conscience to Rebel Against the Queen?* (1872), which had argued for the existence of a seething Muslim discontent against British rule exacerbated by a basic religious fanaticism. In so far as such worries had a focus, they were concentrated on the activities of the Wahabis, an Islamic reformist sect which had become increasingly active in the 1860s, and those of the Kukas, a Sikh organization whose attacks on Muslims in the Punjab had been brutally suppressed by the provincial government in January 1872, including the blowing of forty-nine Kuka prisoners across the mouths of field guns.

Northbrook began making extensive enquiries about the security situation even before he left England and, by the time he reached Bombay, seems to have come to what proved to be the correct conclusion that there was no immediate cause for alarm. In particular he did not believe in a

[20] Mallet, *Thomas George Earl of Northbrook*, 81.

Wahabi conspiracy. Nevertheless, he decided to keep watch over them, and over the Punjabi Kukas as well.[21] Evelyn Baring was directly concerned in this business in two types of ways. First, as Northbrook's private secretary he was in charge of viceregal security, which he found had been greatly increased after Mayo's assassination, for example by the posting of European guards all round Government House. This led him immediately into a close correspondence with Samuel Wauchope, the level-headed Commissioner of the Calcutta police, to arrange matters concerning the Viceroy's personal safety, as well as to seek his general advice about whether it would be all right for Northbrook to make a short tour of some of the districts where the Wahabis and the Kukas had been most active on his way up to Simla. After he and Wauchope had decided that this did not pose too great a risk, Baring took it upon himself to manage matters by ensuring that the Indian spectators were kept at what he thought was a safe distance. His description of his policy to Sir William Muir, the Governor of the North-West Provinces, says a great deal about his own position in the viceregal household:

I take all the steps for ensuring Lord Northbrook's personal safety on my own responsibility without telling him anything about it as I have his general consent that I should do what I think best in the matter: he is personally very fearless and occasionally complains to me of the irksomeness of the measures which I adopt, but between ourselves I never pay much attention to his complaints on this head for, as I tell him, he must submit to them on both public and personal grounds.[22]

A second involvement in security matters was to help Northbrook to set up the first Indian intelligence service, something which followed directly from their joint experience of the War Office reforms in London. To begin with he maintained a secret correspondence with special agents, one that did not go through the Viceroy's office but which he kept to himself using leather pouches with special keys and keeping the letters in a locked box. Expenditure under this head was not subject to audit, and he kept no record of how the moneys were spent.[23] Later they quietly set up what Northbrook was to describe as a 'Detective Police Force for Political Purposes' under Major Edward Bradford, whose appointment as General Superintendent of the existing Department for the Suppression of Thugee

---

[21] Edward C. Moulton, *Lord Northbrook's Indian Administration 1872–1876* (London: Asia Publishing House, 1968), 9–10.

[22] 7 Sept. 1872, *Letters from Capt. Baring*.

[23] Baring to Lee Warner, 19 June 1873, *Letters from Capt. Baring*.

and Dacoity in May 1874 was used as a cover for his intelligence work as well.[24]

The first step to the creation of a military intelligence department was taken a few months later, in October 1874, with the selection of two officers to investigate routes which a body of troops could take 'within and beyond the frontier'.[25] The result seems to have given Northbrook the confidence that, as he was later to write to a correspondent, 'I believe that nothing of consequence can be designed by the disaffected in any of the places where they live without the government hearing it, and that the dangers are known.'[26]

Nevertheless, even if he did not fear immediate armed insurrection, Northbrook was soon convinced that there was a strong underlying discontent in India, a view reinforced by his own interpretation of the views of educated Indian opinion as reflected in the local press or by elite bodies like the British Indian Association. One of the reasons for this was that he believed that 'native opinion has been too much ignored in recent legislation', a situation he tried to improve by inviting Indians to small dinner parties, visiting several in their homes, and appointing a non-aristocratic Indian, Ramanath Tagore, to the Legislative Council, which had been enlarged in 1861 to include unofficial members of both races.[27] A second reason, which had a major influence on all subsequent policy, was that India had gone through several years of what was called 'over-legislation', including the imposition of extremely unpopular measures like income tax and the additions to local taxes associated with Lord Mayo's reform of the system of local government.[28]

Differences of this kind were often regarded as stemming from what Baring and others referred to as different 'schools' of thought about Indian policy, a broad brush for locating policy-makers and their advisers according to whether they emphasized spending or saving, progress or retrenchment. It was useful, too, for painting a highly coloured picture of each viceregal regime in such a way as to demonstrate to British and Indian

[24] Northbrook to William Taylor, 10 Jan. 1878, NP, MS Eur. C144/7.
[25] Captain E. H. H. Collen, 'Report on the Intelligence Branch, Quarter-Master General's Department, Horse Guards', Oct. 1878, PRO, WO 33/23.
[26] Northbrook to Taylor, 10 Jan. 1878.
[27] Moulton, *Lord Northbrook's Indian Administration*, 18.
[28] Dasgupta notes that the main Indian criticism was not of the tax itself but of the unfair and arbitrary way it was collected; Uma Dasgupta, *Rise of an Indian Public: Impact of Official Policy 1870–1880* (Calcutta: BDDHI, 1977), 85–8.

opinion how, for example, Northbrook's was different from that of Mayo before him and Lytton's, which followed.

Northbrook's own approach was guided by a strict adherence to a set of interlocking principles deriving from his interpretation of the tenets of political economy and good government adapted to what he took to be Indian circumstances. These included the need for a balanced budget, minimal taxation, great economy in expenditure, as small an army as possible, and its corollary, a fierce opposition to military adventure. In India these principles were further strengthened by his reiteration of the promises made by Queen Victoria in the Government of India Act of 1858, including that there would be no more territorial acquisitions, and his own promise, given almost as soon as he arrived, that there would be no new taxes.[29] They in turn determined what Baring often called the 'pace of advance', that is, how fast the process of improvement should take place. As he explained to a correspondent in October 1872, 'almost every large question in this country hinges around finance'; although in India it was revenue that dictated the level of expenditure, not the other way round as in Britain. Hence the 'problem of how to obviate the necessity of imposing burdensome and oppressive taxes without quelling the gradual material development of the country' was 'perplexing'.[30]

Finance and Famine

By the time Northbrook and Baring reached India, the budget for 1872/3 had been prepared and presented by the finance member of the Viceroy's Council, Sir Richard Temple. This gave them a little time to acquaint themselves with the situation at first hand, particularly with regard to recent increases in taxation. They were, of course, well aware from their study of recent budgets and blue books of the main outlines of India's unusual financial circumstances. As far as the revenues were concerned, some 40 per cent came from the land tax, which, in most parts of the country, had been fixed by what was called 'permanent settlement', meaning that rates could not be altered for a very long period of time. Of the rest, around 15 per cent came from the receipts of the sale of opium (mostly to China), 10 per cent from the salt monopoly, 5 to 9 per cent

[29] James Routledge, *English Rule and Native Opinion in India: Some Notes Taken 1870–74* (London: Trubner, 1878), 191.
[30] Baring to Tait, 12 Oct. 1872, *Letters from Capt. Baring.*

from tariffs on trade, and another 5 per cent from various excise duties. On the expenditure side, about a third was generally spent on the Army, another third on administration in both India and Britain, 15 per cent on public works, and 10 per cent on interest payments on the Indian debt.[31]

Northbrook's personal commitment to the reduction of taxes was made immediately apparent by the decision he made in January 1873 to veto Sir George Campbell's Municipalities Bill, which he believed would have led to a rise in local taxes in Bengal. He then went a stage further and, in spite of strong opposition from both Temple and the Secretary of State for India, the Duke of Argyll, got rid of the income tax (first introduced in 1861) in the budget for 1873/4. This reduced the expected surplus to a tiny £200,000 (compared with total revenues of just over £50 million). In the event, however, all such calculations were thrown out by the unexpected need to spend many extra millions to fight the 1874 Bengal–Bihar famine, as will be described below.

If taxes were to be reduced, then expenditure had to be cut as well. Given Northbrook's strong liberal principles, the obvious place to begin was with the military. And given the fact that both he and Baring had been so active in the War Office reforms back in London, it seemed sensible to try to combine retrenchment with the introduction of a more efficient use of Indian military resources. As a start, Baring wrote a Native Army Minute, in which he recommended a reduction in troop strength by 120,000 men and the introduction of reserves. Parts of this were then incorporated in the proposals for a large-scale reform which Northbrook sent back to Argyll in July 1873. However, neither Argyll nor Lord Salisbury, the Secretary of State who succeeded him in February 1874, gave them much support, while there was considerable opposition in military circles both in London and from the commander-of-chief of the Army in India, the distinguished general Lord Napier of Magdala.

As Northbrook and Baring were quickly to discover, their attempt at reform of the Indian Army aroused many of the same passions that they had encountered earlier in England. They were soon forced to let the matter drop, contenting themselves with strenuous efforts to prevent any actual increase in military spending in spite of strong pressures from Lord Napier himself, forcefully abetted by Florence Nightingale, whose campaign to improve the sanitary facilities provided for the British troops in

[31] S. Bhattacharyya, *Financial Foundations of the British Raj: Men and Ideas in the Post-Mutiny Period of Reconstruction of Indian Public Finance 1858–1872* (Simla: Indian Institute of Advanced Study, 1971), 10.

India was energetically revived in the mid-1870s.[32] What they did manage successfully was the replacement of most of the Indian soldiers' muzzle-loaders by the much more effective breech-loading rifles, a tricky issue coming so soon after the doubts raised about Indian loyalties by the Mutiny, and also by the fact that breech-loaders had only been provided to British regiments a few years before. But Baring himself was personally defeated in his attempt to persuade any part of the Army to adopt the practice of German-style peacetime manoeuvres he had just helped to encourage in England.

Thoughts of long-term financial planning were then interrupted in October 1873 by confirmation that the monsoon rains had failed in most parts of Bihar and northern Bengal, and then by Northbrook's own on-the-spot discovery that the autumn rice crop, the principal one of the year, was 'failing altogether', making it unlikely that the seed needed for the spring crop would germinate as usual. An estimated 20 million people were now believed to be in danger of starvation. Fortunately, however, the first signs of distress would not appear until the spring.[33] This gave Northbrook, aided by Sir George Campbell, the Lieutenant-Governor of Bengal, a little time to prepare. They did so with memories of government inaction during the previous large famine in Orissa in 1866 very much in mind. It was to be the Viceroy's finest hour.

Within a very short period of time Northbrook had made the major decisions which were to determine not only the policy towards the oncoming famine but also its ultimate success. These included, first and foremost, an announcement in the official *Gazette* that the government itself would undertake responsibility for dealing with the drought. This was something no administration had done before and proved to be a vital first step in reducing panic in the affected provinces and so minimizing the possibility of speculative hoarding. Secondly, Northbrook decided to purchase the 340,000 tons of rice thought necessary to meet the deficit from Burma, where there had been an abundant harvest, and from Madras, although keeping the actual amount secret.[34] A portion of this was to be sold to able-bodied people in exchange for their labour on various public works projects such as the construction of water tanks and roads. The remainder was to be

---

[32] Moulton, *Lord Northbrook's Indian Administration*, 50–1; E. T. Cook, *The Life of Florence Nightingale*, vol. ii (London: Macmillan, 1913), 274–5.

[33] Sir Richard Temple, *Men and Events of My Time in India* (London: Murray, 1882), 393–4.

[34] This was later raised to 480,000 tons in March 1874 as a result of pressure from the home Government; Moulton, *Lord Northbrook's Indian Administration*, 100–1.

given to those unable to work, such as the old, the young, the sick, and those whose caste prevented them from engaging in activities of this kind.

Thirdly, and much more controversially, Northbrook refused to forbid the export of rice from Bengal, arguing that this was only a small amount compared to imports, that it would keep prices a little higher than they might otherwise have been at the beginning of the famine and so help to ensure that scarce food was not wasted, and that it would be wrong to disrupt a trading system which would be much needed once the famine was over.[35] There were many vocal critics of the policy, including Campbell himself. Their numbers increased when people began to notice the strange sight of ships loaded with rice exports passing ships loaded with rice imports on the Ganges. However, the Viceroy was well supported by the Cabinet in London, and stood firm.

The purchase of rice began at once, and by 19 December 1873 Northbrook was able to inform Argyll that enough had already been contracted for to feed 4,200,000 people for four months.[36] Relief works were started in some districts in the New Year. Then the problems began. Campbell's health broke down and most of his work had to be taken over by Richard Temple. There were also great difficulties transporting the rice to the affected areas away from the river, an operation which required not only the construction of a temporary railway but also the hire of some 40,000 bullock carts between mid-February and mid-July.[37] Finally, when the famine had thoroughly declared itself in May, and agricultural and other employment had come to a standstill, the government had to open its own stores, selling grain to those who could afford it at famine rates and supporting the rest of the population with temporary jobs or gratuitous handouts. Famine committees were appointed in every district. Villagers were mustered to determine who could and could not work. Huts had to be visited to make sure that note was taken of those too unfit to present themselves. By great good fortune the monsoon rains came in abundance. Yet even then it was not possible to relax as it was necessary to make large advances to the cultivators to ensure that the next winter crop could be sown in June.[38]

All this required a strong nerve. Journalists from both the British and the Anglo-Indian newspapers were quickly at the scene, some clearly on the

---

[35] For Northbrook's defence of his policy, see his Minute of 30 Jan. 1874, quoted in Mallet, *Thomas George Earl of Northbrook*, 84–5.

[36] Northbrook to Argyll, 19 Dec. 1873, NP, MS Eur. C144/10.

[37] Routledge, *English Rule*, 207.   [38] Temple, *Men and Events*, 398–403.

lookout for evidence that the government was either unprepared or making serious mistakes. This made each month's government figures for deaths by starvation a cause for particular concern. To indicate the seriousness with which he viewed the situation, Northbrook cancelled the summer migration to Simla in 1874, sending Emma home and making a new headquarters for himself in a specially built house at Hazaribagh in Chota Nagpur, closer to the famine and with the added advantage of being situated over 3,300 feet and so much less hot.[39] Meanwhile, Baring was put in charge of the secret purchase of rice, the amount of which was known only to him, to Northbrook, and to Ashley Eden, the Chief Commissioner for British Burma.[40] As Lear, who was still touring India in June, wrote to a friend, it must have been 'no small trial' for Northbrook and Baring to endure the summer climate in and around Calcutta.[41] At about this same time Baring wrote to Lear that he had a fever, but then that he had quickly recovered.[42] Given the huge crisis they faced, he and the Viceroy had no alternative but to soldier on.

By the autumn the crisis was beginning to pass: only twenty-five people were reported to have died from famine, there were few who still needed temporary government employment, and agricultural life had more or less returned to normal.[43] Criticism continued, however, although only from the Anglo-Indian, not the native Indian, press. Now the cry was that government exaggeration of the danger had led it to waste money by buying far too much grain and then being forced to sell it at a loss. Nevertheless, Northbrook himself was completely confident that, as he reported back to Salisbury, if not for his emergency purchases the mortality would have been very high indeed.[44] Most people in both Britain and India seem to have agreed with him.

Baring's Role

Baring's role in these troublesome events was clearly only a supportive one, and there cannot have been many issues on which he had a direct influence on Northbrook's policy-making itself. These, such as they were, were most

---

[39] Buck, *Simla Past and Present*, 38.
[40] Northbrook to Argyll, 23 Jan. 1874, NP, MS Eur. C144/10.
[41] Lear to Lord Carlingford, 12 June 1874, *Edward Lear: Selected Letters*, 241–6.
[42] Ray Murphy (ed.), *Lear's Indian Journey* (London: Jarrolds, 1953), 150, 153.
[43] Moulton, *Lord Northbrook's Indian Administration*, 114–15.
[44] Northbrook to Salisbury, 2 Dec. 1874, NP, MS Eur. C144/11.

likely connected with the few areas where his own experience was at least the equal of that of his cousin, notably certain aspects of military reform. Still, the fact that he lived so close to the Viceroy, and was so much trusted by him, must mean that his advice was often taken to heart, whether in terms of improving a particular approach or in warning of its possible dangers. As he was later to write in his 'Biographical Notes', Northbrook had urged him to play the role of 'Creon's son', that is, to give him 'friendly criticism' which others might have been unwilling to offer. The reference is to Sophocles' *Antigone*, where the King's son Haemon tells his father: 'For your interest, then, I have been accustomed to consider everything that anyone says or does, or has to blame; for your eyes terrify common citizens from using those words which you would not be pleased to hear: but I in the shade hear them.'[45]

Where Baring played a more independent role was in keeping in touch with various strands of Anglo-Indian opinion and in the highly important business of cultivating and managing the press. As far as the first was concerned, he was quick to seek out those officials who seemed to have a particularly insightful knowledge of Indian society and the currents of Indian thought. They included Alan Octavian Hume, then Secretary to the Department of Agriculture, Revenue, and Commerce but later one of the founders of the Indian National Congress, William Hunter, the Director-General of Statistics and editor of the *Imperial Gazetteer of India*, and Alfred Lyall, whose thoughtful writings on Indian religions Baring much admired and who, on his advice, was made Home Secretary to the government of India in 1873. Such contacts were viewed as of particular importance when it came to ascertaining Indian elite reaction to such controversial matters as income tax and the deposition of the ruler of one of the Indian princely states, the Gaekwar of Baroda.

The management of the press was a more complex matter. To speak very generally it had two component parts. The first was to present the Viceroy's policies in the best possible light, both locally and back in London. The second was to prevent leaks, correct mistakes, and warn Indian editors when their criticism of the government was thought to have gone too far. To do this Baring was able to employ a variety of contacts and channels of correspondence. One was the network of other private secretaries ranging from those of the secretaries of state in London to those of the provincial governments in India itself. A second was the editors of the Anglo-Indian

---

[45] This is the translation used in Zetland, *Lord Cromer*, 53 n.

press, who, to make matters easier for Baring, were often the correspondents of major British newspapers as well. And a third was the London-
based editors themselves, for example, the influential Joseph Levy, founder
of Britain's first one-penny daily, the *Daily Telegraph*.

At first sight much of Baring's activity seems perfectly in accord with
what we read of late twentieth-century practices. He leaked information to
a few privileged correspondents. He suggested subjects to friendly journalists. He corrected mistakes. And on one occasion at least he wrote an
anonymous article for *The Times* during the Viceroy's autumn tour in 1872,
although not one of which he felt very proud.[46] Nevertheless, we should
not draw too close a parallel with his time and the present day. The
existence of a public press was still very new in the early 1870s, particularly
in India, where it had only begun to come into its own after the 1840s.
Then again there was, as yet, no consensus about what constituted a
proper relationship between government officials and the press, no Official Secrets Act, no rules regarding the giving or taking of money. Perhaps
because of this, the selection of letters to and from his correspondents in
India which he had privately printed in Simla in 1873 contain items
concerning, for example, payments to journalists, which seem surprisingly
frank, even shocking, to modern eyes. And yet they must have not have
seemed so to those, admittedly privileged, few who read them at the time.
They reflect, it would seem, an epoch when gentlemen felt confident when
dealing with other gentlemen, making clarification of the ethical dimension of the situation seem much less urgent.

However, there is also much evidence that Baring was aware of some of
the problems inherent in the existing situation and wished to see the
introduction of more transparent rules with agreed guidelines as to what
constituted proper practice. Setting out to explain his thoughts on the
matter to G. W. Allen, the editor of *The Pioneer*, he wrote that he was
always glad 'to afford what small help I can to the proprietors or editors of
leading newspapers, but my relations are only based on personal courtesy
and are in no way dictated by the wishes of the government'.[47] This
certainly sounds somewhat disingenuous and tongue-in-cheek. Nevertheless, I think it can also be taken as an attempt to establish the ground rules
for what, today, is known as an off-the-record briefing. A more concrete
initiative came in 1875, when Baring arranged with the private secretary of
the Lieutenant-Governor of Bengal for the establishment of an 'editor's

---

[46] Baring to Routledge, 31 Nov. 1872, in Zetland, *Lord Cromer*.
[47] Baring to Allen, 26 May 1873, *Letters from Capt. Baring*.

room' in Calcutta where copies of those government documents which were not to be printed in the official *Gazette* could be made available to journalists, as well as handouts correcting mistakes about government policy which had already appeared in the local newspapers.[48] This was accompanied in June 1875 by the passage of a law forbidding all connection between officials and members of the newspaper fraternity.[49]

By and large the relationship just described was between Baring and the members of the British and Anglo-Indian press. It was also necessary to develop policies towards the burgeoning local press with its huge array of weeklies, monthlies, and dailies both in Indian languages and in various combinations of English and the vernacular. Like the Anglo-Indian press, it too had a specific concern with the government's legislative and administrative activity. But unlike it, Indian newspapers had a much more direct influence in shaping an emerging public opinion on matters of government policy.[50] These several hundreds of newspapers were monitored by the provincial governments in a somewhat haphazard way. They were also subject, during Northbrook's viceroyalty, to a clear policy laid down by the Viceroy and articulated by Baring. It involved getting local British officials to speak quietly to editors whose comments were thought to have been out of line and then issuing a 'demi-official warning if they persisted'. A second strand was the use of what Baring called the 'respectable portion' of the Indian press 'as an antidote to the somewhat disrespectable portion'.[51] What Northbrook wanted to avoid at all costs was recourse either to a public prosecution or, worse still, to something like the draconian Vernacular Press Act passed by Northbrook's successor, Lord Lytton, in 1878, which both he and Baring deeply deplored.[52]

Baring's contribution came largely in the way he tried to get the Viceroy's ideas to as broad a public as possible, as well as in the skill with which he wove them together to create a larger sense of the purpose and political meaning of the Northbrook years. Only a few days after he and Northbrook first arrived in Calcutta in May 1873 he was writing to James Routledge, the editor of the *Times of India*, to tell him of the two 'dominant ideas' in the Viceroy's mind: the absolute necessity of establishing the finances on a sound basis and of refraining from embarking on any fresh legislation 'without very careful and mature consideration'.[53] And he

---

[48] Baring to Buckland, 2 July 1875, TC, MS Eur. F86/11.
[49] Dasgupta, *Rise of an Indian Public*, 43.   [50] Ibid. 43–51.
[51] Baring to Buckland, 29 June 1875, TC, MS Eur. F86/11.   [52] Ibid.
[53] 17 May 1873, *Letters from Capt. Baring*.

continued to perform this service right through his time in India, ending up with a spirited defence of the whole viceroyalty in his pamphlet *Lord Northbrook's Administration of India 1872–76*, written in April 1876 and printed just after their return to England.[54]

Difficulties with the Gaekwar of Baroda and Even More with Lord Salisbury

One of the keystones of Northbrook's policies was his scrupulous adherence to the assurance given in Queen Victoria's 1858 Proclamation that Britain did not desire any extension of its territorial possessions in India. This was taken to mean that there should be no more annexations of the princely states which many believed had been one of the main causes of the 1857 revolt. The principle was sorely tried in the case of Baroda, the largest independent state in western India, where there was an ongoing struggle between the ruler, the Gaekwar Mulhar Rao, and the British resident, Colonel Robert Phayre, who was trying in his heavy-handed way to make the Gaekwar govern in a less cruel and oppressive manner. Northbrook's first intervention in the matter was to obtain the appointment of a commission of inquiry, consisting of three Britons and one Indian, which produced a full report on the ruler's misdeeds in March 1874, giving him eighteen months to reform, still under the watchful eye of Colonel Phayre. However, matters soon came to a head the following November with a startling report from the Colonel that someone had just tried to murder him by putting a mixture of diamond dust and arsenic in his morning drink of sherbet.

Aware of the extreme sensitivity of the case, the Viceroy replaced Phayre with Sir Lewis Pelly and then, when he was given strong evidence of the Gaekwar's involvement in the poisoning, Northbrook put him under arrest while appointing a new commission, this time consisting of three Britons and three Indians (two of them maharajas), to determine the truth. As Northbrook's biographer Bernard Mallet explained his thinking at this time, he took this novel step as a way of showing his determination to respect the rights of India's hereditary princes.[55] Unfortunately for him, his plan backfired in an extremely embarrassing fashion when the Com-

---

[54] It was printed by the Viceroy's official press in August 1876; copy in CP/2, FO 633/106.

[55] Mallet, *Thomas George Earl of Northbrook*, 93.

mission split along racial lines, with the Britons believing that Mulhar Rao had indeed instigated the poisoning and the Indians saying that the case was not proven. Northbrook himself was convinced of the Gaekwar's guilt and moved to have him deposed by proclamation on 19 April 1875, but only on Lord Salisbury's suggested grounds of 'gross misgovernment' rather than of attempted murder.[56]

Northbrook's action aroused a storm of criticism in both Britain and India. In the Viceroy's favour, however, it could be argued that it did not constitute a breach of the principle of 'no annexation'. And, indeed, he moved quickly to choose a new Gaekwar, a boy of 10 from a distant branch of the ruling family, young enough to allow a British-supervised education while the necessary reforms were being carried out by his ministers in cooperation with Pelly. Northbrook and Baring visited Baroda to attend the new ruler's installation at the end of May. There they were asked to pay a visit to his mother, a woman living in strict seclusion, but one who they were surprised to learn was capable of discussing the state's affairs with what Baring later described as a 'singular intelligence and thorough know-ledge of the facts'.[57]

Salisbury, the Secretary of State, had been largely supportive of North-brook's policies during the crisis. However, he had suffered his own form of embarrassment from the second Commission's report, viewing it, like many in Britain, as tantamount to a 'trial' in which the charge of attempted murder had not been properly proved and so finding its composition, as well as its outcome, difficult to defend in Parliament. More generally, this was just one of many examples of the way in which the differences between Salisbury's London-centred, and Northbrook's Calcutta-centred, view of Indian affairs were becoming more and more pronounced, a division which was eventually to lead to the Viceroy's offer to resign in the spring of 1876, a full year before his five-year term was due to come to an end.

Northbrook had had good relations with Salisbury's predecessor, the Duke of Argyll, who left him very much alone. He also enjoyed a good start with Salisbury after he took office in February 1874 and immediately indicated his warm approval of the Viceroy's famine policy. Nevertheless, there were signs of troubles ahead. Salisbury's longer-term response to the threat of famine was to urge Northbrook to push on with the construction of more railways and irrigation works. Northbrook, for his part, was fearful that such a policy would lead, inevitably, to the need for higher

[56] Moulton, *Lord Northbrook's Indian Administration*, 163.
[57] Quoted in Mallet, *Thomas George Earl of Northbrook*, 95.

taxes. Salisbury then returned to the attack by asserting that Northbrook's preferred programme involved a great waste of money owing to the spend-thrift policies of the senior members of the Public Works Department (PWD)—whom he characterized as 'dreamers of dreams'—and insisting that there should be a special PWD member of the Viceroy's Council to make sure that future allocations were better spent.[58] Northbrook resisted on the public grounds that such an appointment would be a signal that expenditure was going to rise, and on the private ones that the new member would be a Salisbury nominee, most probably someone from what he and Baring believed to be the rival 'camp'.[59]

The dispute soon widened. Salisbury, believing that Northbrook was being unduly influenced by the parochial interests of the other members of council, began a campaign to get him to assert his own authority. North-brook again resisted, saying that he thought it wrong for the Viceroy to have more power and that it was of great advantage to hear his Council's views.[60] Both sides then began to appeal to principle and precedent, a dispute which quickly touched on some of the most basic questions involved in the relationship between Britain and India, many of which had never been properly sorted out after the British government took over direct control from the East India Company in 1858. What was the proper relationship between the two governments? Who had the final responsi-bility? And, even if, as most agreed, this was the Queen in Parliament, how much latitude should be allowed to the Viceroy and his unelected council in India itself?

As in all such disputes, the personalities, as well as the work habits and the strongly held beliefs, of the men involved also played an important role. Salisbury laboured just as hard as Northbrook to master the details of Indian administration but from the point of view of one who believed that it was he, in the last resort, who was responsible to Parliament for what was done and what went wrong. Northbrook, for his part, was bound to be more sensitive to local opinion, both Indian and Anglo-Indian. Salisbury believed that the relationship was best managed through an intimate personal correspondence between Secretary of State and Viceroy.[61] Both Northbrook and Baring disputed this, arguing that, given the speed of

[58] Salisbury to Northbrook, 13 March, 24 July, 1874, NP, MS Eur. C144/11.
[59] Northbrook to Salisbury, 30 July 1874, ibid.
[60] Northbrook to Salisbury, 20 Aug. 1875, ibid.
[61] Lady Gwendolen Cecil, *Life of Robert Marquis of Salisbury* (London: Hodder & Stoughton, 1921), i. 66–7.

communication produced by the new London-to-India telegraph link which had opened in 1870, reliance on such a practice would quickly reduce the position of Viceroy to the equivalent of a mere ambassador sent out to do exactly as he was told.[62]

Nevertheless, all such disagreements might well have been contained if it had not been for two fresh sources of dispute which emerged in 1875. The first was Salisbury's insistence that Northbrook appoint an agent, or agents, to keep an eye on the Amir of Afghanistan, fearful, as he said, that the Russians might attempt to 'throw the Afghans upon us'.[63] Typical of Salisbury, he had studied all the intelligence that Northbrook had sent him relating to those parts of Afghanistan and the land to its north of great strategic importance and concluded that it was 'patchy and unreliable'.[64] Northbrook was equally fearful that such a policy would lead, inevitably, to demands for more military expenditure, particularly as he was sure that the Amir himself would refuse to admit the agents and so have to be subject to coercion. He prevaricated as long as he could until Salisbury obtained direct instructions from the Cabinet ordering Northbrook to make an effort to obtain the Amir's consent. However, by the time these reached India, the Viceroy had already offered to resign, and the matter was carried over for his successor to address.

The second, even more bitter, battle was over tariff reform and, in particular, Salisbury's insistence, under heavy pressure from the Lancashire cotton interests, that India remove the duties placed on British textiles as soon as its finances allowed. Northbrook, as was his usual practice, appointed a special commission to investigate the matter in November 1874. It concluded that the existing 5 per cent tariff was 'not absolutely prohibitive' of the purchase of imported coarse cloth. However, it also proposed a duty on imported raw cotton as a way of meeting another of Lancashire's worries: that the purchase of fine American and Egyptian thread would allow Indian mills to upgrade themselves by learning to weave a superior cloth. This then formed the basis of a new tariff bill which Northbrook introduced in August 1875, without prior consultation with London, which reduced the duties on most imported items but left those on cotton yarn and cotton cloth as 3.5 and 5 per cent respectively.

The result was consternation all round. Salisbury's immediate response was to send a very strong telegram stating that Northbrook's bill was 'at

[62] For example, Baring to Lyall, 8 May 1880, LP, MS Eur. 132/60.
[63] Salisbury to Northbrook, 19 Feb. 1875, quoted in Cecil, *Life of Salisbury*, i. 71–2.
[64] Roberts, *Salisbury*, 145.

variance with our declared policy', and ending with the ominous statement that 'I fear the Act will have to be disallowed.' Northbrook, for his part, was entirely taken by surprise, having firmly believed that the measures taken to reduce tariffs in general would find great favour back home. An abortive attempt was made to patch up the quarrel in November by sending Sir Louis Mallet, an under-secretary of state at the India Office, an economist, and an old friend of Northbrook's, to Calcutta to work out a compromise. He found the Viceroy and his council still adamant, and the best he could do was to get them to agree to reduce the tariff on cotton piece-goods from 5 to 3.5 per cent. The public announcement of North-brook's resignation came just a few days later, on 5 January 1876, as soon as he learned that Salisbury's secret search for his successor had finally come up with Lord Lytton.[65]

Just why Northbrook first offered his resignation on 5 September 1875 remains unclear. One argument is that it was originally for personal reasons. Edward Moulton mentions worries about a liaison between his son Frank and a married woman in Simla, as well as reports that the Viceroy himself was suffering from some 'private grief'.[66] However, as Moulton also notes, Northbrook might have chosen to mention only personal reasons in order to avoid a public debate in the House of Commons, which might have led to serious repercussions on opinion in India itself.[67] A second argument, also mentioned by Moulton, is that North-brook had already come to the conclusion that there were irreconcilable differences between him and Salisbury which could only get worse. However, this obviously flies in the face of his statement to Salisbury in January 1876 that, when he had first offered to resign, 'there were no political questions upon which I felt serious anxiety' but that now there were two: 'the tariff issue and Afghanistan'.[68]

Without more direct evidence it is difficult to go further. Nevertheless, it is possible to hazard a guess that, after the sharp reprimand he had received over the tariff bill in August 1875, the Viceroy found himself locked into a battle with London which, for all his fierce desire to defend what he took to be Indian interests, he believed he could not win, at least as long as Salisbury and the Conservatives were in power. It would also be

---

[65] Mallet, *Thomas George Earl of Northbrook*, 114–15.
[66] The matter is dealt with at length in Moulton, *Lord Northbrook's Indian Administration*, 257–75.
[67] Ibid. 275.
[68] 7 Jan. 1876, NP, MS Eur. C144/12.

typical of him to look for a way out which would not make matters worse. Finally, by agreeing to stay on through the forthcoming royal visit of the Prince of Wales, he may have felt that this would give him another six months or so in which to do what he could to save those of his policies to which he attached greatest importance, notably his refusal to amend a tariff policy which, as he was rightly convinced, was seen in India itself as a defence of Indian industry against a powerful British interest.

Baring's own public thoughts on the matter are also significant. In one of his first responses, a letter to Alfred Lyall on 25 January 1876, he asserts that

all hope of compromise . . . is at an end. Salisbury's notion of a compromise is well illustrated by the Spanish proverb 'Todo para *me* nada para *ti*'—he wants all the concession to be on one side. So there is nothing for it but a big fight . . . It is in some respects a pity but really a practical protest against the recent method of governing India from home has become necessary in the public interests.[69]

These views were then elaborated in later dispatches, and finally distilled many years later in a letter to Bernard Mallet, with whom he was in correspondence about the latter's Northbrook biography. There he wrote of the 'complete revolution' ushered in by the coming of the telegraph to India, which brought Parliament and the British public so much closer to Indian affairs. It was some years, he thought, before the implications of all this were fully realized. Nevertheless, Lord Northbrook's viceroyalty was in fact a 'turning point' in the way India was governed, involving a far more complete subordination of Indian to British interests than ever before.[70]

Such observations, coming from someone so close to Northbrook, would support the view that the Viceroy did indeed recognize the existence of irreconcilable differences and that, having seen the way the new course of things must run, believed that his ability to defend an Indian position was at an end and that the only honourable option was to resign. This may explain, too, why Northbrook, against all Salisbury's expectations, tried so little to win political support for his own position when he reached home.[71]

Baring's private feelings were different again. The same day as Northbrook's decision was made public he sent a telegram to Ethel Errington's sister Venetia in London, who in turn telegraphed Ethel at Sandhoe Hall:

[69] Baring to Lyall, LP, MS Eur. F132/39.
[70] Cromer to Mallet, 2 Aug. 1907, CP/2, FO 633/98.   [71] Roberts, *Salisbury*, 147.

'Telegram from E. Baring this morning. Shall come home this spring probably April tell family Viceroy resigns great good news.'[72]

His anticipated five years of exile from London had been, from his personal point of view, miraculously reduced to just over four. With Sir Rowland Errington's death in March 1875 he and Ethel were now free to marry. But he would also return to a changed London, one without his mother and her Berkeley Square house. He would need to buy somewhere for himself and Ethel to live and, if possible, to find a post which would allow him to build a new career based on the skills, as well as the reputation, he had developed in India.

Leaving India

Given the circumstances, it must have been unusually irksome to have to play host to the Prince of Wales, the future Edward VII, even if Baring's brother-in law Lord Suffield (the husband of his sister Cecilia) was chief of staff of the Prince's entourage. They were in Bombay to meet him at the beginning of December and then returned to Calcutta for an intense round of ceremonies, which began with a state banquet at Government House and continued with a durbar in the throne room the next day, attended by, among others, six maharajas. The following week was devoted to sightseeing, receptions, and race meetings, ending with the Prince presiding over an investiture for the Star of India in a huge marquee on the Maidan, a polo match, a display of fireworks, another banquet at Government House, and finally a performance of one of the Prince's favourite farces, *My Awful Dad*.[73]

Once all this was over, there was still the unfinished business of trying to hammer out a compromise with Mallet over the tariff, as well as the beginning of the series of official events involved with the Viceroy's departure. These included a journey to Allahabad on 6–7 March to take a final leave of the Prince, a public meeting in Northbrook's honour at Calcutta town hall on 8 April, at which he made a vigorous defence of his stewardship, and finally the official transfer of power to his successor, Lord

---

[72] CP/1, Letters and papers of the 1st Lady Cromer.

[73] Philip Magnus, *King Edward the Seventh* (New York: E. P. Dutton, 1964), 138; Lieutenant-Colonel H. A. Newall, *Calcutta: The First Capital of British India* (Calcutta: Caledonian Printing Co., n.d., Introd. 1922), 127–8.

Lytton, before the Viceroy's Council on 12 April.[74] At last Northbrook was ready to board the Indian troopship *Tenasserim* on 15 April, accompanied by Emma, who had come out specially to act as his hostess during the Prince of Wales's visit, Frank, Evelyn Baring, and two aides. They sailed via Ceylon, Aden (where Northbrook, the inveterate walker, led members of his staff up some of the surrounding steep hills), and Egypt to Brindisi in southern Italy, after which he and his children paid a brief visit to Edward Lear in his villa at San Remo near Genoa on 26–7 May.[75] But Baring pressed on ahead, hurrying to London to meet Ethel and to make hasty preparations for their immediate wedding.

Baring at Thirty-Five

Evelyn Baring celebrated his thirty-fifth birthday in Calcutta in February 1876, just over two months before leaving for England. In spite of all the problems with Salisbury, he could be well pleased with himself, having launched a successful post-military career, as well as, at last, being in a position to bring his long engagement to an end. As he wrote in his 'Biographical Notes', it had all been very hard work. During his whole four years in India he had taken only two holidays of two to three weeks each, had practically given up shooting, and had made no effort to fulfil what he called his 'social duties'. Indeed, the legacy he wanted to leave his own children was a sermon on the text 'il faut souffrir pour être belle', for duty and the primrose path of pleasure 'ne se mârient pas'.[76] It was all well worth it, however, because the best education for a young administrator or politician was to be the private secretary to a man occupying a high official position. It took him out of a narrow groove and allowed him to watch the manner 'in which the most important questions of public life are treated'. He himself had gone to India chiefly as an expert on the military. By the time he came away, he had 'laid in a stock of knowledge on a variety of subjects connected with civil administration' which proved of the utmost value in later life.[77] Just as important, his new skills had made a powerful

---

[74] Northbrook's farewell speech as printed as a special pamphlet by the Calcutta newspaper *The Englishman*; copy in CP/2, FO 633/99.
[75] Mallet, *Thomas George Earl of Northbrook*, 21; Lear, 1876 Diary, Houghton Library, Harvard University.
[76] BN 200–1.
[77] BN 196–9.

impression on several influential people in London who were in a position to reward him with more opportunities in the future.

We should note, however, that these words are not to be taken to imply that he was in complete agreement with all that Northbrook had said and done. An important part of the whole process was learning to make up his own mind and to be able to argue his own case. Even in his defence of the viceroyalty written just as he was leaving he was prepared to admit that the choice of people to form the second Baroda Commission of Inquiry had been a mistake.[78] In the years to come Baring revealed himself as quite critical of what he called Northbrook's excessively 'political' approach to certain issues. By this he almost certainly meant the stubbornness with which Northbrook stuck to his initial promises about no new taxes, as well as his determination to keep faith with Indian opinion without regard for the impact this might have on his ability to reach necessary compromises with Lord Salisbury.[79]

Nevertheless, it was the lessons he had learned from Northbrook—the importance of low taxation, of sympathy with the peasant population, of keeping just in advance of local public opinion, and of listening carefully to the uncensored views to be found in the vernacular newspapers—which continued to inform his thinking for the rest of his working life. Northbrook also remained a significant personal example in terms of his integrity and of his unwillingness to be swayed by popular opinion as witnessed by his response to the attacks on his famine policy: 'I hold strongly to not noticing what is said in the papers, an old Whig position and, I believe, a wise one.'[80] Finally, Baring was forever impressed by many of his cousin's administrative skills, such as the ability to reach quick decisions and, more prosaically, his early use of a stenographer for dictating his official correspondence, something which Evelyn was himself to rely on more and more to spare an aching hand.

Such a workaholic approach gave Baring little time for the cultivation of friendships or even the diversions which appealed to his chief such as painting, botany, and long walks. Northbrook had an eye for the Indian landscape, as can be seen from his watercolours as well as the lively accounts of his viceregal travels which he sent dutifully in his reports to the Queen. But for Baring, writing in apology about one of his own few attempts at journalistic reportage, 'I am so much accustomed to what may

---

[78] Moulton, *Lord Northbrook's Indian Administration*, 24–5.
[79] e.g. Cromer to Mallet, 2 Aug. 1907, CP/2, FO 633/98.
[80] Mallet, *Thomas George Earl of Northbrook*, 87.

be termed argumentation, in opposition to descriptive writing, that the former comes by far more readily from my pen.'[81] For him, perhaps even more than most Britons of the official class, the India they ruled cannot have been more than what Amit Chaudhuri has called 'a background for a series of random perceptions, sights, smells and sounds, vivid but indirect, without substance or context, but occasionally oddly beautiful and compelling'.[82]

What Baring did share more obviously with Northbrook, though, was his stiffness, his reserve, his cold correctness, his shortness with subordinates, and his air of rather distant, lofty superiority to all but the very few people he felt comfortable with. Baring is 'abrupt and inclined to be masterful', as Lyall noted in 1873, although '*au fond* [he is] civil to me'.[83] His brusque impact must certainly have been strengthened over time by his growing self-confidence, as well as by the simple fact of his close proximity to the powerful ruler of British India with its population of over 200 million people.

The only letter written to Ethel from India which has survived gives a tantalizingly brief glimpse of Baring off duty. It is dated 20 July 1873 and was penned, he notes, on his knee, at 13,000 feet, after a climb up the valley of a small affluent of the Sutlej River, north-west of Simla on the edge of what is now Kashmir. The party had abandoned the yaks which were their usual mode of travel and he was rather short of breath from increasing years and, he fears, increasing 'bulk'. He is sending her some forget-me-nots which he had picked on the way up, even if 'the delicate hint which their name implies is not necessary to make you remember me'.[84]

Edward Lear provides a few more examples of Baring away from the office: Evelyn helping him up the steps from the steam launch at Barrackpore, taking him for a walk in the Viceroy's garden to jolly him out of a depression, and surrendering his place on an elephant for the ceremonial ride into Lucknow, an offer Lear was forced to decline because his manservant George was too fearful to climb up too.[85] To others he must have appeared most human at the end of the working day, sitting alone with the Viceroy's family or smoking and drinking a last bottle of beer or a sherry and soda with Lear, with whom he was able to talk freely about art, classical

[81] Baring to Routledge, 31 Nov. 1872, *Letters from Capt. Baring*.

[82] Amit Chaudhuri, 'A Feather! A Very Feather Upon the Face', *London Review of Books*, 6 (6 Jan. 2000), 22.

[83] Lyall to Barbara Lyall, 24 Apr. 1873, LP, MS Eur. F132/5.

[84] CP/1, Letters and papers of the 1st Lady Cromer.

[85] 2, 21, 27, 30, Dec. 1873, 3 Jan. 1874, Lear vol. i. Journal in India.

Greek literature, or anything but 'shop'. Given his fond memories of their time in Corfu together, Baring would also have taken particular pleasure in listening to Lear's nonsense poem 'The Akhund of Swat', which Lear copied out for him before he left Government House in January 1874. It begins:

> Why, or when, or which or what
> Or who, or where, is the Akhund of Swat—of WHAT
> Is the Akhund of Swat?

And goes on with verses like:

> Do his people like him extremely well,
> Or do they whenever they can, rebel—or PLOT
> At the Akhund of Swat![86]

This was all very amusing in the privacy of Lear's own rooms. The only problem was that, unlike the Yonghy-Bonghy Bo, the Akhund of Swat was a real person, the revered Muslim ruler of a small but strategically import-ant state on the north-west frontier who was expected shortly on an official visit. There was obviously something of a shock when a copy of the same poem appeared in a local newspaper.[87] How embarrassing this proved to Baring himself is unclear. But it certainly did not stop him trying his hand at similar sorts of nonsense poems in the future where part of the joke is the use of strange-sounding Eastern words like the one written in Cairo sometime in the 1880s beginning 'Twinkle, Twinkle Lewa Parr' (Lewa being a brigadier) and then bringing in a whole list of similar Turkish–Egyptian military titles such as 'sirdar', 'bimbashi', and 'miro-lai'.[88]

---

[86] Noakes, *Edward Lear*, 258.   [87] Mallet, *Thomas George Earl of Northbrook*, 271–2.
[88] Copy in DP, Add. MS 48929.

7

Marriage, the End of a Military Career, and Off to the East Again
1876–1879

Marriage and Married Life

Evelyn Baring returned from India in May 1876 determined to marry and to settle down in England. All the obstacles had now been removed. He had managed to save part of his Indian salary and to this could be added a small legacy from his mother as well as the money Ethel had inherited from her father after his death and then the sale of his Puddington house in June 1875. Just as important, Sir Rowland's death seems to have removed the final obstacle to his daughter marrying a non-Catholic in a non-Catholic church. In these new circumstances it was Ethel who had to make most of the concessions. No Catholics were invited to the wedding. And she also went along with Baring's desire for the children of the marriage to be brought up as Protestants on the grounds, as Baring states in the 'Biographical Notes', that they would otherwise face discrimination in a Protestant country.

The preparations proceeded at great speed. During the four weeks or so between reaching London in late May and the wedding on 28 June, Baring bought a house at 15 Seymour Street, between Marble Arch and Portman Square, a handsome five-storey building which now forms the central part of the Leonard Hotel. He and Ethel also made new wills. Then there were preparations for the wedding itself. In his last days as a bachelor Evelyn was living with his brother Ned, now head of Barings Bank, and his wife in Charles Street, W1. Ethel, meanwhile, had the support of her mother's sister Lady Buller, still living in Bruton Street nearby. The marriage itself took place in St George's, Hanover Square, with General George Buller and a George Baring (possibly a son of Evelyn's uncle George) as witnesses. Evelyn wore a rose, which Ethel later kept in a special envelope marked 'Rose worn by my beloved Mina on our Wedding Day'. According to *The Times*, the noon temperature was a warm 75°F.

After their honeymoon Baring returned to work at his old department in the War Office, renamed, as of April 1873, the Intelligence Branch, with its headquarters in St James's Square. It had only recently been reorganized yet again, with five sections in place of the old three, and an expanded list of duties. Apart from its primary interest in maintaining a mobilization scheme for the British Army and providing updated information on the armies of its main continental rivals, it had a new concern with the Balkans, where an uprising in Bosnia and Herzegovina against its Ottoman rulers the previous year had led to a declaration of war by the Serbs against the Ottomans at the end of June 1876. Given his own experience of garrison life in the Mediterranean, as well as his more recent Indian experience, it was natural that Baring should be asked to write several analyses of the strategic aspect of the situation beginning with one dated 16 October 1876 entitled 'Memorandum on the possible course of action which would be adopted by the Russians in the event of their attempting to occupy Bulgaria and march on Constantinople'.[1]

Baring's reports generally stick very close to matters of routes and the possible speed at which armies could march. But a 'Memorandum on the Central Asian question' dated 8 January 1877 also ventures into geo-strategic matters with its argument that India should be defended at its frontier and not somewhere in Central Asia. There is also a brief comparison at the end between Ottoman and Russian rule which, once again, shows him to be one of the small minority who believed that Britain would defend its interests better by agreement with Russia than by trying to prop up the decaying Ottoman Empire. His argument strikes what, for him, is a new note.

Did I wish to appear as an apologist for Russia I might point out that it is somewhat unworthy to allow our political jealousies to retard the progress of civilization in Central Asia . . . Russia is in a backward condition but I cannot but think that so much as the Bible teaches a purer and more humanitarian religion than the Koran, by so much does Russian civilization bear with it a potentiality for progress . . .

---

[1] Copies of this and other reports which Baring wrote for the Intelligence Department can be found in CP/2, FO 633/16.

superior to any that is possible under the effete and decaying laws and institutions of Mahomedanism.[2]

It was just then that he received an offer to return to the Near East as British commissioner on the newly created Caisse de la Dette Publique set up as part of the complicated international manoeuvres begun in 1875 to deal with Egypt's failure to meet the interest on its growing international debt. The chief financial adviser on the British side was George Goschen, co-author of the Anglo-French Goschen–Joubert financial settlement of November 1876. And it was he, on the advice of Northbrook's former India Office colleague Louis Mallet, who made the final choice. Until then it seems that Baring's plan had been to resign his commission in August 1878, receive his £2,000 gratuity for his twenty years' military service, and go into politics as a Liberal MP. But the offer of a salary of £3,000 a year in Egypt seemed too attractive to turn down and on 2 March 1877 he and his wife arrived in Cairo.

They soon found a house for themselves in the new Ismailiya quarter of the city, a chequerboard of villas, gardens, and small plots of agricultural land, with wide, tree-lined avenues laid out as part of the master plan for Cairo drawn up by the Minister of Public Works, Ali Pasha Mubarak, in the late 1860s. It stretched from the main centre of European activity which was emerging around the newly constructed Azbakiya Gardens, west towards the river Nile, as well as south towards the Khedive Ismail's reconstructed Abdin Palace and the government offices beyond. The gardens themselves suggested the Parc Monceaux in Paris, with green lawns, shady walks, cafés, and regular performances by military bands. Close by were the hotels, banks, shops, theatres, and consulates which served the growing European community of over 20,000 people.[3] Typical of the new amenities was the handsome group of buildings overlooking the gardens put up by the Duke of Sutherland, one of which contained the Khedivial Club, with its salons, dining room, library, and billiard rooms.[4]

The new houses were provided with piped water for those who could afford the cost of installation. The streets had tarred surfaces, drains, and gas lighting. Senior ministers and members of the ruling family rode around the city in well-appointed carriages accompanied by uniformed

[2] Ibid.

[3] Cairo's total population was 350,000 in the early 1870s, of which 19,120 were European; Egypt, Ministère de l'Intèrieur, *Statistique de l'Égypte: Année 1873. 1290 de l'Hégire* (Cairo: Imprimerie Française Mourès, 1873), 20–1.

[4] J. C. McCoan, *Egypt As It Is* (London: Cassell, Petter, & Galpin, n.d.; Preface 1877), 51–8.

guards. Others used the 400 private carriages recorded in the 1875 census or were forced to resort to the somewhat less comfortable service provided by the eccentric collection of 486 carriages for hire.[5] Had he needed to do so, Baring could have made use of the cab stand which *Baedeker* notes as being in the Place Abdin just outside his office in the Ministry of Finance.

There seems little doubt that Ethel Baring, who all the evidence shows was strongly supportive of her husband's career ambitions, was in complete agreement about the move. Nevertheless, she immediately became ill and within a few weeks Baring was seriously considering resigning his post and returning home. Ethel was against it and persuaded him to stay. A month or two later she must have discovered she was pregnant, as her first child, Rowland Thomas (named after his maternal grandfather), was born on 29 November the same year. These events raise the whole question of the nature of Ethel's illness and the impact it was to have on their married life in the twenty years before her death in October 1898.

In the few places where Baring refers to the matter in his public letters during this first period in Egypt he puts her illness down to the heat and to the general discomfort, the summer of 1877 being particularly 'rough on her' even though they spent some of it in the comparative coolness of Alexandria.[6] Later, when they were together in India in 1882, Alfred Lyall referred to Ethel 'suffering greatly from neuralgia'.[7] However, we have it in Baring's own words that what she finally died of was Bright's disease, a condition which was easy to diagnose owing to the presence of albumin and blood in the urine, and so could have become family knowledge whenever it first presented itself, either before or after marriage.[8] It took its name from the doctor at Guy's Hospital who had published one of the first studies of it in the late 1820s. Now known as Nephritic Syndrome, it is the result of a progressive failure of the blood filters in the kidneys and follows a chronic, relapsing course with episodes of acute nephritis and its associated symptoms of what a later sufferer, Winifred Holtby, was to describe as the 'throbbing and pounding' of her pulses, the 'panic and anxiety', and the 'fear of death' it brought.[9] In the nineteenth century it was also believed, correctly, to be associated with high blood pressure and

[5] Ali Mubarak, *Khitat al-Tawfiqiyyah al-Jadidah l-il-Misr al-Qahira* (Bulaq: Al-Matbaah al-Kubra al-Amiriyah, 1304–06h/1886–9), i. 103.

[6] Baring to Lyall, 6 Nov. 1877, LP, MS Eur. F132/39.

[7] Lyall to Barbara Lyall, 7 July 1881, LP, MS Eur. F132/7.

[8] Cromer to (Viscount) Errington (his son Rowland), 20 Oct. 1898, CP/3. See also Clara Boyle, *A Servant of Empire: A Memoir of Harry Boyle* (London: Methuen, 1938), 62–3.

[9] Marion Shaw, *The Clear Stream: A Life of Winifred Holtby* (London: Virago, 1999), 269.

damage to the heart, although whether the kidney condition caused the heart condition or vice versa was a matter of considerable debate from mid-century on.[10] Other recognized symptoms were a general lack of energy and a swelling of the legs and face due to water retention. Doctors usually treated these episodes by ordering bedrest and bleeding, probably the best things to do in the circumstances of the day, and given the fact that there was no possible cure.

The question of when Ethel and then Evelyn Baring learned the full nature of her condition is obviously crucial. There is some evidence that it might have been during the eighth month of her second pregnancy on 15 August 1880, when she wrote to Baring from their Seymour Street home, clearly believing that she was about to die.[11]

My Own Darling,

I leave these few lines simply to tell you what you know already that you have made me the happiest wife in the world. I have always felt that no amount of love on my part could repay you for your great devotion, and great and loving kindness to me, but my own darling it would have been impossible to have given you more love than I gave. You have my whole heart . . . I know in bearing my precious child how you will study his welfare and bestow on him *all* great love and tenderness and this makes me die quite happy. I have no anxiety for his future as long as your dear life is spared. I only implore you my own as he cannot know the happiness of being a Catholic you will teach him to love his religion as I have mine and I pray it may be the same comfort as mine has been to me.

Courage for a little while my darling. We shall meet again in Heaven. Pray to God for me my own.

Such love as ours must last for ever.

God help you and keep you and my blessed child Rowland.

Your most loving happy wife
   Ethel

Baring had fortunately insisted that they would not travel out to Calcutta until November 1880, more than four months after his second

---

[10] See J. S. Cameron, 'Villain and Victim: The Kidney and High Blood Pressure in the Nineteenth Century', *Journal of the Royal College of Physicians of London*, 33/4 (July–Aug. 1999), 382–94.

[11] The letter, in the file marked 'Letters and papers of 1st Lady Cromer' (CP/1) and written on 15 August, does not give the year. Some later editor has pencilled in '1881' but this is clearly wrong. The letter specifically refers to just one child, Rowland, whereas a second son was born on 29 September 1880. This leaves any of the three years 1878–80 as a possibility, with 1880 as a best guess. As it was common Victorian practice to send letters from one person to another in the same house, it is no help to know whether Evelyn was in London when the letter was sent or not.

Indian appointment, to ensure that she could have their second child at home in London. But, from then on, if not before, Ethel's health remained a major concern. One result was a constant tension in their lives as opportunities for service outside England had always to be weighed against the knowledge that there would be serial recurrence of the acute stage of his wife's illness and the very real possibility that she might not be able to come out and live with him for quite long periods of time. In every case, however, it would seem that Ethel pressed him to go and even, when she really was dying in 1898 during the final stages of the campaign to reconquer Sudan, to urge him to remain at work in Cairo rather than come hurrying home to her side.[12]

The letter just quoted also raises the question of the role of religion in the marriage, especially in the light of Baring's often repeated attacks on the Catholic Church. His 'Biographical Notes' contain a litany of anti-Catholic beliefs: the Church did not allow 'liberty of conscience', its priests were not attached to the rest of the population by 'human ties', he had never met one who was 'tolerant', and so on.[13] Much of this was common to many Protestant polemics of the period. However, it is difficult to believe that the strength of his opinions, and the way that they were expressed in a volume which was intended first and foremost for his own family, did not have something to do with his own difficult personal experience, first with the Archbishop of Corfu with respect to his illegitimate daughter, then with Ethel's father about their marriage.

Nevertheless, we also have to make sense of the fact that Evelyn Baring was happily married to a Catholic. From what few fragments exist it would seem that the love and trust and understanding which he and Ethel shared allowed each of them to respect the other's faith while still believing that, somehow or other, they would both end up in the same heaven. His views on the matter are well expressed in a rather desperate letter he wrote to Ethel from Cairo on their ninth wedding anniversary in June 1885. It begins:

I could not help sending you a telegram, my own darling, just to let you see I was always thinking of you and especially today, of all days. Nine happy years have passed since I was lucky enough to marry the best and dearest of wives. God grant that we spend many happy days together, and that then, if as I hope and cannot but

---

[12] See the article by Major Herbert C. Dent, 'The First Lady Cromer', *The Graphic*, 6 Jan. 1923, a copy of which can be found in CP/1 in a file marked '1st Lady Cromer: Letters and papers concerning her death'.

[13] BN 115 ff.

believe, there be any future life, we may be joined together to all eternity. What indeed would any Heaven be without my Angel wife.[14]

Evidence provided by private letters of this kind leaves little doubt that, for Baring, his marriage to Ethel was the bedrock of his life, giving him love, companionship, support, and a refuge from the problems of his public life. It also gave him access to a world of emotions which he seems to have had great difficulty sharing with anyone but his wife, and then sometimes more easily by letter than face to face. 'I often think that you hardly know how much I worship you,' the letter just quoted goes on. 'I am so shy and undemonstrative where my best feelings are concerned.'

Egypt in 1877

Evelyn Baring's move to Egypt was intimately connected with the country's growing international debt. By 1876 this stood at just over £68 million, necessitating annual interest payments of nearly £5,700,000, or some 60 per cent of what were then believed to be the country's yearly revenues.[15] Like the leaders of the Ottoman Empire and many large states in Latin America, Egypt's rulers, Said Pasha (1854–62) and Ismail (1863–79), had taken advantage of the fast-growing capital markets of London and Paris to borrow increasingly large sums of money both in support of their own dynastic ambitions and for the development of their country's infrastructures in terms of the railways, canals, and ports which they believed necessary for future economic progress.

In the Egyptian case there had also been two other powerful stimuli. One was its government's participation in the construction of the Suez Canal, which, as the result of a completely one-sided arbitration carried out by Napoleon III of France in 1864, led to an obligation to pay the Canal Company some £3,360,000 in order just to obtain the return of land and other assets previously ceded in concessions granted in 1854 and 1856. The second was the economic boom of the early 1860s when skyrocketing prices for Egypt's primary export, long staple cotton, during the American Civil War had produced what one economic historian has called a

[14] CP/1, Letters and papers of the 1st Lady Cromer.
[15] Abdel-Maksud Hamza, *The Public Debt of Egypt 1854–1876* (Cairo: Government Press, 1944), Appendices 11 and 111; Earl of Cromer, *Modern Egypt*, vol. i. (New York: Macmillan, 1908), 11.

'Klondike on the Nile', in which both the government and a horde of foreign financiers, speculators, and shady financial operators had tried to make the most of the brief opportunity to get rich quick.[16] To make matters worse, a combination of poor financial management and the ruler's own hand-to-mouth financial expedients had led to the build-up of a large floating debt consisting of some £26 million in short-term government bonds with very high rates of interest.[17]

Major attempts to unify the debt and to consolidate interest payments were made in 1868 and 1873 but without success. Meanwhile, Ismail and his advisers were forced to adopt more and more desperate expedients to meet their obligations to their creditors. These included the one-off scheme known as the *muqabala* ('exchange' or 'compensation') introduced in 1871, by which those subject to the land tax were encouraged to pay a single sum equivalent to six times their annual rate in order to be relieved of half their burden in perpetuity. In spite of this inducement, however, only about half of the anticipated amount was paid into the Treasury, leaving a complex web of obligations and evasions which it took years to sort out. A final effort in this direction was the sale of Egypt's 46 per cent of the ordinary shares of the Suez Canal Company to the British government in 1875 for just under £4 million. This was a signal that Europe's major powers could not ignore, each one anxious to protect the interests of its own citizens who held shares in the Egyptian debt while doing their best to ensure that none of their rivals would be able to establish a more favourable position in Egypt than themselves.

After many months of skirmishing at the end of 1875, and for most of 1876, a partnership between the representatives of the British and French bondholders finally produced the Goschen–Joubert Settlement of 16 November 1876, named after Goschen and Edmond Joubert, its principal architects. This did two things. First, it split the various parts of the Egyptian debt into three main components: a Consolidated Debt of some £59 million, a Privileged Debt of around £17 million, and finally a short-term debt of some £4 million. All three were to be repaid in two annual instalments, known as 'coupons', at 7 per cent interest. Of these, the largest (some £2 million) was that of the Consolidated (or Unified) which was due on 15 July and 15 December each year. Secondly, the terms of the settlement reinforced the existing system of European financial

---

[16] This is the title of chapter 3 of David S. Landes, *Bankers and Pashas: International Finance and Economic Imperialism in Egypt* (London: Heinemann, 1958).

[17] Cromer, *Modern Egypt*, i. 11.

control introduced the previous year with the appointment of two Controllers-General, one British and one French, the former to supervise the collection of revenues, the latter to supervise expenditure. In addition, the British agreed to the appointment of a British representative to the body of four Europeans in charge of the Caisse de la Dette Publique which had been set up in May 1876 to receive the moneys handed over by the Egyptian government on behalf of the British, French, Italian, and Austrian holders of shares in Egypt's debt. This representative was to be Evelyn Baring.

Looked at from Baring's personal perspective, his duties were clear. He was directly responsible to Goschen and to the British bondholders for the proper functioning of the Goschen–Joubert Settlement. This had the great advantage of allowing him to learn much about the principles of international finance, as well as of the management of a national debt, both on the job and through easy access to the man who was acknowledged to be Britain's foremost financial expert. Although nominally a Liberal, Goschen was close to those with most experience in public finance in both of the major British political parties, and so well placed to influence policy towards Egypt as he though thought fit.

Unfortunately, the collection of letters which Baring exchanged with Goschen before mid-December 1877 was lost when he moved from his Seymour Street house.[18] But those for 1878 and the first months of 1879 remain and reveal him writing to his mentor several times a week, and sometimes even several times a day, as he sought to find a way through the problems posed by Egypt's continued difficulty in meeting its various financial obligations. His growing confidence in his own skills can be gauged by the fact that, as the correspondence continued, he was more and more willing to offer Goschen his own advice. He also used the older man, as he was to use many other close correspondents later in his official life, as a person to whom he could grumble and complain as a way of letting off steam.

Beyond that, Baring had two other important working relationships during his nearly three years as a member of the Caisse de la Dette. The first was with the French member of the Caisse, Ernst-Gabriel de Blignières, with whom he was able to achieve an immediate rapport. Unlike Baring, who was a representative of the British bondholders but not of his own government, de Blignières was answerable directly to the

[18] BN 209.

French Consul-General in Cairo, the French Ambassador to the Ottoman Empire in Istanbul, and then to the French Cabinet in Paris. However, he was a man of spirit, with an independent mind, who quickly revealed a willingness to establish the close partnership which both saw as essential to the maintenance of an effective Anglo-French working relationship.

Writing to Goschen on 28 December 1877, Baring described his colleague as having a 'troublesome tongue', but adding that when it came to getting anything done, 'a more loyal and straightforward man I never knew'.[19] Moreover, as the working language of both the Caisse and of the senior officials of the Egyptian government was French, a language which Baring had never had to use so consistently before, he was heavily reliant on de Blignières to provide a polished final draft of all the most important memorandums and dispatches which they had drawn up together. Letters written by his colleague which had begun by addressing him formally as 'Cher Captain Baring' had, by 1879 at least, graduated to the unusually informal 'Mon cher ami'.

Baring's second central partnership was with the British Agent and Consul-General, the Honourable Hussey Vivian, a man, like Goschen, some ten years older than himself, who had served briefly in Egypt in 1873 and then returned to Cairo in May 1876. As it turned out, Vivian proved to have many of the same views about the Egyptian financial scene as Baring himself, and they were soon coordinating efforts to bring pressure to bear in London in support of the various improvements which they were both trying to get introduced. By and large Vivian used the official channels between him and the Foreign Office to press his case, while Baring used Goschen, as well as Northbrook and other members of his own family.

One other significant factor was that Baring was technically an Egyptian government official, wearing the proper uniform of the stambouline, a black frock coat, and a fez, working in the Ministry of Finance and, like all other officials, usually subject to considerable arrears in pay, for example £1,250 by the end of December 1877.[20]

This somewhat anomalous position, part Egyptian civil servant, part representative of the British and foreign bondholders, part agent of a more general British interest, gave Baring a considerable freedom of manoeuvre which he obviously relished. It loosed him from any one set of masters. More importantly, it allowed him to establish an independent position on certain important issues as we shall see. But all this depended on his ability

---

[19] CP/2, FO 633/2.   [20] Baring to Goschen, 31 Dec. 1877, CP/2, FO 633/2.

to manage his three central relationships with Goschen, de Blignières, and Vivian, as well as a host of others, from the ruler of Egypt to the senior members of the local European community and the representatives of the minor European powers. It was a position that took considerable time and effort to maintain, along with considerable powers of diplomacy, perseverance, and persuasion. For all the brusqueness so widely observed in India, Baring seems to have conducted himself with a great deal more tact than might be supposed, remaining patient in public but able to let off steam in his private correspondence and, we must assume, when at home with his new wife.

The Campaign for a Commission of Inquiry

Even before Baring's arrival in Egypt there had been widespread doubts about whether the Goschen–Joubert arrangements could be made to stick. To begin with most worries had focused on the intentions of the Khedive Ismail himself. The weak part of the financial system was that everything depended on the will of one man, as Baring himself observed in a letter to Northbrook written on 12 May, 'and that man very capricious and unscrupulous'.[21] However, as the summer progressed, and the date for the payment of the 15 July coupon on the Unified Debt approached, other worries began to surface. Would it be paid? Would it involve the old practice of collecting taxes in advance? And, even if the money was handed over, would there be anything left over for administrative expenses, the payment of the accumulated arrears in official salaries, and the bills of the government's local creditors, not to mention such extraordinary expenses as the demands made on the Khedive to help defray the cost of the Ottoman government's military campaign in the Balkans.

Vivian took the lead in conveying many of these worries to Lord Derby, the Conservative Foreign Minister in London. Then, after the money for the coupon was finally raised, he began sounding a new note. Without proper information, particularly about the condition of the peasantry, it was impossible to know if the country could bear the burden placed upon it.[22] It was at this stage too that Baring joined in by providing him with figures giving a much more accurate picture of the shortfall between what

---

[21] NP, MS Eur. C144/7.   [22] Vivian to Derby, 12 July 1877, PRO, FO 78/2633.

Goschen and Joubert had estimated various revenues to be and what the government was actually able to collect.[23]

Given the loss of the Baring–Goschen correspondence before December 1877, it is impossible to work out to what extent Baring shared all Vivian's worries at this time. However, he comes forcefully into the picture in September when a crisis blew up following signs that the Khedive Ismail was airing his own opposition to the terms of the Goschen–Joubert Settlement on the grounds of its misleading estimates and saying that he wanted an immediate reduction in the rate of interest. It was enough to cause Baring and de Blignières to hurry off from Alexandria, where they had gone with the government during the hottest part of the summer, to Goschen's country house at Seacox Heath in Kent in order to explain the situation and to win support for their rival plan. This was to announce publicly and unequivocally that there could be no change in the settlement before a thorough inquiry into Egypt's finances, and that, without one, they would be unwilling to agree to any reduction in the level of payments for the creditors.[24] There is a hint here that both Baring and his colleague were aware that they could rely, not just on their own powers of argument and their high-level connections, but also on an implied threat that if they did not vouch for any new arrangement as being in the interests of the creditors they represented it was very unlikely to gain vital acceptance in Europe.

By this time Vivian had also begun to make his own case for an inquiry, supporting his argument with the observation that both the British and the French controller thought it necessary and that 'Captain Baring' believed that it should be conducted by the two controllers themselves as well as the four commissioners of the Caisse de la Dette.[25] However, there was strong official opposition from the Khedive and the French government, while the British government remained merely lukewarm, something which may well account for the increasingly moralistic tone to be found in Vivian's dispatches at this time. With everyone trying to blame everyone else for the need to beat the taxes out of the long-suffering Egyptian peasantry, it was a useful debating point to be able to condemn the Khedive and his cruel collectors or, alternatively, the heartless French.

---

[23] Statement by Baring, 29 July 1877, enclosed in Vivian to Derby, 20 July 1877, PRO, FO 78/2633.

[24] This meeting is described, retrospectively, in Baring to Goschen, 23 Jan. 1878, CP/2, FO 633/2.

[25] Vivian to Derby, 5 Aug. 1877, PRO, FO 78/2634.

Baring himself was obviously made uncomfortable by the implied suggestion that he too might be party to the tax-collectors' attack on the peasants. As he wrote to Lyall in November 1877, the Europeans in Egypt fell into two different classes. One, almost entirely French, took the 'Shylock view, which consists of seizing the Khedive by the throat and extracting the utmost farthing for his creditors'. The other was entirely English—he was obviously thinking of Vivian among others—and 'rather forgets that you can't pass by a stroke of a magician's wand from a system of government by the stick to government without any stick at all'. He saw himself as an 'Egyptian Whig, standing between the extremes and endeavouring to protect the coach from upsetting by compromise'.[26] Nevertheless, however defensive this might sound, it demonstrates that he was beginning to think of a way in which, after the proposed Commission of Inquiry, it would be possible to reduce the burden of debt by demanding an equality of sacrifice from both Ismail and his creditors. This, in turn, would then remove some of the heavy burden from the country's struggling agricultural population.

Meanwhile, the periodic crises as the time for payment of each half-yearly coupon on the Unified Debt approached continued. That due on 15 December had to be postponed, but only as part of a deal whereby the next few deadlines were changed to fit in better with the spring and autumn harvests: 1 May and 1 November.[27] Baring then went off to see the Khedive on 17 December to persuade him to publish an explanation for the creditors as to why the postponement had taken place. As he reported to Goschen, he had no difficulty in obtaining Ismail's agreement, even participating in preparing the first draft, after which the Khedive himself supplied the finishing touches.[28]

In spite of some temporary differences, Vivian and Baring combined forces in December to try to persuade the British government to put pressure on both the French and the Khedive to agree to the proposed Commission, while also engaging in an absorbing struggle with Ismail himself, who proved particularly adept at coming up with schemes to sidetrack the whole business, for example by threatening to appoint a tame commission of his own. Baring, as usual, concentrated on persuading Goschen to back their efforts, sending him a plan of his own devising in

[26] Baring to Lyall, 6 Nov. 1877, LP, MS Eur. F132/39.
[27] As part of this same arrangement the Egyptian government had already paid a small part of the December coupon in advance in November 1877.
[28] Baring to Goschen, 19 Dec. 1877, CP/2, FO 633/2.

December 1877 in which he underlined the importance of making Ismail sell off some of his own property as a way of convincing the bondholders that they too should agree to some sacrifices of their own.

Even though another aspect of the plan, a British-guaranteed loan to Egypt to pay off some of the European creditors, was quickly dismissed as unrealistic by Goschen himself, some of Baring's ideas did provide useful ammunition when it came to the influence that Goschen and Joubert now brought to bear on the Khedive, notably their repeated insistence that only a commission of inquiry could lead to any reduction in the overall debt. Vivian's own dispatches echo many of the same ideas, the result of his close collaboration with Baring and the fact that they showed each other the drafts of whatever they proposed to send back to England.

The necessity for all this was frequently demonstrated by the constant efforts made by the Khedive and the French to water down their proposals so as to place limits on the areas open to proper examination. Every such argument was countered. Each and every alternative had to be shown to be faulty in such a way that the inauguration of a free and unfettered inquiry was left as the only possible way forward. It was obviously tedious, often irritating work. Yet they stuck to it doggedly through the early months of 1878 until a number of developments combined to produce enough European intervention to bridge the gap between the Khedive's own version of a commission of inquiry and something with much more teeth.

One such development was the intervention of Sir Charles Rivers Wilson, a former commissioner of the (British) national debt who had become the Conservative government's principal adviser on Egyptian financial affairs on the strength of a few months spent assisting Ismail in 1876. Now working closely with Ismail's former aide Nubar Nubarian Pasha, who had his own agenda for reforming Egypt's financial system, Rivers Wilson too had begun to try to convince the London Cabinet of the necessity for a thorough outside examination.

The second factor was the growing involvement of Egypt's newly created Mixed Tribunals in matters connected with the debt. These had been set up as the result of lengthy and complex negotiations as a way of providing the country with a single system for trying civil and commercial disputes involving both Egyptian natives and foreigners. The Tribunals employed what was basically a version of French law in a two-tier system of courts of first instance and of a court of appeal presided over by a mixture of European and Egyptian judges.

Among a number of cases touching aspects of both the debt and the Goschen–Joubert Settlement was one in December 1877 involving a European employee of the Egyptian government, a M. Keller, who won a suit for arrears of pay, some of which, according to the court order, was now to be made up to him from funds allocated to the Caisse. Opinions among the four commissioners were divided as to how best to respond. According to Baring, de Blignières was disposed to 'franquer l'huissier par la fenêtre'. He himself advocated taking the matter back to the courts on the grounds that the money did not belong to the government 'but to us' (meaning the Caisse).[29] Then, in February, Baring was instrumental in getting the Caisse more directly involved in the use of the Tribunals by having the Minister of Finance summoned before one of them to provide detailed accounts for some of the revenues assigned to the repayment of the debt, the argument being that there was a gap between the Minister's first estimates and the moneys he had reported as actually having been collected.

On 1 March 1878 the court decided in the Caisse's favour, a point of some importance, according to Baring, as it established the Caisse's position as the legal representative of the creditors.[30] Thereafter, wide use was made of the argument that the Keller case now made it possible for any foreign government to undermine the whole Goschen–Joubert Settlement by supporting the claims of one of its own nationals to a privileged access to Egyptian revenues superior to that of the creditors en masse. It was fears of this type which finally seem to have persuaded London that a full inquiry was the only possible way forward.[31]

There were, however, a couple of last alarms. One concerned the make-up of the proposed Commission. For a few weeks the Khedive had flirted with the idea of appointing Colonel Charles Gordon, a former Governor-General of Sudan, as its president. A brief meeting between Gordon and Baring was enough to convince Gordon that the latter was 'pretentious, grand and patronising' and Baring that, for all the military prowess, Gordon was 'about as much fit for the work in hand as I am to be Pope'.[32] When this proved impossible, Ismail appointed Ferdinand de Lesseps, the distinguished architect of the Suez Canal, whom Baring

[29] Baring to Goschen, 21 Dec. 1877, CP/2, FO 633/2.
[30] Baring to Goschen, 8 Mar. 1878, ibid.
[31] This is the argument of John Marlowe, *Cromer in Egypt* (London: Elek Books, 1970), 27.
[32] Bernard M. Allen, *Gordon and the Sudan* (London: Macmillan, 1931), 209; Baring to Goschen, 8 Mar. 1878, CP/2, FO 633/2.

disapproved of on the grounds of his age. There was then much better news that Rivers Wilson, of whom Baring then had a good opinion, was to be appointed as one of two co-vice presidents together with the Egyptian Minister, Mustafa Riaz Pasha. Finally, the Khedive gave way to the demand that both controllers-general and all four of the Caisse's commissioners should be appointed members with licence to examine the whole of Egypt's financial position including that of the ruler himself. As an exultant Baring wrote to Goschen on 25 March:

My Dear Goschen,

At last! I really think that after five months of incessant labour the inquire [sic] is settled. We have got absolutely everything for which we were contending.[33]

The second alarm came almost immediately after. On 16 April Vivian received a set of instructions from the new British Foreign Secretary, Lord Salisbury, who had just replaced Lord Derby. It demonstrated a most unwelcome swing back to support for the more hardline French position. The key passage read:

French Ambassador has communicated tg. from his Government stating that there is every reason to believe that the Khedive can pay the May coupon if he chooses and that, in the opinion of the French Government, the institution of the Commission should not be made a pretext for postponing the payment of the debts. The French Minister of Foreign Affairs is anxious that you should act with your French colleague in urging this view on the Khedive and Her Majesty's Government authorises you to do so.[34]

As both Baring and Vivian were well aware, this implied de facto endorsement of a policy of more cruel pressure on the taxpaying peasants. They also believed it fiscally irresponsible as it would inevitably mean collecting so much tax in advance as to seriously compromise payment of the next coupon in November. That it should have come from the same Lord Salisbury who had made life so difficult for Northbrook and himself in India must have seemed to Baring to add insult to previous injury. A letter to Goschen of 18 April suggested he was contemplating resignation. After noting that he had never imagined such blatant British support for the bondholders' interests, he continued: 'This is going further than I can go as representing the Bond-holders, or than, as an Englishman, I like to see the English Government go.' Nevertheless, he soon cooled down.

[33] Baring to Goschen, 25 Mar. 1878, CP/2, FO 633/2.
[34] Salisbury to Vivian, 16 Apr. 1878, PRO, FO 78/2851.

After a certain amount of huffing and puffing he ended a letter written to Goschen the next day by adding, rather lamely, that, after all, it was the Khedive's own responsibility and that the Caisse itself could not yet form an opinion as to whether the payment of the coupon in full was legally required or not.

This was not the first time that Baring had threatened resignation. He had already talked of doing so the previous January when faced with the possibility that the Khedive might arbitrarily change the terms of the Goschen–Joubert Settlement and then hand over only a tiny portion of the May coupon to the Caisse. Now he thought that de Blignières and at least one of his other colleagues would do the same.[35] One obvious aim was to put additional pressure on the British government. But it also seems to have been a reflection of his own troubled state of mind. For personal reasons he had desperately wanted the Commission to begin its inquiry before the hot weather so as to be able to accompany Ethel and his young son home for a summer in London. The long delay now made this impossible.

Equally trying was the fact that Baring felt that he had been left too much on his own in a difficult political situation in which it was not at all clear where his official and, just as important, his moral responsibilities might lie. In these uncharted waters he clung fiercely to his belief that a full-scale inquiry, followed by a modification of the Goschen–Joubert Settlement, was in the best interests of all concerned: the bondholders, the British government, and the peasant population who produced the main agricultural wealth of Egypt. Now, after this had seemed momentarily possible in late March, it looked as though he was going to be forced to act in terms of what he believed to be the unprincipled policy of his own government, which clearly favoured bondholder and military interests over those of the poor Egyptian taxpayer.

The same disturbed state of mind may help to explain Baring's apparent willingness to rejoin the Army during the war scare at the end of March 1878, when Britain called up its reserves in anticipation of having to send an expeditionary force to confront the Russian forces advancing on Istanbul. He went so far as to send a letter to the Deputy Adjutant-General of the Royal Artillery placing his services as the disposal of the Duke of Cambridge, still the Army's commander-in-chief, if war was declared.[36] However, such a simple and, to his mind, honourable way out of his

---

[35] Baring to Goschen, 23 Jan. 1878, CP/2, FO 633/2.
[36] Baring to Goschen, 29 Mar. 1878, ibid.

various dilemmas was not to be. The possibility of war was quickly averted by a concerted diplomatic offensive led by Lord Salisbury and others. Unfortunately for Baring, the price Salisbury had had to pay to contain the Russian threat was to become particularly attentive to France's interests in Egypt.

The Commission of Inquiry and its Explosive Consequences

Providentially, some other aspects of Baring's personal situation had begun to improve even before Lord Salisbury's fateful telegram. In a meeting with Rivers Wilson on the very same day, 13 April 1878, that Rivers Wilson had arrived in Cairo to take up his post as co-vice president of the Commission, Baring was able to convince him of his own, and perhaps also his colleagues', wish not to have to work right through the summer. The result was an agreed timetable which would allow a preliminary report with some suggested reforms to be written by August, after which all the members of the Commission bar Rivers Wilson and de Lesseps could depart for Europe, to return in the autumn to complete a final draft. It was understood that work at such a speed could only be accomplished by avoiding any detailed examination of the complex system of Egyptian financial accounts for the first few months, a drawback which the commissioners justified as giving them time to concentrate on some of the broader questions which, in Rivers Wilson's own words, lay 'at the root of the evil and [could] be examined without any great waste of time'.[37]

A better rationale was based on the argument that the Commission would not learn anything very much by going straight to the accounts in which, again according to Rivers Wilson, they would be 'completely lost'. This is almost certainly true. All the European financial experts who came to Egypt at this time were wholly dependent for their knowledge of the figures concerning revenue and expenditures on Egyptian officials, some of whom were not properly aware of what was going on, and others who had personal axes to grind or personal positions to protect. As a result it was almost impossible to reach any realistic conclusion as to the country's taxable capacity except by a painful process of trial and error. Nor, at this stage, was it possible to find out how the official figures were arrived at

[37] Sir Charles Rivers Wilson, *Chapters from My Official Life* (London: Edward Arnold, 1916), 113.

without spending months and months watching the accountants and clerks at work.

Baring, to his credit, realized this just as well as Rivers Wilson. Indeed, given his powerful personality, his confidence of manner, as well as his thirteen months near the centre of the Egyptian financial system, he may even have been the one to persuade Rivers Wilson to adopt this particular course in the first place. Their hand was much strengthened by the fact that the Khedive had chosen Riaz Pasha to be the Commission's Egyptian representative. Mustafa Riaz was one of the most experienced of the new elite of government officials, having served not only as chief treasurer to Ismail himself but also as director of the Departments of Foreign Affairs, Agriculture, Justice, and Education, a career which had given him an unrivalled knowledge of the Egyptian bureaucracy and how it went about its business.[38] Just as fortunate was that Riaz's growing opposition to khedivial policies was turning him into one of Ismail's strongest critics, making him an invaluable resource when it came to the details of tax collection and budgetary evasion.[39] According to Moberley Bell, he was a 'thin, fragile little man of perhaps five foot four' with 'stooping shoulders' and a 'high-pitched, harsh voice'. He was also 'active, busy [and] practical', with a capacity for hard work and a pragmatic approach to government.[40]

The Commission began taking oral evidence on 25 April, starting with Romaine, the British controller, for three hours, and then the Egyptian receiver-general of revenues for the province of Giza, their testimony being taken down by a shorthand writer.[41] All went reasonably smoothly until the commissioners began questioning the Khedive himself on matters of his personal wealth on 19 May. The result, according to Rivers Wilson, was 'a violent scene'.[42] Things continued in this unhappy vein until 22 June, when they all moved to Alexandria to be closer to the European consuls-general, whose ability to apply pressure on Ismail was a very useful asset. The commissioners were back in Cairo again in early

[38] F. Robert Hunter provides a list of all Riaz's government positions; *Egypt Under the Khedives, 1805–1879: From Household Bureaucracy to Modern Government* (Pittsburgh: University of Pittsburgh Press, 1984), table 25, p. 160.

[39] Ibid. 190–1.

[40] Charles Moberley Bell, *Khedives and Pashas: Sketches of Contemporary Egyptian Rulers and Statesmen* (London: Sampson Low, Marston, Searle, & Rivington, 1884) ['by One Who Knows Them Well'] 121–30.

[41] Rivers Wilson, *Chapters from My Official Life*, 120.

[42] Ibid. 126.

July, having achieved, as Rivers Wilson noted, several 'great concessions' from the Khedive. These included the promise to surrender a large portion of those private estates still left in his own hands after about half of them had been taken over by European administrators according to a separate arrangement negotiated by Goschen the previous year. A second concession concerned Ismail's promise to reduce government expenditure by some £1,200,000.[43]

The families of the commissioners began to leave for Europe in late July, some, like Mme de Blignières, being given a 'grand dinner party' at Vivian's lovely Cairo villa to bid them farewell. Food was served on a terrace overlooking the garden, with 'fountains playing, a full moon and much cooling drink'.[44] Baring and his Austrian colleague von Kremer, who had been asked to form a subcommission to examine Egypt's floating debt, signed their own twenty-five-page section of the report in Cairo on 6 August.[45] This left Rivers Wilson, Baring, and de Blignières to complete the rest of the 'Rapport Préliminaire Adressé A Son Altesse Le Khédive' which de Blignières drafted in French.

Now came the difficult problem of getting the Khedive to agree to the report's recommendations, which not only called for sweeping changes in financial practice but also required him to surrender all his houses and properties in exchange for a civil list. Baring, having begged for a 'holiday', was preparing to leave for Europe in the footsteps of de Blignières when he attended an important meeting between the members of the Commission. There, according to Nubar's own *Mémoires* written in the early 1890s, he launched a 'violent outburst against the Khedive', threatening him with 'the thunder of the powers' if he did not accept the report's conclusion in its entirety. 'His violence revolted me,' Nubar goes on, 'but I held myself in and realized that his threats would produce an effect on the Viceroy [Ismail] and would ease [my] task.'[46] True or not, this left Rivers Wilson and Nubar Pasha to orchestrate their own campaign to persuade Ismail to give in. The preliminary report was presented on 20 August, and on 22 August the Khedive announced his acceptance. But only, you might say, with his fingers crossed behind his back while he began to formulate plans

---

[43] Rivers Wilson, *Chapters from My Official Life*, 136, 138, 141–2.

[44] Ibid. 146–7.

[45] France, Ministère des Affaires Étrangères, *Affaires Étrangères: Documents Diplomatiques, Affaires d'Égypte 1879–1880* (Paris: Imprimerie Nationale, 1880), 55.

[46] Nubar Nubarian, *Mémoires de Nubar Pasha*, with introd. and notes by Mirrit Boutros Ghali (Beirut: Librairie du Liban, 1983), 491.

for his next and, as it proved, last great act of resistance to European financial management.

By and large, Baring seems to have worked well with Rivers Wilson notwithstanding a brief initial contretemps when, out of a sense of necessary solidarity, he had taken the side of his colleagues on the Caisse in a dispute with Rivers Wilson and de Lesseps over the choice of the Commission's secretary.[47] As a result he was able to exercise quite an influence over its deliberations, as well as to make use of it as a platform for his own, now well-rehearsed, view that the interests of the Egyptian taxpayers and the foreign bondholders had much in common, in that both would benefit from being able to curb the extravagance and arbitrary rule of the Khedive. He was also more and more convinced that it would only be possible for the Egyptian government to pay its way without oppressive taxation if the principle and practice of ministerial responsibility was properly enforced. This, coupled with a continuation of European assistance, was his personal recipe for meaningful financial reform.[48]

Such ideas were relatively commonplace at the time and had even informed some of the attempts of the Rothschilds to impose a similar type of conditionality on several of their own loans in the belief that countries with constitutional governments and limited royal property were always more likely to repay what they had borrowed.[49] There was one notable dissenter, however, Lord Salisbury, who minuted on one of Vivian's dispatches that the Commission was 'wholly wanting in common sense'. If it wanted to dethrone the Khedive, all well and good. But if it did not, there was no use 'driving him to desperation'. 'It will not increase our hold on him. Those ill-gotten gains are an invaluable screw. But, once dethroned, the screw is gone.'[50]

Baring did not return to Egypt until October, travelling with his wife via Venice, where, on 26 September, she marked the personal significance of the occasion by obtaining a lock of his thin, light brown hair still preserved in an envelope among her effects. Once back, Baring was left very much on his own to complete the Commission's investigations. Rivers Wilson was now Minister of Finance in a so-called European Ministry, with Nubar at its head and de Blignières as his Minister of Public Works. This made the role of the Caisse itself more or less redundant, giving Baring plenty of time for work elsewhere. Perhaps providentially, it also kept him well away from the growing tensions which were to undermine the Ministry and then

---

[47] Rivers Wilson, *Chapters from My Official Life*, 113.   [48] Marlowe, *Cromer in Egypt*, 31.
[49] Fergusson, *The World's Banker*, 132.   [50] Quoted in Marlowe, *Cromer in Egypt*, 33.

to force Nubar's dismissal following an anti-European demonstration by army officers protesting cuts in military expenditure.[51]

While all this was going on, Rivers Wilson and Vivian had fallen out over the question of whether the Nubar Ministry should try to work with the Khedive or not. Vivian, perhaps still under the influence of Salisbury's earlier dispatches, believed that, given Egypt's existing structure of power, the only way to press on with the reforms was in cooperation with the Khedive, a position which Baring also held for some weeks.[52] Rivers Wilson and Nubar held the opposite view that progress was only possible if Ismail was totally excluded from the decision-making process.[53] In the end all lost their positions as a result of Ismail's continuing political counter-offensive. Vivian was recalled to London in March as a first step to moving him to another post in June. And then Rivers Wilson, together with de Blignières, was dismissed from his post in April 1879 a few days after the appearance of the Commission of Inquiry's final report. Yet it was to be a pyrrhic victory. Two months later Ismail himself was deposed on the orders of the Ottoman Sultan responding to British, French, and German pressure.

Baring played a not insignificant role in this train of events through his authorship of large parts of the Commission of Inquiry's final report. The introduction setting out the basic principles upon which a revised financial settlement should be based contains many of the same words and phrases he had been using in his private correspondence in the months before. Egypt had been effectively bankrupt since 1876 and should be openly identified as such by the appointment of a commission of liquidation.

A second theme which was to form the basis of much of Baring's programme when he returned to Egypt in 1879 and again in 1883 was that, as Egypt was an essentially agricultural country, the land tax was its principal resource, rendering most other taxes redundant. Most important of all was the strongly stated position that there could be no sacrifices by the creditors until there had been what he called all 'reasonable sacrifices' by the debtors. These including the restriction of the Khedive's expenses to a civil list of only £300,000 a year, the virtual abolition of the *muqabala* (which would deprive those who had already paid of most of the future advantages they had been promised), and an increase in the taxation levied

[51] Alexander Schölch, *Egypt for the Egyptians! The Socio-political Crisis in Egypt 1878–1882*, trans. Schölch (London: Ithaca Press, 1981), 66–9.
[52] Baring to Goschen, 15 Feb. 1878, CP/2, FO 633/2.
[53] Rivers Wilson, *Chapters from My Official Life*, 177–80.

on what was known as *ushuri* land, which constituted nearly a third of the total cultivated area. To make this last proposal even more controversial, estates in this last category were generally in the hands either of members of the khedivial family or of Egypt's large proprietors and paid only a fraction of the rates levied on the plots owned by the rest of the agricultural population. The counter-sacrifice by the creditors was to be the reduction in the interest on the Unified Debt from 7 to 5 per cent.[54]

All this may have seemed sensible from the point of view of a Gladstonian political economist. However, as John Marlowe correctly observes, it was 'political dynamite' in the contemporary Egyptian context and provided the Khedive with all the ammunition he needed to launch what amounted to his own coup d'état against the growing European control.[55] Although he was not presented with the Commission's final report until April, he had been shown a draft set of proposals written by Rivers Wilson at the end of March and so was able to act in advance of its actual appearance on 11 April.[56]

One of Ismail's main instruments was the chamber of deputies, a consultative body which he had called into session in May 1876. It is certainly no accident that a new, and more radical, tone had begun to characterize its debates in early January 1879 as the deputies became increasingly critical of the actions of the European Ministry, something which neither Nubar nor Rivers Wilson made any effort to bring under control. This was enough to allow Ismail to use the Commission's report as a springboard for an announcement on 7 April that he was replacing the Ministry with a purely 'Egyptian one' headed by Sharif Pasha, a notable politician who had already made a name for himself the previous summer by resigning office rather than give evidence before the Commission of Inquiry.

Ismail's second initiative was to produce his own rival financial plan, which was then backed by many of the most influential men in the chamber. It condemned the abolition of the *muqabala* but said nothing about a civil list or a rise in the tax on *ushuri* land. While there is an ongoing debate among historians of the period concerning the origins of this plan and the extent to which it can be taken as a sign of the notables acting on their own, there can be no doubt that the Commission's report, coming as it did after three years of growing European intervention in the

[54] 'Rapport concernant le réglement provisoire de la situation financière', *PP* (1878–9), 78, 121–63.

[55] Marlowe, *Cromer in Egypt*, 37.

[56] Hunter, *Egypt Under the Khedives*, 218.

administration and the Mixed Tribunals, had aroused sufficient hostility among many sections of Egyptian society to become a focus for all the country's many ills.[57] Both Rivers Wilson and Baring seem to have been blind to all the obvious warning signs. In their elitist view of politics, Ismail was the one and only actor of any importance, and the shouts and murmurs of the Egyptian population, even of its upper class and its army officers, were simply beneath their notice.

With Rivers Wilson and de Blignières out of the way, Sharif asked Baring to take over the function of his Controller of Revenue. He declined on 9 April, informing the Khedive that he could not help execute a plan which he thought 'irréalisable' and absolutely contrary to the interests of the country and its creditors.[58] The next day, 10 April, all the members of the Commission resigned en bloc after issuing a final warning that Egypt's financial arrangements could not be changed unilaterally and that Ismail's counter-plan would never be accepted by the creditors.

Baring's last act was to resign from his post on the Caisse as well, saying that all his hopes for putting Egyptian financial affairs on a 'sound footing' had been dashed to the ground.[59] He was replaced by Auckland Colvin, who had recently arrived from India in order to conduct the cadastral survey which both Wilson and Baring believed vital to the reform of the system of land taxation. For some days in early May there was talk that Baring might be offered the post of Minister of Finance in Istanbul. He allowed his name to be put forward with some reluctance. However, it was soon clear that the Ottoman government was uninterested in pursuing the matter.[60] This left Baring completely free to return to London without further delay.

Back in London Again

Baring left for home on 24 May. It had been a tumultuous two and a quarter years, all spent in Egypt except for the brief visit to see Goschen in September 1877 and the two months in Europe from mid-August to mid-October 1878. It was the first post in which he had had to work almost

---

[57] e.g. ibid. 219–24; Schölch, *Egypt for the Egyptians!*, 85–93.
[58] Enclosure in Lascelles to Salisbury, 11 Apr. 1879, *PP* (1878–9) 78, 90.
[59] Marlowe, *Cromer in Egypt*, 38.
[60] Baring to Northbrook, 10 May 1879, NP, MS Eur. C144/7; Sir Edward Malet, *Egypt 1879–1883* (London: John Murray, 1909), 33–4.

entirely on his own without anyone immediately above him to give day-to-day direction. It encouraged an imaginative approach to rapid problem-solving which suited his impatient, restless mind. It required the mastering of new skills, including the French in which most of his business was conducted. And it took place in an entirely new work environment in which the incipient internationalism of European financial and, to some extent, legal control coexisted with the workings of a highly auto-cratic Egyptian government which was itself in the process of painful transformation.

In these difficult circumstances Evelyn Baring had decided on a course of action early on and then pursued the campaign for a commission of inquiry with single-minded vigour. 'Since I have been here I have led rather than followed,' as he informed Goschen during a tense moment in January 1878, adding somewhat piously, 'and considering the interests I represent, I think I should continue to do so.'[61] It was good training in the ability to marshal arguments, to anticipate problems, to maintain personal and diplomatic alliances, and to find his way through a constantly shifting set of local circumstances. His stance was well described by Sharif Pasha, who, as Baring reported to Goschen, was supposed to have said that he (Baring) was 'bien dur' but reasonable.[62] Nevertheless, we also have to remember that he was only a part of the considerable array of Egyptian and European forces at work in Cairo, that he was not indispensable to any one set of interests, and that he could be sure of only the most general support from his own government and the rest of his colleagues on the Caisse.

Some of the personal stresses and strains which all this produced can be seen in his letters to Goschen recording his weekly, and sometimes daily, ups and downs, as he is constantly trying to define his own position and to work out what to do next. The period between December 1877 and April 1878 was a particular test. As he wrote on 2 February 1878:

The Caisse has been in an extremely difficult position for the last three months. I cannot say if anyone else would have done better. So long, however, as *my* conduct has the approval of the intelligent and well-informed minority, I shall bear the newspaper attacks with equanimity, and shall certainly not attempt to answer.[63]

---

[61] Baring to Goschen, 23 Jan. 1878, CP/2, FO 633/2.
[62] 31 Dec. 1877, CP/2, FO 633/2.
[63] Baring to Goschen, 2 Feb. 1879, CP/2, FO 633/2.

And, true to his word, he did not answer back, in public at least, even if he did write privately to a few editors and correspondents when he though their criticism had gone too far.[64]

Baring's letters to Goschen also provided him with a way of letting off steam. Romaine, the British Controller-General, who had his own plan to solve Egypt's financial difficulties, was described as a 'dangerous lunatic'; a letter sent by the Khedive in January 1878 was a 'string of lies'.[65] There are even a few attempts at black humour. In February 1878 Baring told Goschen of how a man had appeared recently at a masked ball at Alexandria dressed as the 'cushion of the Caisse' with an empty bag on which was written in large letters 'Caisse de la Dette Publique. Versement pour le mois de Janvier P.T. 300 (about three pounds)', an obvious reference to the strong feeling among many members of the local European community that he and his colleagues were not insisting that every last penny be squeezed out of Ismail and his tax-collectors.[66]

Two other themes emerge which were to have important consequences when he returned to Egypt in 1879 and again in 1883. One was the stress Baring began to put on bondholder recognition that they needed to have the 'permanent interests' of Egypt at heart.[67] Read in the context of the times, what this meant was that they should not press the peasantry too hard. A situation in which taxes had to be collected in advance to meet each coupon was, he believed, very obviously counter-productive in that it threatened future agricultural output. Such thinking was also part of a larger attempt to find a way forward in which, in his mind at least, everyone's interests could be reconciled. And this, in turn, implied that he, and perhaps a few like-minded colleagues, knew just what those interests were.

The second theme is the beginning of his growing obsession with the person of the Khedive Ismail himself. Baring had had audiences with the Khedive on a number of occasions in 1877, and so knew something about him at first hand. The initial charm soon wore thin, and Baring came to think of him as a monster to whom almost any crime could be ascribed. Hence, by February 1878, if not before, he had come to the conclusion that it would be a 'monstrous good thing if he [Ismail] should go'.[68] It was almost as though it had become a personal battle between Baring and the

---

[64] e.g. his letter to Palgrave, editor of *The Economist*, 23 Mar. 1878, copy in CP/2, FO 633/2.
[65] Baring to Goschen, 23 Dec. 1877 and 23 Jan. 1878, ibid.
[66] Baring to Goschen, 4 Feb. 1878, ibid.
[67] e.g. Baring to Goschen, 23 Jan. 1878, ibid.
[68] Baring to Goschen, 15 Feb. 1878, ibid.

prince of all evil, a battle which only one of them could win. In April 1878 it was the Khedive who seemed triumphant. However, almost as soon as Baring had got back to London, he learned that Ismail had been deposed and that he himself had been invited by Salisbury to return to Egypt as one of the two new Controllers-General, putting the shoe very much on the other foot.

Nevertheless, the battle was by no means over even then. The shadow of Ismail would continue to haunt Baring after he returned to Egypt in 1883, providing him with a convenient justification for continued European control, yet always there was something that had to be endlessly confronted, abused, and knocked down, like a Mr Punch who could never quite be made to disappear.

Baring's firm intention was once again to settle down in England for good. However, in spite of having retired from the Army, he was still not sure what to try next. As he had written to Lyall the previous November, 'I can scarcely afford parliament, which is what I would like to do.'[69] It is true that this is later contradicted by a note in his *Modern Egypt*, the first draft of which was written in the early 1890s, that it had then been his intention to stand as a Liberal candidate for East Norfolk in the next parliamentary election.[70] No doubt there were various ideas circulating in his mind at the time, including the knowledge that life as an unpaid of Member of Parliament would involve a considerable outlay of personal funds.

Whatever his plans, they are unlikely to have involved service for the Disraeli–Salisbury Government, for which he had a 'profound mistrust' on account of its policies both in India, where he felt it was stirring up needless trouble on the north-west frontier, and of its support for the Ottomans.[71] Nevertheless, this is exactly the direction he took when, in late July or early August, Salisbury offered him the post of Controller-General in Egypt. After some hesitation he accepted, for what must have seemed like a number of good reasons. One was that, with Ismail gone, there was now some real hope of implementing the programme of reforms set out by the Commission of Inquiry. The fact that de Blignières had already agreed to be the other Controller-General must have made this argument still more powerful. The second was that he would go at a salary

[69] Baring to Lyall, 17 Nov. 1879, LP, MS Eur. F132/39.
[70] Cromer, *Modern Egypt*, i. 159 n.
[71] Baring to J. Scott, 30 Dec. 1877, CP/2, FO 633/2; Zetland, *Lord Cromer*, 73.

of £4,000 a year, an increase of £1,000 over his previous one, and approaching that of a British cabinet minister.[72]

Still, even with all these obvious benefits, Baring insisted on the important qualification that he would only serve until Egypt's 'immediate financial difficulties were solved', after which he would request that someone else be nominated to take his place. Worries about Ethel's health and about how much time she and their young son could reasonably spend with him in Egypt must have been a powerful factor in all this. And yet, as ever, there is every reason to suppose that his wife was as supportive of the new offer as she had always been before.

---

[72] Baring to Salisbury, 20 Sept. 1879, CP/2, FO 633/2. In BN 263–4 he mentions that his private income in 1879 was not large enough to allow him to dispense with an 'official' salary.

8

Controlling Egypt's Finances
1879–1880

Putting Things Back in Place: London, Paris, and Vienna

On 25 June 1879 the Ottoman Sultan sent two telegrams to Egypt. One, addressed to Son Altesse Ismail Pacha, 'Ex-Khédive', ordered him to leave the country at once. The other addressed to his son Taufiq made it clear that he was to take his father's place. Five days later, on 30 June, Ismail boarded his personal yacht at Alexandria never to return.

Ismail's departure paved the way for a bout of feverish consultation between Salisbury, in London, and Waddington, his opposite number in Paris, about how best to restart the process of Egyptian financial reform. The British Foreign Secretary also took steps to define his own country's interest in the matter. This included discussions with Baring, Rivers Wilson, and Vivian in July, after which Baring was asked to join with de Blignières in drawing up a draft for the creation of a commission of liquidation to settle the question of Egypt's bankruptcy, as recommended in the final report of the Commission of Inquiry.[1] It was only a week or so later that Baring was also asked if he would go back to Egypt with his old colleague as the new British Controller of Egyptian Finance.[2]

Salisbury met with Baring a number of times in August to work out the details of his new duties in Cairo. They also discussed the proposals which Salisbury was to present to Waddington as a basis for the re-creation on the system of Anglo-French control. According to Baring himself, he and

---

[1] Salisbury to Lord Lyons (British Ambassador to France), 22 July 1879, *PP* (1880) 79, 15.

[2] The exact date on which he accepted the offer is unclear, but it was some time before 6 August, the day Salisbury sent a dispatch to the acting British Consul-General in Egypt with the news; Salisbury to Lascelles, 6 Aug. 1879, *PP* (1880) 79, 46.

Salisbury got on well in spite of past problems and their 'radically different point of view' about Eastern affairs. As Baring summed up the matter in a letter to Northbrook, Salisbury believed that the 'political regeneration of Mohamedism was possible'—at least as far as reform of the Turkish bureaucracy was concerned—but 'I don't agree.'[3] However, they still found it reasonably easy to reach a meeting of minds about Egypt itself. Salisbury, like Baring, had come to the conclusion that it was better to try to exercise an informal, rather than a formal, authority. As he wrote to Baring officially on 11 September, he was to be appointed directly by the British government to exercise powers of 'inspection and advice', not those of direct administration.[4]

What Salisbury and Baring had clearly in mind was the opposition stirred up in Egypt by the presence of Rivers Wilson and de Blignières as cabinet ministers in the Nubar government and its immediate successor the previous spring. Both men were also in complete agreement about the need to share power with the French. Nevertheless, Salisbury, at least, was sure the British would draw ahead of France over time, the result, as he told Goschen, of 'the natural superiority which a good Englishman in such a position is pretty sure to show'.[5]

Two other factors played an important role in their considerations. First, both Salisbury and Baring depended largely on the final report of the Commission of Inquiry itself as a guide as to what to do next. This had raised a number of general questions which it was now necessary to address. They included the designation of a cut-off date after which all new contracts entered into by the Egyptian government became subject to the new arrangements, the size of the fixed expenses of the government which needed to be given first call on Egypt's revenues, and the status of Egypt's bankruptcy in international law. Not surprisingly, these were questions to which Baring had already reached his own, well-considered answers. He had also had the opportunity of coordinating his thinking with de Blignières during their meeting in July, as well as by frequent exchange of letter.

Secondly, Baring was able to exercise his direct personal influence by insisting that he and de Blignières should not proceed to Egypt until the political and legal situation concerning Egypt's indebtedness had been properly settled. It was clear, as he wrote to Salisbury on 19 September, that the recommendations of the proposed commission would have to be

[3] Baring to Northbrook, 21 Sept. 1879, NP, MS Eur. C144/7.
[4] Salisbury to Baring, 11 Sept. 1879, CP/2, FO 633/2.
[5] Roberts, *Salisbury*, 228–9.

promulgated officially by an Egyptian government decree. However, this would make no sense without the prior consent of the fourteen powers who had set up the Mixed Tribunals to the application of any such decree to their own nationals resident in Egypt. If not, the new settlement would immediately by challenged by all and sundry on the grounds that it affected legal rights acquired since 1876.[6] It was Baring's personal opinion that the best way forward would be to set up an international commission on Egyptian legislation to negotiate a general agreement limiting the powers of the Tribunals. But Salisbury for once disagreed, arguing that 'where so many Powers have to be consulted, the resources of obstruction are endless'. He preferred to concentrate on obtaining international agreement for the commission of liquidation, a difficult enough task in its own right.[7]

For some of the time Salisbury was on holiday at Dieppe, although using the occasion to finalize matters with the French. General agreement was reached by mid-September on a number of important issues. The most significant of these from a financial point of view was joint Anglo-French support for the institution of an international commission of liquidation with power to deal with the Unified Debt and all other liabilities. A second area of agreement involved a commitment that, before any money was paid to the creditors, a sufficient sum should be set aside for the government's administrative expenses. And a third was that Baring and de Blignières should meet in Paris to draw up a draft decree for the establishment of the commission, as well as identical instructions to themselves as to their own powers and duties.[8]

When Baring arrived in France on 21 September, he had no trouble carrying out that part of his charge relating to de Blignières and himself. They both agreed that they should offer advice but exercise no administrative functions. They also inserted a clause to the effect that neither of them could be dismissed without the consent of their respective governments. And they now knew each other so well that, although Baring was nominally in charge of the revenue side and de Blignières that of expenditure, they were able to avoid the tricky question of the exact division of labour between them by agreeing to leave the matter entirely to their own discretion once they reached Cairo.[9]

[6] Baring to Salisbury, 19 Sept. 1879, CP/2, FO 633/2.
[7] Salisbury to Baring, 25 Nov. 1879, ibid.
[8] Salisbury to Malet, PP (1880) 79, 1127–8.
[9] Cromer, Modern Egypt, i. 159–63.

Some of the other details involved a longer period of negotiation. Salisbury insisted that Rivers Wilson be the president of the proposed commission, even though the Khedive was against it and Baring lukewarm. It was also necessary to reach a compromise with the French about the commission's terms of reference. Baring, foreseeing the possibility that it might be desirable to reduce the rate of interest on the Unified Debt to 4 per cent, wanted to ensure that, in this one instance at least, the new commission was not restricted simply to repeating whatever the previous commission had suggested. The French, unwilling to open up the possibility of such a reduction, resisted. A final compromise involved a wording which called upon the new commission to take account, 'as far as possible', of its predecessor's recommendations.[10]

With an Anglo-French agreement in place, Baring and de Blignières were free to leave for Cairo. It was decided, however, that they should travel to Vienna first in order to listen to certain demands relative to Austro-Hungarian rights in Egypt, leaving Salisbury and Waddington with the formidable task of obtaining the assent of the eleven other powers represented on the Mixed Tribunals.

Before setting out for Vienna on 20 October, Baring had two more significant tasks to perform. The first involved a meeting with Lord Salisbury, at which, in a further definition of his own role, he put it on record that, even though he had been appointed by the British government, he regarded himself as having responsibilities to the Egyptian government which might well conflict with those of Britain. In such a case, he said, he regarded his Egyptian responsibilities as paramount.[11] Salisbury seemed understanding and wrote to him as he was leaving for Vienna that he was 'quite right to take, in some sort, an independent line in regard to HMG. Your position is not very easy to define, but you have duties to the Egyptian sovereign and people which we have not and you cannot be entirely guided by the political interests of England as we shall be.'[12] This was as clear, or, perhaps better, as unclear, a statement as could be wished, giving Baring a certain freedom of manoeuvre but nevertheless indicating that there must also be some obvious limits to how far he might go.

The second task was a visit to Baron Edmond de Rothschild in order to discuss the loan to the Egyptian government of £8,500,000 which the English and French Rothschilds had agreed to float in an agreement

---

[10] Marlowe, *Cromer in Egypt*, 45–6.   [11] Ibid. 46.
[12] Salisbury to Baring, 29 Oct. 1879, CP/2, FO 633/2.

signed in October 1878. It had been negotiated by Rivers Wilson and its purpose was both to pay off some of the floating debt and to provide a financial cushion against any unexpected revenue shortfall in the short run. According to Wilson, the Rothschilds had initially asked it to be guaranteed by the British government. However, he had managed to persuade them to accept an alternative arrangement whereby the lands offered as security—part of the Khedive's estate known as the Domains—were to be administered by three, British, French, and Egyptian, commissioners jointly responsible for collecting the revenues needed to service the debt.[13] Another part of the agreement permitted the Rothschilds to hand over the loan money to the Egyptian government at staged intervals. This gave them considerable leverage by allowing them to threaten to withhold further payments unless certain new demands were met.

The Rothschilds had already moved to suspend payments in February 1879 until a number of legal matters involving outstanding suits against the Domains had been settled. Whether by design or not this had the further effect of helping to scupper the alternative financial scheme put forward by Sharif Pasha's 'nationalist' government in April, a scheme which relied on Rothschild money to pay off many of the government's more pressing creditors.[14] Further intervention followed in July 1879, when the Rothschilds made it clear during the early stages of discussion concerning the appointment of a commission of liquidation that they would not hand over any more money until the Domains lands should be declared exempt from possible seizure.[15] Their aim was clearly to ensure that, in the new free-for-all opened up by the creation of the Mixed Tribunals, no one would be able to use Egypt's courts to claim a prior legal right either to the Domains lands or to their revenues.

At the meeting with the Baron, Baring agreed to use his best efforts to persuade the Egyptian government to remit that part of the Domains' revenues which it owed to the Rothschilds but had placed in a special temporary account in the Bank of England in an effort to force them to hand over more of the main loan. This he did within a few days of his arrival in Cairo. Nevertheless, the matter was far from over, as we shall see, and soon became a source of considerable annoyance when the

[13] Rivers Wilson, *Chapters from My Official Life*, 172–4.

[14] The matter was generally thought to have been cleared up by the Cairo Tribunal of First Instance in April, but the money continued to be withheld; Lascelles to Salisbury, 4 Apr. 1879, *PP* (1878–9) 78, 90.

[15] M. M. Rothschild, 'Pro-Memorial', 22 July 1879, *PP* (1880) 89, 17.

Rothschilds seemed to renege on their part of the bargain. It was Baring's first, but by no means his last, official encounter with a member of his family's historic banking rivals.

Negotiations with the Austrians proved just as taxing. In a memorandum written on 1 November, Baring asserted that what they wanted was a share in the future financial management of Egypt, an opening which, so he believed, threatened further expansion to include the Germans and the Italians as well. The result would be a type of 'international government', a phrase almost certainly inserted to alarm Salisbury, whom he knew to be dead set against any such idea. It left the British and the French with what he saw as a straightforward decision. Did they, or did they not, want a further expansion of European control? If no, he and de Blignières could proceed to Egypt at once. But if yes, their negotiations with the Austrians would have to go on.[16] Baring's own predilection for a 'no' answer is obvious. As he telegraphed Salisbury's private secretary the next day: 'If British French Governments prepared to withdraw from Tribunals, support us tooth and nail and guaranteed the Khedive against any serious interference by the other powers then no reason why Austrian proposals should not be fully rejected.'[17]

In the heat of the moment Baring was increasingly willing to put forward such simple, even brutal, solutions to the complex problems of managing an Egypt which seemed to him hopelessly entangled in a web of often contradictory international obligations and constraints. Nevertheless, more diplomatic counsels usually prevailed, as they did on this occasion when, with the talks in Vienna getting nowhere, he and de Blignières were simply told to move on, leaving yet another problem for Salisbury and Waddington to finesse. It did, however, have lasting repercussions as far as Baring's attitude to the appointment of a commission of liquidation was concerned. He now came to believe that if the British and French could be persuaded to take a strong stance against the other powers, there would be no need for such a commission at all, leaving the new Egyptian government very much more the master of its own house.

The two Controllers arrived back in Cairo in late November, Baring on the 20th and de Blignières on the 26th. Baring found himself a house in the rue Moughrabi (now Sharia Adly), which ran from the place de l'Opéra next to the Azbakiya Gardens down to the Ismailiya Canal. It was very

[16] 'Memorandum of a Conference Between Major Baring, M. de Blignières, Baron Calice and Baron Schwegel, Vienna, 1 November 1879', a copy of which can be found in CP/2, FO 633/2.
[17] Baring to Currie, 2 Nov. 1879, CP/2, FO 633/2.

close to the English Church (built by public subscription in 1876, and presided over by the redoubtable Dean Butcher), the Shepheard's Hotel, and most of the other major consular offices and European political agencies. Ethel soon joined him. Sadly, her health once again took a turn for the worse, causing Northbrook to observe in January 1880 that he wished that 'Mrs Evelyn and Cairo agreed better'.[18] She was also found herself pregnant again the following spring and it is likely, though there is no direct evidence for this, that she returned to London sometime shortly thereafter to be closer to her English doctor.

The Establishment of a New Triumvirate: Riaz, Baring, and de Blignières

By the time Baring and de Blignières finally reached Egypt, a ministry headed by Mustafa Riaz Pasha had been in existence for just over two months. Riaz himself had been subject to heavy local criticism for having joined the Commission of Inquiry and, under pressure from the Khedive, had been forced to leave the country for Europe at the end of April. Sensing that a new wind was blowing in the months after Ismail's own exile, he returned to Egypt in September and was soon entrusted with forming a new government, secure in the new Khedive's assurance that he was ready to rule with and through his ministers. In addition to presiding over the council of ministers whenever Taufiq was not present, Riaz also took over the key Ministries of Finance and the Interior for himself.

Like Nubar, Riaz was willing to collaborate with the European system of financial control for reasons which seem to have combined realism with a desire for the personal power necessary to secure the regeneration of his country.[19] He believed in honest government. He disliked many of the aspects of Ismail's dictatorial use of khedivial authority, including his frequent resort to arbitrary taxation. He was also a sincere Muslim who was rarely seen without his prayer beads and who lived in an unusually simple Cairene house.[20] And he firmly believed that Islam contained within it the means for its own reform, a view which may well have been reinforced by his association with the Islamic activist Jamal al-Din al-Afghani, whom he had invited to Egypt from Istanbul in 1871.

[18] Northbrook to Baring, 16 Jan. 1880, CP/2, FO 633/2.
[19] Hunter, *Egypt*, 191–2.
[20] Bell, *Khedives and Pashas*, 124.

It was al-Afghani whose activities had done so much to provide the Egyptian movement against European control with many of its most significant weapons, including the use of a burgeoning local press to spread its message of the vital need for Islamic modernization and Islamic self-assertion. Baring was probably right to surmise that Riaz himself regarded the Anglo-French Control as a 'necessary evil' and was looking forward to the time when, in three or four years, he would be able to get rid of it for good.[21] Wilfrid Blunt, who arrived in Cairo in 1880 to study Islam, and who soon got to know many of the members of the Egyptian elite, thought much the same.[22]

Several other events of importance had taken place over the summer of 1879. One was the arrival of Taufiq's firman of investiture from Istanbul in August. This contained some revision of the 1873 Ottoman definition of Egypt's place within the Empire, much of it due to pressure from Britain and France. As far as the work of the Controllers was concerned, the most significant clauses were those stipulating that the Khedive had no right to contract any more loans and that his peacetime army should not exceed 18,000 men.[23]

A second development was the campaign inaugurated by Taufiq, and then carried on by Riaz, against those whose opposition both to European control and khedivial power was judged to have gone too far. Al-Afghani was expelled from the country in the summer and warnings, sometimes followed by a suspension, given to any newspaper which ventured even a mild criticism of the government. Riaz himself continued the practice of issuing warnings and then, in November 1879, banned two journals entirely.[24] Thirdly, Riaz, acting on Anglo-French advice, issued a decree defining the duties of the incoming Controllers in such a way as to limit hostile local criticism by placing particular emphasis on their advisory role and the fact that they were not to exercise official administrative functions of any kind.[25]

The result of all this activity was to pave the way for a period of smooth cooperation between Riaz and the Controllers. Baring and de Blignières

[21] Baring, 'Memorandum on the Present Situation of Affairs in Egypt', 30 Apr. 1880, enclosed in Malet to Salisbury, 5 May 1880, PRO, FO. 78/3142.

[22] Wilfrid Scawen Blunt, *The Secret History of the British Occupation of Egypt* (New York: Alfred Knopf, 1922), 97–8.

[23] Cromer, *Modern Egypt*, i. 155–8.

[24] Schölch, *Egypt for the Egyptians!*, 107–8, 111–12; Lascelles to Salisbury, 31 Oct. 1879, PRO, FO 78/3004.

[25] *Moniteur Égyptien*, 16–17 Nov. 1879, quoted Schölch 104.

were given offices next to his at the Ministry of Finance—a 'huge and ramshackle edifice', built chiefly of lath and plaster and formerly the haramlik of a pasha's palace—and their relations were generally harmonious.[26] What was lost in this arrangement, however, was their access to any sense of the strength of the anti-European feeling still to be found among many sections of Egyptian society and, most importantly, among the native Egyptian officers for whom there could be no place in the small army which was all that Riaz, as well as Baring and de Blignières, thought the country required. This did not matter too much in Baring's own case as he was to leave Egypt for India in July 1880 before any real sign of impending trouble. Nevertheless, he was forced to confront it all again when he returned to Cairo in September 1883, a year after the British military occupation of the country prompted, in part, by an upsurge of popular resentment against European influence in 1881 and 1882.

Baring described how the three of them worked together in a memorandum written in April 1880. The fact that they had contiguous rooms allowed him and de Blignières to be in 'daily and hourly conversation' with Riaz. They also made a point of seeing the Khedive frequently, even though, as Baring pointed out, Taufiq himself took no leading part in public affairs. In addition, the two Controllers had what Baring called a 'voix délibérative' at the council of ministers which allowed them to give their opinion freely but not to vote. They left all the detailed work of financial management to the officials at the Ministry of Finance. Their two names rarely appeared at the bottom of any official paper. However, no document of 'first rate importance' could leave the Ministry without having been prepared under their personal supervision. And no minister could add any extra expense to the budget without the council's consent.[27]

These were the circumstances which allowed Baring and de Blignières to carry out the 'delicate task' of 'controlling, guiding and invigorating' without appearing to govern. It worked, Baring asserted, because the senior Egyptian officials had 'personal confidence' in them and were willing to consult them even on matters not covered by the decree under which they had been appointed. This, in turn, stemmed from the fact that he and de Blignières had been able to convince the ministers that they did not represent any special class or economic interests, that their advice was

---

[26] Ronald Storrs, *Orientations* (London: Nicholson & Watson, 1937), 19–20. The Pasha was the notorious Ismail Sadiq, the Khedive's Minister of Finance, supposedly murdered on Ismail's orders in 1875.

[27] Baring, 'Memorandum on the Present Situation of Affairs in Egypt'.

dictated by a real desire for the welfare of the country, and that, while they were not willing to see legitimate European rights trampled upon, they were equally willing to give the Egyptian point of view a fair hearing when European pretensions were opposed to right and justice.[28]

Baring's language describing what he calls the 'spirit of the Control system' is that of a member of a self-confident administrative elite. It is also the language of Plato's Guardians, echoed, in the second era of modern globalization, by many of the international advisers now sent to help non-European states through another period of financial crisis. There is still the same desire to boast a little in front of their political masters, to make claims for the particular efficacy of their methods, and to argue that theirs was the only effective way to achieve success. There is also the same selective blindness, the same unwillingness to accept criticism, and the same readiness to attempt to build a system based on their relationships with just a handful of irreplaceable local individuals. And yet, as many historical examples amply demonstrate, situations of this type are rarely quite as simple as they are made out to be, and, even more rarely, sustainable for more than a short period by the methods Baring describes.

Managing a Bankrupt Country: From Control to a Commission of Liquidation

Baring started work with his usual energy and application. In the few days before de Blignières arrived, he had already written a report on the findings of an inquiry into the shortcomings of the Alexandria customs administration and begun the draft of what he called a 'Present Programme of Action', which he and de Blignières presented to the first meeting of the council of ministers they attended on 1 December. The Programme of Action sketched out the main features of the Egyptian financial situation and the problems which had to be tackled. It also put forward two basic arguments. First, efforts to deal with the situation so far had only addressed the problem piecemeal while failing to gain binding ('obligatoire') acceptance by the Mixed Tribunals. Hence the only way ahead was by a special law of liquidation, agreed to by the powers, which addressed every aspect of Egypt's bankruptcy and the measures necessary to restore the country to fiscal good health. Secondly, the Commission of

---

[28] Ibid.

Inquiry had already set out elements of a solution. These should now be elaborated into a comprehensive programme of reforms which could either be submitted to the proposed commission—as a 'point de départ'—or, if the commission did not come into being, promulgated straight away on the Controllers' advice so as to put an end to the financial confusion, with European agreement to follow.[29]

It was a bold strategy and one that, as we shall see, ran counter to Lord Salisbury's more cautious approach. Its genesis seems to have lain in the two Controllers' experience in Vienna, which helped to convince Baring and de Blignières that the process of getting international acceptance in advance would take for ever, and that the best way forward would be for Britain and France to present the other powers with what was, in effect, a simple fait accompli. The plan involved two gambles: one, that they could persuade their own governments to follow their lead, and the second, that the reforms could be made to work so well that the rising price of Egyptian bonds and the country's growing prosperity would be enough to disarm criticism by creditors and local European residents alike. With this in mind they urged the Khedive to invite the council of ministers to prepare a budget for the following year.

Acceptance of the Programme of Action by the Khedive, Riaz, and the council paved the way for a period of hectic activity as Baring and de Blignières began work on the details of the forthcoming budget, complemented by a whole range of measures recommended in outline form by the Commission of Inquiry, as well as by new proposals of their own. As far as the former was concerned, they reduced the Commission's estimate of Egypt's potential revenue by £500,000, while dividing the expenditure side almost in half, allocating £4,323,000 to administration and £4,239,000 to repayment of the debt.[30] The discussions and bargaining this involved took up most of December and January. On the revenue side, they managed to get rid of a number of what Baring later called 'vexatious taxes', including the salt tax, the poll tax, and the *muqabala*, to be paid for, in part, by an additional tax, worth £150,000, on *ushuri* land. As to expenditure, they got the Khedive to agree to a reduction in his civil list from the £300,000 recommended by the Commission to £120,000.[31] More

---

[29] A copy of this Programme was enclosed in Malet to Salisbury, 1 Dec. 1879, PRO, FO 78/3005.

[30] Baring to Salisbury, 21 Jan. 1880, CP/2, FO 633/2; Cromer, *Modern Egypt*, i. 168.

[31] Ibid. 168–9.

controversially, they also proposed to reduce the level of debt repayment by lowering the interest on the Unified Debt to 4 per cent.

Looking to the future, Baring and de Blignières obtained the appointment of a commission charged to examine all questions connected with the land tax, including its numerous inequalities, and then to draw up a new set of rules concerning the methods of its collection. Following the publication of its report, decrees were signed in March specifying times of collection and abolishing the unsatisfactory practice of collecting taxes in kind in Upper Egypt. They also prompted the creation of a special department of government headed by Riaz to begin work on a proposed law of liquidation which, if the international attempt to create a commission of liquidation ended in failure, would be presented to the European powers for independent ratification.[32]

The amount of work involved was enormous. Even Baring complained of the load, asking for someone to be appointed as de Blignières's deputy when the latter was forced to leave for Paris on 29 December to visit his dying mother.[33] The process of inspection seems to have been particularly time-consuming, involving as it did an attempt by the two of them to monitor all the work carried out at the Ministry of Finance. There can have been little opportunity for relaxation and not much social life other than the more or less obligatory attendance at official functions, like the dinner given by the Khedive to welcome Edward Malet, the new British Consul-General, on 24 December, at which Baring was seated next to Riaz and opposite Taufiq and the guest of honour.

From the British point of view the two closest observers of the new system of control were Malet and Baring himself. 'Baring is a giant at work,' Malet wrote to his parents on 12 January.[34] Ten days later he waxed even more lyrical: 'I see Baring now pretty well every day, so that I begin to feel that I had a hand in the Liquidation. It takes my breath away to hear him explain the most intricate and extensive financial operations with perfect ease.'[35]

We also have only Malet's and Baring's testimony to how the partnership with Riaz and de Blignières actually worked. Reading their dispatches, you get the strong impression that Riaz was quite happy to allow Baring to take the lead in matters which he himself would have found politically embarrassing, for example, the decision to abolish the *muqabala*. The description

[32] Malet to Salisbury, 14 and 15 Jan. 1880, PRO, FO 78/3140.
[33] Malet to Salisbury, 29 Dec. 1879, PRO, FO 78/3004.
[34] Malet, *Egypt 1879–1883*, 49.   [35] Ibid. 50.

of Baring's relationship with de Blignières is equally one-sided. Baring reported on 30 November that his colleague was 'being conciliatory' by agreeing to a major concession (from the French point of view) involving the 4 per cent reduction of the interest on the Unified Debt.[36] Without knowing de Blignières's side of the story we cannot tell whether this was the result of Baring's powers of persuasion or simply a piece of horse-trading in which Baring offered concessions of his own. Nevertheless, it is clear from some of his letters later published by the French Foreign Minister that de Blignières fully shared his colleague's sense of urgency about the need to settle the question of Egypt's finances as soon as possible, with or without the appointment of a commission of liquidation.[37]

The rapid start to the process of reform took many people by surprise, including Lord Salisbury himself. The Foreign Secretary sounded his first warning note in a telegram sent on 6 January 1880, in which he 'deprecated the issue . . . of any financial decree at present', counselling that a 'provisional attitude' should prevail until the powers of the Mixed Tribunals had expired.[38] Baring's same-day reply was forthright but defensive. Salisbury's telegram, he wrote, placed him in a position of considerable difficulty. He had gone to Egypt on the understanding that in the event of the negotiations concerning the formation of a commission of liquidation being indefinitely postponed, the Khedive was to bring out a plan of his own and act upon it. This had been done in the form of a proposal for the general 'règlement' of the financial situation which had been published in December and a copy sent to London. Now, however, he (Baring) understood that Lord Salisbury did not support either the issue of a financial decree by the Egyptian government or the liquidation plan proposed by the Controllers. What he seemed to want instead was that they draw up such a scheme for their private use only, making provisional payments to the creditors based upon it and doing nothing final until the whole question of the powers of the Mixed Tribunals came up for international review at the end of their first five years, that is, in 1881.

Baring countered with the argument that such a 'provisional' approach was no longer possible. The Controllers had to signify public approval of

---

[36] Baring, Memorandum, 30 Nov. 1879, enclosed in Malet to Salisbury, 2 Dec. 1879, PRO, FO 78/3005.

[37] e.g. de Blignières to Baron de Ring (the French Consul-General), 5 Dec. 1880, Ministère des Affaires Étrangères, *Affaires Étrangères: Documents Diplomatiques, Affaires d'Égypte, 1880–1881* (Paris: Imprimerie Nationale, 1881), 21–2.

[38] Quoted in Baring, 'Confidential Observation on Lord Salisbury's tg of January 6th', 1880, CP/2, FO 633/2.

the Khedive's scheme if it was to gain international assent. Furthermore, their moral influence depended on persuading the Egyptian government that they were advising only what they honestly thought in the best interests of Egypt. Then, in a sentence that was obviously calculated to alarm, Baring put forward the suggestion that, 'as the Powers can't agree, the Egyptian Government should propose its own law for their acceptance'. The dispatch ends on a more mollifying note, an assertion that the Controllers' line would not lead to the series of 'troublesome consequences' which Salisbury seems to have feared. As for the creditors, they had become tired and would accept the Controllers' proposals as the best way out.[39]

There was then something of a stand-off for the next few weeks with Baring trying to show that all was going well and Salisbury, lying sick with acute kidney disease at his home at Hatfield, doing his best to urge caution. Baring also used their correspondence to try to persuade the Foreign Secretary that the appointment of a commission of liquidation was positively 'undesirable' on the grounds that it would undo all the good already done. He had, he wrote on 23 January, always considered such a commission 'an evil', but, while in England, a 'necessary one'. Now, in Egypt, there was a fair chance of being able to settle the whole thing without calling in 'outsiders'.[40] Salisbury was not to be persuaded. Looking at British interests from a larger point of view, he was convinced that the only way to protect the Anglo-French position in Egypt from interference by the other powers was by the passage of a law of liquidation, agreed to by all, and so proof against the use of the Mixed Tribunals to whittle away at any of its provisions. And this, in turn, required the appointment of an international commission to draft such a law.

Many years later Baring was to praise Lord Salisbury for his unique ability to appreciate the interconnectedness of British interests round the world.[41] However, in this particular instance he was concerned first and foremost with his own personal reputation, in terms of both his career and of his ability to advise the Egyptian government in the way he thought fit. It is possible too that part of his unwillingness to act provisionally, and so to wait patiently for the international pieces of the puzzle to come together, was a strong desire to wrap up his business in Egypt as quickly as possible in order to return to London with Ethel for good.

[39] Ibid.   [40] Baring to Salisbury, 23 Jan. 1880, CP/2, FO 633/2.
[41] e.g. Maurice Baring, *The Puppet Show of Memory* (London: Cassell, 1987), 178.

Baring was still arguing against the need for a commission in a dispatch written on 16 February. By then, however, he must have known that the case was near to being lost, for he was also beginning to put forward proposals involving the commission's putative composition and powers. One was that the Controllers themselves should not become members on the grounds that they would be needed to defend the interests of the Egyptian government, which, in his words, would be 'little capable' of defending itself. Another, following from a compromise suggestion made by Salisbury, was that the Cairo government should have a voice in fixing the sum assigned for its own administrative expenses.

Negotiations with the other powers proceeded much more quickly than Baring and de Blignières could possibly have imagined and were finally completed in late March, only a few weeks before Salisbury and the Conservatives left office after their defeat by Gladstone's Liberals in a general election. The Commission was to include two members each from Britain and France and one each from Austria, Germany, Italy, and Egypt. Rivers Wilson was confirmed as its president even though Baring had fought a rearguard action to prevent it on the grounds that Rivers Wilson's alliance with Nubar Pasha could be used to try to undermine the Riaz ministry. Butros Ghali, the Secretary-General of the Ministry of Justice, was nominated as the Egyptian government representative.

Baring's struggle with Salisbury was also unfortunate as it coincided with another fierce conflict with the Rothschilds, who had still not resumed payments on their loan in spite of the compromise negotiated by Baring with Baron Edmond. A letter written to the Baron on 2 December provides testimony to Baring's strong feelings in the matter and how much he personally felt let down.[42] To begin with, the reason for further delay seemed simply a matter of having to wait for the Greek government to sign on to a painfully negotiated international agreement of 15 November that barred all suits against the khedivial estates after the date of their transfer to their new administration in 1878.

However, even when this had been accomplished in late December, new problems emerged. One was the question of what taxes could, or should, be levied on the Domains land, an issue that became still more complicated with the abolition of the *muqabala*, which had been paid for some parts of the Domains estates and not for others, and the heightening of the tax on *ushuri* land, which, again, also applied to some of its possessions but not

---

[42] Baring to Baron de Rothschild, 2 Dec. 1879, CP/2, FO 633/2.

all.[43] This then raised the further question of whether the new system of taxation would, or would not, reduce the value of the lands themselves. A second problem arose from the various attempts by each side to put pressure on the other. Hence, a Rothschild order to the administrators of the Domains to pay less tax than the government had demanded was met, in turn, by counter-pressure from Riaz to get them to transmit the revenues they were collecting, not to the Rothschilds but once again to the Egyptian government's account with the Bank of England.[44]

Meanwhile, various attempts at a negotiated settlement were made by the Rothschilds, by Riaz on the government's behalf, and by Baring and de Blignières. Coordination between Riaz and the Controllers also proved difficult, with the latter forced to veto some of the former's initiatives on the grounds that they reinforced what they strongly believed was an unfair attempt by the Rothschilds to create an extra-privileged position for their own share of Egypt's debt. It was not until April 1880 that the matter was finally settled. A special supplementary convention was signed between the Rothschilds and the Egyptian government by which the former agreed to hand over the balance of the loan in exchange for the latter's release of the revenues from the Domains lands from the special account.[45]

There is no doubt that Baring felt very bitter about the whole affair. The money from the Rothschilds' loan had been urgently needed to meet many pressing obligations, and so the delay in its transfer helped to make the business of debt management more difficult. He had done his best to try to reach a satisfactory compromise, and when this failed had been forced to conclude that his personal authority with the Egyptian government had been seriously undermined.[46] He also felt considerably let down by Salisbury, who, as he wrote to Goschen in March, had taken the Rothschilds' side in the matter against the interests of every other concerned party, including the British government itself.[47]

Once again Baring seemed to be threatening resignation, although whether, as Marlowe surmises, this was the move which finally persuaded the Rothschilds to settle seems doubtful.[48] What was more to the point was his determination to find new ways of keeping up the pressure on the

[43] Note by Baring enclosed in Malet to Salisbury, 19 Jan. 1880, PRO, FO 78/3140.
[44] Enclosures in Malet to Salisbury, 2 Mar., and Salisbury to Malet, 10 Mar. 1880, PRO, FO 78/3141.
[45] Malet to Salisbury, 14 Apr. 1880, PRO, FO 78/3142.
[46] Malet to Salisbury, 2 Dec. 1879, PRO, FO 78/3005.
[47] Baring to Goschen, 19 Mar. 1880, CP/2, FO 633/2.
[48] Marlowe, *Cromer in Egypt*, 48.

bankers, for example by his assertion that if the matter was not settled to the satisfaction of the commissioners of the public debt, they would bring a case against the Rothschilds in the Mixed Tribunals, which they would certainly win.[49]

It was this last threat, as well as the general desire to bring the affair to a close before the arrival of the Commission of Liquidation, which seems to have been the main reason why a settlement was finally achieved. Matters between Baring and the Rothschilds began to be patched up a month later when Alphonse de Rothschild wrote of the Bank's desire for cordial relations with the Egyptian government and of its desire to let or to sell as much of its Domains lands as possible.[50] With growing investor confidence in the economy, and the imminent establishment of a big French mortgage company, the Crédit Foncier Égyptien, in Cairo, it was clear that land prices were going to rise again, making the Domains a particularly attractive asset. In this sense each needed the other: Baring to maintain Egypt's financial health, the Rothschilds to develop its resources and to pave the way for the investment of more and more foreign capital.

Liquidation at Last

The Commission of Liquidation was established by an Egyptian government decree of 31 March 1880 after approval by the local representatives of the six major powers: Britain, France, Germany, Austria, Italy, and Russia. Apart from Rivers Wilson as president, it contained the four commissioners of the Caisse de la Dette, the German Consul-General, Butros Ghali, and a second Frenchman who acted as its secretary. It began its work at the end of April by splitting up into two sections, one to examine the revenue aspect and the other the expenditure side.

Not surprisingly there was some immediate friction between the Commission and the Controllers. It must have been common knowledge that neither Baring nor de Blignières had wanted the Commission in the first place. It was equally clear that they had tried to pre-empt much of its activity by presenting it with a series of faits accomplis affecting many of the central features of any new settlement such as the minimum tolerable level of government expenditure and the rate of interest on the Unified Debt. On top of all this, there was Baring's growing distrust of Rivers

[49] e.g. Malet to Salisbury, 10 Mar. 1880, PRO, FO 78/3141.
[50] Alphonse de Rothschild to Baring, 25 May 1880, CP/2, FO 633/2.

Wilson, as well as his, and de Blignières's, proven willingness to oppose their own governments' stated policy if it contradicted their version of Egyptian interest.

The first sign of possible trouble came on 27 April when the Egyptian government, acting on the advice of the Controllers, informed the Commission that it proposed to issue a decree fixing the interest payments of the 1 May coupon of the Unified Debt at 4 per cent. The Commission, playing for time, replied that, as it was too early for it to form an opinion, the government should use its own discretion.[51] There was then, however, a surprisingly smooth process of agreement about the level of revenue and administrative expenses, with the commissioners giving way to such an extent as to allow both a lower estimate for revenue and a higher one for expenditure than the Controllers had set for their 1880 budget. As this also involved a concomitant acceptance of a 4 per cent rate for the Unified Debt, Baring had every reason to be pleased with what had been achieved thus far.

The main clash came when the Commission began to examine the question of the disposal of any future government revenue surpluses. Riaz, backed by the Controllers, argued strongly that the whole of any surplus should stay with the government in order to speed the development of the country. Rivers Wilson, for his part, wanted it to be used to reduce the debt.[52] Several weeks of heated discussion followed, with Riaz, again supported by Baring, saying that he would not accept any decision which he could not take before his council of ministers, and Baring suggesting to Malet that if he (Riaz) was pushed too far he might resign.[53]

In the end a complicated compromise was worked out by which any surplus on the revenues assigned to the service of the debt was to be used to reduce the debt itself, while any surpluses on the remainder of the revenue account should be applied first to the debt and then, if it reached a certain limit, handed over to the government for its own use. Once this highly controversial matter was out of the way, the Commission was able to proceed quickly towards drafting a Law of Liquidation dealing with all the outstanding matters connected with Egypt's bankruptcy and final settlement. It was finally passed into Egyptian law on 17 July 1880.

Baring, meanwhile, was busy preparing an account of his stewardship, knowing that, once the law was passed, he would be free to return to

[51] Malet to Salisbury, 27 Apr. 1880, PRO, FO 78/3142.
[52] Malet to Granville, 19 May 1880, PRO, FO 78/3042.
[53] Malet to Granville, 19, 25, and 26 May 1880, PRO, FO 78/3142.

England. One aspect of this was his 'Memorandum on the Present State of Affairs in Egypt', dated 30 April 1880, which was clearly timed to coincide with the start of the Commission of Liquidation's own deliberations. It may also have been designed to catch the eye of the members of Gladstone's new Cabinet, which had taken office just a few days before. Parts of this memorandum have already been mentioned, particularly its rosy picture of the working relationship Baring claims he established with de Blignières and Riaz.[54]

For the rest the memorandum contains a detailed account of past achievement and future prospects. There is a spirited and, at times, self-consciously literary account of both the financial reforms themselves and the spirit in which they had been carried out. The commissioners had been concerned with practical innovations and not with an attempt to change the whole system. Their main aim had been to remove abuses and to bring practices into harmony with the already existing regulations. To this end, land taxes had been simplified, reduced, and made more predictable. Meanwhile, thirty small and vexatious other taxes had been removed. As Baring writes in one particularly eloquent passage describing the bad old days, there was 'scarcely an industry or occupation, however humble, there was not an article of food or household use, however necessary, there was scarcely an act of life in which the poorest of the population could engage—which was not liable to the payment of some special tax'.[55]

Furthermore, a regular budget was now being drawn up at the commencement of each tax year, a government account had been opened at a bank with cash balances for sudden extra expenses, and all laws were published openly in *The Moniteur*, the official gazette. The results were there for all to see: the value of shares in the public debt had gone up, interest rates on private loans had gone down, there was an increase in the value of private property, and European capital was 'flowing' into the country. There was, Baring concluded, the usual opposition from those whose interests have been adversely affected by the reforms. However, he was confident that the general attitude of the country was one of 'contentment'.[56]

Baring's thoughts about the future are also of particular interest in the light not only of his current perceptions but also of what we now know of the quite considerable discontent which existed below the apparently calm surface of the Riaz government. 'Years must elapse', Baring argued, before

---

[54] See p. 124–6.   [55] Ibid.   [56] Ibid.

anything like a representative assembly would be possible. The government was, and was likely to remain, 'purely personal' for some time to come. In these circumstances the reforms would only continue if the few 'reformers' like Riaz and Nubar could manage to stay in power. However, if the 'retrograde party' headed by Sharif was able to persuade the Khedive to allow them back into power, all the good work would be abandoned, the country would relapse into anarchy, and this would lead, sooner or later, to some more direct form of intervention by the European powers.

If much of this sounds vaguely familiar, it is because the mid-nineteenth-century European response to the growing indebtedness of non-European states had already produced its own vocabulary and its own justification for what would now be called 'free market' reforms, to be carried through, in the teeth of a strong nativist reaction, by a handful of local politicians identified by their Western financial advisers as the leaders of the 'reform' party. In Baring's case, these were sincerely held opinions, although based, as yet, on quite limited experience, and strongly encouraged, we can be quite sure, by people such as Riaz himself. Like so many other foreign experts, Baring may have felt that he was observing things objectively from outside. Nevertheless, it is also inevitable that advisers like him got drawn into local power struggles between rival local interests, to be manipulated in their turn by those they think they are manipulating. Unlike their local collaborators, however, they can always either leave, if things suddenly go wrong, or, in nineteenth-century terms, call in an army or a fleet.

A final thought concerns the questions of blindness and blame. Even by April and May 1880 there were already signs that all might not be going quite as well as Riaz and the Controllers would have liked to believe. The Controllers seem to have been curiously blind to the resentment caused by the increasing employment of more and more Europeans at salaries which imposed a growing burden on the Egyptian exchequer. According to one estimate, this had reached some 4.5 per cent of total revenues in 1881.[57] Another example is provided by Baring's response to an article written by an anonymous 'Occasional Correspondent' of *The Times*, who argued that, in order to please Egypt's creditors, the 1880 budget had pared expenditure to a minimum, allocating only £430,000 to the military instead of the usual £800,000 to £1 million under Ismail, while skimping on education and public works. Baring countered by pointing out that the Army and Navy had received £40,000 more than it had the year before, adding that,

---

[57] J. C. McCoan, *The Egyptian Problem* (London, 1884), 21.

in his personal opinion the Army and Navy should exist for defensive purposes alone.[58]

Baring's stance may have made good sense from the point of view of sound financial management but posed a threat to future stability at a time when the Egyptian officer corps still constituted a powerful political force. Later, in his *Modern Egypt*, he claims to have been aware of the problem at least as early as December 1880 when, passing through Cairo on his way to India, he warned Riaz that the only serious danger facing the country was the fact that the discipline of the Army had been 'profoundly shaken by the events of 1879'. He then urged him to 'remedy any grievances of which the army could justly complain, but to treat severely any signs of insubordination', only to be told that the warning was 'unnecessary'.[59] However, as this was written well after these same officers had first helped to bring down the Riaz ministry in September 1881, and then played a leading role in the events preceding the British Occupation of 1882, such special pleading must be viewed with some caution.

By and large, it seems that what Baring, Malet, and Riaz were more concerned about in the early summer of 1880 was what Malet described as the 'considerable agitation' against the Commission of Liquidation by the 'Pashas out of office', who included not just the members of what Baring had called the 'retrograde party' but Nubar as well. They had used the abolition of the *muqabala*, he wrote, as a 'stalking horse' and petitioned for a 'Constitutional Government'. Other petitions, including one 'purporting' to be from the army officers, had followed. Yet for Malet, and, I assume, Baring and Riaz as well, all these activities were easy to dismiss as the work of malcontents who did not wish Riaz to benefit from having brought the country through the crisis.[60] Malet could also take comfort from the fact that Riaz soon appeared to have the matter well in hand, giving a stern warning to the eighty-four people who had signed the so-called 'Pasha's Petition' and placing them under police supervision.[61] But, once again, this was to ignore the more deep-rooted manifestations of popular anti-European feeling, as well as the strong sense of injustice to be found among the native Egyptian officers who had either been forcibly retired from the Army or who remained resentful at their continued subordination to senior commanders drawn from the Turco-Circassian elite.

[58] Enclosure in Malet to Salisbury, 16 Feb. 1880, PRO, FO 78/3141.
[59] Cromer, *Modern Egypt*, i. 173–4.
[60] Malet to Granville, 25 May 1880, PRO, FO 78/3142.
[61] Schölch, *Egypt for the Egyptians!*, 128–30.

Not London but India Again

By May 1880 Baring was well placed to enjoy what was to prove his last few weeks in Cairo. He had secured important victories in his struggle with Rivers Wilson and the Commission of Liquidation. At home there was a Liberal Cabinet, including Northbrook and many of his other friends and colleagues, back in power. And he could also look forward to a well-earned long summer holiday in London, and the birth of a new child, whether he was to retire from Egyptian service or not. There is a note of self-satisfaction, even complacency, in the words he wrote to Lyall from Cairo on 8 May:

I don't on the whole regret that I abandoned for a while my Parliamentary activity for my work here now interests me . . . Things are going very well here, but the system is an artificial one and if the natives can soon learn to walk by themselves so much the better. At present the Frenchman and myself have to govern the country and at the same time keep up the appearance of self-government.[62]

However, change was in the air. On 19–20 May Baring went with Malet to accompany the new Viceroy of India, the Marquess of Ripon, from Alexandria to Suez in the khedivial carriage attached to the Indian mail train.[63] Baring was suspicious of a man who had so recently converted to Catholicism in middle age.[64] Nevertheless, he reserved his real spleen for the Viceroy's choice of private secretary, none other than Colonel Charles Gordon, whom he described in a letter to Northbrook as 'very eccentric', given to writing 'foolish, violent letters', and having a very exaggerated idea of his own position and importance.[65] Later he was to offer his opinion that Ripon had only chosen Gordon to cover his flank against attack from the Low Church party in Britain.[66] But this was long after Gordon himself had resigned in a huff only a few days after the viceregal party had reached India.

Whether Ripon used this occasion to discuss the possibility of Baring also coming to India with him as the finance member in his Council is not known. However, the offer was made less than four weeks later and announced in Egypt on 26 June 1880. Again, the 'Biographical Notes' are silent as to why Baring took this decision. It seems to fly against all that he had been saying and planning about a career in British politics. No

[62] Baring to Lyall, 8 May 1880, LP, MS Eur. F132/39.
[63] Malet to Granville, 26 May 1880, PRO, FO 78/3142.
[64] Baring to Lyall, 7 Sept. 1880, LP, MS Eur. F132/39.
[65] Baring to Northbrook, 23 May 1880, CP/2, FO 633/2.   [66] BN 250–1.

doubt considerable pressure was placed upon him by those who realized that Ripon would need all the strong support he could get while facing what would undoubtedly be a hostile majority in his Council. It is also possible that Baring himself saw it as a good way round the problem of becoming an unsalaried MP. Not only were Indian salaries very much higher than those in Britain, but if he could also do well with a Liberal Viceroy under a Liberal administration this might translate into an offer of a well-paid cabinet position on his return. Lastly, there may have been a continuing element of personal competition with some of the leading lights of the Lytton administration, notably the finance member, Sir John Strachey, an old opponent whose financial acumen had just been called in question by the discovery of a huge underestimate of the costs of the Afghan War.[67] What Baring did insist on, however, was that he would not go out with Ethel until November, giving time for her to have her baby in London in late September or early October.[68]

The shock among his colleagues in Egypt was palpable. Riaz seemed to regard the loss of Major Baring as 'little short of a calamity', wrote Malet to Lord Granville, the new Liberal Foreign Secretary, on 26 June. And he went on:

there has never been an instance of so deep seated and general a feeling of regret being felt at the departure of a European official. Major Baring has won the respect and attachment of all and he leaves Egypt a bright example of a typical Englishman in his best attributes—clear in his judgement and swift to form it, he has carried with him the Ministry on all points on which he thought it worthwhile to do so, showing considerable tact in not pressing them in cases which were not especial.[69]

Granted the obvious temptations towards hyperbole, this seems fair comment from a British point of view. Lord Northbrook certainly thought so. As he wrote to Ripon on hearing of Baring's new appointment:

You will find him an extraordinary quick worker, and an excellent writer. He has high courage and you may rely on his giving you his opinion with perfect frankness. He used to be perhaps a little too positive in expressing himself when he disagreed with people, and a little too anxious to conciliate people of whom he did not think much; but he has had, since he served with me, four years of very delicate

---

[67] This could be one reading of the phrase to be found in a letter to Northbrook saying that he had accepted the offer of 'Strachey's place'; Baring to Northbrook, 21 June 1880, CP/1, Northbrook Correspondence 1876–1890, FO 633/2, 26–7. Also, Lady Betty Balfour, *The History of Lord Lytton's Indian Administration, 1876 to 1880* (London: Longmans, Green, 1899), 498–9, 500–1.

[68] Lear, 1880 Diary, 28 June 1880.

[69] Malet to Granville, 26 June 1880, PRO, FO 78/3143.

work in Egypt and has done admirably, and he has got along excellently with his French colleague, M. de Blignières, who is, I am told, by no means an easy man to deal with.[70]

A month later, having been shown Malet's dispatch of 26 June by the Foreign Office, Northbrook immediately asked permission to be allowed to give a copy of it to 'Mrs EB'; and this was done.[71] Baring himself was back in London by 3 July.

[70] Northbrook to Ripon, 25 July 1880, NP, MS Eur. C144/19.
[71] Note from Lord Northbrook, enclosed in Malet to Granville, 27 July 1880, PRO, FO 78/3143.

9

Lord Ripon's Right-Hand Man in India
1880–1883

Preparing for India

Evelyn Baring spent the month of July 1880 in London before going off to
Glenmazaran Lodge, near Inverness in the north of Scotland, for a holiday
some time in early August. Edward Lear was back in London at the time
and records in his diary that Baring visited him for an hour on 11 July.
Then follows the comment: 'I suppose no one could be more unchanging
in 20 years than EB; even if he had no changes of position his remaining so
would be remarkable—still more when his rise in life is considered.'[1]

Even granted Lear's passionate hatred of change, this was certainly nice
testimony to Baring's ease of manner with those he knew and liked well.
Five days later Lear was invited to dinner by the Barings at 15 Seymour
Street, where he was placed on Ethel's left and opposite an unrecognizable
George (now Sir George) Strahan, who drew the following comment:
'I could not have known [him] . . . he has grown immensely large.'[2] Lear
and Baring met once more, at a reception at the Admiralty on 19 July given
by Northbrook, who had just been made First Lord. Lear also paid a last
call on Ethel alone the next day to deliver a folio of twenty birds which he
had drawn specially to help Rowland, then aged two and three-quarters,
with his colours.[3] Most of the drawings are simply of the 'Light Red Bird',
the 'Lilac Bird', etc., but there are also two more fanciful ones, the
'Scrooblous' and the 'Runcible' birds.[4]

---

[1] Lear, Diary 1880.   [2] Entry for 16 July 1880, ibid.
[3] Entry for 20 July 1880, ibid.
[4] The bird pictures are reproduced in Lear, *Queery Leary Nonsense*.

Meanwhile, Baring had begun to prepare for his new post in India, driven on, it would seem, by a sense of guilt that he was not able to join Ripon more quickly. What must have given him particular pause was the shocking news of the British defeat at Maiwand on 27 July, which threatened to undermine the whole military position built up in southern Afghanistan during Lytton's Afghan War. He was not wasting his time, he assured the Viceroy, and was in constant communication with various financial authorities at the India Office.[5]

By 'authorities', Baring almost certainly meant Louis Mallet, a distinguished economist with his own very clear views about the type of reforms he wished the new Ripon administration to introduce. Mallet was a fervent advocate of internationalism and the mutual advantage of free trade, and a strong opponent of British expansionism.[6] He may even have had an important role in Baring's selection as finance member, recognizing him from his visit to India in 1876 as someone who shared many of his own views. Their developing partnership was soon to exercise a significant impact on Indian affairs, making Mallet something of an *éminence grise*, whose influence soon came to be called into question not just by Ripon but by some of the Liberal ministers most closely involved, including Mallet's old friend Lord Northbrook.[7]

As a result of his conversations with Mallet, Baring soon formulated a strategy for the next two years. It was, he informed Ripon, to wait until what he called 'this miserable Afghan affair' was over before making any major changes as far as taxation was concerned. This would involve presenting a very conservative budget in March 1881, and then using the following summer to review the whole situation *pari passu* with the important question of whether 'in some form or other the native element can be introduced into the government of the country to a greater degree than at present'.[8] The same idea was to flower into the scheme for a further decentralization of local finance combined with the greater degree of local self-government introduced in 1882.

Baring left for Scotland in early August. There is some suggestion in a letter to Lyall that he was in bad health.[9] He certainly needed a rest. Ethel,

[5] Baring to Ripon, 29 July 1880, RP, Add. MS 43596, CVI, fo. 1.

[6] Bernard Mallet, *Sir Louis Mallet: A Record of Public Service and Political Ideas* (London: James Nesbit, 1905), 93–7, 155–6.

[7] Lucien Wolf, *Life of the First Marquess of Ripon*, vol. ii (London: John Murray, 1921), 74–5; Ellis to Baring, 8 Dec. 1881 (misdated as 1880), CP/1, India 1880–1883: Letters Received E–Z.

[8] Baring to Ripon, 29 July 1880, RP, Add. MS 43596, CVI, fo. 1.

[9] 18 Aug. 1880, LP, MS Eur. F132/60.

now in the last months of pregnancy, remained in London. What happened next is unclear and must depend on whether or not the disturbing letter of 15 August from Seymour Street, telling him that she thought she was about to die, was sent in that year or another (see p. 93). If it was indeed sent in 1880, this would surely have set him hurrying back to London. Otherwise, he was certainly in Seymour Street on 7 September, well in time for the birth of their second son, Windham (named, perhaps, after William Windham, Baring's brother, who had died in 1876), on 29 September.[10]

There is evidence that, as early as 15 September, Baring was also heavily engaged with Indian business again, writing to Ripon to say that Chapman, the Financial Secretary, whom he believed to have had a major responsibility for the mistakes in the Afghan War estimate, should be made to retire, and suggesting Theodore Hope, a member of the Viceroy's Council, as his replacement. He also argued that it was desirable that a trained accountant should accompany him (Baring) from England to India. It was very important that the new Liberal Chancellor of the Exchequer had full confidence in the Indian accounts. And this could only be achieved if there was a thorough overhaul of Indian finances conducted by people from outside, all Indian officers being 'more or less implicated' in the recent debacle.[11]

Baring had two particularly important sets of conversations at this time. The first was with Lord Hartington, the new Secretary of State for India. They discussed the improvement in the British position in Afghanistan as a result of Lord Roberts's successful march to relieve the garrison in Kandahar under threat since the Maiwand defeat. This facilitated Ripon's decision to withdraw from all parts of Afghanistan except the southern districts of Pishin and Sibi, a compromise which Baring personally opposed as breaking the unwritten rule of no expansion beyond India's present borders.[12]

Hartington and Baring also considered the report of the commission set up to investigate the frequent occurrence of famine during the 1870s, which had argued that another 5,000 miles of railways were urgently needed to make sure that future food shortages could be more easily dealt with. Hartington's point of view was that these extra lines could, and should, be built by private capital and without a state guarantee if at all

[10] This was the date on which he wrote another letter to Lyall, ibid.
[11] Baring to Ripon, 15 Sept. 1880, RP, Add. MS 43596, CVI, fo. 7.
[12] Baring to Northbrook, 4 Oct. 1880, CP/1, Northbrook Correspondence, 1876–1890.

possible.[13] As a result Baring contacted Sir Nathaniel Rothschild, the head of the British branch of the Rothschild Bank, about the possibility of raising capital for the line that the government of Bengal wished to build from Jessore and Khulna to Calcutta. He must have been particularly gratified to receive Sir Nathaniel's response: 'you can be assured that a new company can be formed and the money found at once if the Indian Government will give the new company the land to make the railway with'.[14]

The second set of conversations was with the Prime Minister, William Gladstone. After a discussion of the problems of Indian finance in general they moved on to the vexed question of how and when to remove the Indian duties on imported cotton, a measure for which the Lancashire textile interests were still pressing hard. In Gladstone's view, and Baring's as well, this could only be done when the budget got back into surplus after costs of the Afghan War had been fully met. Baring was also anxious to convince the Prime Minister that there was nothing fundamentally wrong with the financial situation and that India could pay the whole costs of the Afghan War—then estimated at £17,500,000—if called on to do so.[15] While it was probably his firm intention to convince Gladstone that all was well and that everything was in control, Baring was also confident enough of his knowledge of Indian finance to know that he could bring the budget back in balance in spite of the obvious short-term difficulties.

Later, long after he had fallen out with Gladstone over the latter's handling of the Sudan Relief Expedition of 1884–5 and other matters, Baring chose to portray these meetings, and the Prime Minister's advice, in a much more negative light.[16] But, at the time, there can be little doubt that he was still in awe of Gladstone and completely devoted to the idea of using Ripon's viceroyalty as an instrument for bringing Gladstonian liberalism to India.

The theme that Indian finances could well bear the costs of the Afghan War is then repeated in Baring's letters to Ripon, in one of which he comments that the Financial Secretary's estimates for 1880/1 did not

[13] Horace Bell, *Railway Policy in India* (London: Rivington, Percival, 1894), 30.

[14] Quoted in Baring, Notes of the Financial Department, 31 Dec. 1880, NAI, Finance and Commerce (Accounts), A, Proceedings (Feb. 1881).

[15] Baring to Gladstone, 29 Oct. 1880, GladP, Add. MS 44466, CCCLXXXI, fo. 231; L. Mallet to Secretary of the Treasury, 24 Nov. 1880, in 'Failure of the Estimates of the Cost of the War in Aghanistan, 1879–80', NAI, Department of Finance and Commerce (Accounts and Finance), A, Proceedings (Feb. 1881), 340.

[16] BN 314.

frighten him 'overmuch', even though he did anticipate a fight with the spending departments, in which he hoped that the Viceroy would be ranged on his side. The same letter also makes the observation that it was becoming difficult to 'get a hearing for Indian affairs' in London because everyone was entirely occupied with Ireland, by which he meant the furore raised by Parnell's parliamentary speeches in favour of the Irish Home Rule Bill. His further comment—'I devoutly hope that there will not be a split in the Liberal camp'—was heartfelt but quickly overtaken by a series of tumultuous events.[17]

The Barings set off for India towards the end of November with a large party of domestic servants including a French cook. They also took with them enough luggage to excite Evelyn's wry comment when he saw it all laid out on the quayside at Alexandria. There were, he wrote to Mallet, twenty-four 'grand colis' and twenty-one 'indispensable hand-bags', not one of which, according to Ethel, 'could have been spared without seriously impairing our travelling efficiency'.[18] After a week in Egypt in which he visited Riaz and other old colleagues, the Barings left Suez on 9 December and finally reached Bombay on 21 December. There Evelyn met his outgoing predecessor, Strachey, who, as he quickly discovered, was 'dead opposed' to the ideas he had brought from London concerning private finance for some of the new railways.[19]

The Barings then journeyed on to Allahabad, where Lord Ripon was lying seriously ill after a hunting trip in which his son, 'the best shot' in England, had bagged nine tigers.[20] This was not an auspicious start to their collaboration. Baring obviously found the Viceroy's condition as annoying as Ripon must have found Evelyn's own delayed arrival. It is a 'great upset to all business', Baring wrote to Mallet at the India Office, adding tartly that the moral of the whole episode was that a 'middle aged Viceroy of a full habit of body should not go out into the sun and should especially leave tiger shooting to a younger generation'.[21] This was unfair. Whatever the cause, Ripon had been close enough to death to have recommended that his doctor be made a Commander of the Star of India for 'saving the life of a Viceroy'.[22] But the remark was characteristic

[17] RP, Add. MS 43596, CVI, fo. 14.

[18] Baring to L. Mallet, 2 Dec. 1880, CP/1, Mallet Correspondence: India 1875–83.

[19] Baring to L. Mallet, 22 Dec. 1880, CP/1, Mallet Correspondence.

[20] Jonathan Garbier Ruffer, *The Big Shots: Edwardian Shooting Parties* (n.p.: Debrett, 1977), 43–4, 135.

[21] 22 Dec. 1880, CP/1, Mallet Correspondence.

[22] Wolf, *Life of the First Marquess of Ripon*, ii. 66.

of a mutual impatience with each other which was to mark the early months of their relationship.

As later events were to prove, the two men were much too similar in working habits, and much too dissimilar in personality, to cooperate easily. Like Baring, George Frederick Robinson, who became, successively, Earl de Grey and then the Marquess of Ripon, had had no proper schooling and had not gone to university. Like him too, he had made his career on the basis of his considerable administrative skills, marked by a capacity for hard work and quick grasp of essentials. They had also shared many of the major preoccupations of the radical wing of the Liberal Party, from army reform to their opposition to Disraeli's expansionist foreign policy. Indeed, one of the main reasons why Ripon came out of the period of political retirement following his conversion to Roman Catholicism in 1874 was his very strong feelings about the immorality of Lytton's Afghan War.[23]

The differences between the two of them were just as striking. Ripon was more conciliatory to his political opponents than Baring, more of a democrat, more concerned with the pursuit of social justice. He had joined the movement of Christian Socialism as a young man. He had worked hard and with great enthusiasm for the nascent cooperative movement and to promote working-class education. And even after his conversion to Catholicism he continued to believe strongly that his Christianity could be reconciled with his political radicalism.[24] Baring, for his part, was much more forthright, quicker to make decisions, and irritated by Ripon's tendency to vacillate, his acute sensitivity, and what he called Ripon's great sense of *amour-propre*.[25] He was also doubly aggravated by Ripon's religious and moral enthusiasms. Given his own dark views about official Catholicism, he could not have found it easy to collaborate with Ripon's display of Christian social conscience. This was the more so as he was temperamentally inclined to keep his own faith to himself, seeing it as one small part of a larger approach to good government and public morality which, in his case, was much more dependent on the secularized notions of honesty, integrity, industry, and the importance of sticking to one's principles.

[23] Anthony Denholm, *Lord Ripon 1827–1909: A Political Biography* (London: Croom Helm, 1982), 126.

[24] Introd., ibid.

[25] Baring to L. Mallet, 1 July 1881, CP/1, Mallet Correspondence.

How were these two men to work together to promote the programme of liberal reforms which they had brought with them from London? Its main ingredients—good government leading to eventual self-government, decentralization as a way of promoting local initiative, and Gladstonian economy—were part of a consensus they shared with many of the leading Liberal politicians of the day. They had been put forward by Gladstone in his influential Midlothian speeches in November 1879. They informed that part of the Famine Commission's report calling for measures of increased self-government in order to encourage greater local participation in future famine control measures. And they were very much part of the thinking of the major figures involved in Indian affairs, particularly Hartington and Mallet.[26] As it turned out, they also represented a last gasp of a liberal, universalist moment in British political thinking which was soon to be overtaken by the more particularist, racially assertive, aggressive certainties of late Victorian imperialism.

A Whirlwind First Hundred Days

Baring entered Calcutta like a whirlwind, determined to tackle the major financial issues of the moment as well as to make up for lost time. The two most immediately controversial subjects at hand were the continued fall-out from the miscalculations concerning the cost of the Afghan War and Baring's proposals for bringing private capital back as an agent of railway construction. Beyond that, there was the question of the shape of his first budget, due in March. Finally, there was the general problem of how to give the Ripon administration a liberal stamp. It was his bad luck that he had to do all this with the Viceroy ill and in the teeth of a Council packed with Lytton supporters who were uniformly suspicious of the ideas which he and Ripon had brought from London. Within a few weeks he had managed to upset most of the senior officials and, if ever there was a moment for him to cement his reputation for brusqueness and for being 'overbearing', this was it.

Baring's office was in the Department of Finance and Commerce in Harrington Street, a 'tumbling down' building soon to be replaced by the palatial offices which can still be observed just across the street from the old viceregal palace, now the official residence of the governor of

---

[26] e.g. Denholm, *Lord Ripon*, 139–40.

West Bengal.[27] Its role had only recently been redefined in a reorganization of government carried out in 1879 during which the civil administrative departments had been reduced to just two: Home, Revenue, and Agriculture and Baring's own, Finance and Commerce. Under him were five different sections: accounts, mint and paper currency, special revenues (which included all taxes and tariffs bar the land tax), statistics and, finally, public moneys which dealt with leaves, pensions, and ad hoc expenses.[28]

The family lived close by at 43 Chowringhee Road, where a travel-weary Ethel, now with a bad cold, was no doubt left very much on her own to manage their large establishment of nurses, nannies, cooks, and other household servants. It was a far cry from living and working in a vice-regal household as Baring had done under Northbrook. However, it proved a good retreat from all the problems of work. As he wrote to his cousin on 11 January 1881, 'I am fighting all the big departments' but 'thanks to my French cook I am very well'.[29]

Baring had come out to India well primed as to the thinking in London about the Afghan War expenses. An India Office committee had begun taking evidence on the subject in July 1880 and it was already clear what most of its recommendations would be even before its final report appeared the following February. Moreover, many of these same recommendations showed up in a dispatch received from the India Office in January containing the home Government's remarks on the revised estimates for revenue and expenditure for 1879/80, together with its 'Instructions as to the mode of preparing these estimates in future'. This gave Baring a head start in reforming the old system of accounting, enabling him, for example, to anticipate the call for the use of monthly statements until more complete figures were available just before the end of each financial year.[30]

Nevertheless, there were still some early problems. There was heavy pressure from Hartington to provide a figure for the final cost of the war by 10 January, so that he could bring the matter before Parliament for a decision as to how this was to be shared between London and Calcutta.

[27] Baring to L. Mallet, 27 Aug. 1881, CP/1, Mallet Correspondence.

[28] *Guide to the National Archives of India* (New Delhi: National Archives of India, 1982), pt. VIᴀ, particularly pp. 180–1.

[29] Baring to L. Mallet, 11 Jan. 1881, CP/1, Mallet Correspondence.

[30] Government of India to Secretary of State, 14 Mar. 1881, NAI, Department of Finance and Commerce (Accounts and Finance), A, Proceedings (July 1881), 1158.

Continued shortcomings in the system of accounting prevented Baring from meeting the deadline, much to his personal irritation. And it was not until April 1881 that Parliament finally decided to contribute £5 million to the war to be paid in two annual instalments for the financial years 1880/1 and 1881/2.

One related matter concerned the process of house-cleaning in India itself. After extensive internal inquiries as to who was responsible for the accounting failure, a report of 21 May noted that the financial and military members had resigned, that the Controller-General was on furlough, and that the Financial Secretary, Chapman, was about to vacate his post. All this had paved the way for Baring to implement his own system, based on British practice, which involved automatic regular financial reporting rather than, as he put it, relying on the 'vigilance and intelligence of individuals'.[31] Such an assault on traditional methods was bound to put backs up and so increase internal opposition to further manifestations of Baring's new broom.

The second controversial subject was that of the railways. Taking the bull by the horns, Baring initiated a discussion in Council in which, in his own words, his proposal for a Rothschild-financed line in Bengal proved nothing less than a 'bombshell'.[32] He had introduced the matter by saying that, although the arguments which had caused the government to prefer the use of state agency to that of private capital with state guarantees from 1869 onwards were still good, he himself believed that the experiment of trying to attract private capital without guarantees had never been fairly tried. There was now a great amount of capital in the London market. Railways had been built by British capital round the world without guarantee. The Rothschilds were willing and able to undertake the project as Sir Nathaniel's letter, which he produced, clearly showed. And the Secretary of State had given it his enthusiastic support. Then, in a characteristic effort to win over his opponents, he tried to move the argument on, from one based on abstract principles about the rival merits of public versus private enterprise to one about contemporary financial reality. It was not necessary to take sides about the desirability of monopolies in general, he asserted. He was simply concerned with the special case of India, where the only way to build railways above and beyond the Secretary

---

[31] Government of India to Secretary of State, 21 May 1881, and Notes by Financial Member, ibid. 1160 ff.

[32] Baring to L. Mallet, 29 Dec. 1880, CP/1, Mallet Correspondence.

of State's cap of £2 million on government expenditure on public works was to find alternative sources of finance.[33]

Baring's arguments fell largely on deaf ears, as can be seen from the list of senior officials who minuted their opposition: 'B.F.C.' (Chapman), 'J.S.T.' (Colonel Trevor, Public Works), 'F.S.S.' (Stanton, secretary of the Bengal Public Railways Department), and many others.[34] However, Baring was not to be deterred. His own minute of 12 January notes that the objections to acting at once were of 'absolutely no account', and he immediately set up a commission to draw up the terms to be offered to the Rothschilds and other prospective companies.[35] Matters were then somewhat complicated by Hartington's dispatch of the same month laying down that every privately financed railway must be constructed on 'commercial principles' with a fair promise of paying a 4 per cent return within five years of opening to traffic, a target which few new transport enterprises, then or now, could possibly achieve.[36] This first burst of energy culminated in Baring's budget statement of March 1881, in which he reiterated his hope that British capital could be attracted to at least some of the projected lines without guarantee, while also expressing a desire for the investment of native Indian capital as well.[37]

Although most of these battles were fought while Ripon was still recovering from his illness, Baring knew that these were subjects on which he could be sure of his general support. At the same time he and the Viceroy were clearly experiencing the greatest difficulty in establishing the satisfactory working relationship which both knew was vital to the successful implementation of their many grand schemes. One early bone of contention was Ripon's intemperate offer of resignation at the end of January 1881 during a dispute over his failure to obtain cabinet permission for a decision to sanction a broad-gauge railway through the state of Bhopal. Even though he quickly apologized, attributing his unwonted 'vehemence' to his illness, Baring can only have seen it as a sign of the Viceroy's general unsteadiness under political fire, and perhaps even of an irresponsible willingness to let his long-standing personal antipathy to Hartington,

---

[33] E.B., 'Preliminary Discussion in Council', 30 Dec. 1880, in E.B., 'Notes of the Financial Department', 31 Dec. 1880, file: Proposed Construction of the Central Bengal Railway by Messrs Rothschild, NAI, Department of Finance and Commerce (Accounts), A, Proceedings (Feb. 1881), 362–8.

[34] Ibid.

[35] Ibid.

[36] Bell, *Railway Policy*, 30 n.

[37] 'Financial Statement by the Government of India for 1881–82', *PP* (1881) 68, 307.

the Secretary of State, get in the way of the larger need to make his new liberal administration a success.[38]

There was an obvious clash of personalities as well. It cannot have helped that Baring's letters to the Viceroy at this time reveal a readiness to lecture Ripon on the basis of his own superior local knowledge and an unfortunate tendency to remind him of matters which he already knew. There can be little doubt that Ripon, for his part, found Baring's 'bull in a china shop' approach to his local colleagues often ill-considered and counter-productive. He was also disturbed by the fact that Baring maintained his own personal lines of communication with such influential people as Mallet and Northbrook in London.[39] Baring, too, made little effort to hide the fact that he felt the Viceroy was not doing enough to help him in his dealings with what he called the 'napoleonic bureaucrats' who were so stuck in an Indian groove that they failed to grasp 'the real issues at stake' and were 'becoming more and more out of harmony with the principles of Liberal Government which must sooner or later prevail'.[40] As he wrote, sadly, to Northbrook at the beginning of March: 'no doubt I am quite out of harmony with my surroundings. Whether I have shown this too much, of whether they have all made a dead-set against me, I really can't say—perhaps a little of both.' And he went on to note that Ripon was not quite '*firm*' enough and that 'unless I supply him with a little *steam* I doubt if anything will be done here yet a while—and there is plenty to do'.[41]

The experience of the first few months in Calcutta left Baring feeling sorry for himself and yet determinedly combative and upbeat. 'Don't be alarmed at my over-working myself,' he told Mallet on 6 March. 'I have never felt better in my life:

My cook is good. I play lawn tennis every day, and anyone who has worked with Lord Northbrook acquires the power of getting through his work quickly. The only thing that really worries me is that my wife and children are in this beastly climate. But tomorrow we go off to Simla. I do not think that there is a reasonable chance of my health breaking down. I was rather anxious about my eyes at one time, but now I have a short-hand writer who is an immense assistance. Except letters to you and Brett [Hartington's private secretary] & etc., I write very little with my own hand.[42]

---

[38] Quoted in S. Gopal, *The Viceroyalty of Lord Ripon 1880–1884* (London: Oxford University Press, 1953), 216.

[39] Baring to L. Mallet, 27 Feb. 1881, CP/1, Mallet Correspondence.

[40] Baring to L. Mallet, 21 Feb. and 6 Mar. 1881, CP/1, Mallet Correspondence.

[41] Baring to Northbook, 6 Mar. 1881, CP/1, Northbrook Correspondence 1876–90.

[42] CP/1, Mallet Correspondence.

Nevertheless, it was also perfectly clear that Ripon and Baring would sink if they did not learn to swim together. The first tentative understanding which they were able to reach about future policy was well expressed in Baring's budget statement of March 1881, which is best seen as a joint manifesto setting out the principles which were to guide them, and the main goals which they hoped to achieve during the rest of their time in India. There is an argument for the role of private capital in the construction of Indian railways. There is a reference to the fact that native Indian investment was a necessary part of the process of local self-government. There is a commitment to reducing the level of taxation, embellished by one of Baring's favourite maxims about the importance of leaving money to 'fructify' in the pockets of the people where it was 'more advantageously employed'. And there is a thinly veiled reference to a future repeal of Lytton's highly unpopular Vernacular Press Act under the heading of the need to remove all restrictions on that 'free expression of opinion which so materially helps to bring to light the nature of evils to be remedied'.[43]

All this was sufficient to paper over a number of the issues which divided the Viceroy from his chief lieutenant. However, there were still plenty of controversial topics which both knew they would need to thrash out before the main lines of the next budget could be agreed between them. Of these certainly the most significant were their obvious disagreements over the future of the Licence Tax, which Ripon wished removed, and over their strategy with respect to the pressure from London for the removal of the duty on imported cotton.[44]

Retreat to Simla and the Big Budget Debate of 1882–1883

It must have been a great relief to the Barings when they were able to get away to Simla at the end of March 1881, the move being made some days earlier than usual owing to the Viceroy's lingering ill health. As Evelyn was to write to Northbrook a few days after their arrival, his wife and children were 'all looking better for the change'.[45] They had taken the Kennedy House, the first house built in Simla in the 1820s. It stood on the western end of the ridge, close to the Peterhoff, the Viceroy's residence. A sketch of

[43] The Act, which gave the government the power to close Indian-language newspapers without appeal, was finally repealed in February 1882.

[44] e.g. Ripon to Baring, 9 Feb. 1881, CP/1, Ripon Correspondence 1880–1882.

[45] Baring to Northbrook, 3 Apr. 1881, CP/1, Northbrook Correspondence: 1876–1890.

it drawn just after its construction shows a one-storey building with two steep gabled roofs intersecting at right angles surmounted by a high, steeple-like chimney.[46] The senior members of Baring's department were most probably quartered all around, as was the custom. Their offices would have been in rented houses nearby.

Simla had changed a great deal in the five years since Baring was last there. During the Lytton viceroyalty efforts had begun to make it a more habitable place. The roads had been widened and a good carriage road built around the Jakhu (known to Kipling and the local British residents as the Jakko), the hill at the eastern end of the ridge, which gave a sense of a much greater freedom of movement. Most of the houses were now supplied with piped water. Nevertheless, there was still much to do. It was only in 1881 that the problem of providing proper offices for government officials was first addressed, with the Public Works Department buying up private houses and then modifying them especially for this purpose.[47] Meanwhile, the Viceroy was addressing the lack of a hospital especially for Europeans by planning one of his own, opened in 1885. As for his own residence, he contented himself with adding an extra storey to the Peterhoff, as an alternative to Lytton's ambitious plans to construct a much larger and grander building on Observatory Hill to the west, a project undertaken by Ripon's successor, Lord Dufferin.[48]

Simla under Lytton had also become a much more lively place, with many more parties, balls, gymkhanas, and other diversions to add to the usual fare of theatricals, picnics, tennis tournaments, dinners, and the evening promenade along the Mall. There was even a roller-skating rink. Ripon, a much more sober person than his flamboyant predecessor, was anxious to cut down on what he called 'swagger', and, as he told his wife, took to 'walking about in a shooting jacket and dispensing with Body Guards as much as possible'.[49] Nevertheless, the taste for entertainment was now sufficiently well entrenched for this to form an essential ingredient of the summer season and the stuff of many of Rudyard Kipling's early short stories based on the visits he began to make in the early 1880s. As Lady Lytton had observed, Simla society was either 'dowdy' or 'fast'.[50]

---

[46] Buck, *Simla Past and Present*, 5.

[47] Pamela Kanwar, *Imperial Simla: The Political Culture of the Raj* (Delhi: Oxford University Press, 1999), 54.

[48] Ibid. 51.

[49] Wolf, *Life of the First Marquess*, ii. 15.

[50] Quoted in Longford, *A Pilgrimage of Passion*, 152.

For the Barings, there was enough to keep them occupied without having to socialize more than they felt like. There were the usual household crises like the 'anxious week' in early June when little Windham went down with a high fever, prompting his father's heartfelt remark that 'in accepting Indian service, many a man runs the risk of losing more than money can repay'.[51] This was followed almost immediately by the defection of one of the children's nurses, who went off and married a bandmaster, something which, according to Baring's brother Robert, who was visiting at the time, put Ethel 'in despair'.[52] But, by and large, it seems to have been a happy time. Even though, as Evelyn had soon noticed, the Anglo-Indian society of Simla 'looked askance at Liberals' and was 'out of harmony with the prevailing feelings at home', there were enough like-minded people to keep them going.[53] However, their favourite occupation was to camp somewhere out in the nearby hills with Evelyn riding in to work every day and Ethel sketching and painting watercolours until his return. These, he wrote later in the 'Biographical Notes', were the times he most enjoyed in India, 'passed under tents in the magnificent deodar forests beyond Simla'.[54]

Lyall, who freely admitted that he found Simla 'dull as ditchwater', saw a great deal of the Barings at this time.[55] He was in many ways the exact opposite of his friend Baring, cynical, restless, insecure, unhappily married, and full of adulterous fantasies about running off with another woman. He was also a shrewder observer of other men than his friend, and much more interested in the follies and eccentricities of humankind. Nevertheless, they entertained a great respect for each other. Baring admired Lyall's scholarly approach to the study of Indian society, while Lyall seems to have been somewhat in awe of Baring's drive and sense of purpose and ability to get things done. Lyall, sometimes with his wife, sometimes without, was often invited to meals cooked by the Barings' French chef, occasions which he enjoyed reporting to his sister Barbara. 'Evelyn Baring gives very heavy dinners,' he wrote to her in June 1881, 'and is very stuffy if you come late and the soup is spoiled.'[56] Baring was even less relaxed in the homes of others. As Lyall noted to Barbara a fortnight later:

[51] Baring to L. Mallet, 10 June 1881, CP/1, Mallet Correspondence.
[52] Northbrook to Baring, 23 June 1881, CP/1, Mallet Correspondence.
[53] Baring to Northbrook, 3 Apr. 1880, CP/1, Mallet Correspondence.
[54] BN 342.
[55] Lyall to Barbara Lyall, 2 Apr. 1881, LP, MS Eur. F132/7.
[56] Lyall to Barbara Lyall, 24 June 1881, ibid.

I can see that though he is a very shrewd and industrious man he is not a star of the first brilliance—his pluck and honesty are excellent, but his outward manners still so unfinished that he is not appreciated. I was tickled with laughter last night as I watched him shaking hands with a lot of ladies on entering the Hopes' dining room. He gave one of them a finger and looked the other way. We had a rather poisonous banquet, and Baring influenced me to join him at supper immediately after: he said he was starving.[57]

Both Ripon and Baring took the withdrawal of the last British troops from Afghanistan in May 1881 as a sign that they could at last get on with the business of basic financial reform. Much of the summer was spent on addressing the major issues on their agenda, including, most important of all, the changes which were to be set out in the 1882/3 budget statement, a first draft of which had to be sent back to London by 15 December for India Office approval. Baring did an enormous amount of preliminary reading and was also greatly assisted by the new Financial Secretary, Theodore Hope, someone with whom, at last, he could discuss issues involving 'financial principle'.[58]

Apart from the business of the new budget, there were many other matters which required Baring's vigorous attention. One was the fact that, as he put it, the Public Works Department had been 'miraculously converted to private enterprise' as far as railway building was concerned, but was quite incapable of carrying out such a policy itself. His immediate answer was to propose the addition of an extra member of the Viceroy's Council to lead the Department in its new direction, a post which was eventually given to Hope.[59]

The second matter was the difficult question of what approach, if any, the Indian government should take to the Third International Monetary Conference to be held later in 1881 in which, once again, the question of introducing a bimetallic, as opposed to either a mono-gold or mono-silver, currency regime, was to be discussed. This was a matter of great importance for countries like India with silver-based currencies, the value of which had depreciated greatly against gold, and Baring was all for instructing the British delegates to indicate India's interest in efforts to introduce an international bimetallic regime. However, he was unable to obtain

---

[57] Lyall to Barbara Lyall, 8 July 1881, LP, MS Eur. F132/7.

[58] Baring to L. Mallet, 9 Apr. 1881, CP/1, Mallet Correspondence.

[59] It will be remembered that Northbrook had bitterly resisted Salisbury's attempt to get him to appoint just such a representative in 1874–5. But this was to promote a more vigorous policy of works of famine relief, not to encourage private sector investment. See p. 80.

either Ripon's or Hartington's support for his scheme, and, in the end, the two delegates representing the Indian interest (one of whom was Mallet) were mandated to go no further than to offer India's 'practical assistance' to any country planning to join a putative bimetallic union.[60]

It is significant that even this rather anodyne formula was resisted by Ripon himself on the grounds that support for bimetallism was contrary to the principles of political economy and would produce 'mischievous consequences'.[61] It proved to be one of the many skirmishes over their rival economic expertise, as well as over policy in general, which continued throughout the Simla summer. For Baring, Ripon was simply not the man to carry out the changes which the situation required. 'If Indian matters are wanted to *sleep*, he is an ideal Viceroy,' he complained, but vigorous reform 'is not in him'.[62] Baring, it seems, continued to see himself as a lone, embattled warrior. This is well illustrated in his next letter to Mallet, in which he asserts that, while India needed to be governed by a 'cabinet of statesmen', what there was instead was

(1) A Viceroy who carries the love of compromise to a passion.
(2) A Legal Member who is in some respects a clever man but not a statesman.
(3) Four bureaucrats, two civilian, two military.
(4) A Financial Member, who is an English Radical, and therefore hopelessly isolated.

This was undoubtedly his strongest identification with the radical wing of the Liberal Party during the whole of his public life outside England, a position from which he was to spend the next ten years in slow retreat.

Baring's quarrels with the Viceroy were finally to break out into open war when he began to set out his own proposals for the next budget in a series of memorandums which were finally ready for circulation in mid-September. What he proposed was the complete abolition of all import duties, except those on liquor, a general reduction—as well as overall equalization—of the salt tax, and some remission of taxation in two of the poorest regions, Oudh and the North-West Provinces. This was to be offset by a plan to turn the licence tax into a tax on all incomes over Rs 2,000, to be paid by government officials, professionals, and the land-

[60] Report of the International Monetary Conference of 1881, by Sir Louis Mallet and Lord Reay, 14 Feb. 1882, a copy of which can be found in NAI, Department of Finance and Commerce (Accounts), A, Proceedings (June 1882), 571–3.

[61] Quoted in L. P. Mathur, *Lord Ripon's Administration in India (1880–1884 A.D.)* (New Delhi: S. Chand, 1972), 188–9.

[62] Baring to L. Mallet, 1 July 1881, CP/1, Mallet Correspondence.

owners of the Central Provinces and Bengal, who were particularly lightly assessed as far as their land tax commitments were concerned.

Baring used three main arguments in support of these proposals. First, abolition of the customs duties was justified in terms of both the principles of sound political economy and the need to remove what had become a serious bone of contention between Britain and India. Secondly, if these duties were to go, some other 'growing source of revenue had to be found to meet [India's] growing expenditure'. Thirdly, the proposals were aimed at taxing the rich while making things easier for the mass of the population, whose main burden—a huge one in a hot climate—was the salt tax.[63]

Ripon's first comments were not encouraging and precipitated a fierce exchange of correspondence between the two. The Viceroy clearly saw the budget proposals as far too sweeping and urged caution. Baring, for his part, made a strong case for decisive action. Both realized the importance of persuading the Gladstone government to back their own particular view, a strategy which forced them to present their ideas in terms of general principle rather than particular detail. Hence, when Ripon pointed out that Baring's proposals regarding a licence–income tax constituted a complete reversal of Northbrook's policy laid down in 1873, Baring countered with the assertion that times had changed and policy had to be allowed to move on. And when the Viceroy urged delay in order to consult Indian public opinion, Baring relied on a set of arguments, already well rehearsed between him and Mallet, to the effect that, while the elite Indians to be consulted represented only their own class interest, it was the government's duty to look after the poorer classes as well, for example by allowing them to purchase cheaper imported cloth. If in India the country was to suffer from 'manifold evils' arising from the absence of free institutions, 'it should . . . at all events, reap the benefits to be derived from the presence of a strong executive'.[64] Baring's final appeal was to his own strongly held belief that the present government had a 'special duty to deal boldly and comprehensively' with the whole question of Indian financial reform.[65]

The debate moved on to the Viceroy's Council, still meeting in Simla. There Ripon stated his unwillingness to accept two of the main proposals, the abolition of the customs duties and the reimposition of an income tax,

---

[63] e.g. Wolf, *Life of the Marquess of Ripon*, ii. 72; Baring's Memorandum to the Viceroy of 26 Sept. 1881, RP, Add. MS 43546, CVI.

[64] Baring, 'Confidential', 26 Sept. 1881, ibid.

[65] Enclosure in Baring to Ripon, 7 Oct. 1881, ibid.

both of which he thought would be deeply upsetting to Indian opinion. As a compromise he suggested postponing what he saw as the most unpopular parts of the budget for another year. To Baring this was simply 'cowardice'.[66] Meanwhile, the Council itself was divided. However, there was enough support for Baring's draft that the Viceroy was afraid to send it home, a step which, according to Baring, would force Ripon to reveal the strength of his own dissent.[67] Much now depended upon which side the key members of the Cabinet in London would be willing to support. Hartington seemed inclined to favour Baring. Northbrook appeared to be advocating a compromise. It was also a question of whose nerve would hold up the longest.

Perhaps it was just as well that Ripon chose this moment to leave Simla for a shooting trip. Baring, staying with his family in the hills just outside the town, continued to press his case with Mallet, as well as with the Viceroy's private secretary, Primrose, whom he had reason to believe took his own side. Ripon, for his part, felt that he was not being properly supported from London over an issue on which his authority was at stake and was soon hinting to Northbrook that he might have to resign. His letter of 15 October is worth quoting at length as an example of his state of mind at this time:

If Baring and I ultimately differ, I do not at all know what line Hartington is likely to take. Baring's proposals will, I have no doubt, receive Mallet's support and Mallet has great influence with Hartington on matters of this kind . . . You will appreciate how difficult my position would be if I were to be overruled in such a matter . . . It would cost me very little to go home; my wife is not well, and I do not know how far the climate is affecting her injuriously. I have been feeling the pressure of work of late, and if the Government at home does not want me out here any more I should be far from sorry to return to my own *lares* and *penates*; but at the same time if it is thought I am any use here I do not want to run away from my work.[68]

In spite of the alarms this raised in London, the struggle continued on into November as the parties made their way back to Calcutta, Baring taking Ethel on a sightseeing tour of Delhi en route. By this time both Ripon and Baring seem to have come to the conclusion that it was Northbrook, more than anyone else, who held the key to the final decision. This explains the series of letters which Ripon directed towards him in an

---

[66] Baring to L. Mallet, 8 Oct. 1881, CP/1, Mallet Correspondence.   [67] Ibid.
[68] Quoted in Wolf, *Life of the First Marquess of Ripon*, ii. 75.

effort to get him to moderate his cousin Evelyn's stance. As he wrote on 15 November:

on most points we [Baring and I] agree in principle. It may perhaps be said that the great distinction between us is that he is a Doctrinaire and I am not. I think a Doctrinaire policy dangerous in India . . . He came out here with a cut and dried policy arranged between him and Mallet at the India Office without consideration of circumstance or of persons in this country. Mallet is a more utter Doctrinaire than Baring and believes more than he does in the unredeemed wickedness of the Indian Civil Service . . . I suspect that Baring and Mallet thought that I was a much more colourless person without opinions or a policy than I really am.[69]

This is a harsh criticism and not without some truth. Baring was pressing a case with an economic logic which others might well think too harsh for Indian conditions. It was one thing for Mallet and himself to agree in London that India was now ready to be pushed further along the route of modern progress by making the switch from a system of indirect to one of direct taxation. But it was quite another to try and force it through against the combined opposition of Gladstone, Northbrook, and Ripon, all of whom proved to be strongly against this particular transition.[70] It also seems to fly in the face of the political lessons Baring had learned under Northbrook about the strength of local opposition to both the licence and the income tax.

There is evidence that Baring had begun to realize this himself before he left Simla.[71] Then, as he accompanied Ethel on their brief tour, he seems definitely to have begun to think himself into a different frame of mind. The fact that Northbrook now turned out to have been very much more on his side than he initially imagined also helped to make the idea of compromise more palatable. Northbrook, he believed, shared his desire for a 'bold budget'. As for his own position, he told Mallet that he had now come to see the next budget as more 'transitional than final', adding that he was no longer ready to tackle the question of an income licence tax 'this year'. Better to do nothing and bide his time than agree simply to a 'tinkering' which could undermine the possibility of meaningful advance towards direct taxation sometime in the future.[72]

Hence, by the time the Barings had finally reached Calcutta, Evelyn was ready to arrange a compromise. He would keep the licence tax as it was and agree to a somewhat higher estimate for opium revenue than he had

---

[69] Quoted ibid.   [70] Gopal, *Viceroyalty of Lord Ripon*, 202.
[71] Baring to L. Mallet, 23 Oct. 1881, CP/1, Mallet Correspondence.
[72] Baring to L. Mallet, 20 Nov. 1881, ibid.

originally thought prudent, in exchange for the Viceroy's agreement to the complete abolition of the customs duties and a reduction of the duty on salt.[73]

The document containing the revised version of the budget proposals, entitled 'Financial Arrangement for the Year 1882–83', was sent back to London in December and received final approval from the Secretary of State on 2 February 1882. Letters expressing considerable relief that this fierce though still private row was over poured out of London. One, from General Arthur Ellis, also contained a mild rebuke. It was a great pity, he wrote, that Baring had not corresponded with Hartington, or more with Northbrook, and confided mainly in Mallet, whom they all thought a 'frondeur', that is, a malcontent or political rebel.[74] This was fair comment. Although Baring obviously derived much personal comfort from being able to let his hair down with Mallet about his troubles with Ripon and the bureaucrats, it also seems to have encouraged him to pursue his intransigent, all-or-nothing stand over the budget to a point where the whole viceroyalty might easily have been wrecked.

Baring was to write later that he had found the whole episode 'exceedingly painful and disagreeable' as it had brought him into 'apparent conflict' with those in both India and England with whom he had 'so much in common'.[75] Nevertheless, it marked a vital turning point in his relationship with Ripon himself. In the heat of the conflict he had, as he told Mallet, come to realize that the position was 'becoming intolerable', that the 'public interest suffered and my own power for good was crippled'.[76] He repeated the same message after his return from a brief trip to British Burma in the New Year with the strong assertion that he '*must*' manage to get along with Lord Ripon and that he would not 'quarrel any more'.[77] Perhaps part of the pain came from the fact that he had been forced, unwillingly at first, to admit that he could not manage the reform of Indian finances all on his own, that some of the Viceroy's ideas about how the budget proposals should be presented were better than his own, and that to make the remainder of his time in India a success he needed Ripon just as much as Ripon needed him.

[73] Baring to L. Mallet, 4 Dec. 1881, CP/1, Mallet Correspondence.
[74] Ellis to Baring, 8 Dec. 1881 (misdated as 1880), CP/1, India 1880–1883: Letters Received E–Z.
[75] Baring, 'Very Private and Confidential: For the Viceroy Only', 31 Mar. 1883, CP/2, FO 633/99.
[76] 4 Dec. 1881, CP/1, Mallet Correspondence.
[77] Baring to L. Mallet, 9 Jan. 1882, CP/1, Mallet Correspondence.

Creating a Partnership with Ripon

With the dispute behind them, Ripon and Baring entered into something of a honeymoon period in which friendship began to flourish and they found themselves able to work together in increasing harmony. It was helped along by the great kindness shown by the Ripons during February 1882 as Ethel's life hung in the balance as a result of a sharp attack of typhoid fever. The two boys were taken into Government House while Evelyn looked after his wife and the Viceroy took over all his work.[78] This was followed by the 1882/3 budget statement, delivered by Baring on 15 March 1882, which, even more than the previous one, can be seen as a mutual assertion of principle and a statement of joint intent. Apart from the compromise changes in the system of taxation its main innovation was what they called the 'provincialization' of finance and the development of local self-government. This involved the introduction of a new formula by which provincial and other local governments would no longer receive a fixed annual sum from the central government but a proportion of the total revenue amounting to some 60 per cent of the whole, a portion of which they could allocate as they thought fit once approved by a new set of partially elected boards and committees.[79]

A government resolution drafted by Ripon and Baring the previous September had invited the provincial authorities to scrutinize both their own, and the local and municipal, accounts to see what items could be transferred to administration by the same new boards and committees.[80] Much of 1882 was then given up to a renegotiation of the settlements (also known as contracts) between the centre and the provinces, a system which had been originated by Lord Mayo and which was now used to accelerate the shift of financial resources towards greater local control. Baring paid close attention to the whole process while doing his best to prevent the details of the individual contracts being sent back to London.[81] While his stated reason for this is that they would not be understood properly by the India Office, his private motive is much more likely to have been a desire to

---

[78] Baring to L. Mallet, 5 Feb. 1882, CP/1, Mallet Correspondence.

[79] 'Financial Statement of the Government of India for 1882–1883', PP (1882) 48, 301.

[80] Gopal, Viceroyalty of Lord Ripon, 91–2.

[81] See Baring's own minute in file marked 'Secretary of State's observations concerning certain points relating to the detailed provincial arrangements with the local governments and administrations', NAI, Department of Finance and Commerce (Accounts and Finance), A, Proceedings (Aug. 1882), 890.

prevent further outside meddling in what was proving to be a very complicated process.

A central section of Baring's 1882/3 budget speech was devoted to the argument that, in present circumstances, continued reliance on the revenues from exported opium was absolutely vital to the well-being of the local Indian population. Given the great sensitivities involved, and the presence of a strong anti-opium lobby in England, he took great pains to try to make the case as carefully as he could. The abolition of the opium monopoly, he argued, would lead to India's insolvency because no alternative source of taxation was possible given the very low level of India's average annual income, no more than Rs 27 (£2.70) a person.[82] The use of any new tax to try to bridge the gap would be enormously resented. Opium's social effects were no worse than those of liquor, which was highly taxed but remained legal.[83] Ripon's own budget speech followed much the same lines, with its repeated emphasis that it was 'the first duty of the Government of India to consider the peoples of India' (i.e. not of China, where most of the opium was consumed).[84]

If this proved troublesome to Ripon's and Baring's consciences, they could take some comfort from the visit paid to Simla in the summer of 1881 by the Secretary to the Chinese Imperial Commission, Mr Mah Kie Tchong. Speaking to Baring in French, he had tried to sound him out on the attitude of the Indian government to any future negotiations about the trade in opium. Baring gave nothing away. The envoy was more forthcoming in his meeting with the Viceroy when he suggested an agreement by which the Chinese government would be given a monopoly over the purchase of Indian opium for thirty to fifty years ahead, during which time it would seek to reduce imports from India while raising the amount produced in China itself.[85] This suggestion seems to have been based on an attempt to reach a compromise between what the envoy had told Baring were two contending parties in Beijing, one of which was all for growing opium in China, the other for relying on continued imports.[86] Either way, the Chinese government could be presented in Britain as even more

---

[82] This is based on the official exchange rate then in use of Rs 1 = 2s.

[83] 'Financial Statement of the Government of India for 1882–1883', 328.

[84] Quoted in Wolf, *Life of the First Marquess of Ripon*, ii. 78–9.

[85] Gopal, *Viceroyalty of Lord Ripon*, 200.

[86] File marked 'Opium Trade with China', NAI, *Proceedings of the Government of India in the Department of Finance and Commerce: Special Revenues, Statistics and Commerce, July to December 1881* (Calcutta: Office of the Superintendent of Government Printing, 1882), 1598.

exploitative of its own people than the Indian. The matter was then passed on to the Foreign Office in London, which had final responsibility for such treaties, but nothing concrete transpired.

Baring provided some further elaboration of his views about fiscal devolution in the discussion in the Legislative Council that followed his budget statement. It was the firm intention of both governments of Britain and India, he said, to increase the share of the work of the country performed by Indians themselves. He also hoped that the number of Indians in the Covenanted Service would go up as a result of the breaking down of 'social and religious obstacles' between the British and the local elite, a remark which brought an instant rebuke from one of the Indian members, Raja Prasad, who reminded him that no genuinely Orthodox Hindu would ever encourage any such thing. Perhaps by way of a mild counter-attack, Baring delivered a series of comments about the members of India's privileged classes. He had heard a great deal, he said, of India not having representative institutions. But he did not know of any body of people, in India or elsewhere, who were so well represented as those 228,000 people who actually paid the licence tax. 'The Government had always heard of their grievance both in and out of Council.' If the budget had indeed been aimed simply to benefit this small and wealthy community, it might in justice have been said that he and his colleagues 'had sacrificed the interests of India and legislated for class interests'.[87]

There were ideas here which Baring was to continue to develop after his return to Egypt in 1883, as were some of his Indian budgetary initiatives. One was the proposal to introduce post office saving accounts in the Bengal and Madras presidencies, an encouragement to good husbandry he was later to promote in Egypt as well. A second was based on his use of a quotation from the Indian Famine Commission report to the effect that with agriculture providing almost the sole occupation of the mass of the population, 'no remedy for present evils can be complete which does not include the introduction of a diversity of occupations, through which the surplus population may... find the means of subsistence in manufactures or some such employments'. Given the fact that the government already purchased a great variety of local products, he hoped local capital would respond positively to this ever expanding market.[88]

[87] 'Discussion' following 'Financial Statement of the Government of India for 1882–3', *PP* (1882) 48, 293.

[88] Ibid. 319.

Simla in 1882: Financial Decentralization and Preparations for Baring's Last Budget

Given the still precarious state of Ethel's health, the Baring family moved in easy stages up to Simla in late March, only for Evelyn to go down with typhoid the moment they finally arrived. Although the attack was 'relatively slight', he was unable to do much work for two to three months.[89] He wrote to Lyall in May: 'The change has done both my wife and me a great deal of good. I have the fever again slightly, but it weakened me a good deal. Barley water for a month is not an invigorating drink.'[90]

It was also during this summer in Simla that Baring seems to have finally settled affairs concerning his daughter Louisa. It would appear from the correspondence he preserved with the Archbishop and others on Corfu between 1880 and 1882 that he had been sending regular payments—one letter suggests twice-yearly payments of £15 and another that these payments were made through the Ionian Bank—as well as more irregular payments for treatment of a continuing gynaecological problem ('emoragia uttera' in Italian). Then, in February 1882, the Archbishop of Corfu raised the question of making more permanent financial arrangements for Louisa now that she was soon to come of age at 19. Baring's offer of a final lump sum payment of £300 was rejected in July, the Archbishop arguing that he must send £600 to be deposited at a bank at 5 per cent so as to yield the previous £30 a year. Baring replied from the Department of Commerce and Finance offices on 11 August as follows:

My Dear Archbishop,

I have received your letter of July 12th in which you tell me that £300 will not be sufficient dowry to ensure[?] Louisa's making a suitable marriage and in which you request me to send £600.

I have always been afraid that the girl would be brought up with expectations which could not be realised, I think if you will refer to my letters of past years I have occasionally given expression to these fears. However, it is of no use now to press[?] that point any further.

I am by no means a rich man, and have a wife and children to provide for. £600 is therefore a very large sum of money for me to pay, and I consider that, under all the circumstances of the case, I might decline to pay it. I am, however, unwilling not to do my best to ensure the happiness of the girl. I send, therefore, a cheque for £600 and I beg you to dispose of it in such a manner as you may consider most conducive

---

[89] BN 341.   [90] Baring to Lyall, 14 May 1882, LP, MS Eur. F132/39.

to her interests. But, in sending this money, I must beg that it be fully understood that neither now, nor at any future time, shall I be under any consideration[?] to any further appeals for money on her behalf. I consider that I have done not only my duty but more than my duty. The girl must look either look[?] to her husband, if she desires, or to her employment[?] in some honest occupation suitable to her sex, to increase her income any further.

I have now only to thank you again for your kindness in all that you have done throughout the matter. I will ask you to be so good as to acknowledge the receipt of this letter. Our correspondence, which has now extended over 18 years, will then cease, for I shall, of course, discontinue any more[?] half yearly payment.

This troublesome exchange, combined with continued family illness, was not calculated to put him in the best of tempers. In April we find him telling Mallet that he was thinking of coming back to England. 'I have never,' he wrote, 'for a week together, had the doctor out of my house since I have been in India.' What gave him some comfort, though, was his good working relationship with the Viceroy. 'Together', he told Mallet, Ripon and he could do 'almost anything':

Look at this recent self-government business. It is a great move onward. We are quite agreed and so easily beat the bureaucracy. But, once separated, my usefulness is destroyed . . . I am glad to say that *nothing* could be better than our relations now. Perhaps I am rather influenced by the extreme kindness shown by Lord and Lady Ripon during my recent domestic troubles but certain it is that I have a higher opinion of his ability than I did a year ago. Further, I understand his personal character better, and I am careful to do nothing to wound his extremely sensitive nature. He, on the other hand, shows a much greater disposition to consult me and listen to my advice.[91]

The main task before Baring was, as always, work on the next budget, particularly the vexed question of possible reform of the licence tax. However, before this could get properly under way came the disturbing news that the Indian government had been ordered to send a contingent of troops to Egypt to join General Garnet Wolseley's force preparing to crush the revolt against foreign control under the leadership of Colonel Ahmad Urabi. It was soon followed by the unwelcome information that India would be expected to defray the whole cost. Ripon and Baring were at once faced with the prospect that the small surplus of several hundreds of thousand pounds shown in the revised estimates for 1882/3 would be turned into a larger deficit. They sent off an immediate protest to London

---

[91] Baring to L. Mallet, 2 June 1882, CP/1, Mallet Correspondence.

on 26 July, followed by another on 4 August, to the effect that British policy towards Egypt was entirely the responsibility of the home government, that the government of India had never been consulted about the military expedition, and that any benefits which accrued would go mainly to British and not Indian subjects.

This last point was almost certainly one developed by Evelyn Baring, who had particular reason to feel aggrieved by the knock-on effects resulting from the breakdown of what had seemed his own well-ordered management of Egyptian affairs. Coming to India, he had had to cope with the hangover of expenses from the Afghan War. Then, just when things were beginning to look up, he had to cope with a second set of military-related costs over which he had no control.

Baring's obvious irritation is manifest in the long telegram sent by the Government of India to Hartington on 14 August. It began with the assertion that it was impossible to make financial plans until the question of how large the Indian expedition's expenses would be, and then how they might be divided between the two governments, was finally settled. It then made a short *tour d'horizon* of the Indian financial situation to make the point that, although the government was solvent and able to meet ordinary expenses, there were many difficult problems ahead. Chinese competition might damage opium revenue. There could be a further decline in the gold–silver exchange rate, and so a further rise in the real cost of meeting the interest on loans from London. Finally, as a result of the new contracts made between the central government and the provinces, the centre had less in reserve to meet sudden emergencies of this kind. The dispatch ended with a reminder that the Indian people were very poor, that the maintenance of peace was a vital economic interest to them, and that, not living in a democracy, they did not have the usual means of protesting against war-making policies which might lead to a concomitant increase in their own taxes.[92]

In spite of all these clouds on India's financial horizon, Baring still wished to reopen the question of introducing direct taxes. However, Ripon proved unwilling and he does not seem to have tried to push the point very far. A last effort based on the argument that it might be possible to induce the new boards and committees to be set up under Ripon's local government initiative of May 1882 to persuade the Indians to agree to place direct taxes on themselves came to nothing as a result of opposition

[92] NAI, Department of Finance and Commerce (Accounts and Finances), A, Proceedings (Sept. 1882), 1211.

from London.[93] Reform of the licence tax was thus impossible, and Baring had to content himself with producing another do-nothing budget for 1883/4, just as he had had to do for 1881/2. The only slight relief came from Ripon's success in persuading Gladstone to contribute £500,000 to the cost of sending the Indian contingent to Egypt, leaving India to find the remainder of just under £700,000.[94]

The other main activity of the summer was the negotiations with the various provincial governors, who were now required to give flesh to Baring's decentralization of the financial system by creating the boards and committees to manage local financial affairs. The basic outlines had been set out in Ripon's Government Resolution of May 1882. These included the principle that all committees were to have a majority of non-official members and that they should be elected when it was practicable to do so. Franchises and the form which elections might take were to be decided by the provincial governments after discussion with the leading citizens in each locality. The new boards would then be given control over all the local rates and cesses levied in their jurisdiction. In time, they might also be given the right to assess and then to collect the licence tax, a point which Baring tried to use to his own advantage in the initiative just described above.[95]

One of the governors now required to address the issue was Alfred Lyall, who had been moved to the North-West Provinces in April 1882. Based in his summer capital at Nainee Tal, he carried on his usual spirited correspondence, not only with his sisters, but also with Baring himself. Their letters throw an interesting light on the political temper of the times and must be read in the light of the fact that ideas of nationalism and self-government were very much in the air as a result of the Irish Liberal MPs' advocacy of home rule and the Urabi movement's cry of 'Egypt for the Egyptians'.[96]

Lyall was well aware of the significance of what was being attempted and, while supporting it in general, had a number of obvious doubts. As he wrote to his sister Barbara in June:

Ripon and Baring have done more than they know or intend to set the ball rolling by publicly directing a wholesale introduction of the elective system into local

---

[93] Baring, 'Very Confidential: The Licence Tax', Simla, 2 Oct. 1882, CP/2, FO 633/99.

[94] Gopal, *Viceroyalty of Lord Ripon*, 204.

[95] Ibid. 94.

[96] The cry of 'Egypt for the Egyptians' was aimed much more at the local Turkish elite than at the creation of an independent nation-state; Schölch, *Egypt for the Egyptians!*, 310–11.

councils and municipalities. I am not quite sure which way the ball will roll; but as the system spreads and the electorate grows strong and active the burden of managing these vast multitudes will grow rather formidable.[97]

Baring was both more sanguine and more concerned to make the best possible case for the correctness of the path to which he and the Viceroy were now firmly committed. After a long comment to Lyall about the current crisis in Egypt and the popular cry of 'Egypt for the Egyptians', he went on to note that, in his opinion, the cry of 'India for the Indians' might come sooner than most people generally imagined. It was important to recognize that the momentum was building up and to prepare for it. Such a movement was 'controllable' 'if we can only guide it, and prevent any violent transitions'.

I do not think that English statesmen . . . quite sufficiently recognise that the final cause of British rule in India is to teach the people to govern themselves. And Anglo-Indians hardly recognise the depth of change which is going on under their own eyes. This is natural enough. I don't recognise that I am getting older by looking in the glass every morning as I shave, but my friends will recognise it when I get home. You will easily have divined that the motto of the present administration is to prepare gradually for the changes. Let us by all means move carefully and not too fast. but still we must move, or India will move without us.[98]

The reasoning seems quite clear. It is not that Baring was a great believer in popular government. However, given that the demand for it was becoming more intense, at least among the more educated people in both Britain and India, it would be sensible to try and address the issue rather than simply to turn a blind eye. As he wrote to Ripon in August 1882, 'Whether we like or dislike the typical Baboo, the fact of his existence has to be recognised.'[99] The same view was more sharply put in a letter he wrote to Mallet the following month: 'we shall not subvert the British Empire by allowing the Bengali Baboo to discuss his own schools and drains. Rather we can afford him a safety-valve if we can turn his attentions to these innocuous subjects.'[100]

The term 'Baboo' had once been used as a sign of respect, rather like 'Mr', but here it is almost certainly being used with what the *Hobson-Jobson*

---

[97] Lyall to Barbara Lyall, 9 June 1882, LP, MS Eur. F132/7.
[98] Baring to Lyall, 19 July 1882, LP, MS Eur. F132/39.
[99] Baring to Ripon, 3 Aug. 1882, RP, Add. MS 43596, CVI.
[100] Baring to L. Mallet, 25 Sept. 1882, quoted in Gopal, *Viceroyalty of Lord Ripon*, 95.

dictionary calls a 'slight air of disparagement, as characterizing a superficially cultivated but too often effeminate Bengali'.[101]

Lyall, for his part, based his position much more clearly on a version of the social Darwinism then much in vogue. Writing to Baring on 27 July 1882, he stated his strong opposition to the theory that the 'final cause of Britain in India' was 'to teach people to govern themselves'. This, he argued, was

> superseded by the theory of existence terminating in the survival of the fittest, which still applies to people as to plants. And I know of no instance in history of a nation being educated by another nation into self-government and independence; every nation has fought its way up in the world as the English have done, testifying freely for the great principle, and putting out its blood when needed. Our residuary legatees are not the educated Indians, but the next strongest race to ourselves in Asia, whoever they may be, Afghans, Russians or Chinese.[102]

This, of course, was a lesson which the colonized peoples could learn themselves as soon as they too realized that they would have to fight the British for their freedom.

Calcutta, Financial Affairs, and the Shock of the Ilbert Bill

Back in Calcutta, Baring had three major preoccupations: putting the final touches to his 1883/4 budget statement, drafting an ambitious dispatch aimed at providing a general set of principles to guide future railway construction policy, and returning one last time to the vexed question of the licence tax. His renewed interest in railway matters was very much prompted by the promotion of Theodore Hope to be public works member of the Council. Here was someone whose vigorous approach to administration matched Baring's own, and by January 1883 they had drawn up a new set of proposals designed to break the logjam caused by the Secretary of State's veto of a first attempt to sketch out a comprehensive railway policy in September 1881. Their document contained a spirited defence of the decision to award the Rothschilds' Central Bengal Railway Company a limited, five-year government guarantee, and a proposal that 'safe and reasonable guarantees' be offered to other prospective

---

[101] Colonel Henry Yule and A. C. Burnell (eds.), *Hobson-Jobson: A Glossary of Colloquial Anglo-Indian Words and Phrases* (New Delhi: Rupa, 1994; first pub. 1886), 44.
[102] CP/1, India 1880–1883: Letters Received E–Z.

investors. Hartington, who was still insisting that private capital could be found without such inducements, had turned it down flat.[103]

The new Hope–Baring proposal tried to build on the experience of the past two years in which different, ad hoc, arrangements had had to be made with at least four different private companies, all but one of which had been offered some type of guarantee. Now was the moment, they argued, to pre-empt such time-consuming negotiations by returning to general principles. These were nothing short of revolutionary, involving a complete reversal of previous policy by calling upon the state to build only those lines which were not commercially viable ('unproductive', in the language of the time), and to leave the productive ones to private capital without guarantee but with free grants of the necessary land.[104]

Lord Kimberley, Hartington's successor at the India Office, took his time in considering the matter and his reply only arrived on 16 August 1883, just as Baring was getting ready to leave. It put the whole question on hold once again while a parliamentary select committee was appointed to give advice. Clearly the issue was much more complex than Ripon, Baring, and Hartington had first believed. Their case was not improved by the fact that the government surveys on which the Bengal Central Railway flotation had been based had proved much too optimistic, producing great embarrassment when a new contract had to be negotiated in 1887 with yet more government financial support.[105] Nevertheless, it is also possible to agree with a contemporary expert, Horace Bell, that the Baring–Hope recommendation for creating a basic division between the construction of productive and unproductive lines was soon widely used as a guide to Indian government railway policy in the 1890s.[106]

Baring's final tussle with the problem of the licence tax proved equally frustrating. After much effort he produced a long, hand-written draft of some 20,000 words which he labelled 'Very Private and Confidential. For the Viceroy Only, 31 March 1883'.[107] In many ways it was a typical Baring document of this period of his life in which he pares down an issue to its basic essentials before seeking to demonstrate that there is just one way of moving on. In this case, it was the decision to abolish the tariffs which, in

---

[103] Bell, *Railway Policy*, 33–4.
[104] Government of India to Secretary of State, 23 Jan. 1883, in NAI, Department of Finance and Commerce (Accounts and Finance), A, Proceedings (Jan. 1883), 244–6.
[105] Bell, *Railway Policy*, 81.
[106] Ibid. 57.
[107] CP/1, FO 633/99.

his argument, had finally settled the long-standing controversy over direct versus indirect taxation by making transfer to the former inevitable. The question of how to do this remained unclear, even though his personal inclination was still to find a way of introducing such taxes at the local, rather than the central government, level.

The document is also a very personal statement, a *cri de cœur* almost, designed to excite Ripon's sympathies, not to stir up more trouble. Baring writes of his great difficulties in trying to think of a way forward. He goes through the history of his own approach to the matter and the way in which his original scheme was turned down by the India Office Council in 1881. He describes how he had then come up with a new scheme in 1882 which sought to introduce direct taxation more slowly and with less political friction. However, this too had found little favour in London, persuading him and the Viceroy not to press the matter further for 1882/3. There, he wrote, the issue rested. Nevertheless, it is clear from the length of the document, and the care put into it, that Baring was still hoping to persuade Ripon to have one last try.

It was at this moment, just before his summons back to Egypt, that all thoughts of new directions had to be put on hold as a result of the political crisis brought on by the huge Anglo-Indian public outcry which had accompanied the publication of the Criminal Procedures Amendment Bill by the law member, Sir Courtenay Ilbert, on 2 February. Now began one of the most famous or, from an Indian point of view, most infamous, disputes in British Indian history. It concerned the process for trying Europeans in the district courts in areas at some distance from the main centres of provincial government. The right to such a local trial had been accorded to them in 1872 at a time when there were only British magistrates and assessors who might be called upon to adjudicate. However, even then, at a time when there were just four Indian members of the Covenanted Civil Service, it was clear that, sooner rather than later, the question of the role of Indian magistrates in the district courts would arise. Indeed, an effort to anticipate just such an eventuality had been defeated in the Viceroy's Council just before Northbrook and Baring arrived in India in 1872, leaving district adjudication to British magistrates alone.

The question was next addressed seriously in 1881. A discussion in the Viceroy's Council revealed that Baring and one other member, James Gibbs, were in favour of granting the right to try all criminal cases involving Europeans to Indians of the Covenanted Service. However, with four other members against, Ripon felt that further action was 'inopportune'.[108] His hand was then forced by two events in 1882. One was a petition of complaint by an Indian member of the Service, Behari Lal Gupta, that, as a newly appointed sessions judge in Upper Bengal, he was not allowed to try Europeans. The second was the receipt of a letter from the Governor of Bengal, Sir Ashley Eden, in which he pointed to the anomaly that an Indian district magistrate should have less power than either his British subordinate or an Indian colleague in a presidency town who did have such a right.

Eden's letter was then sent around the provincial governments, in the usual routine way, for their comments. All seemed inclined to support the removal of the anomaly, with just a single civilian member of the Madras Council warning that a move of this type might arouse opposition from the Anglo-Indian community. The matter was finally referred to London, where the India Office Council also approved the general lines of the new scheme, with only Sir Henry Maine, who was not present on the occasion but who sent his opinion by letter, sounding a note of caution. Somewhat surprisingly, there was no mention of Maine's letter when Hartington's approval was transmitted to Calcutta, an oversight which Baring was later to blame on the fact that the Secretary of State had stuffed it into the pocket of his greatcoat when setting off for a race meeting at Newmarket and then simply forgotten all about it.[109]

Ilbert was now free to draw up the necessary bill. By all accounts it was not well drafted and went much further than simply attending to Gupta's complaint. Not only did it extend jurisdiction over Europeans in the district courts to Indian magistrates as asked, but it also gave local governments an open-ended discretionary power to grant powers of trial to selected officers of ranks lower than Gupta's.[110] This was immediately seized on by members of the European community, already looking for a fight with Ripon, who were now able to stir up public opinion by appealing to what Sarvepalli Gopal has called 'the unreasoning fear of an Indian judge', and the belief that every member of their community was now at risk.[111]

The first sign of real trouble came at a public meeting at the Calcutta Town Hall on 28 February, when a huge and angry crowd of Anglo-Indians passed a resolution denouncing the bill. So loud was the noise that, according to Mortimer Durand, Ripon himself could hear the 'shouts of applause and wrath from his room at nearby Government House while

[108] Gopal, *Viceroyalty of Lord Ripon*, 127–8.
[109] Zetland, *Lord Cromer*, 79–80.
[110] Gopal, *Viceroyalty of Lord Ripon*, 136–7.
[111] Ibid. 138.

his opponents were denouncing him'.[112] There was an immediate worry as to whether the government could actually maintain order given the fact that there were only seventy British constables on the Calcutta police force.[113]

The matter was discussed again in the Viceroy's Council on 9 March, a meeting at which Baring was uncharacteristically silent. He later explained that this was because he was unused to making speeches and that, anyway, the points he wished to make were expressed more eloquently by others.[114] It seems rather a lame excuse from someone universally acknowledged to be Ripon's right-hand man. It is more likely that the whole event had simply caught him unawares and that he had not had time to make up his mind. As he was to write much later in the 'Biographical Notes', he had initialled his support for the Ilbert draft when it was first sent to him as soon as he had noted that the opinions of local officials had been obtained. However, he also admitted to having done so without studying the proposals with any care in the belief that they were only of 'technical importance'. He also referred to the great pressure of his other work.[115] In further explanation, we may note that the principle behind the bill was one of which he had long approved, probably from at least as early as his first period in India with Northbrook.

Baring seems to have been as surprised as all the rest of his colleagues by the strength of the pent-up Anglo-Indian feeling against Ripon and all his works. His first considered reaction, which he was then to adhere to for the rest of his life, was that he was sorry that the whole question had been raised at all, for 'the benefit of the reform which will be a small one will be more than counter-balanced by the ill-feeling that it creates'. However, once a decision had been taken, the government's own credibility as far as its reputation for impartiality and strength of purpose were concerned 'required that the matter be seen through to its conclusion'.[116] Hence, there was no alternative but to give his support to the Viceroy, whose display of courage he much admired. 'The Ilbert affair has raised Ripon

---

[112] Quoted in Louis L. Cornell, *Kipling in India* (London: Macmillan; New York: St Martin's Press, 1966), 57.

[113] Uma Dasgupta, 'The Ilbert Bill Agitation, 1883', in Ravi Dayal (ed.), *We Fought Together for Freedom: Chapters from the Indian National Movement* (New Delhi: Oxford University Press, 1995), 59.

[114] Farewell Speech of 27 Aug. 1883, quoted in Zetland, *Lord Cromer*, 80–1.

[115] BN 348–55.

[116] Compare Baring to L. Mallet, 27 Feb. 1883, CP/1, Mallet Correspondence, with BN 348–55.

100% in my estimation,' he told Mallet. 'He is firm and determined not to yield.'[117]

The Council met briefly to decide to refer the matter to London for further advice before leaving for Simla, with Ripon arriving there on 17 March, the earliest he, or any of his predecessors, had ever gone before. This was seen by most members of the Anglo-Indian community as an inglorious retreat, a sentiment put into verse by the young Rudyard Kipling in a poem published on 29 March. The last stanzas went as follows:

> For his [Ripon's] notions of natives were curious,
> So India objected, and rose,
> And, when India was properly furious,
> He remarked. 'This discussion I close,
> The heat to my health is injurious,
> I hie to Himalayan snows.
>
> With the tact that belonged to his station,
> With a suavity solely his own,
> He has set by the ears half a nation
> And left it—to simmer alone.
> With his maudlin *ma-bap* legislation,
> He has played merry Hades and—flown.[118]

It was while up at Simla that Baring received the request that he return to Egypt as Malet's successor as British Consul-General. With Ripon's reluctant permission he decided to accept. It was clearly a great blow to the Viceroy and his policies. By this stage Baring's open support for the Ilbert Bill was public enough to excite the attentions of the Anglo-Indian press. According to his 'Biographical Notes', he had been subject to almost as much invective as Ripon himself, one Calcutta newspaper describing him as having 'the oiliness of a Chadband and the malignity of a fiend'.[119]

Nevertheless, Baring must have retained some doubts about his own conduct in the affair. In one of his farewell speeches, to the Bombay Branch of the East Indian Association on 27 August, he felt it necessary not only to offer his lame explanation for his silence at the Council meeting of 9 March but also to assert, unequivocally, that he 'entirely concurred' with the bill as originally introduced and that, as far as the 'essential principles'

---

[117] 6 Mar. 1883, CP/1, Mallet Correspondence.

[118] Rudyard Kipling, 'A New Departure', in *Early Verses*, 184–5. 'Ma-bap' is translated as 'ingratiating'.

[119] BN 348–55.

were concerned, he was still of the same opinion as he had been nine months before.[120]

A longer and better-argued version of the same argument is offered in an article defending the Ilbert initiative which was published in the *Nineteenth Century* in October. This can now be seen as his major public intervention in the affair, one designed to cement support for the Viceroy in London employing arguments which he had frequently discussed with Ripon before leaving. The article characterizes the struggle as one between two opposing groups as to whether India was to be governed in terms of the Queen's Proclamation of 1858 or of the 'retrograde and anti-native policy' proposed by a section of the European community. Baring firmly allies himself with the former position, which he identifies as involving the support of a free press, the promotion of education, and the admission of more Indians into the public service.[121]

Opposition to the Ilbert Bill had intensified over the summer, led in India by the newly formed European and Anglo-Indian Defence Association. Ripon himself stood firm. But the general consensus in government circles was that there would have to be changes in the light of the Secretary of State's long-awaited response to the draft bill on 24 July. It may well be that it was Baring's departure that finally caused the Viceroy to appreciate the need for concessions as it left him with only Ilbert as a strong supporter of the original proposal. After prolonged negotiations a watered-down version of the bill was finally passed in January 1884. It allowed Europeans being tried in district magistrates' courts to insist that no fewer than half the jurors or assessors present be Europeans. Ripon's need to climb down in the face of a well-organized campaign waged by the Anglo-Indians was not lost on educated opinion and is generally credited with encouraging the first stage of the Indian national movement under the leadership of the Indian National Congress founded the very next year.

As for Baring himself, there can be no doubt that the Ilbert Bill controversy cast a considerable pall over his last months in India. If we add that his two largest projects, the attempt to introduce a form of direct taxation and to transform the Indian railway system by an infusion of private capital, remained stalled, and that two of his three budgets had been victims to war expenditures over which he had had no control, it may

---

[120] Quoted in Zetland, *Lord Cromer*, 80–1. The mention of 'nine months' is odd and seems likely to be a slip of the pen: it could only have been six since he had seen the first draft of the Ilbert Bill. However, he may have been referring to some earlier discussion of Eden's letter.

[121] Evelyn Baring, 'Recent Events in India', *Nineteenth Century*, 14 (Oct. 1883), 572, 586.

well have seemed that his impact on the Ripon viceroyalty was very much less than could have been reasonably expected in the heady months after the Liberal victory of 1880. Whatever comfort he may have been able to derive must have come from a solid sense that some of his policies had eased the crippling burdens of India's millions of poor peasants, and that his joint project with Ripon to decentralize both government and finance might bear much useful fruit some time in the future. He certainly would not have appreciated the irony that what he and Ripon are now principally remembered for is for having stirred up so much Anglo-Indian opposition as to excite an Indian counter-reaction to a bill which they had initially regarded as a very insignificant measure of liberal reform.

The Call to Return to Egypt

It was in May 1883, just as the Ilbert Bill controversy was just getting under way, that Baring was asked if he would return to Cairo as Consul-General with the special rank of Minister Plenipotentiary in the diplomatic service. His loosely defined task was to preside over yet another reorganization of the Egyptian administration and then the immediate evacuation of the British troops who had occupied the country in August–September 1882. Baring had, of course, tried to keep in close touch with affairs in Egypt while also being asked for advice by his colleagues in the Liberal Cabinet in London.

Some of his first thoughts on the matter can be found in a letter he wrote to Lyall on 19 July 1882 shortly after Lyall had returned to India via a brief visit to a turbulent Cairo. 'I agree with you that only two policies were possible, viz. Blunt's or Colvin's, and I also agree with you that Colvin's was the one.' This is a reference to the activities of Wilfrid Blunt, the poet and anti-imperialist, who had tried to persuade the Gladstone Cabinet to accept the programme of what he called the 'native government' after Riaz's dismissal in September 1881, and that of Baring's successor as Controller, Auckland Colvin. Nevertheless, Baring was critical of some aspects of Colvin's and also of de Blignières's behaviour. He was 'inclined to think that the former had brusquéd [rushed] the whole thing too much' and that if he (Baring) had still been there he would have given Urabi 'more rope wherewith to hang himself'. He also thought that the two Controllers had 'leant too much on Downing Street and the Quay d'Orsay'. This was certainly true of Colvin, whose 'leaning' involved a sustained campaign to

persuade the Gladstone Cabinet that the Urabi movement posed a fundamental challenge to the whole system of European financial control. But it
was only partly true of de Blignières, who had lost his job in Cairo for
having tried to champion the same line. Still, Baring was charitable enough
to say that, whatever they had done, the outcome would probably have
been the same because, in his opinion, the origins of the problem lay much
earlier, beginning with the Egyptian government's unwillingness to punish
the army officers whose mutinous demonstration in February 1879 had led
to Nubar's dismissal from office.[122]

Baring's views about the policy to be pursued after the military occupation are contained in a long memorandum written on 18 September 1882
in response to a specific set of questions from Lord Granville, the Foreign
Secretary, and Lord Northbrook. The key statement came in response to
their question 'How is order to be maintained?' Baring replied that he
was 'strongly opposed to the establishment of a Protectorate'. Whatever
Urabi's faults, 'I do not see what the Egyptians, considered as a nation,
have done to forfeit their right to self-government.' Moreover, from a
British point of view, such a course would involve a huge responsibility,
including the future of the lands to the south, meaning the provinces of
Sudan. It followed that the Khedive must be left to preserve order himself,
subject to one caveat: if evidence showed that he could not do this, then he
(Baring) would most 'reluctantly' have to admit that a protectorate was the
only alternative. However, if all went well, Taufiq should be allowed to
choose his own ministers, Riaz and Sharif being the best combination.

Baring also advised putting an end to the system of dual control by
replacing all the French with British advisers who, once again, should
exercise only limited powers of direct interference. 'There remains nothing in the area of fiscal reform that can't be done by the Egyptians
themselves,' he asserted in one arresting phrase, and, anyway, 'Europeans
were inclined to go too fast.' Finally, he was in favour of only temporary
British support for the Khedive's reassertion of authority, believing it
'reasonable' to suppose that this need last no more than six to twelve
months at most.

Two other answers had a direct relevance for the policies actually
pursued by the Liberal Cabinet. One was Baring's argument that he was
against handing Urabi over to the Khedive to be tried and shot, preferring
banishment instead. The second was his belief that it was in the best

---

[122] LP, MS Eur. F132/39.

interests of both Britain and Egypt that Egypt be made independent from Turkey. For one thing, this would probably involve the abolition of the Capitulations, the series of treaties creating a protected position for foreigners in the Ottoman Empire, whose passing he regarded as a very good thing so long as local European interests could be safeguarded in some other way. For another, with control over the Suez Canal assured, Britain could watch the further development of the 'Eastern Question' (basically, the future of the Ottoman Empire in Europe) with 'perfect indifference'.[123]

Views of this kind must have commended themselves to Gladstone's principal advisers when it came to the question of who was to oversee what they hoped would be an orderly process of British evacuation from Egypt. A divided Cabinet had sent Lord Dufferin, the British Ambassador at Istanbul, to Egypt in November to advise the Khedive on measures to re-establish his authority. One further step was the abolition of the system of dual control, after difficult negotiations with the French, and the replacement of the two Controllers by a single British financial adviser. Dufferin's subsequent report of February 1883 set out the basic problems to be solved without, however, being able to offer more than a provisional solution. It began:

Had I been commissioned to place affairs on the footing of an Indian state, the outlook would have been different. The masterful hand of a resident would have quickly bent everything to his will and, in the space of five years, would have greatly added to the national well-being of the country. But the Egyptians would have justly considered these advantages bought at the expense of their political independence. Moreover, HMG and public opinion in England have pronounced against this solution. But it is absolutely necessary to prevent the fabric we have raised from crumbling to the ground as soon as our hand is withdrawn.[124]

Dufferin's tentative answer to the conundrum was to begin the reorganization of the Army and the police, the reform of the legal system as it related to native Egyptians, and the replacement of the chamber of deputies by two other representative institutions, a legislative council and a general assembly. It was Dufferin's report, and its recommendations as to the new system which was to be set in place, which were to be Baring's only guide.

[123] Baring, 'Very Confidential Memorandum on the Present Situation in Egypt', 18 Sept. 1882, CP/2, FO 633/99.
[124] Dufferin to Granville, 6 Feb. 1883, PP (1883) 83, 129.

Once again Baring left no public record of why he agreed to take up the post, especially as it meant proceeding straight to Egypt without a short time in London first. We can only imagine the pressure that must have been put on him by his Liberal colleagues in London and by his own sense that the system of control he had helped to institute in Egypt was in need of urgent repair. One other possible explanation is that, as he was to write in an essay completed towards the end of his life, Gladstone had advised him some time in 1880 that there was no longer any point in trying to enter Parliament as the Liberal programme of the past many years was more or less complete.[125]

Lyall's final comment concerning Baring and Egypt is also of considerable interest. After telling Barbara in May 1883 how sorry he was to learn that Evelyn was leaving, he went on: 'I think Egypt suits him better than India—he can grasp the whole situation there, and he has not the uncontrolled power enjoyed[?] by men high in Indian office. This sense of great power, and the shortness of power in office, makes Baring rush at his work out here.'[126]

This was a very thoughtful observation as far as it went. Another colleague was perhaps nearer the mark in a verse he penned about Baring's transfer at just the same time:

> The virtues of patience are known
> But I think, that when put to the touch,
> The people of Egypt will own with a groan
> There's an evil in Baring too much.[127]

[125] 'The Politician Wordsworth', *The Spectator*, 11 Dec. 1915, repr. in Earl of Cromer, *Political and Literary Essays: Third Series* (London: Macmillan, 1916), 261–2.

[126] Lyall to Barbara Lyall, 25 May 1883, LP, MS Eur. F132/8/9a.

[127] This verse must have been widely circulated and is quoted in a number of places. I have taken it from vol. vii of the 11th edition of the *Encyclopaedia Britannica* (1910), 484.

PART III

Governing Egypt
1883–1907

10

---◆---

Egypt: Digging In
1883–1885

Creating a Residence

Baring, now Sir Evelyn Baring, went straight from India to Cairo, arriving on 11 September 1883. He returned to the rue Moughrabi and established both his residence and his office in a house owned by Sir Alexander Baird that was later to become the Turf Club after the Agency moved out in December 1893.[1] Harry Boyle, who came to work in it in August 1885, described it as 'small and rambling', a statement which seems somewhat at odds with photographs of the building itself.[2] 'Small' is, however, a relative concept and the question of whether it was big enough for its purpose soon became a matter of some importance.

From at least as early as February 1886 Baring and his staff were seriously looking for a larger alternative.[3] Hence Baring himself had every incentive to exaggerate its smallness when pressing London to be allowed to build a more comfortable official residence for the British Agency. Towards the end of 1886 he wrote to the Earl of Iddesleigh, then briefly the Foreign Secretary, that the reception rooms were too small for the number of people he was obliged to entertain. 'As regards sleeping apartments, there is only just enough room for my family, which only consists of my wife, two children and a governess. If I have to receive any visitors as was the case when the Viceroy [Lord Ripon] returned from

---

[1] The Turf Club moved again in 1934, and it was this new building that was burned down in the anti-foreign demonstrations of January 1952.

[2] Boyle, *A Servant of Empire*, 39. A photograph of the Agency building can be found in Samir Raafat, 'Bayt Al-Lurd', *Cairo Times*, 29 Apr. 1999.

[3] Letter from R. H. Boyce, Cairo, to the First Commissioner for Works, London, 16 Feb. 1886 (copy in the chancery of the British Embassy, Cairo).

India I am obliged to go to the trouble and expense of sending my children to a hotel.'[4] As for the part of the building which housed his office, he noted that the chancery consisted of only two very small rooms, one originally a pantry and the other so hot as to be almost uninhabitable in summer, into which was 'stuffed' his staff of six persons. Meanwhile, the archives had to be stowed wherever space could be found throughout the rest of the building.[5]

During his first months in Cairo, Baring had no trained diplomat to assist him. However, as the possibility of an immediate British evacuation was put on hold, he was joined first by Edwin Egerton, and then by two more diplomats, Gerald Portal and Francis Elliot. If we add the Military Attaché, a Syrian interpreter, and the chancery registrar, we get to a total of six by July 1885. The interpreter, Nicola Aranghi, was soon too ill to continue and was replaced by Harry Boyle, sent to Cairo from the Embassy in Istanbul.[6]

Given Britain's new position in Egypt following the occupation, the Agency soon became a major centre of power in Cairo, visited regularly by Egyptian cabinet ministers, the consuls-general of the European powers, the representatives of the various local European communities, and others. It was also the site of Baring's meetings with the most important of the British advisers, Clifford Lloyd (under-secretary at the Ministry of the Interior) and Colin Scott Moncrieff (Inspector-General of Irrigation at the Ministry of Public Works), who had been recruited by Dufferin before Baring arrived, and the 27-year-old Edgar Vincent, later Lord d'Abernon, Baring's choice to succeed Auckland Colvin at the Ministry of Finance, who started work in October 1883.

Vincent, who kept an irregular diary, provides an account of some of these Agency meetings as well as, more generally, of Baring's working practices. In one attended by Julius Blum, the long-time Financial Secretary to the government of Egypt, on 21 December 1883, the main item on the agenda was the urgent need to cut back budgetary expenditures to the level of 1880. Baring opened by stating that he intended 'to make himself very disagreeable' to the Egyptian government on the subject. The British were not only in Cairo to give advice 'but to insist on it being carried out'. There was then a general discussion as to how the message should be put

---

[4] Baring to Iddesleigh, 26 Oct. 1886, CP/2, PRO, FO 633/5.

[5] Ibid.

[6] Boyle, *Servant of Empire*, 39. Boyle was not given the newly created post of Oriental Secretary until 8 Dec. 1899, BP, box A, file 3.

across. Baring was all for writing to Sharif, the Prime Minister.[7] But meeting again on Boxing Day, Vincent and Blum found that Baring had changed his mind. He had begun to draft his letter on 23 and 24 December, he told them, yet had soon found that it had begun to assume 'gigantic proportions'. His new plan was that they simply set a target for the overall reduction in expenditure and then appoint a committee consisting of Vincent, Blum, and Fitzgerald (the Director of Accounts) to work out the details. Blum suggested they add the Minister of Finance himself, and this was agreed.[8]

The Agency was also the focus of what became an increasingly elaborate ritual by which the British presence was demonstrated to the local population, as Baring drove out in a carriage escorted by British troops to visit the Khedive at his Abdin Palace, to greet important personages at the main railway station, the Bab al-Hadid, or to attend the regular parades by British troops. Meanwhile, the Barings themselves assumed the position of leaders of the British community, giving dinners and dances for the advisers, the senior military officers, and the increasing numbers of British dignitaries passing through. Apart from members of Egypt's Turco-Circassian aristocracy, few local people were invited, making the Agency a bastion of European, and particularly British, solidarity, and a symbol of Britain's new supremacy.

Ethel, whether she liked it or not, was thrown into the position of first lady, although often in heated competition with Mme Barrère, the English wife of the French Consul-General. One early incident involved Mme Barrère's protest at Lady Baring being asked to collect subscriptions for a local Catholic charity, something which she thought should be the duty of the French as a major Catholic power.[9] Others led to periods of considerable *froideur* between the two agencies. According to Vincent, the French were 'in a fury for a week' after the Barings had invited Mme Barrère to a dance at which Evelyn Baring had shamefully refused to dance with her himself.[10]

It was in his overcrowded agency that Baring spent his first seven hectic months until he was ordered back to London in April 1884 to help prepare for the International Conference on Egyptian Finances. He was later to

[7] Vincent, 'Memo of conversation with Sir E. Baring', Diary, 21 Dec. 1883, DP, Add. MS 48948.
[8] Ibid., 26 Dec. 1883.
[9] Vincent, 'Notes: M. Barrère and the Conference', Diary, 20 July 1884, DP, Add. MS 48948.
[10] Ibid.

write that the first three months of 1884, in which he had to deal with the pressures attendant on the first stages of General Gordon's mission to Khartoum, as the worst period in his life.[11] He was ill, overworked, and increasingly tetchy and bad-tempered. Living and working in one house had its obvious advantages and disadvantages. On the one hand, Ethel was close at hand to look after him and to share his worries and concerns. On the other, his aides could visit him with problems at almost any time, even when he was sick.

Putting the Evacuation on Hold

Baring's instructions from Granville, the British Foreign Secretary, were minimal. He was simply to act on the basis of the instructions previously given to Lord Dufferin. These were to 'advise' the Khedive on the re-establishment of his authority, to reform certain sections of the administration, including the Army, and to oversee the improvement of the local system of justice. The underlying imperative, however, was to ensure that the military occupation would be as short as possible. If Baring himself had been in any doubt as to the overwhelming importance attached to this in London, it was immediately reinforced by letters he received from members of Gladstone's Cabinet, notably Northbrook, who wrote to him on 5 September that the 'main question for us. [the Liberal Cabinet] is, how soon our troops can safely leave Cairo'.[12]

This was a course of action which commended itself to Baring as well, otherwise he would never have accepted the post in the first place. He must also have appreciated, not just Dufferin's outlines for a reformed system of Egyptian government with its small Legislative Council of thirty members, but also the tone and temper of the noble lord's aristocratic distrust of 'paper constitutions' and his disinclination to suggest the creation of a new, unrepresentative assembly which would prove, he wrote, an 'uninstructed and unmanageable mob'.[13]

Baring also possessed particular advantages when it came to the organization of a speedy withdrawal, such as his previous acquaintance with major political figures, notably the Khedive, and Egypt's three leading politicians, Prime Minister Sharif, Riaz, and Nubar, as well as his long experience with Egyptian finance. The tone of his first few dispatches was

[11] Cromer, *Modern Egypt*, i. 417.   [12] Quoted in Zetland, *Lord Cromer*, 87–8.
[13] Dufferin to Granville, 5 Feb. 1883, *PP* (1883) 83, 94, 129.

fairly sanguine. Writing to Granville on 27 September and 14 October, he felt able to recommend a reduction of the British garrison from 6,700 to 3,000 and the withdrawal of all troops from Cairo.[14] It is true that he alarmed some members of the Cabinet by pointing out the extent to which the Khedive's authority had been weakened not only by 'recent events' (the Urabi revolt) but also by the Dufferin reforms, which were, 'in essence', to protect the people against the arbitrary acts of their own government.[15] Moreover, Baring was soon to conclude that Dufferin had painted a somewhat too rosy picture of the local scene, and thus that it was his duty to highlight some of the contradictions necessarily entailed by the British policy of trying to restore khedivial authority while shifting power away from the ruler at the same time.

Ideas of this type soon led Baring to begin to advocate policies that, though based on the assumption that 'we must not stay too long', involved a number of prior steps that he judged were necessary if Egypt were not to relapse into anarchy after the British had left, an argument persuasive enough to convince even Mr Gladstone.[16] These included a return to themes which he had emphasized during his previous period in Egypt, 1877–80. One was his attempt to get Granville to agree to present the other powers with a total package of proposed reforms rather than consulting them one detail at a time. Then, when this was vetoed as too drastic, he turned his attention to trying to persuade the British Government to support two other measures designed to stabilize Egypt's now rickety financial situation. One was to negotiate amendments to the Law of Liquidation. A second was to sanction a new loan to enable Egypt to pay the new debts incurred by the Urabi revolt, notably an indemnity of just over £4 million for property destroyed during the anti-foreign riots in Alexandria following the British bombardment in June 1882. Once again the Cabinet, and particularly Childers, the Chancellor of the Exchequer, was unsympathetic to many of the details of Baring's proposals. But it did agree to the calling of an international conference to discuss these and other matters, an event which finally took place in London in July 1884.

The whole situation was then radically altered by the news of the defeat of the army sent by the Egyptian government under a retired British officer, Colonel Hicks, to confront an uprising in western Sudan.

---

[14] CP/2, FO 633/5.   [15] 8 Oct. 1883, CP/2, FO 633/6.
[16] Baring to Granville, 28 Oct. 1883, CP/2, FO 633/6; Edward Hamilton, *The Diary of Sir Edward Walter Hamilton, 1880–1885*, ed. Dudley W. R. Bahlman (Oxford: Clarendon Press, 1972), 503.

A rebellion against Egyptian rule had been proclaimed in May 1881 by Muhammad Ahmad, an ascetic and religious devotee, who had taken advantage of an atmosphere of heightened religious expectation to proclaim himself the Mahdi, that is, a messianic figure claiming divine guidance whose mission is to restore right government to the Muslim community at a time of great social crisis.[17] His movement had begun to assume a serious dimension when his followers had defeated two much better-armed Egyptian forces sent against him in September 1882. Meanwhile, the rebellion had spread to the Red Sea coast, where the Mahdi's allies were getting uncomfortably close to Suakin, the main Egyptian base and a vital link between Egypt and the Nile town of Berber some 250 miles across the desert to the west. News that Hicks's army had been entirely wiped out reached Cairo on 22 November 1883.

The strength of the revolt not only threatened Egyptian rule over Sudan but also raised the possibility that the Mahdi's armies might soon march on Egypt itself. To make matters worse, it came at a time when Urabi's Egyptian army had been entirely disbanded and when its replacement, plus an associated gendarmerie, was only in the early stages of training and organization. One result was that any prospect of immediate withdrawal of British troops from Egypt had to be postponed. A second was the need to address a set of large and difficult questions concerning policy towards the deepening crisis. How serious was the threat and how could it best be contained? What were the respective roles of the Egyptian government and its British advisers, notably Baring himself and General Sir Evelyn Wood, the sirdar, or commander, of the newly reorganized Egyptian army? Who was to pay the military costs involved? How would this impact on the future of Egypt's own finances? And what was to be the role of the British garrison, either in retaining control of Sudan or simply in ensuring the defences of Egypt proper? To make matters more complex still, the answers to any of these questions were also bound up with yet larger problems, such as the proper exercise of British advice, the allocation of responsibilities between Britain and Egypt, and the protection of British interests in the Near East (however defined), about which the Britons most closely involved were either unsure or in growing dispute.

The dispatches exchanged between Baring and Granville show both men struggling to decide how best to cope with the new situation, with Baring not only developing his own line but also reporting on the official

---

[17] P. M. Holt, *The Mahdist State in the Sudan, 1881–1898: A Study of Its Origins, Development and Overthrow* (Oxford: Clarendon Press, 1958), 22, 42–3.

Egyptian response to the Mahdist threat, a response which he was well placed to shape. Many of the basic issues involved were on display in Granville's dispatch of 25 November acknowledging Baring's report on Egyptian military preparations, and then making the point that, as far as the Cabinet was concerned, the matter was entirely the responsibility of the Egyptian government, relying solely on its own resources.[18]

Baring, for his part, was quick to come to the personal conclusion that Britain was much more deeply involved than the Cabinet was willing to allow. As a result, he devoted a large portion of his dispatches to trying to get London to clarify its position by forcing it to respond to a variety of possible policies, for example, the use of British, Indian, or even Ottoman troops to defend Suakin and the Suakin–Berber road.[19] The result was an ever more categorical set of instructions from Granville, including one on 13 December in which he told Baring to recommend that the Egyptian government abandon all the territory south of Aswan, or at least south of Wadi Halfa on the present Sudanese–Egyptian border.[20]

Baring countered with two extremely significant proposals in a telegram sent on 22 December. The first asked for authority to insist on the total evacuation of Sudan (something which he knew the Sharif ministry would bitterly resist), adding that 'if the present Ministry will not carry it out he must find others to do so'.[21] The second was that it would also be necessary to send a 'British officer of high authority to Khartoum' with full powers to withdraw all the Egyptian garrisons from Sudan and to 'make the best arrangements possible for the future government of the country'.[22] These were considered at a cabinet meeting of 3 January 1884, after which a telegram was sent to Cairo putting a further gloss on Baring's first proposal by laying down the principle that 'in matters affecting the administration and safety of Egypt the advice of Her Majesty's Government should be followed as long as the provisional occupation lasts. Ministers and Governors must carry out this advice or forfeit their offices.'[23]

There was no immediate reference to Baring's other suggestion concerning the 'British officer of high authority'. Nevertheless, within a few weeks this was to mesh with the hasty and ill-considered decision to send General Charles Gordon back to Sudan, something which was to haunt Gladstone, the members of his Cabinet, and Evelyn Baring for the rest of their lives.

[18] Allen, *Gordon and the Sudan*, 204.
[19] Cromer, *Modern Egypt*, i. 376–8.
[20] Ibid. 379–80.   [21] Ibid. 381.
[22] Allen, *Gordon and the Sudan*, 206.
[23] Cromer, *Modern Egypt*, i. 382.

Armed with the Cabinet's telegram, Baring went immediately to see
Sharif Pasha, who, faced with what was in effect a British order to evacuate
Sudan, promptly resigned on 7 January 1884. Acting under advice, the
Khedive then asked Nubar to head a new Cabinet. This produced a classic
situation in which the British, as occupiers, now depended on the only
prominent local politician who was willing to carry out an unpopular
policy in the British interest. Meanwhile, Nubar, who had no power base
of his own, was well aware that he could only stay in office with British
approval. The result was the emergence of a tense working relationship
between Baring and Nubar which was to last, with increasing strain, for the
next four years. Its terms were well understood on both sides. Nubar
would support all the measures necessary to ensure the quick evacuation
of Sudan. In exchange, Baring would allow him a considerable degree of
freedom with respect to his domestic policy, including the power to
prevent further British inroads into the Egyptian judicial system and the
Ministry of the Interior. As Nubar himself put it in an interview with *The
Times* published on 23 May 1884, he was in favour of 'British supervision
but not of British government'.[24]

Nubar was fourteen years older than Baring and so now nearing 60.
Described by one British diplomat as a 'tall, handsome, grey-haired man
with great charm', he had already had a long and distinguished career in
Egyptian government service, including his extended struggle, first to
create, then to amend, the Mixed Tribunals.[25] He was also highly intelligent and intent on doing his best to preserve what he could of Egypt's
vanishing independence. Nevertheless, he had few illusions about either
the practice of international politics or the changed nature of Britain's new
relationship with Egypt. This produced an endless series of bons mots
concerning the main actors on the European stage. The English government is 'very like a cat', he observed to Vincent in September 1884,
apropos of the temporary failure of the London Conference on Egyptian
Finances: 'it dashed at a thing; missed it; fell over again. One thought it
must be dashed to pieces; but at the end it invariably fell on its feet.'[26] And,
more trenchantly: 'The British are easy to deceive. But when you think you
have deceived them, you get a tremendous kick on your backside.'[27] Nubar

[24] Quoted in Jacques Berque, *Egypt: Imperialism and Revolution*, trans. Jean Stewart (London:
Faber & Faber, 1972), 154.

[25] Sir J. Rennell Rodd, *Diplomatic and Political Memories, 1894–1901: Egypt and Abyssinia*
(London: Edward Arnold, 1923), 31.

[26] Vincent, 'Nubar's titbits', Diary, 22 Sept. 1884, DP, Add. MS 48949.

[27] Quoted in Berque, *Egypt*, 155.

also maintained an air of wary amusement about his relationship with Baring and the many differences between them. 'I always say "yes",' he told Vincent a month or so later, 'not because I agree but because I want time to reflect. Baring makes up his mind at once. I can never make up my mind about somebody else's ideas without sleeping over it or invent an idea of my own without thinking over it for a fortnight.'[28]

In personality they were like chalk and cheese, something which Baring took great pains to underline. 'What a curious and emotional man is this unimaginative Southerner,' he noted in his journal for 12 April, after describing how tears had come into Nubar's eyes when he had been told that it was to be the British, not the Egyptian, government which was to take responsibility for a controversial decision to suspend payment of one of the coupons to the Caisse de la Dette Publique.[29] But there was inevitably much more to it than that. Both presented versions of their relationship skilfully tailored to persuade their respective masters that it was they who were manipulating the other.

Both men also referred constantly to the other's obstructionism as a way of transferring responsibility for things they did not wish to do themselves. Baring found this tactic particularly useful. He could invoke Nubar's disapproval of policies which he wished to resist, for example, pressure from Hugh Childers, Gladstone's Chancellor of the Exchequer, to cut the numbers of Egyptian officials at a particularly tense time in March 1884.[30] Or he could argue that Nubar would certainly resign rather than go along with Childers's suggestion of placing a higher tax on *ushuri* land. Everything in Egypt depended on just two men, he told the Chancellor, himself and the Prime Minister, while noting that men capable of playing the latter role were none 'too plentiful'.[31]

Gordon Goes Back to Khartoum

The immediate question facing Baring and the British Government after Nubar's appointment was how to secure the evacuation of the quite substantial Egyptian garrisons scattered throughout the huge land area of Sudan, some 21,000 troops all told, with their large quantities of guns and ammunition, as well as the 11,000 civilians who had also indicated a

[28] Vincent, 'Nubar, Northbrook and Baring', Diary, 24 Oct. 1884, DP, Add. MS 48949.
[29] Journal 1884–5, BA, DEP 11.   [30] 4 Mar. 1884, CP/2, FO 633/5.
[31] Baring to Childers, 30 Jan. 1885, CP/2, FO 633/5.

desire to accompany them.[32] Baring's own preference was to send Nubar's new Minister of War, Abd al-Qadir Pasha, a former governor-general, back to Khartoum to carry it out. However, Abd al-Qadir quickly refused once Baring informed him that, as one of his first duties, he would have to make a public announcement that Egypt was now planning to withdraw from the whole of Sudan. As he rightly pointed out, once the local people heard this, they would have no further interest in cooperation and every reason to pledge their loyalty to the Mahdi and his movement.[33] Meanwhile, back in London there was the beginning of a huge groundswell of opinion in favour of sending Gordon, if not actually to supervise the evacuation, at least to travel to Suakin and to report on how best it might be effected.

The events that led to this idea being melded with Baring's original one of sending a British officer to Khartoum to organize both the evacuation and the skeletal government to be left behind have been the subject of numerous books and the cause of unending controversy. In what follows I will take my cue from Bernard Allen's *Gordon and the Sudan*, whose detailed analysis of these developments was the first to use the official records to provide a precise chronology of the exchange of cables and dispatches between London and Cairo in such a way as to pinpoint both the responsibilities and the confusions involved. My own aim will not be to rehash the old story yet again but simply to highlight Baring's role in these highly dramatic events, and then to compare it with the way he presented it in his later writings, notably his 'Biographical Notes' and *Modern Egypt*.

As far as the British Cabinet was concerned, Evelyn Baring was the man on the spot and, it would seem, well trusted by most of the ministers. It was he who was responsible for coordinating policy with the Egyptian government and he who advised on matters of more purely military policy, after seeking the advice of the two senior British officers present, General Stephenson, the commander of the British garrison, and Sir Evelyn Wood. Baring and the home Government remained more or less in step through the first fortnight of January.

It was only when Abd al-Qadir turned down his request that he return to Sudan that Baring's first really significant intervention in the affair took place with his reversion to his original plan of sending a 'qualified British officer with full military and civil powers'.[34] The telegram of 14 January in which he revived this proposal crossed with one from Granville that

---

[32] These are the Egyptian Minister of War's figures quoted in Allen, *Gordon and the Sudan*, 224.
[33] Ibid.   [34] Ibid. 225.

arrived in Cairo only a few minutes later. It asked Baring's opinion about the possibility of sending Gordon on a brief mission to Suakin to report on the military situation in Sudan.[35] Baring's response was to amalgamate the two proposals, and so to recommend that Gordon not just advise, but also supervise, the actual evacuation. In his words:

Gen. Gordon would be the best man if he will pledge himself to carry out the policy of withdrawal from Sudan as soon as possible, consistently with saving life. He must fully understand that he must take his instructions from the British Representative in Egypt and report to him...I would rather have him than anyone else, provided there is a perfectly clear understanding with him as to what his position is to be, and what line of policy he is to carry out.[36]

The gist of this was then incorporated in Granville's instructions to Gordon. He was to proceed to Suakin to report on the military situation and the best methods of evacuating the Egyptian garrisons from the interior of Sudan. But he would do this under orders from Baring in Cairo and perform 'such other duties as may be entrusted to him by the Egyptian Government' through Sir Evelyn.[37] As Allen notes, this last sentence immediately altered the whole character of the instructions, for, when read in association with Baring's own request for an officer with 'full civil and military powers', it opened up 'vast possibilities of executive action'.[38] Some of these possibilities became immediately apparent when Gordon, while still travelling through France, suggested that he be made the Governor-General of Sudan, a proposal which Baring himself approved in a telegram to London.[39]

The speed at which all this was effected introduces a considerable element of confusion into the story, some of which was made worse by the fact that, once the Gordon mission had failed, many of the participants tried to shift responsibility for its enlarged role either on to their colleagues or back on to Gordon himself. It also raises two important questions about the reasons for Baring's actions at this time. Why did he change his mind over Gordon, having rejected his assistance on 11 January, only three days before? And why did he encourage the expansion of the mission from one of reporting from Suakin to one of temporary government in Khartoum?

The first question is easier to answer than the second. As Baring was to write to Northbrook on 4 April 1884, he had agreed to Gordon because so

---

[35] Ibid. 226.   [36] Ibid.   [37] Ibid. 231–2.
[38] Ibid. 232.   [39] Ibid. 236, 238, 242.

many people were urging that he be sent, and because 'English public opinion seemed to be unanimous on the subject.' This was enough to overcome his doubts about Gordon's character and the fear he had had of his being caught in a trap.[40] Later, in his *Modern Egypt*, he provided a list of those who had supported Gordon, from the Cabinet in London to Nubar and General Wood in Cairo, and offering the explanation that, with 'this array of opinion against me', he had come to mistrust his own judgement.[41]

As for the second question, Granville's instructions to Gordon, and then the Cabinet's validation of Gordon's own suggestion that he be made Governor-General, must certainly have led Baring to believe that the British Government, or at least some of its key members, had now come round to the idea of giving Gordon an expanded role. It is also important to remember that, with Abd al-Qadir's refusal, Baring himself was at a loss as to how to effect an orderly withdrawal of the garrisons and their valuable military equipment. Finally, he had his own particular *idée fixe* about the need to find some way of maintaining a semblance of order on Egypt's southern border after the Egyptian garrisons had gone. All this is probably enough to explain, not just the expansion of the mission itself, but also Baring's own role in making it wider than most of Gladstone's Cabinet had intended.

There the matter might have rested if all had gone well in Khartoum. It is only the failure of the mission, and the continuing recriminations that followed, which make the allocation of responsibility at once necessary and much more difficult. In the case of both Gladstone and Granville in particular, not only did they muddy the waters when alive, but they also left enough evidence to persuade several of their biographers to exonerate them, at least partially, after they were dead.[42]

Baring also shared in some of what, in retrospect, looks very much like a collective amnesia. In writing to *The Times* in November 1905, apropos of the appearance of Lord Edmond Fitzmaurice's *Life of Earl Granville*, he disputed the author's assertion that the terms of Gordon's mission had been changed only when he arrived in Cairo. On the contrary, the change had begun in London and then been continued by Gordon himself on his

---

[40] CP/2, FO 633/4.
[41] Cromer, *Modern Egypt*, i. 437–8.
[42] e.g. Morley, *The Life of William Ewart Gladstone*, ii. 155–64; Philip Magnus, *Gladstone: A Biography* (London: J. Murray, 1954), 326; Lord Edmond Fitzmaurice, *The Life of Earl Granville*, vol. ii (London: Longmans, Green, 1905), 383–6.

journey through France.[43] This is true as far as it goes. However, as Allen notes, Baring completely ignores the role which he had played in asking for an English officer with wide powers in the first place.[44] The strength of Baring's argument also turns on the interpretation of the additional instructions that he and Nubar gave to Gordon in Cairo, which will be described below. Were they a 'change', as Granville later alleged, or simply an expansion of something already agreed?[45]

It is interesting to read Baring's private portrayal of Gordon in his 'Biographical Notes', which were written about the same time as his letter to *The Times*. Here Gordon becomes a drunken fanatic and a criminally impulsive man of violent temper who, if not medically classifiable, was someone whose mind habitually hovered 'between sanity and insanity'.[46] This suggests that a continued uneasiness about the extent of his own personal responsibility is being overlaid by a deliberate exaggeration of Gordon's, admittedly unusual, personality. It is also significant that Baring omitted mention in *Modern Egypt* of his suggestion that it was an 'English' officer he wanted sent to Sudan, an omission which he was later forced to acknowledge in a letter written to a critic of the book.[47] Nevertheless, it is also to Baring's credit that he never attempted to deny that his agreement to the employment of Gordon was a mistake, perhaps even the greatest mistake of his life.[48]

Gordon began his mission at Charing Cross Station, where he was seen off by Granville, who bought his ticket, and the Duke of Cambridge, who opened his carriage door.[49] He then proceeded, as planned, across France and the Mediterranean to Port Said and the Suez Canal. However, as soon as he and his companion Colonel Stewart made landfall in Egypt, they were urged by Granville, at Baring's own insistence, not to travel straight to Suakin but to pass through Cairo instead. This was seen as particularly vital as it offered Baring the opportunity of doing his best to ensure that Gordon, whose judgement and consistency of purpose he continued to mistrust, was in no doubt about the proper conduct of his mission and that

[43] Allen, *Gordon and the Sudan*, 245–6.

[44] Ibid. 245.

[45] This point is dealt with in Lord Elton, *Gordon of Khartoum: The Life of General Charles George Gordon* (New York: Knopf, 1955), 292–5.

[46] BN 243–5.

[47] For the relevant passage, Cromer, *Modern Egypt*, i. 424; for his acknowledgement, Cromer to Captain Atkins, 17 Nov. 1911, CP/2, FO 633/11.

[48] For his thinking at the time, see Baring to Northbrook, 4 Apr. 1884, CP/2, FO 633/4. For his later summing up of the matter, see Cromer, *Modern Egypt*, i. 436–9.

[49] Elton, *Gordon of Khartoum*, 290–1.

he was to take his instructions directly from Baring himself. As Baring wrote to Granville on 21 January, 'it is as well that he [Gordon] should be under my orders, but a man who habitually consults with the Prophet Isaiah when he is in difficulty is not apt to obey the orders of anyone'.[50] This may also be one of the reasons for the particularly effusive tone of the letter that Baring had delivered personally to Gordon as soon as his ship had reached the northern end of the Canal. It began: 'I was exceedingly glad to receive Lord Granville's telegram informing me that you and Stewart were coming to Egypt. I feel confident that you both may render many great services as regards Soudan affairs. I need hardly assure you that you can rely on my most cordial support and assistance.'[51]

The letter had the desired effect and persuaded Gordon to come to Cairo for two days. On his first morning he went to see the Khedive, and then to the Agency, where he went over his instructions with Baring and Nubar. It was agreed that he should take two firmans with him, both signed by the Khedive. One contained a copy of his letter of appointment as Governor-General. The other announced his policy as being one of total evacuation. In addition, Gordon was required to do his best to leave a functioning system of law and order behind. This new desiderata greatly complicated the mission and sat unhappily with the other policy of evacuation, which provided little incentive for Sudanese cooperation. Nevertheless, it was quite in keeping with the spirit of optimism which all seemed to share at this time, based as it was on Gordon's considerable reputation and on his personal belief that it would be possible to persuade the Mahdi to help him with his plans. Later historians have been quick to point out that this huge miscalculation rested on an enormously ill-informed underestimate of Muhammad Ahmad's potential power and influence.[52]

Gordon was put up at the Agency, where the Barings gave a dinner party in his honour, attended by Nubar and many of the Cairo elite. Easily bored by such events, he slipped away from the table at one stage to visit the Barings' sleeping sons in their nursery upstairs. It made for a rare link between him and Baring. 'Tell your little fellow to pray for me,' Gordon was later to write as a PS to a letter written to Baring on his way up the Nile.[53] The next day, at Nubar's house, Gordon bumped into Abd al-Rahman Munir Zubayr (usually Zobeir or Zebehr in British dispatches)

---

[50] CP/2, FO 633/5.   [51] 22 Jan. 1884, GP, Add. MS 51303.
[52] e.g. Holt, *The Mahdist State*, 80–1.
[53] Gordon to Baring, 28 Jan. 1884, CP/2, FO 633/5.

Pasha, a former Sudanese provincial governor and notorious slave trader whose son Gordon had ordered killed for leading a revolt against his government in 1879. In spite of the fact that Zubayr pointedly refused to shake his hand, Gordon took it into his head to suggest that he accompany him back to Khartoum. But Baring thought the enmity between them made the risk too great. Gordon and Stewart left by train for the railhead at Asyut at ten o'clock that same evening, being seen off at Cairo station by Baring and assorted members of the Egyptian Cabinet and of the army of occupation.

Gordon reached Berber by steamer on 11 February. There he took two very significant steps. One was to dismiss all his accompanying Egyptian troops and officials, announcing that, from then on, Sudan was to be governed solely by Sudanese. The second involved an attempt to bolster his local authority by reading the firman stating that he had come to effect the complete evacuation of Sudan.[54] Historians are divided in their judgement, but the majority see all this as constituting yet another grave error. For example, P. M. Holt, who knew Sudan well, argues that Gordon's only hope of carrying out his mission was to get everyone away before the Mahdist enemy was able to appreciate his weakness. As Holt also points out, Gordon himself was sufficiently worried about the implications of what he had done that he did not make the same announcement when he finally reached Khartoum.[55] Here again, Evelyn Baring must certainly bear some of the blame.

The true nature of the situation was immediately apparent in Khartoum. It was clear to all that the loyalties of local shaikhs and other notables had begun to waver as soon as they learned the news of the decision to evacuate. This in turn caused Gordon to focus his immediate attention on the problem of how to create a form of government capable of keeping order after he and the Egyptian troops had left. The answer was, once again, Zubayr. No sooner had he reached Khartoum on 18 February than Gordon wired Baring with a request that Zubayr be appointed his successor. Baring, although still worried about the possibility of bad blood between the two, added his own support when sending the message on to Granville in London. In his opinion, Zubayr was the 'only possible man' for the job.[56] The Government sent its refusal on 23 February, arguing that British public opinion 'would not tolerate' such an appointment. The message reached Gordon three days later. Baring himself then made the

[54] Holt, *The Mahdist State*, 84.   [55] Ibid. 87.   [56] Allen, *Gordon and the Sudan*, 274.

case for Zubayr once again, using language which surprised even the Queen with its 'outspoken plainness':

Whatever may be said to the contrary, Her Majesty's Government must, in reality, be responsible for any arrangements that are now desired for the Sudan . . . It is for Her Majesty's Government to judge the importance to be attached to public opinion in England, but I venture to think that any attempt to settle Egyptian questions by the light of English popular opinion is surely productive of harm, and in this, as in other cases, it would be better to follow the advice of responsible authorities on the spot.[57]

When the British Government tried to prevaricate, saying that it wanted further information as to the real seriousness of the situation, Baring tried one last time. Zubayr, he argued, was the key to the establishment of a centre of authority able to govern Sudan after Gordon left, adding that, in view of the urgency of the situation, he withdrew his previous objection to Gordon and Zubayr working together in Khartoum.[58] However, it was not to be. So strong was the feeling in the House of Commons against the idea of sending such a notorious slave trader back to Sudan that the Cabinet felt it had no option but to turn it down. The news reached Baring in Cairo but never got to Khartoum, as this was just the moment when the telegraph line between Berber and the south was cut by Mahdist forces.

Difficulties in communication now began to have an enormous impact on events. Baring could still send messages as far as Berber. But after that their onward passage depended on local messengers travelling over hostile terrain, so that only one of those sent between March and the last week in July actually got through. To make matters worse, this unhappy state of affairs did not become apparent for another month or so, persuading both Baring and the Government in London that their messages were being ignored. After that they had no way of knowing what Gordon had actually received. Meanwhile, the many more messages sent from Khartoum only reached Cairo in fits and starts, and then rarely in the order originally dispatched.

To compound the confusion still further, Gordon was a man much given to using his dispatches to think through a series of different options out loud, making it difficult to understand what he really intended to do. The practice had already been the subject of complaint even before the telegraph line was cut. On 29 February Baring told Granville that Gordon's messages were 'hopelessly bewildering and contradictory'.[59] On 11 March

---

[57] Allen, *Gordon and the Sudan*, 289.   [58] Ibid. 293.   [59] Cromer, *Modern Egypt*, i. 500.

he informed Northbrook that he wished 'to goodness that Gordon, like Dickens' young lady, could be made to count to twenty before he writes telegraphs'.[60] The members of the Cabinet were equally perplexed, even though Northbrook tried to console them with the thought that although Gordon 'says all the foolish things that pass through his head...his judgment is excellent'.[61]

Baring also contributed to the problem of proper communication, as Bernard Allen notes. Sometimes he sent Gordon's messages on to London by telegraph and sometimes by the much slower ordinary mail, further complicating the difficulty for those in the Foreign Office trying to work out the order in which they had been written. There were also occasions when Baring paraphrased them in such a way that an essential part of their content was misunderstood.

Allen's most significant example concerns two telegrams sent to Cairo by Gordon on 26 February. One informs Baring of his decision to dispatch two expeditions into the districts around Khartoum as a show of strength. Neither fired a shot. But the fact that the second telegram contained the words that they were off to 'attack the rebels' was enough to convince members of Gladstone's Cabinet that Gordon had thrown over the policy of peaceful evacuation and was determined to beat the Mahdi by force of arms. Allen notes that this impression would have been much less severe if Baring had not omitted to send another sentence from the first telegram referring to the fact that the evacuation was still well under way.[62] In these and other ways Baring helped, unwittingly, to worsen relations between Gordon and the Cabinet, perhaps even contributing in some small part to its decision not to send Zubayr, while making it more difficult for Gladstone and his colleagues to dispatch an immediate relief expedition once it became clear that Gordon had become trapped in Khartoum for good.

Baring's personal sense of frustration was heightened by his growing awareness of the dangerous situation developing in northern Sudan. He was also increasingly convinced that, having sent Gordon to Khartoum, the Gladstone Government was morally responsible for getting him out. This led him to send two telegrams to London on 24 March suggesting how it might be done. One was to rely on Gordon to hold out until the autumn, when the rising Nile would allow a military expedition upriver by boat. A second was the immediate dispatch of troops from Suakin to Berber (which Gordon might be able to reach by steamer), a plan that

[60] Zetland, *Lord Cromer*, 112.   [61] Granville to Baring, 8 Feb. 1884, CP/2, FO 633/7.
[62] *Gordon and the Sudan*, 278–80.

Generals Wood, in Suakin, and Stephenson, in Cairo, thought feasible in spite of the 'extraordinary military risks'.[63] On receiving the Cabinet's rejection of the second plan, Baring says he found it difficult to preserve his 'diplomatic calm', the more so as the men in London had used his own words about 'military risk' as an argument against him.[64]

Still Baring refused to give up. On 26 March he wrote again to Granville as follows:

Let me earnestly beg her Majesty's Government to place themselves in the position of Gordon and Stewart. They have been sent on a most difficult and dangerous mission by the English Government. Their proposal to send Zebehr which, if it had been acted upon some weeks ago, would certainly have altered the situation, was rejected. The consequences they foresaw have occurred.

He then went on to urge that Gordon be told to hang on until the end of the summer, when an expedition would be sent to relieve him. And he ended with the highly charged appeal that, having sent Gordon to Khartoum, 'it appears to me that it is our bounden duty, both as a matter of humanity and policy, not to abandon him'.[65]

Granville likened the dispatch to a 'heavy canon-ball', and it was no exaggeration.[66] The use of the emotional word 'abandon' was immediately taken up by all those both inside and outside the Cabinet who were now beginning to demand action. The dispatch also had to be shown to the Queen, who immediately ordered Ponsonby, her private secretary, to telegraph the Prime Minister that 'Sir E. Baring only expresses my own feelings.'[67] She had used even stronger language to Ponsonby himself with respect to an earlier dispatch: 'Sir E. Baring is evidently *not* pleased at what the Queen must call the miserable, weak and too late action of the government.'[68]

Attacks such as these forced Gladstone into an energetic programme of damage limitation, explaining to Queen Victoria that what Baring was actually recommending was a 'reversal of official policy', that he 'overrides the most serious military difficulties', and that he proposes to provide for dangers for which the evidence did not exist, and all this in ignorance of General Gordon's own 'circumstances, opinion and desires'.[69] Baring's

[63] *Gordon and the Sudan*, 311–12.
[64] Cromer, *Modern Egypt*, i. 52–4; Allen, *Gordon and the Sudan*, 313.
[65] Allen, *Gordon and the Sudan*, 313–14.
[66] Granville to Baring, 29 Mar. 1884, CP/7, FO 633/5.
[67] Elton, *Gordon of Khartoum*, 323.   [68] Ibid. 314.
[69] Allen, *Gordon and the Sudan*, 325–6.

dispatch helped cause a commotion inside the Cabinet as well. The decision not to send an immediate expedition was only carried after a very stormy meeting during which the Lord Chancellor threatened to resign if his colleagues did not promise to mount something in the autumn.

For some, Baring's dispatch was also seen to contain an implied threat that he might resign. This was sufficient to provoke a particularly stern reprimand from Lord Northbrook on 27 March:

Pray recollect that the responsibility rests upon us, not upon you, and that while you are right to express your opinion with the utmost freedom, on the other hand, you must remember that it is not only possible, but probable, that we, being removed from the immediate influences which must surround you, are not unlikely to be right; and certainly we must be better able than you to weigh the real importance of Egyptian affairs with the whole interests of the Empire, while we must certainly be better judges as to the feelings of the people of this country and of Parliament by which, so long as England is governed as it is now, the conduct of every Government must be controlled.[70]

Baring's response came on 4 April in what he described as the 'longest document' he had penned since he had been in Egypt. It is clear from his very defensive tone that he realized that he had gone too far. He also struck a rare note of self-pity. He was not personally sore at the rejection of his proposals but he was 'a great deal disheartened and discouraged'. 'It is heartbreaking to go on slaving as I do without apparently doing the least good.' He had the sense of finding himself all alone in the wilderness. The Government should remember that, beyond a few general indications, he had never had any lead given him from home. It had also assumed that the best way of avoiding serious intervention in Sudan was not to interfere at all. He could not bring himself to believe that the results had been successful.

Nevertheless, Baring being Baring, the dispatch contained something of a sting in the tail. By not taking proper responsibility for Sudan, there was a danger that 'we shall gradually drift into governing [it] ourselves'. Much the same lesson might be drawn about Egypt too. If Britain had assumed greater responsibility in September 1882, 'we should by this time be much further advanced . . . towards the attainment of the object which we have in view, viz., . . . to leave Egypt to govern itself'.[71] The parallels between British policy in Egypt and Sudan, and between his role and that of Gordon's, both sent to secure a speedy evacuation, were just too powerful for him to ignore.

---

[70] Zetland, *Lord Cromer*, 115–16.   [71] Ibid. 117–18.

If he had had a mind to do it, Baring could have comforted himself with the thought that he had, at least, helped to stir things up in London. Given the balance of power in the Gladstone Cabinet, there was little chance of a consensus for immediate action in Sudan. However, he had given a significant push to the idea of sending an autumn expedition, which is what eventually transpired. For Baring, and all those of his generation, it was axiomatic that if British officials on difficult missions became trapped far away from home, there would always be pressure to send troops to their rescue. Zubayr was different. Had he been allowed to proceed to Sudan, and then become besieged, no one in England would have lost a night's sleep. But an 'English officer', and certainly someone of Gordon's stature, was quite a different proposition and should only have been sent on the understanding that he would be rescued if things went very wrong.

Recalled to London to Discuss Egyptian Finance

Meanwhile, events had been moving quickly on the financial front as well. Vincent was soon at work with the senior members of his staff on three reports outlining their estimates for the achievable levels of government revenue and expenditure for 1884/5. He was then recalled to London in March 1884 to assist the Government in the difficult negotiations with the French that were a necessary prelude to the promised conference on Egyptian finance. Finally, his input, and that of Baring himself, was incorporated in Granville's circular to the Ottoman Sultan and to the European powers on 19 April. It included two of the major proposals for which Baring had been pressing since the previous autumn. One was an amendment to the Law of Liquidation giving Egypt freedom to deal with any surpluses which might arise as far as either the 'affected' or the 'non-affected' revenues were concerned. The other recommended an internationally guaranteed loan to provide £8 million for immediate payment of the Alexandrian indemnities and the new floating debt which had been accumulating since 1882, with another £1 million for irrigation works to improve the productive (and so taxable) capacity of the rural areas.

Baring himself was now called back to London to give advice. It is not at all clear how willing he was to do this with Gordon trapped in Khartoum. One possible source of comfort was that he would surely be back in Cairo before the next window of opportunity for sending a relief expedition, when the Nile began to rise in September. More positively, he may also

have been anxious to mend his strained relations with his Liberal colleagues in London. He was certainly deadly tired and no doubt quite
happy to get away from Cairo for personal reasons, particularly as it
meant being able to spend more of the summer at home with Ethel and
the children. His second in command, Edwin Egerton, was left in charge
of the agency to bear the brunt of Gordon's gibes and criticisms for doing
nothing to rescue him from Khartoum.

So ended Baring's first seven months in Egypt. Things had begun well
enough, but from December onwards he had been exposed to increasing
strain. The new system of temporary British management of key aspects of
Egyptian affairs was difficult to direct. He had problems, at one time or
another, with all the most important advisers. Some threatened his
working relationship with Nubar by their impatient attempt to interfere
more and more in the workings of the police and the legal system, while all
resented the fact that, after the outbreak of the Sudan crisis, he would not
let them work as a team to effect a concerted programme of reforms.[72]
Clifford Lloyd was a particular problem. Although appreciative of his
knowledge of rural conditions during his first few months, Baring soon
came to regard him as a 'bull in a china shop' as a result of his ability to
upset not only Nubar and his officials but many of his British colleagues as
well.[73]

To make matters worse, Baring lacked the necessary staff to deal with his
heavy workload, having to write much more than he was used to by hand
until he obtained the services of a shorthand writer in January 1884.
Furthermore, we know from Ethel and other sources that he was seriously
ill for at least part of the time. As she wrote to Northbrook on 18 February
1884,

Evelyn has been confined to his bed the last few days with a fever and a sore throat.
I have seldom seen him so ill. I attribute his great prostration to the amount of
work and anxiety he has had lately, and of course it has been impossible to keep his
brain quiet as every matter, great and small, is referred to him.[74]

Baring's own gloss on the matter is equally telling: 'Directly I am laid up,
as I was for a few days last week, everyone sits still and waits for orders,
except a pertinacious few who penetrate my bedroom in spite of a very

[72] e.g. Vincent, 'Note: Clifford Lloyd, Benson Maxwell and Baring', Diary, 20 July 1884, DP,
Add. MS 48948.
[73] Marlowe, *Cromer in Egypt*, 98.
[74] Zetland, *Lord Cromer*, 94–5.

courageous defence on the part of my wife, armed only with a bottle of cough mixture.'[75]

Lastly, there was the question of his role as a liberal anti-annexationist caught up in a situation in which the permanent occupation of Egypt was beginning to seem to many as the only way ahead. As he had also complained to Northbrook in his letter of 4 April 1884,

Surely it is cruel fate that drives me, with all my strong opinions against an extension of territory and the assumption of fresh responsibilities, and with strong anti-Jingo convictions which deepen every year I live, to be constantly making proposals which, at all events at first sight, have a strong Jingo flavour. In this uncongenial political atmosphere I am always having to speak in exactly the opposite way to what I should wish.

Equally unsettling was his growing disenchantment with Gladstone's handling of the Sudanese crisis and his failure to protect government policy from the sudden enthusiasms and prejudices of Parliament and the press. Among many other things, he informed Northbrook, the impact of the Gordon affair was 'to make me very much on my guard against being influenced by English public opinion'.[76]

Soon after he arrived in London, Baring was again in direct correspondence with Gladstone and took the occasion to pose a series of questions concerning policy towards Egyptian finance and what the cabinet minutes for 1 May referred to as 'native government'.[77] This led to his being asked to present his own ideas about Egypt to the cabinet meeting on the afternoon of 14 May. Concerning the timetable for final evacuation he said that he believed that it would take a minimum of five years to get everything in order, although it could also just be managed in three and a half if he were to be given greater freedom from foreign financial control. He was also able to speak out against a rival proposal that there should be a public commitment to leave in 1888. This, he argued, would have a bad effect in England, where it might affect the negotiations for a guaranteed loan, and in Egypt, where it would destroy confidence in the possibility of continuing stable government. While in the room he may also have been informed of the good news that the Cabinet had just decided that his main bugbear among the British advisers, Lloyd, was definitely to be brought home.[78]

---

[75] Zetland, *Lord Cromer*, 96–7.   [76] CP/2, FO 633/4.

[77] H. G. C. Matthew (ed.), *The Gladstone Diaries: With Cabinet Minutes and Prime-Ministerial Correspondence*, vol. xi: *July 1883–December 1886* (Oxford: Clarendon Press, 1990), 140–1.

[78] Ibid. 146–7; Baring to Granville, 31 May 1884, CP/2, FO 633/5.

Baring also had several conversations with Granville at the Foreign Office about the future supervision of Egyptian finances. He set out his own ideas in a letter of 2 June in which he reiterated his view that the Law of Liquidation required modification and that this modification should be final. Another point was the need to keep a powerful check on Egyptian government expenditure. This, he suggested, might be entrusted to the Caisse to carry out, adding that it might also be consulted about the budget and have to assent to any increase over and above the agreed expenditure. Finally, he used the occasion to develop the argument that, while it would be 'wise' for Britain not to assume the permanent management of Egypt (given the fact that its only major interest there was the Suez Canal), it was nonetheless desirable that it ensure that the country was 'reasonably well-governed'.[79]

For the rest, Baring was hard at work in a committee consisting of Rivers Wilson, Blum (brought over from Cairo), and two other British officials drafting a report entitled 'On the Financial Situation in Egypt'. Interestingly, he was given as his own private secretary the young Edward Grey, later to become Foreign Minister, and so Baring's superior during his last years in Egypt, 1906–7. The report was presented to the Cabinet on 21 June.[80] It contained two estimates, one of future expenditure, the other of future revenue. The former estimate was supported by comments from Baring suggesting, first, that the Ministry of Education could be suppressed to save money, and, secondly, that both he and Nubar believed some of the proposed dismissals of new officials hired since 1880 to be unwise. The latter contained a note saying that there was a universal opinion in Egypt that the present level of land tax was too high. Finally, the report confirmed that the floating debt had indeed reached some £8 million.[81]

The International Conference opened on 28 July. It had been preceded not only by intense discussion on the British side but also by a series of preliminary discussions with the French. Given the difficult diplomatic circumstances in which the British had placed themselves as a result of their unilateral occupation of Egypt, political questions were bound to predominate over purely financial ones. The British needed French, and

[79] FO, Further Correspondence Respecting the Finances of Egypt, Egypt, no. 23 (1884), 9, copy in *PP*, (1884) 89, 43 ff.

[80] Matthew (ed.), *Gladstone Diaries*, xi. 162.

[81] 'Report by Sir Evelyn Baring, Sir R. E. Welby, Sir C. Rivers Wilson, and Sir J. Carmichael, on the Financial Situation of Egypt (June 28 1884)', in FO, Further Correspondence Concerning the Affairs of Egypt, Egypt, no. 28 (1884), a copy of which can be found in *PP* (1884) 89, 373 ff.

possibly European, acquiescence for an international loan. The French, for their part, were equally anxious to restore Egypt's financial position, given the fact that French citizens had the largest share in the debt as well as all other foreign investments. However, while they were well aware that immediate evacuation was impossible, they were concerned to get Britain to pledge itself to a fixed date sometime in the not too distant future. And against that day they wanted to see a considerable increase in international financial control, including greater powers for the Caisse.[82]

All this allowed some room for compromise. Both sides were intensely aware of the way in which political uncertainties helped to push down the price of shares in the Egyptian debt. Both were worried that the ideas which inspired the Mahdi's movement might spread elsewhere in North Africa. Nevertheless, there was bound to be a confrontation over short-term goals, with the British trying to confine the discussion to measures designed to ease Egypt's present financial difficulties and the French equally anxious to open it out to include both a British commitment to evacuation and the exact nature of the proposed post-evacuation financial supervision.

The conference met for seven sessions from 28 June to 2 August. Baring's old colleague de Blignières attended all but the first; Baring attended all but the first three. Because of their particular expertise they soon became the two principal, though rival, experts when it came to discussions of the collection of taxes, the proper level of administrative expenses, and, more generally, the powers of the Caisse and whether they were sufficient for the task at hand. Their arguments were laid out in de Blignières's critique of the British commission's report, Baring's rejoinder, and de Blignières's final reply. They clashed in particular over de Blignières's support of the French position that the present system of taxation was satisfactory, as against Baring's position that the land tax was too high and needed to be reduced.[83] At least one observer, Tigrane Pasha, Nubar's son-in-law, thought that it was de Blignières who had got the best of their exchange with his pre-conference appeal to the increasing volume of Egyptian imports as a sign that rural poverty was not as serious as Baring

[82] Samir Saul, *La France et l'gypte de 1882 à 1914: Intérêts économiques et implications politiques* (Paris: Ministère de l'économie des Finances et d'Industrie/Comité pour l'Histoiré conomique et Financière de la France, 1997), 575–83.

[83] 'Protocols of Conference Held in London Respecting the Finances of Egypt', FO, Further Correspondence Respecting the Finances of Egypt, Egypt, no. 29 (1884), 26–9, 32–4, a copy of which can be found in *PP* (1884) 89, 439 ff.

claimed. Nevertheless, as Tigrane also noted, Baring's stand in defence of Egypt's rural inhabitants was much appreciated back in Cairo.[84]

Perhaps because Baring realized the inevitability of a clash with de Blignières, he made no effort to try to smooth the waters by reaching some preliminary understanding, something he would certainly have tried to do when they were working so harmoniously in 1879–80. According to Edgar Vincent, this is what de Blignières had imagined when he had first arrived in London. But Baring had merely made a courtesy call, treating him like an 'acquaintance', not a former 'close colleague'.[85]

The Painful Failure of the Northbrook Mission

The International (or London) Conference was unable to reach a decision and agreed to adjourn. Baring was then asked to attend a cabinet discussion concerning the dispatch of Lord Northbrook as a 'special commissioner' to 'report and advise HMG as to what counsel they should offer the Egyptian government' with special reference to finance.[86] It remains a somewhat mysterious event. It is possible that the point of the exercise was simply to buy time while waiting for a second round of negotiations with the French. It may also be that, with the mounting of a Gordon relief expedition finally agreed upon, Gladstone wished to have one of his senior colleagues in Cairo to give him a reliable report of what was actually going on.[87]

Two things are more certain. One is that Northbrook himself went in good faith and was bitterly disappointed when his report was almost instantaneously rejected after his return.[88] Secondly, both Baring and Vincent thought that they could use Northbrook's presence in Cairo to lobby for their mutual *idée fixe*: the importance of standing up to the French and of reducing international control over Egypt's finances.[89] Indeed, the two points could have been connected. It may well be that Baring and Vincent were able to use the fact that Northbrook was away

[84] Extract from letter written by Tigrane to Nubar, quoted in Vincent, 'Egypt and the New Loan', Diary, 20 July 1884, DP, Add. MS 48948.

[85] Vincent, 'Note: Barrère at the Conference', Diary, 20 Sept. 1884, DP, Add. MS 48949.

[86] Matthew (ed.), *Gladstone Diaries*, xi. 183.

[87] See Gladstone's letter to Lord Northbrook of 14 Aug. 1884 referring to his worries about having heard nothing from Gordon; ibid. 188.

[88] Mallet, *Thomas George Earl of Northbrook*, 229–30.

[89] Vincent, Diary, 15 Sept. 1884, DP, Add. MS 48949.

from Gladstone, Granville, and his other London colleagues to override his better judgement and to push him towards the advocacy of an independent role for Britain in Egypt, in spite of the fact that this was clearly regarded as politically dangerous by the rest of the Cabinet.

Baring and Northbrook travelled to Cairo together with Sir Garnet Wolseley, the newly appointed commander of the relief expedition whom Baring had known since his Staff College days. Once back in Cairo on 9 September the first order of business was to attend to the worsening financial situation in Egypt. In spite of having obtained a £1 million loan from the Rothschilds to tide them over, the immediate demands on the treasury were such that Baring and Vincent were forced to try to buy time by advising the Egyptian government that, just for a month, they should pay the Caisse only enough to service the funded debt, using the rest for administrative purposes rather than to meet the deficits on the loans secured on the two khedivial estates, the Domains and the Daira Saniya, as required by the Law of Liquidation. It was helpful that Northbrook was there to lend his support.

The Caisse then sued the government in the Mixed Tribunals, and won a judgement against it on 15 December 1884. However, the stratagem had served its purpose and was to prove only the first of a long line of hand-to-mouth expedients, mostly devised by Vincent, which were to keep the Egyptian treasury just afloat for the next three years. It is also possible that the decision to take on the Caisse was part of a larger strategy of trying to persuade London of the dangers of French obstructionism, and so to encourage the Cabinet to support Baring's and Vincent's demand for a freer hand. It was certainly Baring's understanding that, however unenthusiastic they might seem, the French would always have to go along with his financial initiatives so long as their own investments remained secure.

Northbrook returned to London at the end of October, writing the bulk of his report on the boat, and then modifying it when it received the instantaneous criticisms from some of his cabinet colleagues.[90] John Marlowe's observation that Northbrook was very largely acting as a mouthpiece for his cousin Evelyn's ideas is well taken.[91] The report highlighted two ideas which Baring, supported by Vincent, had been trying to persuade Gladstone and Granville to pursue for a year: that all previous estimates of Egypt's financial situation had been too optimistic, and that

---

[90] Mallet, *Thomas George Earl of Northbrook*, 191.

[91] Marlowe, *Cromer in Egypt*, 103–4; Northbrook to Vincent, Diary, 30 Oct. 1884, DP, Add. MS 48937.

greater autonomy in the management of its finances was a necessary condition for its return to health. It also contained their specific recommendations that the British Government should guarantee a loan of £8,700,000 secured on the Domains and Daira estates. The greater part would be used to pay off all Egypt's current debts, while leaving the now magical figure of £1 million for improvements in the system of irrigation.[92] Lastly, Northbrook's report was enthusiastically supported by Baring himself in a letter written to Granville on 10 November.

The immediate reaction in London proved how badly Northbrook and Baring had misjudged the current political mood. According to Northbrook, his report caused 'consternation' among his cabinet colleagues.[93] Gladstone was very obviously embarrassed, while Childers, writing to Baring, described it as 'dynamite'.[94] There were two major points of concern. One was that a British-guaranteed loan not only implied more involvement in Egypt's financial future than most members of the Liberal Party could stomach, but could also be construed as giving official support to a highly suspect bondholder interest. The second was Northbrook's explicit statement that the result would 'undoubtedly' be to 'substitute the financial control of England for the international control which was proposed at the London Conference'. All this flew in the face of continuing efforts to negotiate with the French. There was also considerable doubt that there would be enough Liberal votes to get it through the House of Commons.[95] Lastly, both Gladstone and Childers felt that rather than cutting the land tax across the board, as Northbrook suggested, the rich proprietors should actually be required to pay more.[96]

Northbrook battled away in Cabinet for the retention of parts of his scheme, even going so far as to threaten resignation in December 1884 and early January 1885 in an effort to limit the degree of international control. This threat won him a small victory when he and two colleagues were able to block Gladstone's willingness to support a French demand for a second commission of inquiry. Nevertheless, the Government remained firmly intent on a set of compromises which finally reached fruition in the London Convention of 18 March 1885. Britain obtained agreement to an international (not a purely British) loan for £9 million. It also obtained a reduction of one-twentieth in the interest on the funded debt for two

[92] A copy of Northbrook's report can be found in PRO, CAB 37/13/39, dated 9 Aug. 1884.
[93] Mallet, *Thomas George Earl of Northbrook*, 195.   [94] 21 Nov. 1884, CP/2, FO 633/5.
[95] Childers to Baring, 21 Nov. 1884, CP/2, FO 633/7.
[96] Baring to Childers, 30 Jan. 1885, CP/2, FO 633/5.

years, 1885 and 1886, but only with the dangerous proviso that there would be a new commission of inquiry if full repayment were not resumed in 1887. In exchange, Britain had to allow German and Russian representatives to join an expanded Caisse de la Dette, as well as to acquiesce to certain changes in the Law of Liquidation, including what Baring believed to be an 'excessively cumbersome method' for dividing any revenue surpluses between the Caisse and the Egyptian government.[97]

Baring was bitterly disappointed. He had obviously held high hopes that Northbrook could get his report through Cabinet. Now a far less satisfactory document had been signed leaving Egyptian financial policy 'even more at the mercy of the French'.[98] 'I cannot say that I like the financial arrangement,' he wrote to Granville on 3 March, 'but we must try to make the best of it. I hope that the Treasury will not be too exacting.'[99] It is a sign of his enormous resilience that he was already preparing himself for the next stage of the battle to achieve financial equilibrium. In this he was to be just as much at odds with successive Chancellors of the Exchequer, Childers, Lord Randolph Churchill, and then his old friend Goschen, over military and other expenses as he would be with the Caisse and the French.

The Gordon Denouement

Meanwhile, the Gordon Relief Expedition was making its way upriver in the urgent knowledge that the Mahdi himself had arrived outside Khartoum in October and that the town's defences would become much more exposed now that the Nile flood had crested and the river waters were beginning to fall. Baring received one last smuggled message from Gordon on New Year's Day. It was the size of a postage stamp, dated 14 December 1884, and simply contained the words 'Khartoum all right. G. C. Gordon'.[100] This emboldened him to telegraph Wolsley suggesting, once again, a dash across the desert from Suakin. But, once again, it was turned down.[101] Then, on 5 February, came news that the steamers sent ahead by the Relief Expedition had found Khartoum in the hands of the Mahdi's forces and reported that Gordon must be presumed dead.

This was blow enough. It was immediately made worse for Baring by the fact that members of the expedition had returned with the six volumes of a

[97] Baring to Goschen, 7 Feb. 1885, CP/2, FO 633/5.   [98] Ibid.
[99] CP/2, FO 633/5.   [100] Entry for 1 Jan. 1885, Journal 1884–5, BA, DEP 11.
[101] Ibid.

journal (covering the period 10 September to 4 December 1884) which Gordon had been sending back one or two at a time to the British forces on the Egyptian border. Baring was soon to learn not just that the journal contained some extremely unflattering comments on himself (as well as on Gladstone, Granville, and many others), but also that the Government in London regarded them as official documents and so felt duty-bound to publish them without delay.[102]

As Allen reminds us, these writings should properly be regarded as the musings of a lonely, often unhappy, man who, after he had sent Stewart and the last of his British companions north on 10 September 1884, was left with only his daily journal as an outlet for his thoughts.[103] Nevertheless, the fact remains that much of what was written about Baring could be read in a disagreeable light. Gordon makes fun of Baring's enthusiastic offer of support when he had passed through Cairo in January 1884 (19 September 1884). He accuses him of 'indiscretion' (19 September 1884). He upbraids him, quite wrongly, of having failed to support the idea of a relief expedition the previous spring (24 October 1884). He guys him as someone who is far too serious ever to laugh (7 November 1884). And not only does he draw a small cartoon of him, looking like an angry parrot, but he also mocks the idea of Baring and Egerton tut-tutting about his sketches of them when they reach Cairo (17 November 1884):

Baring to Egerton. 'You said *it was too dreadful*; what will you say when I tell you he has made sketches of you and M E? and how, horrible to relate, put them in his demi-official journal; and we can do *absolutely* nothing, for if he is attacked as being a British officer, he says he made the sketches as Governor-General, and *vice versâ*.'

Baring must certainly have been shown copies of the journal sometime before it was published later in 1885.[104] His public view, as expressed in his *Modern Egypt*, was that some passages had then been officially deleted, probably those containing 'a good deal of violent and very foolish abuse of Lord Granville'.[105]

Strangely enough, Baring's own diary contains no hint of his feelings concerning Gordon's violent end. All we do know, from Vincent, is that the

---

[102] The journals were first published in the summer of 1885 with an introduction and notes by A. Egmont Hake as *The Journals of Major-Gen. C. G. Gordon, C.B., at Khartoum*; I quote from the facsimile reprint (London: Darf, 1984).

[103] *Gordon and the Sudan*, 377–8.

[104] For example, he notes in his journal for 21 June 1885: 'have been writing account of Gordon's mission', which sounds very much like preparation of his own rejoinder.

[105] *Modern Egypt*, i. 432.

news was not enough to cause him to cancel the fancy dress ball which he
and Ethel were giving that same evening. Vincent's comment suggests that
he thought that this represented an obvious lack of tact.[106] One British
MP, Sir William Marriott, even asked a hostile question about it in the
House of Commons.[107] However, in Baring's defence it could be argued
that, in the face of what was clearly a humiliating defeat for Britain, its
Army, and its Empire, he felt it necessary to display a traditional stiff upper
lip as a way of demonstrating that Britain's business was still to be conducted as normal. There was certainly the danger of a wholesale loss of
nerve in Cairo, where many thought that the Mahdi's next move would be
to invade Egypt proper. Baring himself noted the general atmosphere of
alarm at this time and was clearly happy to sanction the deportation of
Zubayr to Gibraltar in March after a police pickpocket had found what he
described as 'incriminating letters', clearly reference to Zubayr's being in
correspondence with either the Mahdi or some of his followers.[108]

Reflections at the End of a Bad Ten Months

Baring did not leave for his summer in England until the beginning of July
1885. By then he had learned of the fall of the Liberal ministry and its
replacement by a temporary Conservative one with Lord Salisbury, his old
antagonist, back at the Foreign Office. For all his frustrations with the
Gladstone Government, he could not have looked forward to having to
serve a new set of masters with whose apparent enthusiasm for reinvading
Sudan and for sending yet another temporary commissioner to Egypt he
instantly disagreed.[109] What with this, the failure of Northbrook to obtain
cabinet acceptance of his report, the debacle at Khartoum, and his continued difficulties with the French, his second ten months in Cairo had
proved even more frustrating than his first seven.

Some of the strain shows in the signs of irritability so clearly visible in
his dispatches. It can also be observed even more clearly in the entries to a
journal which he started in late November 1884. Unlike Gordon's, with
which it may have been in unconscious competition, it was obviously not
intended for publication but rather to serve as a private way of letting off

[106] Vincent, 'Cairo society', Diary, 30 Mar. 1885, DP, Add. MS 48949.
[107] Marriott to Baring, 20 Oct. 1887, CP/2, FO 633/6.
[108] Journal 1884–5, 23 Mar. 1885, BA, DEP 11.
[109] Baring to Ethel Baring, 27 June 1885, CP/1, Letters from the 1st Earl of Cromer.

steam. This is clear from the first entry (25 November 1884), which is written in the light of news of the Cabinet's rejection of the Northbrook proposals:

The way the Government has muddled this Egyptian business is perfectly fearful. They have throughout been between the devil and the deep sea, the former represented by Parliament and the latter by the Powers, and they have never had the pluck to choose a decided line which would satisfy either party. I see no issue from the whole thing but war or eating the international leek and the present government will certainly prefer the latter alternative however unpalatable it may be.

Next day, still very annoyed, he writes that he has telegraphed to ask if the Cabinet really mean to reject Northbrook's ideas about granting fiscal autonomy to Egypt. Not, he adds that 'there is much use saying anything': 'The Government never listens to anyone's advice. All they care about is a few votes in the House of Commons.' Baring then asks himself a question that he must certainly have posed many times before: 'In the meanwhile, what is my *duty*? Evidently to help to the best of my ability and carry out their wavering and ill-defined policy. It is an ungrateful task, but I must try to do it as well as I can.'

Baring returns to the same theme on 9 December 1884. He had just been reading Coker's diary with its comment on the Duke of Wellington's sense of duty and the fact that he had the courage to make himself unpopular. 'I wish as much could be said of our leading spokesmen ... The art of Government requires great *moral* courage.' There is more in a similar vein on 13 December 1884 concerning what he described as a 'vile intrigue' by the French, Russian, German, and Austrian Consuls-General to get rid of Nubar as Prime Minister. 'I wish I had more confidence in my tools. But I have to deal with the timid men here and at home the most incapable ministry—as regards foreign affairs—that I believe ever ruled England.'

We have to remember that many diplomats, soldiers, and others habitually expressed equally hostile views towards their political masters. But, in Baring's case, it was all of a piece with his growing frustration, not only with Gladstonian liberalism but also with the influence of the newly enfranchised voters to whom it seemed dangerously beholden. As if to act as compensation, Baring's love of family also comes shining through. For example, he writes of going to Alexandria on 27–8 May to see Ethel and the boys off for their summer holidays and how he missed them 'dreadfully'. He also writes of the letter and telegram he sent on his wedding anniversary on 28 June: 'Nine happy years with my darling wife'.

The letter he wrote on this same occasion, the first part of which has already been quoted (p. 93), speaks of both great love and great personal frustration:

Duckie, I am *very* low politically. The new [Conservative] Government are like the old. They didn't consult me and threw themselves into Wolsley's arms who is imploring them to go to Khartoum. I think it insane. I think of all the precious lives which will be wasted if this mad decision is taken. Much as I like Wolsley, I cannot help seeing that he is no politician and, even if he was, it would be unwise to consult on political matters an unsuccessful general who is under a scar[?] of failure. He looks on it all in too forward a light. He wants to retrieve his reputation. But what can I do? My own opinion is not asked and, if I volunteered it, shall be accused of some trumpery[?] party motive . . . But I shall never do for English political life. I feel it more and more every day. No one understands me and I see around me hardly any one whom I can respect. I look in vain for high-minded patriotism[?] and total effacement of personal views and ambitions. Perhaps my standards are too high. Anyhow it is the only one which I will accept and I shall work up to it regardless of its effect on my personal prospects; but when I die I feel that 'misunderstood' is the epitaph that should be written on my grave.

The letter ends: 'I am longing to be with you . . . Kiss thy blessed cheeks. Oh those beautiful curls! Yours Mina.'[110]

It must have been a wonderful relief when he met up with Ethel in Venice on 12 July and journeyed back to London with her by rail. After a meeting with Salisbury at which he agreed that he would stay on in the diplomatic service, he finally reached the family's rented house in Scotland on 2 August, where he fled to be 'among the pine woods out of the political and social world'. A journal entry of 16 August 1885 describes his holiday routine: 'Get up at 7, short walk, breakfast at 8.30. Music, German, and reading (Taine, *La femme*) until dinner at 1. Long walk at 4, tea at 7, bed at 10.'

---

[110] There is a note on it in Ethel's hand: 'a dear[?] letter from my beloved Mina'.

II

Surviving the Drummond Wolff Mission
and the 'Race Against Bankruptcy'
1885–1887

Yet Another British Mission to Egypt

As Baring prepared to leave for Cairo at the end of the summer of 1885, his main preoccupation was with what was soon to be called the 'race against bankruptcy', the name given by Alfred Milner to the struggle to ensure a return to full payment of the interest on Egypt's funded debt within the two years allocated by the London Convention which followed the London Conference.[1] However, even before he left England for Austria, perhaps to take the waters at Carlsbad (now Karlovy Vary), perhaps to go hunting, he learned that there was to be a significant new development on the international front as well. This was Salisbury's decision to send Sir Henry Drummond Wolff to Istanbul and Cairo, as Envoy Extraordinary and Minister Plenipotentiary, to negotiate with the Ottoman Sultan about the British evacuation of Egypt.[2] Sir Henry, once General Storks's private secretary on Corfu, had had considerable experience of Egyptian–Ottoman relations having been a member of the Goschen–Joubert financial inquiry of 1876 and then British Commissioner for the reorganization of Eastern Roumelia after the Congress of Berlin. He was now a Conservative MP and a member of Randolph Churchill's so-called Fourth Party.

Wolff's official instructions were to 'secure for this country [Britain] the amount of influence which is necessary for its own imperial interests' and,

---

[1] This is the title of chapter 8 of Milner's, *England in Egypt* (London: Edward Arnold, 1892).

[2] Baring must have learned about this at least as early as 23 Aug. 1885 for he wrote to Salisbury a letter asking for more details about the mission on this date; CP/2, FO 633/5.

subject to that condition, 'to provide for a strong and efficient Egyptian Government as free as possible from interference'.[3] Salisbury's position was spelled out more clearly in a private letter of 13 August: 'The end to which I would work is evacuation, but with certain private reservations, e.g. a Treaty right to reoccupy Alexandria when we pleased and predominant control of Egyptian railways.'[4] It was also understood that Drummond Wolff would try to involve the Ottomans in a military role in Sudan.

The news was most unwelcome to Baring for both public and private reasons. The new initiative threatened to reopen the whole question of Egypt's future at a time when he believed the main business at hand was the struggle to avoid further foreign financial control. It would create a marked sense of uncertainty among the Egyptian elite once they suspected a possible return of Ottoman influence, backed, perhaps, by a belated re-establishment of Ottoman control over the Egyptian Army. And, given the fact that Wolff was now in charge of British policy in Cairo, it interrupted Baring's own plans to return to Egypt, leaving him stranded in Austria until the scope of Sir Henry's mission became clearer. A letter from Salisbury in mid-September suggests that Drummond Wolff had already begun to occupy the Cairo Agency and that Baring himself could not proceed further until either he, or Wolff, had been able to find alternative accommodation.[5] Not so Ethel and the children: they seem to have travelled to Cairo on schedule, allowing Ethel to assist the Wolffs to settle in. If there was one small comfort in an otherwise frustrating situation, it could have been that the delay gave him more time in Carlsbad to treat his sciatica. But this is unclear.[6]

Some of Baring's unhappiness at the new turn of events comes through in the reply he sent to Salisbury from Austria acknowledging the receipt of the public instructions given to Drummond Wolff: 'It is impossible to feel sanguine that he will succeed . . . nor am I sanguine about winning the battle against internationalism in Egypt. The movement in this direction began after the break-up of the [London] Conference *without* a distinct

[3] Marlowe, *Cromer in Egypt*, 110.

[4] Roberts, *Salisbury*, 344.

[5] 15 Sept. 1885, CP/2, FO 633/5.

[6] The first mention I have found of Baring's sciatica comes in a letter to Moberley Bell written on 5 May 1891 in which he complains that 'every year a race goes on within me between Carlsbad and sciatica . . . & this year sciatica has unfortunately won'; MBL, TA (1891). But the fact that his visits to Austria-Hungary become so frequent in the 1880s suggests that he had already begun to find a temporary cure there.

declaration of policy from HMG and was greatly accelerated by the breakdown of the Northbrook mission.'[7]

More irritation was caused in late October when Drummond Wolff was able to sign a convention with the Ottoman Minister of Foreign Affairs according to which two high commissioners, Drummond Wolff himself and a distinguished Turkish officer, Gazi Mukhtar Pasha, were to meet in Cairo to discuss arrangements for the further reforms, including the reorganization of the Egyptian Army and the best means of 'tranquillizing' Sudan by pacific means. Then, when they had established the security of the frontiers and the 'good working and stability' of the Egyptian govern-ment, they would present a report to their respective governments, who would conclude a convention 'regulating the withdrawal of British troops . . . in a convenient period'.[8] Not only would this delay agreement on a final settlement, but it also necessitated a further surrender of the Agency to Drummond Wolff.

Baring did not return until 2 November, when he was met at Cairo station by Nubar, Egerton, and Harry Boyle. Then, with an escort of fifty cavalry, he was driven by carriage to the Shepheard's Hotel, where he stayed in a suite until Drummond Wolff finally found a house of his own in mid-January.[9] However, Baring must have gone back to his old office during the day to work because Boyle had a disturbing encounter with him there the day after his return. Baring's first words were 'Can you speak Arabic perfectly?', to which Boyle was forced to reply, 'No Sir, hardly at all.' Baring then retreated into his study, where he could be heard saying to Egerton, 'What the devil does White [the British Ambassador at Istanbul] mean by sending that boy here? He'll be worse than useless.'

Nevertheless, Boyle soon plucked up the courage to ask for time to learn Arabic and was given six weeks.[10] It was just enough to get him started and he was soon to become one of Baring's most trusted aides, as well as his main link with the local elite. A few years later Boyle, a good linguist, offered to teach Baring Turkish, 'mainly as a pastime but also because Boyle had a great admiration for the language'. The lessons went so well that, at one stage in the early 1890s, their daily walks consisted of conver-sations entirely in Turkish.[11]

Mukhtar Pasha arrived in Cairo on 27 December and at once began a series of discussions about the future organization of the Egyptian Army.

---

[7] 19 Sept. 1885, SP, Unbound letters. [8] Cromer, *Modern Egypt*, ii. 373.
[9] Boyle to Mrs Boyle, 2 Nov. 1886, BP, box A, file 2: 1885–7.
[10] Boyle, *A Servant of Empire*, 40. [11] BN 151.

Baring knew that Salisbury regarded Ottoman involvement as a vital ingredient in any settlement involving European consent to a British reoccupation in circumstances still to be defined. Nevertheless, he was particularly irritated by Mukhtar's plan to replace British with Ottoman officers, as well as to enlarge the size of the Egyptian Army without paying proper attention to how this might be financed.

As if the situation were not becoming confused enough, the Conservatives lost the general election held in February 1886 and were at once replaced by a Gladstone government totally preoccupied by the question of Irish home rule. As Northbrook summed it all up, 'the fate of the Egyptian peasant had been decided by the [votes of] the Irish peasant'.[12] The new Foreign Secretary, Lord Rosebery, instructed Drummond Wolff to reject Mukhtar's plan for military reorganization but to continue his general discussions in Egypt and Istanbul. There the matter rested until November 1886, when the Conservatives were back in power again and Lord Salisbury recalled Sir Henry to London for consultation.

Baring seems to have sensed a political ally in Rosebery, whose disagreements with Gladstone over Sudan and other matters were now public knowledge. At any rate, he lost no time in acquainting him with his own views. His first dispatch exhibited his now habitual pessimism, stating that he did not believe that it would be possible for the troops 'to withdraw from Egypt for many years to come'. The only 'faint chance', he added, was the possibility of calling in Turkish aid 'in one form or another'. Then, as if to offset the gloomy side of the picture, he also informed Rosebery that there had been a general improvement in the domestic Egyptian situation during the six months he had been away. The 'Anglophobe' Barrère had been moved on and, in general, the French were less hostile, perhaps because they could no longer count on German support. Meanwhile, payment of the Alexandrian indemnities had 'thrown money' into the country, which also permitted some progress as far as the British-initiated reforms were concerned.[13]

A week later, after another survey of the local scene in which Baring referred yet again to the Khedive's loss of authority, Nubar's lack of local popularity, and the Egyptian Army's unreadiness to maintain order on its own, he returned to the same theme:

I think it a great pity that we came to Egypt and I should be very glad if we could get away. But the facts have to be looked in the face, and looking at the facts as they

---

[12] Quoted in Wolff, *Rambling Recollections*, ii. 304.   [13] 9 Feb. 1886, CP/2, FO 633/6.

are now, I do not see the smallest probability of our being able to get away for the present at all events. If we had stopped the Hicks expedition, the English garrison might have been largely reduced, and perhaps by this time withdrawn altogether. But the Hicks disaster enlarged the whole aspect of affairs. It involved the loss of the Soudan, and the presence on the frontier of a number of war-like tribes converted by a religious fanatic and the hope of plunder. I do not say that our occupation of Egypt need last for ever . . . All I say is that we certainly cannot withdraw at present, and that it would be the highest degree imprudent to fix any time at which we would engage to withdraw.[14]

Here Baring fairly and squarely nails his colours to the mast in adopting a position from which he was never to withdraw. Whether he would have done so quite so quickly if there had not been, from his point of view, the dangerous combination of the Drummond Wolff initiative and the rapid turnover of governments in 1885–6, cannot be said for certain. What does seem clear is that, faced with these challenges, he was forced to develop a set of arguments to which he soon became closely committed and then had to work with all his might and main to defend. Of course, if the Drummond Wolff mission was to succeed, he would have to accept the new situation, however reluctantly. However, until that moment, he was clearly determined to hammer away at his central themes in the hope of postponing the evil day. A letter written to Lyall in November 1886 finds him putting the remains of his old Liberal conscience to rest. 'If a civilised Power takes a quasi-barbarous country it must make up its mind quickly whether to go or stay.'[15] Clearly believing that it was through no fault of his own, he was able to assure himself that that particular moment was now well passed.

Finance and Friction

Given these various preoccupations, much of the day-to-day management of Egypt's finances was left to Vincent. In a survey of the situation written a couple of years later, the financial adviser calculated that, given the rigidities on both the revenue and expenditure side, the range of possible economies was only something of the order of £200,000 a year.[16] Hence

[14] 15 Feb. 1886, CP/2, FO 633/6.
[15] 27 Nov. 1886, quoted in R. V. Mowat, 'From Liberalism to Imperialism: The Case of Egypt 1875–1887', *Historical Journal*, 6/1 (1973), 121.
[16] 'Finance', in draft MS 'Egypt in 1887', DP, Add. MS 48961B.

his main emphasis was on relatively small-scale measures to help bridge the gap. These included persuading the top British officials to accept temporary reductions in their salaries, and then a more complicated scheme for reducing interest payments by a proposed conversion of the Domains–Daira loan. Not surprisingly his efforts precipitated several clashes with Nubar, including a major one in the spring of 1886 when, in a report to the Egyptian government, Vincent seemed to be suggesting that, in the eyes of the British government, the anxiety of Egyptian ministers to get their hands on lands to be released as a result of the proposed Domains–Daira conversion was based simply on 'personal cupidity'. Nubar complained to Baring who, in turn, asked Rosebery to write to Vincent.[17]

A copy of the resulting reprimand can be found in Vincent's personal papers. It refers to two events which had made an 'unpleasant impression'. One was the premature leak of a earlier report that Vincent had assured Rosebery would be kept confidential until it had been shown officially to the Egyptian Cabinet. The second was the suggestion in Vincent's report to Nubar that the allegations concerning personal cupidity represented the British Government's official view. As Rosebery angrily pointed out, this was 'not the first time' that he had had to remind Vincent that his actions were not a manifestation of the 'conciliatory course' that he had advocated in Egypt. He ended with the stern warning that he alone was 'the present mouthpiece of the intention of the British Government towards Egypt'.[18] Baring passed on the message to Nubar, telling him that he had received a telegram from Lord Rosebery saying that there was no shadow of foundation in Vincent's statement as to the opinion of HMG about which he had no authority to speak. He added that the telegram had concluded with the words 'Pray express my personal annoyance to Nubar Pasha. You fully enjoy the confidence and esteem of HMG.'[19]

Baring, for his part, was left with the larger task of persuading the British Government either to contribute more to the military costs of the Sudan campaign and the occupation or to waive some of its right to an annual interest payment of £175,000 on its Suez Canal shares. This led him to take up the cudgels with a series of chancellors of the exchequer, all of whom were much more interested in balancing Britain's budget than in

[17] Baring to Rosebery, 10 May 1886, CP/2, FO 633/6.
[18] Rosebery to Vincent, DP, Add. MS 48937.
[19] Baring to Nubar, 18 May 1886, CP/2, FO 633/5. Also Rosebery to Baring, 21 May 1886, CP, FO 633/7.

pandering to Baring's fear of a second international commission of inquiry.[20]

Baring's other major task was to try to reduce the clashes between the British advisers and the Egyptian ministers. These were an inevitable accompaniment of the extension of some of the administrative reforms to new areas of government, as well as a general understanding that, if the Drummond Wolff mission were to succeed, the days of the occupation must surely be numbered. In some instances, notably the further reform of *ahaliyah* tribunals, the system established for trying cases involving native Egyptians, which became an issue in early 1886, both Baring and Nubar wanted something to be done but differed over exactly what. In others, particularly where the British advisers were pushing on with their own pet projects, there was every incentive for the Egyptian ministers, sometimes encouraged by Nubar himself, to dig in.

As Baring saw it, the working of the system depended not on written instructions but on the personal influence of the British Consul-General on Nubar, the Khedive, and the leading officials. In the vast majority of cases such influence was sufficient:

It has enabled me to exercise a general and sufficiently effective supervision over public affairs, to patch up the numerous quarrels which occur, to smooth down personal jealousies, and to suggest solutions for the frequent questions which arise in this country which is the chosen home for every political and administrative paradox . . . I have never yet come across an Egyptian who was not inordinately afraid of taking responsibility and who, particularly if some slight unpopularity is to be incurred, was not only too anxious to shift the responsibility of coming to a decision on to the shoulders of someone else.[21]

This then was Baring's task as he saw it. It involved a large amount of office work as well as many official and unofficial visits, interviews, and discussions, underpinned by the general assertion of British influence, power, and prestige. It also involved a prolonged and unceasing campaign to convince whoever was in power in London of what he thought to be the basic 'facts' of the case, embroidered now and again by his own vision of an Egypt whose inhabitants were incapable of administering themselves. For this reason, Nubar became one of his prime exhibits. During 1886 and 1887 Baring began to present him to London as, at one and the same time, the only man for the job and yet terribly lacking in certain vital skills and in

[20] Edward Hamilton, *The Diary of Sir Edward Walter Hamilton, 1885–1906*, ed. Dudley W. R. Bahlman (Hull: University of Hull Press, 1993), ii. 45.
[21] Baring to Roseberry, 10 May 1886, CP/2, FO 633/6.

the courage to take unpopular decisions. 'Directly he gets in difficulty he generally comes running to me.'[22]

In the midst of all this stood the Agency itself. Harry Boyle's weekly letters to his mother provide a fresh set of observations of both work and relaxation during the early summer of 1886.[23] On 1 June, for example, he tells her of a Baring family party to celebrate the recovery of one of the boys from illness. It was held in the garden and attended by some of the British diplomats, Dean Butcher from the English church, two doctors, and others whom Boyle described as the 'aristocrats of the foreign colony' who 'surrounded' Ethel to offer their congratulations. A day or so later another large crowd including Nubar, Drummond Wolff, and Mukhtar Pasha, went to the railway station to see Ethel and the boys off to England for the summer, Evelyn accompanying them as far as their boat at Ismailiya on the Suez Canal. This left Baring alone at the Agency until at least 5 July, when Boyle gave his mother details of their working days, 8 a.m. to 6 p.m., during one of which he wrote eight dispatches for Baring, four drafts, and two translations, and sent four cipher telegrams. 'Sir Evelyn is a capital fellow to work with,' he reported. 'His instructions are wonderfully clear and precise.'[24]

Back on the Drummond Wolff Roller Coaster

Baring was present in Britain for at least part of the general election campaign of July 1886 that resulted in a Conservative win and Salisbury's arrival as Prime Minister, with Lord Iddesleigh, the former Stafford Northcote, as his tame Foreign Secretary. Salisbury's return was certainly welcome news as Baring, like Northbrook and a number of former Liberal ministers, had come to believe that he had a far better grasp of Britain's foreign and imperial interests than Gladstone. Nevertheless, all was not smooth sailing. Iddesleigh proved to be an enthusiastic supporter of the revival of the Drummond Wolff mission. He was, as he wrote to Baring in Cairo on 5 November, a firm believer that 'our position in Egypt must be regularised and preparations made for our ultimate withdrawal'.[25] Baring replied in his usual vein that he was against setting such a date. However, if it proved absolutely necessary, it should be ten years without binding commitment.[26]

---

[22] Baring to Roseberry, 10 May 1886, CP/2, FO 633/6. [23] BP, box A, file 2: 1885–7.
[24] Ibid. [25] CP/2, FO 633/7.
[26] Baring to Iddesleigh, 31 Oct. 1886, CP/2, FO 633/6.

Iddesleigh must soon have come to the conclusion that Baring was being difficult and, perhaps, not as fully committed to working towards an eventual evacuation as he had once seemed to be. He was also annoyed by what Zetland calls 'an increasingly vigorous expression' of Baring's feelings. 'Sir Evelyn Baring angry—must be quieted', as he minuted beside one of Baring's more intemperate dispatches.[27] Evidence of Iddesleigh's irritation has led some writers to suggest that this may have been one of the reasons why he supported the idea that Baring return briefly to India to his old post as finance member in Council under the new Viceroy, Lord Dufferin. The facts seem more complicated. Lord Cross, the new Secretary of State for India, clearly felt that Baring's expertise would be useful; while Randolph Churchill, the new Chancellor of Exchequer, felt savings could be made if the Treasury had only to pay Drummond Wolff's salary in Cairo and not Baring's as well.[28] As for Iddesleigh, he wrote to Baring saying that, while he did not like the idea, he was under pressure from Churchill and Salisbury.[29]

Baring told Cross that he would be willing to go to India for a year even though the idea was '*most* distasteful' and he could not see what good he could do.[30] Nevertheless, he also began a correspondence with Dufferin about Indian finance. He planned to leave Egypt in April 1887 for a few weeks in London, he wrote, and to arrive in Simla in May. With a year's leave from Cairo that would give him time to bring out the Indian budget for 1888.[31] It made a welcome Christmas present to hear from Iddesleigh on 28 December that the scheme had been abandoned.[32]

Two other significant events took place in London at this time. The first was Randolph Churchill's dramatic resignation just before Christmas and his replacement as Chancellor by George Goschen in January. The second was Lord Iddesleigh's sudden death from a heart attack on the day he too was leaving office to make room for Lord Salisbury. This left Baring to deal with Salisbury and Goschen as the two key decision-makers during the final stages of the Drummond Wolff mission and the last stretch of the race against bankruptcy.

Salisbury believed just as much as Iddesleigh in the need to ease Britain's diplomatic position in Europe by making a commitment to evacuate Egypt. As he wrote to Drummond Wolff soon after he had sent him

---

[27] Zetland, *Lord Cromer*, 146.   [28] Iddesleigh to Baring, 17 Dec. 1886, CP/2, FO 633/7.
[29] Iddesleigh to Baring, 12 Nov. and 3 Dec. 1886, ibid.
[30] 21 Nov. 1886, CP/2, FO 633/5.   [31] 15 Dec. 1886, ibid.
[32] CP/2, FO 633/7.

back to try once again for an agreement with the Sultan, 'I heartily wish we had not gone into Egypt. Had we not done so we could snap our fingers at the world.'[33] To the Queen he wrote that permanent occupation would mean 'permanent disagreement with France and Turkey'.[34] Baring continued to express his usual doubts. 'No arrangement is better than a bad arrangement,' he cautioned Salisbury on 21 January 1887, while delivering his rote warning against fixing an actual date by which the British troops would have to leave.[35]

Nevertheless, as the weeks went by, Baring reluctantly came to the conclusion that Salisbury's intentions had to be taken seriously, and he began to suggest some measures which would allow a post-occupation Egyptian government to stand up to foreign pressures, for example, by depriving the Caisse of the power to bring suits against it in the Mixed Tribunals.[36] On 23 April he even gave way so far as to express his opinion that, if a date did have to be set, he would recommend that it should be three years before the troops left Cairo, and five before they abandoned their last positions in Alexandria.[37] Finally, on 15 May, he offered a fourteen-point programme designed to secure 'good government' after the soldiers had finally departed.[38]

The long-awaited Drummond Wolff Convention was signed with the Ottoman Foreign Minister in Istanbul on 22 May 1887. It pledged Britain to evacuate its troops within three years provided that, in the meantime, there was 'no appearance of danger' as far as matters interior or exterior were concerned. It also contained a right of reoccupation by British and Turkish troops if one or other of these two dangers were to appear anytime thereafter. Salisbury's last proviso was that the five other European great powers should signal their agreement, thus giving Britain's position the international acceptance it had so far lacked. Sultan Abdul-Hamid was allowed four weeks to consider the matter before giving his final assent.

Baring, making the best of what he still believed to be a bad job, sent a personal message of congratulations to Drummond Wolff, saying that he recognized 'the general diplomatic arguments in favour of going must be allowed to prevail over the local arguments for staying'.[39] In other letters written at this time he speaks of the 'approaching evacuation of Egypt by

---

[33] Cecil, *Life of Salisbury*, iv. 41, quoted in Marlowe, *Cromer in Egypt*, 114–15.

[34] Cecil, *Life of Salisbury*, iv. 39, ibid, 115.

[35] SP, A/52.   [36] Baring to Salisbury, 4 Mar. 1887, SP, A/52.   [37] Ibid.

[38] Baring to Salisbury, 15 May 1887, SP, A/52.

[39] 1 June 1887, CP/2, FO 633/4, quoted in Marlowe, *Cromer in Egypt*, 118.

the British troops'.[40] When he went back to England on leave in mid-June, he must have believed that, if he was to return to Cairo, it would be to a totally different situation.

The French and the Russian governments then moved in to abort the whole process. Neither liked the fact that the Convention gave Britain an automatic right either to stay or to evacuate in circumstances to be decided by London alone. More to the point, the French Prime Minister had come to the conclusion that the existing, unratified situation regarding Egypt provided more room for the defence of his country's financial interests there than one which regularized the British position.[41] The result was that, under intense pressure from the Russians and the French, the Sultan begged Salisbury to allow him to reopen negotiations on some of the most contentious clauses in the draft Convention. Salisbury permitted only a fifteen-day extension and then, when this expired, instructed Drummond Wolff to return home in mid-July. And that, suddenly and unexpectedly, was that.

In the event, all sides now had to make the best of what was clearly a very unusual and irregular situation. What Britain may have won in terms of freedom of action inside Egypt was seriously compromised by the remains of the old, unsatisfactory international regime. According to the Convention, the European powers were supposed to have been invited to consider ways in which 'their subjects can be brought under a local and uniform jurisdiction and legislation'. Now that moment was lost, as it turned out, for ever. As for the French, they were left with great powers of obstruction but with few of those opportunities for influencing the Egyptian government directly that they would have had if evacuation had paved the way for a much larger measure of local independence.

Tensions All Round

In the difficult months leading up to the signing of the Drummond Wolff Convention, Baring also had to wage a constant struggle with his own Government for assistance and diplomatic support. Once again, the dispatches he wrote during this period reveal obvious signs of bad temper, irritation, and overall strain. To make matters worse, February brought a sore throat 'such as I rarely had', which, as he told Goschen, 'took away the

[40] e.g. Baring to Salisbury, 31 May 1887, PRO, FO 141/245.
[41] Saul, *La France et l'Égypte*, 600.

only instrument through which I can keep matters straight here, namely the use of my voice'.[42] The decision that Ethel and the children would go home much earlier than usual in April produced the weary comment: 'I must get a holiday later. I cannot stand the work and worry I have to go through for twelve months this year.'[43] Further annoyance came from criticisms in London of his 'extravagance' for wanting to build a new residency.[44]

The political situation too was tense and unsettled. What with the frequent changes of British government and the on-and-off character of the Drummond Wolff mission, no one, from the Khedive to the humblest peasant, knew quite what the future might bring. Baring betrayed his own uneasiness about the state of local opinion by taking an extremely pro-active approach to any possible manifestation of anti-British discontent, as when he arranged for the presence of British troops when Sharif Pasha's body was brought back from Istanbul to Alexandria for burial in April 1887, 'on the ostensible grounds that we wish to show respect to his memory'.[45] He was also constantly on the lookout for ways to try to make the occupation less unpopular, this being one of the major reasons for his encouragement of efforts to provide more water for Egypt's peasants.

Apart from this general uncertainty about Egypt's future, there were two other matters of central concern. One was the intensification of Baring's long fight with the British Treasury over responsibility for the costs of occupation. Its unwillingness to help, and the sharp language which Goschen, Salisbury's new Chancellor, used to express his position, were a constant irritant and produced frequent accusations that he was not being properly supported. There are signs that Salisbury felt much the same about Baring's own intemperate language as Iddesleigh had before him. He replied with some pointed language of his own:

Mr Goschen takes a strong objection to the sort of vague reliance on the British budget which has, very naturally, prevailed among Egyptian financiers of late. He says that your existing claims are untenable in themselves, and objectionable in that they are evidently destined to be the parents of a long and healthy line of little claims in the future.[46]

---

[42] 28 Feb. 1887, CP/2, FO 633/5. [43] Baring to Goschen, 1 Apr. 1887, ibid.
[44] Baring to Primrose, 5 Mar. 1887, ibid.
[45] Baring to Salisbury, 24 Apr. 1887, PRO, FO 141/245.
[46] Zetland, *Lord Cromer*, 148–9.

Baring, as might be expected, gave as good as he got, complaining to Goschen about the present constitution of the British Parliament, which made it impossible to see through any important business, and of the lack of cohesion among the British ministries, which led to the financiers pushing him in one direction and the military another. This latter situation produced a fine burst of sarcasm. The utterances of the War Office, and especially the Minister's recent letter to General Francis Grenfell, the new commander of British troops, were 'so oracular' that they must have been written with

special reference to the presence of the Sphinx in Egypt...So far as I can understand we are expected to reduce military expenditure but not the army. I cannot read the riddle. *Davus sum non Oedipus*. The process of making bricks without straw has been tried once before on the banks of the Nile, but it was not very successful.[47]

In the end, however, the Egyptian budget was brought into balance without help from Britain. This in turn permitted an announcement of a return to full interest payments on the funded debt for the financial year 1887/8 in March 1887.[48] Baring's insistence on cuts in the army and the police, the ability of Vincent and Blum to find small sums of extra revenue here and there, and an unremitting emphasis on strict economy, plus a certain amount of creative accounting, had allowed them to pull through.[49] Whether this was such a success in Egyptian eyes is another matter. For some, such as Nubar, the activities of Vincent's committee on finance was a constant irritant with its penny-pinching attempts to save very small sums of money by interfering with his own prerogatives to award jobs, pensions, and allowances as he saw fit.[50] Indeed, Alfred Milner, writing only a few years later, went so far as to suggest that Nubar might even have welcomed the idea of another international commission of inquiry which might offer relief from a purely British management of the Ministry of Finance.[51]

Baring's second source of concern stemmed from the Egyptian government's attempt to replace the annual corvée of peasants for the summer cleaning of the canals by paid day labour. This was an idea that had been supported by Nubar and Riaz well before 1882 and could be defended on a number of grounds: the corvée was wasteful of manpower, it took peasants

---

[47] Baring to Goschen, 7 Mar. 1887, quoted in Zetland, *Modern Egypt*, 151.
[48] Sir Auckland Colvin, *The Making of Modern Egypt* (London: Thomas Nelson, n.d.), 177.
[49] Alfred Milner, *England in Egypt*, 11th edn. (London: Edward Arnold, 1904), 205–6.
[50] Ibid. 108–9.   [51] Ibid. 110–11.

away from their own fields too long, and, as a form of tax, it was inequit-able, often cruel, and unfair.[52] Just why it became an issue at this particular moment is less clear, the more so as it required the payment of wages from funds which the government simply did not have. However, it was cer-tainly pressed for by Scott Moncrieff and his fellow irrigation engineers, who, as early as January 1885, were complaining of the difficulty of getting out the corvée without threats of physical violence, and of how, as a result, the cleaning was done much less well.[53]

As for Baring himself, he was able to make use of a train of events which had begun with Lord Northbrook's recommendation that the land tax be reduced by £450,000 a year, a figure which Vincent had incorporated into the budget for 1885/6. This, in turn, encouraged Nubar and the British advisers to suggest that part of the reduction (eventually put at £250,000) should be made in the form of a partial abolition of the corvée. Application was then made to the Caisse to allow £250,000 to be added to the agreed costs of administration in order to pay for an alternative supply of labour.[54] Finally, while the matter was being discussed, first by the commissioners of the debt, and then by the local representatives of the European great powers, Moncrieff simply took matters into his own hands, allocating the £250,000 in advance of international agreement, and so calling out only half the usual number of corvée labourers for 1886.[55]

Baring's particular contribution to what threatened to be a major inter-national incident soon followed. When the French delayed their accept-ance of the new arrangement, he attempted to shame them into doing so by getting the Egyptian government to call out the whole corvée on 3 February 1887. The French, seeing the trap, belatedly agreed to Moncrieff's use of the £250,000, but only in return for British agreement to an expansion of the powers of the Caisse to include supervision of all expenditure on public works.

Under pressure from Baring, the British Cabinet finally stood firm. But it was hard going. Salisbury and Goschen had initially threatened to pull the rug out from under his initiative by cutting into the Egyptian budget so sharply as to raise doubts about whether there would be money to pay for

---

[52] Nathan J. Brown, 'Who Abolished Corvée Labour in Egypt and Why?', *Past and Present*, 144 (Aug. 1994), 124–30; Scott Moncrieff's report of 14 Jan. 1885, quoted in Cromer, *Modern Egypt*, ii. 409.

[53] Ibid. 407.

[54] Milner, *England in Egypt* (1904), 193–5.

[55] Ibid. 411–13.

the extra labour.[56] It required a fierce counter-attack from Cairo before the Cabinet relented with an offer to waive payment of the interest on Britain's Suez Canal shares long enough to allow the Egyptian government to find some alternative source of revenue.[57] This was just enough to allow Baring to rescind the call-out of the corvée and so to be able to move, once and for all, in the direction of the use of paid labour for canal-cleaning. The French finally came round in March to complete a famous victory. It was, Baring informed Salisbury, 'the only really popular measure we have adopted since we have been in Egypt'.[58] The one fly in the ointment was the fact that Salisbury would not allow him to publicize it as widely as he wished for fear of further hurting French susceptibilities at a time of great tension in Europe.

In spite of Baring's firm stand, the affair placed a further strain on his relations with his two chief British lieutenants, Moncrieff and Vincent. Moncrieff believed that he had not been strongly enough supported. 'Baring, though just and honest, is unsympathetic as stone,' he wrote to a correspondent, in explanation of an offer of resignation designed, as he said, 'to stir Baring up to see what a blackguard business it is'.[59] Baring, tired of such threats, put it all down to Moncrieff's being an 'Anglo-Indian', who could not understand that Egypt was not India, as well as to the fact that he belonged to the 'anti-slavery, anti-opium lot', that is, British do-gooders who did not understand the realities of the exercise of imperial power.[60] Nevertheless, he wrote a sufficiently mollifying letter for Moncrieff to withdraw his resignation a few days later.[61]

There was certainly no meeting of minds. Moncrieff, for example, demonstrated an almost complete misunderstanding of Baring's position when he wrote to him to announce that 'where we differ is, I think, on one big principle. I look on it that England has been responsible really for everything in Egypt since Tel el Kebir.'[62] However, Baring was also at fault in not doing more to keep in regular touch with the British advisers so as to ensure they better understood the need to balance long-term goals with shorter-term political considerations.

[56] Salisbury to Baring, 4 Feb. 1887, CP/2, FO 633/7.
[57] Salisbury to Baring, 11 and 13 Feb. 1887, ibid.
[58] Quoted in Marlowe, *Cromer in Egypt*, 131.
[59] Mary Albright Hollings (ed.), *The Life of Sir Colin C. Scott-Moncrieff* (London: John Murray, 1917), 219.
[60] Baring to Salisbury, 7 Feb. 1887, SP, A/52.
[61] Baring to Moncrieff, 6 Feb. 1887, CP/2, FO 633/5; Moncrieff to Baring, 7 Feb. 1887, CP/2, FO 633/7.
[62] 6 Feb. 1887, SP, A/52.

The difficulties over the corvée also explain a serious contretemps with Vincent after the latter had been called back to London yet again for financial consultations in April 1887. A long (eighteen-page) letter written by Baring from Cairo on 29 May accuses him of reneging on their previously agreed tactics by negotiating a solution which gave the Caisse still more of a stranglehold over his Ministry's freedom of financial action as the result of his surrender to the French demand for an annual ceiling on public works expenditure.[63] And this at just the moment when the signature of the Drummond Wolff Convention had given France a major unreciprocated concession in the shape of a firm date for final British evacuation.[64]

The letter to Vincent is also interesting for the light which it throws on Baring's state of mind during the short period when it seemed as though the British occupation was about to come to an end. The tone is one of weary self-pity mixed with a quiet resolve to make sure that things would be done differently in the future. Referring to Vincent's apparent volte-face, he wrote: 'I am much too old an official hack to mind in the very least my opinion being set aside. I shall carry out faithfully whatever official instructions I receive. But do not ask me to approve of the arrangement; that I am unable to do. I think it a bad one.'

Baring went on to assert that all the shortcomings of the 1885 Convention were the work of British Treasury officials who had then 'pitchforked' the difficulties they themselves had created on to 'us'. Hence the lesson he derived from the whole business was that as 'a very large part of the responsibility for meeting any difficulties which may arise will fall on me, I shall take very great care not to say I approve of any plan unless I really think there is a fair chance of carrying it out in practice.' The home Government's policy was very much like that of Wackford Squeers's method of teaching his boys about 'honesty'. First, he spelled the word in the schoolroom. Then he sent the boys to weed the garden. 'You and I', he told Vincent, 'have to weed the garden.'[65]

In spite of all these problems with the British advisers, Baring's most difficult relationship remained that with Egypt's chief minister. The man whom he patronizingly refers to as 'my Nubar' continued to play a particularly vital role during the difficult months of the corvée dispute

---

[63] The reasons for Baring's anger are better explained in Baring to Goschen, 9 May 1887, CP/2, FO 633/5.

[64] Copy in DP, Add. MS 48929.

[65] Ibid.

and the Drummond Wolff negotiations. Nubar, as Baring frequently reported to his colleagues in London, remained 'indispensable'. In spite of his many faults he had been 'the best man for his place, during the last few years'. Indeed, given the very limited number of possible candidates he was, perhaps, 'the only one'.[66] He was, 'as Orientals go', a statesman.[67] He was also the only man in Egypt who 'serves as some connecting link between Eastern and Western ideas'.[68] All this by way of implying that, if there were to be any sudden change in Egypt's international status, Nubar would be the best person to make it palatable to the Khedive and the Egyptian elite. It followed, of course, that Nubar needed his protection against the bullying tactics of Vincent, Moncrieff, and their like.

Reading through this correspondence, it is difficult not to avoid the impression that many other points are being made between the lines. At one level, Baring wants to demonstrate to London that it is he who is in charge, he who is setting the local administrative agenda. Hence, in reply to a request from Drummond Wolff that he find out from Nubar what he thinks about a plan for the future of the Domains and the Daira estates, Baring averred that 'the best plan is not to ask Nubar what he wants but to make up our own minds as to what we want and then ask Nubar what he has to say about it'.[69] Nevertheless, it was equally in Baring's interest to invest Nubar with sufficient power to make what he was thinking or feeling central to the decision-making process. It is true that this was often wrapped up in some phrase like Nubar is 'not now in the best of tempers'.[70] However, it is also very possible that some of the things which Baring says Nubar opposed, he opposed too, but chose not to say so.

What is being described is a partnership, albeit an unequal and, possibly, only temporary one, in which there were real advantages on both sides. These included an implicit division of labour, with Baring confining British reforming activity to just a few areas, such as public works, while making no effort to wrest further control from key ministries like those of justice and the interior. As he had described his thinking to Iddesleigh in October 1886:

The idea that in a few years we can put matters to right, and then leave our work to be continued by native agents is, in my opinion, erroneous . . . a programme with a slightly better chance of success is to leave the major administrative branches alone

---

[66] Baring to Salisbury, 22 May 1887, SP, A/52.
[67] Baring to Goschen, 28 Feb. 1887, CP/2, FO 633/5.
[68] Baring to Iddesleigh, 24 Oct. 1886, CP/2, FO 633/6.
[69] Baring to Salisbury, 2 Feb. 1887, SP, A/52.   [70] Ibid.

and concentrate our efforts on reforms which, in the event of our withdrawal, a native government might wish to continue.[71]

Nubar, too, had his own agenda, parts of which, such as his desire for the abolition of the corvée and for the further amendment to the Mixed and *ahaliyah* courts, overlapped with Baring's. And while, on some occasions, he proved a tenacious defender of Egyptian interests, on others it suited him best to let Baring make all the running, particularly when he had opposition to face from other members of the Egyptian political establishment. What he lacked was the opportunity to send his ideas directly to the Foreign Office, and so the Cabinet in London, being forced to communicate via Baring, a situation with he bitterly resented.[72] Hence, by the summer of 1887 he was forced to adopt the rather desperate procedure of journeying to London to lobby Lord Salisbury and the Foreign Office officials against Baring and Vincent. Unfortunately for him, Baring himself was present during at least one of these interviews to ensure that Nubar, though well received, met with little encouragement for his pains.[73]

Baring at Forty-Six: The Turning Point

The summer of 1887 marks the most important turning point in Evelyn Baring's public life. News of the failure of the Drummond Wolff Convention meant that he would go back to Cairo in the autumn secure in the knowledge that he had many years ahead in which to continue the work of Egyptian reform. It is true that, at this stage, the financial situation had not quite reached the stage where he could proclaim the race against bankruptcy finally won. That would have to wait for Vincent's draft 1888 budget. But he could still be reasonably confident that the end was in sight. It was also true that, as a member of the British diplomatic service, he could be recalled and transferred at any time. Still, if it is possible to date the moment at which he began the serious implementation of what he was later to call 'my work' in Egypt, this was it.

The four years since Baring had first returned to Cairo had resulted in many other important changes. They had seen his personal passage from a

---

[71] 24 Oct. 1886, CP/2, FO 633/6.
[72] Edward Dicey, *The Story of the Khediviate* (London: Rivingtons, 1902), 395–6.
[73] Cromer, *Modern Egypt*, ii. 340–1.

1. CROMER HALL: a lithograph showing the Baring family home *c.*1850 with a distant view of Cromer church and the sea.

2. ORDNANCE SCHOOL, CARSHALTON HOUSE, 1850: the boy cadets dressed in Eton jackets apparently enjoying various forms of recreation.

3. The Sons of Mrs Henry Baring, 1860: Evelyn Baring at right with his brothers (from left to right) William, Richard, Walter, and Edward (Ned). Evelyn was then nineteen and on leave from his regiment in Corfu.

4. Major Evelyn Baring in India: private secretary to the Viceroy.

5. The Viceroy's Household and Staff, Simla 1875: Lord Northbrook with Evelyn Baring (with stick) on his left and what is likely to have been his daughter, Emma, on his right.

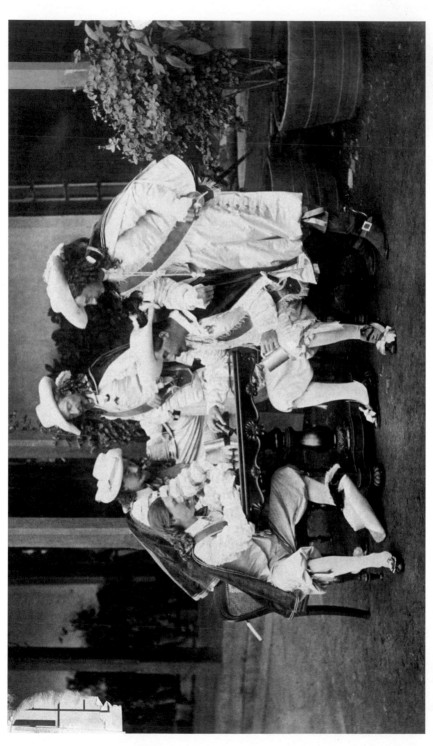

6. Evelyn Baring in Fancy Dress, Simla, 1875: Baring sitting at table on right with tankard in hand posing as one of the Five [sic] Musketeers. Taken in the same studio as the one of the Viceroy's Household.

7. TOWN HALL AND MALL, SIMLA, 1890s: town hall (completed 1888) at far end of mall on right with the Jakhu hill behind it and Christ Church to its left. The open area in front was known as Scandal Point because it was a major meeting point for gossip.

8. OLD COURT HOUSE STREET, CALCUTTA, MID-1860s: part of a street which runs north from beside Government House towards St Andrew's Church with Dalhousie Square further up on the left. When Baring returned to India in 1880 his offices were in a street several hundred yards to the west.

9. GOVERNMENT HOUSE, CALCUTTA: Baring's home, 1872–76.

10. How Britain Managed Egypt according to Abou Naddara: a cartoon from Ya'qub Sannu's Paris-based satirical political journal, *Abu Naddara Zarqa* (The Man with Blue Spectacles) 1885, showing Gladstone giving an order to Granville, who gives it to Evelyn Baring, who gives it to Nubar, who passes it on to the Egyptian ministers, while the representatives of the other European powers look on from the gallery.

11. Ethel, the First Lady Cromer, Cairo 1890s: a studio portrait taken in the year of her death.

12. EVELYN BARING, CAIRO, c.1890: a good illustration of Baring's broad middle-aged bulk and piercing, though somewhat hooded, eyes.

13. LORD CROMER ON AN EGYPTIAN CIGARETTE CARD: a photograph from the early 1890s used as an advertisement for Cousis' cigarettes. Local companies vied with each other to brand their products with names associated specifically with Egypt such as 'Camel', 'Sphinx', etc.

14. KATHERINE, THE SECOND
LADY CROMER: she was
described by her friend, Virginia
Woolf as one of the 'beauties
of her age' and in 1903, as
'an Athena married to Lord
Cromer'.

15. THE KHEDIVE ABBAS AND
HIS COUNCIL IN THE EARLY
1890s: Abbas seated at the end
of the table with Nubar and
Sir Elwin Palmer (Finance) on
his immediate right and
Mustapha Fehmy and Butros
Ghali on his immediate left.

16. The New British Agency, Cairo, Early 1900s: the Cromers' bedroom was on the first floor on the left.

17. Lord Cromer Arriving at the Abdin Palace, Cairo, 29 December 1892: Cromer's mission was to present the young new Khedive, Abbas II, with the British Order of the Bath.

18. British Troops Saluting the Flag at the Queen's Birthday Parade, Abdin Palace, Cairo, 4 May 1899, in the Presence of Lord Cromer.

19. LORD CROMER AFTER HIS RETURN TO LONDON 1907: photograph taken to mark Cromer's being made a Freeman of the City of London.

20. LORD CROMER BY 'SPY': a caricature from a supplement to *The World*. 'Spy' (Leslie Ward) was better known for his work for *Vanity Fair*. As he was to write in his autobiography 'men are often known, remembered and immortalized by some idiosyncrasy selected by the capriciousness of time'.

man who believed in the possibility of a reasonably quick evacuation of the British garrison to one who felt strongly that at least ten years was required to create a regime sound enough to prevent a return of the situation which had led to foreign occupation in the first place. He believed strongly that such a regime was in Egypt's best interests, a point he began to make repeatedly in his dispatches to London.[74] It can also be observed how, over time, he shifted from the assumption that he was the best interpreter of Egypt's financial interests to those of Egypt *tout court*. All that now remained was to persuade the leaders of British elite opinion to make his perceptions their own.

Though he may not have fully realized it at the time, Baring's actions and arguments between 1883 and 1887 had helped to place Egypt on a path along which the only logical destination was not self-government but annexation. In other words, the country would now be subject to the familiar colonial process by which the more reforms were implemented, the more further reform was seen as absolutely necessary; and that the more extensive these reforms became, the more Baring and the British believed that they could only be executed by European personnel. Soon all that differentiated Egypt from a conventional colony was the existence of certain limits imposed by what Baring sometimes referred to as 'internationalism', sometimes simply as the obstruction of certain European powers, notably the French. In spite of any number of victories, Baring's campaign against the restrictions imposed on his freedom to manage Egypt as he saw fit was one that he could never completely win.

As Zetland observes, these same years also involved a split with the Gladstonian wing of the Liberal Party.[75] If Baring described himself to Rosebery in February 1886 as a 'moderate liberal', rather than the 'radical' he had styled himself in India, it was a signal that he now sided with those members of the party who, like Northbrook, had become increasingly certain that Britain's worldwide interests were much safer in the hands of the Conservative Lord Salisbury than anyone else.[76] Like them, Baring was increasingly distrustful of the impact of the era's more democratic politics on the conduct of the House of Commons. And like them too, he remained a convinced believer in low taxes, limited military spending, and free trade.

[74] e.g. Baring to Goschen, 28 Mar. 1887, CP/2, FO 633/5.
[75] Zetland, *Lord Cromer*, 119–26.
[76] Baring to Rosebery, 7 Feb. 1886, CP/2, FO 633/4; Mallet, *Thomas George Earl of Northbrook*, 232.

A photograph of Evelyn Baring, probably taken about 1890, reveals a bulky, broad-shouldered man with thinning brown hair and the tired, peering eyes of someone who probably needs to start wearing glasses. Though seated, he seems tense and ready to spring up at any moment; certainly not a man to be trifled with. If, as W. H. Auden believed, we are all responsible for the look of our face beyond the age of 40, here is a person who appears just as he had willed himself to become: a pugnacious, no-nonsense, public figure defending a considerable personal investment of time and experience in the management of non-European peoples. No wonder Wilfrid Blunt, reporting on a meeting with him in 1883, thought him older than he actually was.[77] No wonder that so many of his visitors seemed so much in awe of him, finding him a formidable presence, brusque, impatient, and with few of the usual social graces. 'Able' but 'with no manners', as the Prince of Wales told James Rennell Rodd in 1889.[78]

In private, however, Baring liked jokes, family horseplay, and funny stories. Christmas Day 1897, for example, saw him playing what Boyle called 'inventive' games until midnight, at one stage lying on the floor next to General Grenfell with both of them banging each other on the head with paper clubs.[79] He also read widely, preferring the classics to contemporary works and prose to poetry, while his comments tended to the cut and dried rather than the literary or the elaborate. He records in his diary for 9 December 1884, that, on rereading *The Odyssey*, he first thought some lines from the third book 'beautiful' but then concluded that what they really meant was that 'we must all die'. 'What do I, and I fancy most people, find to admire in poetry? . . . Chiefly this, I think, that they find occasionally a commonplace idea expressed in pathetic and felicitous language.'

Another indication of what Vincent called his 'prompt and business-like approach' to life was his assertion to the clergyman Dean Butcher that some time ago he had made out a list of various heresies since the first century and that most of them seemed 'of great nonsense'.[80]

But the writer who best captured the Baring of this period is Lytton Strachey. In a famous passage he observes that,

[77] Longford, *A Pilgrimage of Passion*, 198–9.
[78] Sir J. Rennell Rodd, *Social and Diplomatic Memories, 1884–1893* (London: Edward Arnold, 1922), 188–9.
[79] Boyle to Mrs Boyle, 26 Dec. 1897, BP, box B, file 1: Letters to Mother 1896–7.
[80] Vincent, 'Sir Evelyn Baring', Diary, 5 Apr. 1885, DP, Add. MS 48949.

When he [Baring] spoke, he felt no temptation to express everything that was in his mind. In all he did he was cautious, measured, unimpeachably correct . . . His temperament, all in monochrome, touched in with cold blues and indecisive greys, was eminently unromantic. He had a steely colourness, and a steely pliability, and a steely strength. Endowed beyond most men with the capacity for foresight, he was endowed as very few men have ever been with that staying power which makes the fruit of foresight attainable. His views were long, and his patience even longer. He progressed imperceptibly; he constantly withdrew; the art of giving way he had practised with the refinement of a virtuoso. But, though the steel recoiled and recoiled, in the end it would spring forward.[81]

[81] Lytton Strachey, *Eminent Victorians* (first pub. 1918; London: Penguin Books, 1986), 239.

12

Asserting British Control
1887–1891

The Final Attack on Egyptian Administrative Autonomy

Baring returned to Egypt in the autumn of 1887 with two major priorities: the further assertion of British control, particularly in matters concerning the courts and the police, and the inauguration of a campaign to convince party leaders and their followers in London that the British were better governors of Egypt than the Egyptians themselves. Success was still not completely assured. In spite of the breakdown of the Drummond Wolff Convention, there was continued talk of evacuation by certain British politicians, both in and out of power. As late as June 1889 Lord Salisbury himself was willing to use a guarded promise of evacuation as a card in his negotiations with the French Ambassador.[1] And, in general, he remained much more cautious than Baring about upsetting France by any type of interference which might call attention to the role of British power in Egypt. Meanwhile, the Liberal position was bound to remain unclear until tested by the party's possible return to power in the next general election.

Baring's new resolution did not necessarily mean that he intended Nubar to go; certainly not immediately. But it did make it likely that Nubar's opposition to further British inroads into the ministries would be tolerated no longer. Just as soon as Baring had arrived back in October he took the precaution of making sure that Riaz would be available as an alternative should one be needed. Nevertheless, as he wrote to Salisbury, he did not intend to get rid of Nubar at that point, 'mainly because everybody expects me to do this because of his attacks on me in London'.[2]

---

[1] Saul, *La France et l'Égypte*, 611.

[2] Baring to Salisbury, 22 Oct. 1887, quoted in Marlowe, *Cromer in Egypt*, 133.

However, Nubar was clearly living on borrowed time owing to the problems associated with two of the projects with which he was most closely associated: the *ahaliyah* courts, and the commissions of brigandage, which he had been instrumental in setting up in 1884. The activities of the former were under serious attack from various quarters, including the British Army and the Muslim *ulama*. Baring, for his part, blamed Nubar, abetted by his secretary, Butros Ghali, for managing the courts in ways which only added to the general criticism. Nubar's choice of judges, for instance, was said to favour Christians.[3]

The commissions of brigandage had initially been created to compensate for what was seen as the failure of the *ahaliyah* courts to deal with certain forms of rural violence. All the evidence suggests that this had been endemic in the countryside long before the British occupation as a result of many decades of rapid economic and social change, including the forcible appropriation of tens of thousands of peasant plots and the creation of new landed estates called *izbas*.[4] However, the problem achieved a particular salience in 1884, partly because it was important for Nubar to show that Egyptians could keep order in their own country, partly through fear that the Mahdi might be able to exploit various forms of local discontent from across the Sudanese border.

The commissions were first established in each of the Lower Egyptian provinces and then, in 1885, extended to Upper Egypt as well. They were placed directly under the control of the mudirs, bypassing the police and the courts, where foreign influence was much more strongly felt. Complaints about the over-zealousness with which suspects were tortured to extract confessions led to the creation of a central supervisory committee in the Ministry of the Interior but to no real change. Nevertheless, the commissions were left alone by Baring, who had other priorities, and who may even have calculated that their shortcomings might be used as a stick with which to beat the Egyptian administration of justice at some later stage.

In a first trial of strength Nubar had been forced to appoint a Belgian judge, Legrelle, as Procureur-Général in October 1886, because of the numerous complaints against the activities of both the local courts and the commissions. The next trial followed a year later as a result of the sudden

[3] Baring to Salisbury, 14 Dec. 1887, printed as 'Egypt, Confidential, 1168', copy in CP/2, FO 633/98.

[4] Nathan Brown, 'Brigands and State Building: The Invention of Banditry in Modern Egypt', *Comparative Studies in Society and History*, 32 (1990), 265–6.

death of Sir Valentine Baker, the Inspector-General of Police, in November 1887. Nubar, still pursuing his strategy of trying to limit the British presence in the provinces, wished to see him replaced by an Egyptian. Baring resisted, putting forward as a counter-proposal the appointment of a British officer in the Egyptian Army. Nubar then threw down the gauntlet by sending his son-in-law Tigrane to London early in 1888 to lobby for his own plan.

Baring, hurt that the Foreign Office had given Tigrane its permission against his own advice, immediately saw this as a test of his authority, as well as of the strength of British government support. He immediately upped the stakes with a stream of letters to Salisbury designed to ensure that, when it came to a showdown, it was Nubar who would have to give way. In the heat of the moment he even offered his own resignation, but in such as way as to put further pressure on Salisbury to come down on his side. The move succeeded. Although Salisbury told Baring not to do anything precipitate while tensions were running very high with the French—'I should dread any exhibition of our sovereignty in Egypt at this moment'—he did send a telegram of support strong enough to force Nubar to agree that a Briton would indeed be appointed as Baker's successor.[5]

In the event, Nubar was not actually dismissed by the Khedive until the following June. The immediate cause was the breakdown of confidence between the two. Taufiq blamed Nubar for, first, persuading him to stand up to the British in the matter of the inspector-general of police, and then caving in to leave him in humiliating isolation. So ended the more than four-year relationship between Baring and Nubar.

Why did Nubar overplay his hand? Both Salisbury and Baring seemed to believe that it was because he had become convinced that the British still planned to evacuate Egypt. Perhaps Nubar was also pushed into a confrontation by the erosion of his own domestic support. It may also have had something to do with a surge of confidence produced by his temporary alliance with the Khedive, based, according to his confidant Edward Dicey, on his useful diplomatic skills at a time when Taufiq was worried that the Ottomans might use the Drummond Wolff negotiations to press for the return to Egypt of his father, Ismail.[6]

Nubar left behind an important legacy, which was generally acknowledged by the British officials who knew him well. One part of this was his

---

[5] Salisbury to Baring, 17 Feb. 1888, quoted in Marlowe, *Cromer in Egypt*, 146.
[6] Dicey, *Story of the Khediviate*, 438–9.

outline plan for the reform of the Mixed Tribunals contained in an 1886 memorandum. This constituted a blueprint for both Salisbury and Baring in their efforts to reach an understanding with the principal European powers designed to bring foreign subjects more closely under local jurisdiction and to prevent Egyptian legislation affecting Europeans from being challenged in the courts. Baring's dispatches show him to have been floundering around in this discussion without any clear idea as to how to proceed and very much reliant on others for advice.[7]

Another part of Nubar's legacy was his role in the abolition of the corvée, generously acknowledged by the engineer William Willcocks, who dedicated the first edition of his *Egyptian Irrigation* to him in 1893. After that Nubar had fewer defenders, whether British, French, or Egyptian, while his own account of events in his *Memoirs* stops in 1879, leaving the field to Baring and others to dismiss him as a clever but untrustworthy figure of limited historical importance. If his efforts to protect Egypt's administrative autonomy have gained greater recognition in more modern times, it is mainly because of the way his characterization of Baring and his colleagues as hell-bent on establishing an 'Indian' type of administration in Egypt continues to strike a nationalist chord.[8]

Nubar's successor, Riaz Pasha, was largely unsuccessful in his attempt to continue his predecessor's policy of limiting British influence in the face of Baring's renewed attack on the Egyptian administration of justice. 'Honest but tactless', he was not difficult to outmanoeuvre.[9] Armed with Legrelle's damning report on the cruel and arbitrary proceedings of the commissions of brigandage, which appeared later in 1888, Baring soon presented the new Prime Minister with a loaded alternative: either abolish the commissions entirely or make sure that all their prisoners always appeared before a committee of revision containing at least one European member. Riaz chose what he saw as the lesser evil and closed down the commissions in May 1889.[10] He was then subject to further defeat when Baring was able to secure the appointment of a British officer, Herbert Kitchener, as Inspector-General of Police in the spring of 1890.

When negotiations with the European powers over reform of the Mixed Tribunals broke down in 1889, Baring asked for temporary secondment of

[7] Barbara Allan Roberson, 'Judicial Reform and the Expansion of International Society: The Case of Egypt', Ph.D. thesis (London, 1998), 212–17.
[8] e.g. Afaf Lutfi al-Sayyid, *Egypt and Cromer: A Study in Anglo-Egyptian Relations* (London: John Murray, 1968), 70–5.
[9] Berque, *Egypt*, 159.
[10] Brown, 'Brigands and State Building', 277.

a British Indian judge, John Scott, to advise on the reform of the *ahaliyah* courts. Scott's report of December 1890 recommended the appointment of a British inspector-general as well as an increase in the number of the European judges sitting on the bench. Riaz, together with the Khedive, was quick to object. Baring then came back with a suggestion that, instead of a single inspector-general, much the same function be performed by a committee of inspection consisting of Scott, the Italian legal adviser to the Egyptian government, and the Procureur-Général. Once again enough British pressure was applied to persuade Riaz to give way, leaving the Khedive, for a second time, out on a limb. It was this, in addition to Baring's open encouragement of Scott and Kitchener to bypass the Prime Minister by going straight to Taufiq, which finally led him to resign in May 1891.[11]

There is general agreement that, on this occasion, it was Baring who deliberately forced the issue, having decided that Riaz's tenure was no longer in the British interest. Riaz's replacement was Mustafa Fahmi, a long-time Cabinet minister and open supporter of the occupation. He remained president of the council of ministers without a break for the rest of Baring's time in Egypt, apart from the two-year period 1893–5. Baring's own comment on the affair to the editor of *The Times* a day or so later betrays a, perhaps understandable, note of triumph: 'The state of affairs here is now very different to anything with which I so far had to deal during my 14 years connection with this country. The battle is really won. All the important administrations are subject to English influence, and mostly well chosen influence.'[12]

The British officials were equally triumphant. Not only did the fall of Riaz mean the dismissal of certain of their *bêtes noires*, such as Ali Mubarak at the joint Ministry of Public Works and Public Instruction, but they also believed that the way was now open for a thorough going reform of every aspect of Egyptian administration. As Alfred Milner of the Ministry of Finance put it anonymously, in his pamphlet *An Englishman in Egyptian Service: Britain's Work in Egypt*, the Britons in Egyptian government service now realized that 'the best way out of Egypt is to march straight through it, to drive the ploughshare of reform from one end of the administration to another'.[13]

[11] Roberson, 'Judicial Reform', 220–5; Harold Tolufson, *Policing Islam: The British Occupation of Egypt and the Anglo-Egyptian Struggle Over Control of the Police, 1882–1914* (Westport, Coun: Greenwood Press, 1999), 66.

[12] 5 May 1891, MBL, TA (1891).

[13] (London, 1892), 22.

Nevertheless, it is important to note that there were still only 366 Britons employed by the Egyptian government, just thirty-nine of whom occupied high positions, including two in finance, nine in public works, and eight in the police.[14] The numbers were to increase greatly during the remainder of Baring's service in Egypt. But, for the time being, it was this small group of men who, together with Baring and his staff, and backed by a small garrison of some 5,000 British troops, managed the general direction of affairs. Perhaps because of his sense of the weaknesses in this position, Baring placed great emphasis on frequent demonstrations of British strength by way of constant military parades in and around Cairo, Alexandria, and the canal towns, as well as making good use of his smaller army of policemen, spies, and intelligence agents.

Central to Baring's success in gaining control of the main levers of Egyptian administrative power was his working relationship with Lord Salisbury. This took some time to establish. Nevertheless, by the time Salisbury stepped down after his Government's defeat in the 1892 general election, Roberts, his latest biographer, believes that, with Baring, he had created the 'best professional relationship' he had achieved with any public servant.[15] It was not without its stresses and strains, however. Baring was increasingly insistent in his demands, always pushing for more than the cautious Salisbury felt able to allow.[16] Indeed, Baring may even have been one of the subjects of Salisbury's 1888 complaint to Lytton that he felt himself beset by 'Turcophobes and Jingoes who simply desire to annex and object to evacuating in all cases'.[17]

Nevertheless, Baring always took care to argue his case at length, to keep Salisbury well informed of his intentions, to sound him out before taking any major steps, and so, in general, to establish an atmosphere of trust and mutual confidence. As a result, each became better aware of the pressures to which the other was subject. On occasions they were also able to share a mutual distrust of the blandishments of those like the generals who, in Salisbury's words, if allowed full scope, 'would insist on the importance of garrisoning the Moon in order to protect us from Mars'.[18] Once this position had been reached sometime in the early 1890s, it was no longer a question of persuading Salisbury not to evacuate but of providing him with the arguments which would allow him to admit more openly that Britain was in Egypt to stay.[19]

[14] Marlowe, *Cromer in Egypt*, 154–5.   [15] Roberts, *Salisbury*, 532.
[16] Quoted ibid. 531.   [17] Quoted ibid. 530.   [18] Quoted ibid. 532.
[19] This is more or less the chronology adopted by Roberts, ibid. 531.

While all this was going on, the management of Egypt's finances was left very largely to Vincent and then, after the summer of 1889, to his successor, Elwin Palmer. It was Vincent who prepared the ground for the two major conversions, those of the Privileged and the Daira Debts, which were undertaken in the summer of 1890. Taking advantage of the high price of stock in Egyptian debt, they produced savings in the interest payments of £314,000 a year. The initial aim was to use this sum to allow the final abolition of the corvée. As usual, such a move exposed all the ambiguities in the French position, as perhaps it was meant to do. Knowing that these and possible future conversions would make Britain's management of Egyptian finances easier, France felt it necessary to assert its veto powers as far as any new financial initiative was concerned. However, by doing this, the French incurred great odium by appearing to support the continued use of the corvée, as well as running into serious criticism from members of their own community in Egypt.[20] They were finally let off the hook only because Palmer was able to secure the final replacement of the corvée by money obtained from the duty he placed on the increased imports of tobacco consequent on the total ban placed on local production in June 1890.

Agricultural prospects also began to look much brighter, in spite of the continuous decline in the world price of cotton and cereals. This was a result of Scott Moncrieff's repair of the Delta Barrage (originally constructed in 1840), which, when linked to three high-level canals flowing off from it, allowed a great increase in the water available to the agriculturalists of Lower Egypt. The result was a major increase in cotton production, from an average of 2,930,000 qintars a year in 1885/6–1889/90 to 4,760,000 in 1890/1–1894/5 (1 qintar = c.100 lb).[21]

Another significant initiative at this time was the attempt to reduce French cultural influence by recruiting British teachers, and then using a bridgehead in the Ministry of Public Works and Public Instruction to extend the areas in which English was taught. Key to this was Baring's appointment of a Scotsman, Douglas Dunlop, to teach English at various schools in Cairo in 1889, followed by his recruitment as an inspector at the Ministry in January 1890. Dunlop, a graduate of Glasgow University and, latterly, the headmaster of St Andrew's (missionary) School in Alexandria, was a dour, unimaginative, socially uncomfortable pedagogue whose in-

---

[20] Saul, *La France et l'Égypte*, 611–15.

[21] Egypt, Ministère des Finances, Département de la Statistique Générale, *Annuaire Statistique de l'Égypte: 1914* (Cairo: Imprimerie Nationale, 1914), 356.

creasing role in the management of Egyptian education was to make him a target for all the local opposition to British educational policy.

Whether Baring realized what he was letting himself in for is unclear. His priority at this stage was simply to find a way of reducing French linguistic and cultural influence at a time when Britain's hold over Egypt was becoming ever more secure. A new secondary school, the Khidiwiya, was created in Cairo in 1889 as a counter to the French-controlled Taufiqiya, with a teacher-training section designed to produce instructors of English. Dunlop's remit was both to teach and to recruit more teachers from Britain. Baring's larger aim may even have been to use Dunlop as a Trojan horse through which to effect a coup designed to place education under a British director-general at the Ministry of the Interior.[22] Even after this plan had been aborted by French pressure, Dunlop remained as the prime mover of a policy designed, not just to counter the French, but also to impose his own narrow vision of Egypt's educational needs through an increasingly rigid, centralized bureaucratic structure.

Convincing London

Baring pursued a double strategy in his campaign to persuade Salisbury, the British politicians, and the British public to admit the importance of a continued military presence in Egypt. One aspect was to stress the value of British-inspired reforms, the other to develop views of the country and its people, which suggested that Egyptians were incapable of managing their own affairs without European assistance. Such an approach, of course, was not new and had already been long practised in India and elsewhere. What was special about Baring's version was that, having made up his mind about the need for a continued British presence, he followed through the implications with such great thoroughness and consistency and with so clear an understanding of the ways in which domestic opinion might best be manipulated. He was now at the height of his intellectual and physical power. And it is difficult not to believe that the energy he put into his campaign was also motivated by something of a personal crusade in which he had managed to convince himself that it was only he who had the right

[22] French sources cited in David Chapin Kinsey, 'Egyptian Education Under Cromer: A Study of East–West Encounters in Educational Administration and Policy, 1883–1907', Ph.D. thesis (Harvard, 1965), 227.

to speak for Egypt, and that anyone who doubted this, whether British, European, or Egyptian, was a political enemy.

Baring's assault on the notion of Egyptian self-government took shape in 1886–7 in response to two events: the Drummond Wolff negotiations and the reappearance of Wilfrid Blunt as the champion of a revived notion of 'Egypt for the Egyptians'. In October 1886 Baring was already writing to Iddesleigh that the only 'native government' that would provide any prospect of stability would be an 'ultra-fanatical' Muslim one which would get the finances of the country into 'hopeless confusion'.[23] Later, most of the ideas which he was to elaborate in the first draft of his *Modern Egypt*, written sometime in the early 1890s, were presented in two dispatches sent to Lord Salisbury in 1887. The first was written directly in response to a letter from Blunt recommending the formation of a ministry of Muslims, which Salisbury had forwarded to him in April for his comments. Blunt's picture of Egypt as a 'Mohammedan country' best governed by Egyptian Arabs was 'very imperfect', Baring replied. Egypt was, in fact, a 'nondescript country'. Were the Suez Canal, the railways, the telegraph to Europe, the European colonies, trade, the Capitulations, the debt, and the Mixed Tribunals all removed, and Blunt made Consul-General, Blunt's suggested government might be made to work. But it would be more 'rapacious, violent and corrupt' than that of the Turkish aristocracy which it replaced.[24]

The same ideas reappear in more extended form in a second dispatch sent to the Foreign Office in December of the same year. This deals at quite extraordinary length, some 25,000 words, with the arguments put forward in a book written by Salim Faris, the son of a Lebanese Maronite political maverick who was variously the editor of local newspapers in both Istanbul and Cairo. According to Baring, Faris's *The Decline of British Prestige in the East* was worthy of attention because, in spite of its huge faults, it represented the spirit of a 'not inconsiderable' section of Muslim opinion in Egypt. Such people saw the present government of Egypt as being in the hands of strangers: not just the English but also the Armenians (represented by Nubar), the Christians (both Syrians and local Copts), and the Turks.

This, in turn, raised the question 'What is an Egyptian?' The answer, as far as Baring was concerned, was that anyone who lived in Egypt was an Egyptian, a formula which included most of the people whom Faris

---

[23] 31 Oct. 1886, CP/2, FO 633/5.   [24] 1 May 1887, SP, A/52.

deliberately excludes. It is these others who were vital to its proper government. As a result, men like Faris, who were in favour of handing over Egypt to the real Egyptians, were supporting a policy which, so Baring believed, was 'utterly impracticable and contrary to the interests of the Egyptians themselves'. For who were Faris's 'real Egyptians'? They were in fact a 'residue' consisting of three main elements: the mass of the peasant population 'who are sunk in the deepest ignorance'; a certain number of small proprietors, village shaikhs, and so on, 'who constitute the squirearchy of the country'; and a hierarchy consisting principally of the *ulama* of al-Azhar, whose 'incapacity for government has been clearly demonstrated', and whose return to power could only be accompanied by 'corruption, misgovernment and oppression'.[25] Nor would Faris's hidden alternative, a government by Turks either from Istanbul or long resident in Egypt, be much better.[26]

It is easy to see how, in terms of this same argument, Baring can present Nubar as one of his prime exhibits. Faris, who advocated Nubar's replacement by Riaz, was certainly correct to argue that the Egyptian Prime Minister was very unpopular. Nevertheless, this was not because he was an Armenian nationalist, as Faris falsely asserts, but simply because he was a Christian. And, as a Christian, he had given many hostages to fortune, first by introducing the *ahaliyah* courts, which many Muslims alleged were 'wholly at variance' with the shari'a,- and then by showing excessive favouritism to Christian as opposed to Muslim judges. To make matters worse, he was constantly being egged on by Butros Ghali Pasha, another (Coptic) Christian. Not only had Nubar and Ghali shown a great reluctance to discuss these matters with the leaders of Muslim opinion, but they had also acted in a partisan way by dismissing only incompetent Muslim judges, leaving Baring to put the matter to rights by insisting that two incompetent Coptic judges be dismissed as well.[27]

Baring's purpose in this section of his dispatch seems clear. It is to establish the point that Nubar himself can be seen as a symbol of all that was wrong with Egypt. He is portrayed, at one and the same time, as the best of a bad lot and yet also as someone so wholly partial to one of Egypt's many communities that it required someone like Baring to keep him on the right track. What does this say about the rest of the ruling elite? And what does it also say about the impossibility of any one Egyptian being able to transcend his country's basic divisions? Egypt, personified by Nubar, was

<hr />

[25] Baring to Salisbury, 14 Dec. 1887, CP/2, FO 633/98, 2–7.   [26] Ibid. 7–8.
[27] Ibid. 20–2.

manifestly unable to carry out such a difficult task. Only the British, the unprejudiced outsiders, could be relied upon to remain religiously and racially unbiased.

The dispatch as a whole is a good demonstration of how far Baring had travelled away from the policy he had advocated before arriving in Cairo in September 1883. Then he had talked of self-government and a speedy evacuation. Now he had moved on from the position he took up during the Sudan crisis—that it was not possible to leave Egypt because of the chaos that would immediately ensue—to one in which the Egyptians, as he defined them, were too backward and too divided to be allowed to manage a country which had become 'almost part of Europe'. Even if, as he somewhat grudgingly admits, the Urabi revolt was a demonstration of some type of nationalist feelings, things had developed too fast to allow any going back. The population, far from being 'homogenous', was now 'heterogeneous and cosmopolitan to a degree almost unknown elsewhere'. Hence the policy of 'making the Egyptians a really autonomous nation' had become 'utterly impracticable' and also quite wrong. 'I doubt', he observed,

whether any instance can be quoted of a sudden transfer of power in a quasi-civilized State to a class so ignorant and incapable as the pure Egyptians. These latter have for centuries past been a subject race . . . Neither for the present do they appear to possess any of the qualities which would render it desirable, either in their own interests or in those of the civilized world in general, to raise them to the category of autonomous rulers.[28]

The second arm of Baring's campaign was to dramatize British achievements in Egypt in such a way as to make those at home feel proud about what had been accomplished in their name. This took two main forms: the annual reports which he began to mastermind from 1891 on, and the use of members of his staff to write books and articles praising what was soon to be known as England's 'mission' in Egypt.

As far as the first project was concerned, the occasional reports on Egyptian finance gave way to what were now called 'Annual Reports on the Administration and Condition of Egypt and the Progress of Reforms', beginning in March 1891. These provided a well-written account of the main lines of British achievement as far as material, but not what in the Indian context was called 'moral', progress was concerned, the latter being something which Baring himself believed virtually impossible in Egypt

---

[28] Baring to Salisbury, 14 Dec. 1887, CP/2, FO 633/98, 7.

in the short run owing to the presence of polygamy and the absence of family life.[29]

The annual reports were compiled from notes sent in by departments and completed soon after the end of the year in question so as to be ready to send back to England in the spring, when Baring believed their publication would have most effect. The result, as Coles Pasha of the police noted, was that, although they could not be surpassed as literary efforts, they would have been much more properly informative if, as in India, they had been written after all the statistics had been collected much later in each year.[30] They were intended for two different publics, one in England and one in Egypt. As Baring himself pointed out, the former got a 'good deal of archaeology and slavery' while the latter got 'land tax assessment'.[31] And while this may well have been heartening to some readers, it soon provoked a counter-literature designed to show that, far from improving conditions in Egypt, British policies had, in fact, made them worse.

A central role in the second part of Baring's campaign was played by two officials who came to Egypt during the latter part of the 1880s, Eldon Gorst in November 1886 and Alfred Milner in 1889. Gorst spent his first year in Cairo working as a diplomat at the Agency and learning Arabic in his spare time. He quickly earned Baring's confidence and was, in his own words, allowed to take a prominent part in the writing of the 1887 report on Egypt's finances.[32] Alfred Milner started life in journalism on the *Pall Mall Gazette* and then learned about finance as George Goschen's private secretary, helping him to prepare his first three budgets as Conservative Chancellor of the Exchequer, 1886–8.[33] He was recruited by Baring as director-general of accounts after Elwin Palmer was promoted to Vincent's position as financial adviser in 1889. According to Wilfrid Blunt and others, his appointment was not just to make use of his financial expertise but also to allow him to produce *England in Egypt*, a book in praise of British accomplishment, written largely in 1891, and published at a vital moment just before Gladstone and the Liberals returned to power in the autumn of 1892.[34]

---

[29] This argument is made, *inter alia*, in Baring to Nubar, 15 June 1891, CP/2, FO 633/5.

[30] C. E. Coles Pasha, *Recollections and Reflections* (London: St Catherine Press, 1918), 170–1.

[31] Cromer to Villiers, 30 Jan. 1896, PRO, FO 78/4761.

[32] Mellini, *Gorst*, 18–19.

[33] John Marlowe, *Milner: Apostle of Empire* (London: Hamilton, 1976), 15.

[34] Wilfrid Scawen Blunt, *My Diaries: Being a Personal Narrative of Events 1888–1914* (London: Martin Secker, 1932), 44–5; H. S. Deighton, 'The Impact of Egypt on Britain: A Study of Opinion', in P. M. Holt (ed.), *Political and Social Change in Modern Egypt* (London: Oxford University Press, 1968), 247.

Milner's accomplishment was to set out the main themes justifying Britain's role in Egypt, coining phrases such as 'the veiled protectorate', 'the race against bankruptcy', and 'the struggle for water' which were soon to become fixed in the popular consciousness. He also managed to invest the whole business with a sense of both drama and quiet inevitability well calculated to make a late nineteenth-century audience proud of what men exhibiting the best 'qualities of the British race' had managed to achieve. There was also a seductive flattery of his audience. Egypt is presented as a land of paradox, both historically and in terms of the complexities of its contemporary status, which only the British, with their genius for patience, pragmatism, and good sense, could manage to any good effect.

The book achieved instant popular success and went through four editions by 1894, followed by another seven editions in the next ten years. Apart from its impact in Britain, many of its ideas found almost equal resonance in France. It is probably no accident that the duc d'Harcourt's *L'Égypte et les Égyptiens*, the first French work to justify the occupation, appeared in 1893. And that, following the precedent set by *England in Egypt*, it excited considerable hostile comment in Cairo.[35]

There is little point trying to work out which of the ideas found in *England in Egypt* are those of the author and which those of Baring, Boyle, and the rest of the Agency staff. For example, Milner's use of questions, 'Who are the Egyptians?' and 'Where are the Egyptians who can govern Egypt?', or his description of Egyptians as a 'motley mass', are clearly inspired by a reading of some of Baring's dispatches to Salisbury. Milner's personal contribution consisted of his own polished turn of phrase, as well as his unusual ability to present imperialism as both a duty and a drama, a burden and an exciting, if unsought, opportunity. Baring's major role was that of the animator of the project, its driving force, and the person who stood to gain most from its success. As a diplomat, and as someone in day-to-day contact with the Khedive Taufiq and his ministers, there was much he would have liked to say publicly but could not. Part of his task then involved finding others to speak for him. Blunt's mischievous comment was that 'most of it must have been taken down from his [Baring's] own dictation'.[36]

Milner, however, did not simply serve as his master's voice. In a number of sections his treatment of various central topics is both more reasonable

[35] Blunt, *My Diaries*, 84–5; Kassem Amin, *Les Égyptiens: Réponse à M. le duc d'Harcourt* (Cairo: Barbier, 1894).
[36] Entry for 31 Dec. 1892, Blunt, *My Diaries*, 86.

and more nuanced than that to be found either in Baring's comments on Salim Faris or in his first draft of *Modern Egypt*, which Milner read, and gently criticized, in 1896.[37] Milner was not anything like as censorious as Baring in his treatment of the French position in Egypt, for example. Perhaps more to the point, he provided a much more insightful analysis of Egyptian society, paying particular attention to the growing professional class of government officials whom Baring completely ignores in his desire to paint the local Muslims as either rural nobodies or urban religious fanatics.[38]

Managing the News

One of Baring's main motives for encouraging Milner and others to write as they did was based on the lessons he had learned from the Gladstone Government's handling of the Sudan affair and, more generally, from what he regarded as its pusillanimous approach to accepting proper responsibility for Egypt. A basic reason for its failures, so he believed, was its fear of its own parliamentary supporters, urged on by the press and public opinion. His answer was to balance appeals to his political masters with a more direct manipulation of those on whose votes their own power depended. Hence, while some of his arguments were directed at what he identified as the remains of a high-minded, Whiggish, non-partisan, opinion, another set was directed to Britain's growing newspaper-reading electorate.[39] This was a group which, he believed, was both wholly ignorant of foreign affairs and yet too important to be ignored. As he wrote to Milner, working in London on his book, in the summer of 1891,

Foreign policy is predominantly a matter about which the crowd not only should but need to be guided . . . I am sure that as regards Egypt and other matters the only plan is to follow Cobden's Corn Law system—i.e. to go on drumming the same thing into their heads over and over again. You have done your part of the work well.[40]

It was part of this same line of thinking that led Baring to seek channels for getting his ideas into the British press on a regular basis. To begin with

[37] Milner to Cromer, 21 May 1896, CP/2, FO 633/12.
[38] Compare Milner, *England in Egypt*, 324–8, with Baring to Salisbury, 14 Dec. 1887, 6–7.
[39] For his views on the existence of a non-party, Whiggish opinion, see Baring to Moberley Bell, 3 Apr. 1890, MBL, TA (1891).
[40] 27 June 1891, MP, quoted in Deighton, 'The Impact of Egypt on Britain', 247.

he continued his usual practice of working through individual correspondents or, on occasion, placing a particular article in a particular newspaper.
His main local contact was the *Times* correspondent Charles Moberley
Bell, a man he had known since the later 1870s. Bell was the son of a British
merchant family established in Alexandria who went from occasional
journalism to becoming one of the founders of the *Egyptian Gazette* in
1880, before being hired on a regular basis by *The Times* as a result of his
reporting of the events leading up to the occupation of 1882. One of the
many fruits of this relationship was Moberley Bell's pamphlet *Egyptian
Finance*, published in 1887.

An opportunity to make a more regular impact on the British press
occurred when Moberley Bell was called to London to manage *The Times*
in 1890. He wrote immediately to Baring asking for suggestions as to how
to improve the paper after its disastrous mishandling of the Parnell divorce
case. Baring's lengthy reply resulted in a regular exchange of letters in
which they worked together to find a new Egyptian correspondent. Baring's first choice was Gorst, who wrote at least five articles and some letters
before his transfer to the Ministry of Finance in January 1891 made the
task too difficult. Baring's suggestions as to how he might deal with a
newspaper correspondent on his own staff is of considerable interest. In an
early letter to Bell about Gorst he wrote:

I should rely on him to make discreet use of information not available to the
general public, & also I should expect him not to send anything which would be
seriously embarrassing to me or to the English Govt. Otherwise I should not care.
I should not see his letters or telegrams before they went or expect to be consulted
except perhaps on some great occasion when it might be a question of the sort of
thing to suggest to The Times & the public. Secrecy is very important. I should
not tell a soul here, not even the other members of my Chancery.[41]

In later years other channels were opened up as well. One was *The
Spectator*, whose editor and proprietor John St Loe Strachey became a
close personal friend after he and his wife were invited to dine at the
Agency during a visit to Cairo in 1896 at which, according to Strachey,
they discovered a close personal and political 'rapport' which lasted for the
next two decades.[42] Another was the Reuters news agency, which was given
a regular subsidy by the Agency and whose local correspondent, a friend of

---

[41] 11 May 1890, MBL, TA (1890).

[42] John St Loe Strachey, *The Adventure of Living: A Subjective Autobiography* (London: Hodder
& Stoughton, 1922), 367.

Harry Boyle's, was the only man connected with the press allowed free entry to the Chancery, 'where he was always welcome'.[43]

Baring also used his own considerable powers of personal persuasion to get his ideas across. He was particularly successful with visiting politicians; for instance, the influential Joseph Chamberlain, who returned to Birmingham in March 1890 to tell his constituents that he had now changed his mind about Egypt and that Britain had 'no right to abandon the duty which has been cast upon us'.[44] These powers were readily acknowledged by Baring's political enemy Wilfrid Blunt, who wrote of his willingness to listen to arguments, 'however opposed to his own opinions', a characteristic to which Blunt attributed his success 'in converting many English Radical MPs who, arriving in Cairo with the idea of hastening the evacuation, left it persuaded that the proposal was impossible or at least premature'.[45]

Baring's last concern was to find pro-British outlets within the Egyptian press, which was then expanding by leaps and bounds. One early count gives a list of 168 Arabic journals and periodicals founded between 1876 and the late 1890s.[46] Many proved ephemeral. However, their growing numbers were proof of the importance now attached to providing news for a growing middle-class European and local public. General control of the situation was difficult for, in spite of the presence of a press bureau in the Ministry of the Interior with a responsibility for licensing new journals, many remained either unlicensed or else could not be licensed because they were under foreign protection. In this latter category were at least three Arabic language newspapers, including the newly founded, pro-French, Al-Ahram.[47]

Baring's method of trying to mould local public opinion was to work through, as well as to subsidize, two of the most influential pro-British newspapers, first the *Egyptian Gazette*, and then the Arabic-language *Al-Muqattam*, founded in 1889 by Faris Nimr and two other journalists who had moved to Egypt from Beirut some five years earlier.[48] This latter, four-page, paper soon had a circulation of 2,500, large for those times. It gave

[43] Quoted in Clara Boyle, *Boyle of Cairo: A Diplomatist's Adventures in the Middle East* (Kendal: Titus Wilson, 1965), 113–14.

[44] *The Times*, 25 Mar. 1890.

[45] Blunt, *My Diaries*, 30.

[46] Martin Hartmann, *The Arabic Press of Egypt* (London: Luzac, 1899), 52–85.

[47] W. Fraser Rae, 'The Egyptian Newspaper Press', *Nineteenth Century*, 32 (Aug. 1892), 214–16.

[48] Hartmann, *The Arabic Press*, 101.

over part of its front page for translations of articles about Egypt in the European press, including the use of a source which must have been especially pleasing to Baring: *The Times*.[49] The irreverent Harry Boyle, the man directly responsible for day-to-day relations with *Al-Muqattam*, privately referred to its Lebanese–Syrian proprietors as the 'Macatamites'.

The Barings' Larger Cairo Family

Baring's Cairo year had now assumed an unvarying regularity. He and his family were in Egypt from October until the official end of the Cairo season marked by a grand reception following the Queen's birthday parade on 24 May. Ethel then went home, leaving Evelyn to follow a month or so later. At some point in the 1890s he stopped going via the baths at Carlsbad, substituting bottled Contrexéville water instead, which, as he told Salisbury, could be drunk anywhere.[50] As soon as Ethel left, the household was shut down and the chef and retinue of Indian servants sent off on their summer holiday in order to cut down the expense of private entertaining, which Baring generally had to pay out of his own pocket.[51]

In spite of Baring's best efforts the family continued to live in the old Agency, not receiving permission to build a new one by the Nile until 1890, with work only finally completed in the winter of 1893–4. The Barings and their two sons Rowland and Windham lived closely with other members of the diplomatic staff, who tended to be single males and to reside nearby. They all lunched together every day after the morning's work and were often invited to dinner with the Barings as well. Harry Boyle in particular soon became a part of the family, sharing the weekend trips and becoming a kind of high-spirited uncle to the Baring boys. He helped to nurse Rowland night and day during his serious attack of pneumonia in December 1888 and received a warm letter of thanks from Ethel, who had been ill with pleurisy at just this time. It began:

Dear Mr Boyle,
    Please accept this picture of a small boy who will, I am sure, never forget your great kindness to him; I cannot thank you enough for the many hours you have kindly devoted to his amusement and instruction . . .

[49] Rae, 'The Egyptian Newspaper Press', 220–1.
[50] 15 May 1896, CP/2, FO 633/6.
[51] Rennell Rodd, *Social and Diplomatic Memories, 1894–1901*, 10–11.

This photograph will, alas, soon be but a recollection of the past, as I fear 1889 will bring a rude change in a cropped head and schoolboy clothes—sad for his parents, as it also means that Cairo without that cheery little voice will lose much of its charm. Changes must come, however.[52]

As Ethel's letter indicates, 12-year-old Rowland went off to preparatory school in England in 1889, and then on to Eton. He was soon followed by Windham and, after that, they returned to Cairo only for the Christmas and Easter holidays.

For a couple supposedly averse to social life Evelyn and Ethel gave a very large number of parties, dances, and even fancy dress balls. Early in 1887 Evelyn told a correspondent in London that he must have a thousand names on his visiting list and that he gave a party 'almost every week and often a dance'.[53] The guests began to include some of the more distinguished winter visitors who began to return to Egypt from 1886–7 onwards. A few were put up at the Agency itself. Some, like Evelyn's brother Tom, were always welcome visitors. But others proved more of a trial. One such was Bosie Douglas, who, at Oscar Wilde's suggestion, had been sent out for a change of air in Cairo by his mother for three months in the winter of 1893–4.[54] Baring found him a 'useless boy full of all sorts of... wilfull nonsense'.[55] And it may have also been this same young man who incurred his wrath by leaving some 'decadent' illustrated French books in his room, which so scandalized Baring that he threw them into the fire.[56] Nevertheless, even though he felt sure that Bosie would 'never earn his bread and butter', he did make an effort to find him a post as honorary attaché to the British Ambassador in Istanbul.[57] But the Ambassador refused.[58]

Ethel had her own social role as manager of the female members of the British community, doing her best to ensure high standards of behaviour and keeping an eye out for those in trouble or distress.[59] Soon it became more or less de rigueur for the wives of new officials to call on her soon

[52] Christmas Eve 1888, CP/4, box 1, file 1; it is reproduced in Boyle, *Boyle of Cairo*, 82.
[53] Baring to Primrose, 5 Mar. 1887, CP/2, FO 633/5.
[54] Wilde to Lady Queensberry, 18 Nov. 1893, in *The Complete Letters of Oscar Wilde*, ed. Merlin Holland and Rupert Hart-Davis (New York: Henry Holt, 2000), 575–6. Bosie's three months in Egypt allowed Wilde the peace of mind to finish the last three acts of *An Ideal Husband* and most of two lesser-known plays; Richard Ellmann, *Oscar Wilde* (London: Penguin Books, 1988), 387–8.
[55] Cromer to Venetia Pollington, 6 Jan. 1894, CP/1, Letters from the 1st Earl of Cromer.
[56] Storrs, *Orientations*, 52–3.
[57] Cromer to Venetia Pollington, 6 Jan. 1894, CP/1, Letters from the 1st Earl of Cromer.
[58] Ellman, *Oscar Wilde*, 392.
[59] Rodd, *Social and Diplomatic Memories, 1894–1901*, 21.

after their first arrival. She then co-opted them in various ways, including making sure that they joined her in calling on the Khedive's wife, the Vicereine, at the palace at least once a fortnight during the winter season. As Mabel Caillard, one such new wife, described it, they were 'invited to assemble first at the Agency so there could be no backsliding'. They then went off to the palace, where, after they were all seated on chairs in front of the Vicereine's gilded settee, they were welcomed with a few words in French. Afterwards Ethel was unsparing in her criticism 'of one's dress and behaviour'.[60]

As for the Barings' friends, one of their closest was General Sir Francis Grenfell. Apart from being the sirdar of the Egyptian Army, Grenfell was also a busy amateur archaeologist and collector who financed several digs out of his own pocket, including one on the west bank of the Nile at Aswan.[61] His journals show him to have been a regular guest in 1887. It was also at one of the Agency balls that he proposed to his first wife, Evelyn, going round the next day to inform Ethel that he had been accepted. His fiancée then became a regular visitor too, often being taken out for drives with Ethel and the Vicereine in a phaeton. The Barings attended the Grenfell's wedding at Eaton Square in May of the same year, presenting them with a moonstone bangle as their major gift. Grenfell's journal also gives an example of one of the jokes told on these social occasions. Question: 'Why would a clergyman refuse to bury Lord Salisbury?' Answer: 'Because he is not dead yet.' It is a good example of late Victorian humour, which, like the Victorian predilection for huge meals, is now totally baffling to most people reading about these things a century later.

The Barings' main contact with the world of the Egyptian elite was through Princess Nazli Fazil, a niece of the Khedive Ismail, who lived in a large house behind the Abdin Palace. General Grenfell described her as a 'determined champion of female emancipation' who wore a 'remarkably transparent yashmak and was very attached to Lord Cromer'.[62] Although a one-time supporter of the Urabi movement, she had soon turned into an equally firm supporter of the occupation and, as Ronald Storrs was later to point out, 'embarrassingly pro-British'.[63] She gave regular lunches for Egyptian ministers and couples from the diplomatic corps, which provided

---

[60] Mabel Caillard, *A Lifetime in Egypt, 1876–1935* (London: Grant Richards, 1935), 107.
[61] Reverend A. H. Sayce, *Reminiscences* (London: Macmillan, 1923), 240.
[62] GrenP, Diary, 31 Dec. 1898.
[63] Lutfi al-Sayyid, *Egypt and Cromer*, 95; Storrs, *Orientations*, 105.

some of the few social occasions on which Baring and his officials could meet important local dignitaries. She also took it upon herself to provide Baring with the kind of information she thought he might use. A letter of thanks, written on 8 May 1889, mentions cuttings, letters to the press, and gossip about the khedivial family and other important local personalities.[64] She may even have deliberately introduced him to Egyptians whom she believed it would be useful for him to know.

Wilfrid Blunt occupied a more equivocal category between acquaintance and political adversary. He came from much the same class and background as Evelyn Baring and was almost the same age. However, they had diametrically opposed views about empire. Baring clearly believed in the importance of progress at all levels of a society, while Blunt, a social conservative, was much happier to leave non-European peoples to govern themselves undisturbed by the intrusion of all those aspects of European civilization which he abhorred. Over time he also developed an intense hatred of military campaigns against native peoples and what he regarded as the senseless slaughter of large numbers of the Mahdi's followers at the Battle of Omdurman in 1898.

Baring and Blunt had first clashed personally in 1883 when Blunt had gone to the Agency to plead that Urabi be allowed to return to Egypt, something that Baring had told him was 'quite out of the question'. Relations then deteriorated still further when Blunt visited some of the nationalist leaders in prison without waiting for official permission (later denied), and then found himself banned from visiting Egypt for three years, even though the prisoners themselves were soon released as he had asked.[65] He returned to his beloved house at Sheykh Obeyd outside Cairo in 1887. Although he had vowed to keep out of politics, he still visited Evelyn at the Agency from time to time, and also used their acquaintance to send Baring a list of members of what he called a 'fellah' party, that is, a party of Arabic-speaking Muslim Egyptians which he believed should replace Riaz's fading ministry in February 1891. This had been drawn up in consultation with Blunt's old friend Shaikh Muhammad Abduh, who had just been allowed to return from his own exile, and contained, among other names, that of the lawyer Saad Zaghlul.[66] Although this idea too was turned down, Baring still remained sufficiently open-minded to file it away for future use, helping Abduh to become Egypt's Chief Mufti and an appointed member of the Legislative Council in 1899 and inviting Zaghlul

[64] Baring to Princess Nazli, CP/2, FO 633/5.
[65] Longford, *A Pilgrimage of Passion*, 198–9.   [66] Blunt, *My Diaries*, 48.

to become Minister of Education in 1906. Their somewhat uneasy acquaintanceship continued for another fifteen years, with Baring giving Blunt's daughter away at her wedding in Egypt in February 1899 when Blunt was too ill to leave England.[67]

One other aspect of Agency life was the dramatic appearance of runaway slaves. This was a period when it had become quite usual for such fugitives to take refuge in the gardens of British embassies and consulates round the Middle East, particularly in Istanbul. Official policy was to hand them over to the local police, who were then supposed to negotiate with their owners about either their freedom or their better treatment. Increasingly, however, they were simply passed on to some version of what in Cairo was known as the Manumissions Bureau, established after the Anglo-Egyptian Anti-Slave Trade Convention of 1877, whose duty it was to provide the escaped slaves with papers establishing their freedom, and then to prepare them for some type of gainful employment. Baring was content with this gradualist process of dealing with the problem, believing, correctly, that Muslim society was favourably disposed towards manumission but not to an outright ban on slavery which most religious scholars believed to be contrary to the dictates of the shari'a.[68] Given the fact that some 10,000 slaves were manumitted in Egypt between 1883 and 1889, it must be assumed that only those escaping from politically powerful households made their way to the Agency to seek Baring's particular protection.[69]

Harry Boyle tells a story of an occasion in 1887 when Baring was having lunch with two male members of the powerful British and Foreign Anti-Slavery Society from London. A Circassian woman burst in and threw herself at his feet. Questioned by Boyle, she revealed that she had been ill-treated in an aristocratic household and wished for her liberty. At this Boyle took her himself to the Manumission Bureau, where she was officially freed and then sent on to the Cairo Home for Freed Women Slaves established by Baring in 1886 to keep newly liberated female slaves from prostitution.[70]

Summers too had their own routine. The family would spend most of their time at Strathmore Lodge in Caithness in the north-east tip of Scotland, which they rented from a local landowner. The Lodge stood

[67] Blunt, My Diaries, 340–1.

[68] Y. Hakan Erdem, Slavery in the Ottoman Empire and Its Demise 1800–1909 (Houndmills, Basingstoke: Macmillan Press, 1996), 91–2, 161–4, 168–9.

[69] Figure from Memorandum by Mr. Clarke, in FO, Egypt, no. 4 (1889), 44; repr. in PP (1889) 87, 685 ff.

[70] FO, Egypt, no. 4 (1889), 72–3.

above the River Thurso near Halkirk and some 15 miles from the busy fishing port of Wick. Built in the early nineteenth century, and then progressively enlarged, a modern photograph shows a two-storey building with a high front entrance, tall enough to ride in on horseback, and dominated by a circular, three-storey tower topped by a corbelled, conical upper storey under a pointed roof.[71] No doubt the area was chosen for its good hunting and fishing. But the distinctive feel of Caithness, beyond the Scottish mountains and culturally more Scandinavian than Gaelic, may also have had its own appeal.

Windham's letter to Boyle describing an excursion to a hotel on Loch Alsh on the west coast opposite the Isle of Skye in August 1889 gives some small indication of what such holidays involved:

I caught a conger eel two feet long and I caught a lot of cod fish some big and some little.

Papa shot one grouse and one hare with Lord Vaux there are plenty of mush-rooms and in the Hotel plenty of children and two squalling babies that keep me a wake nearly the hwole [sic] night it is a blessing when it goes to sleep.[72]

At some point before this the Barings had sold their Seymour Street house in London and stayed in the capital less and less due to what Evelyn described as the 'discomfort of a London lodging & and still more the twaddle of London society'.[73] Caithness, like Simla before it, was just about as far away as you could get from the hustle and bustle of metropol-itan affairs.

During their last years in the old Agency there were also three other major family events: the Nile cruise taken by Evelyn and Ethel in November–December 1889, Evelyn's fiftieth birthday in February 1891, and, as if to provide a miserable counterpoint to this last event, the crisis which overtook the family bank of Baring Brothers beginning in October 1890. The bank had unwisely become far too closely involved in lending money to certain unsound enterprises in Argentina. For a few weeks it was touch and go whether it could survive. But in mid-November the business was saved by concerted effort involving the Governor of the Bank of England and a number of the private banks, including the Rothschilds. Part of the price was the enforced retirement of Evelyn's older brother

---

[71] Elizabeth Beaton, *Caithness: An Illustrated Architectural Guide* (Edinburgh: Rutton Press, 1996), 104.

[72] Boyle, *Boyle of Cairo*, 83.

[73] Baring to Bell, 30 May 1890, MBL, TA (1890).

Ned, Lord Revelstoke, who was held responsible for the disaster, the lengthy liquidation of the old company, and its replacement by a new one, Baring Brothers and Co. Ltd.[74]

The cruise which, as Ethel wrote to her sister, they had been talking of for twelve years was finally made possible by the Battle of Tushki in August 1889, when Grenfell and the Egyptian Army had annihilated an invasion force of 3,300 Sudanese led by Balaja al-Nujumi.[75] This made it safe to proceed upriver as far as the second cataract, just inside the modern Sudan. The Barings' party boarded Thomas Cook's steamer *Prince Osiris* at Asyut on 16 November and sailed up to Aswan, stopping regularly to inspect courts, schools, and prisons, and to meet with parties of local shaikhs for Turkish coffee and cigarettes.[76]

Those who have sailed up this majestic river themselves can imagine the Barings' experience of the daily programme of magical morning mists, the boat's slow glide past fields and villages, temples and monuments, the sunset's setting the water ablaze with fierce reds and yellows, and the dark velvet peace of an Egyptian night. Ethel was particularly taken by the dawns and sunsets, and her letters to her sister Venetia describe many examples of her attempts to capture their 'glorious colours'.[77] Two dozen or so of the postcard-sized water colours survive and show that she was certainly the equal of the more famous painters like David Roberts and John Frederick Lewis when it comes to reproducing the intense reds and pinks and purples of the Upper Egyptian sky. She later had them framed for Evelyn as a fourteenth wedding anniversary present the following June, calling them 'recollections' of their 'three happy weeks' on the Nile.[78]

Having reached Luxor, they attended a banquet put on in Baring's honour by the local consular agent at which the performance of some local dancing girls demonstrating what Boyle calls 'the prevailing lesbian vices' made his master 'physically sick'. What exactly was going on is, of course, entirely unclear. It could be that the 'vices' to which Boyle refers involved the dancers paying lascivious attentions either to each other or perhaps to Ethel and her female companions.[79]

[74] Ziegler, *The Sixth Great Power*, 244–56.

[75] Ethel to Venetia Pollington, 21 Nov. 1889, CP/1, Letters from Ethel Errington (Cromer) to her sister Venetia Errington (Pollington).

[76] Ibid.; Boyle, *Boyle of Cairo*, 98–9.

[77] 21 Nov. and 5 Dec. 1889, CP/1, Letters from Ethel Errington (Cromer).

[78] Letter of 28 June 1890, CP/1, Letters and Papers of 1st Lady Cromer.

[79] Boyle, *Boyle of Cairo*, 99.

At Armant, some miles south of Luxor, Boyle accompanied Baring on a long walk into the desert, arriving at sunset at a village well out of sight of the river, where they were greeted by the elders, who, according to Boyle, did not know who they were. This makes for a good, if unlikely, story, particularly as these same elders began to speak of the great improvement in their condition 'especially since the English Pasha governed in Cairo'. Then, when Baring and Boyle rose to leave, the old men insisted that they ride back to the boat, but could only find one camel and one donkey to carry them. Baring chose the donkey and was lifted on to its back by some of the elders, only for the poor animal to collapse. So they proceeded on foot, accompanied by the whole village, to find the whole plain near the river dotted with moving lights as Ethel had turned out the entire ship's company, as well the inhabitants of a Nile village, to search for them.[80]

Finally, having transferred to a gunboat and arriving at Sarras at the second cataract they came across groups of Sudanese dying of hunger and exhaustion after a 140-mile journey across the desert. According to Boyle, Ethel and an army doctor tried to revive those still living by putting small pieces of bread soaked in brandy into their mouths, 'but it was too late'.[81] Ethel's own account is somewhat different. She first encountered the refugees, she writes, when she was riding a camel at some distance from the river and came across a naked boy tied to another camel, apparently dead of starvation. Later, having returned to Sarras, she gave some whisky and soda to a 'poor refugee woman' which 'put her to sleep' and so, she was told, saved her life.[82]

The party then returned down the Nile to Luxor, where they were given another dinner at which a shaikh recited a poem in which Ethel was referred to as Evelyn's 'buried jewel'. It was, she told her sister, the cause of 'great jokes'.[83]

How Baring celebrated his fiftieth birthday just over a year later is not recorded. But he must still have been preoccupied by the family's banking crisis as a letter to Moberley Bell a month earlier amply indicates: 'My relations have ruined themselves and their splendid commercial name but they have done no harm to anyone else . . . My pride has received a blow from which it is unlikely to recover.'[84] His comment on Moberley Bell's subsequent commiserations reveals several of the reasons why he was taking it all so hard:

[80] Ibid. 98–9.   [81] Ibid. 99–100.
[82] Ethel to Venetia Pollington, 5 Dec. 1889, CP/1, Letters from Ethel Errington (Cromer).
[83] Ibid.   [84] 15 Jan. 1891, MBL, TA (1891).

Your most kind letter touched me more than I can say. I never knew how many friends my family and myself had until this recent sad business. I suppose that I shall get over it in time, but it has certainly touched me on my most tender point. I hear very good accounts of the liquidation of the old firm, and of the prospects of the new, but I fear that the prestige of the *name* can never be what it was before. Apart from family considerations it is very much to be desired that they should get back some of their old position. Otherwise the Jew [i.e. the Rothschilds] will be as important in the City of London as he already is in every other capital in Europe.[85]

Baring had been kept apprised of the progress of the crisis and of the rescue efforts by his brother Tom in New York. For a while Tom's weekly letters were full of recriminations against Ned for having ruined the family name.[86] Nevertheless, both Tom and Evelyn joined many of their relations in putting money into the new firm, Tom providing £25,000 and Evelyn £10,000.[87] This was to prove financially rewarding in the long run as it enabled them to be placed on the firm's 'red list' of people entitled to first rights to the allocation of shares in the flotation of any large loan managed by the firm.[88] The bank soon revived under the leadership of Ned's son John, later the second Lord Revelstoke. But it proved a bitter as well as humiliating moment. The one good aspect of the crisis was that it prompted Tom's return to the London office, even if this also created some extra confusion among their friends and acquaintances as Evelyn and Tom had now grown to look almost exactly alike.[89]

[85] 5 Feb. 1891, MBL, TA (1891). [86] Ziegler, *The Sixth Great Power*, 251–2.
[87] Ibid. 256–7. [88] Ibid. 294. [89] Ibid. 269.

13

Cracking the Whip
1892–1895

Confronting the New Khedive

Baring, who chose the name of his birthplace as his title when he became Lord Cromer in March 1892, faced two new and related problems which had to be surmounted before he could establish his power in Egypt on a permanent basis. One was the sudden death of the Khedive Taufiq in January 1892, followed by the accession of his new and untried son Abbas Hilmi, now Abbas II. The other was the long-awaited return of what proved to be Gladstone's last Liberal government in the autumn with a majority of ministers who still supported the idea of British evacuation. The two problems were connected by the fact that the new Lord Cromer needed wholehearted support from London to deal with Abbas's challenge to the British position. This was not always forthcoming from the Liberals, although he was helped immeasurably by the fact that Gladstone's Foreign Secretary, Lord Rosebery, was someone with whom he had established a good rapport since his visit to Egypt in 1887. He was also comforted by the knowledge that Rosebery was committed to following Lord Salisbury's policy of advancing British interests in Africa.

In the ten years following the occupation Taufiq had become an ideal partner for the British. A man described by his father, Ismail, as having 'Ni tête, ni cœur, ni courage', it is not surprising to find him characterized by Milner as 'growing more English in sympathy with every succeeding year'.[1] To Berque he was a 'resigned, complaisant fellow, with no great illusions about himself'.[2] Even what was left of his sense of his own dignity

[1] Schölch, *Egypt for the Egyptians!*, 308; Milner, *England in Egypt* (1904), 135–6.
[2] Berque, *Egypt*, 151.

could be used to British advantage when it came to the manoeuvres which had accompanied the dismissal of a minister like Nubar. Cromer's personal view is probably best summed up by a story told by Arthur Hardinge, who arrived at the Agency in 1890. On reading Hardinge's first draft message to the Khedive, which ended with the words that he was convinced that his message would commend itself 'to the enlightened judgement of your Excellency', Cromer burst out, 'No, no, Hardinge, this will never do! You mustn't spoil him; for, as a matter of fact, he hasn't any judgement, and if he had, it would certainly not be enlightened.'[3]

Hence Taufiq's unexpected death, on 10 January 1892, at the age of 40 and after only a very short illness, came as a considerable shock. Baring, who had worked with him on and off since 1879, and who clearly anticipated many more years of easy cooperation, was clearly most upset, telling Salisbury that Taufiq had undoubtedly been killed by 'the incompetence of his native doctors'.[4] Just as important, he realized that a change of khedive was bound to affect the management of Egypt in the short run. However compliant, the ruler remained an important symbol of Egypt's ambiguous international status, nominally part of the Ottoman Empire but sufficiently detached from Ottoman control to allow Britain to manage it as a separate entity in his name. As a result, the Khedive still possessed sufficient power and prestige, if he chose to use it, to disrupt, and perhaps even to reverse, British policy in a number of key areas.

Taufiq's eldest son, Abbas Hilmi, a young man of 17, had been sent to Europe for the bulk of his education. This included visits to a large number of countries, including England, France, Germany, and Austria-Hungary, as well as periods at school in Switzerland (1883–7), and the Academy of the Theresianum in Vienna (1887–92). It was at the Theresianum that he heard the news of his father's death, setting off immediately for Alexandria on an Austrian Lloyd ship placed at his disposal by the Austro-Hungarian Emperor.[5]

---

[3] Sir Arthur Hardinge, *A Diplomatist in the East* (London: Jonathan Cape, 1928), 38.

[4] 10 Jan. 1892, SP, A/53. Baring also blamed Taufiq's death on his venereal disease; Baring to Salisbury, 11 Jan. 1892, CP/2, FO 633/7. The same story is told by the newly arrived British diplomat Horace Rumbold; see Martin Gilbert, *Sir Horace Rumbold; Portrait of a Diplomat, 1869–1941* (London: Heinemann, 1973), 11.

[5] Abbas Hilmi, *The Last Khedive of Egypt: Memoirs of Abbas Hilmi II*, ed. and trans. Amira Sonbol (Reading: Ithaca Press, 1998). These memoirs were dictated to a secretary in French some decades after Abbas was deposed by the British in 1914. Parts of them were published in Arabic in the Egyptian newspaper *al-Misri* in April 1951.

Much has been written about Abbas's first encounters with Cromer, including personal accounts by the two participants themselves.[6] Almost all this writing is of a partisan character, designed to defend the behaviour of one side or the other. It is also, for the most part, written with hindsight in an attempt to explain why the two protagonists found themselves so quickly on a collision course that was to have major implications for future Anglo-Egyptian relations. To make an accurate reconstruction of these first encounters more difficult still, it is hard not to get caught up in the implicit drama of the situation, an uneasy confrontation between a pugnacious British proconsul of 51 and a young man of limited experience who soon developed strong feelings about his own dignity, his father's passivity, and the humiliations heaped upon his country by a British presence that was beginning to look increasingly permanent.

Nevertheless, it seems very clear that, in this matter at least, their rival personalities mattered very much less than their rival positions, each recognizing the other as a very obvious threat to their own private and national agendas. In Cromer's case too, there is good reason to believe that, having imagined, wrongly, that he could train up the new Khedive in the way that another older man, Lord Melbourne, had managed with the young Queen Victoria, he then sought to disguise his failure with an alternative regime of bullying and threats designed to humiliate Abbas and to keep him firmly in his place.

In Abbas Hilmi's memoirs his struggle with Cromer began as soon as he reached Alexandria and the Egyptian national anthem was followed by a British military band playing the Turkish anthem. This, he was sure, was Cromer's way of reminding him that Britain and the Ottoman Porte would always unite 'to hinder the development of Egypt's freedom and independence'.[7] The accusation is somewhat unfair as Cromer was almost immediately involved in defending Egyptian interests against the threat posed by the new Khedive's firman of accession which defined the country's eastern border in such a way as to place most of the Sinai Peninsula in Ottoman hands. Salisbury in London seemed unconcerned. So it was only as a result of Cromer's spirited protest that the firman was amended to return the frontier to its previous position on a line running from El-Arish to the head of the Gulf of Aqaba.[8] Moreover, as soon as it arrived Cromer

---

[6] For Abbas, see Abbas Hilmi, *The Last Khedive*, particularly ch. 14. For Baring, Earl of Cromer, *Abbas II* (London: Macmillan, 1915), chs. 2–4.

[7] Abbas Hilmi, *The Last Khedive*, 69.

[8] Marlowe, *Cromer in Egypt*, 157.

had it read out in front of the Khedive and his people at an Egyptian Army parade outside the Abdin Palace.[9]

As far as Cromer himself was concerned, his first few official meetings with Abbas seem to have encouraged a mood of early complacency. As he boasted to Salisbury in February, 'I am riding my new colt with the lightest of snaffles . . . By degrees he will grow confidence in the English Government and, I hope and believe, confidence in me.'[10] He left for his summer leave without any sense that there might be trouble ahead.

The British general election was held in July while Cromer was staying at Strathmore Lodge. The Liberal victory was a double blow. It not only brought back his *bête noire* Gladstone as Prime Minister but also put an end to his increasingly harmonious working relationship with Lord Salisbury. By the same token, the news was very welcome to the Khedive and his circle, particularly as Gladstone had talked about evacuation in some of his pre-election speeches. There were even rumours, based on the fact that Cromer was forced to delay his return to Cairo as a result of a serious illness, that he might not be coming back at all.[11]

In the event, Gladstone's desire to get out of Egypt was held in check by Rosebery, the new Foreign Secretary, and he was soon manoeuvred into announcing an official position that negotiations with the Ottomans about withdrawal could not be restarted until Egypt had returned to its 'normal' state. As Wilfrid Blunt was quick to point out, if this meant that the whole of Egypt had to be converted to 'Lord Cromer's view', it was 'equivalent to naming the Greek kalends', given that 'an Anglicised administration supported by [Egyptian] public opinion without the necessity of armed force is an Anglo-Egyptian Utopia which none of us will ever live to see'.[12]

Cromer returned to Cairo to find a number of the senior British advisers worried that Abbas was not going to accept the subordinate role assigned to him. Gorst blamed Cromer's long absence and the 'foolish counsels' of Tigrane Pasha, the Minister of Foreign Affairs.[13] Others noted that Abbas had replaced many of his father's courtiers with men who were younger, more assertive, and Anglophobe to a man. It was also suggested that he was being egged on by de Reverseaux, the French Consul-General.[14] Soon

[9] Hardinge, *Diplomatist in the East*, 53–4; *Egyptian Gazette*, 14 Apr. 1892.

[10] 13 Apr. 92, SP, A/53.

[11] Mellini, *Gorst*, 44.

[12] 'Lord Cromer and the Khedive', *Nineteenth Century*, 35 (Jan.–June 1894), 187.

[13] Mellini, *Gorst*, 44.

[14] Mohamed Gamel-El-Din Ali Hussein El-Musaddy, 'The Relations Between Abbas Hilmi and Lord Cromer', Ph.D. thesis (London, 1966), 30, 35.

Cromer himself began to find the Khedive more unfriendly, more sensitive in matters of dignity, and, above all, more visible as far as the Egyptian population was concerned, visiting schools and government departments and sending personal communications to government officials.[15] He was also reported to be expressing public criticism of certain aspects of the occupation and of encouraging anti-British sentiment in the Arabic press.[16] Cromer's response was to give Abbas a stern lecture, after which, as he wrote to Rosebery, he did not envisage having 'much more difficulty with him'.[17] But, once again, he was wrong, as a great crisis erupted only two months later.

Given the increasing tension between Abbas and the British, it was only a matter of time before Egyptian criticism began to focus on the Prime Minister, Mustafa Fahmi. To the Khedive and his advisers he represented all that was wrong with Taufiq's willingness to fill his Cabinet with pro-British puppets. Meanwhile, Fahmi's ill health encouraged a spate of rumours about who might succeed him. On Saturday 14 January 1893 Abbas sent an emissary urging him to resign. Fahmi replied with the suggestion that the Khedive had better consult Cromer first. Abbas, ignoring this advice, immediately replaced him with Hussain Fakhri Pasha, a former Minister of Justice whose anti-British credentials had been publicly established by his opposition to Sir John Scott's legal reforms, for which he had been forced out of office in December 1891 at Cromer's personal insistence.[18] Two other of Fahmi's ministers were also dismissed and replacements named.

Cromer took this as a direct challenge to the British position, as indeed it was. In what was rapidly becoming a zero-sum game between him and the Khedive, any assertion of Egyptian independence was seen immediately as an effort to undermine his own authority. In these circumstances, Abbas's retrospective justification of his actions in his memoirs, that the 'choice of ministers appeared to be left to the Sovereign alone', is unconvincing.[19] He and his advisers must have known that it was a direct challenge to the way Cromer was now expressing Britain's authority. But they may also have calculated that Cromer would not be well supported by the Gladstone Cabinet in London. At the very least, a public confrontation of this magnitude would serve to rally Egyptian opinion to their side.

[15] Ibid. 36–7.   [16] Berque, *Egypt*, 165.   [17] 12 Nov. 1892, CP/2, FO 633/6.
[18] H. D. Traill, *England, Egypt and the Sudan* (London: Archibald Constable, 1900), 138.
[19] Abbas Hilmi, *The Last Khedive*, 79.

Cromer went straight into battle with an assertiveness and lack of sensitivity that almost caused him to overplay his hand. His arguments can be easily followed in the flurry of public dispatches, each accompanied by a private telegram to Rosebery. No sooner had he heard the news of Fahmi's dismissal than he telephoned the palace and made Abbas promise not to issue any official notification of the change of ministers until he, Cromer, had had a chance to contact the British Foreign Secretary.[20] This he did in a telegram which presented the whole thing as such an affront to the British position that London would have no option but to support whatever counter-measures he proposed. The choice as he presented it was stark:

If the Khedive is allowed to carry his point the continuance of the system which I have worked for the past ten years will no longer be possible and we shall very probably have a discussion of the Egyptian question thrust on us prematurely, perhaps in an objectionable form. On the other hand, if the Khedive learns a lesson, he will probably not give much further trouble.[21]

To make sure Rosebery and the Cabinet got the point, Cromer sent two more telegrams the same day stating that the whole affair had been coordinated with the Ottomans, the French, and the Russians, and passing on the rumour that if the Khedive was able to get away with his démarche, 'the next step will be the wholesale dismissal of British officials'.

Rosebery's telegraphed reply was received the next day:

HMG expects to be consulted in such an important event as a change of Ministry. No change appears at present to be either necessary or desirable. We cannot sanction the proposed nomination of Fakhry Pasha.[22]

A second telegram asked what steps Cromer proposed to take if the Khedive refused to give way. Cromer's belligerent reply was enough to set alarm bells ringing. Should the Khedive refuse to back down,

I propose to request General Walker [the commander-in-chief of the British garrison] to take military possession of the Ministries of Finance, Justice and the Interior with instructions that the three ministers who have been named without our consent shall not be allowed to enter. I would then request Palmer, Scott and Settle [the Inspector-General of Police] to take charge of the three departments and to act generally under my instructions until such time as the Khedive has submitted to me the names of ministers whom HMG could accept.[23]

[20] Berque, *Egypt*, 167. [21] 15 Jan. 1893, CP/2, FO 633/6.
[22] 16 Jan. 1893, PRO, FO 141/299. [23] Ibid.

This was too much even for Rosebery, saying that it reminded him of Louis Napoleon's Paris coup d'état of December 1851.[24] It also made things extremely difficult at that day's cabinet meeting, given the deep suspicions which Cromer's proposal had aroused in Gladstone and the rest of his ministers.[25] As Rosebery was to write to the Queen, herself a Cromer supporter, some days later:

Lord Rosebery makes every allowance for the crisis and the strain to which Lord Cromer has been subjected. But he cannot believe that the tone of his telegram was judicious and constituted indeed the greatest obstacle in Lord Rosebery's path. Lord Cromer is gouty, but gout, though a disease by no means incompatible with statesmanship, is an element of the situation which demands vigilance on the part of the sufferer. That is to say, he must watch himself it does not affect his style or manner. The French proverb might be converted into 'Il n'y a que la vérité et la goutte qui piquent': there were traces of both in Lord Cromer's telegrams. Hence the Cabinet was irritated.[26]

Rosebery's relay of the ministerial response had still not arrived by the time Cromer set off for the palace the next morning, forcing him to play for time. He told Abbas that if he reinstated Fahmi there would be no objection to his appointing new Ministers of Finance and Justice. He would return the next day for his answer. There was no mention of troops. Rosebery's telegram arrived the minute he returned to the Agency:

We [the Cabinet] consider the means proposed by you too violent and as such might constitute a breach of International Law. It would be better to inform the Khedive, in case of his refusal, that he must be prepared to take the consequences of his act and that you must refer to HMG for instructions. That would give you breathing space to concert something less violent.[27]

This was blunt enough to force a change of course. As Cromer described the occasion in his *Abbas II*, there was a meeting at the Agency with Tigrane and Butros Ghali that same afternoon when the three agreed on a plan by which Mustafa Fahmi would be replaced by Riaz while the Khedive would declare, in words dictated by Cromer, that he was 'most anxious to cultivate the most friendly relations with England, and that he would always most willingly adopt the advice of Her Majesty's Government on all questions of importance in the future'.[28]

[24] Marquess of Crewe, *Lord Rosebery*, vol. ii (London: John Murray, 1931), 415.
[25] Robert Rhodes James, *Rosebery: A Biography of Archibald Philip, Fifth Earl of Rosebery* (London: Weidenfeld & Nicolson, 1963), 277–9.
[26] Crewe, *Lord Rosebery*, ii. 419.
[27] Ibid. 419.　　[28] Cromer, *Abbas II*, 27.

Cromer's telegram describing his visit to the Khedive the following day does not seek to hide his disappointment at the position in which he had been placed:

In view of the great excitement here and of the fact that your telegrams give little indication of any intention to act vigorously in support of any representations I might make, it appeared to me essential to settle the matter quietly... The Khedive expressed his regret at the recent incident and pointed out that it would humiliate him and make him lose all authority if he were obliged to reinstate Mustafa. He therefore begged HMG not to insist on this ... He proposed to name Riaz in place of Fakhry... I was reluctant not to insist on Mustafa, but at the same time he is ill and will be so for some time. After what happened it is unlikely that his relations with the Khedive will ever be friendly again. Also I think it unwise to humiliate the Khedive too much ... I therefore took it upon myself to say... that I would accept the Khedive's proposal for a final settlement of the matter.

The report ends with what amounts to a demand to be 'put in possession of your views so that I can regulate my conduct accordingly and so I may do nothing which is likely to be rejected'.[29]

Cromer immediately found a way of bouncing back. In another telegram the same day he asked for an additional British infantry battalion. The Khedive had gained enormously in popularity, the Egyptian Army was unreliable, and he wanted to be able to make an immediate announcement that the garrison was being increased.[30] This led to another stormy cabinet meeting on 20 January in which Rosebery found himself in a minority of two against Gladstone and the rest of his colleagues. Gladstone is quoted as saying that they might as well ask him to put a torch to Westminster Abbey as to send more troops to Egypt.[31] Nevertheless, Rosebery's argument, that if they did not agree to Cromer's request, 'they faced the alternatives of leaving Egypt when ordered by the Khedive or sending in an army at a later stage', eventually won the day.[32] Still, it was touch and go. On Saturday 21 January Rosebery telegraphed Cromer that there was to be another cabinet meeting two days later, and that 'if you do not receive the powers you ask by Monday evening the Foreign Office will have passed into other hands'.[33] Cromer replied: 'I need hardly say that if you should unfortunately leave the Foreign Office I will follow your example in my smaller sphere. The result will almost certainly be that

[29] Cromer to Rosebery, 18 Jan. 1893, quoted in Marlowe, *Cromer in Egypt*, 165–6.
[30] Cromer to Rosebery, 19 Jan. 1893, quoted ibid. 167.
[31] Hamilton, *Diary, 1885–1906*, 20 Jan. 1893, 186–7.
[32] James, *Rosebery*, 276.   [33] CP/2, FO 633/6.

many of the high English officials here will resign or be dismissed and in fact the whole machinery will collapse.'[34]

Even though Rosebery had not used the threat of resignation in the Cabinet itself, the combined arguments of Rosebery and Cromer were enough to persuade Gladstone to give in.[35] Indeed, it was his suggestion that an infantry battalion, the Black Watch, then approaching the Suez Canal on its way to India, should be taken off the ship and marched to Cairo, where Cromer had it immediately paraded through the streets as a show of force.

It is not possible to reconstruct Cromer's mood during these tense ten days. We can only imagine the impact of the conflicting pressures from London, from the local European community, and from his own advisers, some urging him to act decisively, others to proceed with greater caution. Meanwhile, the speed of events and the need to clear things with the Cabinet often required an almost instantaneous response. As was often the case, his immediate reactions were much more violent than those which accompanied his second thoughts. We can also get the sense of his enjoyment of managing a difficult situation with its associated exercise of power. As he later boasted to Rosebery, he played tennis at the Khedivial Club every day during the worst of the crisis, an act which 'gave confidence to the English and annoyed the French and others extremely'.[36]

When it was over, Cromer was able to take some comfort from the incident. According to Rosebery, although almost all of the Cabinet were still in favour of evacuation, there was 'never a moment when it was less popular in the country'.[37] This, in turn, had had much to do with Cromer's own campaign to win over people in Britain to his own point of view, notably the publication of Milner's *England in Egypt*, which had come out just before the 1892 election campaign. For these and other reasons he could congratulate himself on having forced the Liberal Cabinet to recognize some of what he took to be the realities of the Egyptian situation, notably the dangers of leaving prematurely and the importance to the British position of the continued presence of British troops.

Nevertheless, there remained considerable cause for concern. If Milner's book had been well received in Britain, its translation into Arabic had just the opposite effect in Cairo, where its insider explanation of the real nature of Cromer's 'veiled protectorate' had confirmed Egyptian suspicions about the realities of the occupation. As Blunt recorded in his

---

[34] 22 Jan. 1893, CP/2, FO 633/6.   [35] James, *Rosebery*, 279–80.
[36] Zetland, *Lord Cromer*, 191.   [37] Rosebery to Cromer, 14 Feb. 1893, CP/2, FO 633/7.

diary, the book had done much to popularize Abbas's increasingly anti-British stand.[38] And this, in turn, had been enough to revive popular feelings that had remained largely dormant since 1882.

Cromer recognized the change in the situation himself and used it to support his argument for more troops. There had been demonstrations by students from the higher schools in Cairo, he reported, while a crowd had unhorsed the Khedive's carriage and pulled it themselves to the mosque where he was to attend Friday prayers. Hostile demonstrations outside the *Muqattam* offices took place the next day, followed by news of expression of anti-British, pro-Abbas sentiments in the provinces.[39] Even if Cromer consciously exaggerated the importance of some of these events, it was clear that the genie of opposition was once again out of the bottle and it would take time before the situation calmed down.

The Final Showdown and Its Consequences

The new spirit of opposition manifested itself in some sustained criticism of the British advisers and British policies. One sign of the times came in December 1893 when the unofficial members of the Legislative Council took the unusual step of refusing to discuss proposals for the next year's budget on the grounds that it had been presented at such short notice.[40] Later, they made a number of detailed amendments including votes to abolish the prisons and slave trade departments, to reduce the grant made for public works and the secret service, and to cut the salaries of leading British officials. Wisely, given the fact that they were engaged in a battle to influence public opinion in London as well as Cairo, the members were careful to choose issues which could be justified in terms of the reduction in peasant income due to a sharp fall in the international price of cotton. But they also revealed their nationalist bent by their demand to lower the state subvention to the European theatre so as to be able to subsidize an Egyptian native theatre as well.[41] Riaz, in Cabinet, induced his ministers to reject the majority of the Council's proposals. Nevertheless, they were taken seriously by Cromer and his colleagues, who saw

[38] Bunt, *My Diaries*, 85–6.

[39] Lutfi al-Sayyid, *Egypt and Cromer*, 111.

[40] Ibid. 119–20.

[41] *Journal Officiel*, 146 (23 Dec. 1893), suppl., copy in Cromer to Rosebery, 24 Dec. 1893, PRO, FO 78/4516.

them as yet more proof of Abbas's ability to stir up Egyptian resentment against them.

The main struggle then shifted to military affairs. Abbas had always made plain his dislike of the presence of British troops in Cairo and of British control over what he regarded as his army. He was also made quickly aware of the considerable resentment among the Egyptian officers, whose pay was less than that of their British colleagues and who had no chance of promotion beyond colonel.[42] Tensions were further heightened, first, by Cromer's increase in the British garrison in January and then by the Khedive's appointment of Muhammad Mahir as Under-Secretary of War in September 1893. Mahir was a former assistant governor of the Frontier Province on the Sudanese border and, according to Abbas, his promotion from bey to pasha was designed to show the Egyptian officers that they could, in fact, be appointed to high posts.[43]

General Walker, the commander of the British forces, and Major Wingate, the head of military intelligence, now realized that they had a serious fight for the loyalty of the Army on their hands.[44] They were also well aware that the issue was sensitive enough in Britain to provide them with an important weapon in the general campaign to curb khedivial influence. Given Britain's imperial memory of the sepoy rebellion in India in 1857, even a whisper of the possibility that native troops might be planning to disobey their European commanders would be enough to cause serious alarm in London. As Grenfell wrote to Wingate on 5 November 1893, Rosebery would support anything they recommended if a crisis arose involving the sirdar and his British officers.[45]

Cromer seems to have been rapidly converted to the same opinion as soon as he returned from his summer vacation in October 1893. He immediately began a campaign to convince Rosebery that Mahir was acting as the Khedive's agent in a secret plan to alienate the Army from its British command.[46] He also tried his best to drive a wedge between Abbas and Riaz, knowing that he would need Riaz's support if and when the opportunity for a final showdown should arise.[47]

The moment came in January 1894 when Abbas, Mahir, and Kitchener went on a tour of Upper Egypt to inspect the troops guarding the frontier with Sudan. Although there is some disagreement about the details, the Khedive seems to have made a number of disparaging remarks about some

[42] El-Musaddy, 'Relations', 72.   [43] Abbas Hilmi, *The Last Khedive*, 82–3.
[44] El-Musaddy, 'Relations', 91.   [45] Quoted ibid. 76.
[46] Zetland, *Lord Cromer*, 208.   [47] Marlowe, *Cromer in Egypt*, 173.

of the British-officered battalions paraded in front of him at Aswan and Wadi Halfa. Even Kitchener admitted that at least one of these complaints was well-deserved.[48] Nevertheless, he was upset enough to offer his resignation, only to be pressed strongly by Abbas to withdraw it a few hours later. Cromer, however, seized on the incident as a perfect opportunity to humiliate the Khedive one final time. Although it is doubtful that Abbas made these particular criticisms as part of a general challenge to the British control over the Egyptian Army, it could easily be portrayed as an attempt to undermine British military authority. As Cromer was later to explain in his own account of the incident 'I determined to choose my own battleground in the struggle which was obviously impending. It was necessary that the quarrel should be brought to a head over an issue which would be comprehensible to the British public and would afford no just ground for intervention by any foreign Power.'[49]

Cromer transmitted Kitchener's telegram announcing his offer to resign to Rosebery, with the recommendation that Her Majesty's Government should insist on the removal of Mahir, to be accompanied by the issue of an order of the day by Kitchener commending the Egyptian Army and the British officers in it.[50] Rosebery at once telegraphed his agreement. Cromer then used this to inform Riaz and Tigrane in Cairo of what had to be done:

Lord Rosebery directs me to inform Khedive that he considered incident very serious. It has become the practice of HH to inflict slights on British officers. It is imposs for HM Govt to allow this conduct to cont unchecked . . . Adequate satisfaction must be given. If not Eg army would come under more direct control. Instructed to propose following reparations. (a) Dismissal of Maher + (b) issue Order of the Day commending Eg army and Brit officers.[51]

The Khedive, who was still on his way back from Upper Egypt, now found himself completely outmanoeuvred and without either local or international support. Riaz was persuaded of the need to follow Cromer's line for fear of what the British might do to establish even further control over what they obviously believed to be a mutinous and xenophobic Egyptian Army. He may also have been influenced by some words from

---

[48] Kitchener's report on these events can be found in Cromer to Salisbury, 28 Jan. 1894, PRO, FO 78/4574; the Khedive's, Cromer to Salisbury, 18 Feb. 1894, ibid.

[49] Cromer, *Abbas II*, 53–5.

[50] Ibid. 56–7.

[51] Cromer to Tigrane, 24 Jan. 1894, PRO, FO 78/4574.

Rosebery that could be interpreted as a threat to establish a protectorate or even annexation.[52] Meanwhile, the French and Russians also made no effort to come to the Khedive's aid. Hence, when Riaz came to bring him the news in the Fayyum, Abbas had little alternative but to agree to the dismissal of Mahir, as well as to the publication of an order of the day under his name confirming his full satisfaction with the appearance and discipline of the Army.

All historians agree that what now came to be called the 'Frontier Incident' marked the end of the Khedive's role as the public leader of the opposition to the British presence. From then on he confined himself largely to encouraging others to oppose while taking great care not to run any serious risks himself. This is not to minimize his influence. Not only did he patronize the new generation of nationalist journalists and politicians, but he also found indirect ways of asserting an Egyptian nationhood, for example, by using his influence over the Waqf administration to promote a neo-Mamluk style of local architecture that stood in such obvious contrast to the *beaux arts* style of public buildings favoured by the Europeans.[53] Nevertheless, there could no longer be any doubt that the 'veiled' aspect of British power was at an end and that it was Lord Cromer who stood revealed as what a visiting British journalist was soon to call 'the ultimate ruler' of Egypt.[54]

A second set of repercussions involved the almost complete demoralization of the old guard of politicians who had spent much of the previous two decades trying to keep European influence at bay. Riaz resigned as Prime Minister in April 1894, telling Blunt that he had lost all confidence in the Khedive since the Frontier Incident.[55] He was replaced by an even more disillusioned Nubar, who had come to believe that the British had gained more during the short period of Abbas's opposition than in all the years of Taufiq's acquiescence. As he wrote in a private letter on 5 April, 'Sensible Englishmen treat ministers, or so-called ministers, as criminals or cowards, because they encouraged the Khedive, then at the last moment crawled at Cromer's feet.'[56]

[52] Lutfi al-Sayyid, *Egypt and Cromer*, 123.
[53] André Raymond et al. (eds.), *Caire: L'art et les grandes civilisations: Les grandes cités* (Paris: Citadelles & Mazenoud, 2000), 401; Donald Malcolm Reid, *Whose Pharaohs? Archaeology, Museums, and Egyptian National Identity from Napoleon to World War 1* (Berkeley: University of California Press, 2002), 239–42.
[54] G. W. Steevens, *Egypt in 1898* (Edinburgh: William Blackwood, 1898), 64.
[55] Blunt, *My Diaries*, 135.
[56] From Nubar's unpublished memoirs, quoted in Berque, *Egypt*, 169.

Poor Nubar was suffering from diabetes and, according to Cromer, looked 'aged and worn out'.[57] Some months later he surrendered control over the last important line of defence against British interference, the Ministry of the Interior. While Cromer had long been looking for a way of increasing British influence there, Gorst, who had supported Nubar's candidature for Prime Minister, now presented a subtle scheme which much impressed the Agency, even though it involved replacing the police officers recruited from the British Army by a new English police inspectorate with responsibility for supervising security and administration down to the village level.[58] As part of the package, Gorst would merely be 'attached' to the Ministry as an adviser, a face-saving compromise which did not fool anybody. Hence Nubar's gloomy conclusion: 'There is no longer an Egyptian government.'[59]

The defeat of the old guard paved the way for new political figures to come forward, many of them encouraged and supported financially by the Khedive himself. They included the fiery Mustafa Kamil, a young law school student who had led the demonstrations outside the *Muqattam* offices in January 1893, and Ali Yusuf, editor of *Al-Mu'ayyad*, the principal nationalist newspaper. The new men soon formed links with the previous generation of militant nationalistic figures, such as Abdullah Nadim, a fierce opponent of European domination from the late 1870s, now back briefly in Egypt as editor of *Al-Ustadh*.[60]

Cromer himself seems to have been well informed of their activities, with the name Mustafa Kamil turning up regularly in his reports, although more as a nuisance to keep an eye on rather than as the harbinger of a new wave of Egyptian nationalism that he soon proved to be.[61] Kamil, for his part, proved adept at thinking up publicity stunts designed to embarrass his British enemy. He wrote a letter to Gladstone, now in retirement, trying to get him to criticize the occupation. He also published an article describing how he had met Cromer's brother Walter on a boat returning to Egypt, who assured Mustafa Kamil that the British were in Egypt to stay.[62]

For the time being, however, Cromer persuaded himself that his victory over the Khedive was still not complete. He wrote to Lord Kimberley,

[57] Cromer to Kimberley, 2 June 1894, CP/2, FO 633/6.

[58] Mellini, *Gorst*, 48–50.

[59] Nubar, letter of 27 Nov. 1894, quoted in Berque, *Egypt*, 169.

[60] Arthur Goldschmidt Jr., 'The Egyptian Nationalist Movement', in P. M. Holt (ed.), *Political and Social Change in Modern Egypt* (London: Oxford University Press, 1968), 311–12.

[61] e.g. Cromer to Salisbury, 28 Jan. 1896, PRO, FO 78/4761.

[62] *Al-Ahram*, 28 Jan. 1896.

Rosebery's successor as Foreign Secretary, in April 1894, that Abbas had in no way changed, suggesting that it might still be necessary to replace him sometime in the future.[63] From then on there were repeated references to the malevolence of the Khedive, as well as to his unfortunate ancestry, stoked up, we may suppose, by Harry Boyle, who, according to Ronald Storrs, made it his business to learn every dark secret about Egypt's ruling dynasty.[64] Typical of this is a letter to Lord Lansdowne in 1900 asserting that the members of Abbas's family were mostly 'degenerate': Ibrahim, his great-grandfather, was 'most certainly a homicidal maniac'; his father had been 'a mass of disease' and a blood relative of his own wife; and his brother had 'epileptic fits'.[65] While this was obviously useful ammunition should another major confrontation occur, it is difficult not to avoid the conclusion that it was one of the many ways by which Cromer persuaded himself, and then tried to persuade others, that Egyptian nationalism was not a real phenomenon but only something got up and encouraged by an unregenerate Khedive.

Rennell Rodd, who arrived to take up a diplomatic post at the Agency in May 1894, found Cromer still 'depressed about the future of Egypt'. There was no visible end in view, he grumbled. All he could do was to develop the resources of the country under the indeterminate conditions which the absence of British policy dictated. And all this would become even more difficult as result of the new Franco-Russian entente exacerbated by a hostile Khedive.[66]

Nevertheless, there was some good news from Egypt during Cromer's Scottish holiday that summer when one of his chief Egyptian critics, Ali Sharif Pasha, the president of the Legislative Council, was arrested with two other men for purchasing female slaves. It had been Sharif who, during the budget debate the previous winter, had pressed for the partial abolition of the anti-slavery department on the grounds that its European officials received excessively high salaries and that it was no longer necessary. Even so, Cromer's comments to Barrington, the Prime Minister's private secretary, were couched in measured tones:

Personally I do not take a very serious view of their offence. Old fashioned pashas cannot be expected to see the harm in buying slaves. At the same time their actions [are] wholly illegal. Moreover, if slavery is to be finally put down in Egypt it can only be done by cutting off the demand which is held up by the Pasha class.

[63] 20 Apr. 1894, CP/2, FO 633/6.   [64] Storrs, *Orientations*, 68.
[65] 9 Nov. 1900, CP/2, FO 633/6.
[66] Rennell Rodd, *Social and Diplomatic Memories, 1894–1901*, 11–12.

Cromer went on to suggest that, when the case was brought before a military court martial, the sirdar be asked to appoint a trustworthy officer, preferably an Egyptian, to watch the proceedings to make sure that the pashas were neither exonerated just because they were pashas, nor received more than a very light sentence.[67] There was no need to do more: the facts spoke for themselves to a British audience, and Egypt's opposition had, once again, appeared to shoot itself in the foot.

Sharif claimed Italian citizenship in order to avoid trial. By the time this was turned down by the Italian authorities, it was too late to allow him to be tried with the others. One of the pashas was sentenced to five months' imprisonment and the other acquitted, while the slave dealers were given five years' hard labour. As for the women, five of them were sent off to the Home for Freed Slaves.[68] Sharif escaped trial on account of ill health, but only in exchange for a confession that he had, indeed, bought three of the females.[69]

The unofficial members of the Legislative Council, now without Sharif, tried one more round of criticism of the new budget in December 1894, returning to what were now some familiar themes: a decrease in the sums allocated to secret expenses, a curb on the use of foreign languages in the bureaucracy, and, as a response to the continuing economic depression, a reduction of taxes.[70] Cromer encouraged Nubar to complain about the tone of certain observations in the Council's report.[71] But he then balanced this by allowing a few concessions in those instances where, as he put it, the criticisms were 'more or less valid'.[72] Most, however, were ignored. Perhaps as a result of these tactics there was no lengthy budget debate in 1895, something Cromer himself put down to the fact that Abbas was no longer interested in trying to stir up trouble.[73] Nor was there much criticism of issues from the Legislative Council after that, with the single exception of British educational policy, which continued to excite strong feelings until Cromer's retirement in 1907.

[67] 31 Aug. 1894, PRO, FO 78/4596.

[68] Eve Marie Troutt Powell, 'Colonized Colonizers: Egyptian Nationalists and the Issue of the Sudan, 1875–1917', Ph.D. thesis (Harvard, 1995), 144–62.

[69] *Egyptian Gazette*, 29 Sept. 1894.

[70] 'Report of Committee of Legislative Council on 1894 Budget', *Journal Officiel*, 151 (31 Dec. 1894), suppl., copy in Cromer to Kimberley, 2 Jan. 1895, PRO, FO 78/4668.

[71] Cromer to Kimberley, 4 Jan. 1895, PRO, FO 78/4668.

[72] Cromer to Salisbury, 2 Dec. 1895, PRO, FO 78/4669.

[73] Ibid.

A Tale of Two Palaces

By an interesting coincidence, Cromer's final victory over the new Khedive came the same winter, 1893–4, that he and his family and staff moved into the new Agency which had just been completed at Qasr al-Dubara on the Nile. It was only a few hundred yards from the main British barracks at Qasr al-Aini and less than a mile from Abbas's Abdin Palace. These two households now came to represent the twin poles of Egyptian political life, one containing a ruler without power, the other Egypt's 'real suzerain', backed by immediate military force and able to call on all the resources of Britain's world Empire.[74] In public style, too, they mimicked each other, entertaining the political elite, handing out medals and other decorations, and showing themselves to the people by constant carriage rides around Cairo or official progresses through the provinces.

The new Agency was designed by the British Office of Works architect R. H. Boyce, and cost just under £40,000 to build and furnish. It was an imposing structure with a long verandah at the front and verandahs on the first and second floors along the western (and therefore cooler) side facing the Nile. The main entrance was towards the city on the east. Inside the entrance, to the left, was Cromer's study, the chancery where the diplomats worked, and the dining room. To the right was a reception room and a ballroom. The Cromers' own living quarters occupied all of the northern half of the first floor and contained a bedroom, two dressing rooms, a bathroom, a workroom, and a large open cupboard or wardrobe. There was a large guest bedroom and sitting room for distinguished visitors, also with a Nile view, and more bedrooms along the front.[75] Much of the Agency was simply, but brightly, decorated with plain white walls and furnished with white woodwork tables and chairs.[76] A two-storey servants' wing was tucked away almost out of sight on the south-west corner.

Unfortunately, it was soon discovered that the Agency had been built too cheaply and at too great a speed, forcing the Cromers to spend several years overseeing efforts to redo faulty work or to add things which had

[74] Steevens, *Egypt in 1898*, 68.

[75] Plan in F. A. Huntley, 'H. M. Diplomatic Agency, Cairo', May 1894 (copy in the chancery of the British Embassy, Cairo). Huntley was the local superintendent of works who acted as surveyor. There is much the same layout today except that the Ambassador's study and the chancery offices are now in a new building next door.

[76] Thomas S. Harrison, *The Homely Diary of a Diplomat in the East, 1897–1899* (Boston: Houghton Mifflin, 1917), 28, 69.

been left out of the original plan.[77] There was more work to be done on the big garden between the house and the Nile, with Ethel supervising its layout and upkeep.[78] For all these reasons the first years of life in the new Agency were not quite as comfortable as that prescribed in Robert Kerr's classic manual *The Gentleman's House: How to Plan English Residences. From the Parsonage to the Palace* (1864) with its emphasis on the creation of a space for 'home comfort' and for being 'at ease'.[79] Too much had had to be sacrificed in the interests of both the public money involved and the need for a new building reflective of Britain's now dominant position in Egypt.[80] Nevertheless, all the evidence points to the fact that the Cromers regarded it as, in every sense of the word, their Cairo home.

It was here that Evelyn and Ethel now conducted both their personal and their official life, treating the diplomats of the Agency staff as part of their extended family. Describing the domestic aspect, Clinton Dawkins wrote to Milner: 'I don't suppose two people live so exclusively for themselves, in themselves, and in their children as Cromer and Lady Cromer.'[81] It was a place in which to relax when official duties were over. Horace Rumbold, who served as an attaché, and then third secretary, between 1892 and 1895, described Cromer as being devoted to his children and fond of music, often to be heard 'hammering out' a Strauss waltz on the piano while waiting for dinner.[82] He also recalled being lent one of Cromer's cummerbunds and some of Ethel's jewellery as part of his costume for one of Kitchener's fancy dress balls.[83] Cromer's nephew Maurice Baring, who stayed at the Agency in November 1896, remembered eating breakfasts of 'tiny eggs and bananas' on the high verandah outside his bedroom overlooking the Nile and then listening to his uncle read aloud some of the 'abuse' written about him in the Egyptian press.[84]

All this catered to Cromer's private and softer side, which was generally hidden from outsiders. Ethel continued to see in him a warmth of sentiment and a sensitivity of which most outsiders were entirely unaware.[85]

[77] e.g. Cromer to Lord Esher, 23 Nov. 1899, CP/2, FO 633/8.

[78] Cromer to Boyce, 12 June 1897, CP/2, FO 633/8.

[79] Quoted in Karen Chase and Michael Levenson, *The Spectacle of Intimacy: A Public Life for the Victorian Family* (Princeton: Princeton University Press, 2000), 159.

[80] Dawkins to Milner, 16 Aug. 1896, quoted in Mellini, *Gorst*, 55.

[81] Ibid.

[82] Gilbert, *Sir Horace Rumbold*, 20–1.

[83] Ibid. 16.

[84] Baring, *Puppet Show of Memory*, 168–9.

[85] e.g. extract from Scott Moncrieff's diary for 26 Oct. 1891 in Hollings (ed.), *Life of Sir Colin C. Scott Moncrieff*, 267.

According to Rumbold, he was 'always charming to his own staff' and confided in them frequently.[86] He also delegated a great deal of the work to them while giving those who remained in Cairo more or less carte blanche to run the Agency as they saw fit while he was away for his long summer holidays.[87] As he made clear to one of them,

Understand my Dear Hardinge, that when I take my holiday you are in sole charge, and that I emphatically decline to answer any questions respecting Egypt. If you write to me to ask what you are to say to the Khedive or Tigrane, I simply reply that I am fishing in Caithness-shire and know absolutely nothing about either of these personages.[88]

Outsiders, however, remained in awe of him, made nervous as much by his reputation for rudeness as by the reality of his own bulky and commanding presence. Even such important personages as Kitchener and General Rundle admitted to Rennell Rodd that they approached the door of Cromer's study with a 'sense of shyness and misgiving'.[89]

Descriptions of the Agency's daily routine emphasize the interplay of the formal and the domestic. In Rennell Rodd's account of a typical day in the mid-1890s Cromer had an early breakfast, then moved to his study, where he drafted telegrams and dictated the gist of dispatches that his staff had to turn into 'coherent English'. Then came the visitors: the British financial adviser who was the Agency's main link with the council of ministers, the heads of various government departments, and finally deputations of provincial notables, religious shaikhs, and members of the Legislative Council, introduced, and then interpreted for, by Harry Boyle. Lunch was eaten by the family and staff together, often followed by a carriage drive out to the countryside by the pyramids or up the Muqattam Hills, where Cromer would walk with Boyle, Rennell Rodd, or one of the other diplomats. He often used this time to think out loud about problems facing him or to engage in free discussion about how he should act.[90] Recreation also included games of tennis at the Gezira Club. Rumbold noted that Cromer hated being beaten, and that tennis also provided him with an opportunity to exercise some of his few words of Arabic by shouting 'Wallad koura' ('Boy, the balls') at the ballboy.[91]

[86] Gilbert, *Sir Horace Rumbold*, 11.
[87] Rennell Rodd, *Social and Diplomatic Memories, 1894–1901*, 59.
[88] Harrison, *Homely Diary of a Diplomat in the East*, 42.
[89] Rennell Rodd, *Social and Diplomatic Memories, 1894–1901*, 5.
[90] Ibid. 59–60.   [91] Gilbert, *Sir Horace Rumbold*, 21.

Many evenings during the Cairo season were spent in various forms of entertainment: receptions, 'at homes', dinners, and fancy dress balls (sometimes with as many as 600 guests). The Agency's kitchen was famous. According to Horace Rumbold, his first meal at the old Agency opened with reindeers' tongues and peach bitters followed by the chef's renowned prawn curry.[92] Thomas Harrison, the American Consul-General, writes of an 1897 dinner with a clear 'golden' soup, a 'fricandeau' of veal, cold breasts of wild duck, a cherry 'bounce' from Norway, and finally an ice and a pastry.[93] Cromer took a deep personal interest in the menus. While on summer leave in London he supervised the purchase of prime items, such as the winter supply of hams.[94] And he always kept a close eye on how much his guests were eating. This habit gave rise to what may be an apocryphal story involving the Prince of Wales, who, on a visit in 1889, is said to have called out to Cromer that he wanted 'some more of that excellent curry of yours', only for his host to reply: 'You had much better not. It is rich as it is, and you have already had two helpings.'[95] In the 1890s meals were served by Indian servants in white turbans and gold-embroidered breastplates. But they were then replaced in 1900 by Egyptians directed by an English butler when their raids on the household accounts became too much for Cromer to tolerate.[96]

The guests were generally European: diplomats, the commissioners of the public debt, judges of the Mixed Tribunals, a few leading advocates, British army officers and officials, and some of the most important of Cairo's winter visitors. There were still very few Egyptians.[97] Many of the guests seemed overawed by the occasion as well as by Lord Cromer's public reputation for lack of small talk, for what might be called his ruthless politeness, and for the way he seemed, as Mabel Caillard put it, to 'reserve his cheerfulness for the end of parties'.[98] Nevertheless, with Ethel's help, Cromer endured a large number of events, even putting on fancy dress on occasions, or staying up for the end of dances, which sometimes lasted until four in the morning.[99]

It was the duty of the third secretary to help Ethel with all social arrangements both inside and outside the Agency.[100] These included the entertainments put on for various of the Cromers' local charities, for

[92] Gilbert, *Sir Horace Rumbold*, 12.   [93] Harrison, *Homely Diary of a Diplomat in the East*, 35.
[94] Rennell Rodd, *Social and Diplomatic Memories, 1894–1901*, 11.
[95] Boyle, *A Servant of Empire*, 58.   [96] Boyle to Mrs Boyle, 10 Sept. 1900, BP, box B, file 3.
[97] Boyle, *A Servant of Empire*, 51.   [98] Caillard, *A Lifetime in Egypt*, 117–18.
[99] Ibid.   [100] Gilbert, *Sir Horace Rumbold*, 12.

example, the amateur theatricals held every year to raise money for the Cairo branch of the Society for the Protection of Animals (established in 1894), usually a performance of one of the Gilbert and Sullivan operettas.[101] Gorst, who was 'an extraordinarily good amateur actor', also helped Ethel with some of these dramatic entertainments.[102]

If the evening was free from visitors, or they were not out at some official function or the opera, the family, personal friends, and embassy staff played cards or engaged Lord Cromer in literary discussion. According to Rumbold, Cromer had an excellent memory for what he had read. He loved Dickens and could have passed an examination on his work. He also liked French novels, memoirs, and English eighteenth-century poetry.[103] Rennell Rodd notes that he could not be induced to read modern poetry and that he particularly detested Browning.[104] Others give a more generous picture of his reading, while his private correspondence shows him to have kept up with much of the biographical writing of his period as well as to have exchanged modern novels with his friends and relatives.[105] Lord Northbrook even had the temerity to lend him Émile Zola's new novel *Rome*, even though he thought the writer 'wallowed too much in mire'.[106]

At the weekend there were longer drives into the desert or to the step-pyramid at Sakkara or the gardens behind the Delta Barrage, which were favourite sites for family picnics.[107]

The Agency, or what Cairenes started to call the 'bait al-lurd' (house of the lord), soon became the centre of a highly personalized system for ruling Egypt. Unlike the diplomatic side of Cromer's work, when it came to the local administration he maintained few written records, keeping most things in his head.[108] Indeed, this was sometimes seen as one of the great strengths of the Cromerian system in that it eliminated the 'delays and misunderstandings of departmental paperwork'.[109] Cromer also made use of just a few of his principal subordinates. As far as direct contact with the Egyptian government was concerned, he preferred to work through a single British official. Eldon Gorst, Elwin Palmer, Clinton Dawkins, and

[101] Caillard, *A Lifetime in Egypt*, 127–8.   [102] Mellin, *Gorst*, 75.
[103] Gilbert, *Sir Horace Rumbold*, 21; St Loe Strachey, *The Adventure of Living*, 370.
[104] Rennell Rodd, *Social and Diplomatic Memories, 1894–1901*, 56–7.
[105] Baring, *Puppet Show of Memory*, 168–9.
[106] Northbrook to Cromer, 11 Nov. 1896, CP/2, FO 633/11.
[107] e.g. Boyle to Mrs Boyle, 17 Jan. 1897, BP, box B, file 1: Letters to Mother 1896–97.
[108] Rennell Rodd, *Social and Diplomatic Memories, 1894–1901*, 29; Mellini, *Gorst*, 99; Boyle to Tommy, 30 Oct. 1899, BP, box B, file 3.
[109] Eldon Gorst, 'Lord Cromer in Egypt' (1905), quoted in Mellini, *Gorst*, 88.

later William Garstin were all used at some time in this way. Dawkins saw it as the result of 'an odd vein of laziness' which led Cromer to want to work through just one man and to hear everything from him.[110]

In this way, Cromer set the main guidelines for Egyptian public policy. Meanwhile, it was the duty of the head of chancery to receive visiting European journalists and businessmen, leaving Harry Boyle as the main conduit to the local Cairo journalists, as well as the recipient of an endless series of petitions and local complaints. As time went on, information about Egyptian political and religious opinion came to be filtered more and more through Boyle and his own contacts, supplemented by the use of a secret service of local agents and informers. It was not an entirely happy situation. By the late 1880s Boyle, still a young man in his twenties, had become Cromer's single most important source of information and advice about popular and, above all, religious opinion. To make matters worse, Boyle deprived himself of any outside perspective by spending his first nine years entirely in Egypt without a break, and then taking only a single home leave until his master retired in 1907.

The new Agency was also used as the base for imposing Cromer's influence on Cairo and the provinces beyond. He was soon a familiar figure driving about the city in an open carriage wearing a grey frock coat and white hat, with brown-liveried servants, and a syce (*qawwas*), who ran before shouting his name and ordering people out of the way.[111] Princess Nazli described a scene in the late 1880s when the Khedive Taufiq turned pale on hearing the shout of Cromer's syce from the street outside, muttering, 'who knows what he is coming to say to me?'[112] Meanwhile, Cromer and Ethel and their staff attended any number of parades and other military ceremonies in the square in front of the palace, events that, once again, can be seen as provocative reminders of just where the real power lay. As the American Consul-General noted of this period, 'No picture of Cairo that does not include the soldier can be considered complete, for the military aspect is in almost aggressive evidence... By company and regiment, soldiers are so frequently marched through the streets that the visitor might believe Cairo to be a vast military camp.'[113]

Something of Cromer's use of the physical presence of British power can also been learned from contemporary descriptions of the celebrations arranged to mark Queen Victoria's Sixtieth Jubilee in June 1897. On the

---

[110] Dawkins to Milner, 16 Aug. 1896, quoted in Mellini, *Gorst*, 55–6.
[111] Rennell Rodd, *Social and Diplomatic Memories, 1894–1901*, 60.
[112] Storrs, *Orientations*, 52.   [113] Frederick Penfold, quoted in Mellini, *Gorst*, 96.

Sunday before, he drove out of the Agency to attend a service at All Saints' Church. Two days later, on the day itself, he attended a military parade in front of the Abdin in a carriage escorted by the 21st Lancers. There he received the royal salute, presented medals and decorations, and presided over the march past of British troops. Cromer then returned to the Agency to act as host for a reception for British subjects. Later in the day he attended the British fête in the Gizeh Garden, followed by a jubilee banquet given by the commander of British forces at the Continental Hotel, before returning to the fête at 10 p.m. Meanwhile, the British had made sure that Cairo was ablaze with lights, with some along the river frontage of the Agency, and a huge 'VR' picked out in coloured lights over the Citadel. A bonfire on the Muqattam Hills completed the scene, along with the firing of salutes.[114] It is impossible to imagine a more complete invasion of khedivial space. Few of Cairo's Egyptian population could have been left in any doubt as to the nature of British presence in their capital.

In this way Cromer's role in Egypt can be seen as completing a full circle, beginning with his participation in the efforts to limit Khedive Ismail's personal rule in the late 1870s, and then proceeding to establish his own form of personal rule as the occupation progressed. Nor was there anything secret about it. Having come to the conclusion that Egypt's particular circumstances demanded it, he referred to it many times in his official correspondence as a necessary, if regrettable, feature of the Egyptian scene.[115] It was also recognized and defended by many other Britons as well. As Fitzroy Bell, a visiting educational expert, put it in 1902, 'despotism is the only possible system [for British rule in Egypt] and those who administer government having no House of Commons, must justify their work at the bar of the civilised world as well as the high court of history'.[116]

Only a few of those who worked closest to Cromer were willing to point out, privately, some of the dangers involved. Clinton Dawkins at the Ministry of Finance observed, 'a man loses something of his best when he begins to consider himself quite indispensable, and he [Cromer] is certainly not as inclined to take trouble and to use his own eyes as his Memoirs show that he used to do'.[117] To Rodd, writing much later, this

[114] *Egyptian Gazette*, 22 June 1897.
[115] e.g. Cromer to Salisbury, 8 May 1896, CP/2, FO 633/6.
[116] R. Fitzroy Ball, 'Education in Egypt', *Nineteenth Century and After*, 52 (July–Dec. 1902), 412.
[117] Dawkins to Milner, 18 Sept. 1896, quoted in Marlowe, *Cromer in Egypt*, 232.

was the time when Cromer's authority became 'too exclusively personal', leading to the further development of the 'autocratic character to which he was temperamentally disposed'.[118]

Just how much Cromer himself was aware of the insidious temptations to which those with great personal power seem inevitably subject is unclear. On the one hand, he must certainly have read much of the huge literature on the subject, from Thucydides and Machiavelli to Shakespeare, Gibbon, and Lord Acton. On the other, he continued to pride himself on taking care to allow his junior colleagues to express themselves freely.[119] It also remained an article of faith that it was only the khedives who exhibited the vices of personal rule, or who would do so if allowed. And he was quick to criticize men like Riaz for failing to see that 'under the reign of law, he could not always have his own way'.[120]

Nevertheless, if we are to judge from his own actions, Cromer does not seem to have been particularly conscious of the dangers of relying on only a handful of people to keep him informed about the lives and aspirations of those he governed. Nor could he have been much aware of the way in which his personal identification with Egypt was making him more and more sensitive to public criticism of any and every aspect of Egyptian policy and administration. Perhaps there is even a hint of his somewhat unbalanced Egypt-centredness in Salisbury's well-known comment: 'If the world was falling to pieces round his ears, but Egypt was left intact, Lord Cromer would not ask for more.'[121]

Ethel, as always, remained a vital part of the Agency's public and private life, the more so as she grew increasingly socially confident with age and experience. It was she who arranged most of the winter entertainment, she who led the fun and games at the parties and dances, she who balanced Cromer's lack of social skills with a warmth and charm of her own.[122] She also provided her own strong judgement behind the scenes, conciliating people with a genuine kindness of heart and doing much to soften the somewhat misanthropic views of the increasingly influential Harry Boyle. A studio photograph of her taken in Cairo in the year of her death (1898) shows her in profile with a pencil in her right hand just under her chin,

[118] Rennell Rodd, *Social and Diplomatic Memories, 1894–1901*, 18–19.

[119] Gilbert, *Sir Horace Rumbold*, 11.

[120] e.g. Cromer, *Modern Egypt*, ii. 345.

[121] Quoted by the French Ambassador to Britain in a dispatch of 3 Oct. 1896, Lutfi al-Sayyid, *Egypt and Cromer*, 127–8.

[122] Caillard, *A Lifetime in Egypt*, 117–18; Rennell Rodd, *Social and Diplomatic Memories, 1894–1901*, 21.

leaning slightly forward to look intently at what we are supposed to take for a menu or a guest list or some other piece of domestic arrangement. Attached to her dress is the heart-shaped locket in which she kept pictures of her husband and children. Her brow is unfurrowed and the absence of wrinkles on her arms or neck, no doubt the result of the photographer's art, makes her look a good deal younger than 55.

Ethel also provided a more benevolent face for the Agency when it came to relations with both the European community and Egyptian society at large, driving about Cairo in a carriage by herself to offer help and condolence to families she knew, and giving liberally to hospitals, asylums, benevolent societies, and other charitable enterprises.[123] In all these ways, consciously or unconsciously, she helped to make the point that European women were freer than their Egyptian counterparts, and European domesticity, with its open mingling of the sexes, superior to that of the sexual segregation to be found in the Muslim world.

[123] Ibid. 106–7; Ethel's obituary notice, *Egyptian Gazette*, 17 Oct. 1898.

14

Sudan Again and the Tragedy of Ethel's Death
1895–1899

The Decision to Reconquer Sudan

Cromer's belief that even a defeated Khedive would continue to make trouble for the British provided the spur for his renewed emphasis on policies designed to ensure Egypt's economic growth. The rationale was well spelled out in a dispatch to Salisbury some years later. He was 'certain', he wrote, that,

as long as the occupation lasts, the Khedive and the small but influential class that look to the Khedive for guidance will maintain a position of irreconcilable hostility... [Hence] it is almost a political necessity that the mass of the people should be in such a condition of material prosperity as to render them proof against appeals to the sentiments of race hatred and religious fanaticism.[1]

The cornerstone of this policy was to be the construction of what was then known as a 'Nile reservoir' at Aswan. In the meantime, Egypt would benefit from the fact that revenues had begun to rise again once cotton prices recovered after the 1894 recession and the impact of the increased summer water from the Delta Barrage had worked its way through the system in terms of higher yields. To derive further advantage, a cadastral survey was begun in 1898, defining ownership rights and fixing tax obligations for the next thirty years on the principle of the Indian land settlements.

---

[1] 15 June 1898, SP, A/111.

The idea of building a water storage reservoir on the upper Nile was one which had been actively pursued since 1891, when the British engineer William Willcocks had been appointed the Director of Reservoir Studies. His investigation of possible sites was completed in 1893, resulting in the choice of Aswan on the grounds that the granite rock formation there provided not only a firm bed for the dam wall but also building materials for the dam itself. The proposal was then confirmed by an international commission called to Egypt for largely diplomatic reasons in order to facilitate a request for finance from the surplus fund held by the Caisse de la Dette.[2] Willcocks's final report summing up the whole matter appeared in 1895, and Cromer was anxious to start construction as quickly as possible in spite of the fact that the scheme involved flooding the ancient temple of Philae just to the south.

It was just at this moment, and to Cromer's considerable annoyance, that Lord Salisbury's new Conservative Cabinet decided, on 12 March 1896, to respond to the Italian defeat by the Ethiopians at the Battle of Adowa by, as Salisbury put it, using a military move designed to take the pressure off the Italians to 'plant the feet of Egypt rather further up the Nile'.[3] Even though Cromer had known for a long time that an expedition against what remained of the Mahdist power would be necessary at some stage, bitter experience had made him well aware how costly it might be. There was thus good reason to suppose such a move would postpone the reservoir project for some years. He was further annoyed that the decision was taken in London without consulting him first and without proper consideration of Egypt's own interest. As Ethel complained bitterly to Lady Anne Blunt, the whole thing had been decided 'over my husband's head'.[4] The result was a series of angry telegrams to London containing words which could well be taken to imply that, yet again, he was again willing to resign if not appeased.[5]

Salisbury now knew Cromer well enough to see that something had to be done. A decision was immediately taken that Cromer himself should be put in charge of the proposed military expedition, receiving his instructions from the Foreign Secretary not the War Office. By the same token, Cromer's own choice to lead the expedition, Herbert Kitchener, the new sirdar of the Egyptian Army, would be directly responsible to him and not to the military authorities in London. It helped that both Salisbury and

[2] William Willcocks, *Sixty Years in the East* (Edinburgh: W. Blackwood, 1935), 128.
[3] Salisbury to Cromer, 13 Mar. 1896, SP, A/55.   [4] Blunt, *My Diaries*, 220.
[5] Marlowe, *Cromer in Egypt*, 202.

Cromer shared a common distrust of the British general staff when it came either to keeping expenditures under control or to taking decisions which had obvious diplomatic ramifications. They may also have wanted to avoid the ambiguities about the chain of command which had dogged the Gordon relief expedition a decade earlier. Finally, Salisbury helped Cromer to mollify the angry Khedive, who was equally upset by the lack of preliminary consultation, and to persuade him to send a message of encouragement to his Egyptian troops.[6]

Once these initial difficulties had been solved, Salisbury and Cromer were able to continue the good working relationship which they had begun in the late 1880s. They trusted each other's competence and good sense, and they understood each other well enough to be able to keep their correspondence to essentials. All in all Salisbury found Cromer's particular combination of administrative, financial, military, and diplomatic skills to be exactly what was required to manage such a difficult campaign, as well as to reassure Parliament that its leadership was in good hands.

Cromer's relationship with Kitchener represented more of a challenge. Kitchener was unpopular with many of the British regular officers and was thought to lack sympathy for his troops. He had gained a reputation for military recklessness during the 1884–5 Sudan campaign. A further worry, from Cromer's personal point of view, was that Kitchener had private lines of communication with Lord Salisbury, first through his friendship with Salisbury's sister-in-law Lady Alice Cranborne, and second via his appointment of Salisbury's son Lord Edward Cecil as an aide-de-camp during the Sudan campaign. Indeed, Cromer had already had occasion to disapprove of Kitchener's lobbying for a march on Dongola while spending his 'annual weekend' with Salisbury and his family at Hatfield House in 1894.[7]

Nevertheless, the advantages clearly outweighed the disadvantages. Kitchener had been hard at work training the Egyptian Army for just such a campaign since 1892. He knew the terrain well. And Cromer had been sufficiently impressed by Kitchener's talent for finance and administration not to dwell on some of the more penny-pinching economies he had introduced, such as refusing to buy any new uniforms for his Egyptian soldiers.[8] Just as much to the point, Cromer felt confident in his own abilities to manage the situation. As he wrote to Lord Salisbury, 'I do not

[6] Blunt, *My Diaries*, 221.

[7] John Pollock, *The Road to Omdurman* (London: Constable, 1998), 88–9.

[8] Philip Warner, *Kitchener: The Man Behind the Legend* (New York: Athenaeum, 1986), 75.

anticipate any difficulty in being able to keep Kitchener in hand.'[9] Kitchener was equally positive, telling Salisbury's private secretary that Cromer was a 'splendid man to serve under; he does everything one can possibly want and has been most kind'.[10]

Now began one of those uneasy partnerships which were such a feature of imperial life. From the outside, Cromer and Kitchener might have seemed to have much in common. Both had a well-deserved reputation for brusqueness, both could be 'rude when bored or shy', both hated making public speeches. Indeed, many of the same stories seemed to circulate about them, illustrating their obvious boredom at parties and their embarrassment at having to make small talk with women.[11] Needless to say, these similarities went unrecognized by the men themselves, each feeling himself an example of quite a different type: the one a diplomat, international financier, and man of the world, the other a rough soldier with no time for frills of any kind and a determination to make his career by engineering the comprehensive defeat of the Mahdist forces. Yet both were keenly aware of how high the stakes were, how much they needed each other, and how neither could afford any of the embarrassments which had dogged the previous march on Khartoum. So each did his best to maintain the partnership, even though grumbling constantly about the other's pigheaded short-sightedness.

Cromer and Kitchener faced two immediate, and related, problems. One was a concern about the fighting ability of the new and largely untried Egyptian Army, particularly when faced with an enemy which would surely make every effort to win the Muslim troops over to its side. They were also concerned that if their army performed badly they might well have to call upon the assistance of regular units from Britain, something which would add enormously to the cost. For this reason both were anxious to make sure that the first engagement was conducted in as favourable a set of circumstances as possible.[12] And both were greatly relieved when the Egyptian troops fought well at Firket on the way to the initial target of Dongola, just over 200 miles south of Wadi Halfa, which was captured while Cromer was on holiday in Scotland in September.[13] The second worry was financial, made even more pressing by the fact that Cromer had managed to persuade Salisbury that the reservoir scheme was now even more important than ever as a way to ensure Egypt's future agricultural

[9] 17 May 1896, SP, A/55.   [10] Kitchener to Barrington, 21 May 1896, KP, 30/57/9.
[11] Pollock, *Road to Omdurman*, 287.
[12] Cromer to Salisbury, 13 June 1896, CP/2, FO 633/6.   [13] Cromer, *Modern Egypt*, ii. 90.

prosperity and hence its ability to pay for both the expedition itself and the administration of whatever parts of Sudan that it might recapture. The key to both problems was the approval of the Caisse to release money out of its now quite considerable reserves.

As it turned out, the way the first stage of the financial problem was solved proved highly gratifying. The application to the Caisse for the immediate release of £500,000 was approved by four of the commissioners against the dissent of the French and the Russian. Then, no sooner had the money been handed over than the transaction was challenged by the dissenting commissioners in the Mixed Tribunals. Finally, when the decision went against Cromer and the Egyptian government, and the money had to be returned, the British government was persuaded to step into the breech with a loan of £800,000, enough, in Kitchener's estimate, to allow the troops to push on to Berber in 1897 and the accompanying railway lines to be laid as far as Abu Hamad.[14] Kitchener himself was credited with doing much to influence the Chancellor of the Exchequer's decision while he was back for a brief visit to England in November, although it was Cromer who persuaded the Chancellor to lower the proposed rate of interest from 3.5 to 2.5 per cent.[15]

So far so good, but the next year's campaign proved much more difficult, as military success took the expedition further away from its Egyptian base. The move forward began, as always, in late summer, when the rising Nile allowed boats to negotiate the cataracts south of Wadi Halfa. Abu Hamad was captured at the end of July and Berber a month later. This in turn allowed the railway to be built across the desert to Abu Hamad, while opening up the alternative route between Berber and Suakin on the Red Sea.

It was then, however, that Kitchener's real troubles began. On the local front there was a real worry that the Khalifa's army's sudden evacuation of Berber with hardly a fight might be simply a feint to allow it to cut off the desert railway line. This, in turn, raised the question of if and when it might be necessary to call for British reinforcements to help fight the still undefeated enemy force thought to be lurking nearby. To make matters worse, it was just at this moment that the War Office announced the appointment of Grenfell as GOC Egypt, a move that could easily be interpreted as implying that he was to take over command of the combined army as soon as the first British troops arrived. Finally, Kitchener was

---

[14] Marlowe, *Cromer in Egypt*, 207.   [15] Ibid.

engaged in an increasingly acrimonious correspondence with Palmer in Cairo, who had much reduced the sum of money he had requested to garrison Kassala, a strategically important town recently evacuated by the Italians which commanded the plain between Khartoum and the Red Sea.

This accumulation of worries, combined with tiredness and overwork, drove Kitchener near to collapse. As he wrote to Clinton Dawkins on 6 November,

You have no idea what a continual anxiety, worry, and strain I have through it all. I do not think that I can stand much more, and I feel so completely done up that I can hardly go on and wish I were dead. Before next year's work in the field begins I must get some leave, or I shall break down.[16]

It was in this state that he sent a telegram to Cromer tendering his resignation on 18 October.[17] Cromer was not too worried, assuring Salisbury that Kitchener was subject to fits of depression from which 'he rapidly recovers'.[18] No doubt he was well able to remember moments in his own life when acute frustration had led him to offer his resignation for what, in retrospect, seemed largely tactical purposes. Nevertheless, he recognized the situation as sufficiently grave as to instruct Kitchener to hand over his command to his deputy for a month and return to Cairo.

Just how much Cromer may have contributed to the worsening situation is still a subject for debate. It was he, just as much as Palmer, who was responsible for vetoing the provision of sufficient money for a Kassala garrison. And, more generally, he was now much less keen than Kitchener to press on to Khartoum, warning Salisbury that such an effort was beyond the military and financial resources of Egypt.[19] Magnus also asserts that Cromer had been made aware that Grenfell's appointment was not intended to affect Kitchener's position, but had failed to pass on the information, thus needlessly adding to Kitchener's anguish.[20] Nevertheless, by inviting him back to Cairo, and then sending him off to Massawa to confer with the local Italian governor about the future of Kassala, Cromer not only allowed him some time to relax but was also able to use the occasion to address some of Kitchener's anxieties with considerable sympathy and tact. Above all, he was able to reassure him that he would remain in command whatever might happen, that funds to allow the garrisoning of

---

[16] Quoted in Pollock, *Road to Omdurman*, 111.   [17] KP, 37/57/11.
[18] Pollock, *Road to Omdurman*, 112.   [19] 22 Oct. 1897, SP, A/110.
[20] Philip Magnus, *Kitchener: Portrait of an Imperialist*, (London: John Murray, 1958), 107–8.

Kassala would now be forthcoming, and that he could call for a British brigade whenever he wanted.[21]

The moment Kitchener returned to active duty at Wadi Halfa, the whole situation changed yet again. Having been informed by Wingate, incorrectly as it turned out, that the whole of the Khalifa's army was about to march on Berber, he telegraphed Cromer to say that he and the Army would not be able to survive such an attack without the aid of British troops.[22] This was enough to cause Cromer to abandon all caution and to request immediate reinforcements in order to round off the campaign without further delay. More than this: riding the tide of enthusiasm in Britain, Cromer was able not just to ensure that the new troops would be under Kitchener's command but also that Britain would bear most of the cost.[23]

Meanwhile, another series of very important developments demanded Cromer's attention in the closing month of 1897. Anticipating correctly that the administration of the new Sudan would cost more than could be raised in revenue for some time to come, he looked around energetically for schemes to raise money, such as an abortive plan to borrow against the sale of the future rights to run the Sudanese railways. However, his main hope for increased revenues remained the rapid completion of the Nile reservoir, and here too he was adept at finding a way forward. When the British government refused his 1896 request for a £2 million grant or loan for the scheme, he turned to the private sector, sending Palmer to London for secret negotiations with the London engineering firm of Messrs Aird and Co. in February 1898.

The outcome was a complicated agreement by which Airds agreed to construct both dam and reservoir within five years, without receiving any money until the work was completed in 1903, and then accepting payment in instalments over the next thirty years.[24] This had the great advantage of circumventing a demand from the Caisse de la Dette that the contract be put out for international public tender, a measure that would not only have delayed matters for some years but might also have taken the whole business out of British hands.[25]

For reasons that remain unclear, but which probably have to do with the fact that the Egyptian government was forced to permit competitive bids

---

[21] Ibid. 112.   [22] Cromer, *Modern Egypt*, ii. 96.   [23] Zetland, *Lord Cromer*, 232–3.
[24] Cromer to Salisbury, 5 June 1897, SP, A/110; Saul, *La France et l'Égypte*, 641.
[25] Kurt Grunewald, ' "Windsor-Cassel": The Last Court Jew', *Leo Baeck Institute Yearbook*, 14 (1969), 135; Cromer to Revelstoke, 2 Feb. 1898, CP/2, FO 633/8.

in London, it was then necessary to borrow money in order to allow Airds immediate payment.[26] Letters to Salisbury and to Cromer's nephew Lord Revelstoke reveal some of the problems involved. The London market would not look at a public offering which was not backed by an unconditional guarantee. An approach to Barings was out of the question for reason of propriety. The Rothschilds also required a government guarantee which could not be granted, and was quite probably illegal under the various international treaties governing Egyptian finance.[27]

In this hour of need Cromer then turned to Sir Ernest Cassel, an independent financier, who had been coming to Egypt for his health for some years and who was quick to recognize that a close association with both the dam project in particular, and the British administration in general, could bring rich rewards.[28] Cromer and Cassel speedily negotiated a deal in which Cassel assumed financial responsibility on behalf of Airds, paying them off immediately and then being repaid himself by an Egyptian government loan over thirty years in half-yearly instalments, the equivalent of a forty-year loan at 6 per cent.[29] There was immediate British cabinet agreement allowing the contract between Airds and the Egyptian government to be signed on 20 February 1898.[30] Cassel, meanwhile, ceded the Egyptian government's drafts issued in advance to cover the cost of Airds' work to a new company, the Irrigation Investment Corporation Ltd. The Corporation raised the £4,700,000 needed to pay off the drafts by issuing shares at 4 per cent, before going into voluntary liquidation in 1902.[31] It was a sound investment all round.

Triumph and Tragedy in 1898

In February 1898 the Cromers and the Grenfells took a cruise up the Nile. The purpose was twofold: to see something of the newly reconquered parts of northern Sudan and to meet Cassel at Aswan. Unfortunately, their steamer ran aground on a reef at Nag Hamadi on the way south and,

[26] Helen E. Jeffries, 'Sir John Aird', *DBB* i. 18.
[27] Cromer to Revelstoke, 2 Feb. 1898, to Salisbury, 4 Jan. 1898, CP/2, FO 633/6.
[28] Brian Connell suggests that Cromer had recognized Cassel's financial acumen when he visited Egypt on behalf of Bischoffsheims Bank in the 1870s; *Manifest Destiny: A Study of the Rise and Influence of the Mountbatten Family* (London: Cassell, 1953), 71.
[29] Grunewald, 'Windsor-Cassel', 135.
[30] Marlowe, *Cromer in Egypt*, 227.
[31] Saul, *La France et l'Égypte*, 641.

although it was refloated with the help of what Boyle called a 'levée en masse' of 600 local men and five steam tugs, they decided to go back to Cairo without having seen Sir Ernest.[32] The major reason for the sudden change of plan was the return of Ethel's old illness.[33] She had already been ill enough the previous year to send her husband instructions concerning what she had thought was her approaching death. If she died in Cairo, she wrote on 9 April 1897, she wanted a Bahinia tree planted over her grave with a plain white cross and the simple words 'Ethel Stanley, the Devoted Wife of Evelyn Baring, Lord Cromer . . . So it may require little care.' And if in England, not with her father and sister in Kensal Green, but far away from any large town. Perhaps in the churchyard at Hooton, near the old family home in Cheshire? At any rate, not in a closed vault but in the sunshine among the flowers.[34]

Now that her sense of imminent death had returned, she wrote again on 31 March 1898: 'My Own Darling: final parting cannot be far off.' The children had no better example than their father, 'for there never was a character like yours'. If she died in Egypt, she wanted to be buried in England with the chain and locket 'with your dear face and those of the children' and the gold crucifix 'you gave me'.[35] Soon after, she returned to London to see a medical specialist. His official diagnosis was that her health had improved and she would be able to return to Cairo after a prolonged rest. But Major Herbert Dent, the doctor she consulted next, was convinced that she had brought pressure to bear to ensure that Cromer would not have to leave his post at such a critical time when Kitchener's Anglo-Egyptian army was beginning its move towards Khartoum. Dent concluded that she had only a few months to live. He was called several times in the night to administer injections of what was probably morphine to ease the heart-pain which was a major symptom of her Bright's disease.

In these grim circumstances Dent felt that he should write to inform Evelyn. However, when he showed her the letter, she tore it up saying, 'it would bring my husband home'. A few nights later, after a particularly alarming attack, he took matters into his own hands, talking to Cromer's sister Cecilia, who was staying nearby. It was Cecilia's letter that finally brought Cromer home in July. At Ethel's request, they both travelled to their house in Scotland.[36]

---

[32] Boyle to Mrs Boyle, 23 Feb. 1898, BP, box B, file 2.
[33] Cromer to Cassel, 26 Feb. 1898, CP/2, FO 633/6.
[34] CP/1, Letters and papers of 1st Lady Cromer.   [35] Ibid.
[36] Major Herbert C. Dent, 'The First Lady Cromer', *The Graphic*, 6 Jan. 1923.

Meanwhile, back in northern Sudan, events were moving towards their climax. On the military side, the fact that the British troops had started to arrive in January meant that it was going to have to be a summer campaign. The advance began again in March and the army soon encountered a large force of the Ansar under Uthman Diqna camped near the point where the River Atbara joins the Nile. For a few days Kitchener was unable to make up his mind how to proceed and begged Cromer for advice. After a rapid exchange of telegrams seeking other opinions Cromer first suggested caution and then that Kitchener attack.[37] Perhaps emboldened by this advice Kitchener order an advance on Good Friday, 8 April, and routed the enemy.

The way was now open to Khartoum, less than 200 miles to the south. Kitchener spent the next four months in summer camp receiving further reinforcements and preparing for the final advance. By the time the Anglo-Egyptian army set off again in late August it contained some 25,800 men, nearly a third of whom were British. Its finances were also assured after the June decision in London that the previous £800,000 advanced as a loan could now be treated as a grant, and that another £750,000 should be made available to meet the costs of the rest of the campaign.

On the diplomatic front, the key intervention was made by Salisbury, who, in a telegram to Cromer on 3 June, proposed that the whole of Sudan, from Wadi Halfa to Wadalai (on the present Sudan–Uganda border), should be treated not as de jure Egyptian territory dominated temporarily by rebels but as an independent and sovereign Mahdist state.[38] The distinction was of the greatest importance. Not only did it suggest a way of detaching Sudan from the Ottoman Empire, its previous suzerain, but it also created a separate Anglo-Egyptian position by right of conquest. This, in turn, would help to deter the other European powers with designs on parts of Sudan, notably the French, who had already dispatched an expedition under Colonel Marchand to establish a post on the Nile at Fashoda, some 400 miles to the south of Khartoum.

To make the point absolutely clear, Salisbury also proposed that when Khartoum was finally captured, the British and Egyptian flags would fly side by side, 'as a symbol of the judicial equality of the two conquerors'.[39] Cromer had some initial doubts about the plan, perhaps because it involved a continuation of the ambiguities that had dogged his policies in Egypt. But a week later was telling Salisbury that he now liked the idea 'very much'.[40]

[37] Magnus, *Kitchener*, 119–20.   [38] PRO, FO 78/5050.   [39] Ibid.
[40] 11 June 1898, CP/2, FO 633/7.

Cromer was still nursing Ethel when the next round of discussions about the future of Sudan took place at a cabinet meeting of 25 July which he was asked to attend. It had before it a memorandum sent by Cromer himself from Cairo the month before. The 'two-flags' policy was formally agreed with the proviso that, as Cromer had suggested, the Khedive be informed that 'HMG consider they have a predominant voice in all matters connected with the Sudan'. The Cabinet also adopted Cromer's suggestion that, following the capture of Khartoum, two flotillas of gunboats be sent south. One was to sail up the Blue Nile to hoist the two flags at Roseires on the putative border with Abyssinia. A second, larger, one, under Kitchener's command, was to proceed up the White Nile to establish whether the French expedition had arrived at Fashoda, and, if so, to lay claim to the territory, making a formal protest, and establishing posts upstream and downstream of the French position.[41]

Early in August Cromer received a telegram from Kitchener warning him that he should be back in Cairo by 1 September.[42] However, Ethel's health did not allow it and they were still in Caithness when the Queen sent a messenger with news that the Battle of Omdurman had been fought and won on 2 September.[43] The Cromers returned to Egypt together, against Dr Dent's advice, and were back in Cairo by 4 October. Ethel survived the journey in spite of a bad moment in rough seas.[44] But she took to her bed in the great late summer heat and by 12 October was showing signs of collapse. She stopped taking any nourishment, her heart attacks became more frequent, and on Sunday 16 October she died at six in the evening, just after a Catholic chaplain had finished saying the prayers for the dead.[45] The death certificate gave 'heart failure' as the cause of death, but, as Cromer informed his son Rowland, it was kidney disease that 'really killed her'.[46]

Boyle, writing to his mother on 14 October, described how Cromer's self-control was 'almost too painful to see . . . But at times he goes out into the garden with me and allows his heart and grief a little flow.'[47] On the same day Cromer had written to Ethel's sister:

[41] Roberts, *Salisbury*, 696–7; Marlowe, *Cromer in Egypt*, 216.
[42] Cromer, *Modern Egypt*, ii. 103.
[43] Ibid. 103–4.
[44] Dent, 'First Lady Cromer'; Rennell Rodd, *Diplomatic and Political Memories, 1894–1901*, 239.
[45] Ibid. 239–41.
[46] Cromer to Rowland (Viscount Errington), 20 Oct. 1898, CP/4.
[47] BP, box B, file 2.

My Dearest Venetia,
    It is nearly all over. She cannot speak but is a bit conscious and recognizes me. She kissed me for you and sent her fondest love before she was ill. There is absolutely no hope, but it is impossible to say how long it may last. It is, however, inconceivable that she should be alive when this reaches you.
    Affectionately, Cromer.[48]

    Cromer was too overcome by grief to attend either the Requiem Mass at St Joseph's Church on 19 October or the Memorial Service at All Saints' Church the following Sunday. Dean Butcher, the British chaplain, preached the All Saints' sermon, in which he begged that Cromer and his two sons be supported by those four consolers: 'sympathy, memory, time and that belief in a future life which shone out in every act and word of the wife and mother who has gone before them to her rest'.[49] Kitchener, who was back in Cairo from his confrontation with Marchand at Fashoda, visited the Agency the day before Ethel's death, moving Cromer to write:

Like most Englishmen I find it difficult to express my feelings when I am really moved and I do not think that I adequately expressed to you on Saturday how deeply I have been touched by your sympathy & consideration in my present crushing sorrow. I know it is heartfelt.

He then went on say that 'all the credit of the [Sudan] campaign is due to you', and concluded:

all my interest in public affairs is now gone but I shall go round[?] the mile[?] & not give up. That further distinction awaits you I cannot doubt. Whatever happens you will always find in me a true friend.[50]

    Ethel's body was sent back to England on 20 October as she had wished. She was buried on 11 November in the Wimborne Road Cemetery in Bournemouth in the presence of her two sons. It was not quite the country churchyard she had mentioned in the letter to her husband—her Victorian desire to sleep 'within the church's shade' being difficult to arrange for Catholics—but still peaceful enough even today with the graves scattered under tall umbrella pines.[51] There was a white cross, as she had instructed,

---

[48] CP/1.
[49] The text can be found in CP/2, FO 633/35.
[50] 19 Oct. 1898, KP, 30/57/14.
[51] Quotation from Elizabeth Stone, *God's Acre; or, Historical Notices Relating to Churchyards* (1858), in Michael Wheeler, *Death and the Future Life in Victorian Literature and Theology* (Cambridge: Cambridge University Press, 1990), 57.

and the simple inscription: 'Ethel Stanley, Wife of Evelyn, First Viscount Cromer, Died at Cairo, October 16th 1898'. An adjacent plot was purchased at the same time for her sister Venetia, who was laid to rest next to her only two years later.[52] According to Cromer's 'Biographical Notes', Bournemouth was chosen because it was where 'she had passed some happy months with her children'.[53]

Friends and relatives did what they could to comfort him. One couple with whom Cromer found particular solace was the Grenfells, who had always been very close to Ethel. Returning from Sudan, Francis Grenfell had gone to see him on 25 October to find him 'broken and much altered'. A month later Grenfell wrote in his diary that 'we have seen a great deal of him lately. He likes to come quietly to us as he knows the great friendship which existed between my wife and Lady Cromer.'[54] It was quickly arranged that Cromer's niece Nina Baring, the daughter of his brother Walter, should come out within a month to act as the temporary mistress of the Agency.

Rowland and Windham also came out to Cairo for Christmas and must have provided great comfort for their grieving father.[55] On 27 December they all went with Gorst and Boyle to Luxor, where they toured the Valley of the Kings, and then on by steamer to Aswan and Wadi Halfa, a journey that must have been a painful reminder of the two cruises with Ethel, the second only eleven months before. They took the newly built desert railway to Khartoum, arriving there on 3 January. The next day they toured the adjacent town of Omdurman in the morning, examining the houses of the Mahdi and the Khalifa, while Cromer made a number of speeches to British soldiers and officials, as well as to one gathering of local shaikhs, at which he told them that they would now be ruled by the Queen of England and the Khedive of Egypt.[56] More controversially, and in order to allay their fears of Christian domination, Cromer also announced that there would be no interference with their religion. Later, in answer to a question, he replied that this promise included the continued application of the Muslim 'Sacred Law', as well as the principle of 'Quieta non movere'

---

[52] Information from the Wimborne Road Cemeteries Office kindly provided by Father Terence Healy of the Church of the Sacred Heart, Bournemouth, at which Ethel's funeral service was held.

[53] BN 370–1.

[54] GrenP, entries for 29 Oct. and 19 Nov. 1898.

[55] The day after Ethel's death Cromer had written to Rowland, 'I am so lonely and none but my beloved children can cheer me'; 17 Oct. 1898, CP/4.

[56] Mellini, Gorst, 71; Blunt, My Diaries, 310–11.

('Let sleeping dogs lie') as far as slavery was concerned.[57] 'God knows what they made of it,' wrote Gorst, referring both to the speech itself and to Boyle's somewhat free and easy, sentence by sentence, translation.[58] But it was certainly enough to cause great concern in anti-slavery, missionary, and other circles in Britain, something which contributed to Cromer's insistence that missionaries be kept out of Sudan until the situation had stabilized.

The party visited the battlefield in the afternoon, and the next day Cromer laid the foundation stone for Kitchener's pet project, Gordon Memorial College. As Boyle described the scene to his mother,

There was a big show of troops and the whole ceremony was done which much state and pomp. Our costumes were quaint, especially the dear old 'Lord's', for he was in a helmet, khaki riding breeches, and coat with insignia and ribbons of the Bath across it. I sported my usual riding kit and top boots.[59]

Cromer never really recovered from Ethel's death. He had loved her deeply for thirty-five years and been happily married to her for twenty-two. She was his partner, his companion and confidante, and the only person, apart from his children, with whom he felt emotionally comfortable and able to express the kinder side of his nature. Their marriage was his 'school of affection'. Their love was forever strengthened by her repeated illness and a sense that they were living on borrowed time. Her memory was ever with him. The annual anniversary of her death was always full of 'the saddest memories of the past'.[60]

Ethel is referred to in 'Nunc Dimittis', one of Cromer's paraphrases of Greek verse written in the early 1900s:

> Holding my husband's hand with ebbing breath,
> I praised the gods of Marriage and of Death,
> These that I gave my love to such as he.
> Those that he lives our children's stay to be.[61]

She is also twice mentioned anonymously in *Modern Egypt*, as the one 'who inspired it to be written', as well as the partner who helped him

---

[57] Zetland, *Lord Cromer*, 218–19; Taj Hargey, 'Festina Lente: Slavery Policy and Practice in the Anglo-Egyptian Sudan', *Slavery and Abolition*, 19/2 (Aug. 1998), 251.

[58] GrenP, entry for 4 Jan. 1899.

[59] Quoted in Boyle, *Boyle of Cairo*, 103.

[60] Cromer to Katherine Cromer, 16 Oct. 1903, CP/5, box 1, file 1.

[61] The Earl of Cromer, *Paraphrases and Translations from the Greek* (London: Macmillan, 1903), 98.

introduce a 'high standard of morality' into Egyptian social life.[62] Long after her death he continued to turn to her memory for strength and for guidance. And, in spite of the fact that he remarried in 1901, he was buried next to Ethel in the Bournemouth cemetery, an unusual arrangement but one which reflects the conventional Victorian desire that a husband and wife should lie together until the Resurrection.[63]

Sudan

It was decided that Salisbury's two-flags formula should be set out in the form of a convention between the British and Egyptian governments. Cromer sent a draft prepared by the judicial adviser under his direction to London on 10 November. It was then subject to some revision as a result of a meeting between Salisbury and Kitchener in which Kitchener objected to the fact that it suggested too much control from Cairo, particularly over the expenditure of money.[64] One of the key words in Kitchener's argument was the use of the bogey of 'centralization' to condemn Cromer's attempt to exert total control, a point that was then passed on to Cairo by Salisbury in a dispatch warning against 'that mania for paper piling which is the endemic pest of British Departments'.[65]

The convention was signed by Cromer and Butros Ghali, the Egyptian Foreign Minister, on 19 January, as soon as Cromer returned from his Nile trip. Supreme military and civil command was vested in a governor-general appointed by khedivial decree on the recommendation of Her Majesty's Government. He could make laws provided they were notified to the British Agent and the Egyptian Prime Minister. Egypt and Sudan were to constitute what would now be known as an economic customs union with a common external tariff, but would remain politically separate. Hence no Egyptian law would apply to Sudan unless specifically proclaimed by the Governor-General. Furthermore, there were to be no special privileges for the subjects of foreign powers, nor were they to be considered within the jurisdiction of the Egyptian Mixed Tribunals.

[62] Cromer, *Modern Egypt*, ii. 104, 322–3.

[63] Wheeler, *Death and Future Life*, 2, 48, 55.

[64] M. W. Daly, *Empire on the Nile: The Anglo-Egyptian Sudan 1898–1934* (Cambridge: Cambridge University Press, 1986), 16–17.

[65] Salisbury to Cromer, 9 Dec. 1898, quoted in Marlowe, *Cromer in Egypt*, 218.

The convention was not popular with either the Khedive or Egyptian opinion in general. The members of the Cabinet were particularly embarrassed as, according to Blunt, they had been going around saying that Sudan had been conquered for Egypt.[66] Meanwhile, the Legislative Council attached a statement to its annual budget report stating that Sudan was part of Egypt.[67] The British obsession with avenging Gordon also called for some trenchant comment from Mustafa Kamil. 'Is the blood of one Englishman of higher price,' he asked rhetorically in December 1898, 'while the blood of thousands has no price and gets nothing but oblivion?'[68] To add insult to injury from an Egyptian point of view, Egypt had to make good Sudan's annual deficits of some £E1,500,000 until 1914, as well as financing all its capital expenditure.

Cromer sent Kitchener a copy of the convention together with an official letter setting out his view of the new relationship between Cairo and Khartoum. He wanted to 'control the big questions', he wrote, 'but to leave all the detail and execution to be managed locally'.[69] In a second, private letter he offered Kitchener some instructions and advice, which, however honestly given, must have been regarded by Kitchener as gratuitous and unnecessary. 'Pray encourage your subordinates to speak out and tell you when they do not agree with you,' keep a 'sense of proportion', and 'pray keep me informed and consult me fully'.[70]

Cromer did his best to defend Kitchener's conduct of the last stages of the battle and the attack on Omdurman itself. News had rapidly reached London of the killing of some of the Ansar wounded, the failure to provide medical attention to many others left on the battlefield to die, the destruction of the Mahdi's tomb, and the throwing of the Mahdi's skeleton, less the skull, into the Nile.[71] The *Manchester Guardian* led the charge together with Ernest Bennett, who wrote a highly critical piece in the *Contemporary Review*.[72] Questions were asked in Parliament, and there was some opposition to the proposal to award Kitchener a parliamentary grant of £30,000 from a 'grateful nation'. Even the Queen was upset. Although she was pleased that Gordon had been avenged, the 'destruction of the poor body

[66] Blunt, *My Diaries*, 310.

[67] Abd al-Rahman al-Rafi'i, *Mustafa Kamil ba'ith al-haraka al-wataniya* (Cairo: Maktabat al-Nahda al-Misriya, 1962), 370–4.

[68] Speech of 23 Dec. 1898, quoted in Powell, 'Colonized Colonizers', 170–1.

[69] 19 Jan. 1899, KP, 30/57/11.

[70] Ibid.

[71] e.g. Wilfrid Blunt's letter to *The Times*, 10 Sept. 1898.

[72] Ernest Bennett, 'After Omdurman', *Contemporary Review*, 75 (Jan. 1899), 18–33.

of a man who, whether he was very bad or cruel, after all was a man of a certain importance . . . savours in the Queen's opinion, too much of the Middle Ages'.[73]

Cromer forwarded a letter from Kitchener to Salisbury denying that his troops had carried out any massacres of the wounded.[74] Cromer, for his part, told Salisbury that he thought the destruction of the Mahdi's tomb was 'not only justifiable, but necessary'.[75] But he was more cautious about the treatment of the Mahdi's bones, saying that, if they had been reburied in the ordinary cemetery, 'no one would have said a word'.[76] When the Government published a short, three-page, White Paper in March designed to quieten public opinion, two of Cromer's letters were used in Kitchener's defence.[77] Whether these reflect his real views, or stem from his usual habit of defending his subordinates, it is impossible to say.

For a while Cromer did nothing to discourage Kitchener's extravagant rebuilding of Khartoum, defending him against his own Cairo officials, who were quick to condemn such excess. However, such support became increasingly difficult as Kitchener not only refused to consult him before making his decisions but also neglected to provide details of how the annual subvention from Cairo was being spent.[78] There was more friction in March when, by abolishing the extra allowances awarded to all ranks of the Egyptian Army serving in Sudan, Kitchener seemed to be privileging British junior officers over their Egyptian colleagues. Cromer tried to get the order cancelled but Kitchener refused.

Martin Daly is certainly correct that the valley of the Nile could scarcely contain 'two such imperious and ambitious men'.[79] Cromer's constant grumbling in private gives a sense that all his initial respect for Kitchener was slipping away. Kitchener did not see with sufficient clearness the 'difference between governing a country and commanding a regiment', he told Salisbury in April 1899.[80] In May he persuaded Kitchener to come to Cairo to discuss yet another contentious issue, Kitchener's refusal to allow trade in grain with the famine-stricken areas south of Khartoum on

[73] Quoted in Magnus, *Kitchener*, 135.

[74] Enclosure in Cromer to Salisbury, 17 Feb. 1899, quoted in Daly, *Empire on the Nile*, 3.

[75] 17 Feb. 1899, quoted in Daly, *Empire on the Nile*, 5.

[76] Cromer to Salisbury, 2 Mar. 1899, quoted in Daly, *Empire on the Nile*, 6.

[77] 'Dispatches from Her Majesty's Agent and Consul-General in Egypt respecting the conduct of British and Egyptian troops following the Battle of Omdurman', *PP* (1898) 112, 921–3.

[78] Magnus, *Kitchener*, 149; Kitchener to Wingate, 1 Feb. 1899, quoted in Daly, *Empire on the Nile*, 32.

[79] Daly, *Empire on the Nile*, 30.

[80] Cromer to Salisbury, 22 Apr. 1899, CP/2, FO 633/7.

the grounds that they still contained the remains of the Mahdist forces. But when Cromer begged Kitchener to remember that he was a civilized Christian ruler who was dealing with human beings, not blocks of wood, Kitchener exploded, saying that he had had enough of Sudan and would seek employment in India.[81] No wonder that, as Boyle wrote to his mother, 'the Lord sees Sudan like Sisyphus', and that just as Cromer thought he saw some prospect of getting his Egyptian stone to the top, the Gods threw him another 'and told him to roll that one too'.[82]

Cromer and Kitchener both went back to Britain for the summer. While Cromer must have experienced a very painful return to the home he had shared with Ethel in Caithness, Kitchener made a triumphal tour of English country houses, lobbying Lord Salisbury for a job in either India or South Africa. The two men had another, more friendly, discussion about Sudanese finance in Cairo on their return. However, the problem of their vexed relationship was only put to rest by Kitchener's appointment to take command of British troops fighting the Boers in South Africa in December. He was succeeded by Wingate, whose first task was to put down a brief mutiny by a Sudanese battalion against its British officers, prompted, so Cromer believed, by Kitchener's neglect of the Egyptian and Sudanese troops.[83] Cromer's relations with Wingate proved very much easier, although not without their particular stresses and strains whenever he believed Wingate was trying to run Sudan without reference to Egyptian interests. 'The only reason why the British flag is flying [in Khartoum] . . . is to avoid the Capitulations,' Cromer told him in March 1904, after Wingate had imposed a 10 per cent export duty on cattle to Egypt. 'Pray get all these ideas of independence out of the heads of your officials.'[84]

Cromer summed up his feelings about Kitchener in a letter written to Revelstoke shortly after his departure. Kitchener was a good military organizer, he allowed, but he had a mania for economy and was the 'most arbitrary and unjust man I ever met'. His only touch of human nature was when he 'wept like a child at my wife's funeral'. As for Sudan, the only thing which appears to have interested him was 'a ridiculous palace wherewith he entertains the Duchess of Portland, Lady Cranborne, etc. This—I mean the construction of a huge public building before anything else—is what the French do before they begin to misgovern a new colony. I hate it.'[85]

[81] Cromer to Salisbury, 19 May 1899, CP/2, FO 633/7; Magnus, *Kitchener*, 151.

[82] 6 Apr. 1899, BP, box 2, file 2.   [83] Magnus, *Kitchener*, 153–4.

[84] Cromer to Wingate, 25 Jan. 1904, CP/2, FO 633/8.

[85] 22 Feb. 1900, BA, 203076, Partners' File: Supplementary Set.

15

Years of Economic Success
1900–1904

The Advantages and Disadvantages of European Investment

The year 1898 marked a famous victory not only over the Khalifa's army but also over the French. In the first place France had been outmanoeuvred in its attempt to use the Caisse to prevent Egypt's reserves from being spent on both the military expedition and the proposed dam at Aswan. Secondly, the appearance of Cassel, as well as his ability to work with local bankers like the Suarès brothers, who had formerly been closely identified with French capital, opened up the way for British investment in a way that Cromer had long been trying to promote.[1] One of the first fruits of this was the creation of the National Bank of Egypt, an institution designed by Cromer and Palmer as a counter to the Caisse, as well as to the pretensions of the French-dominated Imperial Ottoman Bank to play an important role in Egypt's financial affairs.[2]

The importance of Cassel's role in all this cannot be overemphasized. He had good connections not only with the Rothschilds but also with the local Jewish bankers in Egypt, who were already playing an important role in financing public works schemes.[3] Most significant of all, he had won Cromer's confidence during his winter visits to Egypt in the 1890s, while also fostering a close association with Elwin Palmer which was to bring

---

[1] Saul, *La France et l'Égypte*, 649, 651; Cromer to Carver, 18 Dec. 1895, CP/2, FO 633/8.

[2] Cromer to Lord Hillingdon, 21 May 1898, CP/2, FO 633/8; J. Thobie, 'European Banks in the Middle East', in Rondo Cameron and V. I. Bovykin (eds.), *International Banking, 1870–1914* (New York: Oxford University Press, 1990), 411–12.

[3] Robert Vitalis, *When Capitalists Collide: Business Conflict and the End of Empire in Egypt* (Berkeley: University of California Press, 1995), 33–8; Gudrun Krämer, *The Jews of Modern Egypt, 1914–1952* (Seattle: University of Washington Press, 1989), 39–41.

them both rich rewards. Hence, when Cromer needed money for the Nile expedition and the dam, Cassel was well placed to help, and then to promote other enterprises of his own.

It is not clear how much attention Cromer himself was able to pay to the details of the schemes negotiated between Cassel and Palmer, notably the creation of the National Bank of Egypt and the sale of the remaining 300,000 feddans (1 feddan = approximately 1 acre) of Daira Saniya land, both of which were announced towards the end of June 1898. He was personally preoccupied with the final drive towards Khartoum, as well as, from February onwards, with Ethel's failing health. Nevertheless, the schemes undoubtedly had his overall blessing. It was only later that he began to understand that, from an Egyptian government point of view, too much had been given away.

The concessions for both the bank and the sale of the Daira Saniya properties had first been obtained by Ralph Suarès, who travelled with them to Europe looking for financial support. He was advised to see Cassel, who immediately realized their importance.[4] The bank would provide him with significant influence, while the Daira Saniya estates offered the prospect of large profits once land prices began to rise in anticipation of impact of the Aswan Dam and its related canals on agricultural productivity.

The National Bank was a private company with an initial capital of £E1 million, half of which was provided by Cassel on behalf of himself and a group of London financiers.[5] It was to act as the government's treasurer, holding all its balances except those designated for the Caisse. It also had a monopoly over the right to issue banknotes. Later, in 1899, it opened an agricultural loans department, as Cromer wished, and in 1902 this was hived off as a separate company, the Agricultural Bank of Egypt, with Cassel again as an important shareholder. Cromer's official interest in the Agricultural Bank is shown by the fact that he agreed to a government guarantee of a minimum return of 4 per cent on its capital, while allowing tax inspectors to assume responsibility for the collection of the principal and interest on its agricultural loans.[6]

[4] Grunwald, 'Windsor-Cassel', 135–6.

[5] Ibid. 136; A. E. Crouchley, *Investment of Foreign Capital in Egyptian Companies and the Public Debt*, Ministry of Finance Technical Paper, no. 12 (Cairo, 1936), 32.

[6] Samir Saul, 'European Capital and Its Impact on Land Distribution in Egypt: A Quantitative Analysis (1900–1914)', in Gregory Blue, Martin Bunton, and Ralph Crozier (eds.), *Colonialism and the Modern World* (Armonk, NY: M. E. Sharpe, 2002), 135.

The formation of the Daira Estates Company was a more complicated scheme, and this may be one of the reasons why Cromer took some time to comprehend its implications. At root it involved the purchase of the Daira's remaining properties for just over £E6,400,000, the amount outstanding on the loan for which they still stood as security. Furthermore, although the properties were not actually to be handed over to the new company until February 1905, sales were allowed to begin at once.[7] The company set up to perform these operations involved a consortium put together by Cassel in London and Suarès in Egypt.[8] Meanwhile, the sugar factories and associated light railways, which were also part of the Daira Saniya estates, were sold off to another local company, the Société Générale des Sucreries et de la Raffinerie d'Égypte, in 1902.[9] In these circumstances it must have been extremely difficult for anyone outside Cassel's small circle to work out how much money had actually been made. Nevertheless, Cromer became firmly convinced that the Government had sold off one of its prize assets on the cheap. As he wrote to Revelstoke in December 1903, 'I tear my hair over having allowed Cassel to make such scandalous profits.'[10]

The privatization of state institutions and assets has always been something of a hit-and-miss operation, especially when it comes to the calculation of a 'fair' price. In turn-of-the-century Egypt the practice was still in its infancy, with the largest sale so far, that of the Khedivial Steamship Company in 1897, worth only £E150,000. Administrators worth their salt have to learn from their mistakes. They also have to deal with the consequences of the fact that some of their top officials leave for better-paying jobs in the expanding private sector. Palmer's move to become the first Governor of the National Bank was followed by officials of the quality of Victor Hariri and many others.[11] The result was not only a drain of skilled personnel but also a worry about possible conflicts of interest. Similar ethical problems were raised by the use made by some irrigation engineers of their advance information about the height of the Nile to influence the cotton futures market for private profit.[12] At least as early as 1900 Mu-

[7] Saul, *La France et l'Égypte*, 648.

[8] Pat Thane, 'Sir Ernest Joseph Cassel', *DBB*, i. 607.

[9] Roger Owen, 'The Egyptian Sugar Industry, 1870–1914', in Bill Albert and Adrian Graves (eds.), *Crisis and Change in the International Sugar Industry Economy, 1860–1914* (Norwich: ISC Press, 1984), 221–3.

[10] 6 Dec. 1903, BA, 203076, Partners' File: Supplementary Set. Cromer must also have been aware of the fact that no sooner had shares in the Daira Saniya Company been put on the market than they appreciated enormously in value; Saul, *La France et l'Égypte*, 677.

[11] Cromer to Windham (Baring), 23 June 1904, BA, 203076, Partners' File: Supplementary Set.

[12] Boyle to Mrs Boyle, 12 Apr. 1900, BP, box B, file 3.

hammad Abduh was telling Blunt that, although he had a good opinion of Cromer personally, 'there are a number of shady things done by his subordinates'.[13]

Cromer, for his part, was clearly aware of the need to maintain his own reputation for financial integrity. As he wrote to Revelstoke in 1905 to explain why he could not use Barings to sell bonds in Egypt, he lived in a 'glass house' where any suspicion of impropriety would bring immediate opposition from all those 'he has refused to bribe, every corrupt official whose illicit income he has curtailed . . . and every unofficial scamp in this putrid heterogeneous society whose infamous practices have in one form or another been checked by my instrumentality'.[14] It is also possible to document occasions on which he reprimanded public officials for abusing their position for their own gain, for example, Harry Crookshank, the British director of the Daira Saniya, who was told that it was 'highly improper' that he should have purchased Daira land himself.[15] Nevertheless, as Cromer admitted in 1907, he had been unable to devise guidelines to prevent British officials from speculating in land.[16] As a result, he could only try moral exhortation or, in the case of someone like Palmer, whose willingness to grant large overdrafts to the National Bank's directors both Cromer and Cassel found questionable, the appointment of a 'strong successor'.[17] It was an approach which won the approval not only of Muhammad Abduh but also of Wilfrid Blunt, who described Cromer as the 'only guarantee we have at present against a new era of speculation and financial jobbery'.[18]

As the years went by, Cromer also began to express a certain disenchantment with Cassel himself. Apart from the evidence of Cassel's 'good pile' from the Aswan loan, and that he had outwitted Cromer over the Daira Saniya properties, he was also closely connected with the new King, Edward VII, who was known to dislike Cromer on account of the fact that he and his wife had refused to see the King's favourite mistress, Mrs Keppel, when she visited Cairo in 1902–3.[19] Cassel owed this connection to the fact that he had acted as investment adviser to both the King and

[13] Entry of 15 Feb. 1900, Blunt, My Diaries, 349–50.

[14] 15 Nov. 1905, BA, 203076, Partners' File: Supplementary Set.   [15] CP/2, FO 633/8.

[16] AR 1906, PP (1907) 100, 668–9.

[17] Cromer to Revelstoke, 16 Feb. 1906, BA, 203076, Partners' File: Supplementary Set. The largest of these overdrafts was said to be the huge sum of £E400,000.

[18] Diary entry for 17 Mar. 1905, quoted in Longford, Pilgrimage of Passion, 359.

[19] Cromer to Bell, 11 Nov. 1902, MBL, TA (1900–10); Hardinge to Grey, 13 Apr. 1906, PRO, FO 800/92.

his lady.[20] Soon he was doing the same with the Khedive, making him a loan of £E500,000 in 1904 in 'exchange for certain concessions'. Cromer was furious as this threatened to undermine his own policy of keeping Abbas on as short a financial rein as possible so as to prevent him from being able to subsidize anti-British activity.[21] Still, as he told Revelstoke in 1905, he preferred Cassel to the Rothschilds.[22] Cassel was easier to deal with and more willing to consider a much wider variety of schemes. He might have added that, after the Anglo-French Agreement of 1904, Cassel was less able to play London off against Paris at the highest level.[23] Above all, Cassel remained an important link to the type of French capital investors whom Cromer wished to encourage because they helped to support the political status quo in Egypt.[24]

Cromer found an admirable adjutant in Eldon Gorst. There had been a short period before 1898 when Gorst had been out of favour, with Cromer switching to Palmer as his main confidant.[25] But then, when Palmer decided to opt for the easier and more rewarding post of governor of the new National Bank, Gorst seemed his obvious successor. Cromer, back in London to be with Ethel, informed him of his appointment on 21 July. He used the occasion to give what Gorst recorded as 'a little homily on my future conduct'. 'The two points which he criticized were my relations with the fair sex, which were apparently too conciliatory, and those with my own sex, which were apparently not conciliatory enough.'[26] Fortunately, Gorst was able to take such criticisms in his stride and to subordinate everything to the business of making himself indispensable. As he was to describe the new working relationship in 1900,

The Financial Adviser can be practically the Prime Minister of the country with Lord Cromer as a very easy going sovereign when once his confidence is attained . . . Nothing is done without my approval, and without boasting I may say that subject to the *influence* rather than the direction from Lord Cromer (which I do not in the least wish to minimize), I practically run the internal government of the country—I trust wisely.[27]

[20] Diana Souhami, *Mrs Keppel and Her Daughters* (London: HarperCollins, 1996), 53–7.

[21] Pat Thane, 'Financiers and the British State: The Case of Sir Ernest Cassel', *Business History*, 28/1 (Jan. 1986), 92.

[22] 15 Nov. 1905, BA, 203076, Partners' File: Supplementary Set.

[23] Saul, *La France et l'Égypte*, 669.

[24] Cromer to Revelstoke, 6 Dec. 1903, BA, 203076, Partners' File: Supplementary Set.

[25] Mellini, *Gorst*, 55–6.

[26] Quoted ibid. 67.

[27] Ibid. 72.

It was Cromer and Gorst together who formed the vital partnership that helped to solidify the British economic position in Egypt. A series of successful negotiations with the Caisse over the release of reserve funds for the completion of the Aswan Dam and for new railway construction were followed by the Franco-Egyptian commercial convention of 1902 and then the Anglo-French treaty of 1904, which gave Britain carte blanche as far as control over Egypt's finances was concerned. Their initial plan had been to try to marginalize what was left of the power of the Caisse by another huge conversion of the Unified Debt. But Cromer was soon to come to the conclusion that the high-level Anglo-French diplomatic manoeuvrings over Morocco, a process with which he himself was closely involved, provided an even better opportunity for persuading the French government to abandon what was left of its veto rights over the way Egypt spent it revenues.

The lessons drawn by Cromer and Gorst from the concessions awarded to Cassel and his associates in 1898 were also of great importance. In 1899 Gorst was instrumental in preventing Cassel from pushing though the same kind of scheme for the Domains land as he had for the Daira Saniya, choosing, instead, to sell the land directly to the profit of the government itself. Subsequently, both Gorst and Cromer also turned down a variety of schemes to privatize the Egyptian railways, on the grounds that, where there was a natural monopoly, private enterprise, deprived of the stimulus of competition, had no obvious advantage over state management.[28] In both cases, this had the additional advantage of providing a sop to the French by way of a continuation of the existing Anglo-French management of the railways and the Domains, a strategy of conciliation now possible once all the major instruments of French official intervention had been removed.

Cromer's Notion of an Egyptian State Interest

It was, perhaps, inevitable that the new situation should also encourage a more clearly defined notion of state interest, albeit one in which it was Cromer himself who continued to decide what was best for the Egyptian economy. An important aspect was his developing distrust of the excesses of private capital and of its ability to get in the way of his own schemes. The

[28] Saul, *La France et l'Égypte*, 660 ff.

merchant, as he was later to write, needed to be 'kept under control.[29] This, in turn, implied a return to a question which he had previously confronted with respect to the construction of Indian railways: what can the state can do most effectively and what the private sector?

Even more significant was his appreciation of the complexity of an economy which was not only growing much faster than ever before but also encouraging investment in a whole host of enterprises and new ways of making money. Thinking about matters economic was no longer simply a matter of how to raise sufficient revenues to pay off the public debt. It now involved questions of the management of the banking sector, of the balance between industry and agriculture, of employment and unemployment, and of policy towards major private concerns experiencing temporary economic difficulty. Some of these subjects, like banking, Cromer was reasonably well equipped to deal with. For instance, he began to think about the possibility of turning the National Bank into a proper state bank, a 'bank of banks' as he called it. which would exercise a general oversight over the sector and make sure that the other banks kept enough in cash or at short call to be able to meet any sudden demand for extra liquidity.[30] An opportunity presented itself as a result of Palmer's death in January 1906. But plans for changing the status of the bank had not been completed by the time of the financial crisis of March 1907 and had to be put on hold.[31] Other interventions, like his decision to offer government assistance to the failing Société Générale des Sucreries et de la Raffinerie in 1905, required significant amendment to long-held principles about what a government should and should not do.

It is noticeable that Cromer also began to make more use of statistics, notably the information contained in the 1897 census, to underpin large statements about the economy and the welfare of the Egyptian people. During his first years in Cairo he had shown no particular interest in this form of knowledge, and had even allowed the statistical bureau to be wound up in 1883. However, once the occupation became more permanent, his interest in numbers revived. He re-established the bureau in 1905 and used its data to return to that central tool of British Indian economic analysis, the balance between a country's population and resources. In Egypt, as he wrote in his 1906 Annual Report, there were 'no semi-

[29] Cromer, 'The Government of Subject Races', repr. in the Earl of Cromer, *Political and Literary Essays 1908–1913* (London: Macmillan, 1913), 51.

[30] Cromer to Revelstoke, 22 Feb. 1906, BA, 203076, Partners' File: Supplementary Set.

[31] Saul, *La France et l'Égypte*, 684, 688.

insoluble problems, such as a congested population normally living on the edge of starvation'.[32] Nevertheless, there were some worrying signs: evidence of overpopulation in one or two of the Delta provinces and over-dependence on a single export crop, cotton. Such thinking was behind his growing advocacy of technical education as a way of finding alternative employment for the agricultural population, as well as his support for sugar production in the interests of agricultural diversification.[33]

There were also areas were Cromer's thinking had definite limits, the more so when he had only his Indian experience to go on. The two most significant, both at the time and in terms of subsequent criticism of his policies, were his attitude to the development of factory industry and his failure to provide the educational facilities required by a growing Egyptian middle class. As far as the former was concerned, the issue was first raised in 1895 when Cromer had a meeting with a Briton, Matthew Wilks, who had obtained permission from the Public Works Department to establish a cotton mill in Cairo. Cromer was immediately concerned that, if the project succeeded, it would be followed by many similar enterprises. And this, as he reported to Lord Kimberley, would have 'serious consequences both in respect of the finances of Egypt and the huge trade in cotton now carried on between England and this country'.[34] There would be an immediate decline in revenue raised from the 8 per cent duty on imported cotton, while protests would most certainly be forthcoming from Britain's Lancashire textile exporters. Hence, as he informed Wilks, one of two measures would eventually become necessary: 'either the removal of the cotton duties or the imposition of a [countervailing] excise tax on home-made [cotton] goods'.[35]

In the event Wilks did not proceed further. However, the issue was revived when his rights were transferred to a second group of British businessmen with plans to found a new company, Egyptian Cotton Mills Ltd, in 1898. They found Cromer's attitude unchanged. In reply to their request for an assurance that no countervailing duty would be imposed on their products, Cromer instructed Gorst to say that this was impossible. As Gorst explained, 'the system under which you wish to establish cotton mills in Egypt would be a protective one, and the policy of the Egyptian

---

[32] *AR 1905, PP* (1906) 100, 500.

[33] Ibid. 503.

[34] 15 Apr. 1895, PRO, FO 141/311.

[35] Ibid. Also E. R. J. Owen, 'Lord Cromer and the Development of Egyptian Industry, 1883–1907', *Middle Eastern Studies*, 2/4 (July 1966), 282–301.

government has never been favourable to protection in Egypt'.[36] The promoters were not so easily deterred and went ahead with their plans, encouraged by their belief that the imposition of such a duty would be a violation of their capitulatory rights and so open to challenge in the Mixed Tribunals.[37] Work on building the new mill began in 1900, managers and technical staff were recruited in Lancashire, and a start made in training Egyptian workers to operate the new machinery.

Just before operations were to begin in March 1901, the company's chairman made one last effort to prevent the imposition of a countervailing duty but without success. Cromer indicated that he must fight them for, if he exempted them from duty, Lancashire would be up in arms.[38] True to his word, a decree imposing a duty of 8 per cent on all cotton goods produced in Egyptian factories (but not in workshops) was promulgated the following month. The company then appealed to the Mixed Tribunals and won. Still Cromer would not give up. Although believing that he and Gorst were the only two people in the country who thought that the government had a case, he ordered the administration to appeal.[39] To everyone's surprise, the higher court upheld the government's case. From then on both Egyptian Cotton Mills and its Alexandria-based competitor, the Anglo-Egyptian Spinning and Weaving Company, had to pay the 8 per cent duty on all their finished products.

Whether Cromer himself was able to influence the Tribunal's decision cannot be known for sure. Nor is it certain how much the imposition of the duty contributed to the overall difficulties of the two companies. Egyptian Cotton Mills rarely made a profit and went into liquidation in 1907. The Anglo-Egyptian Spinning and Weaving Company staggered on to 1908 and was then too far gone to be helped by the decision taken by Gorst, Cromer's successor, to suspend the countervailing duty for five years. The companies themselves put forward a number of reasons for their lack of success, including low productivity and a difficulty in finding local retail outlets for their products at a time when it was more profitable for Egyptian shopkeepers to sell known-quality imported goods. Neverthe-

[36] Gorst to Little and Johnson, 8 Oct. 1898, enclosed in Cromer to Salisbury, 29 Oct. 1898, PRO, FO 141/335.

[37] For a copy of the relevant legal opinion, see de Wiart to Garfallo, 4 May 1896, to be found in Egyptian Cotton Mills Ltd, 'Copy of the Correspondence with the Egyptian Government Relating to the 8% Duty', enclosed in Lansdowne to Rennell Rodd, 9 Aug. 1901, PRO, FO 141/361.

[38] Atherton to the Directors, 8 Mar. 1901, in 'Copy of Correspondence with the Egyptian Government Relating to the 8% Duty'.

[39] Cromer to Bergne, 2 May 1901, CP/2, FO 633/8.

less, the fact that both were operating at the margin must have meant that the duty played some role in their demise. More generally, Cromer's determination to fight the companies so hard may well have discouraged a number of other would-be manufacturers from even making the effort.

The controversy also says something important about Cromer's view of colonial government, as well as of empire in general. First, he was not against factory industry as such, believing that it would develop naturally over time in both India and Egypt. Indeed, on occasions he was actually anxious to promote it himself, witness the encouragement he gave to the Sornaga Factory to produce locally made pipes for the Cairo drainage system.[40] However, like all free traders, he did not believe that this should be at the expense of the cheap imports which helped to clothe the large numbers of very poor people living in these predominantly peasant societies.[41] Secondly, as a imperial administrator, he was unwilling to admit that there could be any basic contradiction between the interests of Britain and those of its colonies. As he was to write later in retrospective defence of the policies he and Ripon had pursued in India, 'they foresaw that the rival commercial interests of India and Lancashire would cause a rankling and persistent sore which might do infinite political harm'.[42] In this argument, free trade was expected to play a political, as well as an economic, role by preventing the emergence of dangerous inter-Empire disputes. Here, as elsewhere, it was all too easy for his opponents in India and Egypt to make just the opposite case: that local interests were being sacrificed to British ones and industrial interests to the notion that large parts of the Empire were, and should remain, predominantly agricultural economies.[43]

Cromer was even less prepared to rethink his views when it came to policy towards Egyptian education. There are various reasons for this, although it is difficult to put them in any order of importance. Perhaps the best place to begin is by pointing out that, while he was growing up, education in England (though not Scotland) was largely in private hands and there was no tradition of using the educational system as an instrument of state policy.[44] Hence, it was natural for an imperial administrator to turn

---

[40] M. E. Yapp (ed.), *Politics and Diplomacy in Egypt: The Diaries of Sir Miles Lampson, 1935–1937* (Oxford: Oxford University Press, 1997), 231–2.

[41] Baring, 'Recent Events in India', 687.

[42] 'The Fiscal Question in India', in Cromer, *Political and Literary Essays 1908–1913*, 331.

[43] e.g. 'Report of the Organizing Committee for the First Egyptian National Congress', pt. III: 'The Economic Situation', in *Minutes of the Proceedings of the First Egyptian National Congress* (Alexandria, 1911), 30–1.

[44] Kinsey, 'Egyptian Education Under Cromer', 79, 213–15.

to India for an example of what such a system might be. But then it became all too easy to be trapped in the British Indian notion that the education of more than a small Indian elite was leading to the production of a surplus of over-educated, underemployed agitators. So strong was this prejudice that Cromer continued to believe that Egypt too was educating potential troublemakers even after it had become absolutely clear that the system was not turning out even enough teachers for its own narrow purposes.[45]

A second influence which derived directly from late nineteenth-century India was the increasing pessimism about the possibility of using a British type of educational training to produce Indians with the European norms of character and morality then thought necessary as the basis for effective administration. The British saw this as a failure of the earlier assimilationist model promoted by Macaulay and others. However, it would seem just as reasonable to view it as a, possibly unconscious, reaction to the increasingly powerful late nineteenth-century notions of racial difference, with their stress on the difficulty, if not the impossibility, of native peoples making constructive use of a British type of education.[46] It is typical of the language of the time that Milner should describe the 'assimilation' of European ways by the Egyptian upper class as 'only skin-deep', while criticizing members of this class for their lack of 'backbone'.[47]

What we find then is a haphazard collection of, mostly Indian, prejudices reinforced by two other, more local concerns: a desire to increase the British component of the system and to spend as little money as possible. Such were the principles (if that is not too grand a word) which guided Cromer's thinking through the 1890s, to be given some limited coherence when, under pressure from the Legislative Council and the nationalist press, he was forced to lay out his basic aims in his Annual Report for 1902.[48] This envisaged a state system consisting of two parts. First, Europeanized education for a small number of pupils in the higher primary and secondary schools, plus the three colleges designed to prepare them for government service, their numbers limited by the need to pay fees. Secondly, a system of mass education in the village schools (or *kuttabs*) involving only what Cromer once called 'the three R's in the vernacular language; nothing more'.[49] The best of these were to be given a small grant in aid to improve their performance in return for becoming subject to government

[45] Kinsey, 'Egyptian Education Under Cromer', 195–213.   [46] Ibid. 86–7.
[47] Milner, *England in Egypt*, 321, 328.   [48] PP (1903) 87, 1008–14.
[49] Cromer to Freemantle, 17 Dec. 1896, CP/2, FO 633/8.

inspection, a scheme which was to be expanded as soon as money and qualified teachers became available.

The justification for this approach produced some particularly tortured logic. Good government required good bureaucrats. But it would be wrong either to produce more candidates for government service than the openings available for them, or to give the impression that the schools of higher primary education were simply a preparation for passage through the system towards government employment. Hence the use of fees to limit entry. Hence, too, Cromer's frequent exhortation to Egyptian parents to consider whether secondary education was really in the best interests of their sons and if they would not be better employed as skilled artisans. To Britons, who saw everything in terms of a logic based on a combination of public security and good administration, this must have made good sense. But to educationalists who saw value in education for its own sake, or to members of an expanding Egyptian middle class anxious to find good jobs for their sons, it was a provocative challenge.

Cromer was content to leave Dunlop in charge of executing his educational policies. He did not have a high opinion of his abilities but realized that he was useful to him, particularly in the way he bore the brunt of much fierce criticism.[50] Cromer must also have accepted Dunlop's methods of choosing British teachers even though they too began to excite criticism from 1903 onwards, when a new policy of recruiting university graduates was put in place. The new recruits were soon found to lack any commitment to Egyptian education, many of them simply making use of the service as a stepping-stone to better-paid posts elsewhere in the bureaucracy.[51] Nevertheless, enough of them remained in the educational service to alter its balance entirely. Hence, while the number of British teachers in the secondary and professional schools increased from 57 to 120 between 1896 and 1906, the number of Egyptians fell from 128 to 98.[52] Meanwhile, Dunlop made little effort to encourage Egyptians to take greater responsibility for the management of the system, fearing that this would have a deleterious effect on what constituted his exceedingly narrow notion of administrative efficiency.[53]

It is, of course, impossible to know whether another imperial administrator would have paid more attention to increasing educational opportunities for young Egyptians. Certainly, in Cromer's case there is no evidence

[50] Kinsey, 'Egyptian Education Under Cromer', 250–1.
[51] Humphrey Bowman, *Middle East Window* (London: Longmans, Green, 1942), 38–41.
[52] Kinsey, 'Egyptian Education Under Cromer', 308.   [53] Ibid. 398.

that he was under pressure either from Dunlop or from his close colleagues to do more.[54] Milner, for example, hid the few pages he devoted to education in *England in Egypt* in a chapter entitled 'Odds and Ends of Reform'. Nevertheless, the fact remains that, at a time of unprecedented economic development, and with the urban population increasing by at least 125,000 a year, the numbers of students in the state primary and secondary schools grew from 6,800 in 1892 to 8,520 in 1905 with the latter only graduating around some 100 pupils in 1902.[55] Cromer's Annual Report for 1902 admits that only 1 per cent of the budget was being spent on education.[56]

Little wonder that Egyptians of all types joined together to criticize Cromer's policies. Educational opportunity was restricted to a tiny number of children from well-to-do families. They were being educated in the state schools in foreign languages without any reference to their own history and culture, while the bulk of the population had to make do with the rudimentary training provided by the *kuttabs*. For Mustafa Kamil, the aim of such a policy was to destroy 'tout sentiment patriotique'.[57] For Muhammad Abduh, its purpose was to provide training for bureaucrats rather than a good general education with proper moral and spiritual training.[58] For Ahmad Lutfi al-Sayyid, although he was ready to praise Cromer's attempt to expand a more open type of *kuttab* education, there was no 'Egyptianness' in the state school system and no study of the real political world all around.[59]

Loneliness and Remarriage

By all accounts, Ethel's death, and what Cromer described as 'my solitary and joyless life', made the Agency a particularly unhappy place.[60] Cromer took refuge in official business and in translating Greek verse for a small volume he circulated privately among friends in 1903. Boyle provided a vivid description of his master's work habits at this time: 'The Lord has on

[54] Kinsey, 'Egyptian Education Under Cromer', 202–3.

[55] Milner, *England in Egypt*, 303; Marlowe, *Cromer in Egypt*, 290; Reid, *Cairo University and the Making of Modern Egypt*, 18.

[56] Ibid.

[57] Mustafa Kamil, *Égyptiens et Anglais* (Paris: Perrin, 1906), 28.

[58] Charles C. Adams, *Islam and Modernism in Egypt: A Study of the Modern Reform Movement Inaugurated by Muhammad 'Abdouh* (London: Oxford University Press, 1933), 196.

[59] *Al-Jarida*, 15 Sept., 23 Nov., and 6 Dec. 1908.

[60] Letter to Rennell Rodd, Apr. 1900, quoted in Zetland, *Lord Cromer*, 287.

his table 3 large baskets marked respectively, "For disposal", "Chancery" and "To Wait", and 20 times a day the Chancery basket is emptied out and he begins to fill it up again.' There was a bell on the table which Cromer used to summon the attention of those working in the chancery next door to his office, once ringing it eighteen times in an hour and a half, according to Boyle's somewhat bitter calculation. He would also walk into the chancery from time to time himself, to 'communicate a joke' or to consult.[61]

Apart from suppers with his niece Nina and his sons, when present, Cromer spent many of his evenings dining alone, and then smoking and playing patience until midnight.[62] He also turned even more towards Harry Boyle as one of the few people who seemed able to comfort him.[63] Horace Rumbold, returning to Cairo in 1900, noted that Cromer was not anything like as accessible as before, with Boyle standing more and more 'between us and our chief'.[64] He also missed Ethel's guiding hand, noting that, since her death, Cairo society had split up into 'absurd sets'. In these difficult and gloomy circumstances there was considerable pressure on Cromer to remarry. He must have felt this pressure still more keenly when, in a relatively short space of time, Nina got married in October 1900, Venetia, his sister-in-law and close confidante, died in November 1900, and finally, to everybody's great surprise, his brother Tom also got married for the first time in 1901, at the age of 62.

Perhaps all this also explains the speed at which Cromer himself got engaged and married in the autumn on 1901. His bride was Lady Katherine Thynne, the daughter of the fourth Marquess of Bath. She was in fact a distant relative with whom Ethel had been friends.[65] According to Blunt, it must also have been a sudden decision. Cromer was supposed to go down to Bournemouth to lay a wreath on Ethel's grave in mid-September, and then on to Paris to meet Gorst, when the engagement suddenly intervened.[66]

It sounds from his hurried notes to Katherine at this time that Cromer was very much in love. One, of 20 September, ends 'I worship the ground you tread on. My Katie! My darling! My dear wife that is to be! I shall think of you all night. Your own Mina.'[67] And another, the evening before their wedding, 'I want you to get just a line for first thing tomorrow to tell you once more that I love you with all my heart & soul and that you shall never

[61] 23 Mar. 1900, BP, box B, file 3.   [62] Boyle to Mrs Boyle, 29 Sept. 1901, BP, box B, file 3.
[63] Zetland, *Lord Cromer*, 287.   [64] Quoted in Gilbert, *Sir Horace Rumbold*, 40.
[65] Boyle, *Boyle of Cairo*, 148; Charles Douglas-Home, *Evelyn Baring: The Last Proconsul* (London: Collins, 1978), 18–19. Cromer's cousin Harriet Ashburton had married Katherine's grandfather, the third Marquess of Bath, in 1830.   [66] 4 Oct. 1901, Blunt, *My Diaries*, 425.
[67] CP/5, box 1, file 1.

regret the step you are going to take! Goodnight, my own darling! Mina.'
Cromer was then just 60, his bride 36.[68]

The marriage took place at St Thomas's Church, Portman Square, in
London. The bride wore a dress of white ivory satin. There was no best
man, bridesmaid, or pages. Guests included Katherine's widowed mother,
her brother and sisters, Tom and his new wife, Constance, Nina and her
new husband, the Earl of Granville, Cromer's son Windham, his sister
Cecilia, Lord Northbrook and his daughter Emma, and Cromer's old
friends from his Indian days Sir Alfred and Lady Lyall.[69] Among the
wedding gifts on display at the reception at Katherine's mother's house
in Manchester Square were a silver inkstand from the King and Cromer's
own special presents for Katherine, a diamond tiara, a single-stone diamond necklace, a diamond pin, and a pearl-head pin with a 'K' on it in
diamonds.[70] The couple spent their first three nights together at Tom's
house at Hookham in Norfolk, and then left Charing Cross Station for
Brindisi, where they joined the steamship *Isis* en route for Port Said.

The Agency staff seem to have been delighted at this turn of events.
According to Rumbold, his immediate reaction to the news of Cromer's
impending marriage was one of 'great relief'. As he wrote to his father, 'he
[Cromer] will be ever so much happier and it will make everything easier'.
Another advantage, from Rumbold's point of view, was the probable
decline in Boyle's influence, making it much easier to obtain Cromer's
attention and, so, his confidence.[71] Boyle himself noted that the couple
seemed 'devoted' to each other and that, as a result of Katherine's arrival,
the Agency was 'more like its old self again' with the 'Old Lord ... busting
out no end again and making things hum'.[72] One thing the Cromers
shared was a love of walking, 'tearing along the dykes' by the Nile,
according to Boyle, with Katherine tucking up her skirts and striding
through the deep dust and sand at a pace which left Harry and her husband
'panting behind'.[73]

Nevertheless, things were definitely not the same as before. On a
personal level, Rumbold, who had met Lady Katherine at an English
house party before her engagement, remained unimpressed, recalling
later that she was 'rather narrow-minded, very obstinate and extraordinarily tactless, on occasion'.[74] Storrs found her 'noble in spirit and appear-

[68] CP/5, box 1, file 1.   [69] *The Times*, 23 Oct. 1901.
[70] Ibid.; *Daily News*, 22 Oct. 1901.   [71] Gilbert, *Sir Horace Rumbold*, 43.
[72] Boyle to Mrs Boyle, 31 Oct. and 6 Nov. 1901, BP, box B, file 3.
[73] 23 Nov. 1901, BP, box B, file 3.   [74] Gilbert, *Sir Horace Rumbold*, 42–3.

ance' but caring little for 'diplomatic or social life'.[75] It is also said that she ran the Agency 'inefficiently, if not chaotically', that she fell asleep during dinner like her mother, and that she refused to talk to many Cairenes, whom she said were all fools except one, Sir Edward Grigg.[76]

It could not have been easy for Katherine to take over the management of the household of a former and obviously well-loved first wife, in which, as Boyle noted, nothing could be changed, with all Ethel's pictures, photos, and other mementoes remaining exactly as before.[77] She was also now the stepmother to two young men, as well as being responsible for meeting the Cromers' social obligations to an enormous array of Britons, Europeans, and Egyptians. And although she had her detractors, others found her charming, lively, and interested in local charities. One such person was Ernest Richmond, a young man in the Public Works Department, who was invited to have tea with her on 28 May 1906 to discuss the dispensaries she had opened for poor Egyptians in different parts of Cairo and the best way to educate mothers in child-rearing.[78] He returned in the evening of 2 June and, finding her sitting alone in the garden, talked until eight. 'She is such a splendid woman,' he wrote back to his fiancée in England. 'I love talking to her, she is always above petty things and always in sympathy with them too—a very noble woman.'[79]

What Cromer himself thought about it all is more difficult to determine. He must have known all about Katherine's somewhat eccentric upbringing, with a father who used to take her alone to Venice for Christmas away from the family, and a mother who forbade her three daughters to look in the mirror, something which is supposed to have accounted for their exceptionally 'scruffy' appearance.[80] He also knew that, in the years before her marriage, she had been happiest when living in retreat at her cottage near St Albans, and that, as her brother once observed, she had 'no education', and a passion for philanthropy which included working in London Boys' Clubs.'[81] Nevertheless, she was rich, with a dowry which was probably worth some £10,000, and well-connected.[82] Cromer must have also believed that she could manage the social side of his official life

---

[75] Storrs, *Orientations*, 53.   [76] Douglas-Home, *Evelyn Baring*, 19.

[77] Boyle to Mrs Boyle, 31 Oct. 1901, BP, box B, file 3.

[78] Letter to Muriel Lubbock, 29 May 1906, RL. Cromer believed that Egyptian mothers did not know how to look after their children; Cromer to Graham, 14 Oct. 1910, CP/2, FO 633/14.

[79] Richmond to Muriel Lubbock, 3 June 1906, RL.

[80] Douglas-Home, *Evelyn Baring*, 17–18.

[81] Alexander Thynne to Katherine Cromer, 28 Jan. 1902, CP/5, box 1, file 2.

[82] Douglas-Home, *Evelyn Baring*, 18.

without too much fuss. Just as important, there is more than simply Boyle's evidence that his marriage lifted his spirits and gave him a new lease on life. Something of this is also evident in one of his translations of a Greek poem by Marcus Argentaris published in 1903. Entitled 'Love and the Scholar' it goes:

> As over Hesiod's page I pore,
> Comes tripping in my lovely Katie.
> I fling the book upon the floor,
> And cry, 'Old Hesiod, how I hate ye!'[83]

The inevitable tensions seem to have been managed by a process of mutual teasing. Katherine chided him for drinking too much. He poked fun at her bad spelling and her unwillingness to put the date on her letters. All this is present in a verse entitled 'To My Wife', probably written towards the end of 1902:

> Dearest Katie, when you tease
> Do you think I really mind?
> Love, remember if you please,
> Can be deaf as well as blind.
> No! I glory in my fate,
> Let the merry humour flow:
> You may play at being Kate—
> I won't be Petruchio![84]

The Cromers spent their first winter in Cairo, and their first summer at their new London house at 26 Wimpole Street, with time in Scotland and visits, at least for Cromer himself, to Oxford to obtain an honorary degree at the end of June and to Aix-les-Bains in August, where he may have gone to take the waters once again for his gout. He also went with Gorst to look at a public display of his portrait by John Singer Sargent begun the previous autumn.[85] It shows him sitting next to a desk containing a line of leather-bound state papers in what could be a dark corner of his Wimpole Street study. His eyes seem tired and unfocused, his moustache and hair are now white, and, altogether, he seems to have begun to look like an old man.

Sadly, Gorst does not record what Cromer thought of it. It was certainly not to everyone's liking. One of Sargent's biographers says it makes

[83] Cromer, *Paraphrases and Translations from the Greek*, 8.
[84] Cromer, 'Occasional Verses', CP/5, box 5.
[85] Gorst, Diary, 24 Sept. 1902, GD. The portrait is at present on loan from the National Portrait Gallery to the British Embassy in Cairo.

Cromer look like a 'business executive'.[86] And a reviewer for *The Spectator* took Sargent to task because 'it lacked the genius to explain the secret of the qualities of mind and character that enabled this square-built English-man to become the greatest ruler that Egypt has had since the days of the Pharaohs'.[87] Only Wilfrid Blunt seemed wholly pleased, writing in his diary that his old enemy was portrayed as having 'bloated cheeks, dull eyes, ruby nose and gouty hand, half torpid, having lunched heavily', and concluding 'Truly my quarrel with him avenged'.[88]

During their second Egyptian winter the Cromers attended the opening of the Aswan Dam by the Duke and Duchess of York (later George V and Queen Mary) in December 1902, and then went on to Khartoum for Christmas, although missing Christmas dinner itself when the steamer on which they were making a short day trip up the Blue Nile ran aground and was only towed off by a gunboat towards midnight. Those guests who had remained behind had all the food to themselves, as well as licence for such fun and games as speeches in the manner of the absent VIPs, Gorst taking the lead with a 'lifelike imitation of Lord Cromer'.[89]

The Cromers' party then proceeded up the White Nile on a boat with Wingate, Rowland and Windham, and a number of friends and officials including, of course, Boyle. In Boyle's words: 'It was a most charming party, and the nonsense we all talked, the foolish poems we all wrote to each other, and the general frivolity which prevailed as a background to everything cannot be described.'[90] Perhaps his mood had something to do with the fact that it was on the same trip that he became engaged (although only briefly) to one of the other passengers, Katherine's friend the Countess Valda Gleichen. When they reached Gondoroko on the southern frontier, Cromer wrote that 'elephants gaze at us from either bank, hippopotami sport round the steamer, and only yesterday a herd of giraffes came down to drink and to stare at the intruders'. The only problem was with what he called 'the smaller animals': 'never in my life have I met a greater host of biting, stinging and crawling insects'.[91] Another memory was of

---

[86] Charles Merrill Mount, *John Singer Sargent: A Biography* (New York: W. W. Norton, 1957), 190.

[87] Quoted in William Howe Downes, *John S. Sargent: His Life and Work* (Boston: Little, Brown, 1925), 209.

[88] 16 May 1903, Blunt, *My Diaries*, 469.

[89] Boyle, *Boyle of Cairo*, 111–12.

[90] Quoted ibid. 106.

[91] Quoted in a memoir entitled 'Evelyn: Earl of Cromer', for the British Academy, by Lord Sanderson, *Proceedings of the British Academy* 8, 25 n., copy in CP/2, FO 633/43.

members of a 'cannibal tribe' coming on board to ask if they could see the faces of the white women.[92]

The Cromers' only child, Evelyn, was born on 29 September 1903, at Katherine's mother's house in London. Kate had gone home in May in mid-pregnancy and Cromer's letters to her are full of eager anticipation, as well as serious discussion about the relative merits of different types of milk.[93] In the end Evelyn was bottle-fed and came out to Cairo with his mother in November, before being sent back home again with his nanny when the temperatures heated up the following May. One of Cromer's poems attempted to describe how he and Katherine felt about 'baby's departure':

> With baby we were wont to play,
> But here alas he could not stay,
> And now that he has gone away,
> > We miss him.
> He went and left us in the blues,
> We lived upon the weekly news,
> Meanwhile exchanging parental views,
> > Vicissim.[94]

The same sad process of sending little Evelyn back to Britain at the start of the hot season in April continued throughout their stay in Egypt. At Easter 1906 Katherine wrote to him in Scotland:

My Darling Little Baby,

We miss you so much that we can hardly bear the house without you. The nursery and bedroom are so quiet and Papa shaves all alone & and always wears a red tie, even a red and yellow tie . . . It has been nice and cool and you could easily have stayed till now.[95]

The Anglo-French Agreement of 1904

The resolution of the Fashoda crisis had raised fresh hopes that it might be possible to obtain complete financial freedom by putting an end to the French veto over the use of Egypt's now considerable cash reserves. As Cromer asked Salisbury in November 1898, 'has the time not arrived when

---

[92] Address to dinner of the Royal Geographical Society, 26 Sept. 1911, CP/2, FO 633/28.
[93] Letters in CP/5, box 1, file 1.   [94] Douglas-Home, *Evelyn Baring*, 15–16.
[95] BP, Durham University, file GRE/I/153.

we might tell the French that the constant heckling we have to endure from them in Egypt will not be tolerated?'[96] The problem remained that the British had nothing to offer the French by way of a quid pro quo. The alternative was to render the Caisse more or less redundant by working towards the conversion of most of the public debt as soon as it became legally possible in 1905. Cromer hoped that even the threat itself might be enough to get the French to modify their stance.[97]

In the end the break came via France's growing interest in Morocco. Anglo-French discussions of this and other colonial questions had already begun in 1902. But it was not until the French Foreign Minister, Cambon, included Egypt on his list of questions to be discussed during an important meeting with the new British Foreign Secretary, Lord Lansdowne, in July 1903 that a real opening occurred. Cromer, quick to see the possibilities, urged Lansdowne to take advantage of 'the opportunity now offered'.[98] He was in London at the time, waiting for his baby's birth, and wrote two crucial memos which became the basis for Lansdowne's future negotiating tactics. Being close at hand, he was also able to 'coach' Lansdowne for the approaching meeting, getting him to list what Britain wanted in Egypt and what it was prepared to surrender over Morocco.[99] It was, he told the Foreign Secretary, 'by far the most important diplomatic affair that we have had in hand for a long time past'.[100]

On his return to Cairo, Cromer arranged for Gorst to go to London in December 1903, and then on to France, to assist in the financial side of the negotiations. He then had to wait and watch impatiently while Gorst shuttled between London and Paris with drafts involving colonial matters few of which concerned Egypt, worried all the time that the French community in Egypt might suddenly get wind of what was going on and trigger an explosion among public opinion in France.[101] The final sticking point proved to be the wording of the official French acknowledgement of Britain's right to remain in Egypt without limit. Gorst came up with a formula which he hoped would be to Cromer's liking. However, by the time his letter of explanation reached Cairo, the agreement had been signed, on 8 April 1904, and though Cromer's reply suggests that he found the wording unsatisfactory, it was too late to do anything about it.[102] Nevertheless, the French promise that it would not 'obstruct the

[96] 28 Nov. 1898, SP, A/55.   [97] Cromer to Lansdowne, 17 July 1903, CP/2, FO 633/6.
[98] 17 July 1903, quoted in Marlowe, *Cromer in Egypt*, 247.
[99] Roberson, 'Judicial Reform', 239–40.   [100] 1 Nov. 1903, CP/2, FO 633/6.
[101] Zetland, *Lord Cromer*, 280.   [102] Ibid. 281–4.

action of HBMG [in Egypt] by asking that a limit of time be fixed for the British occupation' was generally deemed to count as a solid recognition of Britain's right to stay as long as it wished.[103]

As far as the financial situation was concerned, the French also gave their approval to a draft khedivial decree attached to the agreement as an annex. By repealing, or partially repealing, all the existing decrees governing Egyptian finance, it allowed the Egyptian government free use of all its revenues other than those required for the annual repayment of the debt. It also released all the money in the two Caisse-controlled reserve funds, less a small sum retained against any shortfall in the revenues needed for debt repayment. This produced a windfall of some £E6 million, or nearly half a year's total government receipts.[104]

The Egyptian section of the Anglo-French entente was generally perceived as very much Cromer's own achievement. However, great credit must also go to Gorst, who had done most of the diplomatic donkey-work in Paris. His reward was a senior appointment at the Foreign Office, something very much in line with Cromer's plan that Gorst should leave Egypt for a while in order to gain wider experience and stature in the larger British official world before returning to Cairo as his successor.[105]

---

[103] 'Declaration Respecting Egypt and Morocco', PRO, FO 371/68; Zetland, *Lord Cromer*, 284; Marlowe, *Cromer in Egypt*, 251.
[104] Ibid. 252.
[105] Mellini, *Gorst*, 73–4.

16

Things Fall Apart
1904–1907

A Multitude of Afflictions

Cromer rightly saw the Anglo-French Agreement of 1904 as a great personal triumph. It also seemed to pave the way for the accomplishment of his ultimate goal: the abolition of the Capitulations as the last international barrier to unfettered British control. This was to become his main preoccupation during what proved to be his final three years in Egypt, 1904–7. He was also fortunate, at least in the short run, to preside over an explosive economic boom in which land prices and rents soared as the result of what the American Consul-General called the 'profuse introduction of loanable capital'.[1]

Unfortunately for Cromer, these were also years in which his freedom of action came to be severely circumscribed by a new set of factors, some accidental, some very much of his own making. One stemmed from his increasing age and declining health. In April 1905 he wrote to Lansdowne to say that he had consulted 'numerous doctors', who all told the same story, that there was

nothing organically wrong with me, and that with care I may perfectly go on for some years. But also all say that I am, so to speak, living on my capital and that I cannot stand for long the sort of work I have to undertake for nine months and in this climate . . . Work tends to increase rather than diminish.

---

[1] 'Report on the Present Prosperity of Egypt', in Iddings to Bacon, 12 Jan. 1906, United States National Archives, II, Washington, DC, State Department, RG/59, T41/24.

Cromer ended with the observation that by taking four months' summer leave instead of the usual three he planned to stay in Egypt for another six years but then to retire from government service.[2]

Signs of what seem like intimations of his own mortality can be found during the long summer he spent at Strathmore Lodge in 1905. In July he wrote to Rowland saying that he had begun to think about how to allocate his property to his descendants. Then, in August, he began to compose just over 400 pages of 'Biographical Notes' with the aim, he wrote in the Preface, 'that the children should know something of their father's career'.[3] They contain a combination of memories, anecdotes, and moral instruction, as well as a guide to some of the important figures, both good and bad, in his life. Storks and Northbrook were in the former category, Ismail ('a spendthrift, a thief and a murderer'), Gladstone ('ignorant of facts about Egypt which were within knowledge of any ordinary newspaper reader'), and Gordon (a 'drunkard' whose mind 'wandered between sanity and insanity') in the latter.[4] There is also an attempt to shape his life itself in terms of a moral lesson: that of a reformed prodigal, a wild, badly educated boy and pleasure-loving youth redeemed by hard work and the desire to be worthy of Ethel's love.

Worries about his health become more obvious after his return to Cairo, when he used it as his main reason for turning down Campbell-Bannerman's offer of the post of Foreign Secretary in his new Liberal Cabinet in December. As Cromer explained the situation to his nephew, Lord Revelstoke, 'I am quite unable to grapple with the work of the Foreign Office, and I do not think that I shall be able to grapple with my Egyptian work for much longer.' He was down with dengue fever, he wrote, which has 'completely prostrated me'.[5] Two weeks later he told his son Rowland that it was not the dengue but a high temperature brought on by a doctor's injection of an anti-diphtheria serum designed to cure the neuritis in his arm.[6]

Matters became worse in 1906 when Cromer began suffering from what sounds like an irritable bowel or colon, aggravated by worry, overwork,

---

[2] Cromer to Lansdowne, 30 Apr. 1905, quoted in part in Zetland, *Lord Cromer*, 288–9.
[3] BN 370–1.
[4] BN 242–3, 312.
[5] 15 Dec. 1905, CP/3, Barings: Partners' Files, Lord Cromer, 1899–1908.
[6] Cromer to Rowland (Errington), 29 Dec. 1905, CP/1, Letters from the 1st Earl to the 2nd Earl, 1905–1906.

and the growing criticism of his administration in both Egypt and Britain.[7] It was also becoming more obvious that the system of one-man rule which he had created was not only an inefficient method of directing Egyptian affairs but also one that placed a near-impossible burden on his own shoulders. There was Sudan to manage. There was the inevitable increase in the complexities of administration as more money became available from the reserve funds released by the Caisse as a result of the Anglo-French Agreement, and as demands for more social spending multiplied. There was the work to be done on his plan to secure the abolition of the Capitulations. All this could be managed after a fashion with the help of the industrious and reliable Gorst. But when Gorst went back to the Foreign Office in 1904, his replacement, Vincent Corbett, proved much less satisfactory. Indeed, Cromer was later to describe him as 'by no means a capable man' who did not afford him loyal support.[8] Nor was he willing to allow the Egyptian ministers to play any role in linking the administration to the larger society. Mustafa Fahmi and most of his colleagues had been in office since 1895 and, as far as anybody could see, were bent only on 'dying in their seats'.[9] A few of the British officials like Rennell Rodd and Storrs were beginning to be aware of the system's shortcomings.[10] But, like Cromer himself, they could grumble about it without having any realistic ideas about how to make it work better.

Nor were things much better at the Agency itself. Rumbold gave Cromer's illness and more brusque manner, and Lady Cromer's reluctance to give Agency officials the family status they had known before, as reasons for wishing to find another post.[11] Later he notes Boyle's attempt to revive his influence: he was trying to usurp the duties of head of chancery and had 'access to Lord Cromer at all times'. 'How Lady Cromer hates Boyle.'[12] Katherine's rather haphazard approach to social functions only made things more uncomfortable. In spite of Cromer's strong feelings for her, and the fact that she was very obviously trying to protect him from the longer social engagements, he must have been made daily

---

[7] His stomach condition may also have been aggravated by the salicyclic acid he took for his gout; Cromer to Rowland (Errington), 24 Nov. 1905, CP/1, Letters from the 1st Earl to the 2nd Earl, 1905–1906.

[8] BN, Insertion 1, 2 Aug. 1910.

[9] This phrase was used by an editorialist in *al-Ahram*, 11 Nov. 1908.

[10] Mellini, *Gorst*, 103.

[11] Gilbert, *Horace Rumbold*, 55.

[12] 31 Oct. 1905, ibid. 52.

aware that things no longer ran as smoothly as they had while Ethel was alive.[13]

What must have seemed like the last straw was a misunderstanding between Katherine and Rowland in London in the autumn of 1906 that seemed to him to reveal an underlying antipathy between them of which he had been 'wholly unaware'. Rowland's letter about the incident, he wrote in reply, had 'distressed' him more than anything that had occurred since his 'great sorrow' (Ethel's death). He had always feared that such a thing might happen but had 'hoped and believed that the danger had been averted'. Katie was sometimes 'careless and forgetful' but she had a heart of gold, was devoted to both Rowland and his brother, 'and would do nothing to hurt you'.[14] This painful situation was patched up but never properly solved, a situation which was to be revealed by the events following Cromer's death just over ten years later.

Cromer's position in Egypt took a dramatic turn for the worse at just the same time. First, the return of a Liberal ministry in December 1905 was followed by a huge Liberal victory in the general election in January 1906, bringing into Parliament a number of men who, though not against empire as such, were stern critics of the way it was often conducted, as well as advocates of the steady political development of its inhabitants.[15] Hence, although Cromer was well acquainted with the new Foreign Secretary, Edward Grey, he was quickly made aware that Grey had to be very careful in dealing with the other members of the Cabinet, as well as with those Liberal radicals who were beginning to ask hostile questions about his Egyptian policy in Parliament. No longer could Cromer practise what he had told Revelstoke in 1903 was a kind of Egyptian 'home rule', rarely referring anything to London and, when he did, telling them 'what they have to do'.[16]

Secondly, Egyptian popular criticism of his policies was greatly stirred up by two events which took place in 1906: the confrontation with the Turks about the boundary between Egypt and the Ottoman Empire (known either as the 'Aqaba' or the 'Taba' crisis), and then the harsh punishment meted out to the peasants accused of attacking British officers shooting pigeons near the Delta village of Dinshawai. Both unleashed a

---

[13] Caillard, *A Lifetime in Egypt*, 117.
[14] 8 Nov. 1906, CP/1, Letters from the 1st Earl to the 2nd Earl, 1905–1906.
[15] Bernard Porter, *Critics of Empire: British Radical Attitudes to Colonialism in Africa, 1895–1914* (London: Macmillan, 1968), 294–5, 314.
[16] 7 May 1903, BA, Partners' Files, Lord Cromer, 1899–1908.

torrent of attacks in the Egyptian press, creating a situation which was as puzzling to Cromer and his colleagues as it was alarming to many members of the foreign communities. Even though those at the Agency did their best to blame it all on a combination of local agitators and meddlesome British troublemakers, it became clear that not only was some change in British policy towards Egypt required but also that Cromer was too old and tired and ill to effect it himself.

How to End the Capitulations

As far as Cromer was concerned, the link between the Anglo-French Agreement and ending the Capitulations was to be found in the general assumption that France had now granted Britain a free hand in Egypt, as well as, more specifically, in two secret clauses included at his personal insistence. One contained a French acknowledgement that Britain would be free to act unilaterally as far as the Capitulations were concerned if the other capitulatory powers could not agree. The second committed France to 'examine' British proposals regarding them.[17] The problem was that there was no understanding about when negotiations should begin. While Cromer was ready to press ahead as quickly as possible, Grey, in particular, was anxious for the French to gain complete control over Morocco first.[18] As he reminded Cromer in one of his first dispatches to him after assuming office, it was necessary to 'nurse' the new entente 'carefully'.[19]

An early pointer to Cromer's approach to the ending of the Capitulations is provided by his farewell speech to Gorst on 22 April 1904. In it he praised him as one of the small band of Europeans who had been engaged in carrying out a policy of 'Egypt for the Egyptians' in the only sense that that policy was practicable and beneficial to all interests concerned. This was not a policy that implied that Egypt was to be governed solely by native Egyptians. But it did imply that 'the touchstone to be applied to every Egyptian question is to inquire how far that proposal is in the true interests of the dwellers of Egypt, of whatsoever nationality or creed

[17] Cromer to Lansdowne, 12 and 14 Mar. 1904, copies in PRO, FO 800/124. See also G. P. Gooch and H. Temperley (eds.), *British Documents on the Origins of the War 1898–1914*, vol. i (London: HMSO, 1927), 354–5, 385–95. Cromer mentions the clauses in his letter to Sir John Rees, 24 Nov. 1911, CP/2, FO 633/20.

[18] Roberson, 'Judicial Reform', 248.

[19] 20 Dec. 1905, PRO, FO 800/46.

they may be'.[20] Henceforward the notion of a common interest shared by all the 'dwellers of Egypt' regardless of race or nationality was to become the key to persuading the European powers to surrender their capitulatory rights to a British-dominated Egyptian government.

Cromer used his Annual Report for 1904 (written in early 1905) to air two of the basic elements of his plan. First, the powers should be persuaded to transfer the legislative powers they exercised over their own citizens through the Mixed Tribunals to the British government alone. Secondly, there should be some new local 'legislative machinery' to make laws for 'all the dwellers of Egypt' both native and foreign.[21] These ideas were then amplified in a set of 'Rough notes to serve as a basis for further discussion of the question of revising the system of legislation at present in force in Egypt' sent to the Foreign Office in April. What was necessary, Cromer argued, was the creation of some machinery which would offer guarantees to the European community in Egypt while maintaining the 'autonomous' rights of the Egyptian government. This could probably best be done by the establishment of a new legislative body just for the Europeans.[22]

To set the ball rolling, and also to get the European communities, particularly the British and the French, on his side, he asked for Grey's permission to use his next Annual Report to set out his proposals for local discussion.[23] Grey, worried about how this might be received in Paris, consulted the Prime Minister and the new Liberal Cabinet before giving a qualified agreement, while insisting that nothing be said to suggest either that the British government was committed to the plan or that it felt obliged to take action.[24]

So it was that, in early 1906, Cromer laid out a set of suggestions about which, he said, he wished to have the views of the local European chambers of commerce and other communal institutions. It is significant that he also took steps to make sure that the Annual Report was available in French translation, at government expense.[25] His key proposal was the creation of a separate council 'composed wholly of subjects or protected persons of the powers who were parties to the treaties under which the judicial reforms of 1876 were accomplished'. Legislation proposed by the majority of its members, and then promulgated by the Egyptian government, would

---

[20] Quoted in Mellini, *Gorst*, 79–80.   [21] *PP* (1905) 103, 1097, 1100.
[22] PRO, FO 881/8616.   [23] Cromer to Grey, 25 Nov. 1905, PRO, FO 800/46.
[24] Grey to Cromer, 20 Dec. 1905, PRO, FO 800/46.   [25] *AR 1905, PP* (1906) 137, 485.

be binding on all non-native foreign residents.[26] This council should coexist with the existing Egyptian Legislative Council and assembly. It should also be small, with no more than twenty-five to thirty members, the majority to be elected. He was aware, he wrote, of no precedent for such an arrangement involving two legislative bodies side by side. But at least it had the virtue of being easier to establish than a joint European and Egyptian chamber.[27]

Secondly, to open the discussion as to what the new council could and could not do, Cromer put forward his own list of reserved subjects over which it was to be denied legislative powers.[28] Thirdly, the council, together with the British and Egyptian governments, should take over the responsibility presently exercised in civil and criminal affairs involving Europeans by their individual national consular authorities, again subject to a whole set of reservations.[29]

It requires a complete suspension of belief to imagine that Cromer really thought that such a strange and ambitious scheme would be taken seriously, let alone made to work. It required the European communities to believe that their interests would be better protected by the British in Egypt than by their own governments. It also required them to put pressure on these same governments to allow it to be put it into effect. And it required the Egyptian people to acquiesce to what was manifestly a huge and permanent reduction in their own country's sovereignty. Proof of just how unrealistic this was soon appeared in the shape of the rejection of the idea of an international legislative council by both the British and Italian chambers of commerce.[30]

Further insight into Cromer's thinking at this time is provided in a remarkable letter he sent to one of his major British confidants, St Loe Strachey, the editor of *The Spectator*, in May 1906. Wilfrid Blunt was quite wrong, he wrote, to believe that Egypt was simply a Muslim country. 'For me all the dwellers in Egypt are Egyptians: Muslims, Copts, Syrians, Levantines as well as the Europeans who represent the civilising elements in the country.'

My aim and endeavour, ever since I have been here, has been to fuse all these classes into one, and to move somewhat in the direction of making a nation of them. Of course, it is absurd to believe that this ideal can be realised in the life of one man. All that is possible is to take some steps in the desired direction.

---

[26] Ibid. 486.   [27] Ibid. 486–7.   [28] Ibid. 487–8.   [29] Ibid. 488–9.
[30] Cromer to Grey, 1 Dec. 1906 and 12 Jan. 1907, PRO, FO 800/46.

The 'steps' taken so far had been to end Egypt's administrative and financial difficulties and provide orderly government, to instil a liberal spirit into the bureaucracy, to end Anglo-French rivalry, and to get rid of the Caisse. The next step would be to deal with the Capitulations. It would be a long business and 'if I accomplish this work my contribution to Egyptian regeneration will, I think, have been finished, and the matter must be taken up by some younger man'. He was going to Alexandria the following week to lay the foundation stone of Victoria College and would take the opportunity to allude to his notion of 'fusing together all the races of the Valley of the Nile' in 'guarded terms'. To a great extent this was a new idea as far as the Egyptian public were concerned. But 'I have long had it in my head.' He wanted Strachey to publicize it in Britain.[31]

Once again, it is difficult to exaggerate the extraordinary, and mis-guided, ambition behind this exercise in what would now be called 'nation-building'. Even more striking than the unreality of the whole project is the megalomania involved. That Cromer really believed that one man could persuade the different groups in Egypt to fuse themselves into a single cosmopolitan society with common interest is testimony to a system of personal rule that had become significantly divorced from major local developments. It also demonstrates how the original strength of someone who gets himself into a position of almost unbridled power can become weakness when freed from all restraint. An iron logic had now convinced him that, because the Egyptians were neither a nation nor capable of administering themselves, and that because the Europeans would only abandon the Capitulations if they received a special status in Egypt, the only way forward was to persuade them all to become some-thing new. Similarly, a vision of man as primarily an economic actor had convinced him that a shared interest in material progress would be enough to overcome all the religious and linguistic forces that divided people not into classes but into separate cultural communities.

On a more prosaic level, Cromer also failed to read the local signs right. In his view, as he told Strachey, it was a 'favourable moment' to throw out his new ideas. Not only had the Anglo-French accord 'softened' inter-national rivalry, but what he called the 'recent display of Muslim fanati-cism' had also caused the local Europeans to rally round the British, putting an end to any notion of a 'purely native political development' along the lines suggested by Wilfrid Blunt. Here he is referring to the use

[31] 18 May 1906, CP/2, FO 633/8.

made by Mustafa Kamil and others of the Taba incident to rally support for the Ottoman sultan Abdul-Hamid II; and the response to it by others, like the Europeans, who were disturbed by its pan-Islamic overtones, and the more moderate Egyptians close to the Agency who viewed the matter in Egyptian territorial rather than in Islamic terms. There is some literal truth here. However, a wiser course would have been to recognize the implications of the fact that latent opposition to the occupation had proved easily mobilized by such incidents. As it was, Cromer's heavy-handed attempts to reassure the Europeans by displays of British military force, something he believed vital to the success of his scheme to get rid of the Capitulations, ended up by provoking many Egyptians into just the type of anti-colonial nationalism that he was trying to avoid.

Taba and Dinshawai

The Taba incident had its origins in British concerns about the possibility of the Ottomans building a spur of the Hijaz railway down to Aqaba, thus greatly increasing the strategic value of the southern section of the still undefined Egyptian–Ottoman border. A small force under the command of W. E. Jennings-Bramley, a British frontier administration official, was sent, first to probe the border and then, in late January 1906, ordered by Cromer to occupy strategic positions on the Sinai side of the Gulf of Aqaba, just a few miles south of Aqaba itself.[32] When this force reached Taba, it found it already occupied by a small Turkish garrison and was moved a little further down the coast on a British warship.[33] There followed a long process of diplomatic exchange accompanied by a press campaign in support of the Sultan's position led by Mustafa Kamil's *al-Liwa*. An editorial of 22 April supported the Ottoman claim to the Sinai Peninsula over that of Egypt, and another, of 8 May, called upon every Egyptian to support Turkish rights.[34] Kamil also organized a strike at the law school, which was only ended by Cromer's personal mediation between the striking students and the French director, who was refusing to allow them back.[35]

---

[32] Findlay to Grey, 25 Jan. 1906, PRO, FO 371/60. Cromer was ill in bed at the time.

[33] For Jennings-Bramley's own account, General Sir James Marshall-Cornwall, 'An Enigmatic Frontier', *Geographical Journal*, 125/3–4 (Sept.–Dec. 1959).

[34] Quoted in Lutfi al-Sayyid, *Egypt and Cromer*, 167.

[35] Ibid. 169; Goldschmidt, 'Egyptian Nationalist Movement', 319.

Rashid Khalidi suggests that it might have been local opposition of this type that encouraged Cromer to try to persuade the Foreign Office that the dispute had wider international ramifications, including possible German involvement on the Ottoman side.[36] It is also credible that he saw it as a way of encouraging the recently created Committee of Imperial Defence to put military pressure on Grey and the other civilians in the Liberal Cabinet. Meanwhile, the Ottomans continued to resist the British demand that they abandon Taba as a prelude to a boundary arbitration. In a characteristic letter of this period Cromer informed Grey that, though diplomatic measures were 'preferable', should they fail it might be useful to send a British fleet 'steaming towards Constantinople'.[37] Evidence of the general air of belligerence in the Agency at this time can also be found in Boyle's comment to his mother a few days later: 'It is years since we have had such a jolly old time as we are having about the Akaba frontier and the Lord is like a thrush on the lawn from gaiety and happiness at having a fight again. Nothing cheers him up like a row, especially if it is with our old pal at Constantinople.'[38]

Finally, Cromer managed to wear Grey and the Cabinet down with his appeals to the need to bolster British prestige, to protect imperial communications, and so forth. The result was a stiff ultimatum to the Sultan in early May demanding the withdrawal of his troops from Taba within ten days, backed up by orders to British warships to proceed in the general direction of the Dardanelles, seizing 'island after island' on the way.[39] This was sufficient to force the Ottomans to capitulate, pulling out their troops and then taking part in a joint delimitation of the frontier, which was finally signed on 1 October. According to Ronald Storrs, Egypt had always been 'the father of improvisation and its first cousin, bluff'.[40] In this case at least, Cromer would certainly have concurred. As he admitted to Grey in May, if the Turks had acted more diplomatically themselves, it would have been very difficult 'to justify strong action on this small incident'.[41] Nevertheless, it does not seem that he got everything he wanted: what the British now saw as an international frontier, the Ottomans themselves called only

[36] Rashid Khalidi, *British Policy Towards Syria and Palestine 1906–1914* (London: Ithaca Press, 1980), 32–3.
[37] Dispatch of 7 Apr. 1907, quoted ibid. 35.
[38] 11 Apr. 1907, quoted ibid. 40.
[39] Grey to Cromer, 3 May 1906, PRO, FO 800/46.
[40] Storrs, *Orientations*, 22.
[41] 16 May 1906, PRO, FO 800/46.

a 'separating administrative line'.[42] And so it was that the issue continued to trouble the successor states until it was finally settled when the Israelis agreed to cede their Taba Hotel to the Egyptians in the early 1980s.

Cromer's bluster can also be seen as having an important Egyptian domestic component. On the one hand, the plans he was just unfolding for reform of the Capitulations required convincing the European communities that, in spite of all their fears about a general Islamic rising, their security was safe in British hands. Hence his demand for a second increase in the garrison in April based on the 'absolute necessity to establish confidence that public order can be maintained'.[43] Hence too the marching of troops through the 'native quarter' of Cairo and the disarming of the Egyptian police in Buhaira.[44] On the other, Cromer believed it important to deflate the pan-Islamists as a way of encouraging what he had identified as the more moderate Egyptian national elements associated with Shaikh Muhammad Abduh and his circle. Egyptians, he informed Grey, must be convinced that 'we have got the best of it' and that it is the Turks 'who have had to climb down'.[45] Much the same thinking informed his response to the next significant incident, the attack on some of the officers of a British mounted infantry battalion involved in a military show of force from Cairo to Alexandria in mid-June.

The battalion reached a military camp in Khamshish in the Delta province of Minufiya on 13 June 1906 in time for five of its officers and its doctor to set off to shoot pigeons at the neighbouring village of Dinshawai as they had done the two previous years. What happened next was subject to some dispute. However, on the basis of the report of the subsequent trial, it seems that the British started their shooting in two groups outside the village before receiving official permission from the *umda*, or officially appointed headman.[46] The correspondent of *The Times* even suggested that one of the five villagers they approached had told their guide, in Arabic, to 'be careful' or to 'watch out'.[47]

The trouble began when, as one of the officers, a Lieutenant Porter, started to shoot, fire broke out in the grain pile of a nearby threshing floor causing the owner, Muhammad Abd al-Nabi Muazzin, to try to seize

---

[42] Marshall-Cornwall, 'Enigmatic Frontier', 461.

[43] Cromer to Grey, 21 May 1906, PRO, FO 141/397.

[44] Richmond to Muriel [Lubbock] May 1906, RL.

[45] 28 Apr. 1907, PRO, FO 800/46.

[46] 'Correspondence Respecting the Attack on British Officers at Denshawai', *PP* (1906), 137. 703–5.

[47] *The Times*, 5 July 1906.

Porter's gun. In the struggle the gun went off, wounding five villagers including Muazzin's wife. There may even have been a moment when it was thought that she was dying. The leader of the expedition, a Major Pine-Coffin, rushed across to see what was going on and, in order to try to calm things down, ordered the rest of the group to give up their guns and to walk back to their carriages. Then, when a crowd of angry villagers attacked them and prevented them from getting away, the Major told a Captain Bull and the doctor to run back to camp for help. Bull collapsed from a combination of a blow to the head and sunstroke and died that same evening. The others were eventually rescued by some policemen and village guards. Finally, soldiers arrived and randomly arrested some seventy villagers.

Cromer's instant response to the news was to order the assembly of a special tribunal to try the case under a decree which he had had passed in 1895. As he had written to the Foreign Secretary at that time, he wanted to have some machinery to hand that would deal 'swiftly and summarily' with attacks on British soldiers and sailors with the power to inflict 'severer punishment' than was possible in the *ahaliyah* courts.[48] Swift and summary it was. After three days of hearings the court of five, consisting of two Britons and two Egyptians under the presidency of Butros Ghali, the acting Minister of Justice, pronounced sentence on the morning of 27 June. It ordered four of the alleged culprits to be hanged for the 'intentional' murder of Captain Bull, and eight flogged, with the punishments to be carried out the next day in front of their fellow villagers. Muazzin and another man were sentenced to penal servitude for life, and ten others to between one and fifteen years.[49]

Cromer had himself left Egypt for London before the trial began, taking much longer than usual to make the journey as Katherine's sudden attack of measles forced them to sail home across the Bay of Biscay rather than by train through France. By the time they arrived on 30 June, Mansfeld Findlay, Cromer's new deputy, had confirmed the sentences and begun to make a case both for their severity and for the justice of the proceedings, telling Grey that 'I am informed [by the two British judicial officials who acted as judges] that any British jury would have found the six [main] prisoners guilty of murder.'[50]

[48] 24 Feb. 1895, a copy of which appears in 'Correspondence Respecting the Attack on British Officers', 689.

[49] Ibid. 704–5.

[50] Findlay to Grey, 27 June 1906, PRO, FO 141/404, and 8 July 1906, PRO, FO 800/46; Parl. Deb., vol. 159, col. 1111 (28 July 1906).

As soon as he heard the news, Cromer realized that a mistake had been made. Grey describes how he came to see him saying that he was greatly 'disturbed', that it would have a bad effect on public opinion, and that if he had had any notion that such things might happen, 'he would never have left Egypt before the trial was over'. Nevertheless, once the sentences had been announced, they could not be rescinded.[51] Cromer's public position, expressed in a hastily written memorandum, was that he considered the sentences, 'though severe, just and necessary'.[52] But even this document reveals some of his sense of embarrassment at the fact not only that public hangings had been officially abolished in Egypt some years before, but that his annual reports had always placed heavy emphasis on the British role in putting an end to the use of the kurbash (*kurbaj*), or heavy whip used to flog the taxes out of the rural population.

Writing from Cairo, Boyle, confessed to his mother: 'The sentence was rather a staggerer for, between ourselves, we had not expected any capital punishments.'[53] Storrs later commented that 'some of us felt that a mistake had been made'.[54] Humphrey Bowman, a newly appointed British school inspector, tried to justify matters to himself with the argument that, while it had been necessary to hang someone, it had also been impossible to stop at just one because the evidence did not point to any one person being any more responsible than anyone else.[55]

None of this was any help when it came to the storm of criticism stirred up by the sentences in both Britain and Egypt. Whereas there had only been twenty questions about Egypt during the winter and spring of 1906, fifty-two were laid down during the rest of the year just about Dinshawai.[56] The Liberal MP John Mackinnon Robertson also brought up the matter during the summer adjournment debate in early August, using information from Egypt to argue that the attack on the officers was not premeditated, as the House had first been told, that Major Pine-Coffin could hardly have believed that Captain Bull's injuries were serious when he sent him to run 6 miles to get help, and that 'the great deeds of Lord Cromer were no reason for permitting under his control

[51] Lord Grey of Falloden, *Twenty-Five Years: 1892–1916* (New York: Frederick A. Stokes, 1925), i. 134.
[52] Memorandum by Lord Cromer, 12 July 1906, PRO, FO 141/404.
[53] 6 July 1906, BP, box C/3.
[54] Storrs, *Orientations*, 64.
[55] Entry for 27 Sept. 1906, Journal, Sept. 1905–Mar. 1910, BowP, box 3A.
[56] Mellini, *Gorst*, 116–17.

acts of mere revenge which were unworthy of the traditions of the British Empire'.[57]

It was Grey who bore the brunt of the attack, trying to steer a course midway between attempting to cut off debate entirely, as Cromer and Findlay seemed to urge, and allowing his backbenchers to voice their legitimate concerns. Moreover, he did it with a decreasing lack of conviction. In particular he felt that he had been forced into making misleading statements on the basis of the early reports that he had received from Cairo, and that 'when the full facts were before me I felt that what had been done was open to question'.[58] This probably explains his very half-hearted defence of British policy during the adjournment debate, admitting that public executions were 'a very doubtful expedient except in the rarest cases', and that public flogging should 'never be resorted to'.[59]

Meanwhile, outside Parliament, Wilfrid Blunt was orchestrating a campaign of articles, pamphlets, and visits of Egyptian nationalist politicians designed to discredit the occupation. His main effort was the publication in mid-September of what he called his 'Atrocity' pamphlet, an account of Dinshawai written with the help of the detailed reports in Egyptian newspapers.[60] Its aim, he wrote, was to show that Dinshawai was no 'exceptional error of judgment but part of a system in which every principle of civilised law has been for years past made subservient to what has been considered political advantage'. More specifically, the system of justice was dominated by Lord Cromer and, in political cases, no local court had the 'smallest independence'.[61] Then, after a survey of a number of cases involving disputes between Egyptians and members of the army of occupation, and a sharp criticism of the conduct of the Dinshawai trial, he laid the entire blame on Cromer and demanded that he be called to account for his actions.

The pamphlet was translated into Arabic and published in two Cairo newspapers in early October.[62] A leader in the *Manchester Guardian* used its comments to point out that the original decree setting up the Special Tribunal referred only to attacks on soldiers going about their military

[57] Parl. Deb., vol. 162, cols. 1822–9 (4 Aug. 1906).

[58] Quoted in Mellini, *Gorst*, 271 n. 66.

[59] Parl. Deb., vol. 162, cols. 1831–5 (4 Aug. 1906).

[60] Wilfrid Scawen Blunt, *Atrocities of British Justice Under British Rule in Egypt* (London: T. Fisher Unwin, 1906); Longford, *A Pilgrimage of Passion*, 360–1.

[61] Blunt, *Atrocities*, 6.

[62] Blunt to Meynell, 2 Oct. 1906, Houghton Library, Harvard University, W. S. Blunt, bMS Eng. 1235.

duty. It also wondered how Cromer's scheme for the abolition of the Capitulations could ever commend itself to members of the European communities so long as Cromer himself showed so little trust in the Egyptian courts.[63]

It was left to Bernard Shaw, briefed by Blunt, to have what are the most famous last words on the affair. In the preface to his play *John Bull's Other Island*, entitled 'The Denshawai Horror', he asked his audience to

Try to imagine the feelings of an English village if a party of Chinese officers suddenly appeared and began shooting the ducks, the geese, the hens and the turkeys and carried them off, asserting that they were wild birds as everybody in China knew, and that the pretended indignation of the farmers was a cloak for hatred of the Chinese, and perhaps for a plot to overthrow the religion of Confucius and establish the Church of England in its place.[64]

In Egypt, Dinshawai provided the catalyst for the latent anti-British feeling to express itself in many quarters. According to Mustafa Kamil, the Khedive had felt so insulted that a pardon for the Dinshawai prisoners was refused in his name without consultation that he deliberately stayed in Alexandria to avoid attendance at the King's birthday parade.[65] Meanwhile, popular outrage orchestrated by the nationalist press helped to turn a group of individual critics of the occupation into a popular movement with its own parties and programmes. The temperature was further raised by an exchange of fierce polemics between the pro-government and opposition press, with the latter attacking the Egyptians who had taken the government side in the trial, and then themselves being attacked for their dangerous and divisive comments. There was also an almost instant production of novels, one entitled *The Maiden of Dinshawai*, a play, *Masrahiyat Dinshaway*, which was banned in 1908, and numerous poems which did much to bring the affair to the attention of Egyptians living outside the major cities.[66] One poem, attributed to Muhammad Ajaj, has Cromer turning up at Dinshawai demanding 'excessive restitution' and including flogging for the lesser sentences. It ends:

[63] *Manchester Guardian*, 12 Sept. 1906.

[64] George Bernard Shaw, 'Preface for Politicians', in his *John Bull's Other Island and Major Barbara; also, How He Lied to Her Husband* (London: Archibald Constable, 1907), xliv–xlv.

[65] Blunt, entry for 19 Dec. 1906, *My Diaries*, 575–6.

[66] *The Times*, 27 Aug. 1906; Findlay to Grey, 20 July 1906, PRO, FO 371/67; Pierre Cachia, *Popular Narrative Ballads of Modern Egypt* (Oxford: Clarendon Press, 1969), 247–57.

Those who were hanged have died, and from the lashes blood ran, Something that indeed brings tears to the people, the sons of the Fatherland.[67]

In the memoirs of Egyptians alive at the time, news of the Dinshawai punishments is generally portrayed as the blackest moment of their lives.[68]

To Cromer, trying to nurse his health in Caithness, it must have been a particularly trying time. Many of his old bugbears had returned to haunt him: a Liberal Party whose leaders spent too much time appeasing their radical followers, Wilfrid Blunt still capable of exercising a considerable influence, and regular news from Findlay and Boyle in Cairo of the continuing torrent of criticism in Cairo and its impact on the morale of their own small band of local supporters. Mustafa Kamil had become a 'tribune of the people', Boyle wrote to him in September, 'and is full of abuse for the *Muqattam*'. And he went on to marvel at the difference between the small number of agitators and the 'vast amount of turmoil and unrest they are creating'.[69] Then, just before returning to Egypt, Cromer had what was obviously quite a difficult meeting with some newspaper editors in London, at which, according to the leader writer of *The Tribune*, 'he showed great emotion and [was] quite upset about the Denshawai business'.[70]

All Cromer and Findlay could do was to hammer away at Grey on the theme that the Egyptian 'agitation' would have been impossible if its leaders had not been able to count on finding supporters in the House of Commons.[71] In August Cromer was still harping on the same theme, arguing that Mustafa Kamil and his followers, 'such as they are', had been greatly 'heartened' by the speeches of a 'certain MP' (Robertson) with the result that a 'native patriotic party is spinning into existence'.[72] Repeated almost ad nauseam, this belief offered a crumb of comfort, as well as a very obvious way of shifting the blame.

The other crumb of comfort was the emergence of opposition to Mustafa Kamil from inside the nationalist movement itself. Hence, Cromer must have taken great pleasure when he read Findlay's dispatch of 5 August reporting the efforts of two Egyptian gentlemen of 'high social and official standing'—certainly Muhammad Mahmoud, a future Prime Minister, and

[67] Ibid. 255, 257.
[68] e.g. Salamah Musa, *The Education of Salamah Musa*, trans. L. O. Schuman (Leiden: Brill, c.1961), 32–3.
[69] 'Review of Week's Press Activity', 10 Sept. 1906, HP, VIII.
[70] Blunt, entry for 6 Oct. 1906, *My Diaries*, 568.
[71] Findlay to Grey, 20 July 1906, PRO, FO 371/67.
[72] 26 Aug. 1906, PRO, FO 371/67.

Ahmad Lutfi al-Sayyid, a lawyer who had helped to defend the Dinshawai peasants—to found a new newspaper called *al-Jarida*. They proposed, he said, to create a healthy public debate concerning religious understanding and reform based on the assumption that the system of government should be accepted as it actually was, and that no objection would be allowed to the part played by His Majesty's Government or the presence of British advisers.[73]

Meanwhile, Cromer was politician enough to recognize that changes needed to be made. Some clues to this thinking can be found in his 'Memorandum on the Situation in Egypt', completed at Strathmore Lodge on 8 September. Part of it was defensive—'the only people who take an interest in the welfare of the people are British officials'—and part a restatement of previous positions such as the need for the 'fusion' of the dwellers in Egypt. Nevertheless, he did suggest three new initiatives. One echoed the conventional imperial response to demands for greater partici-pation in government with a proposal that Egyptians be allowed to involve themselves more fully in local and provincial affairs and to spend money allotted from new taxation. Secondly, he was actively encouraging the small class of 'moderates' to start a newspaper, 'by all possible means short of granting pecuniary aid'. And, thirdly, he proposed to address some of the problems of personal government by finding a way to bring the heads of department 'more systematically together'. One thing he was not prepared to suggest, however, was any attempt to revivify either the general assembly or the Legislative Council, both of which he professed to hold in low esteem.[74]

Cromer's Last Seven Months in Egypt

Cromer returned to Cairo in October. His first letters to Grey were upbeat. On 27 October he wrote that the situation was better than he had expected and Mustafa Kamil discredited, and on 2 November that he had heard on all sides that 'Denshawai is forgotten.'[75] This was now to be the Agency line: that Egyptian feeling had largely subsided, and that if

[73] Findlay to Grey, PRO, FO 371/67; Charles Wendell, *The Evolution of the Egyptian National Image: From Its Origins to Ahmad Lutfi al-Sayyid* (Berkeley: University of California Press, 1972), 215–6 n.; Lutfi al-Sayyid, *Egypt and Cromer*, 188.
[74] PRO, FO 371/68.
[75] CP/2, FO 633/13.

agitators like Kamil continued to make trouble it was only because they felt well supported by their friends in London. It was not an easy line to sustain, however, and any advantage he might have obtained from his summer in England was soon dissipated by the combination of work and worry.

In spite of having increasing problems with his digestion, Cromer threw himself into a number of new initiatives, as well as seeking to make further progress over the Capitulations. The first of the initiatives was the upgrading of the Department of Education to a ministry and the appointment of one of the 'moderates', Saad Zaghlul, as its new head in early November. Zaghlul was someone he had known of for many years, a protégé of Princess Nazli, who, at her encouragement, had learned French, attended the law school in Cairo, and had then become her legal adviser. He was something of a political loner but loosely associated with Ahmad Lutfi al-Sayyid and the would-be founders of *al-Jarida*. As Cromer made the case to Grey, he was anxious to encourage the cooperation of Egyptians in high positions. Owing to what he called 'force of circumstances', the present ministers had 'drifted rather into a position of ciphers'. Zaghlul would not be such a person.[76] What must also have been on his mind was that the appointment would do something to mollify the critics of his educational policy while also helping to quieten the disturbances at the law school and elsewhere. It was certainly approved of by Blunt, particularly after Mustafa Kamil had told him that Zaghlul was asserting his authority against Dunlop.[77]

Christmas seems to have gone well, and Cromer was gratified by the number of Egyptians who came to pay a call on what, he told Grey, they regarded as Britain's national fête. He took it, he wrote, as a sign that the occupation was not so unpopular after all.[78] But then, in late January, came an upsetting fact-finding visit to Egypt by J. M. Robertson. Cromer took the precaution of obtaining a report on him from a 'trustworthy police agent', who found him 'ignorant and vain'.[79] He then had three interviews with Robertson, who reported various things he had learned during his stay, among them that he had been told by a few Egyptians that they would be willing to pay heavier taxes if the money were to be spent on education.[80]

[76] 2 Nov. 1906, CP/2, FO 633/13.
[77] Entry for 19 Dec. 1906, Blunt, *My Diaries*, 577.
[78] 26 Dec. 1906, CP/1, file marked 'Typed copy of private correspondence with Sir Edward Grey over Dinshawai'.
[79] 12 Jan. 1907, ibid.
[80] Cromer to Grey, 1 Feb. 1907, CP/2, FO 633/13.

Robertson told Blunt that he had found Cromer 'very nervous and sensitive about public opinion in Britain'.[81] Cromer told the Reverend Rennie MacInnes of the Church Missionary Society that Robertson had shown himself to be the 'most narrow-minded man he had ever met' and that he had 'swallowed everything he was told by the Nationalists'.[82] Six weeks later Cromer invited MacInnes to a second interview to complain about some statements which Robertson had made in the House of Commons concerning missionary activity in southern Sudan, telling him that it was monstrous that a European should 'endeavour to excite Moslem fanaticism in this manner' and urging him to get the Society's spokesman in Parliament to warn the House of Commons against listening to such foolish and irresponsible criticisms.[83] Even if one makes allowance for the fact that Cromer was now a very ill man, there is more than a touch of political paranoia here.

Cromer's other main preoccupation remained the abolition of the Capitulations. By now he had come to the conclusion that his scheme would only work if it was accompanied by a clear statement concerning the permanency of the occupation. This, in his eyes, was made the more important by the extra need to reassure the foreign community after the near-panic triggered by fears of Egyptian violence following the sentences at Dinshawai. As he put it baldly to Grey on 17 January 1907, unless the Government made a move, 'we may bid goodbye to any idea of modifying the Capitulations'. Moreover, if there were the least idea of any concessions to Mustafa Kamil, the local opposition to modifying the Capitulations, 'already strong', would become irresistible, and all the resident Europeans would have their governments cordially behind them.[84] Grey, worried about the reaction of the Cabinet, cut out the words 'perpetual and 'permanent' from the statement Cromer hoped to use to the British Chamber of Commerce, permitting him to say no more than that 'there is no reason for allowing the prospect of reform . . . to be prejudiced by any doubt as to the continuance of the British occupation which it is the settled intention of the British government to maintain'.[85]

[81] Entry for 19 Feb. 1907, Blunt, *My Diaries*, 578–9.
[82] MacInnes to Baylis, 12 Apr. 1907, quoted in Mellini, *Gorst*, 126. The interview took place on 4 Mar. 1907.
[83] MacInnes to Baylis, 11 May 1907, quoted in Mellini, *Gorst*, 127. The interview took place on 25 Apr. 1907, after Cromer's resignation.
[84] CP/2, FO 633/13.
[85] Grey to Campbell-Bannerman, 18 Jan. 1907, C-BP, Add. MS 41218; Grey to Cromer, 18 Jan. 1907, quoted in Roberson, 'Judicial Reform', 251.

The same formula was repeated in the Annual Report for 1906, which Cromer wanted to use not only as a reply to his critics but also to promote further discussion of his ideas among the foreign communities. By now he was ill again or, as he told Grey, 'desperate from strain of work', and some of the report had to be written while he sailed up the Nile for a rest.[86] To add to his difficulties, an Egyptian Committee had been formed to watch Egyptian affairs in the House of Commons—Grey believed it had been 'got up by Blunt'—and was pressing both him and Grey hard on a number of matters, including education and the absence of any preparation for eventual Egyptian autonomy.[87] Cromer was compelled to make several last-minute changes in the text of the new Annual Report in response to each new critical thrust.[88] Sometimes this took the form of alterations to the budget as well. As he grumbled to Gorst in late February, it had become necessary to spend larger sums of money on education during the next financial year, 'because the demand here is universal', and because it had become the chief point of attack of Robertson and his friends. Just how annoying he found this type of politics is revealed in the comments that followed:

If we are to take up the line that some abuse is to be abolished at once, merely because it is an abuse, or that some reform, however costly, is to be carried out because it is required, it will, I need hardly say be a complete reversal of the policy which has been carried out with great success for the last twenty years and more, and moreover would land us in very serious financial embarrassments.[89]

The Annual Report was, always, the work of many hands. Cromer's own contribution can be seen in his remarks on the nature of Egyptian nationalism, as well as in his restatement of the basic lines of future education policy. By now his views must have been very well known, at least in official circles, and much of what he wrote was simply an echo of his previous memorandum 'The Present State of Egypt'. There were, he wrote, various 'currents of thought' that were moving in the direction of creating a local public opinion favourable to 'Egyptian Nationalism'. The first current was 'deeply tinged with Pan-Islamism'. And a second, the Egyptian National Party (of Mustafa Kamil), consisted merely of 'a few noisy individuals . . . who in no way represent the real wishes and aspirations of their fellow countrymen'. Its aim, an immediate extension of parliamentary institu-

---

[86] 6 Feb. 1907, PRO, FO 800/46.
[87] Grey to Cromer, 1 Nov. 1906, CP/2, FO 633/13, and 1 Mar. 1907, ibid.
[88] Cromer to Grey, 1 and 9 Mar. 1907, PRO, FO 800/46.
[89] 28 Feb. 1907, ibid.

tions, would produce a 'chaotic' situation in which intrigue would be rife, while any attempt to exert financial control would inevitably lead to national bankruptcy. Hence the one nationalism worth the name was the solidarity of all the dwellers in Egypt, and the formation of an Egyptian 'national spirit in the only sense in which that spirit can be evoked without detriment to the true interests of the country'.[90] As for education, the Report indicates that, while more money would be made available, there would be no move in the direction of more free education or more Arabic language until more teachers had been trained. The other major goal remained the extension of elementary education in the vernacular.[91]

In London members of the Egyptian Committee continued to ask about a 'dozen or so questions a week' in Parliament.[92] Apart from Cromer's educational policy, there was continued concern about the use of the special courts and the long gaol sentences passed on the Dinshawai prisoners. Cromer, now severely weakened from his digestive problems, defended himself as best he could while clearly becoming more and more irritated with Grey for not supporting him more strongly against the pack 'barking and snarling at my heels'. His difficulties were not local, he argued, but stemmed entirely from the 'supposed sympathy in England with the ultra-opposition here'.[93] By the same token, his attacks on the foolishness of his British critics become more and more extreme. Robertson's plan to advance rapidly in the direction of Egyptian autonomy was 'hopelessly impossible'. 'To suppose that, whilst the occupation lasts, we can leave these extremely incompetent Egyptians to do what they liked about local affairs is little short of madness.'[94] And five days later, after complaining that 'Robertson and Co.' were annoying him like 'mosquitoes', and that they were now arguing that there was no moral progress in Egypt, he countered with the gloomy prediction that 'it will not take years, but probably generations, to change the moral character of the Egyptian people. They are heavily weighted by their leaden creed and by the institutions which cluster around the Koran.'[95]

Cromer also found himself engaged in another round of tense discussion with Grey, who wanted to appease his parliamentary critics by 'revising' some of the harsher Dinshawai sentences.[96] Although he admitted that 'most people consider that severity, though necessary, was carried

[90] *PP* (1907) 100, 627–32.   [91] Ibid. 711–19.
[92] Grey to Cromer, 1 Mar. 1907, PRO, FO 800/46.
[93] Cromer to Grey, 3 Mar. 1907, CP/2, FO 633/13.   [94] Ibid.
[95] Cromer to Grey, 8 Mar. 1907, PRO, FO 800/46.   [96] 1 Mar. 1907, CP/2, FO 633/13.

somewhat too far', Cromer still wanted the matter postponed for another two or three years.[97] But he was forced, reluctantly, to give ground over the special courts and to agree that most offences against British troops should, once again, be left to the *ahaliyah* process.[98]

Grey replied as best he could, giving Cromer some of what he wanted, notably another increase in the size of the army of occupation. Grey also assured him that there had been no hesitation in backing him up when necessary. This had included taking a very strong line over Dinshawai the previous year, when Grey had defended all that had been done 'without qualification', even though some of his statements could hardly be sub-stantiated in the light of later and fuller information.[99] Whether he could have done more to assuage Cromer's larger concerns seems doubtful. On 22 March Cromer informed him that he was confined to his room but hoped to get up in two or three days.[100] Just over a week later, on 28 March, he tendered his resignation. By this time, according to Boyle, his health had totally given way. His digestion was 'entirely gone': 'he can take nothing, suffers torments of dyspepsia and generally is in so weak a state owing to want of nourishment and to constant pain that he is totally unfitted to grapple with the terrific work of this place, more especially now our life here is one long struggle and contention with hostile parties'. For months past he had taken only Bengers food for infants and now was 'unable to digest even that'.[101]

Cromer's letter of resignation lists a wholly litany of problems begin-ning with the deterioration of his health in 1898, which he traced to 'a domestic cause, the force of which none, unfortunately, are more able to appreciate than yourself', a reference to the fact that Grey's wife had been killed in a carriage accident just a year before.

Moreover, in spite of all my efforts to decentralise, the tendency is to throw the work and responsibility more and more on my shoulders. Gorst's departure made a great difference to me. I have now absolutely no one here except Garstin who is not departmental in the somewhat narrow sense of the term. If I were younger I should rather enjoy fighting the Khedive, Mustafa Kamil and their[?] English allies, and moreover, I think I should beat them.

---

[97] 7 Mar. 1907, PRO, FO 800/46.
[98] Grey to Cromer, 15 Mar. 1907, PRO, FO 371/246; Cromer to Grey, 22 Mar. 1907, PRO, FO 800/46.
[99] 9 Mar. 1907, ibid.
[100] Ibid.
[101] 27 Mar. 1907, BP, box C, file 3.

However, his local doctor, a man of decided ability, was 'quite clear on the necessity of my going'. To avoid the possibility of disturbances, or a slump in Egyptian securities, he wanted Grey to stress that his leaving was the result of ill health, not of political causes, and to emphasize that a change of man did not mean a change of policy.[102]

Grey replied that he had been 'shocked' when the news arrived by telegram and begged him to reconsider.[103] But on receipt of the letter of 28 March he realized that Cromer had no choice after listening to his doctor's opinion. He felt sure that Gorst was the best man to succeed him, even though he might have difficulties at first, owing to his lack of personal ascendancy over the 'British element and the officials'.[104] Writing privately to Hardinge, his permanent under-secretary, a few days earlier, Grey noted that 'it has been unspeakably disturbing to see him [Cromer] struggling against complete physical exhaustion & to see him nervously shrinking from opposition the existence of which a short time ago he would not have deigned to notice'.[105]

Grey made the official announcement of Cromer's resignation in the House of Commons on 12 April. Although he took care to stress that it was for reasons of health not politics, this was discounted by the Egyptian nationalist leaders, who preferred to believe that he had been asked to resign as result of their campaign and of the British government's disapproval of his blunders.[106] This was the point made by Mustafa Kamil in *al-Liwa*. Cromer's health, he wrote, had been broken by the opposition to him since Dinshawai. Though a model of personal integrity, he had lost the love of the Egyptian people, whom he had not educated politically as he should.[107] The same point, soon to become an essential feature of Egyptian nationalist lore, was repeated in the major Egyptian school history textbooks until the 1930s.[108]

Lutfi al-Sayyid's comments in the recently established *al-Jarida* made several other points which continued to inform Egyptian thinking for several decades. In an article entitled 'Lord Cromer Before History' he made a sharp distinction between the 'magnificent results' of his financial

[102] 28 Mar. 1907, CP/2, FO 633/13, copy in C-BP, Add. MS 41218, vol. XIII.
[103] 5 Apr. 1907, ibid.
[104] 7 Apr. 1907, ibid.
[105] 30 Mar. 1907, PRO, FO 800/46.
[106] El-Musaddy, 'Relations', 392.
[107] 14 Apr. 1907.
[108] Barak Aharon Salmoni, 'Pedagogies of Patriotism: Teaching Socio-Political Community in Twentieth Century Turkey and Egypt', Ph.D. thesis (Harvard, 2002), 853-4, 918.

policies and the fact that he had earned no praise in Egypt for his political opposition to British withdrawal. Moreover, in spite of 'enlarging the domain of personal freedom', Cromer had failed to establish the foundations of a 'productive and serviceable' system of public education, he had used Britons rather than Egyptians to effect his reforms, and he had ignored Egyptian nationality in favour of trying to create an 'internationalist' nationality in Egypt.[109]

Reaction in Britain was much more polarized. Grey, in making the announcement, called Cromer's retirement 'the greatest personal loss which the public service of this country could suffer'.[110] Balfour, the leader of the Conservative opposition, talked of the 'magnitude' of Cromer's work and the 'patience' with which he had carried through the 'great task committed to him'.[111] The leader writer in *The Times*, after expressing his regret, went on to observe that Cromer's name had become 'synonymous with Modern Egypt'.[112] For the *Daily Telegraph*, he was 'the administrator who has piloted the state barque through innumerable shoals into the sea of prosperity'.[113] As for Cromer's critics, the news made Wilfrid Blunt shout 'Whoo-whoop', and leave London for the country 'feeling like a huntsman at the end of his day's sport with Cromer's brush in my pocket'.[114] Ten days later he wrote some more considered criticism in the *Manchester Guardian*. Under the title 'A New Régime for Egypt', Blunt argued that Lord Cromer had what the French call 'the defects of his qualities':

His long success upon certain lines of administration has narrowed the range of his political vision to the point of making him unable to see the plain facts a little left or right of it. His strong personality, too, has hypnotized the British nation into a blindness almost equally abnormal with his own. It is time that this should cease if we are to retain hold upon our political reason. The opportunity is ours. The spell is broken. We must awake to reality and see Egyptian things for what they are.[115]

Edward Dicey, writing in the *Empire Review* for May 1907, was equally to the point. Egypt, he wrote, was less fitted for self-government than it had been twenty-five years before and it was a great blunder to have excluded the native Egyptians from all important posts.

[109] 13 Apr. 1907, quoted in Wendell, *Evolution of the Egyptian National Image*, 298, 300–1.
[110] Parl. Deb., vol. 172, col. 391 (11 Apr. 1907).   [111] Ibid., cols. 391–2.
[112] *The Times*, 12 Apr. 1907.   [113] *Daily Telegraph*, 12 Apr. 1907.
[114] Entry for 11 Apr. 1907, Blunt, *My Diaries*, 581.
[115] *Manchester Guardian*, 23 Apr. 1907.

17

Return to England
1907–1908

Last Days in Egypt

Cromer continued to try to direct policy until Gorst and his wife arrived to take over on 24 April 1907. Having made his decision, he was anxious to go as quickly as possible, writing to Rowland that 'I cannot tell you how much I am looking forward to a little peace and quiet'.[1] It was a confused and difficult time. One factor was the impact of the United States stock market crash in March, which produced immediate restrictions in local bank and mortgage credit leading to what *The Economist*'s correspondent called a 'wave of demoralisation... without parallel' on the Alexandria stock exchange.[2] Given his own preoccupations, Cromer seems to have missed the obvious international source of the crisis, believing the local stock market's troubles to be the result of the 'over-speculation' that he had been warning of for several years, made worse by nationalist agitation and the uncertainty following his own decision to leave.[3]

A second cause for concern was an outbreak of a series of strikes by local workers, including one by 7,000 to 8,000 Cairo cab drivers on 18 April in protest against the strict way in which the police, urged on by the Cromer-sponsored SPCA, inspected their horses, removing many of those deemed unfit for work. Hoping to bring the city's transport system to a halt, the cabbies smashed a tram, as well attacking carts and buses carrying children to school. Many returned to work the next day, but only after obtaining a number of concessions, including the sacking of four particularly hated

[1] 6 Apr. 1907, CP/1, Letters from 1st Earl to 2nd Earl 1905–1906.
[2] *The Economist*, 23 Mar. 1907, 504. Also Crouchley, *Investment of Foreign Capital*, 64–5.
[3] Cromer to Grey, 13 Apr. 1907, CP/2, FO 633/13.

government officials.[4] Next came the striking carters, who went even further, damaging forty-three trams. British troops were then paraded through the Bulaq quarter, where many of the strikers stabled their horses. Finally, it was the turn of the silk-weavers, the mat-makers, and, in May, the butchers.[5]

Although the timing of the strikes owed as much to the end of the winter tourist season as anything else, they were believed by many Britons to be the result of a nationalist campaign, contributing greatly to the general air of uncertainty and causing the authorities to take enormous precautions to prevent hostile demonstrations during Cromer's farewell speech at the Cairo Opera House on 4 May. In the event, although it was attended by friends and all the leading lights of the European community, it was boycotted by all but three of the leading Egyptian politicians: Mustafa Fahmi, who spoke briefly of Cromer's great contribution to Egyptian progress, the elderly Riaz Pasha, and Saad Zaghlul. Cromer's carriage passed through empty streets, but there were no signs of popular disturbance.

The speech itself was mainly a restatement of what had become his usual list of British achievements but with a significant change of emphasis. He now offered the abolition of the kurbash and the corvée, the end of major corruption, and lower taxes as examples of Egypt's 'moral', rather than 'material', progress, in an effort, it would seem, to meet the widespread criticism that he had only concerned himself with the latter. There was also a re-emphasis of the hardline position taken in his last Annual Report. The British occupation would continue for an indefinite period. And while it did the British government would be responsible for the main lines on which the administration was conducted. Gorst, his 'very able successor', would guide it along similar lines while he (Lord Cromer) would return to Britain to urge that 'this wholly spurious manufactured movement in favour of the rapid development of parliamentary institutions be treated for what it is worth' as it did not really represent the 'voice of the intelligent dwellers in Egypt, European or Egyptian'. Finally, while his opponents in England wished policy to gallop, he proposed a 'steady jog trot'.[6] All this was too much for Egypt's leading poet, Ahmad Shauqi, who wrote a

---

[4] John Chalcroft, 'The Striking Cabbies of Cairo and Other Stories: Crafts and Guilds in Egypt, 1863–1914', Ph.D. thesis (New York, 2001), 409–33.

[5] Ibid. 433–56.

[6] Earl of Cromer, *Speeches and Miscellaneous Writings*, vol. i (London: privately printed, 1912), 142–6.

'Goodbye to Lord Cromer' in which he accused him of using his Opera House speech to announce Egypt's 'lasting enslavement and unending humiliation | and a state that would never see change'.[7]

Cromer left Egypt with Katherine two days later. Once again, to avoid any chance of disturbance, all traffic was stopped and troops lined the entire route from the Agency, via Opera Square, to the station. According to the *Egyptian Gazette*, all hotel verandahs, windows, and balconies of houses were crowded with sightseers, while 'thousands of native sightseers preserved a most respectful demeanour throughout'.[8] As the train pulled out, the crowd of well-wishers broke out into 'Auld Lang Syne', and there was a fifteen-gun salute. On arrival at Folkestone a week later, the Cromers took a special train to Victoria Station, where they were met by Rowland with their little son Evelyn, as well as the Prince of Wales, the Prime Minister, and Edward Grey. They were then whisked off by carriage to the nearby Buckingham Palace.

Such had been the speed of his departure that Cromer had had to leave a 'vast pile' of private papers, behind which took Boyle several months to sort through, burning some of them, including the original manuscript of *Modern Egypt*.[9] Cromer had given a few of his books away to his staff, for example, presenting Storrs with Ricardo's collected works.[10] But a large number remained, some of which were sold by his half-sister Dorothea when she came to Egypt after his death in 1917.[11]

England and Scotland

Cromer spent his first six weeks back in England in a nursing home, then convalescing with Katherine in Caithness and at her sister Alice's home, a large Georgian house on the Ardgowan estate built on a high promontory at the mouth of the Clyde, just outside Glasgow. Zetland suggests that he derived much extra comfort from the huge numbers of letters he received from colleagues, well-wishers, and friends.[12] These may also have helped him face his next personal trial: the opposition expressed in and out of

[7] Hussein N. Khadim, 'The Poetics of Postcolonialism: Two Qasidahs by Ahmad Shawqi', *Journal of Arabic Literature*, 28 (1997), 180–2.
[8] *Egyptian Gazette*, 7 May 1907.
[9] Boyle to Cromer, 19 Aug. 1907, CP/2, FO 633/11; Boyle to Mrs Boyle, 20 Aug. 1909, BP, C/3.
[10] Storrs, *Orientations*, 54–5.
[11] *Al-Ahram*, 6 July 1990.
[12] Zetland, *Lord Cromer*, 299–302.

Parliament to the Government's proposal that he be awarded a grant of £50,000 in recognition of his services. The main reason for this somewhat unusual suggestion—such grants were usually given only to military men—was the discovery that, although his final salary had reached £6,500, his official pension would only be £900 a year.[13]

Opposition came from those who believed that there was no precedent for such generosity, that he should not be rewarded for failing to carry out the policy of evacuation that he had been sent to do, and that, in the words of William Redmond, Dinshawai was a 'savage and ruthless miscarriage of justice'.[14] However, he was well defended by Grey, the Prime Minister, and the leader of the Opposition, Arthur Balfour. Making the case for Cromer's great achievements, Grey noted that, as a result of his work, the occupation had been accepted at home and abroad, and that the British taxpayer had good reason to be indebted both for what he had done and for what he had avoided.[15] There was also an influential speech from John Robertson, in which he argued that the British, having created an autocracy in Egypt, and having backed the system of which Lord Cromer was the representative, were not entitled to 'haggle over the business of giving a grant'.[16] In the end, the vote was carried by 254 votes to 107, with many Liberal MPs abstaining. Blunt was delighted to discover that the Government was only saved from defeat by the Conservative vote.[17]

Cromer was well enough by October to receive the freedom of the City of London. In his acceptance speech at the Guildhall he attacked those in both England and Egypt who had misled the Egyptians into thinking that British public opinion favoured their rapid political development. These were the 'extremists' who existed in Cairo as well as Calcutta and Dublin, and any attempt to conciliate them would spell political suicide in India and Ireland and cause Egypt to relapse into the misgovernment and disorder of the past. Then, after praising Gorst, he added the slightly barbed comment that he would do well if he did not allow himself to be hurried by 'faddists' in England and the numerous tribe which sympathized with them in Egypt.[18]

Cromer's main activity was to put the finishing touches to the manuscript of *Modern Egypt*, including criticisms of passages in Wilfrid Blunt's recently published *Secret History of the English Occupation of Egypt* (1906),

---

[13] Marlowe, *Cromer in Egypt*, 275–6. [14] Parl. Deb., vol. 179, col. 863 (30 July 1907).
[15] Ibid., cols. 875–83. [16] Ibid., col. 886.
[17] Entry for 1 Aug. 1907, Blunt, *My Diaries*, 590.
[18] *The Times*, 29 Oct. 1907, copy in CP/2, FO 633/25.

and replacing his original conclusion with a new one entitled 'The Future of Egypt'.[19] He then obtained assent to its publication from the Palace and the Foreign Office, but only after Grey had made some 'problems' by insisting that he remove an extract from a letter by Queen Victoria.[20] Finally, he was given help with reading the page proofs by Boyle and Gorst in November 1907.

The two volumes of *Modern Egypt*, some 1,200 pages in all, were published in early March 1908. Its stated aims were to provide a narrative of some of the principal events in Egypt from bankruptcy in 1876 to the death of Taufiq in 1892, and then to explain the 'results which accrued to Egypt from the British occupation'.[21] Although Cromer had also completed an account of his early confrontations with the Khedive Abbas, he thought it improper to publish it until after Abbas's deposition in 1914. Two other aims are mentioned. One, he wrote, was to counter certain historical 'inaccuracies' which had crept into public perceptions about British policy in Egypt. The other was to offer the book as a guide to some of the general problems of 'Oriental administration' where the broad lines of reform are 'traced out by the commonplace requirements of European civilisation'.[22] For Cromer, Egypt is thus seen as part of the East but with certain special features. It was a country, he asserted, where one alien race (the British) had to control a second (the Turkish) in the government of a third (the Egyptian). And it had to be reformed without changing the 'condition of government' that had existed before the occupation began.[23]

The historical part consists of thirty-three chapters with a particular emphasis on the nature of the Urabi revolt, the reasons for the occupation, and then the abandonment and later reconquest of Sudan. Much of it involves a root-and-branch criticism of Ismail's financial mismanagement, followed by a detailed and quite technical account of the efforts made by Cromer and his colleagues to put the finances to rights. But the main weight of argument concerns, first, an analysis of the character of the Egyptian 'quasi-national' movement under Urabi, and then a detailed examination of the varying degrees of responsibility for the decision to evacuate Sudan, the Gordon mission, and the long delay in launching the

[19] Zetland, *Lord Cromer*, 303, 307.
[20] Cromer to Rowland (Errington), 6 Nov. 1907, CP/1, Letters from 1st Earl to 2nd Earl, 1905–1906.
[21] Cromer, *Modern Egypt*, i. 1–2.
[22] Ibid. 2–5.
[23] Ibid. 5–6.

Gordon relief expedition. Here the main protagonists are revealed not to be the Egyptians, nor the Sudanese, but Cromer's three major British *bêtes noires*: Blunt, Gladstone, and Gordon. Reference to Blunt becomes the occasion to repeat the now standard Cromerian judgement that the Arabic-speaking Muslims, whose capacities Blunt touted, would never have been able to run the country properly on their own. Not only had they been a 'subject race' for many centuries past, but the first thing they would have done had they been allowed to come to power would have been to eliminate the only people with proper administrative skills: the Europeans, the Turks, the Khedive Taufiq, and the Syrians and Armenians.[24] This was more or less the same argument that Cromer had presented to Salisbury in 1887, but extended in such a way that it was now supposed to apply as much to the situation before 1882 as it was to the years just after.

As for Gladstone and Gordon, it is easy to imagine how the disparaging references to them in some early drafts had been toned down as a result of correspondence with Gladstone's biographer John Morley and others. Nevertheless, what remains is still a 'flighty' Gordon, completely unsuitable for the task assigned him, and of a pusillanimous Gladstone unwilling to recognize the approaching danger, and so very much at fault for not sending an expedition to rescue Gordon before it was too late.[25] It is to Cromer's great credit that he also admits that he too made a great mistake in agreeing to send Gordon to Khartoum, even if he excuses it a little with his suggestion that he allowed himself to be carried away by the enthusiasm for Gordon shown by Northbrook and practically everybody else whose judgement he valued.[26]

The sections on contemporary Egypt begin with an account not of the country's natural resources but of the many different types of peoples who lived there. Their heterogeneity is demonstrated by offering the reader the same lesson that Kipling's lama provides Kim on his journey along the Great Trunk Road, an 'ethnological' description of a random set of passers-by in an imagined Cairo street each defined in terms of his facial features, clothes, and manner.[27] There is one whose 'headgear, dress and aquiline nose' proclaims him a Beduin. And another whose small height, dreamy eyes, and far-away look suggest a Coptic clerk in a government office. And so on. Who then, Cromer ask rhetorically, is Mr Wilfrid Blunt's 'true Egyptian'?[28] There follows an equally essentialist account of the social

---

[24] Ibid. 323–8.   [25] Ibid. 429–35, 582–92.   [26] Ibid. 436–9.
[27] Rudyard Kipling, *Kim* (New York: Doubleday, Page, 1901), 96–9.
[28] Cromer, *Modern Egypt*, ii. 127–8.

role of Islam, which leaves the reader in no doubt that, in Cromer's eyes, the Muslim Egyptians are not only different from Christians but also inferior. Islam keeps women in a position of 'marked inferiority', it subjects Muslims to a law based on 'antique principle', it tolerates slavery, and is intolerant of all members of other religions.[29] The result is an insurmountable barrier between the Muslim and the Christian. Christians, or, as they now become, 'Europeans', practise accuracy, scepticism, concern for the future; Muslims, in Cromer's world-view, do just the opposite.[30]

It is no defence of writing of this type to say that the same prejudices were probably held by the vast majority of Europeans and North Americans at this time. Nor to point out that, some thirty years earlier, Cromer himself had imagined both Egyptians and Indians as much better able to administer themselves than he now believed. What we can say is that the vast expansion of the European empires into the non-European world at the end of the nineteenth century practically demanded such views. Not only could this essentially despotic form of rule be justified in terms of racial difference, but the notion of difference itself also allowed the deployment of a whole host of politically self-congratulatory terms to laud such rule as a 'mission' or as Britain's 'work' in Egypt.[31] Looked at from this perspective, what becomes special about Cromer's version of the white man's burden is not just its emphasis on race as a biological category, but also the energy he puts into confronting Wilfrid Blunt's counter-arguments about Egypt's right to national independence. And all the while defending his own policies as being both in British interests and in the interests of the vast majority of Egyptians, whether or not they were capable of understanding it themselves.

It also has to be said that Cromer's remarks about Islam were deeply offensive to most Muslims. Perhaps this is what Harry Boyle meant when he wrote to his mother in November 1907 that, in his opinion, 'the Lord is going to get himself in to the most appalling trouble with this blessed book' and that 'I am doing my best to get him to cut out some of the worst, from the local point of view, parts.'[32] But he could equally well have been referring to certain other characteristics of Cromer's expository style. One was the use of thumbnail sketches of real (though recently deceased) Egyptians he had known to exemplify what was wrong with the different sections of Egyptian society. Hence Shaikh Muhammad Abduh is used to make the point that an orthodox Muslim's attention to the letter rather

[29] Ibid. 134–40.   [30] Ibid. 145–50.   [31] Ibid. 124.   [32] 18 Nov. 1907, BP, III/B.

than the spirit of his faith tends to make him an 'Agnostic'.[33] And Shaikh Muhammad Bayram is mentioned as an example of the pain felt by a would-be religious reformer who realized that there was no way of arresting Islam's decay.[34] Nor do Cromer's Christian acquaintances fare much better. Nubar is described as the 'peculiar type of Oriental' who can weave a series of 'half-truths, bordering on fiction' into the appearance of truth.[35] While Tigrane, his son-in-law, possessed the Armenian national characteristic of a 'Franco-Byzantine' mind.[36]

Another characteristic rhetorical device was to proceed from a series of anecdotes designed to indicate the 'muddleheadedness' of the 'ordinary uneducated Egyptian' to the much larger claim that 'somehow the Oriental generally acts, speaks, and thinks in a manner exactly opposite to the European'.[37] This is Herodotus' notion of Egypt as the land of paradox writ large. But what for the Greek traveller was simply an entertaining way of exaggerating difference—for example, Egyptian 'women buy and sell while men stay at home and weave'—for Cromer it becomes a marker of Eastern backwardness and so the justification for long Western tutelage.[38] Muslim Egyptians are instantly recognizable by their clothes, their actions, and their physical features, and no matter what they might do or say, they have an essentialized identity imposed upon them.[39]

The political purpose of this method of presenting the non-European population as a collection of disparate classes and communities greatly in need of foreign moral and administrative guidance is also revealed in Cromer's closing paragraphs, in which these same classes and communities are listed in terms of how they viewed the first years of the British presence. Some, like the Turco-Circassian pashas, the Muslim hierarchy, and the Europeanized Egyptians, were hostile. Others, like the Copts, the Syrians, and the Levantines, 'hovered between friendship and hostility'. Finally, the mass of the population, the peasants, were friendly from the first, but also so politically speechless, as well as so credulous and ignorant, that, had they attempted to make their voices heard, 'they would just as likely as not have fallen into the hands of frothy demagogues or unprincipled newspaper editors, who would have made them say the opposite of what they really thought'.[40]

---

[33] Cromer, *Modern Egypt*, ii. 179–80.   [34] Ibid. 181–8.   [35] Ibid. 337–8.
[36] Ibid. 223.   [37] Ibid. 151–64.
[38] Herodotus, *History*, ed. J. Enoch Powell, book VIII (Oxford: Clarendon Press, 1939), 125–6.
[39] Faisal Fatehali Devji, 'Hindu/Muslim/Indian', *Public Culture*, 5/1 (Fall 1992), 11–12.
[40] Cromer, *Modern Egypt*, ii. 257.

Cromer's picture of the Egyptian class structure is that of a predominantly agricultural society with a governing class, or aristocracy, of predominantly Turco-Circassian officials, a religious 'corporation' of learned men centred on the Azhar, a 'squirearchy' of village shaikhs and *umdas*, and then a mass of peasants at its base. It is significant that each group is defined primarily in terms of its attitude to the British occupiers, and also that there is no mention of native Egyptian merchants, professionals, or entrepreneurs, and so no sense of how such a stratum might develop in the future as part of an unstoppable process of urbanization and industrialization.[41]

Cromer's evaluation of Egypt as a mélange of different religious and racial communities then sets the stage for the rest of the book, with its description of how the British reformers, led by Cromer himself, managed to convince most of the members of this awkward crew that the benefits conferred were so palpable that they could not be denied.[42] Once again this is done by means of a skilful rhetorical device in which the 'machinery' of Egyptian government is introduced via a comparison between the European factory and a system of 'mechanical chaos'. By analogy, the former is likened to a 'civilised' state administration in which 'we [the readers] know what despotism means and we know what constitutional government means', whereas 'the political dictionary may be ransacked in vain for any terse description of the Government of Egypt'.[43] Hence this government is not really a government, the Khedive not really a ruler, the executive power all over the place, and the judicial system a tangle of conflicting jurisdictions.[44]

Whatever motive power this ramshackle enterprise may have is provided by the British officials, while Cromer himself appears, somewhat improbably, in a chapter entitled 'The Workers of the Machine'. In his role as British Agent he had 'vague but preponderant power', which he used sometimes to spur the 'unwilling Egyptian along the path of reform', sometimes to curb the impatience of the British reformer.[45] More generally, he had to assist in the government of the country, 'without the appearance of doing so and without any legitimate authority over the agents with whom I had to deal'.[46] As for the other 'workers', three of those he mentions, the Khedive Taufiq, Nubar, and Riaz, are described as providing useful, although occasionally unhelpful, collaboration, while a fourth, Mustafa Fahmi, was 'statesmanlike enough to see that the interests

[41] Ibid. i. 289, 325, and ii. 171–98. [42] Ibid. ii. 258. [43] Ibid. 260–2.
[44] Ibid. 262–3. [45] Ibid. 321, 323. [46] Ibid. 326.

of his country would be served by working loyally with the British officials instead of opposing them'.[47]

It should be clear even from this brief description that one of the 'workers' is more important than all the rest, although how much more important is not fully spelled out. Taken just at his own word, it would seem that Cromer saw his role as at least that of a manager, deciding very largely on his own not only how fast the machinery was to run but how much to invest, whom to employ, and what to produce. However, there is more to it than that. The analogy of the malfunctioning factory run on ad hoc lines is a nice way of avoiding the charge that he too might have exhibited dictatorial tendencies. Moreover, by explicitly concentrating on the situation before Abbas's succession in 1892, his account ignores the further concentration of power in the Agency during the next fifteen years.

As for the question of whether Cromer was being deliberately disingenuous about his own position, this obviously cannot be known for sure. At the very least, it seems to have suited his own self-image to imagine himself a manager hemmed in by problems not of his making. It is probably possible to go further and to argue that this perception provides an essential clue to one of the major shortcomings of his role. The model he presents is one akin to that of the engineer, albeit a social engineer, operating in a world where everything is planned for the long run, everything controlled, but leaving no room for everyday political accident, no means of anticipating future problems except in the crudest possible terms, such as his insistence on policies designed to prevent the overproduction of educated Egyptians.

The remaining chapters of *Modern Egypt* list the major reforms under the general headings of finance, irrigation, the interior, justice, education, etc., which, in Cromer's summing up, are presented as the seeds of 'true civilisation' and proof against anything that the forces of reaction in Egypt might do to destroy them. Such claims were well calculated to appeal to a European audience, as well as to many of the members of Egypt's ruling elite. What members of the same elite found much more difficult to stomach was his concluding view of 'The Future of Egypt', in which the occupation should go on indefinitely, while the passage of 'one or more generations' would be required before the question of Egyptian self-government could even be 'usefully discussed'.[48]

---

[47] Cromer, *Modern Egypt*, ii. 327–46.   [48] Ibid. 567.

Even worse was to come from the forceful repetition of his argument that Egypt would only achieve a meaningful autonomy after the abolition of the Capitulations and the fusion of all the dwellers in 'cosmopolitan Egypt' into 'one self-governing body', once again the work of years or 'possibly' generations.[49] This was an affront even to the friends of the occupation, as well as an actual incitement to the students and young professionals represented by Mustafa Kamil. Not surprisingly, these latter now began to challenge even the most obvious achievements of Cromer's rule, a process soon to be summed up by a root-and-branch indictment of Cromerian policies by the *Egyptian Standard*'s London correspondent, Theodore Rothstein, entitled *Egypt's Ruin*.[50]

The British reviews of *Modern Egypt* were mainly laudatory. In a leading article *The Times* described its publication not just as a literary event but as a 'contribution of first rate importance to the applied science of states-manship'.[51] Meanwhile, the author of a two-part review in the *Times Literary Supplement* could 'recall no instance of a great Captain of State telling so fully and reservedly and with such lucidity and candour...the story of great events quorum paes maxima fuit'.[52] For Sidney Low, the historian and literary editor of the *Standard*, it was a 'great book' by a 'great pro-consul'.[53] And for the anonymous reviewer in *The Spectator*, undoubt-edly its editor, St Loe Strachey himself, the book would prove a 'guide and inspiration to all those who are engaged in the work of establishing and keeping secure the Empire and of maintaining the character of British rule for justice and good government'. Strachey also had special praise for Cromer's 'diagnosis' of the 'Mohammedans and their creed', for no man 'has ever obtained a clearer insight into the Mohammedan and Eastern mind, and into the Mohammedan and Eastern social organism, than he has'.[54] The Indian writer S. M. Mitra agreed. Cromer's views on Orientals were wholly correct with one wicked exception: he was wrong to try to demonstrate their 'lack of intelligence' by means of the suggestion that an

[49] Ibid. 568–9.

[50] Blunt, *My Diaries*, 581; Theodore Rothstein, *Egypt's Ruin: A Financial and Administrative Record* (London: A. C. Fifield, 1910).

[51] *The Times*, 5 Mar. 1908.

[52] 'A Great Page of History', *Times Literary Supplement*, 5 Mar. 1908, 73. The reviewer's only criticism was that the index was 'deplorably inadequate and slovenly', *Times Literary Supplement*, 12 Mar. 1908, 84.

[53] Sidney Low, 'Lord Cromer on Gordon and the Gladstone Cabinet', *Nineteenth Century and After*, 63 (Apr. 1908), 674.

[54] John St Loe Strachey, 'Lord Cromer's Record of His Trust', *The Spectator*, 1 (7 Mar. 1908), 874, and 2 (14 Mar. 1908), 420.

Egyptian asked to point to his left ear would use his right rather than his left hand, not realizing that the use of the left hand was taboo.[55]

Wilfrid Blunt, not surprisingly, was much more lukewarm. In a set of first impressions he offered to the *Manchester Guardian* on 3 March 1908, he averred that the only interesting part of the first, historical, volume consisted of Cromer's personal comments on Gordon based on private letters and unpublished memorandums. As for the second volume, on the 'dwellers in Egypt', this was a 'brutal challenge to all native Egyptian sentiment'. Blunt returned to the attack in his *Gordon at Khartoum* (1911), with its avowed aim of persuading 'those in power with us to adopt an attitude towards the Mohammedan World less antagonistic to its thoughts and feelings'.[56]

Cromer's views on Gordon reignited the old controversy about Gordon's character. They inform about half of the *Daily Telegraph*'s review of 3 March 1908, and almost all of the two-part review written by W. T. Stead in his own *Daily Chronicle* a week later. Stead had a particular reason to be involved as it was he, as the editor of the *Pall Mall Gazette*, who had been the main advocate of sending Gordon to Khartoum in the first place. Criticizing what he calls Cromer's 'impeachment' of Gordon, he turns much of what Cromer writes on its head, arguing, for example, that what Cromer describes as Gordon's 'chopping and changing' was a wise tactical response to the ever changing circumstances in which he found himself in Khartoum. There is also a considerable sting in the tail when he likens Cromer to Uncle Remus's Brer Terrapin outwitted by Gordon's 'swift and brilliant' Brer Rabbit, but without even the saving grace of Brer Terrapin's sense of humour.[57] The controversy continued into the quarterlies. Lord Esher, for example, found Cromer's comments 'grudging'.[58] Meanwhile, Cromer had to field a great deal of private correspondence on the matter, including a letter from Gordon's nephew asking if he was suggesting that Gordon drank when he wrote that he had lacked 'self-control'.[59]

[55] S. M. Mitra, 'Lord Cromer and Orientals', *Nineteenth Century and After*, 63 (May 1908), 749–50. Mitra is referring to the practice of many peoples who use their left hand to wipe themselves after defecation.

[56] W. S. Blunt, *Gordon at Khartoum: Being a Personal Narrative of Events in Continuation of a 'Secret History of the English Occupation of Egypt'* (London: S. Swift, 1911), preface, v.

[57] W. T. Stead, 'Lord Cromer on General Gordon', *Daily Chronicle*, 10 Mar. 1908.

[58] Lord Esher, 'Conversations with Zobeir Pasha at Gibraltar', *Nineteenth Century and After*, 63 (June 1908), 936.

[59] Major A. Nelson to Cromer, 25 Mar. 1908, CP/2, FO 633/12.

Another set of views which provoked some criticism in England, and more in Egypt and the rest of the Muslim world, was Cromer's trenchant observations on the future of Islam. Theodore Morrison saw no reason for accepting Lord Cromer's dictum that 'Islam as a social system is moribund'.[60] Blunt saw them as 'written in a tone of contemptuous official superiority' and an attack on the 'Mahomitans' destined to give the 'gravest offence both in Egypt and in India'.[61]

In Egypt, *Modern Egypt* provided the country's leading politicians and intellectuals with an opportunity to comment not just on the book itself but also on the whole gamut of Cromerian policies. One significant review appeared in the leading journal *al-Manar*, of 1 April, almost certainly written by its editor, Rashid Rida. After acknowledging that Cromer's knowledge of the country exceeded that of any other of its rulers, Rida went on to criticize his characterization of the Egyptian mind, asking why Cromer drew his examples from uneducated rather than educated Egyptians.[62] Cromer receives further criticism for basing his views on Islam on European, rather than Islamic, voices like those of Shaikh Muhammad Abduh.[63] Finally, there is a rather confusing passage concerning Cromer's real view of Muhammad Abduh, in which Rida engaged both with *Modern Egypt* and with another review of the same work in Shaikh Ali Yusuf's *al-Mu'ayyad*. While agreeing with *al-Mu'ayyad* that Cromer's harsh comments on Abduh seemed at odds with the compliments he had paid him in his 1905 Annual Report, Rida was anxious to characterize this as an example of vacillation rather than as a use of the book to make an out-and-out attack on Abduh's faith. Rida, it seems, was unwilling to do anything to undermine the strength of Cromer's support for Muhammad Abduh, while at the same time arguing that Abduh's influence over him would have been greater if he, Abduh, had been able to obtain greater popular backing for his proposed reforms.[64]

The matter was obviously a highly contentious one, involving Abduh's relationship not just with Cromer himself but also with both religious reform and Egyptian nationalism, and discussion of it has continued until the present day. On the basis of the historical record at the time, it would seem fair to say that Cromer did, indeed, exaggerate the nature of their friendship, that both needed and, in large measure, respected each other, and that Abduh's deep opposition to the occupation was tempered by his

[60] 'Can Islam Be Reformed?', *Nineteenth Century and After*, 64 (Oct. 1908), 549.
[61] *Manchester Guardian*, 3 Mar. 1908.   [62] *Al-Manar*, 2 (1 Apr. 1908), 81, 84–7.
[63] Ibid. 87–8.   [64] Ibid. 90–104.

realization that it would be folly to oppose it directly, a position also adopted by many of his compatriots.[65]

Cromer's friends and relatives soon began to send him letters of praise or reports of people they had met who considered the work a classic, like a dining companion who had told Maurice Baring that his uncle's book was the 'best of its kind since Caesar's Gallic Wars'.[66] Others tempered their remarks with a few mild corrections. In this vein, Moberley Bell suggested that Cromer's point about the Oriental's inability to tell the truth might better be described as a habitual courtesy, giving as an example Nubar's reply to his question of how long he was going to stay: 'mais je ne viens que pour vous dire'.[67]

Modern Egypt was an immediate success in the bookshops, selling over 9,000 copies in Britain in its first two and a half years and 4,000 in the United States. This had increased to 15,000 of the 'dear' edition and 17,000 of the 'cheap' by early 1915, producing royalties of just under £4,000.[68] Just why a book of such great length should have been so popular can only be a matter of speculation. Most likely it was the unusual subject, the Egypt of the Khedives not the Pharaohs, combined with its author's global reputation and a readable style which illuminates the story of the successful government of an ancient people with nice literary touches based on a wide reading and an easy classical learning. But, most of all, it must have reflected the spirit of its age: a pride not only in empire but also in the management of subject races with all the skills and fortitude and knowledge that Edwardians were persuaded went with it.

Modern Egypt was clearly written with an English-speaking audience in mind. But Cromer was also anxious to see it translated into Arabic and to learn how it was received in Egypt itself. This was not the case with a smaller companion piece, 'The Government of Subject Races', which appeared in the *Edinburgh Review* in January 1908. The article presents material removed from earlier drafts of *Modern Egypt* in the guise of a review of a book by an Oxford academic on the decline of the Roman Empire. It allowed Cromer to speak generally about the government of 'child-like' subject peoples without breaking his own self-denying ordin-

---

[65] Adams, *Islam and Modernism*, 96–101. Also 'The Future of Egypt' by 'An Egyptian Nationalist', 1910, PRO, FO 141/492. The author describes himself as a teacher in the Egyptian government schools since 1903.

[66] 23 Aug. 1908, CP/2, FO 633/8.

[67] 1 Mar. 1908, CP/2, FO 633/8.

[68] BN, Final Addition, 15 Feb. 1915.

ance about comments on an Egypt now managed by his successor, Gorst. It also allowed him to trumpet British imperialism's superiority to the Roman Empire due to its foundation on the 'granite rock of the Christian moral code'.[69] The significance of this is less clear. On the basis of the text itself, the moral code seems to be associated with the not particularly religious virtue of the role of wise financial policies in securing the contentment of the subject races.[70] But, in the light of Cromer's own thinking at this time, he also seems to have viewed Christianity as a check on the behaviour of the Empire's governors, who had wielded power with so little obvious external constraint.

Another aim appears to have been to use his thoughts about empire to say something significant about Britain itself. Like Curzon and many of his contemporaries, he identified imperial possessions as a central aspect of Britain's global standing, while viewing their possible misgovernment as a step in the direction of 'national decay and senility' or, in another phrase, 'the nemesis which attended Roman mis-rule'.[71] The article is also remarkable for its attempt to condense his own imperial experience into a few general maxims. Good government consists very largely of what an administrator thinks is in the interests of the people he rules. The attempt to establish representative institutions may even get in its way. However, if good government fails, then the 'sword' will be powerless to defend the British position for long. 'It is said', he notes, echoing arguments he had used in his younger days, that representative institutions are a remedy to the evils attendant on personal government, and a way of learning the view of the natives and of providing them with political education. But this is misguided. The administrator's primary duty is not to introduce a system which will enable a 'small minority of natives to misgovern their countrymen but one that will enable the mass of the population to be governed according to the code of Christian morality'.[72]

Public utterances of this kind automatically made Cromer a participant in the Edwardian political discussion about the nature of imperialism. Critics of imperial expansion like Hobson and Robertson had been stimulated by the occupation of Egypt and the South African war to produce what they believed Gladstone had never managed to achieve, a theory of

---

[69] Cromer, 'The Government of Subject Races', repr. in his *Political and Literary Essays 1908–1913*, 53.
[70] Ibid. 52–3.
[71] Ibid. 3–4.
[72] Ibid. 28.

empire.[73] Not that they were against empire as such. But they were certainly against both mindless expansion, as well as the theories that men like Cromer and Curzon used to justify it; for example, the parallel between Britain and Rome and the role assigned to an imperial version of Christianity as an antidote to national decline.[74] Though not persuasive enough to win a large number of Edwardian converts, the critique of imperialism had enough bite to account for the somewhat defensive tone adopted at this time by the British trio of returned proconsuls Lords Cromer, Curzon, and Milner.[75]

[73] Hobson, *Imperialism*; John M. Robertson, *Patriotism and Empire* (London: Grant Richards, 1899), pt. III: 'The Theory and Practice of Imperialism'.

[74] Robertson, *Patriotism and Empire*, 151–7.

[75] e.g. Lord Curzon, 'The True Imperialism', *Nineteenth Century*, 63 (Jan. 1908), 151–65.

PART IV

———— ◆ ————

Reimmersion in British Political Life
1907–1917

18

An Active Retirement
1908–1914

Re-entering British Political Life

Once he felt he had fully regained his health in the spring of 1908, Lord Cromer decided to enter British political life by taking up his seat in the House of Lords. He was now 67. He spent the next four years in the energetic pursuit of a wide variety of causes until his health began to break down again in 1912, when he was too ill to go to Scotland for the summer. This was followed by a fainting fit in the autumn of 1913, and then another serious illness, a stroke, in the spring of 1914, after which he was convinced that, for all practical purposes, his political life was over.[1]

Like other returning imperial officials, Cromer found that British politics had been greatly transformed while he was away. Not only was there a wholly new set of issues, such as the naval arms race with Germany, the stand-off between the House of Commons and the House of Lords, trade union militancy, women's suffrage, and dangerous developments in the Irish question, but also new ways of conducting politics, ranging from press campaigns to strikes and direct action of the type soon to be used by the militant suffragettes. Cromer too had changed: he was now thirty-five years older than when he had first gone to India, and habituated to giving orders rather than going through the troublesome business of seeking popular or parliamentary support.

His initial approach was inevitably conditioned by imperial concerns, notably the challenges which German naval building and other developments posed to Britain's international position. This gave new importance

---

[1] BN, Insertion, 15 Feb. 1915.

to the Empire as the country's major international resource. As he told the Unionist Free Trade Club in June 1908, it would be folly to abandon Ireland when the world trend was towards confederation and agglomeration.[2] Nevertheless, even high-level initiatives of this type required a return to the type of politics he had not practised since the Army reform debates of the early 1870s: the making of speeches, which he still did not like, the negotiation of compromises, the forming of tactical alliances. To begin with, he tried to operate on the cross-benches of the Lords and in association with above-party groups like the Unionist Free Trade Club, and then the Constitutional Free Trade Union, the Centre Party Union, and the Anti-Suffrage League. However, it was not long before he was forced to recognize the central role of parties in British political life, and that, in the highly charged political atmosphere of the time, with its frequent general elections, the attempt to create, and to maintain, above-party institutions was becoming increasingly difficult.[3]

To his credit, Cromer was quick to see the need to reorder his political priorities, as well as to elaborate, and in some cases to amend, long-held political positions. Changing circumstances sometimes pushed him in a more conservative direction, for example, ending his principled support for freedom of the press in the colonies, about which, as he confessed to the Imperial Press conference in 1909, he had been too optimistic.[4] On other issues, he became noticeably more liberal, as evidenced by his recognition of the utility of trade unions and his conversion to the cause of 'reasonable social reform', particularly after Lloyd George had found an important new source of public revenue through his introduction of a graduated income tax.[5] It is also noticeable that he resorted less and less to examples drawn from his own experience abroad. A similar trend can be seen in his growing concern with electoral tactics, a good example being his speech to businessmen in Sheffield in December 1909, when he urged the Unionist Free Traders in his audience to vote for Unionist candidates on the grounds that they were the lesser of two evils and so more likely to promote national defence, to prevent any disruption of the Empire, to protect religious education, and to maintain the existence of an efficient second chamber.[6]

[2] Copy in CP/2, FO 633/26.
[3] Cromer, 'Memorandum on work done 1907–1911', CP/2, FO 633/28.
[4] See speech to Imperial Press Conference, 18 June 1909, copy in CP/2, FO 633/26.
[5] e.g. Cromer's speech on the Finance Bill, 23 Nov. 1909, H.L. Deb., vols. 5–6, col. 823 (23 Nov. 1909).
[6] The Times, 18 Dec. 1909.

Cromer made his maiden speech on 6 February 1908 in support of the recently concluded Anglo-Russian Agreement, which he praised for removing one source of European competition in the East, and so making it easier for Britain to deal with Indian unrest.[7] Like most of his other efforts, the speech looks good on paper. But, according to Edmund Gosse, the House of Lords librarian, he was not easy to follow when tired, having the 'sad trick' of dropping his voice at the end of sentences and so failing to understand how to 'fill a large space with his voice'.[8] Altogether he made another thirteen speeches or short interventions in 1908. However, he never lost his nervousness about speaking in public and often tried to calm himself by spending an hour or so in the library beforehand, talking to Gosse, and 'examining new books and making suggestions'.[9]

For all Cromer's self-confessed 'cross-bench frame of mind', it proved impossible not to become affected by the growing spirit of political animosity as the policies of the new Liberal Government began to come under attack from the huge Conservative majority in the House of Lords.[10] The first confrontation had taken place with the Lords veto of the Government's flagship Education Bill in 1906, and by 1908 the only measures which the Liberals could be sure of passing were those involving money, a subject which parliamentary convention dictated was the responsibility of the Commons alone. In this highly partisan atmosphere Cromer was soon driven towards the Conservative ranks, stimulated by Lloyd George's 1908 Old Age Pension Bill, which he attacked on 20 July as 'rash and opposed to the principles of sound finance'.[11] It could only be paid for, he argued, by a policy of protection, and would make it more difficult for the Government to perform its main duty, that of preparing the country's defences for the European conflict which would probably be forced on Britain 'before many years have elapsed'.[12] Nevertheless, he had second thoughts when he contemplated the dangers of the complete rejection of the Lloyd George bill. So on 28 July he tried simply to amend the scheme by giving it a 'provisional stamp' such that it would automatically have to be reviewed on 31 December 1915 before any more pensions would be paid.[13] When this too was rejected as infringing the

---

[7] Parl. Deb., vol. 193, cols. 1023–6 (6 Feb. 1908).

[8] Edmund Gosse, 'Lord Cromer as a Man of Letters', *Fortnightly Review*, 107 (Mar. 1917), 2.

[9] Ibid. 3.   [10] BN 276–7.

[11] Zetland, *Lord Cromer*, 327–8; Parl. Deb., vol. 192, cols. 1359–60 (20 July 1908).

[12] Ibid., cols. 1353–6.   [13] Ibid., vol. 193, cols. 1086–91 (28 July 1908).

Commons privileges with regard to money bills, he responded that it was what he had expected but he had felt it his duty to try.[14]

Another sign of Cromer's concern about a possible constitutional crisis came when he was one of just ten Unionist peers who opposed outright rejection of the Liberal Licensing Bill on 24 November, only to find himself on the losing side when the rejectionists voted not to give the bill a second reading.[15]

Given his views on how government should be properly conducted, it is perhaps not surprising that Cromer occasionally gave vent to his feelings about what was happening to British parliamentary procedure. Considerations of important pieces of legislation started off with a 'plethora of talk', he noted on one occasion, and then 'rushed from the extreme of procrastination to the other extreme of precipitation' in the Commons, where the guillotine was so ruthlessly applied that many important bills reached the Lords with their most important provisions undiscussed.[16] He was also one of a small band of regular attendees at the Lords, as a result of which he was made the chair of two private bill committees, as well as being asked to act as an arbitrator in the dispute between the Midland Railways and its staff in 1909.

The Cromers' London base was now their house at 36 Wimpole Street, a large establishment with a butler, a chauffeur, and several servants, as well as a secretary, who came in to help Lord Cromer with his growing political and literary correspondence. Summers were spent either with Katherine's family at Ardgowan or at Thurso Castle, which they had begun to rent after Strathmore Lodge became too expensive. It seems that, in the first winters, Cromer often spent considerable periods on his own, while Katherine, who believed little Evelyn to be consumptive, took him off to the healthier climes of Broadstairs in Kent.[17] This may even have included some Christmases, though not that of 1910, which they spent with Katherine's family at Longleat. Writing to Gertrude Bell, Cromer describes how he had suggested plum pudding as the cause of his little son's indisposition. 'No, Papa,' Evelyn replied, 'it was not the plum pudding: it was the plum pudding, *and* the turkey, *and* the sausages, *and* the chestnuts.'[18]

Evelyn made some irregular appearances at a Portman Square kindergarten in 1908 and 1909 before being sent off to a preparatory boarding

[14] Ibid., vol. 193, col. 1911 (28 July 1908).
[15] Roy Jenkins, *Mr. Balfour's Poodle: Peers v. People* (New York: Chilmark Press, 1954), 61–2.
[16] Parl. Deb., vol. 193, col. 1088 (28 July 1908).   [17] Douglas-Hume, *Evelyn Baring*, 20.
[18] Cromer to Gertrude Bell, 14 Jan. 1911, CP/2, FO 633/20.

school in Sussex. From then on he remained a somewhat distant observer of his parents' lives, writing from school in May 1914: 'I am very glad to hear that father was better. *I do hope that he will live,*' the last passage underlined twice.[19]

In April 1908 Cromer's older son Rowland married Ruby, the daughter of Lord Minto, the Viceroy of India. They came to live nearby, producing granddaughters in 1909 and 1910. What Rowland described as Katherine's 'angelic' welcome to Ruby seems to have led to some temporary easing of the tensions between her and her stepson.[20] Windham came back to London in 1910 and, in 1913, married Lady Gwcneth Ponsonby, the daughter of the eighth Earl of Bessborough, with two grandsons born in 1914 and 1916. The fact that Windham became a partner in Barings as soon as he returned, and that Rowland had a year at the firm in 1913. strengthened Cromer's connections with the family business, which, once again, had become a highly remunerative enterprise, making annual profits of 27.1 per cent in 1900–9.[21] He was now a wealthy man with an annual income that had reached £6,691 by 1915 and an estate worth £117,608, or around £7 million in 2002 values.[22]

The House of Lords Crisis

Confrontation between the two houses of Parliament reached a new level of bitterness as a result of Lloyd George's budget introduced at the end of April 1909, with its controversial proposal to introduce a tax on land. Although well supported by the Liberal majority in the Commons, it was not sent to the Lords until the beginning of November. After a relatively short debate a large majority of peers voted to reject it unless it was submitted to the country in an election. It was the first time the Lords had vetoed a finance bill for 250 years. Cromer informed the House on 23 November that, as he could neither vote for a measure of which he disapproved, nor vote against, because of the gravity of the constitutional issues raised, he was going to abstain. He was worried, he said, that a prolonged debate would cripple the nation in the event of any great

[19] Douglas-Home, *Evelyn Baring*, 22.
[20] Rowland (Errington) to Cromer, 10 Sept. 1907, CP/5, box 1, file 4.
[21] Robert Skidelsky, Review of Niall Fergusson, *The World's Banker, New York Review of Books*, 16 Dec. 1999.
[22] Accounts, CP/1.

national emergency. Parliament's major duty was to provide for the country's defence. It was also a vital necessity to preserve the power of the Lords as a barrier to Irish home rule, to socialism, by which he meant Lloyd George's plans to tax and spend, and to the Liberal plan to secularize the educational system.[23] Lords Lytton and Rosebery also abstained on the grounds that, if there were an election, the Liberals would use their expected victory to remove the veto powers of the House of Lords.[24]

The election was held in January 1910 and, although the Unionists made some large gains, the Government was still able to command a majority of 124 in the Commons with the help of the votes of the Irish, the Independent Labour Party, and others. The Lords took this to be the country's assent to the Lloyd George budget and passed it when it was re-presented without a division. Nevertheless, everyone now realized that a Liberal attack on either the powers of the House of Lords or its composition had become inevitable.[25] Asquith, the Prime Minister, had also dropped a number of hints that, should the attempt to reform the Lords be blocked, he would ask the King to create enough new peers to ensure its passage. The government bill to amend relations between the Commons and the Lords was then presented on 1 March. At just this time the Lords began to debate suggestions for its own reform put forward by a committee under the chairmanship of Lord Rosebery. The main element was the proposition that 'possession of a peerage should no longer of itself give the right to sit and vote in the House of Lords'.[26] Cromer gave his support: he was willing to see a diminution in the number of hereditary peers, and the election of some outsiders, provided a reformed Lords 'maintained its powers intact'.[27]

Discussion was brought to a sudden halt by the death of King Edward VII on 6 May. Various attempts were then made to reach a compromise so as not to embarrass the new King. Cromer was just one of many who continued to think of ways around the impasse, for example, amendments to the Parliament Bill followed by a referendum. When all this proved fruitless, Asquith called a second general election in November 1910, which kept a Liberal majority intact.

Battle was rejoined in February 1911 when the Government, having obtained the King's reluctant, and secret, assent to the use of the Royal Prerogative to create new peers, submitted the same Parliament Bill that it

[23] H.L. Deb., vol. 4, cols. 825–9 (23 Nov. 1909).   [24] Jenkins, *Mr. Balfour's Poodle*, 96–7.
[25] Ibid. 138.   [26] Ibid. 139–40.
[27] H.L. Deb., vol. 5, cols. 308–10 (16 Mar. 1910); Jenkins, *Mr. Balfour's Poodle*, 141–2.

had presented a year earlier. The bill was passed by a substantial majority in the Commons but 'massacred' by the Lords, in a direct challenge to the wish of the electorate.[28] It was at this point, at the end of July, that Asquith made public the King's promise to create new peers.[29]

The struggle then switched to the Lords itself, pitting those Unionists who thought further resistance counter-productive against the fifty or so hardliners who proclaimed their willingness to fight to the last ditch. Cromer was in the forefront of the attempts at compromise, tabling a short-lived amendment to the Parliament Bill aimed at making the definition of what constituted a money bill more explicit.[30] He was then asked by Lord Crewe, the leader of Unionists in the Lords, to help to persuade his fellow Unionists not to vote against the bill once discussion had come to an end. In Cromer's own account, written some days later, he called a meeting at Lord Bath's house, which led to a letter being sent to Crewe enquiring how many votes he thought he needed, for on this would depend the number of new peers which the King would have to create if the Parliament Bill was finally rejected. When Crewe proved unable to send a formal answer, the moderates decided not to vote as a bloc for fear that this might encourage their opponents to get out more of their own supporters.[31]

In the event, the denouement was something of a personal anticlimax. The Lords debate began in August 1911 in sweltering heat with the temperature reaching 100°F at Greenwich. The country was also in the middle of the Agadir crisis with Germany, there was a dock strike in progress, and fears of a first national railway strike to come. Cromer intended to speak but was unable to get to the Lords, being laid up in bed with gout. Meanwhile, he sent word that he would have voted for the bill in order to prevent the creation of hereditary peers, and urging others to do same.[32] The bill itself was finally carried by 131 votes to 114 on 10 August. A letter written to Gosse a few days later shows him well pleased with the final outcome: 'All's well that ends well ... The peril is now past, but it was rather a near thing.'[33]

---

[28] Jenkins, *Mr. Balfour's Poodle*, 210–11.

[29] Ibid. 219.

[30] H.L. Deb., vol. 5, cols. 1047–53 (28 June 1911).

[31] Cromer, 'Memorandum of proceedings in connection with passing of Parliament Bill', 11 Aug. 1911, CP/2, FO 633/28.

[32] Zetland, *Lord Cromer*, 337–9; Jenkins, *Mr. Balfour's Poodle*, 250.

[33] 12 Aug. 1911, quoted in Zetland, *Lord Cromer*, 339.

Against Women's Suffrage

Lord Cromer's other great political preoccupation of these years was his role as a major opponent of women's suffrage, a movement that had made great strides under the Asquith Government and was believed to have at least the tacit support of the vast majority of Liberal MPs. Among those who took the lead in encouraging women to found a Women's National Anti-Suffrage League, inaugurated in July 1908, were Lady Jersey and the well-known novelist Mrs Humphry Ward.[34] Cromer gave the movement his active support, joining the Men's Committee for Opposing Suffrage in December 1908 and becoming president of its successor, the Men's League, in September 1909.

He set out the reasons for his position in a speech in the Queen's Hall in March 1909. Giving some women the vote, he argued, would constitute not just a grave constitutional matter but also a political and social revolution that would affect the Empire as much as the United Kingdom. Was it 'Imperial', he asked, to

dethrone woman from that position of gentle yet commanding influence she now occupies . . . and substitute in her place the unsexed woman voting at the polling booth, declaiming on the platform and in Parliament, and possibly sitting at the desk of the Cabinet Minister to decide some question affecting the destinies and interests of her fellow-countrymen and women in the Antipodes?

It would be the thin end of the wedge, and there was no knowing where it would stop. The consequences of the argument that every human being had the right to vote would be little short of ridiculous. 'Let us improve the lot of women by education.' But we must stoutly resist the 'battle of the sexes', lest it carry 'discord and confusion into every family in the country'.[35] A further gloss on the 'thin end of the wedge' argument is provided in a letter written to Mrs Humphry Ward a few years later. It was impossible to conceive of giving votes to a small number of women, he told her; it was all or nothing. And if to all women, then to all men, 'which would be disastrous'.[36]

Here is one version of the mainstream Edwardian attitude to women's suffrage: fear of the unpredictability of a greatly expanded electorate, fear that giving women the vote would hamper efforts to stand up to Germany,

[34] Janet Penrose Trevelyan, *The Life of Mrs Humphry Ward* (New York: Doodad, Mead, 1923), 230.
[35] Speech against votes for women, 26 Mar. 1909, *The Times*, 27 Mar. 1909.
[36] 19 July 1915, CP/2, FO 633/24.

and a strong belief that the separation of the spheres of the two sexes was ordained by God.[37] Much of this is expressed in Cromer's rhetorical question addressed to a Manchester audience in October 1910. As the 'German man is manly [and] the German woman is womanly... can we hope to compete with such a nation as this if we war against nature and endeavour to invert the natural role of the sexes?'[38]

Cromer shared such public views with many of his friends among the leading women Antis, such as Violet Markham and Gertrude Bell.[39] Other aspects he found difficult to discuss. Some of his sense of embarrassment can be discerned in his somewhat edgy jokes, such as his mock fear of the thunderbolts of Mrs Pankhurst's 'man-opposing Amazons'.[40] And it seems clear that, for him, as for many other Edwardian males, the whole business had touched a raw nerve. As he explained to Violet Markham in 1913, the Suffragists 'infuriate me' because 'they have raised a storm of perfectly useless discussion upon the fundamental bases of sex relations which had better not be discussed at all'.[41] It is equally clear that he found it very uncomfortable to have to talk in public about such matters as gender differences in human physiology, once the debate turned to the issues of women's role in relation to child-rearing and public health.[42]

It would be interesting to know how much his feelings and beliefs were shared by Katherine, his wife. They were in general agreement about many things, such as questions of empire, of the threat of socialism, and of the importance to scientific research of the use of animal vivisection. However, it may also be of some significance that she did not appear with him on the platform during any of his major anti-suffrage speeches, even though she occasionally did this when other subjects were under discussion.[43] Biographers should be aware of Wilfrid Blunt's addiction to malicious gossip, but there may still be something in his March 1909 comment that 'Lady Cromer has become a suffragette in opposition to her Lord.'[44]

[37] Brian Harrison, *Separate Spheres: The Opposition to Women's Suffrage in Britain* (London: Croom Helm, 1978), 33–4, 56.
[38] Quoted ibid. 34.
[39] Violet Markham, *Return Passage: The Autobiography of Violet R. Markham, C.H.* (London: Oxford University Press, 1953), 96.
[40] Speech at anti-suffrage meeting in Cambridge, 3 Mar. 1911, *Anti-Suffrage Review*, X (Apr. 1911), 8.
[41] 5 Nov. 1913, CP/2, FO 632/22.
[42] Harrison, *Separate Spheres*, 60.
[43] Katherine did appear with him at an 'at home' for members of the United States Women's League for Opposing Suffrage in May 1914; *Anti-Suffrage Review*, X (May 1914).
[44] Blunt, *My Diaries*, 648.

The Men's Committee had a tiny staff with offices in Bridge Street, Westminster. Its many activities included the circulation of petitions, the recruitment of new members, and the organization of public meetings aimed at stirring up what it believed to be the apathetic male majority against votes for women. Cromer and his colleagues had to get used to the receipt of offensive mail, to being subjected to ridicule, one of the militant suffragettes' main weapons, and to the constant heckling of their speeches. The *Times* report of a Queen's Hall meeting in London on 11 July 1910 gives something of the flavour of those times. Cromer was greeted with 'cheers and hisses', and then subject to a 'considerable interruption' while several men and women were ejected by some of the 800 male stewards.

Cromer and Curzon then used the Men's League as a springboard for a takeover of the Women's League in the autumn of 1910, dissolving their own organization and persuading the women to join them in a new National League for Opposing Women's Suffrage, with Cromer as president and a seven-man, seven-women executive committee.[45] Their reasons were both practical and political. They feared that a majority of MPs were now in favour of giving votes to women householders.[46] They also observed that the Women's League had run out of funds and that it was only men like themselves who could use their contacts to raise the money which an extended campaign would require.[47] In the event, both men and women Antis saw advantages in working together. Nevertheless, the successful amalgamation required all Cromer's diplomatic and administrative skills. There were difficulties to sort out concerning the new name, the ratio of men to women on committees, and even the organization of the office itself.[48] Cromer, who obviously found it difficult to collaborate with independent-minded women, reported that he found Lady Jersey particularly 'difficult'.[49] However, it is also said that he could recognize ability in women.[50]

Running the National League soon brought Cromer face to face with a number of contentious problems. For one thing, the women members were much more aware than the men of the need not just to oppose

---

[45] Harrison, *Separate Spheres*, 128.

[46] 'Announcement of Men's League for Opposing Woman Suffrage', *Anti-Suffrage Review*, 10 (Sept. 1909), 8.

[47] Earl of Ronaldshay, *The Life of Lord Curzon*, vol. i (London: Ernest Benn, 1928), 190.

[48] Harrison, *Separate Spheres*, 128–9.

[49] Ibid. 129; Martin Pugh, *The March of Women: A Revisionist Analysis of the Campaign for Women's Suffrage, 1866–1914* (Oxford: Oxford University Press, 2000), 154–5.

[50] Harrison, *Separate Spheres*, 130.

women's suffrage but also to promote alternative activities for public-spirited women. For another, the mere fact that women took part in the leadership of the movement seemed to suggest that they were quite capable of playing the political game.[51] For these and other reasons it proved difficult to remain a single, above-party organization once the League entered the political arena. One early example is its intervention in the second 1910 election and the pressure it tried to place on MPs not to support Kemp's Conciliation Bill proposing the enfranchisement of some 1 million women heads of household. Even more dangerous to the integrity of the movement was the fact that many of its leading members were in favour of encouraging women's participation in local government, a course to which Cromer himself was opposed.[52] On this occasion Mrs Humphry Ward was his main opponent. She was a firm believer in increasing the role of women in municipal affairs and held that the League should do more than occupy itself with 'opposition and denial'.[53] The result was a short-lived compromise which led to the formation of a separate women's Local Government Advancement Committee.

This was not enough to prevent a major row from breaking out in 1912, when some women members offered their support to a woman candidate of discreet pro-suffrage views standing in the West Marylebone local government election. It was Cromer himself who forced them to back down in what Mrs Humphry Ward described as a 'flood of fury on Dear Lord Cromer's part'.[54] 'Men of political experience', he argued, had warned that it was impossible to mix opposition to women's suffrage with the promotion of the steps needed to encourage the entry of women onto the municipal councils. Not that he was against the councils themselves. But it was tactically impossible to push both ideas in the same association.[55]

Cromer was surely correct in his belief that any attempt to promote wider women's issues could be politically divisive. Nevertheless, his resignation as president in May 1912 is certain testimony to the difficulties he experienced in holding this particular line. He was also simply worn out by the intensity of the campaigning with the constant disruption of meetings like one he had attended in Bristol in the previous February when a

[51] Pugh, The March of Women, 145.

[52] Ibid. 155–6; Julia Bush, Edwardian Ladies and Imperial Power (London: Leicester University Press, 2000), 172–3.

[53] Trevelyan, Life of Mrs Humphry Ward, 230–1.

[54] Quoted in Pugh, The March of Women, 156.

[55] Cromer to Violet Markham, 9 Feb. 1912, CP/2, FO 633/21.

suffragette suddenly appeared on the platform from behind the huge concert organ, an event which resulted in a mass attack by the male stewards on all the other suffragettes in the rest of the hall.[56] As he explained to Curzon, he had not the 'health, strength, youth, and I may add, the temper to go on dealing with these infernal women'.[57] Curzon took over the presidency, with Lady Jersey and another woman colleague as co-vice-presidents.[58]

Egypt and Empire

Lord Cromer, together with his colleagues Lords Curzon and Milner, represented some of the Edwardian period's most high-profile spokesmen for the notion that, as Cromer himself put it, empire was the main title which made Britain 'nationally great'.[59] They supported measures aimed at greater imperial cohesion, they worried about the German threat, and they were becoming concerned with how best to deal with the rising tide of nationalism in both India and Egypt. Evidence for Cromer's own approach to such matters is provided by the speech he made in favour of the Indian Councils Bill (introducing what were later known as the Morley–Minto reforms) in February 1909. He had less objection, he said, to appointing an Indian to the Viceroy's Council than to giving Indians wider legislative powers. He knew, he said, that the legislative experiment had to be tried, but he had 'little confidence in the result'.[60] His private advice to his successor, Gorst, was on much the same lines: pressure for greater political representation was inevitable, but it should be guided from above, and, if possible, diverted away from the centre by the creation of provincial and local assemblies.[61]

Cromer also used his 1910 presidential address to the Classical Association to set out his ideas in a larger historical perspective. Entitled 'Ancient and Modern Imperialism', it was concerned to trace parallels between the ancient empires and those of today. Athens was an example of the 'fatal

[56] John Sutherland, *Mrs Humphry Ward: Eminent Victorian, Pre-Eminent Edwardian* (Oxford: Oxford University Press, 1991), 319.

[57] Quoted in Harrison, *Separate Spheres*, 134.

[58] A letter from Lady Jersey to Cromer suggests that she would have preferred to be co-president; 24 Feb. 1912, CP/2, FO 633/21.

[59] Speech at a dinner of the Unionist Free Trade Club, 21 Nov. 1907, CP/2, FO 633/26.

[60] Zetland, *Lord Cromer*, 312–13.

[61] e.g. Cromer to Gorst, 12 Mar. 1908 and 12 May 1910, CP/2, FO 633/14.

effects of democracy run mad'.[62] So his main comparison was with Britain and Rome, a theme he explored in terms of similar pressures for expansion as a result of the need for defensible borders, and of a similar lack of gratitude among those it had rescued from previous oppression.[63] There were significant differences as well, notably the fact that, unlike the Romans, Britain discouraged intermarriage with its subject peoples, believed that administrative and commercial exploitation should be in different hands, and possessed dangerous European rivals.[64]

A final section, entitled 'Quo Vadis?', provided an occasion to set out what must certainly have been Cromer's last thoughts about the future of colonial empire. India was not a homogeneous nation, he argued, and to leave it would lead to the 'most frightful anarchy'.[65] Britain might at some future distant time be justified in handing over the torch of civilization and progress to those it had had civilized. But all that could be said at present was that, 'until human nature changes, and until racial and religious passions disappear from the face of the earth, the relinquishment of that torch would almost certainly lead to its extinction'.[66]

Egypt would also have been very much on Cromer's mind at this time. But he still considered himself bound by his self-denying ordinance about public utterance on the subject. As he had informed the Eighty Club on 15 December 1908, he felt his best service to Egypt was to 'hold his tongue'.[67] Of course this did not prohibit a substantial private correspondence with Grey at the Foreign Office about Egyptian affairs, and also with Gorst, who often sought his advice. By and large he supported Gorst's policies, although he was occasionally unhappy about changes which called in question some of his own politics, such as Gorst's revision of the Dinshawai sentences.[68] Cromer even held his tongue when he realized that Gorst was making no apparent effort to pursue his idea of a bicameral legislature as a way round the Capitulations. The most he seemed able to achieve was a somewhat makeshift arrangement involving the creation of an assembly of Mixed Tribunal judges with powers to enact civil legislation affecting foreigners.[69]

[62] Cromer, *Ancient and Modern Imperialism* (New York: Longmans, 1910), 7–8.
[63] Ibid. 29–31.   [64] Ibid. 69, 114.
[65] Ibid. 121–4.
[66] Ibid. 127.
[67] Cromer, *The Situation in Egypt* (London: Macmillan, 1908), 5–8.
[68] Grey to Cromer, 2 Aug. 1907, and Cromer to Grey, 2 Aug. 1907, quoted in Mellini, *Gorst*, 161.
[69] Roberson, 'Judicial Reform', 273; Mellini, *Gorst*, 229.

Cromer continued to support Gorst privately until the Egyptian political crisis which broke out as a result of his attempts to raise money for
Sudan in exchange for a lengthy extension of the Suez Canal Company's
concession. This resulted in the assassination of Butros Ghali, Gorst's own
choice as president of the council of ministers, in February 1910, as well as
the rejection of the plan by the Egyptian general assembly. Humiliation on
this scale was enough to convince many in England, as well as Gorst
himself, that the policy of trying to encourage greater Egyptian participation in government had failed. Cromer, for his part, was fearful that, as
Grey told Lord Crewe, 'all his work will be undone'.[70] Something of his
general unhappiness and sense of betrayal is revealed by an addition to his
'Biographical Notes' written while on holiday in Scotland in August 1910.
He had 'trained' Gorst and 'thought that he had entirely agreed with me'.
But, while pretending to carry on his policy, Grey and Gorst 'have entirely
given it up'. Cromer did not think that his 'work of a lifetime' had been
'altogether wrecked'. But he did believe that the edifice which had taken
him twenty-five years to build had been to a great extent 'undermined', and
that, in many directions, 'the work has to be begun again'.[71]

A second insertion in the 'Biographical Notes' a year later notes that his
'poor dear friend' Gorst was dying of cancer.[72] And a third that, as soon as
he had learned of his death, Cromer hurried off to the Foreign Office to
recommend Kitchener as his successor. For a time the authoritarian Kitchener seemed the answer. But then he too began to be criticized for a
variety of initiatives of which Cromer disapproved. A letter written to
Strachey in March 1913 speaks of a 'feeling of deep anxiety and disappointment' at the tinkering to which the edifice it had taken him twenty-five
years to build was being subjected. First, Gorst had gone to one extreme,
now Kitchener was going to the other. He had warned both about some of
their mistaken policies, but Kitchener paid even less heed than Gorst.[73]

One of the major bones of contention was Kitchener's refusal to implement Cromer's pet scheme for amending the Capitulations, having decided, like Gorst, that there was neither local nor international support for
it.[74] This led Cromer to try to revive interest in the scheme in an article
entitled 'The Capitulations in Egypt', published in 1913. As before, he
argued that government for those who shouted 'Egypt for the Egyptians'
was impossible until the Capitulations were removed. Once again, he put

[70] Quoted in Mellini, *Gorst*, 216.   [71] BN, Insertion, 2 Aug. 1910, 5–7.
[72] BN, Insertion, 26 July 1911.   [73] 26 Mar. 1913, CP/2, FO 633/22.
[74] Mellini, *Gorst*, 229; Kitchener to Grey, 24 May 1912, PRO, FO 371/1362.

forward a plan by which Egyptian and foreign elements could be fused together to such an extent as to render them capable of 'co-operating in legislative effort'. What was needed was international confidence in the duration of the occupation.[75] Then all would see that Egypt's future lay in an 'enlarged cosmopolitanism'.[76]

Man of Letters

The range of Cromer's public activities seems unusually large. Apart from his work in the Lords and in the National League for Opposing Women's Suffrage, he was also an active, and often embattled, president of the Research Defence Society defending animal vivisection, a vocal member of the Society for the Prevention of Cruelty to Animals, which, rather like some members of the royal family, he used to head off attacks on blood sports, and the chair of the small committee which produced the draft plan for the creation of the School of Oriental Studies in London. Nevertheless, he also found time to make a small reputation for himself as a man of letters, reading widely and making extensive notes, some of which found their way into a series of four printed commonplace books which he then circulated among friends like Gertrude Bell, Curzon, and Gosse.

Cromer's tastes remained very much unchanged. According to Gosse, he continued to read regularly in Greek and Latin, but never the works of Church Fathers in those languages, for 'he had not an ecclesiastical mind'.[77] He also chose books that threw light on the social and political manners of antiquity.[78] He liked prose to be 'clear and stately', and so was put off by the richness and complications of style of some leading Victorians like Walter Pater.[79] According to his own list, the books he turned to most often were *The Iliad*, the book of Job, *Tristram Shandy*, *The Pickwick Papers*, *Lycidas*, and the Tenth Satire of Juvenal.[80]

Friendship with Strachey also encouraged an outpouring of essays and reviews for *The Spectator*, particularly after he had to curtail his public appearances in 1912. Twenty-two of these appeared between November

---

[75] Cromer, 'The Capitulations in Egypt', *Nineteenth Century and After* (July 1913), repr. in his *Political and Literary Essays 1908–1913*, 161–2, 167.

[76] Ibid. 171.

[77] Gosse, 'Lord Cromer as a Man of Letters', 3–4.

[78] Ibid. 6.

[79] Ibid. 7–8.

[80] Ibid. 13.

1912 and September 1913, including five in July and six in August. About half consisted of reviews of books with imperial or political themes, with much of the rest involving works on literature, the classics, and the writing of history. Cromer's reviews were full of anecdote, much of it from his own life. He seems most excited by books either written by or about his friends, or containing accounts of incidents which he had witnessed at first hand. He maintained a good memory, but he often sent drafts to old colleagues to check. His thoughts were always balanced and clearly expressed, though sometimes sententious and, inevitably, as he grew older, more and more repetitious. As for his style, it never achieved any particular elegance but remained as clear as ever, flowing along slowly and steadily with many qualifications and dependent clauses in a quiet river of words.

The reviews and essays contain a great deal of common sense, such as his comments on the necessary role which subjectivity plays in the writing of history. There is also much grinding of familiar axes about free trade, the 'spurious' nature of most non-European nationalisms, and the fact that educated Indians and other colonial peoples retained all the customs and prejudices of their own people under a 'top-dressing' of Western learning. Praise is heaped on the books written by people of whose opinions he approved, like Gertrude Bell, and the occasional brickbat lobbed in the direction of his old adversaries Blunt and Gordon. Interesting too are the few references to his own mistakes or to changes in his own strongly held ideas, one of the most significant being his admission that his attempt to treat female suffrage as a non-party question had not, so far, 'yielded any very satisfactory or encouraging results'.[81]

Once enough essays and reviews had accumulated, they too were printed up and circulated in three collections, the first published by Macmillan in 1913.[82] If we add the commonplace books, the volumes of speeches, and the annual collections of the more general parts of his private correspondence, divided into the 'political' and the 'literary', we can see a considerable urge to leave a remarkably full account of his public life for his children, as well as for use by a future biographer.

All this certainly constituted an energetic use of retirement by an Edwardian gentleman in his late sixties who suffered from repeated attacks of gout, sciatica, and a nervous stomach. A memorandum he wrote to himself headed 'Work done 1907–1911' reveals something of his con-

---

[81] Cromer, 'Lord Milner and Party', *The Spectator*, 24 May 1913.
[82] Cromer, *Political and Literary Essays 1908–1913*.

tinued desire to fill his days with work and other useful activity.[83] It begins with figures for the sales of *Modern Egypt*, over 9,000 in Britain and over 4,000 in the United States by 30 June 1910, with royalties of £3,880. It then goes through a long list of books 'read and re-read', before finishing with reference to a number of his major speeches, accompanied by an explanation for the way he was being drawn more and more from the cross-benches towards the Conservative, or what he continued to term the 'Unionist', Party.

[83] CP/2, FO 633/28.

19

The First World War, the Dardanelles Commission, and Death
1914–1917

Revived by the Outbreak of War

In the early months of 1914 Lord Cromer came close to death. According to his daughter-in-law Ruby, he was suffering greatly, his digestive organs were not working, and one day he was heard to murmur, 'I feel as if I had severed my connection with one world without entering into communication with another.'[1] Then, suddenly, his health improved, and by the summer he seemed to have obtained a new lease of life. The outbreak of war in August played an important role. Indeed, it seems to have provided a great sense of relief. Not only did it reveal the Germans in what he believed to be their true colours, but it also allowed Britons to transcend their bitter party differences. It dampened the growing tensions over Ulster, and it provided an occasion, as he saw it, for the inhabitants of the Empire to show their true loyalty by rallying to the British cause.[2] As an additional bonus, the war brought old colleagues into new positions of power, and so enabled Cromer to return to old correspondences about political strategy, particularly in the Middle East.

Both his older sons volunteered for military service, Rowland becoming a second lieutenant in the Grenadier Guards, Windham joining the Royal Naval Volunteer Reserve. Rowland then went out to India as private secretary to the new Viceroy, Lord Hardinge, but only after Cromer had

[1] Ruby Baring, Memo, 'Lord Cromer', 29 Jan. 1917, 1, CP/1.
[2] 'Lord Curzon's Imperialism', introd. to Earl Curzon, *Subjects of the Day*, repr. in his *Political and Literary Essays: Third Series*, 1–2, 6.

had to write to Kitchener at the War Office to get round some troubles with his son's medical board.[3] In 1916 Rowland was back in England as assistant private secretary to King George V. As for Cromer's immediate family, Katherine occupied herself with the promotion of many wartime charities while their young son, now in his last years at The Wick preparatory school in Sussex, initiated an animated correspondence with his father about the course of military operations full of questions about strategy and weapons.[4] The Cromers stayed more in London as they had to forgo their usual summer holiday at Thurso Castle when that part of the north Scottish coast became off limits owing to its proximity to the principal base of the British Home Fleet under Lord Jellicoe.

As soon as he had regained his strength, Cromer started writing for *The Spectator* again. It was, he told Strachey, the 'bounden duty of anyone who can gain the public ear and who, by reason of age or other causes, is unable to do other and perhaps more valuable work, to use his vice or pen to hammer the truth'.[5] Apart from articles, he also wrote reviews of some of the many books which were beginning to be published about both the war itself and the shape of the post-war world. Cromer's general argument was that the Germans would only change their militaristic system of government, their 'Junkerdom', as a result of their total defeat.[6] He certainly did not want them crushed out of existence because that would lead to pan-Slavic predominance in Europe, something he told his sister-in-law was only 'one degree better than pan-slavism'.[7] Nor would it be right, should the Allies be victorious, to dictate internal changes in the government of Germany and Austria, a matter which might 'safely be left to the Germans and the Austrians themselves'.

Cromer's main aims would be to see the end of the Habsburgs and Hohenzollerns as rulers, while making sure that the Germans were disabled from disturbing future European peace.[8] It was only the Germans who had kept the continent in fear of war for twenty-five years, making it necessary for every nation to bear 'enormous armaments'.[9] These themes were then elaborated in a number of small books and pamphlets, such as

---

[3] Kitchener to Cromer, 10 Feb. 1915, CP/1.

[4] Douglas-Home, *Evelyn Baring*, 22.

[5] Cromer to Strachey, 5 July 1915, CP/2, FO 633/24.

[6] 30 Aug. 1915, CP/2, FO 633/24; Cromer's letter to *The Times*, 11 Apr. 1916, CP/2, FO 633/33.

[7] Cromer to Alice Shaw-Stewart, quoted in Zetland, *Lord Cromer*, 343.

[8] Cromer to Herbert Warren, 22 Nov. 1914, CP/2, FO 633/23.

[9] Cromer to Strachey, 10 Aug. 1914, quoted in Zetland, *Lord Cromer*, 343–4.

Germany Contra Mundum (1915) and *Pan-Germanism* (1916), with its argument that in the battle for global supremacy Germany was 'extending its tentacles round the world'.[10]

The Middle East Again

Cromer naturally took a special interest in the Middle East theatre of the war. For one thing, it provided an opportunity to settle an old score by publishing the manuscript of his *Abbas II*, most of which had been written at the time of his first collisions with him in the early 1890s but shelved as long as Abbas remained Khedive.[11] Now, with Egypt declared a Protectorate in November 1914 and Abbas deposed, he could go ahead, with the aim, as he told Rosebery, of letting 'our doctrinaire politicians, of whom we have a goodly supply, see what the government of Easterns really means', as well as that of exposing 'the iniquities of the ex-Khedive'.[12]

Cromer's other main line of thinking was to take advantage of war with the Ottoman Empire to pursue ideas current in Cairo before 1914 about encouraging the Arabs to free themselves from the Turkish yoke. Hence, in October 1914 he advised Lord Crewe that if a few British officers who spoke Arabic were sent to Arabia, they could 'raise the whole country against the Turks'.[13] A follow-up memorandum on the same subject mentions the possibility of also stirring up the Armenians and the Kurds.[14] But progress was slow. In September 1915 Cromer noted that it should have been possible to raise the Mesopotamian tribes against the Turks but that the Germans got in first with money.[15] A month later he was arguing for support for an alliance with the Sharif of Mecca aimed at taking Baghdad and handing it over to Arabs.[16]

Many of these ideas were, of course, becoming common currency at the time, and were equally strongly supported by Cromer's Middle Eastern correspondents such as Gertrude Bell and Wingate, soon to become Kitchener's replacement as High Commissioner in Egypt. Indeed, it seems likely that his main role was as a public spokesman for the Middle East experts, for example, talking in the House of Lords in the spring of

[10] (London: Darling, 1916), 14–15.   [11] Cromer, *Abbas II*, preface, p. v.
[12] 9 Jan. 1915, CP/2, FO 633/24.   [13] Cromer to Boyle, 5 Oct. 1914, CP/2, FO 633/23.
[14] 16 Oct. 1914, ibid.
[15] Cromer to Bevan, 20 Sept. 1915, CP/2, FO 633/24.
[16] Cromer to Curzon, 21 Oct. 1915, ibid.

1915 of the possibility of an 'Arab Kingdom', and the more remote possibility of a 'politically independent' Arab caliphate.[17] He even had views on the Zionist movement, something which, before long, as he wrote in *The Spectator* in July 1916, politicians would be unable to brush aside as the 'fantastic dream of a few idealists'.[18]

The Dardanelles

Cromer's writings about the Middle East were often written, or dictated, from bed. He was ill again in the early part of 1915 with a gouty toe which he said bore a strong resemblance to a 'red billiard ball'.[19] He was then well enough to return to the House of Lords in the spring, but found it a great strain on his weak heart and was ill again towards the end of the year.[20] Given his chronic stomach problems, Katherine often prepared his invalid food herself, causing young Evelyn to write to his father from school: 'When mother wrote to me she said you did not want to eat what she had cooked. I quite agree with you, cince [*sic*] I would do a great many things rather than eat a meal cooked by her.'[21]

Not surprisingly Cromer took a close interest in the Dardanelles expedition, hoping for the best at the beginning, but soon coming to the conclusion that it had been a 'colossal blunder'.[22] As a result he also became involved in the question of what type of parliamentary inquiry there should be, and of what evidence it should be allowed to see. The two central figures in the whole affair were Asquith, the Prime Minister, who was anxious that the confidential papers should not be put before Parliament and Winston Churchill, who had been dismissed as First Sea Lord in May 1915 and who, having been made the scapegoat for all that had gone wrong, was equally determined that they should. Cromer's contribution was to join with Milner and five other peers in sending Asquith a letter in early November warning him that if he allowed a putative committee of inquiry to be composed simply of the ministers who were responsible for

[17] *The Times*, 23 Apr. 1915, and Cromer's letter to *The Times*, 24 Apr. 1915.
[18] Quoted in Blanche E. C. Dugdale, *Arthur James Balfour: 1906–1930* (New York: G. P. Putnam's Sons, 1937), 166.
[19] Cromer to Lord Mersey, 17 Feb. 1915, CP/2, FO 633/24.
[20] Cromer to Lord Sydenham, 13 Nov. 1915, CP/2, FO 633/24; 'Evelyn, Earl of Cromer', memoir by Lord Sanderson, *Proceedings of the British Academy*, 8, 30.
[21] 2 Feb. 1916, BP, E.B.'s letters to parents, 1916–1917, GRE/I/158.
[22] Cromer to Lord Mersey, 2 Sept. 1915, CP/2, FO 633/24.

overseeing the expedition, its composition would certainly be 'challenged in public debate'.[23]

Asquith chose to deal with this difficult situation by appointing a tame commission which would take evidence in secret and so avoid having to present the confidential papers to Parliament as a whole. He asked Cromer to act as chairman in the spring, although the official public announcement had to wait until 20 July.[24] Other members included Admiral Sir William May, Field Marshal Lord Nicholson, a Lord Justice of Appeal, and four MPs. Cromer's friends and relations feared the strain it would impose on him. He answered them by saying: 'I know that it will kill me, but young men are giving their lives for their country, so why should not I who am old?'[25] It was to be his last official act. And so brought his public career full circle by returning his attention back to the eastern Mediterranean, where he had first worked and travelled nearly sixty years before.

The Commission began work in August, going through the evidence with particular reference to the Admiralty telegrams.[26] It was also necessary to decide what to do with Churchill's request to be present throughout the inquiry, to put forward his evidence in a certain form, and to call his own witnesses.[27] In the event, none of this was allowed. The most Cromer and his fellow members would permit was that witnesses could be given copies of the evidence of other witnesses and might also be recalled to make such further comments as they might wish.[28] In the event, Churchill appeared only once but was furnished with a sometimes daily report of the testimony of others on which he was free to comment by letter.[29]

The Commission sat from 19 September to 4 December, hearing thirty-three witnesses in all, as well as from Asquith and Churchill. Cromer was kept at home with influenza in early December and the last of the sittings was held at his Wimpole Street house. Rowland and Ruby, just back from India, went to visit him when it was over. They found that he had great difficulty in hearing and speaking. But they did overhear him say of his

---

[23] Martin Gilbert (ed.), *Winston S. Churchill: Companion* (London: Heinemann, 1972), iii/2. 1248–9.

[24] Zetland, *Lord Cromer*, 344.

[25] Ruby Baring, 'Lord Cromer', 2.

[26] Martin Gilbert, *Winston S. Churchill*, iii: *The Challenge of War 1914–1916* (Boston: Houghton Mifflin, 1971), 809.

[27] Ibid. 804.

[28] Cromer to Churchill, 19 Sept. 1916, ibid. 808–9.

[29] Ibid. 809, 814, 1817–18.

colleagues: 'They're all so hard, so hard. I tell them, "Gentlemen, I am an old man and have had more experience in my life than most of you, and I find I have made so many mistakes myself, that I cannot afford to be hard".'[30]

The Commission's first report was published after Lord Cromer's death in early 1917.[31] It dealt with the inception of the plan and the conduct of operations in the Dardanelles from the outbreak of the war on 4 August to 23 March 1915 when the idea of a purely naval attack was abandoned. It divided responsibility between the War Council, Churchill and Fisher at the Admiralty, and the late Lord Kitchener. In spite of Churchill's three days of presentation, which one of his biographers describes as a tour de force, the Commission's majority opinion was critical of his failure to present the views of his Admiralty colleagues 'clearly' before the War Council.[32] A minority report, written by Walter Roch MP, was even more critical, accusing Churchill of 'failing to present fully. . . the opinions of his naval advisers', most of whom were much less enthusiastic than he.[33] The Commission's findings were finally presented to the Government in February, three weeks after Cromer's death, and debated in Parliament on 20 March. As Asquith intended, the report made little impact and the full proceedings were never published.

Lord Cromer Dies

Cromer took to his bed shortly after the Commission's formal sessions came to an end. Curzon came to call every morning to enquire about his old friend and to comfort Katherine, often staying to dine with her well.[34] On 29 January Cromer was just well enough to sign the first portion of the report just arrived from the printers with what Ruby described as a 'straggly Cromer'. In the evening of the same day, as Katherine was bringing in a bowl of soup, he announced that he could see a man standing in front of him with a ladder. He then suffered a stroke and died before

[30] Ruby Baring, 'Lord Cromer', 2.

[31] A copy is published in Tim Coates (ed.), *Lord Kitchener and Winston Churchill: The Dardanelles*, pt. 1: *1914–15* (London: Stationery Office, 2000).

[32] Robert Rhodes James, *Churchill: A Study in Failure* (London: Weidenfeld & Nicolson, 1970), 89; Coates (ed.), *Lord Kitchener and Winston Churchill*, 157.

[33] Coates (ed.), *Lord Kitchener and Winston Churchill*, 211.

[34] The Very Reverend W. R. Inge, *Diary of a Dean: St Paul's 1913–1934* (London: Hutchinson, 1949), 59.

Rowland could reach him.[35] Little Evelyn wrote from school the next day: 'Dear Mother, I was so sorry to hear of father's death. I got your telegram in the break today. I am glad he passed peaceably. I saw in the paper it was from a stroke about 10 o'clock.'[36]

Lord Cromer's last wish was to be buried in Bournemouth.[37] His funeral was held there on 3 February with Katherine and most of the members of his close family present. But not little Evelyn, who had the flu.[38] A memorial service took place in Westminster Abbey the same day. His favourite hymn, 'Abide with me', was sung on both occasions.

The Times printed a five-column obituary under the headlines 'Death of Lord Cromer. A Great Ruler. Maker of Modern Egypt'. 'No man', it said, 'has in our times been so directly responsible for the transformation of the whole condition of life for so many millions of down-trodden toilers.'[39] 'A Friend', writing in the same paper a few days later, referred more personally to the 'quality of mental balance in Cromer's writings' which gave the impression of a learned judge who, having satisfied himself on all circumstances, had sat down to pass sentence upon all facts and persons including himself.[40] Strachey, in *The Spectator*, dwelt on his realism about what could and could not be done for Eastern peoples.[41]

Sadly, there were soon 'bitter squabbles' between Katherine and Rowland, leading to Katie moving out of the Wimpole Street House into a place of her own in St John's Wood.[42]

[35] Ruby Baring, 'Lord Cromer', 1.   [36] Douglas-Home, *Evelyn Baring*, 24.
[37] Zetland, *Lord Cromer*, 345.   [38] *The Times*, 5 Feb. 1917.   [39] Ibid., 30 Jan. 1917.
[40] Ibid., 3 Feb. 1917.   [41] *The Spectator*, 3 Feb. 1917.
[42] Douglas-Home, *Evelyn Baring*, 19.

20

Conclusion:
A Life in Government

Horace Rumbold reports seeking out Lord Cromer in London in August 1901 to congratulate him on his earldom. His host, who was talking to somebody else, glared at him and asked him what he wanted. 'I only came to congratulate.' 'That's all right,' Cromer replied. 'Good-bye.'[1] It is a typical story of Cromer's later Egyptian years. We are led to imagine a bulky, imperious, overly self-confident figure who seemed to enjoy his own reputation for brusqueness while only showing a more human side when at home in the small circle of family and close colleagues. This is also the Cromer of the famous caricature by the cartoonist 'Spy', looking somewhat balefully at the world through narrowed eyes like a bull at bay, a caricature in which, as Max Beerbohm once advised, 'whatsoever is salient must be magnified, whatsoever is subordinate must be proportionately diminished'.[2] And this is how most people think of him now.

Yet this commanding figure was only the creation of Cromer's final years in Egypt. Few Britons knew much about him before then. Few such stories, few such cartoons, had found their way into print. The Captain and Major Baring of London and India, or the Sir Evelyn Baring of his first decade back in Egypt, appears in the historical record as a much greyer figure, a workaholic administrator whose 'almost inconvenient zeal' was known at the time to only to the few who had worked with him closely, first in his War Office days, then in Calcutta, Simla, and Cairo.[3]

[1] Gilbert, *Sir Horace Rumbold*, 42.
[2] N. John Hall, *Max Beerbohm: Caricatures* (New Haven: Yale University Press, 1997), 15.
[3] G. D. Hogarth, 'Evelyn Baring', *Dictionary of National Biography: 1912–1921* (London: Oxford University Press, 1927), 20.

Nevertheless, the description of a public reputation is not the story of a life. It gives a false appearance of cohesion to what is, inevitably, a much more accidental series of coincidences, contrivances, and paths taken and not taken. Cromer may have been a Baring, with all that that entailed in terms of wealth, position, and social connection. But the varied lives of his brothers and half-brothers should be enough to disabuse anyone of the idea that just to be a Baring implied anything by way of a good schooling or a successful public career. All that can probably be said is that if Cromer had not forced himself into a process of self-education beginning in Corfu, he would have made a successful career for himself, first in the Army, and then somewhere in British administrative or political life.

Cromer himself was also complicit, late in life, in giving his own existence another type of cohesion. It is true that his 'Biographical Notes' contain many lively stories of his home life and unhappy schooling. But they seem chosen largely to demonstrate how an unruly, badly educated, irresponsible boy transformed himself into a dutiful, hard-working government official, husband, and father, with passing mention of a larger picture composed of the Baring family connections, the political atmosphere in mid-century England, and the opportunities to people of his class for careers in the East. Much, however, has to be read between the lines. And much, inevitably, is lost without reference to Cromer's accounts of his day-to-day life contained in his missing correspondence with Ethel, his brother Tom, and other close friends and relatives. As it is, we have to search elsewhere for occasional glimpses of the slim young man dancing the night away in Naples in 1865, or giggling with Edward Lear over their postprandial brandy and cigarettes in the government houses in Corfu and Calcutta.

The material which is left points mainly to the public man whose life was given shape and direction by opportunities stemming first from his accidental association with the government of Corfu, then from a growing recognition of his administrative, financial, and diplomatic skills, and finally from his increasingly confident exploitation of the confused situation in Egypt from 1883 onwards to create the conditions for his own indispensability through his successful campaign to impress London that the country was subject to a complex form of international government which only he could manage. Of great importance too was the on-the-job training he was able to obtain from important figures like Sir Henry Storks and Lords Northbrook and Goschen.

Much of this was a conventional enough trajectory for an ambitious young man growing up during the great period of mid-Victorian imperial consolidation and expansion. However, Cromer was also able to make a more personal mark as a problem-solver, as a confident man of decision, and, above all, a tyro publicist who understood better than many of his colleagues the necessity of presenting colonial policies in ways which were readily understandable not only by the London elite but also by an ever expanding electorate of newspaper-reading males. All was not plain sailing, though. Easily frustrated when he was unable to get his way, he contemplated resignation on a number of occasions. At times intense irritation, or the iron logic of his method of presenting his ideas, threatened to betray him. At others, and particularly during his second period in India, his contempt for the members of the Indian Civil Service, his inability to work in harness with Ripon, and his over-ideological approach to Indian government in general, threatened to undermine the Ripon viceroyalty before his own wiser counsels, and no doubt those of his wife, Ethel, as well, prevailed.

As his friend Alfred Lyall pointed out, Cromer never understood India.[4] But he was certainly very quick to see his way ahead in Egypt on two separate occasions. On the first, from 1877 to 1880, he became one of the architects of both a financial settlement and a programme of administrative reform implemented by Egyptian officials which, had it been pursued with a greater degree of political skill, might just have prevented a second round of European intervention in 1882. On the second, he reversed himself, seeking more and more direct British control, while obtaining sufficient support in London to be allowed to invent his own special job as manager of a permanent occupation. This allowed him a huge measure of independence which he was then able to exploit further, secure in the knowledge that successive British Cabinets were only too willing to leave almost the whole responsibility for governing Egypt to him, until the contradictions inherent in acting as a virtual one-man band finally brought him down.

It is here that he made his own individual contribution to both British and Egyptian history. It is easy to imagine other Britons running the Agency in Cairo but not any who would have done it in the same way, with such important consequences for so long. Cromer was not your usual 'man on the spot'. The unofficial ruler of a country of ambiguous

[4] See p. 179.

status—part Ottoman, part colony, part independent nation with imperial aspirations of its own in Sudan—he was called upon not just to manage its economy and administration but also to defend its borders and to help to define its status vis-à-vis the rest of the international community. That he did so for so long, with such competence and with such a small staff, puts him in a category of one; somewhere between a long-serving viceroy, a provincial governor, an international banker, and an ambassador, and yet with a different relationship to the people he governed than any of these.

Nevertheless, it is also clear that Cromer's singular position in Egypt was achieved at much cost. Of some of this he himself was well aware. Hence his somewhat disingenuous defence against charges of unchecked despotism with the argument that, if by this his critics meant an absence of control, he was, in fact, answerable to London and 'held in check by the play of a free press in Egypt'.[5] For further peace of mind, he needed to cling on tight to the pretence that he was still acting in terms of a consistent set of personal principles—running all the way from being open to the advice of his subordinates to preparing subject peoples for some measure of self-government—which became increasingly otiose over time.

In such circumstances it was probably inevitable that Cromer came increasingly to blur the boundary between what he saw as his defence of the interests of Egypt and his own *amour-propre*, making him more and more intolerant of criticism, as well as more and more out of touch with the lives and aspirations of those he governed. Hence his blindness about the importance urban Egyptians attached to education. Hence his wildly mistaken belief that he could solve the problems posed by the Mixed Tribunals and the Capitulations by the pretence that the foreign communities had just as much a claim to representation as the local population.

Much of this, it might be argued, can be explained in terms of the inevitable contradictions involved in any form of modern imperial rule. Like all the more perceptive of the great proconsuls, Cromer understood the nature of the central truths: that it was impossible to win the affection of the governed and that British-led progress was destined to undermine itself. Nevertheless, this was all too often undermined on a personal level by a desire to believe that the Egyptians did indeed love, or at least respect, him; and on a public one by an anxiety to control and manage the process in such a way that it could be slowed down to an extent far beyond what was reasonably possible. It might sound fine to create a 'conservative class'

[5] *AR 1905, PP* (1906) 132, 494.

that would be sufficiently content to prevent [the people] from becoming easy prey to either the nationalist demagogue ... or that of some religious fanatic'.[6] But, as later events were quickly to show, such a class provided no bulwark against the emergence of a powerful nationalist movement in 1919.

One thing Cromer lacked, like almost every member of his generation, was a model of capitalist development in a non-European setting which might act as his guide. With his eyes firmly focused on the interests of the rural population, he could not understand the speed and intensity with which increasing agricultural prosperity, combined with the huge growth in foreign investment in Egypt during the decade 1897–1907, helped to created an expanding middle class of bankers, investors, merchants, and would-be entrepreneurs. Nor, perhaps, did he want to envisage such a phenomenon. Far easier to present his British audience with the picture of a mongrel nation full of peasants and shaikhs so stuck in their traditional ways that only a European outsider could bring them the law, order, water, and regular taxation they needed to make best use of their simple assets. In this way, a general understanding of the inevitability of change became mired in a set of polemical positions which became more and more his own, for example, his regularly repeated appeal to Egyptian incompetence, the immorality of Egypt's ruling dynasty, and so to the need to preserve this benighted people from the follies of another Ismail and Urabi. Like the British in India, he was caught, in David Washbrook's trenchant phrase, 'between inventing an Oriental society and abolishing it'.[7]

In fact there were many highly competent Egyptians willing to work with Cromer so long as this meant a proper preparation for political independence. For some, they were simply continuing an agenda pioneered by the likes of Nubar, Ali Mubarak, and Yacoub Artin in the 1860s and 1870s. Others, like Muhammad Abduh and the members of Lutfi al-Sayyid's *al-Jarida* group, focused on the new possibilities provided by the occupation itself, for example, Abduh's use of his position as Chief Mufti to draw up his 1899 proposal for an innovative reform of the procedures used in the *ahalīyah* courts. Hence, while there were areas of considerable dispute between Cromer and the Egyptian elite, most notably over education and the slow recruitment of native Egyptians into high positions in

---

[6] Cromer to Millet, 19 May 1913, CP/2, FO 633/22.

[7] David Washbrook, 'India, 1818–1860: The Two Faces of Colonialism', in Andrew Porter (ed.), *The Oxford History of the British Empire*, iii: *The Nineteenth Century* (Oxford: Oxford University Press, 1999), 419.

government, there was also a considerable overlap between their two agendas including, first and foremost, a shared authoritarianism which insisted that the vast majority of the people needed disciplined guidance from above before they could be become full citizens of a modernizing state. To judge by their comments at the time, Cromer's putative Egyptian partners were often more than willing to see him, not just as an alien presence, but also as a necessary evil in the sense of someone destined to preside over a transitional period during which Egypt was prepared to take its place in the modern world.

Failure to create more than a limited partnership with this elite was only one of the factors which led to Cromer's enforced departure from Cairo in 1907. The return of the Liberals to power was another, providing as it did the possibility of a link between his critics in Cairo and those in London. It also has to be said that it was Cromer himself who provided much of the ammunition that was used against him, from the material in his annual reports to his overreaction to the wave of Muslim support for the Ottoman Sultan after the Taba affair, and the stubborn way he defended the Din-shawai tribunal and its harsh sentences thereafter. Poorly advised by Boyle, Findlay, and his other close colleagues, and still suffering from the death of his first wife, he allowed his critics to get to him in ways that not only made him increasingly tetchy and short-tempered but also seriously undermined his health.

Summing up his own achievements after leaving Egypt, Cromer noted the 'conciliation of tension' with France (represented by the Anglo-French Agreement of 1904), the aversion of bankruptcy, the 'relief of taxation', and the recovery of Sudan.[8] In this view, diplomacy, politics, finance, and military success all combined to rescue the Egyptians from the folly of their rulers, to secure their independence from the Mahdi and the Turks, and to allow the British to put them on the road to a well-governed, prosperous future. But this, as Robertson noted of the panegyric which greeted Cromer's return to London in 1907, could not possibly be the 'verdict of history'.[9] What is required is the much more complex task of assessing Cromer's personal impact in terms of both the larger story of the British occupation and the much larger one of Egypt's modern history.

Within a few years of returning to Cairo in 1883 Cromer had accumulated sufficient power for himself to exercise a considerable influence over

[8] Cromer, 'The Capitulations in Egypt', repr. in his *Political and Literary Essays 1908–1913*, 158–9.
[9] Parl. Deb., vol. 179, col. 883 (30 July 1907).

most sectors of Egyptian life for the next two decades. The general path he followed was one that he had already helped lay out in 1879–80, that is, timely payment of the debt, followed by successive conversions as Egypt's credit improved. This was accompanied by a reform of the system of both assessing and collecting the land tax, as well as such Indian-inspired reforms as improvements in irrigation and, eventually, a thirty-year 'permanent' settlement designed to give landholders the predictability thought necessary to encourage good husbandry. Given a series of competent and well-selected British subordinates, it was usually enough for him to set out the general guidelines and let them get on with the job.

Nevertheless, it was Cromer himself who was largely responsible not only for the overall success of the programme in meeting its own goals, but also for some of its more permanent consequences. Two proved of particular long-term importance. First, without being really sure of the impact of what he was doing, he presided over one of the world's first modern green revolutions, in which a temporary surge in yields and output based on a combination of extra water and more prolific strains of cotton was bought at a longer-term cost in terms of waterlogging and an intensification of pest attacks beginning in the early 1900s. Secondly, he directed the last stages of the establishment of a rural property regime dominated by large landowners with considerable political, as well as economic, power over their tenants and the peasants in the nearby villages.

Cromer was much less sure-handed when it came to following up his early agricultural successes. As far as the other sectors of the economy were concerned, he believed that growth was generally supposed to look after itself, with the state only taking a limited role in the creation of the associated institutional and legal framework. Here he might be blamed for doing too little rather than too much, the one exception being his dogged determination not to allow any protection for a nascent factory textile industry, even though he himself had begun to be aware of the need to find alternative employment for a growing surplus of agricultural labour. These were still very early days in the management of what would now be called a modern economy, and, as had been the case throughout the nineteenth century, growth was still seen as largely a matter of securing an ever more favourable balance between population and resources.[10]

[10] Roger Owen, 'The Population Census of 1917 and Its Relationship to Egypt's Three 19th Century Statistical Regimes', *Journal of Historical Sociology*, 9/4 (Dec. 1996), 468.

Cromer's political influence was just as important. Apart from his significant role in persuading successive British governments to continue the occupation, his major impact was felt in two connected areas. One was the way in which his policies helped Egypt detach itself from both international and Ottoman control, albeit at the expense of increasing British domination. The other, the mirror image of this, was the stimulus his policies gave to a growing sense of Egyptian nationalism by means of the slights he offered to the country's ruling elite and to its small but growing educated class. Here his Victorian paternalism and watered-down Christianity combined with an appeal to a global hierarchy of race to act as a focus for those who found the occupation increasingly offensive on religious, national, and personal grounds.

Even so, it is important to remember that much of the detailed criticism of the Cromerian programme only crystallized after he had left Egypt, and after its economic component appeared to have been seriously compromised by the financial crash of 1907 exacerbated by the crisis in the agricultural sector due to a further dramatic fall in cotton yields in 1908 and 1909. It was these dramatic events which provided the basis for the systematic critique of Cromerian-cum-British policies developed by the nationalist elite, to be given formal shape by the programme of the Egyptian National Congress at Heliopolis in 1910 and the appearance of Theodore Rothstein's *Egypt's Ruin*. Here criticism began to provide its own antidote in the shape of a call for industrialization, economic diversification, and an Egyptian bank which was to provide much of the economic agenda for Egyptian governments from the 1920s to most of the first decade after the revolution of 1952.

Though unwilling to admit it, Cromer was driven out of Egypt by his critics. Clearly he had stayed much too long. As is the case with many powerful men towards the end of a long and successful career, his judgement, perspective, and political good sense began to desert him. But once he had recovered both his health and his natural élan, his activism during the first years of his retirement seems quite remarkable. Not for him the fate of those returning proconsuls 'cut down to size' by the country's 'self-absorbed' political class.[11] Part elder statesman, part politician, he did his best to exert an influence on most of the major political questions of the day. Forced to learn new political skills, humble enough to work in the small, understaffed offices of underfunded pressure groups like the Na-

[11] J. A. Gallagher, *The Decline, Revival and Fall of the British Empire* (Cambridge: Cambridge University Press, 1982), 79.

tional League for Opposing Woman Suffrage, sometimes subject to considerable public ridicule by his opponents, he underwent the chastening experience of a latter-day Rip Van Winkle learning to confront a society and its social practices which had changed out of all recognition from the one he had left in the early 1870s. His capacity to do all this to some effect is testimony to his energy, his sense of duty, and his need to find meaningful occupation. It also placed him firmly in the camp of those for whom the Empire had become an emotionally charged political entity constantly in need of protection from enemies without, notably the Germans, and enemies who threatened its integrity and proper management from within, such as the Irish, the socialists, and the suffragettes.

Cromer's world was almost entirely transformed by a series of momentous events just after his death, from the issue of President Woodrow Wilson's Fourteen Points, through the Bolshevik revolution, to the creation of the League of Nations and the Middle Eastern mandate system. Perhaps, if he had survived the war, like his colleagues Curzon and Milner, he might have been able to adapt to what Mark Sykes and other architects of the post-war system were to call the new 'spirit of the time'.[12] But it seems more likely that his views would actually have proved closer to those of his wife, Katherine, who, in the early 1920s, blamed the First World War for the fact that the Empire was 'dwindling away' with the loss of Ireland and Egypt and the approaching loss of India.[13] Certainly his reputation experienced what his friend Lytton Strachey described as a 'blind spot', something which was also recognized by his official biographer, Lord Zetland, who, as one reviewer wisely noted, had taken Cromer 'as an archetype of a fading attitude of mind, a symbol of a now vanishing desire imperiously to rule'.[14]

With this loss of reputation went any influence that his *Modern Egypt* might possibly have had as a practical guide to the government of Eastern peoples. Such methods simply did not work any more, a point amply proved by the career of one of the very few post-war proconsuls who tried to follow in his footsteps, Lord Lloyd, whose heavy-handed attempts to manage a now partially independent Egypt on Cromerian lines produced enough official embarrassment in London to ensure his early recall.

[12] Roger Adelson, *Mark Sykes: Portrait of an Amateur* (London: Cape, 1975), 253, 322 n.

[13] Inge, *Diary of a Dean*, 74.

[14] John St Loe Strachey, *The Adventure in Living: A Subjective Autobiography* (London: Hodder & Stoughton, 1922), 373; Harold Nicolson, 'Current Literature', *New Statesman and Nation*, 10 Sept. 1932.

For all that, Lord Cromer occupies a singular place in British imperial history. No other proconsul of his era was called upon to manage a country like Egypt in such a way for so long. No other proconsul was left so reliant on his own experience, political skills, conscience, and beliefs to provide guidance to the way ahead. That he continued to do all this with great personal integrity and with a practical concern for the economic well-being of the poorer Egyptians was freely acknowledged in Cairo as well as London. That he was in a position to make large mistakes as well as to provide large benefits, that he directed matters with an increasing disregard for Egyptian sensibilities, that he seemed to relish his exercise of personal power, was also perceived at the time, although by a much smaller circle. That it would have been better for him, as well as for Egypt, to have left well before he actually did was only recognized by a few critics and then, a little belatedly, by Cromer himself.

Most of this made perfect sense to his Edwardian audience. Cromer was seen as a great proconsul among great proconsuls, someone whose high-profile performance in his difficult role in Egypt seemed perfectly tailored to the sensibilities of the times, a larger-than-life figure, easily recognizable, easily tricked out in that most flattering of garbs, the toga of the stern, unbending, Roman governor bringing peace and justice to those he ruled. But what to think of him now when much more is known about him, when his anomalous position in an anomalous late nineteenth-century Egypt seems to make his role much more *sui generis*?

The notion of economic globalization, rather than empire per se, may help to provide an answer. It was international bankruptcy that first brought Cromer to Egypt to work in the type of multinational administration established by the major European powers in highly charged political contexts, where no one of them could afford to allow their partners an exclusive interest. And it was his ability to find a way to make use of the different national, financial, and, in the case of the Mixed Tribunals, legal interests involved that allowed him to play such a significant role, first in drawing up an agenda for dealing with Egypt's bankruptcy, then in overseeing the first period of its implementation, 1879–80. Even at this stage of his career the range of skills required was formidable, while their exercise required great tact, judgement, persistence, and self-confidence, as well as an imaginative and often subtle approach to difficult problems.

Much the same skills were then required when Cromer returned to Cairo in 1883, although, on this occasion, the need to take account of a more purely British national interest came more and more to the fore. It was this that convinced him that it would be dangerous to end the occupation before a whole new series of policy initiatives had taken root, and then that the work of reform should be left almost entirely in British hands. One result was the creation of a set of institutionalized practices used in the management of the irrigation system and Egypt's finances which lasted more or less intact until the 1950s. The other was a sharp move towards a form of direct colonialism, with a progressive reduction in the sphere allocated to Egyptian self-government; but still within the boundaries set by the internationalism represented by the Capitulations, the Suez Canal concession, and the mixed administrations which, try as he might, Cromer was unable to destroy. It was in this special context that he flourished, and here that the limitations of his highly personal style of government were finally exposed. This is how he should now be remembered.

What can also be said, though rarely alluded in his time, is that Cromer's career in government gave him not just honours and rewards but a great deal of personal satisfaction. At the start of his career it was the quiet exercise of power he enjoyed. But over time the public performance of his position, whether in the residence or driving ostentatiously around Cairo, assumed an equal importance. As Clinton Dawkins observed from Egypt in 1896, 'Cromer exults in his strength and success here.'[15] Much of this was shared with Ethel, his friend and confidante since the age of 22, and his wife and partner during most of his years in the East. It was she who provided the stable homes in which he could work or relax, the warmth, comfort, and understanding missing from his early years with his mother, the access to his more sensitive, more vulnerable, inner life. Though he loved his second wife greatly, she seems unable to have contributed anything like the same level of sympathy and support.

Running through the whole of Cromer's adult life is a single thread of temperament which provided the backbone to his character. Always opinionated, strong-minded, purposeful, and stubborn, he was also correct, patient, self-controlled, and, though an optimist, possessed of a great distrust of enthusiasm. For most of his career this was balanced by an openness to new ideas, a willingness to listen to other points of view, an ability to think round problems and not to allow himself to become stranded in untenable positions. Often plain and direct in speech, his written dispatches tended to build up their case in a much more qualified

[15] Dawkins to Milner, 16 Aug. 1896, MP, box 190.

way, assessing the various options in some detail before arguing forcefully for the choice of just one.

Cromer was also a man of decision who believed that too much thought inhibited action, and that it was often better to have any opinion rather than no opinion at all.[16] His huge confidence in his own judgement rarely wavered. This was bolstered by a faith anchored not so much in religion, about which he remained quite sceptical, nor in scientific progress, which does not appear to have interested him a great deal, but much more in exemplary stories derived from the classics in which wise rulers make the most of a Cobdenite world where free trade and laissez-faire allow all differences, whether between nations, classes, or rulers and ruled, to be reconciled by steady men of good will. We can imagine that a conscience, almost always at ease with itself, allowed him a good night's sleep.

Given such a temperament, it was perhaps inevitable that with age and time Cromer became more combative, more pugnacious, more pompous, and more sententious in the sense identified by Gore Vidal as 'something that can happen when one means exactly what one says with no iron door to escape through like quotation marks'. But always with the saving grace that he was aware that his reputation was something different from his real self, that his public performances contained a great element of show. His health too gave him increasing trouble as the 'vigorous physical constitution' that one obituarist identified as essential to the deployment of his various talents began to let him down.[17] Even so, he seems to have managed to continue his vigorous life of walking and tennis-playing until the end of his time in Egypt, supplemented by the many days of hunting and fishing during his Scottish holidays, until his stomach rather than his chronic gout finally let him down.

How did Cromer view this same life from within? As it drew to a close, we could say, with Lois Potter, that he might have thought of himself as one of those happy people able to make themselves remembered 'in a shape as possible to their own conception of themselves'. And that that is the 'closest thing to immortality that most people can hope to achieve'.[18] But for most of the rest of it he chose to live very much in the shadow of the classical world where, at least in his own estimation, the key categories were those of love, literature, religion, nature, and the family, all subject to

---

[16] e.g. Cromer, 'Sir Alfred Lyall', *Quarterly Review*, repr. in his *Political and Literary Essays 1908–1913*, 83; Zetland, *Lord Cromer*, 348.

[17] Hogarth, 'Evelyn Baring, 21.

[18] Lois Potter, 'The Immortal Pointilliste', *Times Literary Supplement*, 11 Oct. 2002.

fate and change, all enlivened by the inevitability of eventual death.[19] As Cromer puts it in his own paraphrase of Palladas' 'The Voyage of Life',

> The bark of life puts out from port,
> We hoist the mast and trim the sail,
> Under the summer sky we sport,
> At times we feel the wintry gale.
> We know not where our lot is cast,
> Our pilot, Chance, may wreck or save;
> What're betide, the voyage past,
> All cast their anchors in the grave.[20]

[19] Cromer used these notions as section headings for his *Paraphrases and Translations from the Greek*, p. ix.
[20] Ibid. 169.

BIBLIOGRAPHY

PRIVATE PAPERS

Lord Cromer and the Baring Family

Cromer and Baring Papers, Durham University Library.

Cromer Papers, Middle East Centre, St Antony's College, Oxford.

Cromer Papers, PRO, FO 633.

ING Barings Historical Archives, 60 London Wall, London EC2M 5TQ.

Papers in private possession of Cromer–Baring family, incl. Lord Cromer's Biographical Notes.

Other

Alfred Lyall Papers, Oriental and India Office Collections, BL.

Charles Gordon Papers, BL.

Charles Greville Correspondence, BL.

Charles Moberley Bell Papers, TA

Earl Kitchener Papers, PRO.

Edward Lear Diaries, Houghton Library, Harvard University.

Ernest Tatham Richmond Letters, in private possession of Richmond family.

General Sir Francis Grenfell Papers, Middle East Centre, St Antony's College, Oxford.

Harry Boyle Papers, Middle East Centre, St Antony's College, Oxford.

Humphrey Bowman Papers, Middle East Centre, St Antony's College, Oxford.

Lord Milner Papers, Bodleian Library, Oxford.

Lord Northbrook Papers, Oriental and India Office Collections, BL.

Lord Ripon Papers, BL.

Lord Salisbury Papers, formerly in Christ Church Library, Oxford.

Sir Charles Hardinge Papers, Cambridge University Library.

Sir Eldon Gorst Papers, Diaries, Castle Combe, Wiltshire.

Sir Edward Grey Papers, PRO.

Sir Richard Temple Collection, Oriental and India Office Collections, BL.

Viscount D'Abernon Papers, BL.

W. E. Gladstone Papers, BL.

Wilfrid Blunt Papers, Houghton Library, Harvard University.

GOVERNMENT PUBLICATIONS

Egypt

Ministère de l'Intérieure, *Statistique de l'Égypte: Année 1873. 1290 de l'Hégire* (Cairo: Imprimerie Française Mourès, 1873).
Ministère des Finances, Département de la Statistique Générale, *Annuaire Statistique de L'Égypte: 1914* (Cairo: Imprimerie Nationale, 1914).
Journal Officiel.

France

Ministère des Affaires Étrangères, *Affaires Étrangères: Documents Diplomatiques, Affaires d'Égypte 1879–1880* and *1880–1881* (Paris: Imprimerie Nationale, 1880–1).

India

Guide to the National Archives in India (New Delhi: National Archives of India, 1982).

UNPUBLISHED THESES

CHALCROFT, JOHN, 'The Striking Cabbies of Cairo and Other Stories: Crafts and Guilds in Egypt, 1863–1914', Ph.D. thesis (New York, 2001).
KINSEY, DAVID CHAPIN, 'Egyptian Education Under Cromer: A Study in East–West Encounters in Educational Administration and Policy, 1883–1907', Ph.D. thesis (Harvard, 1965).
EL-MUSADDY, MOHAMED GAMEL-EL-DIN ALI HUSSEIN, 'The Relations Between 'Abbas Hilmi and Lord Cromer', Ph.D. thesis (London, 1966).
ROBERSON, BARBARA ALLAN, 'Judicial Reform and the Expansion of International Society: The Case of Egypt', Ph.D. thesis (London, 1998).
SALMONI, BARAK AHARON, 'Pedagogies of Patriotism: Teaching Socio-Political Community in Twentieth Century Turkey and Egypt', Ph.D. thesis (Harvard, 2002).

PUBLISHED BOOKS AND ARTICLES

By Evelyn Baring, Lord Cromer

Staff College Essays (London: Longmans, Green, 1870).
Rules for the Conduct of the War Game (London: War Office, Topographical and Statistical Department, 1870).
The Elementary Tactics of the Prussian Infantry (London: HMSO, 1870).
Letters from Capt. Baring to Persons in India (Simla: Private Secretary's Office Press, 1873).

Lord Northbrook's Administration of India (Simla: Private Secretary's Office Press, Aug. 1876).

'Recent Events in India', *Nineteenth Century*, 14 (Oct. 1883).

Paraphrases and Translations from the Greek (London: Macmillan, 1903).

Modern Egypt, 2 vols. (New York: Macmillan, 1908).

'The Government of Subject Races', *Edinburgh Review*, x (Jan. 1908).

The Situation in Egypt (London: Macmillan, 1908).

Ancient and Modern Imperialism (New York: Longmans, 1910).

Speeches and Miscellaneous Writings, vol. i (London: privately printed, 1912).

Political and Literary Essays 1908–1913 (London: Macmillan, 1913).

'The Capitulations in Egypt', *Nineteenth Century and After*, 74 (July 1913).

Abbas II (London: Macmillan, 1915).

Pan-Germanism (London: Darling, 1916).

Political and Literary Essays: Third Series (London: Macmillan, 1916).

By Other Authors

ADAMS, CHARLES C., *Islam and Modernism in Egypt: A Study of the Modern Reform Movement Inaugurated by Muhammad 'Abdouh* (London: Oxford University Press, 1933).

ADELSON, ROGER, *Mark Sykes: Portrait of an Amateur* (London: Cape, 1975).

ALLEN, BERNARD M., *Gordon and the Sudan* (London: Macmillan, 1931).

AMIN, KASSEM, *Les Égyptiens: Réponse à M. le duc d'Harcourt* (Cairo: Barbier, 1894).

ANSTEAD, D. N., *The Ionian Islands in the Year 1863* (London: W. H. Allen, 1863).

BALFOUR, LADY BETTY, *The History of Lord Lytton's Indian Administration, 1876 to 1880* (London: Longmans, Green, 1899).

BALL, R. FITZROY, 'Education in Egypt', *The Nineteenth Century and After*, 52 (July–Dec. 1902).

BARING, MAURICE, *The Puppet Show of Memory* (London: Cassell, 1987).

BEATON, ELIZABETH, *Caithness: An Illustrated Architectural Guide* (Edinburgh: Rutton Press, 1996).

BELL, CHARLES MOBERLEY, *Khedives and Pashas: Sketches of Contemporary Egyptian Rulers and Statesmen* (London: Sampson Low, Marston, Searle, & Rivington, 1884) ['by One Who Knows Them Well'].

BELL, HORACE, *Railway Policy in India* (London: Rivington, Percival, 1894).

BENNETT, ERNEST, 'After Omdurman', *Contemporary Review*, 75 (Jan. 1899), 18–33.

BERQUE, JACQUES, *Egypt: Imperialism and Revolution*, trans. Jean Stewart (London: Faber & Faber, 1972).

BHATTACHARYYA, S., *Financial Foundations of the British Raj: Men and Ideas in the Post-Mutiny Period of Reconstruction of Indian Public Finance 1858–1872* (Simla: Indian Institute of Advanced Study, 1971).

BIDDULPH, GENERAL SIR ROBERT, *Cardwell at the War Office: A History of His Administration* (London: John Murray, 1904).

BLUNT, WILFRID SCAWEN, *Atrocities of British Justice Under British Rule in Egypt* (London: T. Fisher Unwin, 1906).

—— *Gordon at Khartoum: Being a Personal Narrative of Events in Continuation of a 'Secret History of the English Occupation of Egypt'* (London: S. Swift, 1911).

—— 'Lord Cromer and the Khedive', *Nineteenth Century*, 35 (Jan.–June 1894).

—— *My Diaries: Being a Personal Narrative of Events 1888–1914* (London: Martin Secker, 1932).

—— *The Secret History of the British Occupation of Egypt* (New York: Alfred Knopf, 1922).

BOND, BRIAN, *The Victorian Army and the Staff College 1854–1914* (London: Eyre Methuen, 1972).

BOWMAN, HUMPHREY, *Middle East Window* (London: Longmans, Green, 1942).

BOYLE, CLARA, *A Servant of Empire: A Memoir of Harry Boyle* (London: Methuen, 1938).

—— *Boyle of Cairo: A Diplomatist's Adventures in the Middle East* (Kendal: Titus Wilson, 1965).

BROWN, NATHAN J., 'Brigands and State Building: The Invention of Banditry in Modern Egypt', *Comparative Studies in Society and History*, 32 (1990).

—— 'Who Abolished Corvée Labour in Egypt and Why?', *Past and Present*, 144 (Aug. 1994).

BUCK, E. J., *Simla Past and Present*, 2nd edn. (Bombay: Times Press, 1925).

Bulmer's History and Directory of Northumberland (1886).

BUSH, JULIA, *Edwardian Ladies and Imperial Power* (London: Leicester University Press, 2000).

CACHIA, PIERRE, *Popular Narrative Ballads of Modern Egypt* (Oxford: Clarendon Press, 1969).

CAILLARD, MABEL, *A Lifetime in Egypt, 1876–1935* (London: Grant Richards, 1935).

CAIN, P. J., and HOPKINS, A. G., *British Imperialism: Innovation and Expansion, 1688–1914* (London: Longman, 1993).

CAMERON, J. S., 'Villain and Victim: The Kidney and High Blood Pressure in the Nineteenth Century', *Journal of the Royal College of Physicians of London*, 33/4 (July–Aug. 1999), 382–94.

CECIL, LADY GWENDOLEN, *Life of Robert Marquis of Salisbury* (London: Hodder & Stoughton, 1921).

CHADWICK, OWEN, *Victorian Miniature* (London: Hodder & Stoughton, 1960).

CHASE, KAREN, and LEVENSON, MICHAEL, *The Spectacle of Intimacy: A Public Life for the Victorian Family* (Princeton: Princeton University Press, 2000).

COATES, TIM (ed.), *Lord Kitchener and Winston Churchill: The Dardanelles*, pt. 1: *1914–15* (London: Stationery Office, 2000).

COHN, BERNARD, *Colonialism and Its Forms of Knowledge: The British in India* (Princeton: Princeton University Press, 1996).

COLES PASHA, C. E., *Recollections and Reflections* (London: St Catherine Press, 1918).

COLVIN, SIR AUCKLAND, *The Making of Modern Egypt* (London: Thomas Nelson, n.d.).

CONNELL, BRIAN, *Manifest Destiny: A Study of the Rise and Influence of the Mountbatten Family* (London: Cassell, 1953).

COOK, E. T., *The Life of Florence Nightingale*, vol. ii (London: Macmillan, 1913).

CORNELL, LOUIS L., *Kipling in India* (London: Macmillan; New York: St Martin's Press, 1966).

CREWE, MARQUESS OF, *Lord Rosebery*, vol. ii (London: John Murray, 1931).

CROUCHLEY, A. E., *Investment of Foreign Capital in Egyptian Companies and the Public Debt*, Ministry of Finance Technical Paper, no. 12 (Cairo, 1936).

CURZON, LORD, 'The True Imperialism', *Nineteenth Century*, 63 (Jan. 1908).

DALY, M. W., *Empire on the Nile: The Anglo-Egyptian Sudan 1898–1934* (Cambridge: Cambridge University Press, 1986).

DASGUPTA, UMA, 'The Ilbert Bill Agitation, 1883', in Ravi Dayal (ed.), *We Fought Together for Freedom: Chapters from the Indian National Movement* (New Delhi: Oxford University Press, 1995).

—— *Rise of an Indian Public: Impact of Official Policy 1870–1880* (Calcutta: BDDHI, 1977).

DEIGHTON, H. S., 'The Impact of Egypt on Britain: A Study of Opinion', in P. M. Holt (ed.), *Political and Social Change in Modern Egypt* (London: Oxford University Press, 1968).

DENHOLM, ANTHONY, *Lord Ripon 1827–1909: A Political Biography* (London: Croom Helm, 1982).

DENT, MAJOR HERBERT C., 'The First Lady Cromer', *The Graphic*, 6 Jan. 1923.

DICEY, EDWARD, *The Story of the Khediviate* (London: Rivingtons, 1902).

DOBIE, EDITH, *Malta's Road to Independence* (Norman: University of Oklahoma Press, 1967).

DOUGLAS-HOME, CHARLES, *Evelyn Baring: The Last Proconsul* (London: Collins, 1978).

DOWNES, WILLIAM HOWE, *John S. Sargent: His Life and Work* (Boston: Little, Brown, 1925).

DRUMMOND WOLFF, SIR HENRY, *Rambling Recollections*, vol. i (London: Macmillan, 1908).

DUFFERIN AND AVA, MARCHIONESS OF, *Our Viceregal Life in India: Selections from My Journal 1884–1888* (London: John Murray, 1890).

DUGDALE, BLANCHE E. C., *Arthur James Balfour: 1906–1930* (New York: G. P. Putnam's Sons, c.1937).

ELLMAN, RICHARD, *Oscar Wilde* (London: Penguin Books, 1988).

ELTON, LORD, *Gordon of Khartoum: The Life of General Charles George Gordon* (New York: Knopf, 1955).

ERDEM, H. HAKAN, *Slavery in the Ottoman Empire and Its Demise 1800–1909* (Houndmills, Basingstoke: Macmillan, 1996).

ESHER, LORD, 'Conversations with Zobeir Pasha at Gibraltar', *Nineteenth Century and After*, 63 (June 1908).

FATEHALI DEVJI, FAISAL, 'Hindu/Muslim/Indian', *Public Culture*, 5/1 (Fall 1992).

FERGUSON, NIALL, *The World's Banker: The History of the House of Rothschild* (London: Weidenfeld & Nicolson, 1998).

FITZMAURICE, LORD EDMOND, *The Life of Earl Granville*, vol. ii (London: Longmans, Green, 1905).

GALLAGHER, J. A., *The Decline, Revival and Fall of the British Empire* (Cambridge: Cambridge University Press, 1982).

GILBERT, MARTIN, *Sir Horace Rumbold: Portrait of a Diplomat, 1869–1941* (London: Heinemann, 1973).

—— *Winston S. Churchill*, iii: *The Challenge of War 1914–1916* (Boston: Houghton Mifflin, 1971).

GODWIN-AUSTIN, BREVET-MAJOR, A. R., *The Staff and the Staff College* (London: Constable, 1927).

GOLDSCHMIDT, ARTHUR, JR., 'The Egyptian Nationalist Movement', in P. M. HOLT, (ed.), *Political and Social Change in Modern Egypt* (London: Oxford University Press, 1968).

GOOCH, G. P., and TEMPERLEY, H. (eds.), *British Documents on the Origins of the War 1898–1914*, vol. i (London: HMSO, 1927).

GOPAL, S., *The Viceroyalty of Lord Ripon 1880–1884* (London: Oxford University Press, 1953).

GORDON, C. G., *The Journals of Major-Gen. C. G. Gordon, C. B., at Khartoum*, ed. A. Egmont Hake (Boston: Houghton Mifflin, 1885; repr. London: Darf, 1984).

GOSSE, EDMUND, 'Lord Cromer as a Man of Letters', *Fortnightly Review*, 107 (Mar. 1917).

GREVILLE, CHARLES, *Greville Memoirs: Reign of Queen Victoria 1837–1852*, vol. iii (London: Longmans, Green, 1885).

GREY OF FALLODEN, LORD, *Twenty-Five Years: 1892–1916* (New York: Frederick A. Stokes, 1925).

GRUNEWALD, KURT, ' "Windsor-Cassel": The Last Court Jew', *Leo Baeck Institute Yearbook*, 14 (1969).

GUGGISBERG, CAPTAIN F. G., *'The Shop': The Story of the Royal Military Academy*, 2nd edn. (London: Cassell, 1892).

HALL, N. JOHN, *Max Beerbohm: Caricatures* (New Haven: Yale University Press, 1997).

HAMILTON, EDWARD, *The Diary of Sir Edward Walter Hamilton, 1880–1885*, ed. Dudley W. R. Bahlman (Oxford: Clarendon Press, 1972).

—— The Diary of Sir Edward Walter Hamilton, 1885–1906, ed. Dudley W. R. Bahlman (Hull: University of Hull Press, 1993).

HAMZA, ABDEL-MAKSUD, The Public Debt of Egypt 1854–1876 (Cairo: Government Press, 1944).

HARDINGE, SIR ARTHUR, A Diplomatist in the East (London: Jonathan Cape, 1928).

HARGEY, TAJ, 'Festina Lente: Slavery Policy and Practice in the Anglo-Egyptian Sudan', Slavery and Abolition, 19/2 (Aug. 1998).

HARRISON, BRIAN, Separate Spheres: The Opposition to Women's Suffrage in Britain (London: Croom Helm, 1978).

HARRISON, THOMAS S., The Homely Diary of a Diplomat in the East, 1897–1899 (Boston: Houghton Mifflin, 1917).

HARTMANN, MARTIN, The Arabic Press of Egypt (London: Luzac, 1899).

HEIMANN, MARY, Catholic Devotion in Victorian England (Oxford: Clarendon Press, 1995).

HERODOTUS, History, ed. J. Enoch Powell, book VIII (Oxford: Clarendon Press, 1939).

HILMI, ABBAS, The Last Khedive of Egypt: Memoirs of Abbas Hilmi II, ed. and trans. Amira Sonbol (Reading: Ithaca Press, 1998).

HOBSON, J. A., Imperialism: A Study (London: James Nesbit, 1902).

HOGARTH, G. D., 'Evelyn Baring', Dictionary of National Biography: 1912–1921 (London: Oxford University Press, 1927).

HOLLINGS, MARY ALBRIGHT (ed.), The Life of Sir Colin C. Scott-Moncrieff (London: John Murray, 1917).

HOLMES, RICHARD, Coleridge: Darker Reflections, 1804–1834 (New York: Pantheon Books, 1998).

HOLT, P. M., The Mahdist State in the Sudan, 1881–1898: A Study of Its Origins, Development and Overthrow (Oxford: Clarendon Press, 1958).

HUNTER, F. ROBERT, Egypt Under the Khedives, 1805–1879: From Household Bureaucracy to Modern Government (Pittsburgh: University of Pittsburgh Press, 1984).

INGE, VERY REVEREND W. R., Diary of a Dean: St Paul's 1913–1934 (London: Hutchinson, 1949).

JAMES, ROBERT RHODES, Churchill: A Study in Failure (London: Weidenfeld & Nicolson, 1970).

—— Rosebery: A Biography of Archibald Philip, Fifth Earl of Rosebery (London: Weidenfeld & Nicolson, 1963).

JEFFRIES, HELEN E., 'Sir John Aird', in Dictionary of Business Biography, vol. i (London: Butterworths, 1984).

JENKINS, ROY, Mr. Balfour's Poodle: Peers v. People (New York: Chilmark Press, 1954).

JERVIS-WHITE, H., History of the Island of Corfu and of the Republic of the Ionian Islands (Chicago: Argonaut, 1970; first pub. London, 1852).

KAMIL, MUSTAPHA, *Egyptiens et Anglais* (Paris: Perrin, 1906).

KANWAR, PAMELA, *Imperial Simla: The Political Culture of the Raj* (Delhi: Oxford University Press, 1999).

KHADIM, HUSSEIN N., 'The Poetics of Postcolonialism: Two Qasidahs by Ahmad Shawqi', *Journal of Arabic Literature*, 28 (1997).

KHALIDI, RASHID, *British Policy Towards Syria and Palestine 1906–1914* (London: Ithaca Press, 1980).

KIPLING, RUDYARD, *City of Dreadful Night* (New York: H. M. Caldwell, 1899).

—— *Early Verses by Rudyard Kipling 1879–1889: Unpublished, Uncollected and Rarely Collected Poems*, ed. Andrew Rutherford (Oxford: Clarendon Press, 1986).

—— *Kim* (New York: Doubleday, Page, 1901).

KIRKWALL, VISCOUNT (ed.), *Four Years in the Ionian Islands: Their Political and Social Condition with a History of the British Protectorate*, vol. ii (London: Chapman & Hall, 1864).

KRÄMER, GUDRUN, *The Jews of Modern Egypt, 1914–1952* (Seattle: University of Washington Press, 1989).

LANDES, DAVID S., *Bankers and Pashas: International Finance and Economic Imperialism in Egypt* (London: Heinemann, 1958).

LEAR, EDWARD, *Edward Lear: Selected Letters*, ed. Vivian Noakes (Oxford: Clarendon Press, 1988).

—— *Queery Leary Nonsense: A Lear Nonsense Book*, ed. Lady Strachey (London: Mills & Boon, 1911).

—— *Views in the Seven Ionian Islands* (London, 1 Dec. 1863).

LEVI, PETER, *Edward Lear: A Biography* (New York: Scribner, 1995).

LEWIS, SAMUEL (ed.), *A Topographical Dictionary of England*, 7th edn., vol. i (London: Samuel Lewis, 1848).

LONGFORD, ELIZABETH, *A Pilgrimage of Passion: The Life of William Scawen Blunt* (London: Granada, 1982).

LOW, SIDNEY, 'Lord Cromer on Gordon and the Gladstone Cabinet', *Nineteenth Century and After*, 63 (Apr. 1908).

LUTFI AL-SAYYID, AFAF, *Egypt and Cromer: A Study in Anglo-Egyptian Relations* (London: John Murray, 1968).

LUVAAS, JAY, *The Education of an Army: British Military Thought, 1815–1940* (Chicago: University of Chicago Press, 1964).

LYTTON, EDWARD, *England and the English*, new edn. (Chicago: Chicago University Press, 1970).

McCOAN, J. C., *Egypt As It Is* (London: Cassell, Petter, & Galpin, n.d.; Preface 1877).

—— *The Egyptian Problem* (London, 1884).

MACK, JOHN, *A Prince of Our Disorder: The Life of T. E. Lawrence* (Boston: Little, Brown, 1976).

MAGNUS, PHILIP, *Gladstone: A Biography* (London: J. Murray, 1954).

—— *King Edward the Seventh* (New York: E. P. Dutton, 1964).

—— *Kitchener: Portrait of an Imperialist* (London: John Murray, 1958).

MALET, SIR EDWARD, *Egypt 1879–1883* (London: John Murray, 1909).

MALLET, BERNARD, *Sir Louis Mallet: A Record of Public Service and Political Ideas* (London: James Nesbit, 1905).

—— *Thomas George Earl of Northbrook G.C.S.I.: A Memoir* (London: Longmans, Green, 1908).

MARKHAM, VIOLET, *Return Passage: The Autobiography of Violet R. Markham, C.H.* (London: Oxford University Press, 1953).

MARLOWE, JOHN, *Cromer in Egypt* (London: Elek Books, 1970).

—— *Milner: Apostle of Empire* (London: Hamilton, 1976).

MARSHALL-CORNWALL, GENERAL SIR JAMES, 'An Enigmatic Frontier', *Geographical Journal*, 125/3–4 (Sept.–Dec. 1959).

MATHUR, L. P., *Lord Ripon's Administration in India (1880–1884 A.D.)* (New Delhi: S. Chand, 1972).

MATTHEW, H. G. C. (ed.), *The Gladstone Diaries: With Cabinet Minutes and Prime-Ministerial Correspondence*, vol. xi: *July 1883–December 1886* (Oxford: Clarendon Press, 1990).

MELLINI, PETER, *Sir Eldon Gorst: The Overshadowed Proconsul* (Stanford, Calif. Hoover Institution Press, 1977).

MILNER, ALFRED, *England in Egypt* (London: Edward Arnold, 1892; 11th edn. 1904).

—— *An Englishman in Egyptian Service: Britain's Work in Egypt* (London, 1892).

MITRA, S. M., 'Lord Cromer and Orientals', *Nineteenth Century and After*, 63 (May 1908).

MORLEY, JOHN, *The Life of William Ewart Gladstone*, 3 vols. (New York: Macmillan, 1903).

MORRISON, THEODORE, 'Can Islam Be Reformed?', *Nineteenth Century and After*, 64 (Oct. 1908).

MOULTON, EDWARD C., *Lord Northbrook's Indian Administration 1872–1876* (London: Asia Publishing House, 1968).

MOUNT, CHARLES MERRILL, *John Singer Sargent: A Biography* (New York: W. W. Norton, 1957).

MOWAT, R. V., 'From Liberalism to Imperialism: The Case of Egypt 1875–1887', *Historical Journal*, 6/1 (1973).

MUBARAK, ALI, *Khitat al-Tawfiqiyyah al-Jadidah l-il-Misr al-Qahira* (Bulaq: Al-Matbaah al-Kubra al-Amiriyah, 1304–06h/1886–9).

MURPHY, RAY (ed.), *Lear's Indian Journey* (London: Jarrolds, 1953).

MUSA, SALAMAH, *The Education of Salamah Musa*, trans. L. O. Schuman (Leiden: Brill, c.1961).

NEWALL, LIEUTENANT-COLONEL H. A., *Calcutta: The First Capital of British India* (Calcutta: Caledonian Printing Co., n.d.; Introd. 1922).

NOAKES, VIVIAN, *Edward Lear: The Life of a Wanderer* (Boston: Houghton Mifflin, 1969).

NUBARIAN, NUBAR, *Mémoires de Nubar Pasha*, with introd. and notes by Mirrit Boutros Ghali (Beirut: Librairie du Liban, 1983).

OWEN, E. ROGER J., 'Lord Cromer and the Development of Egyptian Industry, 1883–1907', *Middle Eastern Studies*, 2/4 (July 1966).

—— 'The Egyptian Sugar Industry, 1870–1914', in Bill Albert and Adrian Graves (eds.), *Crisis and Change in the International Sugar Industry Economy, 1860–1914* (Norwich: ISC Press, 1984).

—— 'The Influence of Lord Cromer's Indian Experience on British Policy in Egypt, 1883–1907', *St Antony's Papers*, 17: *Middle Eastern Affairs*, 4, ed. Albert Hourani (London: Oxford University Press, 1965).

—— 'The Population Census of 1917 and Its Relationship to Egypt's Three 19th Century Statistical Regimes', *Journal of Historical Sociology*, 9/4 (Dec. 1996).

POLLOCK, JOHN, *The Road to Omdurman* (London: Constable, 1998).

PORTER, BERNARD, *Critics of Empire: British Radical Attitudes to Colonialism in Africa, 1895–1914* (London: Macmillan, 1968).

PUGH, MARTIN, *The March of Women: A Revisionist Analysis of the Campaign for Women's Suffrage, 1866–1914* (Oxford: Oxford University Press, 2000).

RAE, W. FRASER, 'The Egyptian Newspaper Press', *Nineteenth Century*, 32 (Aug. 1892).

al-RAFI'I, ABD al-RAHMAN, *Mustafa Kamil ba'ith al-haraka al-wataniya* (Cairo: Maktabat al-Nahda al-Misriya, 1962).

RAYMOND, A., *Égyptiens et françaises au Caire, 1798–1801* (Cairo: Institut Français d'Archéologie Orientale, 1998).

—— *et al.* (eds.), *Caire: L'art et les grandes civilisations: Les grandes citées* (Paris: Citadelles & Mazenoud, 2000).

REID, DONALD MALCOLM, *Cairo University and the Making of Modern Egypt* (Cambridge: Cambridge University Press, 1990).

—— *Whose Pharaohs? Archaeology, Museums, and Egyptian National Identity from Napoleon to World War 1* (Berkeley: University of California Press, 2002).

RODD, SIR J. RENNELL, *Social and Diplomatic Memories, 1884–1893* (London: Edward Arnold, 1922).

—— *Diplomatic and Political Memories, 1894–1901: Egypt and Abyssinia* (London: Edward Arnold, 1923).

RIVERS, WILSON, SIR CHARLES, *Chapters from My Official Life* (London: Edward Arnold, 1916).

ROBERTS, ANDREW, *Salisbury: Victorian Titan* (London: Weidenfeld & Nicolson, 1999).

ROBERTSON, JOHN M., *Patriotism and Empire* (London: Grant Richards, 1899).

RONALDSHAY, EARL OF, *The Life of Lord Curzon*, vol. i (London: Ernest Benn, 1928).

ROPER, MICHAEL, *The Records of the War Office and Related Departments 1660–1964* (London: Public Record Office Publications, 1998).

ROTHSTEIN, THEODORE, *Egypt's Ruin: A Financial and Administrative Record* (London: A. C. Fifield, 1910).

ROUTLEDGE, JAMES, *English Rule and Native Opinion in India: Some Notes Taken 1870–74* (London: Trubner, 1878).

RUFFER, JONATHAN GARBIER, *The Big Shots: Edwardian Shooting Parties* (n.p.: Debrett, 1977).

SANDERSON, LORD, *Evelyn: Earl of Cromer, Memori by Lord Sanderson* (London: Oxford University Press, nd).

SAUL, SAMIR, 'European Capital and Its Impact on Land Distribution in Egypt: A Quantitative Analysis (1900–1914)', in Gregory Blue, Martin Bunton, and Ralph Crozier (eds.), *Colonialism and the Modern World* (Armonk, NY: M. E. Sharpe, 2002).

—— *La France et l'Égypte de 1882 à 1914: Intérêts économiques et implications politiques* (Paris: Ministère de l'Économie des Finances et d'Industrie/Comité pour l'Histoire Économique et Financière de la France, 1997).

SAYCE, REVEREND A. H., *Reminiscences* (London: Macmillan, 1923).

SCHÖLCH, ALEXANDER, *Egypt for the Egyptians! The Socio-political Crisis in Egypt 1878–1882*, trans. Schölch (London: Ithaca Press, 1981).

SCHUMPETER, JOSEPH ALOIS, *Imperialism and Social Classes*, trans. Heinz Norden (New York: A. M. Kelley, 1951).

SEMMEL, BERNARD, *Jamaican Blood and Victorian Conscience: The Governor Eyre Controversy* (Westport, Conn: Greenwood Press, 1976).

SHAW, GEORGE BERNARD, 'Preface for Politicians', in his *John Bull's Other Island and Major Barbara: Also How He Lied to Her Husband* (London: Archibald Constable, 1907).

SHAW, MARION, *The Clear Stream: A Life of Winifred Holtby* (London: Virago, 1999).

SOUHAMI, DIANA, *Mrs Keppel and Her Daughters* (London: HarperCollins, 1996).

SPENCER, EDMOND, *Travels in European Turkey in 1850*, vol. ii (London: Colbourn, 1851).

STEEVENS, G. W., *Egypt in 1898* (Edinburgh: William Blackwood, 1898).

STORRS, RONALD, *Orientations* (London: Nicholson & Watson, 1937).

STRACHEY, JOHN ST LOE, *The Adventure of Living: A Subjective Autobiography* (London: Hodder & Stoughton, 1922).

STRACHEY, LYTTON, *Eminent Victorians* (first pub. 1918; London: Penguin Books, 1986).

SUTHERLAND, JOHN, *Mrs Humphry Ward: Eminent Victorian, Pre-eminent Edwardian* (Oxford: Oxford University Press, 1991).

TEMPLE, SIR RICHARD C., *Men and Events of My Time in India* (London: Murray, 1882).

THANE, PAT, 'Financiers and the British State: The Case of Sir Ernest Cassel', *Business History*, 28/1 (Jan. 1986).

—— 'Sir Ernest Joseph Cassel', *Dictionary of Business Biography*, vol. i (London: Butterworths, 1984).

THOBIE, J., 'European Banks in the Middle East', in Rondo Cameron and V. I. Bovykin (eds.), *International Banking, 1870–1914* (New York: Oxford University Press, 1990).

TOLUFSON, HAROLD, *Policing Islam: The British Occupation of Egypt and the Anglo-Egyptian Struggle Over Control of the Police, 1882–1914* (Westport, Conn.: Greenwood Press, 1999).

TRAILL, H. D., *England, Egypt and the Sudan* (London: Archibald Constable, 1900).

TREVELYAN, JANET PENROSE, *The Life of Mrs Humphry Ward* (New York: Dodd, Mead, 1923).

TROUT POWELL, EVE MARIE, 'Colonized Colonizers: Egyptian Nationalists and the Issue of the Sudan, 1875–1917', Ph. D. thesis (Harvard, 1995).

VINCENT, JOHN, *The Formation of the Liberal Party 1857–1868* (London: Constable, 1966).

VITALIS, ROBERT, *When Capitalists Collide: Business Conflict and the End of Empire in Egypt* (Berkeley: University of California Press, 1995).

WARNER, PHILIP, *Kitchener: The Man Behind the Legend* (New York: Athenaeum, 1986).

WASHBROOK, DAVID, 'India, 1818–1860: The Two Faces of Colonialism', in Andrew Porter (ed.), *The Oxford History of the British Empire*, iii: *The Nineteenth Century* (Oxford: Oxford University Press, 1999).

WENDELL, CHARLES, *The Evolution of the Egyptian National Image: From Its Origins to Ahmad Lutfi al-Sayyid* (Berkeley: University of California Press, 1972).

WHEELER, MICHAEL, *Death and the Future Life in Victorian Literature and Theology* (Cambridge: Cambridge University Press, 1990).

WILDE, OSCAR, *The Complete Letters of Oscar Wilde*, ed. Merlin Holland and Rupert Hart-Davis (New York: Henry Holt, 2000).

WILLCOCKS, WILLIAM, *Sixty Years in the East* (Edinburgh: W. Blackwood, 1935).

WOLF, LUCIEN, *Life of the First Marquess of Ripon*, vol. ii (London: John Murray, 1921).

XENOS, STEFANOS, *East and West: A Diplomatic History of the Annexation of the Ionian Islands to the Kingdom of Greece* (London: Trubner, 1865).

YAPP, M. E. (ed.), *Politics and Diplomacy in Egypt: The Diaries of Sir Miles Lampson, 1935–1937* (Oxford: Oxford University Press, 1997).

YULE, COLONEL HENRY, and BURNELL, A. C. (eds.), *Hobson-Jobson: A Glossary of Colloquial Anglo-Indian Words and Phrases*, (New Delhi: Rupa, 1994; first pub. 1886).

ZETLAND, MARQUESS OF, *Lord Cromer* (London: Hodder & Stoughton, 1932).

ZIEGLER, PHILIP, *The Sixth Great Power: A History of One of the Greatest of All Banking Families, the House of Barings, 1762–1929* (New York: Alfred Knopf, 1988).

INDEX